Practical Techniques, Strategies, and Interventions

How to Reach & Teach Children & Teens with

ADD/ADHD

THIRD EDITION

Sandra F. Rief

JB JOSSEY-BASS™

A Wiley Brand

Published by Jossey-Bass
A Wiley Brand

One Montgomery Street, Suite 1000, San Francisco, CA 94104–4594—www.josseybass.com

Jossey-Bass books and products are available through most bookstores. To contact Jossey-Bass directly call our Customer Care Department within the U.S. at 800-956-7739, outside the U.S. at 317-572-3986, or fax 317-572-4002.

Wiley publishes in a variety of print and electronic formats and by print-on-demand. Some material included with standard print versions of this book may not be included in e-books or in print-on-demand. If this book refers to media such as a CD or DVD that is not included in the version you purchased, you may download this material at http://booksupport.wiley.com. For more information about Wiley products, visit www.wiley.com.

Library of Congress Cataloging-in-Publication Data
Names: Rief, Sandra F.
Title: How to reach and teach children and teens with ADD/ADHD / Sandra F. Rief.
Description: Third edition. | San Francisco, California : Wiley, 2016. | Includes bibliographical references and index.
Identifiers: LCCN 2016018130 (print) | LCCN 2016019274 (ebook) | ISBN 9781118937785 (paperback) | ISBN 9781118937808 (pdf) | ISBN 9781118937792 (epub)
Subjects: LCSH: Attention-deficit-disordered children--Education--United States--Handbooks, manuals, etc. | Attention-deficit-disordered youth--Education–United States–Handbooks, manuals, etc. | Hyperactive children–Education–United States–Handbooks, manuals, etc. | Classroom management–United States–Handbooks, manuals, etc. | BISAC: EDUCATION / Special Education / General.
Classification: LCC LC4713.4 .R54 2016 (print) | LCC LC4713.4 (ebook) | DDC 371.94–dc23
LC record available at https://lccn.loc.gov/2016018130

9781118937785 Paperback
9781118937808 ePDF
9781118937792 ePub

Cover image: © Caiaimage/Robert Daly/Getty Images, Inc., © Alistair Berg/Getty Images, Inc.
Cover design: Wiley

Printed in the United States of America
THIRD EDITION

PB Printing   V10008595_030419

About the Author

Sandra F. Rief, MA, is an internationally known speaker, educational consultant, and author, specializing in practical and effective strategies for helping students with ADHD and learning disabilities succeed in school. She has written several books and presented numerous seminars, workshops, and keynotes nationally and internationally on this topic. Sandra has trained thousands of teachers in the United States and throughout the world on best practices for helping students with ADHD, and has worked with many schools in their efforts to provide interventions and supports for students with learning, attention, and behavioral challenges.

Among some of the other books she has authored (published by Jossey-Bass/Wiley) are *The ADHD Book of Lists: A Practical Guide for Helping Children and Teens with Attention Deficit Disorders, Second Edition* (2015), *The Dyslexia Checklist: A Practical Reference for Parents and Teachers* (coauthored with J. Stern, 2010), *The ADD/ADHD Checklist: An Easy Reference for Parents and Teachers, Second Edition* (2008), *How to Reach and Teach All Children Through Balanced Literacy* (coauthored with J. Heimburge, 2007), and *How to Reach and Teach All Children in the Inclusive Classroom: Practical Strategies, Lessons, and Activities, Second Edition* (coauthored with J. Heimburge, 2006).

Sandra also authored these laminated guides (published by National Professional Resources, Inc.): *Executive Function: Skill-Building and Support Strategies for the Elementary Classroom* (2016), *Executive Function: Skill-Building and Support Strategies for Grades 6–12* (2016), *Dyslexia: Strategies, Supports & Interventions* (2010), *Section 504: Classroom Accommodations* (2010), and *ADHD & LD: Classroom Strategies at Your Fingertips* (2009).

Sandra developed and presented these acclaimed educational DVDs as well: *ADHD & LD: Powerful Teaching Strategies and Accommodations (with RTI)*; *How to Help Your Child Succeed in School: Strategies and Guidance for Parents of Children with ADHD and/or Learning Disabilities*; *ADHD: Inclusive Instruction and Collaborative Practices*; and, together with Linda Fisher and Nancy Fetzer, *Successful Classrooms: Effective Teaching Strategies for Raising Achievement in Reading and Writing* and *Successful Schools: How to Raise Achievement and Support "At-Risk" Students.*

Sandra is formerly an award-winning special education teacher from San Diego Unified School District (California Resource Specialist of the Year), with more than two decades of experience teaching in public schools. Presently, Sandra is an instructor for continuing education and distance learning courses offered through a few universities on instructional and behavioral strategies and interventions for reaching and teaching students with ADHD, LDs, and other mild to moderate disabilities. She received her BA and MA degrees from the University of Illinois. For more information, visit her website at www.sandrarief.com.

Acknowledgments

My deepest thanks and appreciation to

- My precious, beautiful family (which has grown and blossomed since the first and second editions of this book): Itzik, Ariel, Anna, Jackie, Jason, Maya, Jonah, Ezra, Gil, Sharon, Daniella, and Raquel. You are everything to me, and I love you all so much.
- All of my former students and other wonderful children who have touched my heart and inspired me throughout the years to keep learning what we can do to better reach and teach them.
- The special families who have shared with me their struggles and triumphs and allowed me to be part of their lives.
- All of the amazing, dedicated educators I have had the great fortune to work with and meet over the years; thank you for sharing with me your creative strategies, ideas, and insights.
- The extraordinary parents (especially the wonderful volunteers in CHADD and other organizations worldwide) whose tireless efforts have raised awareness about ADHD and, as a result, have improved the care and education of our children.
- All the researchers and practitioners in the different fields dedicated to helping children and families with ADHD, LDs, and other disabilities, from whom I have learned so much.
- Diana Anderson-Goetz for writing the extraordinarily powerful family story found in Section 5.1 of this book. I am so grateful to Diana and her wonderful husband and children (Vincent and Victoria) for so courageously and generously sharing their very personal and poignant story that is a must-read for teachers, clinicians, and parents of children with ADHD.
- Karen Easter, one of the mothers I was privileged to meet and befriend at one of my workshops, for sharing her wonderful original poems in this book and earlier editions.
- Decker Forrest, an incredibly talented former student of mine, who was in the eighth grade at the time he drew the illustrations in this book (first published in the 1993 edition).
- Dan's mother, Jill, for writing and sharing her son's story on the value of mentorship, which was first published in the original edition (1993) of this book, and Dan, for generously providing his update, in Section 1.9.
- Christine Kreider, Shannon Prior, Itzik Rief, and Julie Heimburge for creating and sharing some of the charts and forms found in the appendix.
- Beverly Shorter and T. Cohen for writing and sharing their wonderful student case studies found in Section 5.2.
- Beth Black for sharing her exemplary high school writing strategies in Section 4.4.
- Joe, Susan, Mike, Amy, Joseph, John, Brita, and Brad, who allowed me to interview them and share their experiences, insights, and tips in excerpts throughout this book.
- Marjorie McAneny, my wonderful editor at Jossey-Bass/Wiley in San Francisco, for her guidance and expertise and for making it a pleasure to write this book and the others we have worked on together over the years. To all of the team I'm privileged to work with at J-B/Wiley . . . you're the best.

Dedication

This book is dedicated in memory of my beloved son, Benjamin, and to all of the children who face struggles in their young lives each day with loving, trusting hearts, hope, and extraordinary courage. I also dedicate this book in loving memory of Levana Estline—dear friend, exceptional teacher, and a blessing to all who knew her.

Contents

Preface * xxv

PART 1: KEY INFORMATION FOR UNDERSTANDING AND MANAGING ADHD

Section 1.1: Understanding ADHD * 3

Clarifying Terms and Labels * 3

Descriptions and Definitions * 3

Signs and Symptoms * 4

- Symptoms of Inattention and Associated Problems * 4

- Symptoms of Hyperactivity and Impulsivity and Associated Problems * 5

- Other Common Difficulties Experienced by Children and Teens with ADHD * 7

Three Presentations of ADHD * 8

- Predominantly Inattentive * 9

- Predominantly Hyperactive-Impulsive * 9

- Combined * 9

Statistics and Risk Factors * 9

ADHD and Coexisting Disorders * 10

- Common Coexisting Conditions and Disorders * 11

- Other Disorders and Conditions * 11

- Identifying and Treating Coexisting Disorders * 11

ADHD Look-Alikes * 12

What Is Currently Known about ADHD * 13

ADHD Brain Differences * 14

- Delayed Brain Maturation and Structural Differences * 14

- Diminished Activity and Lower Metabolism in Certain Brain Regions * 15

- Brain Chemical (Neurotransmitter) Inefficiency * 15

Causes of ADHD * 15

- Heredity * 15

- Birth Complications, Illnesses, and Brain Injury * 16

- Maternal or Childhood Exposure to Certain Toxins * 16

- Other Environmental Factors * 16

Girls with ADHD * 17

- What We Have Learned * 17

Positive Traits and Strengths * 18

ADHD and the Impact on the Family * 19

Section 1.2: ADHD and Executive Function Impairment * 21

Definitions of Executive Function (EF) * 21

EF Analogies and Metaphors * 21

EF Components * 22

EF Dysfunction in ADHD * 23

Models Explaining Executive Function Impairment in ADHD * 23

    – Barkley's Model of EF and ADHD * 23

    – Brown's Model of EF and ADHD * 23

Other Information about Executive Functions * 24

What Parents and Teachers Should Keep in Mind * 24

Section 1.3: Making the Diagnosis: A Comprehensive Evaluation for ADHD * 27

Clinical Evaluation for ADHD * 27

    – DSM-5 Criteria * 27

    – Three Presentations of ADHD * 28

    – Changes in the DSM Criteria * 28

Components of a Comprehensive Evaluation for ADHD * 29

    – Clinical Interview * 29

    – Rating Scales * 29

    – Physical Exam * 30

    – Observations * 30

    – Academic and Intelligence Testing * 30

    – Performance Tests * 31

Pursuing an ADHD Evaluation * 31

    – Who Is Qualified to Diagnose ADHD? * 31

    – Finding a Professional to Evaluate Your Child * 32

    – Working with the School in the Evaluation Process * 32

What Teachers and Other School Professionals Need to Know * 32

    – Information about Current School Functioning * 32

    – Information about the School History * 33

    – Points to Keep in Mind * 33

Section 1.4: Multimodal Treatment for ADHD * 35

Multimodal Intervention * 36

    – Parent Training * 36

    – Medication Therapy (Pharmacological Intervention) * 36

    – Behavioral Therapy * 37

    – Other Psychosocial Interventions * 37

    – Educational Interventions * 37

    – Complementary Interventions * 38

Additional Points to Keep in Mind * 41

Caution about Alternative Treatments * 41

Section 1.5: Medication Treatment and Management * 43

Stimulant Medications in the Treatment of ADHD * 43
- How Stimulants Are Believed to Work * 44
- Stimulant Medications Prescribed for Treating ADHD * 44
- Side Effects of Stimulant Medications * 45
- The Titration Process * 45

Nonstimulant ADHD Medications * 46

Other Medications * 46

Additional Information * 46

If a Child or Teen Is Taking Medication: Advice for School Staff and Parents * 47
- What Teachers Need to Know * 47
- What Parents Need to Know * 49

Interview with Mike * 50

Section 1.6: Behavioral Therapy for Managing ADHD * 51

General Principles of Behavior Modification * 52

Home-Based Behavioral Treatment * 52

School-Based Behavioral Treatment * 53

Child-Based Behavioral Treatment * 54

Interview with Joe * 55

Section 1.7: Critical Factors in the Success of Students with ADHD * 57

Interview with Spencer's Mother * 61

Section 1.8: ADHD in Preschool and Kindergarten * 63

Developmental Signs and Symptoms in Young Children * 63

Red Flags for Possible Learning Disabilities * 64

What the Research Shows * 65
- PATS 2006 * 65
- PATS Six-Year Follow-up * 65

Evaluation, Diagnosis, and Intervention * 66
- AAP Clinical Practice Guidelines for Diagnosis, Evaluation, and Treatment of Preschool Children * 66
- Parent Concerns and Recommendations * 66
- Child Find and School District Evaluation * 67

More Strategies and Tips for Parents * 67

Kindergarten Academic Skills and Expectations * 68

Research-Supported Intervention Programs for Preschool and Kindergarten * 69
- First Step to Success * 69
- Tools of the Mind * 69

Strategies and Tips for Preschool and Kindergarten Teachers * 69

Strategies and Tips for Early Childhood Teachers * 71
  – What to Do About . . . * 71
Interview with Joe * 72

Section 1.9: ADHD in Middle School and High School * 73

For All Kids This Age * 74
  – Challenges of Adolescence * 74
  – What All Adolescents Need * 74
ADHD-Related Challenges and Needs * 74
Addressing Coexisting Disorders * 75
School Supports * 75
Aiding the Transition to Middle or High School * 76
Transition Plans * 76
Warning Signs (Red Flags) in Middle School and High School * 77
Warning Signs of Learning Disabilities in Teens * 78
Understanding Their ADHD and Self-Advocacy * 78
The Value of Mentorship * 79
Dan's Story * 79

Part 1: References * 83

Part 1: Additional Sources and Resources * 89

PART 2: MANAGING THE CHALLENGE OF ADHD BEHAVIORS

Section 2.1: Proactive Classroom Management * 97

Classroom Management Tips * 97
  – Create a Climate for Success * 97
  – Establish Classroom Rules (Behavioral Standards) * 98
  – Teach Procedures and Routines * 99
  – Use Auditory and Visual Cues and Prompts * 99
  – Positively Reinforce (Reward) Desired Behavior * 100
  – Use Your Proximity and Movement * 102
  – Accommodate Students' Need to Move * 102
Environmental Supports and Accommodations in the Classroom * 102
  – Student Seating * 102
  – Space, Materials, and Minimizing Environmental Distractions * 103
  – Using Music * 104
Other Important Strategies and Tips * 104
Common Triggers or Antecedents to Misbehavior * 104
Address Student Misbehavior * 105
Parent Tips: Behavior Management at Home * 107
Interview with Brad * 108

Section 2.2: Preventing Behavior Problems during Transitions and Less Structured Times ∗ **111**

    Parent Tips: Preventing Behavior Problems Outside the Home ∗ *113*

Section 2.3: Class (Group) Behavior Management and Incentive Systems ∗ **115**

Positive-Only Group Reinforcement Systems ∗ 115

    – Praise and Positive Attention ∗ 115

    – Table or Team Points ∗ 115

    – Daily or Weekly Target Goals ∗ 116

    – Tokens in a Jar ∗ 116

    – Chart Moves ∗ 116

    – Raffles or Lotteries ∗ 116

    – Individual Stamp Cards ∗ 117

    – Unsolicited Compliment Rewards ∗ 117

    – Lottery Grid, 100 Chart, or Class Bingo Board ∗ 117

    – Mystery Motivator ∗ 118

Reinforcement Systems That Also May Involve Fines or Deductions ∗ 118

    – Token Economy System ∗ 118

    – Group Response Cost ∗ 119

    – Good Behavior Game ∗ 119

    – Electronic Feedback Point System—Class Dojo ∗ 119

    – Scoreboards, T-Charts, Teacher-Student Points ∗ 120

What to Do about Students Whose Behavior Interferes with Group Success ∗ 121

Points to Keep in Mind ∗ 121

Section 2.4: Individualized Behavior Supports and Interventions ∗ **123**

Target Behaviors ∗ 123

Individualized Interventions ∗ 123

    – Goal Sheets ∗ 124

    – Contingency Contracts ∗ 124

    – Token Economy and Token Programs ∗ 125

    – Daily Report Cards (DRCs) ∗ 125

    – Check-In Check-Out (CICO) ∗ 130

    – Direct Behavior Ratings ∗ 131

    – Other Behavior Charts and Monitoring Forms ∗ 131

    – For All Positive Incentive Programs ∗ 131

    – Other Individualized Behavioral Interventions ∗ 132

Understanding the ABCs of Behavior ∗ 135

Functional Behavioral Assessments (FBAs) and Behavioral Intervention Plans (BIPs) ∗ 136

    – What Is an FBA? ∗ 136

    – What Is a BIP? ∗ 137

Section 2.5: Strategies to Increase Listening, Following Directions, and Compliance * 139

Strategies and Tips for Teachers * 139

*Parent Tips: Getting Your Child to Listen and Follow Your Directions * 140*

Increasing Compliance * 141

Oppositional Defiant Disorder and ADHD * 142

Section 2.6: Managing Challenging Behavior: Strategies for Teachers and Parents * 143

Strategies for Addressing Impulsive and Hyperactive Behaviors * 143

*Parent Tips: More Strategies for Managing Your Child's Hyperactive-Impulsive Behavior * 146*

Strategies for Emotional Regulation and Control * 146

   – Prevention Strategies for Teachers * 146

   – More Teacher Strategies to Aid Calming and Avoid Escalation * 148

*Parent Tips: Prevention Strategies for Frustration, Anger, and Melt-Downs * 149*

Dealing with Argumentative and Oppositional Behavior * 150

Section 2.7: School-Based Social Skills Interventions * 153

ADHD-Related Difficulties * 153

Skill Deficits versus Performance Deficits * 154

The Impact on Children and Families * 154

Classroom Interventions * 155

Schoolwide Programs and Interventions * 156

   – Schoolwide Positive Behavior Supports (SWPBS) and Positive Behavior Intervention and Supports (PBIS) * 156

   – Social Skills Programs and Materials * 157

   – Social-Emotional Learning Programs * 158

Goal-Setting Tips * 158

Social Skill Lesson Plan * 160

Report Form: Social Skills * 163

Part 2: References * 165

Part 2: Additional Sources and Resources * 169

PART 3: INSTRUCTIONAL, LEARNING, AND EXECUTIVE FUNCTION STRATEGIES

Section 3.1: Attention!! Strategies for Engaging, Maintaining, and Regulating Students' Attention * 177

Getting and Focusing Students' Attention * 177

   – Auditory Techniques * 177

   – Visual Techniques * 177

   – The Tech Advantage * 178

   – Arousing Students' Curiosity and Anticipation * 178

   – Liven It Up * 178

– Make It Personal * 178

– Organize Student Thinking * 179

Maintaining Students' Attention through Active Participation * 179

– General Tips for Keeping Students Engaged * 179

– Questioning Techniques to Increase Student Engagement and Response Opportunities * 180

Keeping Students On-Task During Seatwork * 183

Teacher Tips for Helping Inattentive, Distractible Students * 184

Parent Tips: Helping Your Inattentive, Distractible Child * 186

Self-Monitoring Attention (Self-Regulatory Techniques) * 188

Section 3.2: Research-Based Instructional Approaches and Interventions * 191

Universal Design for Learning (UDL) * 191

Differentiated Instruction * 192

– A Word about Multisensory Instruction, Learning Style Preferences, and Multiple Intelligences * 193

– Explanation to Students Regarding Differentiation * 194

Student Learning Style/Interest Interview * 194

Response to Intervention (RTI) * 196

– Essential Components of RTI * 197

– The Three-Tiered Model of Intervention * 197

– A Word about RTI and the Individuals with Disabilities Education Act (IDEA) * 199

Peer-Mediated Instruction and Intervention * 199

– Classwide Peer Tutoring * 199

– Cooperative Learning * 200

Blended Learning * 203

– Models of Blended Learning * 204

– The Technology * 204

Designing Interventions for Struggling Learners: Key Instructional Components * 204

Interview with Amy * 205

Interview with Brita * 206

Section 3.3: Organization and Time Management * 207

What Teachers Can Do to Help with Organization * 208

Parent Tips: Helping Your Child with Organization * 211

What Teachers Can Do to Help with Time Management * 213

– Time Awareness * 213

– Assignment Sheets, Student Planners, and Calendars * 214

– Schedules * 215

– Long-Term Projects * 215

– Other Ways Teachers Can Help with Time Management * 215

Parent Tips: Helping Your Child with Time Management * 216

Section 3.4: The Homework Challenge: Strategies and Tips for Parents and Teachers * 219

Homework Tips for Parents * 220
- Create the Work Environment * 220
- Develop a Homework Routine and Schedule * 220
- Organize Homework Supplies * 220
- Prepare and Structure * 221
- Help during Homework * 221
- Increase Motivation and Work Production * 222
- Communicate with Teachers about Homework Issues * 223
- Other Ways to Help * 223

Homework Tips for Teachers * 223
- Communicate Clearly * 224
- Provide Monitoring and Support * 224
- Increase Motivation * 226
- Keep Things in Perspective * 226
- More Tips * 227

Section 3.5: Learning Strategies and Study Skills * 229

What Are Learning Strategies? * 229

Metacognition and Metacognitive Strategies * 229
- Definitions * 229
- Metacognitive Questions * 230
- Metacognitive Strategies * 230

Cognitive Learning Strategies * 231
- Definition * 231
- Cognitive Strategies * 231

More Learning and Study Strategies * 233
- Note Taking * 233
- Graphic Organizers * 235
- Resource Materials * 235
- Review Games * 235

*Interview with Susan * 236*

Section 3.6: Memory Strategies and Supports * 237

Definitions and Descriptions of Working Memory * 237

Working Memory Deficits and ADHD * 238

Difficulties Associated with Poor Working Memory * 238

Supports and Accommodations for Memory Weaknesses * 239

Cognitive Working Memory Training (CWMT) Programs * 240

Mnemonics ❋ 241
– Keyword Mnemonics ❋ 241
– Pegword Mnemonics ❋ 241
Music and Rhyme ❋ 242
Other Memory Strategies and Tips ❋ 242
Multimodal and Memory Techniques for Learning Multiplication Tables ❋ 243
– Auditory ❋ 243
– Visual and Tactile ❋ 244
– Verbal ❋ 245
– Mnemonic (Memory) Devices ❋ 245
– Conceptual ❋ 246
Memory Techniques for Other Hard-to-Remember Information ❋ 246

Part 3: References ❋ 247

Part 3: Additional Sources and Resources ❋ 251

PART 4: STRATEGIES AND SUPPORTS FOR READING, WRITING, AND MATH

Section 4.1: Common Reading and Writing Difficulties ❋ 257
The Reading Process: What Good Readers Do ❋ 257
Coexisting Learning Disabilities ❋ 258
– Definition of Dyslexia ❋ 259
– Instruction for Students with Dyslexia ❋ 259
Tips for Parents: If You Suspect Your Child Has a Reading Disability ❋ 260
Common Reading Errors and Weaknesses in Students with ADHD ❋ 261
– Inattention-Related Reading Errors and Difficulties ❋ 261
– Impulsivity-Related Reading Errors and Difficulties ❋ 261
– Working Memory–Related Errors and Difficulties ❋ 261
– Metacognition-Related Errors and Difficulties ❋ 262
– Other Executive Function–Related Difficulties ❋ 262
– Processing Speed–Related Errors and Difficulties ❋ 262
Steps of the Writing Process and Potential Problems ❋ 263
Why Writing Is a Struggle ❋ 263
– Planning and Organization ❋ 264
– Attention and Inhibition ❋ 264
– Working Memory and Retrieval ❋ 264
– Shifting and Cognitive Flexibility ❋ 264
– Self-Monitoring ❋ 264
– Speed of Written Output and Production ❋ 265
– Language ❋ 265
– Graphomotor Skills ❋ 265
– Spelling ❋ 265

Section 4.2: Decoding, Fluency, and Vocabulary * 267

Word Recognition and Decoding * 268

Fluency * 269

- Factors That Contribute to Fluency * 269
- Fluency-Building Strategies * 269
- Additional Fluency Strategies * 270
- Remediation Challenge * 271
- Tips for Oral Reading in the Classroom * 271
- Tips for Independent Reading * 271

Vocabulary * 272

- Strategies for Vocabulary Development and Working with Words * 272
- Points to Keep in Mind * 273

*Parent Tips: Reading Strategies * 274*

Section 4.3: Reading Comprehension * 277

Strategies throughout the Reading Process * 277

- Before-Reading Strategies * 277
- During-Reading Strategies * 278
- After-Reading Strategies * 279

The Importance of Teacher Modeling of Strategic Reading * 280

Graphic Organizers * 280

More Key Comprehension Strategies * 281

- Summarizing * 281
- Narrative Text Structure * 281
- Expository or Informational Text Structure * 281
- Close Reading * 282

Other Reading Comprehension Strategies * 283

- Anticipation Guide * 283
- Directed Reading-Thinking Activity (DRTA) * 283
- Imagery and Visualization * 283
- KWL (and Variations) * 283
- GIST * 283
- PASS * 284
- Reciprocal Teaching * 284
- Question-Answer Relationships (QAR) * 284
- Journal Entries * 285
- Literature Logs * 285
- Retelling * 285
- Hot Seat * 285
- Readers Theater * 285

Classroom Book Clubs * 285
   – What Is a Classroom Book Club? * 285
   – The Benefits of Book Clubs * 286
   – Book Club Folders * 287
*Parent Tips: Strengthen Comprehension and Motivate Your Child to Read * 287*
*Interview with John * 288*

Section 4.4: Writing: Strategies, Supports, and Accommodations * 291
Prewriting, Planning, and Organizing * 291
   – Prewriting Techniques in the Classroom * 291
   – Using Planning Forms and Visual Organizers * 292
   – Apps and Software * 293
   – Thinking and Questioning * 293
   – Mnemonic Strategies * 294
   – Other Instructional Techniques in the Prewriting Stage * 294
*Parent Tips: Help Your Child with Prewriting * 295*
Strategies for Building Skills in Written Expression * 296
   – Instructional Approaches * 296
   – Teaching Sentence Structure and Expanded Word Choices * 297
   – Teaching Students to Compose a Draft * 298
   – Teaching Self-Monitoring * 298
   – Apps and Software * 299
*Parent Tips: Help Your Child in the Drafting and Composing Stage * 301*
Strategies for Revising and Editing * 302
   – Strategies for Helping Students with Revision * 302
   – Strategies for Helping Students with Editing * 303
Mnemonic Proofreading Strategies * 304
Other Tips for Teachers * 304
Strategies to Bypass and Accommodate Writing Difficulties * 305
   – Tips for Teachers * 305
   – Assistive Technology * 306

Section 4.5: Spelling and Handwriting * 309
Helping Children with Spelling Difficulties * 309
   – Spelling Challenges * 309
   – Spelling Instruction * 310
   – Motivating, Multisensory Techniques to Practice Spelling * 311
   – Other Techniques for Spelling * 312
   – Additional Spelling Tips * 313
Improving Handwriting and Legibility of Written Work * 313
   – Dysgraphia and Other Handwriting Struggles * 313
   – Handwriting Tips and Strategies * 314

– Handwriting Programs and Apps * 315
– Tactile-Kinesthetic Techniques to Motivate Practice * 315
– Additional Tips * 316

Section 4.6: Mathematics * 319

Math Difficulties Associated with ADHD and Learning Disabilities * 319
– Attention Weaknesses * 319
– Memory Weaknesses * 319
– Other Executive Skill Weaknesses * 320
– Sequencing Weaknesses * 320
– Visual-Motor, Fine Motor, and Spatial-Organization Weaknesses * 321
– Language Weaknesses * 321
– Written Expression Weaknesses * 321
Mathematics: Standards and Student Expectations * 321
– National Council of Teachers of Mathematics (NCTM) Standards * 321
– Common Core State Standards (CCSS) * 323
– Key Shifts in Mathematics Instruction * 323
– The Challenge for Students with ADHD * 323
Mathematics Instruction * 324
– Word Problems * 324
– Instructional Formats and Routines * 325
– Instructional Tips * 326
More Math Strategies, Supports, and Accommodations * 327
Parent Tips: Strengthen Your Child's Math Skills * 329
Connecting Math to Writing and Literature * 330

Part 4: References * 333

Part 4: Additional Sources and Resources * 337

PART 5: PERSONAL STORIES AND CASE STUDIES

**Section 5.1: A Parent's Story . . . What Every Teacher, Clinician, and Parent of a Child with
          ADHD Needs to Hear * 343**

Vincent (Seventeen Years Old, High School Senior) * 343
– Medical History * 343
– Social/Educational History (Narrative) * 344
– Diagnosis, Part I * 347
– First- Through Third-Grade Educational Supports * 347
– Fourth and Fifth Grades and Diagnosis, Part II * 349
– Sixth through Twelfth Grades * 350
– Discipline * 351
– Avoiding Power Struggles * 352
– Assistive Technology * 352

– Note Taker in Math * 353

– Drama * 353

– Creativity, Empathy, Care, and Concern in Teaching * 353

– Medication * 354

– Good Communication * 354

– Behavioral Plan * 354

– High Expectations for Success * 356

– Therapeutic Interventions * 356

– The Saga Continues * 357

Everything Ripples: The Education of Vincent and Victoria * 358

– Everything Ripples * 358

– Handwriting and the Generation Gap? * 359

– YOU Will Have FUN Whether You LIKE It or NOT! * 360

– Are We Having FUN Yet? * 362

– Readiness Is Everything, Except . . . * 364

– Goodness of Fit and Dead Meat * 365

– College and Professional Development * 367

– Learning Strategies Ripple, Too . . . * 369

Notes on Section 5.1 * 372

Section 5.2: Student Case Studies and Interventions * 375

Chloe (Seven Years Old, First Grade) * 375

– Student Profile * 375

– Current Performance Levels * 375

– Desired Outcomes for Chloe * 376

– Intervention Plan * 376

– Teaming with School Staff * 378

– Teaming with Parents * 379

Anne (Eleven Years Old, Sixth Grade) * 379

– Student Profile * 379

– Intervention Plan * 381

– Follow-up (Reported Spring Trimester of Sixth-Grade School Year, Provided by Mrs. Shorter) * 383

– Follow-up (Tenth-Grade School Year) * 383

Part 5: References * 385

PART 6: COLLABORATIVE EFFORTS AND SCHOOL RESPONSIBILITIES IN HELPING STUDENTS WITH ADHD

Section 6.1: Teaming for Success: Communication, Collaboration, and Mutual Support * 389

The Necessity of a Team Approach * 389

The Parents' Role in the Collaborative Team Process * 390

– Know Your Child's Educational Rights * 391

– Be an Effective Advocate at Team Meetings * 391

– Maintain Records ✳ 392

– If Requesting an Evaluation from the School District ✳ 392

– Ensure the Right Care from Doctors and Other Clinicians ✳ 393

– More Advocacy and Communication Tips for Parents ✳ 393

The Educators' Role in the Collaborative Team Process ✳ 394

– Establish Communication and a Positive Relationship ✳ 394

– Be Proactive ✳ 395

– Give Teachers the Supports and Training They Need ✳ 396

– Keep in Mind ✳ 397

The Clinicians' Role in the Collaborative Team Process ✳ 397

Cultural Sensitivity in Communication with Parents ✳ 398

Section 6.2: The Role of the School's Multidisciplinary Team ✳ 399

The Student Support Team (SST) Process ✳ 399

– The Role of the School ✳ 400

– The Role of Teachers ✳ 401

Multi-Tier System of Supports (MTSS) ✳ 401

– Response to Intervention (RTI) ✳ 402

– Positive Behavioral Intervention and Supports (PBIS) ✳ 402

– More about MTSS ✳ 402

– Additional Points ✳ 402

If You Suspect a Student Has ADHD: Recommendations for Teachers and Other School Personnel ✳ 403

– Caution and Tips for Teachers ✳ 404

School-Based Assessment for ADHD ✳ 404

– Interpreting the Data and Next Steps ✳ 405

Section 6.3: School Documentation and Communication with Medical Providers and Others ✳ 407

Communication with Physicians ✳ 407

– School Letter to Steven's Physician ✳ 408

– School Letter to Lucas's Physician ✳ 409

– School Letter to Christina's Physician ✳ 410

Communication between Schools ✳ 411

– Letter Regarding Damien ✳ 411

Teacher Documentation ✳ 413

– Letter Requesting Teachers to Complete ADHD Behavioral Rating Forms ✳ 413

– Sample Letters for Parents Requesting an Evaluation from the School District ✳ 413

Section 6.4: Federal Laws and Educational Rights of Students with ADHD ✳ 415

Individuals with Disabilities Education Act (IDEA) ✳ 415

– Overview ✳ 415

– The IEP Process ✳ 417

– Eligibility for Students with ADHD under OHI or SLD Categories ✳ 419

Section 504 of the Rehabilitation Act of 1973 ✳ 420

Americans with Disabilities Act Amendments Act of 2008 (ADAAA) ✳ 421

– Changes to Section 504 as of ADA Amendments Act of 2008 (ADAAA) ✳ 421

– Additional Important Information about Section 504 ✳ 421

– 504 Accommodations ✳ 422

Which Is More Advantageous for Students with ADHD: An IEP or a 504 Plan? ✳ 422

Disciplining Students with Disabilities under IDEA 2004 ✳ 423

– Removal from School (Suspensions and Expulsions) ✳ 423

– Manifestation Determination Review ✳ 424

– FBA and BIP ✳ 424

– More Rights and Requirements under the Law ✳ 424

– Protections for Students Who Do Not Have IEPs ✳ 425

Part 6: References ✳ 427

Part 6: Additional Sources and Resources ✳ 429

APPENDIX: FORMS ✳ 433

A.1: ___'s Daily Report ✳ 434

A.2: My Behavior Report ✳ 435

A.3A: Daily Report ✳ 436

A.3B: Daily Report Card ✳ 437

A.3C: Daily/Weekly Report Card ✳ 438

A.3D: Daily Behavior Report ✳ 439

A.4: Daily Monitoring Report ✳ 440

A.5: Self-Monitoring Behavior Log ✳ 441

A.6: Notebook Check ✳ 442

A.7: Homework Assignments ✳ 443

A.8: Homework Tracking Sheet ✳ 444

A.9: Book Club Roles ✳ 445

A.10: Book Club Culminating Activities ✳ 447

A.11: Five-Paragraph Persuasive Essay Rubric ✳ 449

A.12: Research Log ✳ 450

INDEX: ✳ 451

Preface

This book offers comprehensive guidance to everyone engaged in the positive education of children and teens who have been diagnosed with ADHD or who show signs and symptoms of this disorder. Whether you are a classroom teacher or a parent; a special education teacher, counselor, or psychologist; or a school or district administrator, this book will be a valuable resource. You'll find information, techniques, and strategies to help these students succeed. While the book addresses the specific needs of students with ADD/ADHD, the strategies are also appropriate and recommended for all children and teens who appear to have executive function weaknesses or who are experiencing any learning, attention, or behavioral difficulties.

This third edition has been completely revised and updated since the second edition, which was published a decade ago. Because much of the information and strategies are for teens as well as children, I revised the title as well, to reflect the inclusion of adolescents. When I wrote the first edition of this book (then titled *How to Reach and Teach ADD/ADHD Children*) back in 1993, awareness of attention-deficit/hyperactivity disorder, as well as information and resources available to parents and teachers, were minimal at best. There were no other published books at that time addressing the educational needs of students with ADD/ADHD, providing practical strategies to implement at home and school to help these children succeed in school.

Since that time, a tremendous amount of information has become easily accessible, and far more resources than ever before are available to parents, educators, and those who work with and treat children and teens with ADHD. However, there is still a great deal of misinformation and many myths surrounding this disorder. There are still countless children and teens who have ADHD and who have been suffering and experiencing school failure due to their lack of identification or treatment and misinterpretation of their behaviors by teachers and others, who don't understand this brain-based disorder and its impact.

For easy use, this resource is organized into six parts providing comprehensive, up-to-date, practical guidance on a variety of topics relevant to parents and educators, as well as reproducible tools in the appendix, and additional resources. There are thirty-four sections filled with useful information and strategies within these categories:

Part 1: Key Information for Understanding and Managing ADHD
Part 2: Managing the Challenge of ADHD Behaviors
Part 3: Instructional, Learning, and Executive Function Strategies
Part 4: Strategies and Supports for Reading, Writing, and Math
Part 5: Personal Stories and Case Studies
Part 6: Collaborative Efforts and School Responsibilities in Helping Students with ADHD

A lot of the content of this book has been adapted not only from the 2005 edition but from my other books published by Jossey-Bass/Wiley, particularly these sources (which you may be interested in exploring for further information, tools, and strategies):

The ADHD Book of Lists: A Practical Guide for Helping Children and Teens with
    Attention Deficit Disorders, Second Edition (2015)
The Dyslexia Checklist: A Practical Guide for Parents and Teachers (coauthored
    with Judith Stern, 2010)
The ADD/ADHD Checklist: An Easy Reference for Parents and Teachers,
    Second Edition (2008)

For even more information and tools, find the bonus content as well as the appendix materials provided online at this link: www.wiley.com/go/adhdreach. The password is the last five digits of the ISBN, which is 9781118937785. See the table of contents for bonus content topics. Some of the management charts and forms in the appendix can be customized to your needs when accessed online before printing.

A number of strategies and recommendations in this book come from what I have learned from my many students with ADHD and learning disabilities, their families, and my colleagues during the twenty-three years I was teaching in public schools. In addition, I have had the privilege of observing hundreds of classrooms and working with scores of educators across the United States and internationally. I am grateful for the openness of the many wonderful teachers and parents, who so willingly shared their ideas, strategies, struggles, and successes. Their stories and insights have inspired me and taught me so much.

I have been very fortunate to meet extraordinary people over the years who have generously and openly shared with me their experiences and insights. Throughout this book, there are excerpts of some interviews I have conducted with teens and adults from across the country who grew up with ADHD, authentic case studies from teachers, and the powerful personal story (Section 5.1) written by a friend of mine and mother of two (now adult) children with ADHD. I urge you all to read them. These interviews and accounts illustrate the positive difference that a single caring adult (particularly a teacher) can make in the life of a child or teen with ADHD. The writing on a plaque my friend saw years ago (author unknown) beautifully summed it up this way:

"Teachers affect eternity. One can never tell where their influence ends."

It is always preferable to be able to identify children with ADHD or any special needs early and then initiate interventions and supports at a young age in order to avoid some of the frustration, failure, and subsequent loss of self-esteem. However, it is never too late to help a child. In many cases, the kind of help that makes a difference does not take a huge effort on our part. Sometimes even small changes (such as in the way we respond to our child or teen) can lead to significant improvements. If I am able to convey any single message with this book, I wish for it to be one of hope and optimism. When we work together—providing the necessary structure, guidance, encouragement, and support—each and every one of our children can succeed!

Sandra F. Rief

Key Information for Understanding and Managing ADHD

Section 1.1: Understanding ADHD

Section 1.2: ADHD and Executive Function Impairment

Section 1.3: Making the Diagnosis: A Comprehensive Evaluation for ADHD

Section 1.4: Multimodal Treatment for ADHD

Section 1.5: Medication Treatment and Management

Section 1.6: Behavioral Therapy for Managing ADHD

Section 1.7: Keys to School Success for Students with ADHD

Section 1.8: ADHD in Preschool and Kindergarten

Section 1.9: ADHD in Middle School and High School

1.1

Understanding ADHD

Clarifying Terms and Labels

ADHD (attention-deficit/hyperactivity disorder) is the umbrella term or diagnostic label established by the American Psychiatric Association. It is inclusive of three presentations (or kinds) of the disorder: predominantly inattentive, predominantly hyperactive-impulsive, and combined (meeting diagnostic criteria for both inattentive and hyperactive-impulsive ADHD). Many people prefer to use the term ADD when referring to individuals with predominantly inattentive ADHD, and that presentation is also referred to as such in federal education law (IDEA). Although I use ADD/ADHD in the title of this book, as I have done since the first edition was published in 1993, throughout the remainder of this book, I will be using only the label of ADHD, which is inclusive of all three presentations of this disorder.

Descriptions and Definitions

Some of the definitions and descriptions of ADHD have been changed or refined as a result of all that we have learned in recent years from neuroscience, brain imaging, and clinical studies, and likely will continue to change in the future. Until recently, ADHD was classified as a neurobehavioral disorder, characterized by the three core symptoms of inattention, impulsivity, and sometimes hyperactivity.

It is now recognized that ADHD is a far more complex disorder, involving impairment in a whole range of abilities related to self-regulation and executive functioning. This more recent understanding of ADHD is reflected in some of the following descriptions, as shared by leading ADHD authorities and based on the most widely held beliefs of the scientific community at this time:

- ADHD is a neurobiological disorder characterized by chronic and developmentally inappropriate degrees of inattention, impulsivity, and in some cases hyperactivity, and is so pervasive and persistent that it interferes with a person's daily life at home, school, work, or other settings.
- ADHD is a disorder of self-regulation and executive functions.
- ADHD is a brain-based disorder involving a wide range of executive dysfunctions that arises out of differences in the central nervous system—both in structural and neurochemical areas.
- ADHD represents a condition that leads individuals to fall to the bottom of a normal distribution in their capacity to demonstrate and develop self-control and self-regulatory skills.

- ADHD is a developmental impairment of the brain's self-management system. It involves a wide range of executive functions linked to complex brain operations that are not limited to observable behaviors.
- ADHD is a neurological inefficiency in the area of the brain that controls impulses and is the center of executive functions.
- ADHD is a dimensional disorder of human behaviors that all people exhibit at times to certain degrees. Those with ADHD display the symptoms to a significant degree that is maladaptive and developmentally inappropriate compared to others at that age.
- ADHD is a common although highly varied condition. One element of this variation is the frequent co-occurrence of other conditions.

Signs and Symptoms

In making a diagnosis of ADHD, a qualified clinician does so based on the criteria set forth in the fifth edition of the *Diagnostic and Statistical Manual of Mental Disorders* (*DSM-5*), published in 2013 by the American Psychiatric Association, which is discussed further in Section 1.3. The *DSM* lists nine specific symptoms under the category of **inattention** and nine specific symptoms under the **hyperactive-impulsive** category. Part of the diagnostic criteria for ADHD is that the child, teen, or adult often displays a significant number of symptoms of *either* the inattentive *or* the hyperactive-impulsive categories *or* in both categories.

Following are lists of behaviors or observable symptoms that are common in children and teens with ADHD. Those symptoms that are found in the *DSM-5* criteria are *italicized* and listed as the first nine bullets in each category. Additional symptoms associated with ADHD are also included; they are not italicized.

Most people display some of the following behaviors at times and in different situations to a certain degree. Those who have the disorder have a history of frequently exhibiting many of these behaviors beyond the normal range developmentally when compared to their peers, in multiple settings (such as home, school, social, and workplace), and

to the degree that they interfere with or reduce the quality of their functioning. Such a history is a red flag that an evaluation for ADHD by a well-qualified professional should be considered.

Symptoms of Inattention and Associated Problems

- *Often fails to give close attention to details or makes careless mistakes in schoolwork, at work, or with other activities.*
- *Often has trouble holding attention on tasks or play activities.*
- *Often does not seem to listen when spoken to directly.*
- *Often does not follow through on instructions and fails to finish schoolwork, chores, or duties in the workplace (for example, loses focus, side-tracked). Note: This is not due to oppositional behavior or failure to understand instructions.*
- *Often has trouble organizing tasks and activities.*
- *Often avoids, dislikes, or is reluctant to do tasks that require mental effort over a long period of time (such as schoolwork or homework).*
- *Often loses things necessary for tasks and activities (for example, school materials, pencils, books, tools, wallets, keys, paperwork, eyeglasses, mobile telephones).*
- *Is often easily distracted.*
- *Is often forgetful in daily activities.*
- Has difficulty concentrating and is easily pulled off task.
- Tunes out, daydreams, may appear "spacey."
- Requires a lot of adult prompts and refocusing to complete tasks.
- Has many incomplete assignments and unfinished tasks.
- Has difficulty working independently; needs a high degree of supervision and redirecting of attention to task at hand.
- Exhibits poor listening: not following directions, being pulled off topic in conversations, not focusing on the speaker.
- Makes many errors with academic tasks requiring attention to details and accuracy

DECKER
FORREST

(such as math computation, spelling, and written mechanics).

- Cannot stay focused on what he or she is reading (loses place, misses words and details, needs to reread the material).
- Exhibits poor study skills, such as test-taking and note-taking skills.
- Goes off topic in writing, losing train of thought.
- Makes many written errors in capitalization and punctuation; has difficulty editing own work for such errors.
- Makes numerous computational errors in math due to inattention to operational signs (plus, minus, multiplication, division), decimal points, and so forth.
- Appears to have slower speed of processing information (for example, responding to teacher questions or keeping up with class discussions).

- Misses verbal and nonverbal cues, which affects social skills.
- Does not participate in class, or participates minimally.

Symptoms of Hyperactivity and Impulsivity and Associated Problems

- *Often fidgets with or taps hands or feet, or squirms in seat.*
- *Often leaves seat in situations when remaining seated is expected.*
- *Often runs about or climbs in situations where it is not appropriate (adolescents or adults may be limited to feeling restless).*
- *Often unable to play or take part in leisure activities quietly.*
- *Is often "on the go" acting as if "driven by a motor."*
- *Often talks excessively.*

- *Often blurts out an answer before a question has been completed.*
- *Often has trouble waiting his or her turn.*
- *Often interrupts or intrudes on others (for example, butts into conversations or games).*
- Has difficulty keeping hands and feet to self.
- Knows the rules and consequences, but repeatedly commits the same errors or infractions of rules.
- Has difficulty standing in lines.
- Gets in trouble because he or she cannot stop and think before acting (responds first, thinks later).
- Does not think or worry about consequences, so tends to be fearless or to gravitate toward high-risk behavior.
- Is accident prone and breaks things.
- Has difficulty inhibiting what he or she says, making tactless comments; says whatever pops into his or her head and talks back to authority figures.

- Begins tasks without waiting for directions (before listening to the full direction or taking the time to read written directions).
- Hurries through tasks, particularly boring ones, and consequently makes numerous careless errors.
- Gets easily bored and impatient.
- Does not take time to correct or edit work.
- Disrupts, bothers others.
- Is highly energetic, in almost nonstop motion.
- Engages in physically dangerous activities (for example, jumping from heights, riding bike into the street without looking); hence, has a high frequency of injuries.
- Cannot sit still in chair (is in and out of chair, rocks and tips chair over, sits on knees, or stands by desk) or sit long enough to perform required tasks.
- Engages in a high degree of unnecessary movement (pacing, tapping feet, bouncing leg, tapping pencil, drumming fingers).

- Seems to need something in hands; finds or reaches for nearby objects to play with or put in mouth.
- Intrudes in other people's space; has difficulty staying within own boundaries.
- Cannot wait or delay gratification; wants things immediately.
- Is constantly drawn to something more interesting or stimulating in the environment.
- Hits when upset or grabs things away from others (not inhibiting responses or thinking of consequences).
- Becomes overstimulated and excitable and has difficulty calming himself or herself or settling down.
- Appears to live in the moment, acting without foresight or hindsight.
- Is easily pulled off task, affecting work performance and class participation.
- Is a greater challenge to motivate and discipline (not responding as well to typical rewards or punishments effective for most students).

Other Common Difficulties Experienced by Children and Teens with ADHD

In addition to symptoms related to inattention, hyperactivity, and impulsivity, other challenges related to executive function and self-regulation weaknesses as well as common coexisting conditions (such as learning disabilities) are often evident in individuals with ADHD. Some include the following:

Social and Emotional

- Experiences a high degree of emotionality (for example, has temper outbursts, is quick to anger, gets upset, is irritable or moody)
- Is easily upset or frustrated and has a hard time coping with or managing his or her anger and other negative emotions
- Is overly reactive; is easily provoked to engage in fighting and inappropriate means of resolving conflicts
- Has difficulty with transitions and changes in routine or activity
- Displays aggressive behavior

DECKER FORREST

- Receives a lot of negative attention and interaction from peers and adults
- Has difficulty working in cooperative groups or getting along with peers in work or play situations
- Gets along better with younger children
- Has immature social skills

Organization and Time Management

- Is disorganized—frequently misplaces or loses belongings; desks, backpacks, lockers, and rooms are often messy and chaotic
- Is unprepared with materials and books needed for schoolwork and homework
- Has poorly organized work, such as writing assignments
- Has little or no awareness of time; is chronically late; often underestimates the length of time a task will require to complete or how long it takes to get somewhere

- Has great difficulty with long-term assignments and projects, scrambling at the last minute to complete important assignments
- Misses deadlines and due dates

Other Executive Skills

- Has forgetfulness/memory issues (not remembering or following all parts of the directions, not remembering to turn in homework even when he or she completed it)
- Has difficulty with planning and follow-through (failing to think through all of the steps or components of a task and having particular difficulty with long-term assignments and projects)
- Has difficulty with tasks requiring a heavy memory load
- Plans poorly for assignments and projects
- Has difficulty prioritizing
- Has difficulty initiating or getting started on tasks

Learning, Language, Academic

- Has learning and school performance difficulties; is not achieving or performing to the level that is expected given his or her apparent ability
- Has language and communication problems (for example, not sticking to topic, not fluent verbally)

- Employs inefficient learning strategies
- Has poor handwriting and fine motor skills
- Experiences problem-solving difficulties
- Performs inconsistently: one day can perform a task, next day cannot
- Takes a lot longer than average time to process information or complete tasks and assignments
- Has difficulty with reading comprehension, written expression, mathematical problem solving (or other complex or lengthy academic tasks that require a heavy working memory load, planning and organization of thoughts and information, and self-monitoring or self-correction throughout the process)
- (If learning disabilities, such as dyslexia, coexist) Has more significant difficulty with basic reading skills (word recognition and fluency, writing, spelling)

Note: *Academic difficulties related to inattention, impulsivity, and executive dysfunctions will be discussed in depth in Part 4 of this book.*

Three Presentations of ADHD

As noted earlier, there are three types or what are now called "presentations" of ADHD, based on the symptoms. Although all people will exhibit these behaviors at times to a certain degree, for those with ADHD, the symptoms far exceed that which is normal developmentally (in frequency, level, and intensity), have been evident and problematic in multiple settings for at least the past six months, and interfere with the person's functioning or development. There are other diagnostic criteria that must be met as well, which will be described in more depth in Section 1.3.

Predominantly Inattentive

This presentation is what some people prefer to call ADD, because those who receive this diagnosis do not have the hyperactive symptoms. They may show some of them, but not a significant amount. These children and teens often slip through the cracks and are not as easily identified or understood. Because they do not exhibit the disruptive behaviors associated with ADHD, it is easy to overlook these students and misinterpret their behaviors and symptoms as "not trying" or "being lazy." Many girls have the predominantly inattentive presentation of the disorder.

Be aware that people with ADHD who have significant attention difficulties are often able to be focused and to sustain attention for long periods of time when they play video games or are engaged in other high-interest, stimulating, and rapidly changing activities. In fact, many hyper-focus on such activities and have a hard time disengaging from them.

Predominantly Hyperactive-Impulsive

Individuals with this presentation of ADHD have a significant number of hyperactive-impulsive symptoms. They may have some inattentive symptoms that are developmentally inappropriate, but not a significant number of them.

Hyperactive-impulsive ADHD (without the inattention) is most commonly diagnosed in early childhood. Children receiving this diagnosis are often reclassified as having the combined presentation of ADHD when they get older and the inattentive symptoms emerge more and become developmentally significant.

Combined

This is the most common presentation of ADHD—a significant number of symptoms exist in both the inattentive category and the hyperactive-impulsive category.

Please note: More information on signs and symptoms of ADHD is found in other sections of this book, such as those describing executive function difficulties, symptoms in girls, and what ADHD looks like at different grade levels or ages (preschool through high school).

Formula ONE for Disaster
take ONE impulsive child
add ONE forbidden object
multiply by ONE minute
to equal
ONE predictable trip to the emergency
room . . .

Karen Easter ©1995

Statistics and Risk Factors

The number of people estimated to have ADHD varies, depending on the source, which can be confusing. Here are some of the reported prevalence rates:

- Conservatively 5–8 percent of school-age children have ADHD (Barkley, 2013).
- Approximately 11 percent of children four to seventeen years of age (6.4 million) have been diagnosed with ADHD as of 2011, according to the results of surveys that asked parents whether their child received an ADHD diagnosis from a health care provider (Centers for Disease Control and Prevention [CDC], n.d.).
- Based on the CDC analysis of data from the National Survey of Children's Health, which has been collected every four years since 2003, the percentage of children diagnosed with ADHD increased from 7.8 percent in 2003 to 9.5 percent in 2007 and to 11.0 percent in 2011 (CDC, n.d.).

- The worldwide prevalence of ADHD for children is approximately 5 percent, based on a review of over one hundred studies comprising subjects from all world regions (Polanczyk et al., 2007).
- Studies throughout the world have reported the occurrence of ADHD in school-age children as being between 5 and 12 percent. This means that on average, there are at least one to three children in every class with ADHD (Centre for ADHD Awareness, Canada, n.d.).

ADHD is associated with a number of risk factors. ADHD places those who have this disorder at risk for a host of serious consequences, which increases the urgency of early identification, diagnosis, and proper treatment. Numerous studies (Barkley et al., 2002; Barkley, 2013) have demonstrated the increased risk of negative outcomes associated with those who have ADHD. Compared to their peers of the same age, youth with ADHD experience

- More serious accidents and hospitalizations, and significantly higher medical costs than those children without ADHD
- More school failure and dropout
- More delinquency and altercations with the law
- More engagement in antisocial activities
- More teen pregnancy and sexually transmitted diseases
- Earlier experimentation with and higher use of alcohol, tobacco, and illicit drugs
- More trouble socially and emotionally
- More rejection, ridicule, and punishment
- More underachievement and underperformance at school or work

Dr. Russell Barkley (2013), one of the world's leading ADHD experts and researchers, has also found the following to be true:

- Up to 58 percent of youth with ADHD may be retained in a grade in school at least once.
- As many as 35 percent fail to complete high school.
- For half of children with ADHD, social relationships are seriously impaired.

- More than 25 percent of ADHD youth are expelled from high school because of serious misconduct.
- More than 30 percent of youth with ADHD have engaged in theft.
- More than 40 percent of youth with ADHD drift into early tobacco and alcohol use.
- Adolescents and young adults with a diagnosis of ADHD have nearly four to five times as many traffic citations for speeding, two to three times as many auto accidents, and accidents that are two to three times more expensive in damages or likely to cause bodily injuries as young drivers without ADHD.

Note: Compared to the general population, people with ADHD are at greater risk than others for negative outcomes (as described). However, when children with ADHD are provided with supports and effective treatments and intervention, the risks are reduced substantially.

ADHD and Coexisting Disorders

ADHD is often accompanied by one or more other conditions or disorders—psychiatric, psychological, developmental, or medical. Because symptoms of these various disorders commonly overlap, diagnosis and treatment can be complex. The word *comorbidity* is the medical term for having coexisting disorders (co-occurring and presenting at the same time as ADHD).

Approximately two-thirds of individuals with ADHD have at least one other coexisting condition, such as learning disabilities, oppositional defiant disorder, anxiety disorder, conduct disorder, Tourette Syndrome, or depression (MTA Cooperative Group, 1999; National Resource Center on AD/HD, 2015). The most common conditions comorbid with ADHD in childhood are oppositional defiant disorder (ODD) and conduct disorder (CD). In adulthood, the most common comorbid conditions with ADHD are depression and anxiety (Goldstein, 2009).

Coexisting disorders can cause significant impairment above and beyond the problems caused by ADHD. It can take time for all the pieces of the puzzle to come together, and parents, teachers, and clinicians need to monitor the child's development and any emerging concerns. Effective intervention will require treatment for the ADHD and the other conditions.

Common Coexisting Conditions and Disorders

The reported prevalence of specific coexisting conditions and disorders accompanying ADHD varies depending on the source. Most sources indicate the following ranges:

Oppositional defiant disorder (ODD). Approximately 40 percent of children and teens with ADHD develop ODD (National Resource Center on AD/HD, 2015). It occurs eleven times more frequently in children with ADHD than in the general population (Barkley, 2013).

Anxiety disorder. Up to 30 percent of children and up to 53 percent of adults with ADHD have this disorder (National Resource Center on AD/HD, 2015).

Conduct disorder (CD). Approximately 27 percent of children, 45–50 percent of adolescents, and 20–25 percent of adults have this disorder (National Resource Center on AD/HD, 2015).

Bipolar. Up to 20 percent of people with ADHD may manifest bipolar disorder (National Resource Center on AD/HD, 2015).

Depression. Approximately 14 percent of children with ADHD and up to 47 percent of adolescents and adults have this disorder (National Resource Center on AD/HD, 2015).

Tics, Tourette Syndrome. About 7 percent of those with ADHD have tics or Tourette Syndrome, but 60 to 80 percent of Tourette Syndrome patients also have ADHD (National Resource Center on AD/HD, 2015).

Learning disabilities. The reported range is from 20 to 60 percent, with most sources estimating that between one-quarter and one-half of children with ADHD have a coexisting learning disability (such as dyslexia). "Up to 50 percent of children with ADHD have a coexisting learning disorder, whereas 5 percent of children without ADHD have learning disorders" (National Resource Center on AD/HD, 2015, p. 2).

Obsessive-compulsive disorder (OCD). Up to one-third of people with ADHD may have OCD (Goodman, 2010; Kutscher, 2010).

Sleep disorders. One-quarter to one-half of parents of children with ADHD report that their children suffer from a sleep problem, especially problems with falling asleep and staying asleep (National Resource Center on AD/HD, 2015).

Other Disorders and Conditions

- Between 12 and nearly 20–30 percent of children and teens with ADHD also have some form of challenge in the area of speech and language (National Resource Center on AD/HD, 2015; Spencer, 2013).
- Autism spectrum disorder (ASD) is now recognized as a possible coexisting disorder with ADHD and was added to the *DSM-5* as such.
- ASD symptoms are more common in children with ADHD than in the general population. In some studies, nearly 50 percent of youth with ASD meet diagnostic criteria for ADHD (Goldstein, 2010).

Identifying and Treating Coexisting Disorders

Most children with ADHD have some school-related achievement, performance, or social problems. It is important that they receive the educational supports and interventions they need.

Because a high percentage of children with ADHD also have learning disabilities, such as dyslexia, the school district should evaluate the student when a possible learning disability is suspected. Parents are advised to request an evaluation if they are concerned that their child may have coexisting learning disabilities.

Parents, educators, and medical and mental health care providers should be alert to signs of other mental health disorders that may exist or emerge, often in the adolescent years, especially when current strategies and treatments being used to help the child or teen with ADHD are no longer working effectively. Anxiety disorder and depression can easily go unrecognized and overlooked. There is a high rate of these internalized disorders, particularly among teenage girls.

ADHD Look-Alikes

Not everyone who displays symptoms of ADHD has the disorder. There are a number of other conditions and factors (medical, psychological, learning, psychiatric, emotional, social, and environmental) that can cause inattentive, hyperactive, and impulsive behaviors that resemble ADHD or that may coexist with ADHD, such as

- Learning disabilities
- Sensory impairments (hearing, vision, or motor problems)
- Substance use and abuse (of alcohol and drugs)
- Oppositional defiant disorder
- Conduct disorder
- Allergies
- Posttraumatic stress disorder (PTSD)
- Anxiety disorder
- Depression
- Obsessive-compulsive disorder
- Sleep disorder
- Bipolar disorder
- Thyroid problems
- Rare genetic disorders (for example, Fragile X syndrome)
- Seizure disorders
- Sluggish cognitive tempo

- Lead poisoning
- Hypoglycemia
- Anemia
- Fetal alcohol syndrome and fetal alcohol effects
- Chronic illness
- Language disorders
- Auditory processing disorders
- Visual processing disorders
- Tourette Syndrome
- Autism spectrum disorder
- Developmental delays
- Sensory integration dysfunction
- Low intellectual ability
- High intellectual ability or giftedness
- Chronic ear infections
- Severe emotional disturbance
- Side effects of medications being taken (such as antiseizure or asthma medication)

Emotional and environmental factors that have nothing to do with ADHD can also cause a child or teen to be distracted and unable to concentrate, or to exhibit acting-out or aggressive behaviors—for example, if the child or teen is experiencing high-stress circumstances, such as the following:

- Experiencing or witnessing abuse or violence
- Family stresses (for example, divorce and custody battles, death of a loved one, financial difficulties)
- Bullying or peer pressure and other social issues
- A chaotic, unpredictable, unstable, or neglectful home life with inappropriate expectations placed on the child

Inattention and disruptive classroom behaviors can be school related (having nothing to do with ADHD). Students may display those behaviors if they are in a school environment with these characteristics:

- A pervasive negative climate
- Poor instruction and low academic expectations
- Nonstimulating and unmotivating curriculum
- Ineffective classroom management

What Is Currently Known about ADHD

ADHD has been the focus of a tremendous amount of research, particularly during the past three decades. Literally thousands of studies and scientific articles have been published (nationally and internationally) on ADHD. All of the advances in neuroscience and the sophisticated brain imaging technologies and genetic research in recent years have dramatically increased our knowledge of ADHD—the brain differences and probable causes of the disorder.

What We Know

- ADHD is not a myth. It has been recognized as a very real, valid, and significant disorder by the US surgeon general, the National Institutes of Health, the US Department of Education, the Centers for Disease Control and Prevention, and all of the major medical and mental health associations.
- ADHD is not new. It has been recognized by clinical science and documented in the literature since 1902 (having been renamed several times). Some of the previous names for the disorder were *minimal brain dysfunction, hyperactive child syndrome,* and *ADD* with or without hyperactivity.
- There is no quick fix or cure for ADHD, but it is treatable and manageable. Proper diagnosis and treatment can substantially decrease ADHD symptoms and impairment in functioning and greatly increase positive outcomes.
- ADHD is not just a childhood disorder. Up to 80 percent of children diagnosed with ADHD continue to have the disorder into adolescence, and 50–65 percent will continue to exhibit symptoms into adulthood (Barkley, 2013).
- ADHD is a neurobiological disorder that is a result of different factors, the most common cause by far being genetic in origin. Heredity accounts for most cases of ADHD, but there are other problems and factors that occur prenatally, during birth, or in childhood that might interfere with a child's brain development and be contributing causes of ADHD.
- Regardless of the underlying cause, there are on average differences in both the size and function of certain areas of the brain in individuals with ADHD (Wolraich & DuPaul, 2010).
- ADHD exists across all populations, regardless of race, ethnicity, gender, nationality, culture, and socioeconomic level. Many children, teens, and adults with ADHD slip through the cracks without being identified or receiving the intervention and treatment they need.
- ADHD can be managed best by multimodal treatment and a team approach. We know that it takes a team effort on the part of parents, school personnel, clinicians, and other professionals to be most effective in helping children and teens with ADHD. No single intervention effectively manages ADHD for most people with the disorder, and intervention needs change over time.
- ADHD is diagnosed at least two to three times more frequently in boys than girls, although many more girls may actually have ADHD than are identified.
- ADHD is *not* the result of poor parenting. ADHD is *not* laziness, willful misbehavior, or a character flaw. The challenging behaviors that children with ADHD exhibit stem from neurobiological differences. Their behaviors are not deliberate. Children with ADHD are often not even aware of their behaviors and their impact on others.
- Although ADHD is most commonly diagnosed in school-age children, it can be and is diagnosed reliably in younger children and adults.
- Most children who are diagnosed and provided with the help they need are able to manage the disorder. Parents should maintain a positive mind-set and be optimistic about their child's future. ADHD does not limit their child's potential. Countless highly successful adults in every profession and walk of life have ADHD.

- Medication therapy and behavioral therapy are research-validated, effective treatments for ADHD. Medications used to treat ADHD are proven to work effectively for reducing the symptoms and impairment in 70–95 percent of children diagnosed with ADHD. Use of a token economy or daily report card system between home and school are among the behavioral interventions and programs that help in the management of ADHD. (See Sections 1.5, 1.6, 2.3, and 2.4 for more on these topics and tools to use.)
- The teaching techniques and strategies that are necessary for the success of children with ADHD are good teaching practices and are typically helpful for all students.
- There is still need for better diagnosis, education, and treatment of this disorder that affects so many lives.

We Do Not Yet Know Enough about . . .

- All of the causes
- How to prevent ADHD or minimize the risk factors and negative effects
- Diagnosing and treating the disorder in certain populations (very young children, females, adults, and racial and ethnic minorities), and cultural variables that may exist—as the majority of research in past decades was studying ADHD in school-age white boys
- Long-term treatment effects
- The inattentive type of ADHD
- What may prove to be the best, most effective diagnostic tools, treatments, and strategies for helping individuals with ADHD

ADHD Brain Differences

The evidence from hundreds of well-designed and controlled scientific studies (metabolic, brain imaging, and genetic) indicates that in people with ADHD, there are brain differences: abnormalities in size, maturation, and levels of activity in the regions of the brain involved in executive functions and self-regulation.

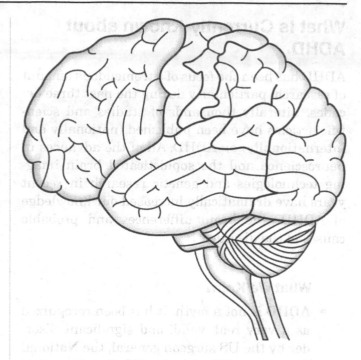

Recent brain imaging research also suggests weaker connections in some important networks (brain regions that activate together to perform a complex task) in individuals with ADHD, including the cognitive control and salience networks, reward and motivation networks, and the "default mode" network (DMN) (Norr, 2015).

Note: *Although imaging tests and brain scans such as functional magnetic resonance imaging (fMRI), single photon emission computed tomography (SPECT), positron emission tomography (PET), and electroencephalograms (EEGs) are used in researching ADHD, they are not used in the diagnosis of ADHD.*

Delayed Brain Maturation and Structural Differences

Recent research has shown that delayed maturation in specific areas of the brain plays a significant part in ADHD.

According to Dr. Thomas Brown (2013b), "Individuals with ADHD have been shown to differ in the rate of maturation of specific areas of the cortex, in the thickness of cortical tissue, in characteristics of the parietal and cerebellar regions, as well as in the basal ganglia, and in the white matter tracts that connect and provide critically important communication between various regions of the brain." Recent research has also shown that the brains of those with ADHD tend to have different patterns in functional connectivity, patterns of oscillations that allow different regions of the brain to exchange information.

Dr. Philip Shaw and other researchers at the National Institute of Mental Health used brain imaging technology to study the brain maturation of hundreds of children and teens with and without ADHD and reported their findings in 2007. They found that in youth with ADHD, the brain matures in a normal pattern, but there is approximately a three-year delay in some regions compared to other children, particularly in the frontal cortex (American Psychological Association, 2008; Shaw et al., 2007).

Neuroimaging studies have found that on average, children with ADHD have about a 5 percent reduction in total volume and a 10–12 percent reduction in the size of four or five key brain regions involved in higher-order control of behavior (Nigg, 2006).

Diminished Activity and Lower Metabolism in Certain Brain Regions

Numerous studies measuring electrical activity, blood flow, and brain activity have found differences between those with ADHD and those without ADHD:

- Decreased activity level in certain regions of the brain (mainly the frontal region and basal ganglia). These underactivated regions are responsible for controlling activity level, impulsivity, attention, and executive functions.
- Lower metabolism of glucose (the brain's energy source) in the frontal region.
- Decreased blood flow to certain brain regions associated with ADHD.
- Less electrical activity in these key areas of the brain.

Brain Chemical (Neurotransmitter) Inefficiency

There is significant evidence that those with ADHD have a deficiency or inefficiency in brain chemicals (neurotransmitters) operating in certain brain regions associated with ADHD. The two main neurotransmitters involved in ADHD are dopamine and norepinephrine. Other brain chemicals also play a part in the disorder and are being studied.

Dopamine is involved in regulating, among other things, attention, inhibition, motivation, motor activity, and emotional responses. It plays a major role in ADHD. Genetic research has found that some of the dopamine receptor and transporter genes are altered or not working properly.

Neurotransmitters are the chemical messengers of the brain. The neurons in the brain are not connected; they have a synapse, or tiny gap, between them where nerve impulses are sent from one neuron to another. The neurotransmitters help carry messages between two neurons by being released into the synapse and then being recycled or reloaded once the message gets across. It is believed that with ADHD, those essential brain chemicals may not be efficiently releasing and staying long enough in the synapse in order to do their job of getting the message across effectively in those key regions and circuits of the brain. Research indicates that individuals with ADHD may have disturbances in their dopamine signaling systems.

Brown (2013a) explains that the problem with ADHD is not one of a generalized chemical deficiency or imbalance: "The primary problem is related to chemicals manufactured, released, and then reloaded at the level of synapses, the trillions of infinitesimal junctions between certain networks of neurons that manage critical activities within the brain's management system" (p. 8).

Causes of ADHD

Heredity

According to the evidence, heredity is the most common cause of ADHD, accounting for approximately 75–80 percent of children with this disorder (Barkley, 1998, 2013).

- ADHD is known to run in families, as found by numerous studies (of identical and fraternal twins, adopted children, families, and molecular genetics). For example, in studies of identical twins, if one has ADHD, there is as high as a 75–90 percent chance that the other twin will have ADHD as well (Barkley, 2013).

- It is believed that a genetic predisposition to the disorder is inherited. Children with ADHD will frequently have a parent, sibling, grandparent, or other close relative with ADHD—or whose history indicates they had similar problems and symptoms during childhood.

- ADHD is a complex disorder, which likely involves multiple interacting genes.

- Genetic research involving several methods have so far identified at least nine genes that link to ADHD—at least three involving the regulation of dopamine levels (two dopamine receptor genes and a dopamine transporter gene). Other genes have also been identified that affect brain growth, how nerve cells migrate during development to arrive at their normal sites, and the way in which nerve cells connect to each other (Barkley, 2013).

- The genetic contribution to ADHD has been thought to reflect differences in certain brain structures and in brain chemistry, as well as the interaction of the two (Goldstein, 2007).

- Research suggests that certain genes or alterations in some genes may be inherited and influence the development or maturation of certain areas of the brain or affect the regulation or efficiency of certain brain chemicals. Other researchers suggest that children who carry certain genes may be more vulnerable than other children to various environmental factors associated with ADHD symptoms.

Birth Complications, Illnesses, and Brain Injury

These are other factors that raise the risk for ADHD and may lead to its development:

- Premature birth and significantly low birth weight
- Trauma or head injury to the frontal part of the brain
- Certain illnesses that affect the brain, such as encephalitis
- Birth complications, such as toxemia

Maternal or Childhood Exposure to Certain Toxins

Certain substances the pregnant mother consumes or to which she exposes the developing fetus increase risk factors and may be a cause for ADHD in some children. This includes fetal exposure to alcohol, tobacco, and high levels of lead.

Other Environmental Factors

- It is generally believed in the scientific community that environmental factors (for example, lack of structure in the environment, stress, diet) influence the severity of ADHD symptoms, but are not the cause of ADHD.

- "Research does not support the popularly held views that ADHD arises from excessive sugar intake, excessive television viewing, poor child management by parents, or social and environmental factors such as poverty or family chaos. Of course, many things, including these, might aggravate symptoms, especially in certain individuals. But the evidence for such individual aggravating circumstances is not strong enough to conclude that they are primary causes of ADHD" (National Resource Center on AD/HD, n.d.).

- Of concern to many people are the unknown effects of all the chemicals in our environment and other toxins. Many are as yet not studied. It is reasonable to assume that future research may identify chemicals and other toxins that affect brain development or brain processes in children and possibly contribute to ADHD or other disorders.

Girls with ADHD

Girls most commonly have the inattentive presentation (type) of ADHD. Many girls do not receive diagnoses or treatment because they do not have the typical hyperactive and disruptive symptoms seen in boys that signal a problem and lead to a referral. Girls also tend to be teacher pleasers and often put a lot of effort into trying to hide their problems. Girls being evaluated for ADHD also may not receive a diagnosis because the *DSM* criteria until very recently required that significant symptoms be evident by age seven. We now know that symptoms may emerge later, particularly in girls. Fortunately, the *DSM-5* has acknowledged this later onset of symptoms and changed the criteria so that now symptoms must occur by age twelve, instead of seven.

Many girls are labeled and written off as being "space cadets," "ditzy," or "scattered." The unrecognized struggles of girls with ADHD and their need for proper diagnosis and treatment place them at high risk for a number of serious negative outcomes (academic and learning problems; social, behavioral, and emotional problems; demoralization; low self-esteem; and more).

Many girls don't receive an evaluation for ADHD because parents, teachers, and physicians are often unaware that ADHD symptoms manifest differently in girls than in boys. When they are evaluated (often in their preteens and teen years), girls may receive a misdiagnosis, or a coexisting condition (commonly anxiety disorder or depression) may be identified, missing the primary disorder of ADHD that existed first.

Most of the research on ADHD over the years has been on boys or has had very few girls participating in the studies. In recent years, much more attention has been paid to gender differences, thanks to the work, leadership, and advocacy of Drs. Patricia Quinn, Kathleen Nadeau, Ellen Littman, and others. The scientific community is now looking at gender issues in ADHD, with some significant studies on ADHD in females, such as by the research teams of Drs. Joseph Biederman and Stephen Hinshaw. Much more research still needs to be done to understand the impact of ADHD in females and the best ways to help girls and women with this disorder.

What We Have Learned

According to Nadeau (2000a, 2000b, 2004a, 2004b); Quinn (2008, 2009, 2012); Littman (2000, 2012); Nadeau, Littman, and Quinn (2015); and Quinn and Nadeau (2000, 2004), girls with ADHD present symptoms in these ways:

- Often have impaired social skills
- Often experience academic difficulties and underachievement
- Often experience peer rejection (generally more so than boys with ADHD) and are more devastated by rejection from their peers
- Often unleash frustrations at home that were kept hidden at school; parents may see behaviors in their daughter, such as temper tantrums and meltdowns, that she would never exhibit at school
- Are self-critical and often feel a sense of shame
- Have more internalized and less externalized (observable) symptoms, such as biting nails or pulling hair
- Have verbal expression and processing problems that are more problematic than they are in boys because so many of girls' interactions rely heavily on verbal communication and demands
- Experience a lot of difficulty with executive function impairment (disorganization,

prioritization, poor time management, working memory difficulties, emotional regulation)

Girls with the inattentive presentation of ADHD often present with these characteristics:

- Shy, timid, withdrawn, introverted
- Passive, daydreaming
- Reluctant to participate in class
- Quick to give up when frustrated
- Often overwhelmed

Girls with hyperactivity and impulsivity often present with these symptoms:

- Hyperverbal and hypersocial behavior (cannot stop talking, chatting, commenting on everything)
- Much giggling, "silly" and immature behavior
- Emotional overreactivity (lots of drama)
- Disruptive behavior (as is also seen in boys with ADHD)

These girls

- Stand out, because their behavior is significantly out of norm (compared to other girls their age)
- Show hyperactive and impulsive symptoms that often look different from what is commonly seen in boys
- Begin to have social problems as early as preschool
- Are at greater risk for consequences stemming from poor self-control combined with lower self-esteem; impulsivity in girls can lead to high-risk activities, such as smoking, drinking, drugs, sexual promiscuity, engaging in unprotected sex, or binge eating
- Are at a much higher risk for self-harm—suicide attempts and self-injury (Hinshaw et al., 2012)

We also know that for girls the following are often true:

- Symptoms get worse at puberty with hormonal changes. Premenstrual syndrome, for example, presents additional problems, worsening ADHD symptoms by adding to

irritability, low frustration threshold, mood swings, and emotionality.
- They often work exceptionally hard (compulsively so) to achieve academic success and cover up their difficulties.
- Low self-esteem is evident and begins at a young age.
- They commonly develop anxiety disorder or depression by their teen years. Quinn (2008) reports that girls with ADHD are four to five times more likely to be diagnosed with a major depression and three times more likely to be treated for depression prior to their ADHD diagnosis.
- They tend toward addictive behaviors offering immediate gratification in terms of self-medication and peer acceptance (Littman, 2012).

Positive Traits and Strengths

Parents and teachers must recognize, appreciate, and nurture the many talents and positive qualities our children possess. To develop their self-esteem and enable them to become resilient, successful adults, we must help our children value their areas of competency and strengths. The following are some common positive characteristics and traits that many of those with ADHD possess:

- Energetic
- Spontaneous
- Creative
- Persistent
- Innovative
- Imaginative
- Tenacious
- Big-hearted
- Accepting and forgiving
- Enterprising
- Ready for action
- Inquisitive
- Adventurous
- Resilient
- Resourceful
- Risk-taking
- Entrepreneurial
- Inventive

- Observant
- Empathetic
- Charming
- Full of ideas and spunk
- Intelligent
- Enthusiastic
- Outgoing, gregarious
- Optimistic
- Charismatic
- Playful
- Passionate
- Willing to take a chance and try new things
- Good at improvising
- Able to find novel solutions
- Good in crisis situations and thinking on their feet
- Talented (artistically, musically, athletically)

And they typically

- Know how to live in and enjoy the present
- Are independent thinkers
- Have a good sense of humor
- Are never boring

ADHD and the Impact on the Family

It is important to be aware of the challenges that exist in the home when one or more children (and possibly a parent) have ADHD, as this disorder significantly affects the entire family. Unfortunately, teachers are generally unaware of or underestimate the struggles that families face. Typically, in homes of children with ADHD, there is a much higher degree of stress than the average family experiences, along with depression or other pathology in one or more family members.

Living with a child who has ADHD often takes a heavy toll on marriages. It is common for parents to be in different stages of a "grieving process" about having a child who struggles compared to other children. For example, one parent may be in the denial or anger stage, and the other parent has progressed to acceptance and is eager to begin a course of intervention for the child. It is common for parents to disagree about treatment, discipline, management, structure, and other issues. There are generally major issues

surrounding the battle with homework as well as with morning and evening routines (getting ready for school and bedtime).

Parents may blame one another for the child's problems or be highly critical of one another in their parenting role. This discord causes a great deal of marital stress. Often it is the mother who must cope with the brunt of the issues throughout the day, which is physically and emotionally exhausting. As any parent of a toddler knows, having a child who needs constant supervision and monitoring is very time-consuming and interferes with the ability to get things done as planned (for example, housework and other chores). In single-parent homes, it is even more challenging.

Parents of children who have ADHD are constantly faced with needing to defend their parenting choices as well as their child. They must listen to negative press about this disorder and reject popular opinion in order to provide their child with necessary interventions and treatment. Parents must deal with criticism and "well-meaning" advice from relatives, friends, and acquaintances regarding how they should discipline and parent their child. They may feel unsupported by extended family and also experience social isolation. This causes a lot of parental self-doubt and adds to the stress they are already living with day in and day out.

The family must frequently deal with social issues, such as the exclusion of the child from out-of-school activities. It is painful when your child is not invited to birthday parties or has difficulty finding someone to play with and keeping friends. Siblings are often resentful or even jealous of the central role their ADHD sibling plays in the family's schedule, routines, and activities, as well as the extra time and special treatment this child receives. In addition, siblings feel hurt and embarrassed when their brother or sister has acquired a negative reputation in the neighborhood and school.

Parents of children with ADHD have a much higher degree of responsibility than is typical for other parents in working with the school, communicating closely with teachers, and advocating for the needs of their child. There is also the financial impact of treatment costs that may or may not be covered by insurance. All of these issues can be stressful for families.

It is likely that more than one family member (a parent or sibling) also has ADHD. In many cases, other family members who have ADHD were never diagnosed and have been struggling to cope with their own difficulties without proper treatment and support. That is why the clinicians who specialize in treating children with ADHD say it is important to view treatment in the context of the family. Learning about the family (for example, the ways the members communicate

and their disciplinary practices) helps in designing a treatment plan that is most effective for the child.

Commonly a parent recognizes for the first time that he or she has been suffering with undiagnosed ADHD for years when a son or daughter receives an ADHD diagnosis. This realization can result in a positive change in the family dynamics.

Without question, families of children with ADHD need support and understanding. Fortunately, there are many supports available and ways to help.

ADHD and Executive Function Impairment

Extensive research has led to ADHD now being recognized as a disorder in the development of *executive functions*—a person's self-management and self-regulatory abilities. People with ADHD experience a wide range of executive dysfunction issues that can vary from person to person.

What are executive functions, and how is executive function (EF) impairment related to ADHD? Dr. Russell Barkley (2012) explains:

> ADHD is a disorder of self-regulation. Self-regulation requires that a person have intact executive functions (EFs). The EFs are specific types of self-regulation or self-directed actions that people use to manage themselves effectively in order to sustain their actions (and problem-solving) toward their goals and the future. (p. 7)

Definitions of Executive Function (EF)

EFs have been described in many ways:

- The management functions (overseers) of the brain
- The self-directed actions individuals use to help maintain control of themselves and accomplish goals

- The range of central control processes in the brain that activate, organize, focus, integrate, and manage other brain functions and cognitive skills
- The higher-order cognitive processes involved in the self-regulation of behavior
- Cognitive processes or brain functions that enable a person to engage in problem-solving and goal-directed behaviors
- The broad set of cognitive skills used to organize, self-monitor, control, and direct our behavior toward purposeful goals

EF Analogies and Metaphors

Executive function and EF impairment are sometimes explained using the following analogies and metaphors:

Conductor of a symphony orchestra. Dr. Thomas E. Brown and others use this popular analogy of EFs having a role like that of the conductor of a symphony orchestra, responsible for integrating and managing all of the different components for a successful performance. If the conductor fails to do his or her job well, even with very skilled musicians, the performance will be poor.

Chief executive officer (CEO). Many experts explain the role of executive functions as being similar to that of a successful corporate CEO: analyzing a task, planning, prioritizing, being flexible, making midcourse corrections as needed, being able to assess risk, being able to delay immediate gratification to achieve long-term goals, keeping an eye on the big picture, making informed decisions, and completing tasks in a timely way (Silver, 2010; Willis, 2011).

Iceberg. Chris A. Zeigler Dendy (2002, 2011), Martin Kutscher (2010), and others have described ADHD as an iceberg, with the visible core symptoms (inattention, impulsivity, hyperactivity) as just the tip. Looming under the surface are often the most challenging aspects of ADHD: the EF impairment (and co-occurring conditions).

Air traffic control center. Just as the air traffic control center coordinates all of the different planes coming and going, the executive functions involve managing a lot of information, resisting distractions, exercising inhibitory control and mental flexibility, and so forth (Center on the Developing Child, Harvard University, n.d.).

EF Components

It has not as yet been determined exactly what constitutes all of the executive functions. However, most experts agree that they involve the following:

Inhibition (controlling impulses, being able to stop and think before responding, being able to resist temptations and distractions). This is considered by many to be a primary executive function because inhibitory control is necessary for all of the other EFs to adequately develop.

Working memory (holding information in mind long enough to act on it, complete a task, or do something else simultaneously; a mental desktop for holding information active while working with other information)

Planning and prioritizing (thinking through what needs to be done, structuring an efficient approach to accomplish those tasks, making good decisions about what to focus on)

Organization (imposing order and structure to manage information, efficiently communicate one's thoughts, and carry out goal-directed behavior)

Arousal and activation (being able to arouse effort and motivation to start or initiate tasks and activities, particularly those that are not intrinsically motivating)

Sustaining attention (maintaining alertness and focus and resisting distractions, especially when the task is tedious or not of interest)

Emotional self-control (modulating or self-regulating one's frustrations and emotions)

Time awareness (being aware of how much time has passed and how long things take, keeping track of time, planning and acting accordingly)

Goal-directed persistence (persevering, maintaining the effort and motivation to follow through with actions needed to achieve goals)

Shifting and flexibility (being adaptable and making adjustments when needed, mentally shifting information around, making transitions, ending one task to move to the next)

Self-monitoring and metacognition (being aware of and self-checking one's own behavior, thought processes, strategies, and comprehension; evaluating one's own performance, monitoring strategy, and revising)

Self-talk and private speech (using your inner voice, mentally talking to yourself to control and guide your behavior or work through a problem)

EF Dysfunction in ADHD

Research has found that children and teens with ADHD lag in their development of EF skills by approximately 30 percent compared to other children their age. So, expect that a ten-year-old with ADHD will have the EF maturity of a seven-year-old, and a fifteen-year-old to have some EF skills more like those of a ten- or eleven-year-old. It is very important for teachers and parents to be aware of this developmental delay and adjust their expectations for self-regulation and self-management accordingly. EF weaknesses can also be expected to cause some academic and work-related challenges to varying degrees (mild to severe), irrespective of the child's intelligence.

The frontal lobes (particularly the prefrontal cortex and extended neural networks) are the primary center of executive functions. This region of the brain has been found to be underactive, smaller, and less mature in people with ADHD than in those without ADHD.

For all people, the prefrontal cortex (PFC) matures and develops gradually from childhood into adulthood (the late twenties), with the most rapid development occurring during the school years. The PFC is the last part of the brain to fully mature, and for those with ADHD, it is delayed in development by a few years. It is not just the PFC that is involved in executive functions. The brain's executive system is complex, as other regions of the brain and neural networks interact with the PFC.

Models Explaining Executive Function Impairment in ADHD

Drs. Russell Barkley and Thomas E. Brown, two world-renowned researchers and authorities on ADHD, have been key leaders in the field, and their work and teachings have fundamentally changed our understanding of ADHD to being that of a disorder of executive functioning—our self-management system. Both Barkley and Brown have developed their own conceptual models of ADHD as a disorder of executive functions, which are best understood by going directly to their books, websites, and other resources, some of which are provided in the references and the Part 1 Additional Sources and Resources.

Barkley's Model of EF and ADHD

According to Barkley, each of the executive functions is actually a type of self-regulation—a special form of self-directed action that people do to themselves (usually mentally and not visible to others). These self-directed actions are what people do in order to modify their own behavior so that they are more likely to attain a goal or change some future consequence to improve their welfare.

Barkley says that there are things people do to themselves for self-regulation:

1. Self-direct their attention (self-awareness)
2. Visualize their past to themselves
3. Talk to themselves in their minds
4. Inhibit and modify their emotional reactions to events
5. Restrain themselves (self-discipline)
6. Play with information in their mind (take it apart, manipulate it in various ways, and recombine it to form new arrangements)

See Barkley's resources at the end of Part 1 and on his website (www.russellbarkley.org).

Brown's Model of EF and ADHD

Brown's conceptual model is that of six clusters of executive functions that are impaired in ADHD. These symptoms of impairment often appear and work together in various combinations in people with ADHD.

1. *Activation.* Organizing, prioritizing, and activating work
2. *Focus.* Focusing, sustaining, and shifting attention to task

3. *Effort.* Regulating alertness, sustaining effort, and processing speed
4. *Emotion.* Managing frustration and modulating emotions
5. *Memory.* Using working memory and accessing recall
6. *Action.* Monitoring and self-regulating action

See Brown's resources at the end of Part 1 and on his website (www.drthomasebrown.com).

****

Both doctors have also developed executive function assessment tools: the Barkley Deficits in Executive Functioning Scale—Children and Adolescents (BDEFS-CA) and the Brown ADD Rating Scales for Children, Adolescents and Adults. These and other EF inventories and tools, such as the Behavior Rating Inventory for Executive Function (BRIEF) and Comprehensive Executive Function Inventory (CEFI), are listed in Section 1.3.

Other Information about Executive Functions

- Executive dysfunction is not exclusive to ADHD. EF impairment to some degree is also common in learning disabilities, ASD, OCD, bipolar, and some other developmental and psychiatric disorders, and can also be acquired by damage to the PFC, such as by traumatic brain injury or stroke.
- Studies have shown that self-discipline has a bigger effect on academic performance than does intellectual talent (Duckworth & Seligman, 2005; Tangney, Baumeister, & Boone, 2004).
- A growing body of research has demonstrated that children's EFs (along with their skills in modulating emotion) are central to school readiness in early childhood (Raver & Blair, 2014).
- EFs may be a better predictor of school readiness than one's IQ or entry-level reading or math skills (Diamond, Barnett, Thomas, & Munro, 2007).

- There is growing evidence that because of the brain's neuroplasticity, a person's environment, supports, and opportunities to practice skills have direct, beneficial effects on the way in which the PFC develops; in other words, self-regulation and executive skills can be strengthened with practice.
- Tools of the Mind is an example of one early childhood school program that has been studied by researchers and has shown impressive results. In this program, teachers spend most of each day promoting EF skills with their preschool and kindergarten children (Diamond et al., 2007). See www.toolsofthemind.org and Section 1.8.

What Parents and Teachers Should Keep in Mind

EF weaknesses cause academic challenges to some degree (mild to severe), irrespective of one's intellectual and academic capabilities. Every individual with ADHD will be affected differently in EF areas of strength and weakness. Many highly intelligent, gifted children and teens with ADHD (even those who manage to get good grades) struggle in their daily functioning because of their EF impairment. Most students with ADHD will need supportive strategies and some accommodations to compensate for their deficit in EF, whether they are part of a formal plan (IEP or 504 accommodation plan) or not.

Every aspect of schooling involves a student's EFs. From the beginning of a school day to the end, children and teens need executive skills in order to get to school and classes on time, respond appropriately to peers and adults, follow directions, find and organize materials, get started and follow through to complete assignments, and much more.

When students have executive dysfunctions, support from teachers and parents and efforts to teach and strengthen EF skills are critical for school success. There are many proactive strategies and interventions that can be helpful—supporting the development of students' EFs as well as compensating for their weaknesses.

Many students with ADHD manage to do well in elementary school because of the high degree of support provided by teachers and parents (who often take on the role of the younger child's PFC). But by middle and high school, the executive demands for organizing, planning, time management, problem solving, and other EF skills can become overwhelming. As students with ADHD move up through the grades, the expectations for self-management and independence are often unrealistic, and many teens who did well in elementary school fall apart at this time.

Dendy (2011) reminds us that, unfortunately, kids with ADHD and EF deficits are often mistaken for being lazy,

> because it can seem as if he or she has chosen not to get started on or complete work; and they are often admonished to try harder. In reality, these children and teens may work very hard, but because of attention and executive function deficits, their productivity does not match their greater level of effort. (p. 39)

Numerous strategies, supports, and accommodations for helping students with ADHD compensate for their EF impairments and strengthen skill development are found throughout this book. The following points describe a few general ways to help:

- Environmental structuring to provide a great deal of external structure, such as visual and auditory cues, prompts, reminders, and clear organization of the classroom and home environment.
- Explicit teaching of executive skills to model and provide a high degree of guided and independent practice with clear feedback and reinforcement. Executive skills such as planning, organizing, time management, goal setting, and self-monitoring need to be taught, with lots of practice opportunities. The same applies for explicit teaching of learning strategies and study skills that are typically affected by EF weaknesses, such as note taking, test-taking strategies, and memorization.
- Management techniques and strategies that enable procedures, routines, and transitions to become smooth and automatic; clear rules and expectations that are effectively taught, practiced, and reinforced.
- Supports and accommodations to compensate for memory weaknesses, such as use of checklists, recorded messages, visual aids, and technology.
- Academic assistance or intervention in areas affected by working memory or other EF weaknesses.
- Reenergizing the brain by providing frequent breaks in activities (brain breaks) and physical exercise to avoid cognitive fatigue.
- Strategies and supports for focusing attention, initiating tasks, and maintaining on-task behavior.
- Supports and strategies for dealing with and managing emotions and for teaching, practicing, and motivating use of self-control.
- Supports and accommodations as needed for organization, time management, classroom work production, and homework difficulties, particularly for long-term projects and assignments.

1.3

Making the Diagnosis:
A Comprehensive Evaluation for ADHD

The diagnosis of ADHD is not achieved through a simple or quick process. There is no laboratory test or single measure to determine if a person has ADHD, and no particular piece of information alone can confirm or deny the existence of ADHD. Nevertheless, ADHD can be diagnosed reliably.

Clinical Evaluation for ADHD

The cornerstone of an ADHD diagnosis is meeting the criteria described in the fifth edition of the *Diagnostic and Statistical Manual of Mental Health Disorders* (*DSM-5*), published by the American Psychiatric Association in 2013. The *DSM* is the source for diagnosing ADHD as well as other developmental and mental health disorders, and it has been updated and revised over the years. The fifth edition (*DSM-5*) is the most current at this time, replacing *DSM-IV* (1994) and text-revised *DSM-IV-TR* (2000).

When evaluating for ADHD, the doctor, mental health professional, or other qualified clinician must collect, synthesize, and interpret data from multiple sources, settings, and methods to determine if there is enough evidence that *DSM-5* criteria for ADHD have all been met. This cannot be done in a short office visit. An appropriate evaluation for ADHD takes substantial time and effort.

In 2011, the American Academy of Pediatrics (AAP) published guidelines for primary care doctors for the diagnosis, evaluation, and treatment of ADHD. These guidelines were revised and updated from the initial guidelines of 2000. The current guidelines (AAP, 2011) for primary care physicians state the following:

- Doctors should evaluate children four through eighteen years of age for ADHD if they present with academic or behavioral problems and symptoms of inattention, hyperactivity, or impulsivity.
- To make a diagnosis of ADHD, all *DSM* criteria must be met.
- Any alternative cause for the symptoms (other than ADHD) should be ruled out, and the evaluation should include, if indicated, assessment for other conditions that might coexist with ADHD (emotional, behavioral, developmental, physical).

DSM-5 Criteria

- The *DSM-5* (as in previous editions) lists nine specific symptoms under the category of inattention and nine specific symptoms under the hyperactive-impulsive category. These eighteen symptoms are listed in

Section 1.1 (italicized under the categories of inattention and hyperactivity-impulsivity).

- For someone to be given a diagnosis of ADHD, the evaluator must determine that the person often presents with a significant number of symptoms in either the *inattentive* category or the *hyperactive-impulsive* category or in *both* categories. What constitutes a significant number varies by age: six out of nine symptoms (in either or both categories) must occur often for children through age sixteen; only five symptoms out of the nine is the requirement for individuals seventeen years old and above.
- Several symptoms need to be present in two or more settings (for example, at both home and school).
- The symptoms are inappropriate and out of norm for the individual's developmental level (compared to others his or her age).
- The symptoms are not new. They must have been present for at least the past six months.
- Symptoms are to the degree that they interfere with or reduce the quality of the person's functioning (for example, academic, social, work) or development.
- Other conditions or disorders (such as anxiety or depression) do not better account for these symptoms.

Three Presentations of ADHD

As noted in Section 1.1, a person may receive a diagnosis of one of these three different presentations of ADHD, depending on the specific symptoms:

- *Predominantly inattentive presentation.* If enough symptoms of inattention but not hyperactivity-impulsivity were present for the past six months.
- *Predominantly hyperactive-impulsive presentation.* If enough symptoms of hyperactivity-impulsivity but not inattention were present for the past six months.
- *Combined inattentive and hyperactive-impulsive presentation.* If enough symptoms in the category of inattention and in the

category of hyperactivity-impulsivity were present for the past six months.

Note: Because symptoms can change over time, a person's type or presentation of ADHD may change at some time during his or her life.

Changes in the *DSM* Criteria

Although much remains the same in *DSM-5* as in earlier editions, there have been some significant changes to the diagnostic criteria:

- In the previous editions of the *DSM,* the criteria were designed to help clinicians diagnose ADHD in children. As the research has proven that ADHD is not just a childhood disorder, it became clear that the criteria did not adequately reflect the experiences of teens and adults with the disorder. The *DSM-5* has adapted the criteria to more effectively diagnose ADHD in teens and adults, as well as in children.
- ADHD is no longer in the "Disruptive Behavior Disorders" section of the *DSM.* It is now found in the "Neurodevelopmental Disorders" section.
- As symptoms tend to be reduced with age, *DSM-5* accounts for this by reducing the number of required symptoms for diagnosis in individuals over seventeen to five out of nine (rather than six out of nine).
- The age of onset changed in the criteria, reflecting our understanding that not all symptoms are evident at a young age. Now symptoms need to occur by age twelve, instead of the previous requirement that symptoms must occur before seven years of age.
- The impairment criteria and wording has been changed. It used to be a requirement that symptoms must cause *impairment* in at least two settings. This has been changed to "clear evidence that the symptoms *interfere with, or reduce the quality of,* social, academic, or occupational functioning" [emphasis mine].
- Although the nine symptoms in each category remain the same, *DSM-5* has added further descriptions to the

symptoms—including what the symptoms may look like in teens and adults. Examples in *DSM-IV* were only of what symptoms may look like in children.

- Instead of being referred to as the three *types* of ADHD, the wording is now three *presentations* of ADHD.
- Now people with Autism Spectrum Disorder (ASD) can also receive a diagnosis of ADHD. It is now recognized that ASD can be a coexisting disorder with ADHD.
- There is now a severity level of ADHD (mild, moderate, severe) that is to be specified under the new *DSM-5* criteria.

Components of a Comprehensive Evaluation for ADHD

Clinical Interview

This is the single most important feature of the evaluation process, during which the clinician spends a significant amount of time speaking with parents to obtain the following information:

- The child's *medical history* (for example, during pregnancy and fetal development, birth, illnesses, injuries), developmental history (approximate dates of milestones reached in language, motor, self-help, learning skills), and school history
- The *family history* (of medical, psychiatric, psychological problems and diagnoses of parents and other family members—particularly looking for known or possible ADHD and coexisting conditions in parents, siblings, grandparents, or other relatives)
- Information about any *significant family circumstances or stressors* (which may be causing some of the symptoms), such as death or serious illness in the family, parental separation or divorce, and so forth
- *Parents' perceptions, insights, and observations* regarding, for example, the following:
  — The child's difficulties in learning, behavior, health, and social relationships
  — The child's strengths, interests, and motivators

— The child's responses to discipline and disciplinary techniques used in the home
— How the child responds when upset, angry, or frustrated
— How the child gets along with siblings, neighborhood children, and others
— The child's feelings (worries, fears, frustrations)

The interview also involves *talking with and observing the child*. The length of the interview with the child or teen, and what questions are asked will vary, of course, depending on the child's age.

An *interview with the teacher* is also recommended. By directly speaking with the teacher, the evaluator will be able to obtain a much better picture of the child's functioning and performance at school (academic, behavioral, social-emotional) and can hear the teacher's observations of the child compared to other students in the classroom.

Questionnaires (such as Barkley's home and school situations questionnaires) or rating forms that may have been sent to parents and teachers prior to the evaluation may be reviewed with further questions asked of parents, the child, or teachers during the interview process.

Note: *It is helpful if, prior to the evaluation, parents are prepared by having the information (particularly the child's history) readily available to share.*

Rating Scales

Rating scales are very useful in determining the degree to which various ADHD-related behaviors or symptoms are observed in different key environments (for example, home and school). Not only teachers and parents but also others who spend time with the child, such as the school counselor, special education teacher, child care provider, or other relative, can fill out rating scales.

The evaluation typically involves filling out one or more rating scales. A variety of scales and questionnaires can be used as part of the diagnostic process for obtaining information from parents and teachers. Scales that provide information specific to the *DSM* diagnostic criteria for ADHD should be used. These include the Vanderbilt

Parent and Teacher Assessment Scales; Conners Parent and Teacher Rating Scales; Attention Deficit Disorders Evaluation Scale (ADDeS); Swanson, Nolan, and Pelham (SNAP-IV-C); and the ADHD Rating Scale-IV.

There are other broadband rating scales that may be used *in addition to,* but not instead of, the ADHD rating scales. These broadband scales may pick up on anxiety, depression, and other possible mental health disorders (which may coexist with ADHD).

There are also scales for executive functioning that the clinician may use for obtaining additional information, such as the Comprehensive Executive Function Inventory (CEFI), Behavior Rating Inventory of Executive Function (BRIEF), Barkley Deficits in Executive Functioning Scale—Children and Adolescents (BDEFS-CA), and Brown Attention Deficit Disorder Scales (BADDS).

Rating scales list a number of items that teachers or parents rate according to the frequency with which they observe the child exhibiting those specific behaviors or problems. Sometimes the ratings range from "never" to "almost always" or from "not at all" to "very much." Some rating scales are numerical (ranging from 1 to 5 or 0 to 4). The scales are standardized, enabling the evaluator to compare a child's behavioral symptoms with those of other children of that age or developmental level.

In some of the instruments, various situations in the home or school are described, and parents or teachers rate whether they see the child presenting difficulty in any of those situations and to what degree (mild to severe).

Teachers may be asked to rate the student in comparison to others in the class on the existence or degree of disruptive behavior, moodiness, oppositional behavior, distractability, organization skills, forgetfulness, on-task behavior, activity, aggressiveness, ability to display self-control, paying attention, and so forth.

Physical Exam

A clinical evaluation for ADHD generally includes a routine examination to rule out other possible medical conditions that could produce ADHD symptoms or that may require medical management. The routine exam may include measuring the child (height, weight, head circumference), screening to rule out poor vision or chronic ear infections, screening for gross motor skills or neurological signs of a developmental disorder.

The child's physical exam and medical history (through interview and questionnaire) may prompt a physician to look for evidence of other possible causes for the symptoms or additional issues that may need to be addressed, such as sleep disturbances, allergies, bed-wetting, or anxiety.

Other medical tests (blood work or imaging scans such as CT, SPECT, PET, EEG) are not done in an evaluation for ADHD. It is the doctor's responsibility to determine the need for additional medical testing or referral to other specialists if indicated.

Observations

Directly observing the child's functioning in a variety of settings can provide helpful diagnostic information. Most useful are observations in natural settings where the child spends much of his or her time, such as school. How a child behaves and performs in an office visit is not indicative of how that same child performs and behaves in a classroom, on the playground, in the school cafeteria, or in other natural settings.

Academic and Intelligence Testing

An evaluator should have at least a general indication of a child's academic achievement level and performance, as well as a rough estimate of his or her cognitive (thinking and reasoning) ability. Some means of obtaining this information include a review of the student's report cards, standardized test scores, classroom work samples, or curriculum-based assessment, or informal screening measures. Information can also be gleaned from the interviews with the child, teacher, and parents.

If there are indications of possible learning disabilities, a psychoeducational evaluation should be considered, which assesses the child's cognitive, processing, and academic strengths and weaknesses—providing information about how the child learns and his or her educational needs.

Parents may seek a professional in the community or request an evaluation from the school district. See Part 6 for more on this topic.

Performance Tests

Additional tests are sometimes used by some evaluators to obtain more information about how a child functions on various performance measures. Some clinicians use computerized tests that measure the child's ability to inhibit making impulsive responses and to sustain attention to tasks. However, these tests are not standard practice or routinely conducted in ADHD assessments; they are not necessary for making the diagnosis.

More Tips and Information

- A thorough history is critical in making an accurate diagnosis of ADHD, which is obtained through the interview, use of questionnaires or rating scales, and a review of medical and school records. With regard to the school history, a great deal of useful data is located in the student's school records, which might include past report cards, IEPs, district and state achievement testing and other school evaluations (such as psychoeducational and speech-language), referrals to the school team, and so forth. Parents may provide some of this information, or it can come from the school.
- *An appropriate assessment for ADHD cannot be made* if the school has not been communicated with and has not provided the evaluator with information about the student's current functioning, and if teacher input and observations have not been provided.
- When indicated, evaluation of the child should include screening or assessment for conditions that mimic (produce similar-looking symptoms) or that may coexist with ADHD.

Pursuing an ADHD Evaluation

Some children have significant behavior problems and ADHD symptoms as early as preschool. For others, the symptoms become of concern in the early elementary grades, when the child must function all day in a classroom with twenty to thirty other children. For many other children, it is not until third or fourth grade that they start to struggle in school as the academic demands become much harder, and expectations for on-task behavior, work production, and self-control intensify.

There are many children with ADHD who manage to perform adequately in an elementary school setting with a high degree of support and structure provided by parents and teachers, but who then fall apart in middle school and high school with the increased academic demands and high expectations for self-management and executive skills, and the challenge of multiple classes and teachers.

At whatever point parents decide to pursue an ADHD evaluation for their child, it is a very important step. A proper diagnosis is key to getting the necessary help and intervention that a child with ADHD needs in order to achieve success and minimize risks of any negative outcomes. Parents are advised not to wait and see when they have concerns, especially if the child is struggling in learning, behavior, or social skill competence.

Who Is Qualified to Diagnose ADHD?

A number of professionals have the qualifications to evaluate children for ADHD: child psychiatrists, pediatricians, neurologists, psychologists, social workers, family practitioners, nurse practitioners, and other licensed medical and mental health professionals. Specialists in childhood medical and mental health, such as child psychiatrists, child psychologists, child neurologists, and developmental or behavioral pediatricians, have the most training and are recommended for complex cases.

A key qualification is the professional's knowledge of and experience in evaluating children and teens for ADHD. If the child is being evaluated by his or her pediatrician, that doctor should be following the American Academy of Pediatrics clinical practice guidelines for the diagnosis, evaluation, and treatment of ADHD (AAP, 2011) and *DSM-5* diagnostic criteria. Not all primary care doctors are aware of or follow these, and in such cases, parents should seek another professional to evaluate their child.

Finding a Professional to Evaluate Your Child

Parents are advised to share concerns with their child's pediatrician or other primary care physician and let the doctor know that you want your child evaluated and why. You may request a referral to a specialist, or the primary care doctor may inform you that he or she can do the evaluation.

Parents need to be proactive and not be embarrassed to ask the doctor about his or her experience evaluating for ADHD and what will be involved in the diagnostic process. If parents feel they are being hurried and not listened to carefully or if their concerns are brushed off and their questions are not satisfactorily answered, they should seek a different professional to evaluate their child.

When it comes to finding a professional, it helps to have recommendations. Your community's chapter of CHADD (www.chadd.org) is an excellent resource, as other parents of children with ADHD who have already been through the process can best recommend local professionals who have expertise in diagnosing and treating ADHD. School nurses and school psychologists are also good resources and are generally knowledgeable about health care providers in the community who have expertise in diagnosing ADHD and coexisting conditions. Local university medical hospitals and children's hospitals are often good resources you may want to explore as well.

Working with the School in the Evaluation Process

It is always important to communicate with your child's teachers regarding any of your concerns. You likely have been doing so prior to reaching this decision to pursue an evaluation for ADHD. If not, the first step should be to set up an appointment and have a conference with the teacher.

The next step is often a school multidisciplinary team meeting to discuss your child and your concerns, and to strategize a plan of support and intervention. This team goes by various names, such as student support team (SST), student assistance team (SAT), or child study team (CST). It may also be the Response to Intervention (RTI) team in your child's school.

At the meeting, share your concerns and ask for input regarding your child's performance from teachers and other staff who know your son or daughter and observe his or her functioning in the classroom and other settings.

The SST meeting is especially helpful when considering an evaluation for ADHD because the school can share with you its role in the assessment and obtain your written permission to begin gathering relevant data from school for the evaluation (such as records, reports, observations, and behavior rating scales). It is more likely that efforts will be coordinated when a school team is informed and involved.

As parents, you have the right to request a school-based evaluation at any time to determine if your child is eligible for special education, related services, or accommodations under federal laws protecting children with disabilities (IDEA and Section 504). See Sections 6.2 and 6.4 on this topic. Sometimes a school evaluation to determine educational needs and possible services and supports is initiated concurrently with a clinical evaluation for ADHD.

What Teachers and Other School Professionals Need to Know

Information about Current School Functioning

As described earlier, the diagnosis of ADHD is dependent on gathering sufficient information from multiple sources to get a clear picture of how ADHD symptoms are affecting a child's functioning in more than one setting. School is a key setting; it's where the child spends much of his or her life. No one is in a better position than the teacher to report on the child's school performance compared to other students of that age and grade. This includes the teacher's observations and objective information indicating the student's academic productivity and social, emotional, and behavioral functioning.

In an appropriate evaluation for ADHD, teachers will be asked to report their observations about the student through standardized behavior rating scales, questionnaires, narrative statements, phone interviews, or other measures. The teacher should be prepared to share information regarding the student's ability to exhibit self-control, stay focused and on-task, interact with peers and adults, initiate and follow through on assignments, and other behaviors.

Other indicators of a student's current school performance (academic and behavioral) may be helpful as well—for example, disciplinary referrals (among the records of guidance counselors or administrators) and work samples.

Information about the School History

Data indicating the existence of symptoms in previous school years, when those symptoms started to become apparent, and difficulties the student experienced in prior grades can generally be obtained from the school records, which might include past report cards, district and state achievement testing, other evaluations (such as psychoeducational and speech-language), referrals to the school's multidisciplinary team, and any school-based support or intervention plans.

Points to Keep in Mind

- It will be necessary for parents to sign a release-of-information form before school personnel are permitted to communicate with other professionals outside of school or provide documentation and data regarding the student. Teachers need to make sure this form is on file with the school district before sharing information requested by a doctor or other evaluator.

- The school is responsible for determining educational impairment due to a suspected or known disability. Schools have the responsibility of initiating and following through with a comprehensive evaluation if the student is suspected of having ADHD or any other disability impairing educational performance. (This includes behavioral, not just academic, performance.) If the student meets eligibility criteria, the school is then responsible for providing supports and services under either of the two federal laws: IDEA or Section 504 of the Rehabilitation Act of 1973 (which are discussed in Section 6.4).

- Up to 50 percent of students with ADHD also have coexisting learning disabilities. If a student with ADHD is struggling academically (for example, in learning to read or write), the school should consider the probability of learning disabilities (such as dyslexia or dysgraphia) and provide a more comprehensive evaluation to determine the child's learning needs.

1.4

Multimodal Treatment for ADHD

Once a child receives an ADHD diagnosis, there are many ways to help the child and the family. It is important to realize that ADHD is not something that can be cured, but it can be treated and managed effectively. The best way of doing so is through a multifaceted approach—a "multimodal" plan that combines medical, behavioral, educational, and other interventions.

ADHD is recognized as a chronic condition (like asthma or diabetes) and follows a chronic care plan of action (American Academy of Pediatrics [AAP] & National Initiative for Children's Healthcare Quality, 2002; AAP, 2011). This means looking at the long-term picture. Various supports and treatments may be needed throughout the individual's lifetime or employed at different times in life as needed. In addition, because of the long-term management involved, the treatment plan requires vigilance on the part of parents, educators, and health providers in monitoring and following up on the effectiveness of the plan, and adjusting as needed.

There are a variety of medical and mental health professionals (physicians, psychologists, social workers) who may be involved at different points in the child's life. The school team also may comprise a number of different school professionals (classroom teachers, guidance counselors, school nurse, administrators, special educators, and other special/related service providers). Parents may bring in to their team anyone who spends much time interacting with the child or teen (extended family, child care providers, tutors, coaches).

A primary intervention is education—particularly of parents and teachers (and the child or teen)—about ADHD. Awareness and understanding of the disorder and of how to structure and modify the environment and employ strategies to manage and respond to the ADHD-related behaviors are extremely important and come with education and training.

When their child receives the diagnosis, parents, as their child's case managers, must do everything they can to learn about ADHD. This is the start of the parents' journey of becoming "ADHD experts"—equipping themselves with the knowledge that will enable them to make the best-informed decisions regarding their child's care and the management of his or her ADHD.

The AAP (2011) established clinical guidelines for the diagnosis, evaluation, and treatment of ADHD in children and adolescents. According to the AAP guidelines, the primary goal of treatment is to maximize the child's functioning at home, at school, and in the community. The guidelines recommend that the treating clinician, the parents, and the child, in collaboration with school personnel, should specify appropriate target outcomes to guide management. Examples of target outcomes include

- Improved relationships with parents, siblings, teachers, and peers
- Improved academic performance (particularly in volume of work, efficiency, completion, and accuracy)
- Increased independence in self-care or homework
- Improved self-esteem
- Fewer disruptive behaviors
- Safer behavior in the community (for example, when crossing streets or riding bicycles)

Important Points to Keep in Mind

- The most positive outcomes for youngsters with ADHD are achieved when parents, teachers, other involved school professionals, and treating medical and mental health providers have good communication and collaborate well.
- The two research-validated interventions known to be most effective at this time are *medication* and *behavioral therapy*. One, the other, or a combination of both is the main treatment for ADHD. The scientific evidence clearly shows that these are the treatments that make the biggest difference with regard to improvement of symptoms and degree of impairment. These interventions have been extensively tested with controlled studies and proven effective in managing ADHD.
- Educational supports and interventions addressing the child's areas of weakness are also a critical component in the success of students with ADHD.
- There are additional complementary supports and interventions to enhance the plan and benefit the individual with ADHD.

Multimodal Intervention

Parent Training

As noted, education is a crucial component of ADHD treatment. Parents must be provided with the following information to best help their child:

- Accurate and reliable information about ADHD in order to understand the impact and developmental course of the disorder, the treatment options, and available resources
- A new set of skills for managing their child's challenging behaviors
- Training in effective behavioral techniques and how to structure the home environment and other aspects of their child's life
- How to best navigate the educational and health care systems

Note: *The Parent to Parent training program offered through CHADD is highly recommended. See www.chadd.org.*

Medication Therapy (Pharmacological Intervention)

Pharmacological treatment is the use of medication to manage ADHD symptoms. This has been proven by an abundance of research to be a highly effective intervention—the most effective as a single intervention—for managing symptoms and improving the functioning of children and teens with ADHD (Adesman, 2003; MTA Cooperative Group, 1999). Stimulant medications have been proven effective in treating approximately 70 to 90 percent of children with ADHD (Barkley, 2013; Brown, 2005).

These medications work to increase the action of the neurotransmitters (brain chemicals) available in certain brain regions and circuits that are not working efficiently in individuals with ADHD. Some FDA-approved nonstimulant medications are also used successfully in ADHD treatment. Appropriate medical treatment requires well-managed and carefully monitored use of medication(s) for ADHD. When there are coexisting disorders, various medications may be prescribed in the treatment of those other conditions as well. See Section 1.5 on medication therapy.

Behavioral Therapy

Behavior modification and specific behavioral strategies implemented at home and school are also research-validated interventions for children with ADHD, and another key component of the overall treatment plan. This involves parents and teachers learning skills and strategies to manage the behaviors of children with ADHD, such as how to provide clear, consistent structure and follow-through, and effective use of rewards (to increase desired behaviors) and negative consequences (to decrease unwanted, undesirable behaviors).

Behavioral therapy provides specific techniques and interventions adults can implement, such as a token economy system or home-school daily report cards (DRCs), and help in recognizing and adjusting the antecedents or triggers to problem behavior. Behavioral interventions for children with ADHD include those learned through parent training and implemented at home, those provided at school by teachers and other school personnel, and skills and strategies that the child learns to improve his or her behavior and interactions with others. See Section 1.6 on behavioral therapy and strategies throughout Part 2 for much more on this topic.

Other Psychosocial Interventions

Social skills training. This training is usually provided in small groups with curriculum addressing specific skills that children with ADHD tend to have difficulties with in their interpersonal relationships (for example, how to disagree respectfully, share and take turns, and play a game and accept losing appropriately). The children are taught through role playing and other techniques, and then practice in natural settings the skills they have learned, receiving feedback and reinforcement. See more on this in Sections 1.6 and 2.7.

Parent counseling. This is the parent training described earlier, which is a vital part of any treatment plan.

Family counseling. The whole family is often affected by issues relating to ADHD. Family therapy can address concerns that affect parents and siblings and improve family relationships.

Individual counseling. The child may work with a therapist in learning coping techniques, problem-solving strategies, and ways to deal with stress, anger, or frustration.

Psychotherapy. This counseling (for teens or adults) helps the person with ADHD who has a history of school, work, personal, or relationship problems talk about his or her feelings and deal with self-defeating patterns of behavior.

Vocational counseling. This can be a helpful intervention for teens and adults.

Educational Interventions

Differentiated instruction. Teachers who recognize that one size does not fit all embrace the challenge of using multiple approaches in teaching the curriculum and enabling students to demonstrate their learning.

Accommodations. Teachers should provide accommodations (environmental, academic, instructional, behavioral) as needed to enable students to succeed, whether those accommodations are provided informally or as per a student's IEP or Section 504 accommodation plan.

Special education and related services. Some students with ADHD qualify for special education and receive an IEP and related services provided through the school district.

Other school interventions. Various supports and safety nets may be available at the school that students in general education are able to access, such as homework or organizational assistance, mentoring, peer or adult tutoring, school counseling, and Response to Intervention (RTI) tier 1, 2, and 3 academic and behavioral interventions.

Tutoring or academic supports. Parents may pursue private tutoring or other academic interventions to help their child in specific areas of academic weakness or with study skills. Learning specialists and educational therapists are recommended for working with students with learning disabilities because of their training and expertise in teaching children with learning challenges and disorders.

Teacher (and other school staff) training about ADHD. Such training to understand the disorder and learn effective instructional and management strategies and supports for helping students with ADHD is a key educational intervention.

See Part 6 for information about Section 504, IDEA, and educational rights of students with ADHD under these two federal laws, as well as more about IEPs, 504 plans, and other school-based educational interventions.

Complementary Interventions

Complementary treatments for ADHD are those that are used *in addition to* the standard treatment of FDA-approved ADHD medication and behavioral therapy for added benefit and improved functioning. As noted, decades of research and scientific evidence have proven medication and behavioral therapy to be most effective in the treatment of ADHD, and these treatments are, therefore, the primary ones recommended by the experts and the major national professional organizations and associations. But there are several complementary interventions and supports that may be helpful for individual children and teens as part of their multimodal treatment plan.

ADHD coaching. This is a service that many teens and adults find beneficial in learning and applying strategies to be more focused and productive and to help them with organization and time management. Coaching generally assists with planning, scheduling,

breaking work tasks down into reasonable short-term goals, checking in regularly (for example, over the phone, by text or email, or via Skype or other webcam format), and keeping the ADHD client accountable and on target with his or her individual short- and long-term goals. ADHD coaches assist their clients in understanding ADHD and its impact on their life while developing skills and strategies that draw on their strengths and aim to bypass their weaknesses. See the Part 1 Additional Sources and Resources for more information about coaching.

Exercise and physical activity. It is important for children and teens with ADHD to engage in sports, dance, or other physical activities. Studies suggest a link between physical activity and the behavioral and academic performance of children with ADHD—regular exercise boosts their functioning and performance (Ratey, 2008). Research shows that exercise improves the attention system by increasing the levels of the brain chemicals dopamine and norepinephrine. There are numerous benefits of exercise, such as enhancing mood, alertness, and self-regulation. Sports and dance not only are fun and motivating activities but also teach and provide opportunities to practice focused attention, self-discipline, and self-control.

The key is to find the sports or physical activities that are right for the individual child. Some children with ADHD have difficulty in team sports, especially those that have a lot of downtime and require having to wait patiently for their turn to participate. Many children with ADHD do best in individual sports, such as swimming, diving, tae kwon do or other martial arts, gymnastics, track and field, tennis, skating, or horseback riding. According to Ratey (2008), for those with ADHD, highly structured exercise that requires complex movements, such as martial arts, gymnastics, ballet, figure skating, or rock climbing, have a greater positive impact than aerobic exercise alone. As mentioned, team sports are not the best for some children with ADHD, but others do fine or excel in them, and they are perfect activities for learning and practicing social skills, such as cooperation.

Neurofeedback (EEG biofeedback). Neurofeedback has been used as a complementary or alternative treatment for ADHD for a number of years, but has been controversial because of limited scientific support from controlled studies and random assignment of subjects. In recent years, there has been more controlled research support, and a number of experts in the field believe that neurofeedback does hold promise as a complementary treatment. EEG biofeedback involves brain exercises that take place during a series of treatment sessions in which the child wears headgear lined with electrodes and performs video games and computerized tasks while brainwave activity in the frontal lobe (the part of the brain that is underaroused in those with ADHD) is measured. The treatment is supposed to increase the activation of brain waves in that part of the brain and train patients to eventually produce on their own the brain wave patterns associated with focus.

Other brain-training technologies. In recent years, various software programs and technologies have been developed to help train and strengthen certain cognitive skills that are weak in children with ADHD. Although still in their infancy, and requiring much more research to validate their positive effects, these types of programs show promise as possible useful complementary interventions. The most well known and well researched of these programs at this time is Cogmed Working Memory Training Program (www.cogmed.com). Some others include the Activate program (www.c8sciences.com), Play Attention (www.playattention.com), Jungle Rangers (www.focuseducation.com), and Brainology (www.mindsetworks.com/brainology).

Meditation practices and mindfulness. Practices involving meditation and attention to one's breathing have been used for centuries. Recent research has been looking at the positive effects of such practices on people with ADHD. According to Lidia Zylowska (2012), codeveloper of UCLA's Mindful Awareness Program for ADHD, mindfulness awareness practices help improve a person's ability to resist distractions, manage emotions, and notice an impulse arising without acting on it. According to the website of UCLA's Mindful Awareness Research Center (http://marc.ucla.edu), the practice of mindful awareness can guide students to improve relationships, create relaxation and calmness, self-soothe, increase memory, enhance focus, reduce stress, manage reactions and emotions, increase self-acceptance, and feel more at ease with test taking. Children may benefit as well from learning and practicing yoga, progressive relaxation, and visualization techniques.

Diet. All children and teens should have a well-balanced diet, high in nutrition (plenty of protein, fruits, and vegetables). Certain dietary factors may affect some children, and parents should discuss with their doctor or a nutritionist any concerns they have that their child's diet may be a factor—worsening his or her ADHD symptoms. For example, omega-3 fatty acids are important in brain and nerve cell function and increase the level of dopamine in the brain. There may be some evidence supporting omega-3 fatty acid supplements as beneficial for individuals with ADHD (Barrow, 2008). Protein is digested more slowly than carbohydrates and can prevent surges in blood sugar, which may increase hyperactivity. Protein for breakfast in the morning is highly recommended ("Special Report: Diet Matters," 2008). Deficiencies of certain minerals (zinc, iron, and magnesium) may worsen symptoms of inattention, impulsivity, and hyperactivity, which may be improved through diet or a multivitamin that contains the recommended daily allowance of key vitamins and minerals. Some children have food sensitivities, such as to gluten, eggs, or dairy. If parents suspect that to be the case, they may wish to try an elimination diet of certain foods under the supervision of their child's doctor. Food sensitivities do not appear to be a specific problem for most children with ADHD, but more recent studies suggest a small effect for all children regardless of whether or not they have ADHD (Goodman, 2008). *Note:* It is strongly advised that parents consult with their child's doctor before giving their child any supplements or trying an elimination diet.

Other healthy lifestyle choices. Getting a good night's sleep is very important but often problematic for many children and teens with ADHD. Parents are advised to discuss sleep problems with their child's physician. More outdoor activities as opposed to indoor ones (glued to a screen of some type) are good choices for everyone and may be even more important for those with ADHD. A few studies have shown that exposure to green, outdoor settings can be beneficial for children with ADHD, with improved symptoms, particularly in attention.

Music therapy and music lessons. Music is well known to have many positive benefits for people. Brain imaging shows that music stimulates and activates certain brain regions, and neuroscience is learning more and more about the effects of auditory stimulation on the brain. "The rhythm and structure of music may be helpful in regulating the ADHD brain. It can be used as a tool to help train the brain for stronger focus and self-control" (Rodgers, 2012, p. 47). Studies have shown that musical training can enhance reading-related skills and language abilities (McGavern, 2015). Recent studies (Hudziak et al., 2014; McGavern, 2015) showed evidence that early music instruction also positively affected prefrontal regions in the brain associated with emotional

regulation and inhibitory control. "Although speculative, it is possible that music training's influence on cortical maturation, particularly in the prefrontal regions, may serve to mitigate aspects of ADHD symptomology" (Hudziak et al., 2014).

Parent support groups. Having the opportunity to share and network with other parents who have children with ADHD is very helpful. CHADD (www.chadd.org) is the nation's main ADHD organization, with local chapters across the United States. CHADD is an excellent source of reliable information and support for parents of children with ADHD. Some communities have other ADHD groups with informational meetings and networking as well. There are also online chat groups that parents in the ADHD community may find helpful.

Developing and nurturing the child's strengths and interests. Very important to the child's happiness and successful future is enabling him or her to participate in such activities as arts and crafts, music, dance, sports, creative and performing arts, or scouts. This is a very important part of a multimodal therapeutic plan for children with ADHD—to help them find their strengths and have areas in their life in which they shine.

Other. See the bonus section "Healthy, Fun, and Therapeutic Ways to Help Manage ADHD Symptoms," available online at www.wiley.com/go/adhdreach (password 37785), for more information on activities that may be of benefit in a multimodal treatment plan—for example, yoga and other controlled exercises, breathing and progressive relaxation techniques, and music and art therapy.

Note: See the resources list in the Part 1 Additional Sources and Resources for much more on these standard and complementary interventions and supports.

Additional Points to Keep in Mind

Children, especially teens, should be included as active partners in their treatment program. For them to be motivated to actively cooperate and participate in the treatment, they need to understand the disorder, the reason for various interventions, and how those treatments are intended to have a positive effect on their daily lives.

As mentioned earlier, interventions need to focus not just on improving the child's areas of weakness but also, just as important, on helping the child or teen recognize, develop, and build on his or her strengths.

Caution about Alternative Treatments

Although complementary interventions are those used *in addition to* the standard ADHD treatments, alternative treatments are those that are used *instead of* the proven ADHD treatments of medication therapy and/or behavioral therapy.

Many parents are reluctant to treat their child with medication, or are outright opposed to doing so. The many advertisements in magazines, TV, radio, or the Internet making claims about various alternative products or treatments that cure ADHD symptoms can sound very convincing and believable. Parents need to be cautious and informed consumers when considering alternative treatments. Be aware of the following:

- Most make their claims based on a small sample of people supposedly studied.
- Most tend to use testimonials in their advertisements and do not have reputable scientific evidence to support the product's effectiveness or to back up their claims.
- Although they may cite a few studies as evidence, these studies are not controlled research that meets the scientific standards for evaluating treatment effectiveness. This would require, among other things, proper controls and random assignment of test subjects, measurement techniques enabling the scientific community to evaluate the findings, peer reviews by other professionals prior to publication of results in scientific journals, and replicated studies by other teams of researchers to see if they achieve similar results.
- Various so-called natural products may be harmful because they have not been through rigorous scientific testing for safety.
- Any treatment that is advertised as miraculous or groundbreaking is generally bogus.
- Some of these treatments have been discredited, some lack the scientific evidence to back up their claims, and some show promise but warrant further study and for now remain unproven.
- It is very important to talk to your doctor about any alternative treatment you are considering for your child.
- A number of alternative treatments have been claimed to be effective in treating ADHD. Those without scientific evidence or that have been disproven include supplements of megavitamins and antioxidants, chiropractic adjustment and bone realignment, optometric vision training, anti–motion sickness medication, vestibular stimulation, herbal remedies, and treatment for candida yeast infection, among others.

For reliable information regarding alternative and complementary interventions, go to these websites: National Resource Center on AD/HD (www.help4adhd.org) and National Institutes of Health, National Center for Complementary and Alternative Medicine (http://nccam.nih.gov).

Medication Treatment and Management

> An Optic View of ADD
>
> If corrective lenses did not exist
> No well-meaning parent could hope to resist
> A pill that enabled their child to see
> And increase that child's ability
> For better sight and clear vision
> No, this would not be a tough decision.
> Then why wouldn't the same analogy
> Apply to the problem of ADD?
> For brains are a lot like eyes, I believe . . .
> They both need to focus in order to see!
> Medication as treatment might be prevented
> If ADD lenses were someday invented.
>
> Karen Easter, 1996

Medications have been used safely for decades to treat ADHD. They do not cure the disorder, but do help in controlling and reducing the symptoms. The most commonly used medications for treating ADHD are stimulants.

There continues to be much attention (media sensationalism and public controversy) regarding the use of stimulant medication in treating children with ADHD. A great deal of misinformation exists, which makes it difficult for parents trying to make an informed decision.

Parents need to consult with their physician or other medical professionals about any medication issues, questions, or concerns. The information presented in this section is meant only as a general reference.

Stimulant Medications in the Treatment of ADHD

Stimulant medications (the methylphenidates) have been regularly used since the 1960s in the treatment of children and adolescents with ADHD (although it was not called ADHD at that time). There are two main classes of stimulants: the *methylphenidate* formulas (for example, Ritalin, Concerta, Methylin, Daytrana) and the *amphetamine* formulas (Adderall, Dexedrine, Vyvanse).

Methylphenidates are among the most carefully studied drugs on the market. Thousands of children have been involved in research evaluating the use of these drugs in the treatment of ADHD, and they have been used safely with millions of children for at least fifty to sixty years.

Stimulants have been studied more extensively than any other psychoactive drug prescribed for children. Hundreds of controlled scientific studies demonstrating their effectiveness in treating children with ADHD have been conducted. Stimulants have been proven to work for 70 to 90 percent of children with ADHD. They are also effective in adults. There are very few people with ADHD who do not respond to stimulant medications, and the results can be very dramatic. Because the scientific evidence so strongly supports the effectiveness of stimulants in managing the symptoms and reducing impairment, they are recommended as the first choice of medications used in treating children with ADHD.

How Stimulants Are Believed to Work

Researchers suspect that stimulant medications act to normalize biochemistry in the parts of the brain (primarily the PFC and frontal-subcortical systems) that are underactive and not working efficiently in those with ADHD. These are the regions of the brain responsible for attention, inhibition of behavior, regulation of activity level, and executive functions.

Stimulants increase (or stimulate) the production of neurotransmitters (brain chemicals) to a more normal level in these key brain regions. The brain chemicals involved are dopamine and norepinephrine. Scientists believe that medications that increase the availability of these neurotransmitters help nerve-to-nerve communication, thereby boosting the signal between neurons.

The stimulants are thought to be working within the system involved in the release of these brain chemicals into the synapse (the gap between two neurons), and their reuptake or reabsorption out of the synapse. They are believed to act by helping keep the proper level of these neurotransmitters in the synapse long enough to efficiently transmit messages from one neuron to the next.

Stimulant Medications Prescribed for Treating ADHD

There are several stimulant medications. In the following list, the italicized name is the generic name, and the names in parentheses are the brand names. Also, SR stands for "sustained release," LA is "long acting," and ER and XR mean "extended release."

- *Methylphenidate* (Ritalin, Ritalin LA, Ritalin SR, Concerta, Metadate CD, Metadate ER, Methylin, Methylin ER, Quillivant XR, Daytrana patch)
- *Dexmethylphenidate* (Focalin, Focalin XR)
- *Dextroamphetamine* (Dexedrine, Dexedrine Spansule, DextroStat, ProCentra)
- *Mixed amphetamine salts* (Adderall, Adderall XR)
- *Lisdexamfetamine dimesylate* (Vyvanse)

Some of the stimulant medications come in tablets or capsules to swallow whole, some are chewable or can be dissolved in liquid, and others can be sprinkled on food. Daytrana is a patch adhered to the skin, and ProCentra is a liquid.

The different stimulant prescriptions vary in their onset (when they begin working), how they are released into the body (immediately or over an extended or sustained period), and how long the medication effects last. Each of the stimulants has a high response rate. A child who does not respond well (in symptom improvement) to one stimulant medication will often respond well to another. The initial choice is generally a matter of doctor and parent preference.

The **short-acting and immediate-release formulas** of the stimulants (such as Ritalin or Methylin)

- Start to work about twenty to thirty minutes from the time the medication is taken
- Metabolize quickly and are effective for approximately three to four hours
- Reach their peak effect within one to three hours
- Generally require an additional dosage to be administered at school

- May require a third dose (often a smaller one) to enable the child to function more successfully in the late afternoon and evening hours
- May be prescribed as an additional booster dose later in the day when a longer-acting stimulant wears off (to provide symptom relief in the late afternoon and evening)

The **longer-acting, extended release** stimulants have a time-release delivery system. These stimulants

- Take longer for the effect to begin
- Vary from approximately five to eight hours of coverage for some of the medications to ten to twelve (and even longer) for others
- Provide a smoother, sustained level of the drug throughout the day
- Minimize fluctuations (peaks and troughs) in blood levels
- Minimize rebound phenomena (a worsening of symptoms as the effects of the drug wear off)
- Eliminate the need for a midday dose at school, which is very beneficial for many children and teens, particularly those who are forgetful or who are embarrassed to take medication at school

About Stimulant Medications

- Stimulants take effect quickly (generally within thirty to sixty minutes).
- For some children, their initial prescription and dosage will work well. Many others require adjustments in dosage or trying others among the stimulant medications and formulas to get the best effect.
- For most children with ADHD taking a stimulant medication, once the optimal dosage has been found, they experience improvement (often very significant) in behavior and symptoms.
- Stimulants are found to improve the core symptoms (hyperactivity, impulsivity, inattention) and many of the secondary or associated problems these children experience (for example, oppositional behavior, difficult

interpersonal relationships, and lack of work production and school performance).

- On a therapeutic dosage of stimulant medication, there are many positive effects that often occur: reduced disruptive behavior and emotionality; improved ability to get started on and complete assignments, pay attention, stay focused, produce work, follow directions, interact with others, and tolerate frustration; and improved handwriting and academic accuracy.

Side Effects of Stimulant Medications

The side effects that are most common are appetite suppression, weight loss, and mild sleep disturbances. Some children may also experience headaches, stomachaches, irritability, moodiness, agitation, an emergence of tics, and a rebound effect (a worsening of symptoms as the medication wears off, such as irritability, less compliance, more activity). Most side effects from stimulant medications are mild, and they tend to diminish over time and respond to changes in dosage or the particular stimulant prescribed.

A small number of children develop or unmask latent tics (involuntary muscle movements) in the form of facial grimaces, sniffing, coughing, snorting, or other vocal sounds. *Note:* These are rare, and in most cases tics do not continue if the medication is stopped.

The Titration Process

Medication treatment begins with a titration phase: a trial period when the physician is trying to determine the appropriate medication and dosage. The correct dosage of a stimulant is determined not by the child's weight or age but according to how efficiently his or her body metabolizes the medication, which varies in every child and teen.

The titration process involves the following steps:

- Starting with a very low dosage and raising it gradually while observing the effects

- Closely monitoring symptoms and behavioral changes (at home and school) while progressively changing the dosages and sometimes adjusting their timing
- Trying to achieve the most improvement in symptoms and optimal effects from the medication with a minimum of side effects

Parents and teachers must communicate with the physician and provide the feedback necessary for the doctor to determine the child's response to the medication so that benefits are being achieved at each dosage level and side effects are minimized.

Nonstimulant ADHD Medications

Atomoxetine (brand name Strattera) is the first nonstimulant ADHD medication approved by the Food and Drug Administration and was released in 2002. This drug works differently from stimulants. It is a selective norepinephrine reuptake inhibitor, believed to work by blocking the reuptake or recycling of norepinephrine and increasing the availability of this brain chemical in the affected areas of the brain. Whereas stimulants mostly work to improve the level of dopamine, Strattera works on increasing the norepinephrine level and activity.

Atomoxetine has demonstrated effectiveness for improving ADHD symptoms in children and adults and may also help with oppositional and defiant behavior and anxiety.

It has the advantage of providing smooth, continuous coverage for twenty-four hours, and can therefore help functioning around the clock. This nonstimulant medication is also easier to re-order because it is not a controlled substance.

Whereas the stimulants take effect immediately once they enter the bloodstream, Atomoxetine takes weeks of daily use before it shows its benefits. The most common side effects are upset stomach (nausea, vomiting), sleep problems, fatigue, nervousness, and dry mouth.

Other Medications

Antihypertensives (alpha agonists) are another type of drug that is sometimes used in the treatment of ADHD. They include *guanfacine* (Tenex) and extended-release guanfacine (Intuniv) and *clonidine* (Catapres) and extended-release clonidine (Kapvay). Intuniv and Kapvay are more commonly prescribed for children. These medications may improve oppositional and defiant behavior, anxiety, aggression, and tics as well as ADHD symptoms. Intuniv was FDA approved in recent years in the treatment of ADHD in children. It is taken once a day and used along with a stimulant to help children who don't respond well to a stimulant alone.

Certain *antidepressants* have also been found effective in treating ADHD, particularly if a child is not responding to the stimulant or nonstimulant or shows signs of depression, anxiety, or tics, as well as ADHD. They are not, however, FDA approved as an ADHD medication. These antidepressants include the tricyclic antidepressants *imipramine* (Tofranil), *amitriptyline* (Elavil), *desipramine* (Norpramin), and *nortriptyline* (Pamelor and Aventyl), and the atypical antidepressant *bupropion hydrochloride* (Wellbutrin).

The tricyclic antidepressants take some time to build up in the bloodstream and reach a therapeutic level. Besides helping improve symptoms of hyperactivity and impulsivity, they also help with insomnia, mood swings, anxiety, depression, tics, sleep disturbances, and emotionality.

Some side effects of the tricyclic antidepressants are fatigue, stomachache, dry mouth, rash, dizziness, accelerated heart rate, and possible risk of cardiac arrhythmias. *Note:* These are not all the possible side effects of the various medications mentioned here. Parents need to discuss risks and side effects of any medication with their doctor.

Additional Information

- Every child has a unique response to medication, and it takes fine-tuning and patience to get it right.
- It is important that the medical professional whom parents choose to treat their child is very knowledgeable about ADHD and the various medications used in treatment for this disorder.

- Children with ADHD and coexisting disorders require more complex medical treatment, which may involve use of a combination of medications. Generally a specialist with expertise in treating these complex cases, such as a child and adolescent psychiatrist, is recommended.
- All medications can have adverse side effects. Parents need to be well informed of the risks versus the benefits in any medical treatment.
- Kalikow (2013) offers this advice to parents in making a decision about whether or not to try medication:
  — Start with a good evaluation by a trusted professional.
  — Consider how your child might benefit from medicine.
  — Get accurate information regarding the side effects.
  — Don't feel rushed to make a decision. You have time to do your research and consider your decision.
  — Know that your decision is reversible. If your child does not benefit from a trial of medicine, or experiences intolerable side effects, the medicine can be stopped.
- There are excellent resources about medication treatment for ADHD, including those listed at the end of Part 1, such as those from CHADD and the National Resource Center on AD/HD.

Note: For all matters related to medications, consult with your physician or other medical professionals.

If a Child or Teen Is Taking Medication: Advice for School Staff and Parents

What Teachers Need to Know

- Parents do not easily make the decision to try their child on medication. They often are fearful of the long-term effects. In addition, they are frequently made to feel guilty by well-meaning relatives, friends, or acquaintances who are uneducated about proven treatments or biased against the use of medication because of misinformation.
- The school's role is to support any student receiving medication treatment and to cooperate fully. School personnel need to communicate their observations so that the doctor can determine the child's response to the medication. These observations and frequent feedback to the doctor are necessary particularly in the titration process when a new medication is started, assisting the physician in determining the right medication and dosage—one that is providing the desired symptom improvement with minimal side effects. During the titration stage, in which medication dosage is increased every few days until the optimal dosage is determined, teachers will be asked for their feedback each time the dosage is adjusted or the timing is changed.
- The teacher is an integral part of the therapeutic team because of his or her unique ability to observe the child's performance and functioning (academically, socially, and behaviorally) on medication during most of the day. Teachers will need to carefully monitor and observe students on medication and report any changes (positive or negative) they observe.
- All students on medication for ADHD (regardless of how long they may be on the medication) need to be monitored for the effects of the medication during school hours. This is necessary to ensure that the child or teen is benefiting from the medication. For these students, teachers should also be prepared to share their feedback on the student's functioning (which will occur much less frequently than during titration periods).
- Physicians (or their office personnel) should be initiating contact with the school for feedback on how the treatment plan is working. Generally this is done through follow-up behavioral rating scales or other observational forms teachers are asked to complete. The

doctor's office may send the teacher rating forms directly, or parents may deliver the rating scales or medication forms to the school.

- Generally it is the school nurse who acts as the liaison between the parent and teacher in helping manage the medication at school as appropriate. Coordination and communication between all parties involved are important for optimal results.

- Medications, dosages, and times to be administered are often changed or adjusted until the right combination is found for the child. It is important to communicate with parents and report noticeable changes in a student's behaviors. Sometimes parents do not disclose to the school that their child has started taking medication (or has had a change of medication or dosage) and are waiting to hear if the teacher notices any difference.

- Children metabolize medication at different rates. To ensure that the medication is providing coverage throughout the school day, teachers should take note of changes of behavior or problems occurring at certain times of the day (for example, in the afternoon).

- Teachers need to let parents (and the school nurse, if available) know about any concerns that may indicate side effects of a medication. Children taking ADHD medications should be showing improved functioning and behavior and not experience a change in personality or appear sedated or lethargic. If they do, the dosage may be too high, or the child needs a different medication. It is important to share these observations so that the parent can let the physician know.

- Stimulant medications suppress appetite, and students with ADHD who take stimulants may not be eating much breakfast or lunch. They may get hungry at different times and would benefit from being allowed a snack if needed.

- Most students with ADHD who are prescribed medication are now taking the longer-acting, sustained-release forms—no longer needing a second dose of medication to be administered at school. This has helped significantly in terms of school responsibility and management of ADHD medications.

- For students who do take a short-acting stimulant, it is important that the second dose that is administered during school hours is given on time (as prescribed by the doctor). Be aware that some children experience a rebound effect when the medication wears off. When the next prescribed dose is not given on time, these children may be found crying, fighting, or otherwise in trouble on the playground or in the cafeteria, and disruptive on returning to the classroom. It takes approximately thirty minutes for the next dose of medication to take effect. Careful timing to avoid this rebound effect helps considerably.

- Students with ADHD have a hard time remembering to go to the office at the designated time for medication because of the very nature of ADHD and executive function impairment. It is the responsibility of the teacher or other members of school staff to help remind them discreetly. Strategies for doing so may include a beeper watch or vibrating alarm, private signals from the teacher, pairing the medication time with a natural transition (for example, on the way to the cafeteria), coded verbal reminders, as well as a sticker chart where the medication is dispensed, rewarding the child for remembering.

- Schools have specific policies and procedures for administering medication—for example, a signed consent form on file; medication in the original, labeled prescription container stored in a locked place; and maintenance of careful records of the dosage, time of dispensing, and person administering the medication.

- It helps if parents are notified well before the school's supply of medication runs out so that they have plenty of time to renew the prescription and deliver it to school.

What Parents Need to Know

- If your child or teen is taking medication, it is important that he or she receive it as prescribed in the morning—on time and consistently—under your supervision. Close monitoring and management of the medication are crucial. If it is administered inconsistently, the child is better off without it.

- Because appetite suppression is a common side effect, it is best to seek advice from the doctor regarding how to manage this—for example, by planning for breakfast and other meals at times your child is most likely to have an appetite.

- When your child is on a long-acting medication and the school isn't involved in administering a midday dose, you may be tempted not to inform the school that the child is taking a medication for ADHD. This is not advised. It is best to inform the school of any medical treatment for the disorder and not keep it a secret.

- It requires teamwork and close communication among the family, school staff, and physician for a child to receive the most benefits from medication treatment. Be prepared to lead this communication effort to make sure that the doctor receives the necessary feedback from the school regarding your child's functioning on medication.

- Follow-up visits with the child's doctor are necessary for monitoring the medication's effectiveness.

- For appropriate medical care, the doctor needs to obtain feedback from you *and the school* when your child is on medication. You may need to facilitate this connection. Follow-up ADHD rating scales (such as the Vanderbilt scales) filled out by you and teachers are helpful in monitoring treatment effects. A free downloadable form that can be used is one created by David Rabiner, PhD, found at www.helpforadd .com/monitor.pdf.

- As discussed earlier, when a child is started on medication therapy, there is always a trial period when the physician is trying to determine the most effective medication and dosage. Some children are fortunate to have a brief and successful trial period, experiencing significant symptom improvement quickly. Others will take longer, and some will not benefit from or be able to tolerate the medication. However, for 70 to 90 percent of children with ADHD, medication is found to be effective. Be prepared for this process to take some time to get right, and therefore be patient. If one of the medications doesn't seem to work, chances are that another one will.

- Because the commonly prescribed stimulants are classified by the Drug Enforcement Administration as schedule II medications, there are strict laws regarding how they are prescribed and dispensed. The FDA has restrictions that pharmacists must follow. This makes it more difficult for refilling prescriptions. For example, the medication cannot be called in, and doctors can write a prescription for only one month at a time. It is important that you pay close attention and communicate with the school nurse to make sure the school has the medication on hand if it is a short-acting stimulant prescription.

- Children should be counseled about their medication and why they are taking it. They should be aware that the medication is not in control of their behavior—they are—but that medication helps them (pay attention, get school and homework done, put on the brakes so they can make better choices, and so forth). There are various resources available that can help children better understand ADHD and why they are taking medication to treat it. Some wonderful books geared for children and teens that explain ADHD in kid-friendly, age-appropriate ways are those by Dendy and Zeigler (2015), Nadeau and Dixon (2004), and Quinn and Stern (2009), found in Part 1 Additional Sources and Resources.

INTERVIEW WITH MIKE
Graduate Student in Colorado

Mike was in his twenties when he received an ADHD diagnosis and began treatment.

What are your memories of school?

"Grade school through high school, I rarely did my homework. I got through on my test scores. On all of my scholastic aptitude tests, I scored above the 90th percentile. I was lucky to be an avid reader. I could get the course syllabus and do the reading without even attending class. But I had a very hard time coping in school. I was highly frustrated, and considered by most of my teachers as a 'problem child.' I wasn't shy about challenging teachers."

Which teachers did you do best with?

"Those who had interesting things to say, lectured well, would go with the flow, and had a sense of humor. I did well with teachers who appreciated an original or challenging thought, who gave latitude for originality, and who weren't rigid."

What is your advice to teachers?

"Kids with ADHD are going to need structure. When you find a kid is not making it, start lending a little structure and see if it will help. I still need a little more structure from my bosses than my co-workers do."

What was it like for you, once you received the diagnosis and started treatment?

"When I started medication, it was a revelation to me that I can start something and be able to accomplish it within a reasonable amount of time—even something like cleaning my apartment. If only I'd been caught at eighteen or even eight."

Behavioral Therapy for Managing ADHD

Behavioral therapy is one of the two research-validated interventions proven most effective in the management of ADHD. Behavioral therapy combined with medication therapy is often the optimal intervention for many children with ADHD, providing the greatest improvement in the child's functioning, behavior, and relationships. For any child not receiving medication, behavioral therapy is essential to treat and manage the disorder.

According to the American Academy of Pediatrics (AAP, 2011) guidelines for treating ADHD in children, primary care physicians should prescribe behavioral therapy as the first line of treatment for preschool-age children (four through five years of age); for children ages six through eleven, the physician should prescribe FDA-approved medications for ADHD or evidence-based behavioral therapy (administered by parents and the teacher) as treatment for ADHD—preferably both.

Behavioral therapy requires training of the parent and teacher in behavior modification techniques and the commitment of the adult to implement strategies learned. This is not easy; it takes time and effort, but the benefits are well worth it.

Behavioral therapy helps adults improve children's behavior by teaching the adults behavioral principles and strategies to implement in managing and responding to problem behavior, with professional guidance. Behavioral treatments work by teaching new skills to parents, teachers, and the children for handling problems and interacting with others.

Behavioral interventions for ADHD may include the following:

- Proactive parenting and classroom management, and effective discipline practices at home and school
- Parents and teachers using behavior modification techniques effectively
- Communicating in ways to increase compliance—that is, helping the child listen to and follow parent and teacher directions
- Structuring the environment and being aware of antecedents or triggers to misbehavior to prevent problems at home and school
- Using strategies to best deal with the challenging behaviors associated with ADHD and poor self-regulation in school, home, and other environments
- Classroom and schoolwide behavioral and social-emotional learning programs and supports
- Improving the child's peer interactions and social skills

- Use of well-designed behavioral programs, such as daily charts and school-to-home report cards, token economy programs, and individual behavioral contracts

Note: A variety of behavioral charts and examples are found in Part 2 and in the appendix. Some of the behavioral charts and daily report cards that are in the appendix are also online at www.wiley.com/go/adhdreach.

General Principles of Behavior Modification

Behavior modification techniques are a cornerstone of behavioral intervention for ADHD. They are based on the three-part "ABCs" of behavior: **a**ntecedent, **b**ehavior, and **c**onsequence. In general, the *antecedent (A)* is the situation, event, or stimulus that triggers the *behavior (B)*. The *consequence (C)* is what occurs immediately after the behavior (B) is demonstrated. The consequence either increases or decreases the likelihood that the behavior will reoccur.

Behavior modification is based heavily on learning how to recognize and adjust the antecedents or triggers that set off behavioral problems, and thereby reduce or avoid them. It also teaches the effective use of consequences to increase those positive behaviors we want to continue and encourage, and to decrease those negative, undesirable behaviors we want to reduce or eliminate.

Behavior modification techniques use incentive systems (such as points or token systems). Rewards are very important in improving behavior. They are particularly necessary for children with ADHD, who require more external motivation than other children typically need. Children and teens with ADHD also need more frequent rewards because their internal controls are less mature, and they have trouble delaying gratification. When they are implemented correctly and judiciously, negative consequences or punishments—particularly use of time-out procedures and loss of privileges—are also effective in changing behavior.

Home-Based Behavioral Treatment

Parents of children with ADHD must become far more knowledgeable and skilled in behavior management principles and techniques than other parents. They need training in how to handle the daily challenges and behavioral difficulties resulting from the child's disorder.

Parent training is key to understanding ADHD and how to best manage it. Parent training programs incorporate techniques to improve parent-child interactions, decrease noncompliance, reduce behavior problems, and facilitate family communication patterns (Teeter, 2000). Parents learn preventive strategies (adjusting or manipulating the antecedents to misbehavior), instructive strategies (directed at providing the child with different and more appropriate ways to accomplish a goal), and consequence-based strategies, including effective use of rewards and punishments (Wolraich & DuPaul, 2010).

Behavior modification training is typically for parents managing the behaviors of preschool and elementary school children. With adolescents, other techniques and skills, such as behavioral contracting and problem solving, are taught to parents and the teen (Wolraich & DuPaul, 2010).

Parent education can be conducted in a group format or with individual sets of parents in training sessions over a series of weeks. Parent trainings are generally provided in eight or more weekly or biweekly sessions, with specific strategies parents are to implement as homework between sessions.

Parents typically learn such strategies as establishing daily routines, organizing and structuring for success at home, praising and giving positive attention for appropriate behaviors, giving effective directions and commands to increase compliance and cooperation, effectively using rewards and negative consequences, avoiding power struggles and conflicts, and using incentive systems (daily charts, point and token systems, school-home note systems).

In order to effectively change their child's behavior, parents must also understand how behavioral principles operate on their own behavior. For example, frustrated parents often respond to children's misbehavior by giving consequences that actually increase rather than decrease that problem behavior's occurrence.

CHADD (www.chadd.org) offers a unique educational program called Parent to Parent (P2P), which is given in the community, online, and on demand, and is facilitated by a P2P trainer.

See Barkley's book *Taking Charge of ADHD* (2013b) for an excellent summary of his recommended steps in parent training, and his program for clinicians in *Defiant Children: A Clinician's Manual for Assessment and Parent Training* (2013a).

The following are some other parent training programs:

- COPE (Community Parent Education Program) (Cunningham, 2005; Cunningham, Bremner, Secord, & Harrison, 2009)
- Triple P (Positive Parenting Program) (www.triplep.net/glo-en/home/)
- Incredible Years Parenting Program (http://incredibleyears.com/programs/parent/)
- Parent-Child Interaction Therapy (www.pcit.org/)

School-Based Behavioral Treatment

There are a number of school-based behavioral approaches that have been found effective in decreasing problem behavior in children. School-based behavioral interventions are implemented by the teacher in most cases and involve the following actions:

- Proactive classroom management
- Creating an ADHD-friendly classroom environment
- Preventing behavior problems during transitions and other challenging times of the school day
- Using class (group) behavior management systems
- Implementing individualized behavioral programs, supports, and interventions, such as daily report cards and behavioral contracts
- Implementing targeted strategies to help students with inattentive, off-task, impulsive, or hyperactive behaviors

- Effectively managing students' anger, frustration, and poor self-regulation

Note: All of these topics will be addressed in Part 2 of this book.

School districts throughout the United States are shifting their focus toward promoting positive behavior and away from reacting to negative behavior, initiating a systematic and structured whole-school effort. This involves modeling and teaching—in all classrooms and schoolwide—the rules and expected behaviors, creating a supportive and consistent environment for all students, and employing a number of early intervention strategies ("Early Intervention," 2014).

Many schools are now implementing a multi-tiered system of support (MTSS), which is a continuum of increasingly intense supports for students. Schools that use a Response to Intervention (RTI) model and a Positive Behavioral Interventions and Supports (PBIS) model, which are both MTSS models, are well structured to provide effective behavioral treatment to students in need. PBIS schools, for example, teach and reinforce prosocial behaviors as a tier 1 intervention for all students, and provide more targeted and intense supports (tier 2 and tier 3) as needed by individual students, with close monitoring of student responses to the interventions to ensure that all students receive the level of help they need. See www.pbis.org and the other resources for implementing schoolwide behavioral interventions listed in the Part 1 Additional Sources and Resources.

An effective program for preschool is Teaching Pyramid, developed at Vanderbilt University Center for Social and Emotional Learning (http://csefel.vanderbilt.edu). It promotes the healthy social-emotional development of young children.

For an outstanding program and model proven highly effective in transforming public schools in communities with high levels of needs, see Turnaround for Children (http://turnaroundusa.org/). Turnaround creates a partnership with schools that accomplishes the following:

- Builds a high-capacity student support system that gets all children, including those with intense needs, help either in school or in partnership with a community-based mental health provider

- Trains all teachers in proven classroom strategies that foster a safe, engaging learning environment and strong student-teacher relationships
- Works with school leaders to drive school-wide improvement, aligned to Common Core State Standards and district guidelines, and creates a high-performing culture that involves the entire school community

Another very useful school-based behavioral intervention, and one that should be provided for students whose behavior is impeding learning, is a functional behavior assessment (FBA), which is a procedure to gather and analyze data to determine the ABCs of the student's problem behavior. Then, based on that information, a behavioral intervention plan (BIP) is designed. Strategies in the BIP will address the antecedents (such as adjustments made in the environment, skill performance demand, or teacher-student interactions) in order to prevent problems. The plan also addresses the consequences of the problem behavior (changing the responses or reactions to the behavior) and more appropriate replacement behaviors to teach the student to use instead of what he or she is doing. See Section 2.4 for more on FBAs and BIPs.

Child-Based Behavioral Treatment

Child-based interventions focus on peer relationships. They usually occur in group settings, such as classrooms, small groups at school, office clinics, and summer camps. Research-validated child-based interventions involve teaching, practicing, and reinforcing social skills and behaviors that improve peer relations. They do not include play therapy or talk therapy approaches.

Some children with ADHD have social skills deficits. They may lack the knowledge of or have not yet learned certain social skills, in which case they may benefit from being taught specific social skills. These are usually taught within small groups of children in the same age range with use of social skills curricula, such as *ACCEPTS: The*

Walker Social Skills Curriculum (Walker et al., 1983), *Skillstreaming the Elementary School Child* (McGinnis & Goldstein, 1999), *Stop and Think Social Skills Program* (Knoff, n.d.), and *Second Step* (Committee for Children, 2008).

Social skills training programs are designed to systematically teach specific social skills for getting along with other children, such as sharing and taking turns. Social skills training typically involves the following:

- The trainer provides a brief introduction to the skill (and the rationale for learning it), defines it clearly, and demonstrates the appropriate skill and inappropriate behavior through positive and negative examples.
- Children role-play and rehearse the appropriate skill with adult and peer feedback.
- The bulk of the session involves actually playing an indoor or outdoor game or engaging in some other activity. Children are prompted and coached in the use of the skill.
- There is a short debriefing with feedback and reinforcement for demonstrating the use of the targeted skill, and children are encouraged to self-monitor their use of the skill.

Quite often children with ADHD have learned social skills and know what to do, but their ADHD-related impairments interfere with their ability to perform the skills with consistency or at an acceptable level. For these performance deficits, they don't need social skills training programs, but do need prompting, cueing, and reminders about the appropriate behavior and consequences. They need lots of practice of the social skills, with feedback and reinforcement of the use of these skills in activities and environments where they have problems (for example, the playground, at the bus stop, in the cafeteria, and when playing competitive games with siblings or friends).

Often a child with ADHD is not socially accepted because of poor skills in playing games and sports. It is a helpful intervention for parents to build their child's skills and competencies in playing sports and games to raise their status with other children. Provide opportunities to learn and practice general sportsmanship and the strategies, rules, and skills of those sports and games, so that their peers will want to include them in their play.

Developing the interpersonal skills for forming and keeping friendships is an important child-based intervention that can be facilitated by parents and teachers (for example, through planned play dates, partnering with compatible classmates for paired and cooperative group activities). Parents often need to be their child's friendship coach.

Barkley (2013b) recommends that parents set up a home reward token program focusing on one or two social behaviors to work on over a week or two, which are posted on a chart. The child is reminded about the rewards and consequences (earning or losing a point or token) for demonstrating (or not demonstrating) the target skills when interacting with other children. Then, as the child is playing with others, parents monitor discreetly, and when observing their child's use of the appropriate skills, find an opportunity (when the playmate is not aware) to praise and reward with the token. Mikami (2011) suggests that when coaching, parents should keep feedback brief (for example, "Nice job of letting your friend go first") and specific ("If you lose, you can say 'good game' to the winner").

There are some highly effective summer camps and summer treatment programs designed for children with ADHD that have a strong focus on teaching, practicing, and reinforcing social skills throughout the day while children participate in fun activities and interactions with one another. For information about such programs and a listing of some camps and summer programs, see www.additudemag.com/directory.asp.

See information from CHADD and the National Resource Center on AD/HD for more expert advice on this topic.

A leading authority on psychosocial (behavioral) interventions for children with ADHD is Dr. William Pelham Jr. I recommend listening to or reading the transcript of his CHADD "Ask the Expert" chat (Pelham, 2014) and view the free resources that Pelham and his team have developed, available online at http://ccf.buffalo.edu /resources_downloads.php.

For additional behavioral resources, see those listed in the Part 1 and Part 2 Additional Sources and Resources.

INTERVIEW WITH JOE
Forty-one Years Old, California

Joe received a diagnosis of learning disabilities and ADHD as an adult.

"Watch Joseph. He's one of the most intelligent children I've ever seen." This was the comment made to Joe's parents when he and his siblings were tested at a young age by their neighbor, a professor of psychology in New York—Joe, who never received higher than a D from sixth grade through high school. Joe, who was constantly ridiculed by his teachers and was a "big disappointment to his parents."

Joe was "left back" in the seventh grade while living in Connecticut. He remembers the trauma of having all his friends moving on to another school when he repeated seventh. He flunked algebra four times. He graduated from high school "dead last" in his class. "After a while I had defaulted into a discipline problem. You gravitate toward those students who have absolutely no respect for the system. Otherwise you have to agree that the only other thing that could be wrong is YOU."

Community college was an uphill battle all over again. He saw his classmates "cruise through all their subjects" to get their degrees. "The only difference between them and me was that I never knew what to do with numbers. Reading is extremely difficult for me. I have to do it very slowly and put everything into my own translator to assimilate the material and have it make sense."

Joe's adult life has been "a patchwork of jobs." Up until a few years ago, the average time he stayed with a job was one year. "There were so many days I was beaten to a pulp, and completely down and out until I was thirty years old. I knew there was something wrong with me, but no one knew what it was."

One significant change came in his adult life when a friend took him "under his wing" and mentored him for three years in his business. "Now I have a good job as a technician in a good company. But it never lets up. I can't get a reprieve. In the real world of high tech, it requires constant training and schooling."

What would have made a difference for you growing up?

"No one saw or was interested in my strengths. The spoken word came easily to me; the written word was very difficult. I was able at a young age to take an engine apart and put it back together. I have an excellent understanding of mechanical things. I was always musically talented . . . and I knew everything there was to know about reptiles and amphibians.

"If one person would have interceded on my behalf. If one person would have said, 'This is not a stupid person we're dealing with . . . There's something more involved here that we need to get to the bottom of,' the weight of the world would have been lifted from my shoulders."

Critical Factors in the Success of Students with ADHD

Knowledge and Understanding of ADHD. It is essential that teachers be aware that students with ADHD have a problem that is physiological and neurobiological in nature. Training about the disorder itself is very important so that adults working and interacting with these students every day at school understand what is underlying the challenging behaviors the children often exhibit and realize that the behaviors are not deliberate in intent. In fact, most of the time children with ADHD are oblivious to the impact their behaviors are having on those around them. A better understanding helps teachers, other school personnel, and parents maintain their patience, tolerance, sense of humor, and ability to deal with the student and his or her behaviors in a positive way. Every school (elementary, middle, and secondary) needs professional development devoted to educating all school personnel about ADHD. All educators need to understand how the disorder affects students' learning and school functioning and to be trained in effective strategies and interventions.

Teacher Flexibility and Positive Attitude. Placement with a teacher who has a positive mind-set and attitude about teaching *all* students in the classroom (including those with learning and behavioral challenges) is essential to the success of students with ADHD. The teacher needs to be flexible in working with the individual student, parents, and other teachers and service providers, and to understand the necessity of making adaptations and accommodations. The teacher also must be willing to put forth the extra time, energy, and effort it takes to provide the supports and implement the strategies needed to help the child or teen succeed.

Clarity and Structure. Students with ADHD need a structured classroom. Some people may have the misconception that a structured classroom is one that is "traditional" in room arrangement and teaching style (as adults remember from their school days). What appears to an observer as a structured teacher and classroom may very well not be.

The key structural components to be looking for in any classroom are clear communication, expectations, rules, consequences, and follow-up; academic tasks with clear directions and standards; long-term, lengthy assignments structured, for example, by breaking them into shorter, manageable increments with feedback after each part; assistance with structuring of students' materials, work space, group dynamics, handling of choices, and transitional times of the day; and a school day structured with alternating active and quiet periods. No matter what the particular teaching style or the physical environment of the classroom, any teacher can and should provide structure for student success.

Powerful, Research-Based Teaching Strategies. Instruction that enables students to be highly engaged, involved, and interacting with their peers is critical in the classroom—especially for students with ADHD. All students need and deserve a curriculum that is enriching and motivating, and that employs a variety of research-validated approaches. In order for teachers to be successful in enabling all students to achieve and acquire the skills, standards, and content mastery for the grade level, they must be adept at differentiating instruction. Teachers need to be trained and skilled in the use of strategies that offer a high degree of active learning and student response opportunities. They also need a large repertoire of strategies and techniques that draw on the diverse learning styles and strengths of students in the classroom. All students need to be given the daily opportunity to work in a variety of formats (for example, with partners, in small groups, individually, and in large groups) and to be instructed through a combination of motivating techniques and methods.

Effective Classroom Management and Positive Discipline. All students deserve to be in classrooms in which there is a positive, respectful climate. Fundamental to school success is creating an environment in which everyone feels part of a caring, supportive community. Students with ADHD are in particular need of a classroom placement in which the teacher structures the classroom environment, procedures, routines, and instruction with a focus on problem prevention. Teachers must be aware of what may trigger behavioral problems and avoid those triggers through careful planning. They need to teach and reinforce appropriate behavior and to employ positive, proactive discipline practices.

Close Communication between Home and School. It is critical for teachers and parents to make every effort to establish a good working relationship and maintain open lines of communication. Early in the school year, it is best to discuss which avenues of communication are preferred by both parties (for example, phone calls, emails, text messaging, home-school notes, journals, daily/weekly reports). This population of students needs far more frequent and regular contact between home and school than is necessary for most other students in the class. The success of students with ADHD depends strongly on the mutual support, communication, and cooperation between home and school.

Environmental Modifications and Accommodations. Classroom environment is a very important factor in how students function. To accommodate a variety of learning styles, there should be options for students as to where and how they work in the classroom. Where the student sits can make a significant difference. Lighting, furniture, seating arrangements, visual displays, color, areas for relaxation, and provisions for blocking out distractions during seatwork should be carefully considered. Teachers should organize the classroom with the awareness that most students with ADHD need to be within close proximity to the teacher (to enable easy prompting and cueing) and to be seated in less distracting, low-traffic areas near and among well-focused students. There are many environmental factors that can be adjusted to improve the functioning and performance of students with ADHD.

Collaboration and Teamwork. The partnership that is developed between parents, educators, and clinicians is a key element in the successful management of ADHD. This disorder affects many aspects of the child's or teen's life, and it takes a team approach to improve his or her functioning—not just at school but at home and in other settings. Parents are truly the leaders of the team. They have the main role in seeking out and trying to assemble the optimal team for treating, caring for, and educating their son or daughter. The team may involve medical and mental health professionals, the teacher and other school personnel, before- or after-school caregivers, tutors, coaches, and so forth.

What about other teaming for school success? Many teachers find that team teaching is extremely helpful. Being able to switch or share students (particularly very challenging ones) for part of the school day may reduce the behavioral problems and minimize the teacher's stress level. Switching or sharing also provides for a different perspective on each child. Various student support services, such as those provided by guidance/school counselors, are often very helpful for students with ADHD. Some of those supports might include working with the teacher in the implementation of behavior modification techniques and training and practice in conflict resolution, peer mediation, social skills, and anger management.

Of course, if the student is receiving special education or related services, successful outcomes involve communication and collaboration among classroom teachers, special educators, and other service providers. There is an IEP team involved when students are being evaluated for and receiving special education services.

The school's multidisciplinary team (which may be called the student support team, teacher assistance team, Response to Intervention team, or something else) can be a great resource and provider of direct and indirect help to the teacher and student. The team often includes the school psychologist, school nurse, and other school-based support professionals. Administrators can be instrumental in obtaining extra intervention and support for the student, as well. You are all part of the same team! Everyone's focus needs to be on the best interests of the student and on ways all parties can help that child or teen experience school success.

Developing and Bringing Out Students' Strengths. Many children with ADHD are gifted and talented (intellectually, artistically, musically, athletically). It is very important for teachers to draw on and foster these children's strengths and interests. Teachers need to provide numerous opportunities—particularly for students who struggle in school—to be able to showcase their strengths and demonstrate to their peers what they do well. Unfortunately, their classmates are all too familiar with the ADHD student's areas of weakness and his or her vulnerabilities. It is important for parents to provide as many opportunities as possible outside of school to help their child discover areas of interest and participate in activities that develop those skills and give him or her a source of motivation, self-esteem, and joy.

Help and Training in Organization and Study Skills. Students with ADHD commonly have major problems with organization, time management, and study skills. They will need direct help and additional intervention to make sure that assignments are recorded correctly, their work space and materials are organized, notebooks and desks are cleared of unnecessary collections of junk from time to time, and specific study skills are learned to enable them to achieve academic success. There are numerous strategies and study skills that will improve the performance of children and teens with ADHD, and teachers and parents can do much to help build these skills.

Limiting the Amount of Homework. If the parent complains that an inordinate amount of time is spent on homework, teachers should be flexible and reduce the homework to a manageable amount. Teachers need to be aware of the terrible homework hassles and stress in many homes of children with ADHD. This, of course, has to do with all the executive function–related difficulty with sustaining the attention, mental effort, and motivation to get through work, such as the average homework assignment. Students with ADHD typically take much longer than the average student to complete homework tasks, and they need more supervision and monitoring than most children of that age to complete homework assignments.

In addition, students with ADHD, who may be medicated and therefore more productive during school hours, often are not receiving medication benefits in the late afternoon or evening hours. It depends on the medication and how long the therapeutic effect. Many teachers have the practice of sending home any incomplete class work. It is important for teachers to keep in mind that if the student was unable to complete the work during an entire school day, it is unlikely that he or she will be able to complete it that evening. Instead of piling on all the incomplete work, teachers should prioritize, communicate closely with parents, set realistic goals, make accommodations, and find ways to modify the homework assigned without compromising the student's learning.

Modifying Assignments and Written Workload. What takes an average child twenty or thirty minutes to do may take a student with ADHD hours to accomplish (particularly written assignments). There is no need to do every problem on the page to practice a skill or reinforce new learning. Teachers need to be open to adapting or modifying assignments when needed for certain students. Remember that ADHD is a disorder that affects performance, production, and output. These students typically cannot produce the same amount of work at the same rate as the average child of the same age or grade. Teachers must be willing to make accommodations so that the amount of work assigned is reasonable for that particular student (for example, every other problem, half a page) to learn the material and demonstrate his or her knowledge. The following are some suggestions for teachers:

- Accept methods of demonstrating learning through means other than in writing (for example, allowing the student to answer questions orally, having the student dictate and a scribe write or record, doing hands-on projects and demonstrations).
- Seek other more fun, creative, and artistic ways for the student to practice skills and show his or her mastery of concepts.
- Ease up on handwriting demands for students if they struggle with the physical task of writing.
- Be sensitive to the extreme effort it often takes children with ADHD and learning disabilities to put down in writing what appears simple to you and what other students can do with ease.

More Time, More Space. To compensate for the difficulty many students with ADHD have with speed of output, providing more time is often a necessary accommodation. This may mean extra time to complete assignments or exams. Some students with ADHD also have slower processing speed. They may, for example, need extra time to process and think about a question and what to say before responding.

Students with ADHD often have a tendency to intrude in others' space. They frequently need more room to themselves (for example, table top or desk space, and more distance and buffer space when sitting on the carpet) in order to stay better organized and reduce problems interacting with their peers. Of course, teachers in upper grades and crowded classrooms have fewer options in how to provide more space without getting very creative.

Support of Administration. It is critical that administrators also be aware of the characteristics and strategies for effectively managing and educating students with ADHD and support the teacher in dealing with disruptive children. Some students are extremely difficult to maintain in the classroom and require highly creative interventions. In these cases, administrative support is very much needed in assisting the teacher. Such support can come in many forms (for example, student time away from the classroom—in other classrooms or settings; more push-in adult help at certain times of the day in the classroom; facilitating meetings with parents and other team members; helping with developing a proactive plan of behavioral intervention).

Administrators need to be sensitive to and receptive of input from parents and teachers regarding classroom placement each year. As instructional leaders of their schools, they must help teachers develop their skills and learn effective strategies for working with and instructing students with ADHD or learning disabilities, and others with diverse learning needs. This can be done by providing the necessary professional development and training. The school climate for academic and social/behavioral success is best established when the administrator takes the lead in setting, modeling, and reinforcing positive expectations in the building (for staff and students).

Valuing and Respecting Learning Styles and Differences, Privacy, Confidentiality, and Students' Feelings. Teachers who are going to be successful in reaching and teaching students with ADHD, and all the diverse learners in the classroom, must value and respect the different learning styles and differences each child possesses. These are part of what makes each student unique. Teachers and other school personnel must also be very conscious and respectful of privacy and confidentiality issues (evaluation results, medication issues, test scores and grades, family information). Self-esteem is fragile in students with ADHD. Because of the high degree of negative feedback they commonly receive over the years, many students with ADHD perceive themselves as failures. We must avoid ridicule and never humiliate any child or teen. Preservation of students' self-esteem is critical in truly helping them succeed in life.

Belief in the Student—Doing What It Takes. Students with ADHD need teachers, parents, and other adults who are on their side, who believe in them and their ability to succeed. These supportive adults must also realize that it takes vigilance and willingness to frequently come back to the "drawing board" to reexamine or revise the original plan. When Plans A, B, and C no longer seem to be working well, there are always Plans D, E, F, and so forth. These students are worth the extra time and effort, and we must never give up!

INTERVIEW WITH SPENCER'S MOTHER
Colorado

What are some of the hurtful comments you remember from Spencer's teachers?

"One teacher told me, 'If he gets enough F's, he'll learn how to do what is expected of him in fifth grade,' referring to his homework. Another teacher said, 'He slipped a few times and has shown us how bright he is. He's just playing games with us.'"

Tell me about his best teacher.

"Spencer's third-grade teacher was wonderful. She read to the class with the lights off . . . made sure there wasn't a lot of clutter on the board or his desk. She seated him to reduce distractions . . . right up front near her. She spoke softly to him, and every criticism was coupled with something positive."

ADHD in Preschool and Kindergarten

Most children with ADHD are not diagnosed until the elementary school grades. With very young children, it is harder to distinguish between what is normal rambunctious, inattentive, and uninhibited behavior from what is abnormal and symptomatic of ADHD. Inattention and high activity level are typical behaviors of preschoolers, but of course, most do not have ADHD.

Although most children do not receive a diagnosis of ADHD until they are six years or older, those youngsters exhibiting significant difficulties with ADHD symptoms are now being identified at a younger age, enabling them to receive earlier intervention. Recent and ongoing research as well as the American Academy of Pediatrics (2011) revised guidelines for the diagnosis, evaluation, and treatment of ADHD in preschool-age children and how to best treat the disorder in this population.

Early identification of ADHD or any related developmental problems and early intervention can make a huge positive difference in the life of the child and family. They can significantly minimize the social, behavioral, or learning difficulties the child experiences as a result of the disorder and prevent a lot of struggle down the road.

Preschool and kindergarten teachers are in the best position to catch children early who are showing signs and symptoms of a developmental delay or disability, or who are at risk for struggles in learning and school. Teachers need to be aware of symptoms—sharing observations and concerns with parents and other school specialists (such as members of the school's multidisciplinary team). Through screening, evaluation, and targeted interventions, many learning and behavioral problems can be prevented.

Developmental Signs and Symptoms in Young Children

Teeter (1998) summarized the research regarding key characteristics of ADHD during the preschool stage, some of which are the following:

- Parental stress is at its zenith.
- The child is often difficult to toilet train.
- The child responds impulsively.
- The child exhibits hyperactivity during structured activities.
- Inattention to tasks and distractibility are high.
- The child shifts from one activity to another.
- Peer rejection is common.

Mahone (2012) describes these additional symptoms of ADHD that are common in preschool children:

- Dislikes or avoids activities that require paying attention for more than a minute or two (such as playing with a toy or listening to a story)
- Talks a lot more and makes more noise than is typical of other children the same age
- Is nearly always restless
- Has gotten into dangerous situations because of fearlessness and has been injured because of moving too fast or running when not supposed to
- Is aggressive with playmates

Schusteff (2007, p. 49) explains that with ADHD in preschoolers, "the tipping point in diagnosis is usually a matter of degree." These kids are much more extreme in their behaviors than the average three-year-old.

If a child receives an ADHD diagnosis in the preschool or kindergarten years, the symptoms are typically quite severe and are persistent over time and across settings. The child experiences many behavioral, social, and interpersonal difficulties. It is not uncommon for these children to be kicked out of one or more early childhood programs—often because of aggressive and oppositional behavior.

If a child has ADHD, the preschool or kindergarten teacher will find the behaviors to be very problematic and excessive in comparison to other children. The teacher should share observations and concerns with parents and support staff and implement strategies and supports to address the needs of the child. Almost all of the teaching and parenting techniques recommended throughout this book are applicable and effective for children in this age bracket as well.

 ## Red Flags for Possible Learning Disabilities

Commonly, a child with ADHD may have other developmental weaknesses or delays in some areas (for example, speech-language, motor skills, or acquiring academic readiness skills—such as learning and remembering ABCs, numbers, shapes, and letter-sound associations). It is important to be aware that children with ADHD often have coexisting learning disabilities, such as dyslexia. Some warning signs of learning disabilities in preschool and kindergarten (Inland Empire Branch of the International Dyslexia Association, 2003; "LD Basics," n.d.; National Joint Committee on Learning Disabilities, n.d.) include the following:

Language

- Slow development in speaking words or sentences ("late talkers")
- Pronunciation problems
- Difficulty learning new words; slow vocabulary growth
- Difficulty finding the right word to use when speaking
- Difficulty understanding and following simple (one-step) directions
- Difficulty understanding questions
- Difficulty expressing wants and desires
- Difficulty recognizing or learning rhyming words
- Lack of interest in storytelling
- Immature grammar (syntax)
- Infrequent or inappropriate spontaneous communication (vocal, verbal, or nonverbal)

Emergent Literacy Skills

- Slow speed for naming objects and colors
- Limited phonological awareness (for example, rhyming, syllable blending)
- Difficulty understanding that written language is composed of phonemes (individual sounds) and letters that make up syllables, words, and sentences
- Minimal interest in print and limited print awareness
- Difficulty recognizing and learning the letters of the alphabet
- Slow learning of the connection between letters and sounds

Cognition

- Trouble memorizing the alphabet or days of the week

- Poor memory for what should be routine (everyday procedures)
- Difficulty with cause and effect, sequencing, and counting
- Difficulty with basic concepts such as size, shape, and color

Motor Skills

- Clumsiness
- Poor balance
- Difficulty with fine motor skills and manipulating small objects (for example, stringing beads, tying shoes, buttoning)
- Awkwardness with running, jumping, or climbing (delayed gross motor skills)
- Difficulty or avoidance of drawing, coloring, tracing, or copying

Social Behavior

- Has trouble interacting with others; plays alone
- Is prone to sudden and extreme mood changes
- Is easily frustrated
- Is hard to manage, has temper tantrums
- Has difficulty following directions and routines

Attention and Behavior

- Distractibility and inattention
- Impulsivity
- Hyperactivity
- Difficulty changing activities or handling disruptions to routines

Note: Many of the listed behaviors are also indicators of some other developmental disorders.

What the Research Shows

PATS 2006

The first long-term comprehensive study of ADHD treatment in this population was the Preschool ADHD Treatment Study (PATS), sponsored by the National Institute of Mental Health,

conducted by researchers at six sites. The study included more than three hundred preschoolers with severe ADHD symptoms, ages three to five. All children and their parents first participated in a ten-week behavioral therapy and training course in behavior modification techniques, such as consistent use of positive and negative consequences.

More than a third of those children were treated successfully with behavior modification and did not proceed to the medication stage of the study. The children who did not improve after the behavioral therapy course were included in the medication part of the study. They were given low doses of methylphenidate (stimulant medication), monitored very closely, and compared to those taking a placebo. Although most of the children tolerated the drug well, 11 percent had to drop out of the study as a result of intolerable side effects.

The findings were that those children taking the medication had a more marked reduction of their ADHD symptoms compared to children taking a placebo. The conclusion of this 2006 PATS was that preschoolers with severe ADHD benefit when treated with behavior modification only or a combination of behavior modification and low doses of methylphenidate. Although medication was found to be generally effective and safe, preschoolers appear to be more prone to side effects than older children and need close monitoring for side effects (National Institute of Mental Health [NIMH], 2006).

PATS Six-Year Follow-up

There was a six-year follow-up to the PATS (Riddle et al., 2012). Approximately 70 percent of the original children participated in the follow-up study, and most all still met criteria for ADHD. ADHD in preschoolers was found to be a relatively stable diagnosis over a six-year period. The course is generally chronic, with high symptom severity and impairment in very young children with moderate to severe ADHD, despite treatment with medication. Development of more effective ADHD intervention strategies is needed for this age group.

Evaluation, Diagnosis, and Intervention

Parents should discuss concerns with their pediatrician or other developmental specialist and their child's preschool or kindergarten teacher. When ADHD symptoms are problematic and exceed what seems normal for other children their age and when symptoms are persistent and observable in different settings (such as home and the preschool or day-care environments), an evaluation should be considered.

Any developmental disorder, such as ADHD, is best identified early so that appropriate intervention can be started. A wait-and-see approach is typically not in the child's best interest. When a child has ADHD, behaviors that affect social and academic performance generally do not improve by just providing more time for the child to mature. In addition, children who have specific developmental delays benefit from early intervention, such as speech-language therapy, occupational therapy, or other needed services.

Wolraich (2007) recommends that parents of preschool children who exhibit symptoms of ADHD take the following steps:

1. Begin with a parent training program: a group program, such as the CHADD-sponsored Parent to Parent program (see www.chadd.org) or an individual program for more intense training, such as Parent Child Interaction Training (www.pcit.org), which works with the child and parent or other caregiver together to improve overall behavior and to reduce parenting stress. The child does not need a diagnosis of ADHD for parents to participate in these programs and learn the skills. *Note:* Other parent training programs are listed in Section 1.6.

2. If parent training does not sufficiently address the problems, parents should have their child evaluated by their pediatrician (if the doctor is knowledgeable about ADHD in young children) or other clinician, such as a child psychiatrist, child psychologist, or developmental behavioral pediatrician.

3. Depending on the results of the evaluation, parents can consider a more intense behavior modification program, treatment with stimulant medication, or a combination of both.

AAP Clinical Practice Guidelines for Diagnosis, Evaluation, and Treatment of Preschool Children

The American Academy of Pediatrics (AAP) wrote and published clinical practice guidelines for the diagnosis, evaluation, and treatment of ADHD in children and adolescents (AAP, 2011), which expanded on those written a decade before. The 2011 AAP guidelines take into account what was learned from the research about the benefits of diagnosis and treatment of ADHD for children who are younger than six, and now include these recommendations for treating children ages four and five with ADHD:

- The primary care clinician should prescribe evidence-based parent- or teacher-administered behavioral therapy as the first line of treatment and may prescribe methylphenidate if the behavioral interventions do not provide significant improvement and there is moderate to severe continuing disturbance in the child's function.
- When behavioral therapy is not available, the clinician needs to weigh the risks of starting medication at an early age against the harm of delaying treatment.

Parent Concerns and Recommendations

Parents should have a general idea of what is typical development. Particularly when the child is their first, it is difficult for parents to know what may or may not be normal development. There are checklists available of developmental milestones for children at different ages—what most children are able to do or demonstrate by the time they are three, four, or five years old. These address social, emotional, language and communication, and cognitive (learning, thinking, problem solving) skills, and movement or physical development. See, for example, such online checklists published by the National Center on Birth Defects and Developmental Disabilities, Centers for Disease Control and Prevention (2014a, 2014b, 2014c).

Parents should talk with their child's doctor if concerned that their son or daughter is not meeting developmental milestones for his or her age. The child may then be screened by the doctor using a standardized, validated developmental screening tool, such as the Battelle Developmental Inventory/Screening Tool, 2nd ed. (BDI-ST), Brigance Screens-II, Child Development Inventory (CDI), Denver-II Developmental Screening Test, or Parents' Evaluation of Developmental Status (PEDS).

If screening indicates that there may be a delay, parents may request a referral to a specialist, such as a developmental pediatrician, to conduct a more in-depth evaluation of the child.

For more information about ADHD evaluations, see Section 1.3, which applies to young children as well as to older children, teens, and adults.

Child Find and School District Evaluation

A young child (even before school age) suspected of having a disability may also be evaluated by the local school district. There is a component of the federal law IDEA that requires states and local education agencies (school districts) to identify, locate, and evaluate all children with disabilities who reside within their state. This is called "Child Find." The process begins with a review or screening of available information about the child. When screening indicates the possibility of an educational disability, the child is evaluated in relevant areas. When results indicate that a child has a disability and is in need of special education services, an Individualized Education Program (IEP) is developed.

Young children found eligible for special education or related services receive those educational interventions at no cost to parents. To inquire, parents should contact their local school district or office of special education and can self-refer for an evaluation. See Section 6.4 for more on IDEA, IEPs, and educational rights of children with disabilities under federal law. For more on Child Find, see http://www.wrightslaw .com/info/child.find.index.htm.

More Strategies and Tips for Parents

Share any of your concerns with your child's pediatrician. Discussing concerns and asking for the input and observations of the teacher or child care provider are also important and helpful in determining how your child is developing and functioning compared to other children of his or her age.

It is difficult for many parents to decide whether or not their children (particularly those with late birthdays) are ready to start kindergarten. Be aware that boys are typically later in their development than girls, and children with ADHD are developmentally behind their peers in self-regulation and executive skills. Visit the kindergarten classes at the school, speak with teachers, ask to see the district's academic performance standards and expectations, seek advice from your child's pediatrician or others, and try to make the most informed decision you can—based on your knowledge of your own child and his or her needs. There are many kinds of early childhood programs and, of course, teaching styles. Some are better suited for certain children than others. Your gut feeling after doing your research is probably your best guide.

As noted earlier, when a child has ADHD or learning disabilities, behaviors that have a negative impact on social and academic performance generally do not improve by just allowing the child more time to mature. Other interventions will be necessary to specifically target the child's areas of weakness and build his or her skills, and early intervention is best.

There are social, emotional, and behavioral competencies that preschool and kindergarten children need to develop in order to do well in school. These include being able to

- Listen
- Follow rules and the teacher's directions
- Share and take turns
- Display reasonable self-control

- Interact appropriately and cooperatively with children and adults
- Function in large and small groups
- Work on tasks independently
- Handle mild frustrations or minor disappointments, such as sharing teacher's attention and waiting
- Cope with the structure of a school day

It is highly recommended that children with ADHD experience preschool (a program appropriate to their needs) and start learning these skills early.

You can help your child in his or her development of self-regulation and social and behavioral skills. It is important to clearly teach your young child what is acceptable and unacceptable behavior and to consistently enforce limits calmly and respectfully, yet firmly. You can prepare your child by exposing him or her to a number of social situations and settings in which you can observe from a distance how the child interacts with other children. Is she bossy or cooperative? Is he too physical or aggressive? Can she take turns and accept losing a game without crying? Does he speak to others with friendly words and tone of voice? You can and should teach all these social behaviors through modeling, role playing, frequent practice with feedback, and reinforcement. It is very important to praise children frequently when observing their display of positive behaviors. "I noticed how nicely you shared your toys with Michael. That's being a good friend."

To build a sense of independence and accomplishment, enable your child to do things for himself or herself that the child is capable of (simple chores, tasks). You can also help your children use words to express feelings and solve problems— for example, "I'm angry," "I don't like that," "That makes me feel sad," " I'm worried." Coach the child in problem-solving language—for example, "What could you say to Lisa if that bothers you?"

Many children, not just those with ADHD, have difficulty adjusting to a classroom environment, the hours away from home, the structure and expectations of their preschool or kindergarten teacher, and relating to the other children. Sometimes it just takes time for them to make the adjustment, learn the routine and structure, and feel comfortable in the new environment with their new teacher and peers. But if behaviors remain problematic and do not diminish much after a reasonable adjustment period, you should investigate further and seek help.

Kindergarten Academic Skills and Expectations

Kindergarten today has a much more academic curriculum than in past years—even five to ten years ago. In many ways, kindergartners are now expected to demonstrate skills that had not been expectations until first grade. Parents should be familiar with the kindergarten grade-level standards in their school district, which may or may not be Common Core State Standards (CCSS). To view all of the Common Core State Standards (the learning goals or expectations for kindergarten and other grade levels), see www.corestandards .org.

It is particularly important to be aware of the standards and expectations in the area of English Language Arts (ELA) for kindergarten students. Children who struggle in learning foundational reading, writing, and language skills (such as alphabet recognition, letter-sound association, writing a simple sentence with phonetic spelling) need to receive more direct and intensive instruction and practice. Dyslexia—a language-based learning disability—is a common coexisting condition in children with ADHD. Early intervention is critical for children who show signs of dyslexia in order to prevent or minimize their reading and writing struggles.

There are numerous ways that parents can help their young child build foundational and language-related skills, and resources to guide parents in doing so, including my books *The Dyslexia Checklist: A Practical Reference for Parents and Teachers* (Rief & Stern, 2010), *Alphabet Learning Center Activities Kit* (Fetzer & Rief, 2002), and *Ready, Start, School: Nurturing and Guiding Your Child through Preschool and Kindergarten* (Rief, 2001). For more information, see the Part 1 Additional Sources and Resources.

Research-Supported Intervention Programs for Preschool and Kindergarten

Two intervention programs that researchers have found of benefit for preschoolers with ADHD have been reviewed by Dr. Mark Katz (2009a).

First Step to Success

This program, developed under the direction of Hill Walker, is recognized nationally as an effective early intervention for reducing aggression in children who display such behaviors during their early school years. Researchers also are finding this program helpful for young children who exhibit symptoms of ADHD. The preschool version of the First Step program is a home-school intervention for teaching sharing, cooperation, following rules, and other social skills. It is proven to reduce serious behavior problems, such as aggression and opposition-defiance, and to improve school readiness and interpersonal skills. For more information, see First Steps to Success Preschool Edition by Voyager Sopris Learning at www.firststeptosuccess.org or www.voyagersopris.com.

Tools of the Mind

This program teaches preschoolers how to use different mental tools to gain greater control of their social, emotional, and cognitive behaviors (Katz, 2013). A 2007 study conducted by neuroscientist Adele Diamond showed that children enrolled in preschool classrooms using Tools of the Mind improved in their ability to resist distractions and temptations (inhibitory control), mentally hold information in mind (working memory), and flexibly adjust to change (cognitive flexibility). According to Katz (2009b, p. 7), "Tools of the Mind is currently being implemented in more than 450 preschool and kindergarten regular education and special education classrooms throughout the United States. Schools are finding the program compatible with Response to Intervention." For more information, see www.toolsofthemind.org.

Strategies and Tips for Preschool and Kindergarten Teachers

In preschool and kindergarten, every behavioral expectation and social skill must be taught. Teachers need to explain, model, and role-play each desired behavior and provide practice until all students know precisely what is expected of them, such as how to line up, stand in line, walk in line, move to groups and learning centers, sit on the rug or at the table, raise a hand to get the teacher's attention, and use indoor voices.

Behavior management techniques for children with ADHD in preschool and kindergarten are similar to those in higher grades: establishing clear rules, procedures, and routines; supplying visual prompting and cueing; offering a high degree of feedback and proximity control; setting up group positive reinforcement systems; consistently applying corrective consequences; and providing individualized behavioral supports. (See strategies throughout Part 2.)

Teaching, practicing, and monitoring behavioral expectations. Have children practice expectations with teacher observation and feedback—for example, "Show me what to do when you have something you want to say." "Who wants to show us how we get our lunch boxes and line up for lunch?" Check for specific behaviors. Ask, "Are your eyes on me?" "Are your ears open and on full power?" "Where should you be sitting right now?" "Are we sitting 'criss-cross applesauce'?"

Literature that has manners and appropriate behavior, such as sharing and being a good friend, as a theme is helpful in teaching behavioral expectations and social skills. So are puppets, music, games, visual display, role playing, and other such means.

Schedules and consistency. Children need the security of knowing their schedule and what they can expect to have happen throughout their school day—which for young children is presented graphically by referring to pictures depicting the flow of the day's activities. A predictable schedule and sequence of activities and consistent routines are necessary parts of the structure for school success.

Quiet space. Sometimes children with ADHD are on sensory overload and can become agitated or disruptive. It is important to allow them time and space to settle, regroup, and get away from some of the overstimulation. It helps to have an area that is designed for this purpose, with pillows, stuffed animals, and calming music they can listen to with headphones, for example. Teachers may ask, "Do you need to move?" or "Is there a better place to do your work?" Or they can redirect the child to a quieter, calmer area by whispering to him or her, "Go to the pillow area and read [look at] a book."

Diversionary tactics. The perceptive teacher will watch for signs of children beginning to get restless or agitated and try diverting their attention (for example, "Sara, come help me turn the pages of this book") to redirect their behavior. Most young children love to be the teacher's helper. They can be given a task such as wiping down tables, putting up chairs, or passing out papers.

Positive attention from the teacher. Watch for positive behaviors and recognize children for what they are doing right. "I see how nicely Coby and Jason are taking turns. Thank you for working so cooperatively." "Emma, I noticed that you are really catching yourself from yelling out in class. I am very proud of you." "Noah, I like the way you came over here and sat down next to Marcus even though someone else took your chair."

Positive attention from classmates. Besides specific praise from teachers, positive recognition and appreciation from peers is important as well: "Let's give a big round of applause to . . ." (children clap finger-to-finger

in a large circular movement). "Let's give ourselves a pat on the back" (children reach over and pat themselves on the back). "Let's give the silent cheer for . . ."

Visual prompts. Use these for all behavioral expectations. For example, make class charts with pictures depicting the behaviors you want students to demonstrate. Point to and refer to those visuals frequently. Keep your camera handy and take photos of children who are sitting appropriately or raising their hand to speak, for example, and use those photos as reminders of appropriate behaviors.

Environmental structuring. Children with ADHD often have difficulty knowing and understanding their physical boundaries. They tend to invade other people's space and react adversely to being crowded or bumped into. They are helped by having concrete visual structuring of their space, such as with colored duct tape to indicate their boundaries on the carpet area or at tables. Also, placing them in the front or back of the line (not in the middle) can avoid some problems when walking in lines.

Behavior charts and rewards. Some children need individualized behavior modification charts for working to improve one or two specific behaviors, such as staying in their assigned place or keeping hands and feet to themselves. Young children need to be reinforced frequently; short time frames of appropriate behavior can earn the child a star, a smiley face, a sticker on a chart, or other reward. When using behavior charts and incentive systems, it is important to identify what an individual child will find to be motivating and reinforcing. Some children have no interest whatsoever in earning a sticker or tangible reward, but would love to work hard for the chance to play with bubbles, use certain "special materials or equipment," or care for the class rabbit.

Movement and exercise. Children—particularly young ones—need numerous opportunities to move. Teachers build movement into the day at frequent intervals. Some teachers have a regular routine of stretching, warm-up, jogging, and cool-down every morning—as well as physical education and motor skills training. In the classroom, there are songs and rhymes with motions (hand and whole body) that are integrated throughout the day. Early childhood programs need to provide children with many opportunities to engage in large and small muscle movements in fun ways throughout the curriculum.

Strategies and Tips for Early Childhood Teachers*

What to Do About . . .

Handling Disappointments. Kindergarten children can become very upset if they are not chosen for certain privileges or responsibilities. Many do not deal well with the disappointment of not being selected or having to wait their turn. One kindergarten teacher teaches her students an "Oh well" signal. With a snap of the fingers in a big, sweeping motion, she leads her children in saying, "Oh well . . . maybe next time." The class has practiced this technique repeatedly in response to disappointments. When students use the "Oh well" response, the teacher reinforces with much praise, telling them: "You are so grown up. I am very proud of you."

The Tactile-Defensive Child. There are some children, especially among those with neurobiological disorders, who have poor tolerance for the feel of anything rubbing or touching the body, such as certain textures or clothes, or being crowded in line. Many overreact to being bumped into or may refuse to wear

---

* Note: See Section 5.1 describing Vincent's developmental history - problems he experienced during his preschool and kindergarten years, as well as strategies found to be helpful for him at home and school.

socks because the seam across the toes is bothering them. These children have what is called "tactile defensiveness." For some children, this means that sitting on the carpet may be almost intolerable. It is highly recommended that teachers consult with an occupational therapist if a child is showing signs of being tactile defensive or having unusual reactions to various sensory stimuli. There are many strategies to help.

The Child Who Has Trouble Sitting. Most young children can sit still for only a relatively short amount of time. Teachers and parents sometimes forget this, and inadvertently place unreasonable expectations regarding the length of time the child is asked to sit quietly and pay attention. For children with ADHD, the length of time they can sit is substantially shorter than their peers; some cannot sit for more than a few moments. Teachers may permit the child to get up and walk around quietly, and try to redirect when possible. Sometimes it is necessary to provide the child space and ignore when he or she lies down, rolls around on the rug, or engages in other behaviors.

Sometimes a child's inability to sit is blamed on behavior when in reality the child does not have the physical tone to sit up on the carpet with his or her legs crossed (a common sitting position in early childhood classrooms). Again, an occupational therapist or adapted physical education teacher should be consulted.

One teacher said that she tries to have an adult sit down with the child, with a gentle hand on the shoulder or back—some physical contact to help keep the child seated and focused. It often helps when a child has trouble (for example, sitting on the rug listening to a story) to give him or her some object that he or she can hold while sitting.

The Perception That a Certain Child Is Being "Bad." Children generally have a real sense of understanding and compassion, and they almost always take the teacher's lead.

Sometimes there is one child who is so disruptive or aggressive that children think of him or her as "bad." One kindergarten teacher shared how she always corrects and softens, for example, by saying, "There are no bad children. Sometimes Michael has trouble remembering the rules. It doesn't mean he is bad. Sometimes he can't help it. We need to help him. How do you think we can help Michael remember the rules?"

INTERVIEW WITH JOE
Fifteen Years Old, Minnesota

Joe received a diagnosis of ADHD and LD at a young age.

Tell me about your favorite teacher in elementary school.

"My second-grade teacher was my favorite. When I was held back a grade, she always checked on me and asked how I was doing. I still go back and visit her."

I understand you have seen many different doctors over the years. How do you feel about that?

"Yeah. I saw all kinds of doctors, including different psychologists and psychiatrists. I took those psychological tests so many times, but the doctors didn't really talk to me. I went to two doctors at the same time, one who took care of my medication, and one because of my psychological problem. I didn't like him. He talked down to me, and I didn't like that."

How did you get along with other kids?

"I'm really good with adults. It's kids who were kind of tough for me. I took offense at what they said. I tried to ignore it, but it took a while. I realize that those kids I had trouble with were just jerks. I'm getting much better now. I've learned that it doesn't happen overnight. It takes a while—everything takes time."

What do you want teachers to be aware of?

"Teachers should be as respectful of kids as kids are to be respectful of them. Class should not be stressful, but relaxed. Teachers shouldn't ever make fun of students. I like active things like research, projects, and reports (especially oral reports)."

What do you want to tell parents?

"Parents need to be aware that kids have a tough time, too, and don't need problems at home. Parents may have had a hard time at the office. Well, we have a hard time, too. My dad (a lawyer) does every day what he learned to do and likes to do. In school we're learning new things, and we have to do what we've never done before, and reach our teacher's expectations. It's tough. Parents have to be aware and know what their kid is doing in school . . . be involved and make teachers tell you more."

section

1.9

ADHD in Middle School and High School

For most children with ADHD, the symptoms continue into adolescence to varying degrees. Some symptoms may diminish, but other problems may emerge or intensify during middle school and high school. For example, hyperactivity in adolescence generally manifests more as restlessness rather than as the overt hyperactivity seen in younger children.

Many preteens and teens find these years to be the most difficult and stressful for them and their families. Impulsivity can be more problematic during the teen years. As noted earlier, poor self-control and lack of inhibition in adolescence are associated with many risk factors, including significantly more than the average number of traffic violations, accidents, and teen pregnancies, as well as conduct that results in conflict with school authorities, parents, and law enforcement.

Many children with ADHD who were able to cope and stay afloat academically in elementary school find themselves overwhelmed and unable to do so with the heavy workload and high executive function demands of middle and secondary school. For some students with ADHD—particularly those with the predominantly inattentive presentation—this is the time they first receive the diagnosis of the disorder.

These are years when it is very difficult for parents and teachers to find the proper balance between teaching the child to assume responsibility for his or her own learning and behavioral choices, and intervening as we guide and support the child to success.

73

For All Kids This Age

All adolescents have certain needs and experience many unique challenges, regardless of whether or not they have ADHD.

Challenges of Adolescence

- Transitioning and adjusting to a different school environment with many new adults and students
- Getting to know and manage the expectations of several teachers
- Learning their way around campus
- Needing to feel accepted and "fit in"
- Undergoing physical changes and raging hormones
- Dealing with the pressure of high academic and cognitive demands and heavy homework load
- Facing enormous social and peer pressures and sometimes having to cope with being the victim of teasing, bullying, and social isolation

What All Adolescents Need

Adolescents need the feeling of "connection" and of being valued. They are seeking a sense of community and belonging. Protecting their image and being treated with respect are of utmost importance. They need to feel safe and comfortable in their classroom environment, knowing that they will be treated with dignity and not deliberately criticized or humiliated in front of their peers.

This is a critical time for students to learn how to learn—how to study and access information and take advantage of their own best learning styles. Adolescents often complain about school being boring, and they don't see the connection between what is being taught in school and their own lives. Instruction at this level must be meaningful, challenging, and relevant—eliciting students' active participation and involvement. The curriculum and schedule at this level have to provide for options and variety. Teachers must be able to motivate and tap into the interests and strengths of their students. They must stimulate their students' curiosity and desire to think, work

hard, challenge themselves, and take risks as learners.

Adolescents still require structure and frequent monitoring both at home and school (even as they complain and resist). During the middle school and high school years, many youngsters are vulnerable and insecure. Students of this age may appear mature enough to need less adult guidance. However, this is the stage when there is probably a greater need for guidance, interaction with caring adults, and open channels of communication than ever before. This is especially true given all of the outside pressures and influences to which our children are exposed. Parental involvement at school and presence on campus frequently decline during these years, but should be strongly encouraged. Schools must explore ways to make parents feel comfortable and welcome on campus.

In addition to the aforementioned common challenges of adolescence, preteens and teens with ADHD must also contend with several other struggles and issues related to their disorder, which makes these years even harder.

ADHD-Related Challenges and Needs

Executive function weaknesses typically become much more problematic in middle and high school, impairing academic performance for many students with ADHD. As discussed in Section 1.2, poor executive skills (for example, planning, organizing, time management, and working memory) greatly interfere with school success. Adolescents with ADHD may appear physically mature and grown up, but looks are deceiving. They are typically far less mature behaviorally and emotionally than their same-age peers. They do not act their age because they have a developmental delay of approximately 30 percent in their self-regulation and executive skills. A fifteen-year-old with ADHD will likely behave like a ten- or eleven-year-old in some respects, and a twelve-year-old may behave more like an eight- or nine-year-old because of this developmental lag. Do not let their intelligence and physical maturity mislead you.

Although these children may be of an age when the expectation is for them to demonstrate more independence, responsibility, and self-control, the reality is that preteens and teens with ADHD take longer to exhibit those behaviors. They need more adult monitoring, supervision, and direct supports than their peers.

Key to school success is teacher flexibility and willingness to put in the extra time and effort to support and work with the student with ADHD. Unfortunately, middle and high school teachers often receive little or no training in ADHD, resulting in less understanding of the disorder, and therefore less empathy and willingness to accommodate these students' individual needs.

Middle and high school students with ADHD need the following from parents and teachers:

- Awareness and understanding of ADHD, and strategies to help them deal with their challenges at this age
- Reasonable and realistic expectations
- Use of a positive discipline approach rather than punishment as the primary mode of dealing with behavior
- Monitoring and supervision (although they may fight this bitterly)
- Open channels of communication with mutual problem solving and involvement in decision making
- Lots of encouragement and support
- A plan to prepare them for whatever their goals are once they graduate high school

Addressing Coexisting Disorders

It is very important for parents and teachers to be aware that at least two-thirds of children and teens with ADHD have or will develop at least one other coexisting disorder—for example, anxiety disorder, oppositional defiant disorder, conduct disorder, or sleep disorder. Any coexisting disorder needs to be diagnosed and treated in addition to the ADHD. The preteen or teen needs the support and treatment for these or other conditions or disorders from medical and mental health professionals.

Learning disabilities (LDs), such as dyslexia, are very common coexisting disorders. Students with LDs need educational interventions (specialized instruction and related services, as well as academic supports and accommodations) to do well in school. Many students with ADHD are never evaluated for LDs, and many with known LDs have undiagnosed ADHD. It should always be suspected that a child or teen with ADHD who is struggling in learning (reading, writing, or math) also has LDs and should be evaluated to determine their learning and academic needs.

It is very important to reevaluate when other conditions are suspected or current treatment is not working well, and to implement whatever interventions may be necessary at this time: academic assistance, medical treatment or adjustment in medication, counseling, or something else.

School Supports

One of the advantages in middle and high school is the availability of more options in scheduling. Sometimes the best intervention is a change of classes or teachers. Other times, rescheduling a class with the same teacher but at a more optimal time of day makes a difference (for example, scheduling the hardest classes in the morning when the student is most alert and energetic).

It is helpful when there is an adult at school who is willing to be a case manager (officially or unofficially)—someone who will be able to monitor progress, advise, and intervene in school situations. For students on IEPs, the special education teacher (for example, the resource teacher) is generally that case manager. Sometimes it is a school counselor, one of the classroom teachers (for example, the advisory or homeroom teacher), or a coach who serves this function.

It also helps if middle and high schools have in place supportive interventions available to students in need, such as mentors, homework and organization assistance, study skills and learning strategies classes, and tutoring. Students with ADHD would benefit from such school supports, as well as the opportunity to participate in clubs, sports, and electives to build on their interests and showcase their areas of strength.

Essential to the success of adolescents with ADHD is the teacher's

- Training, awareness, and understanding of ADHD
- Use of effective classroom management strategies
- Monitoring of behavior and academic progress
- Willingness to work with the student and parents to provide extra support and follow-through (for example, daily or weekly report cards, contracts, checking of the assignment calendar, and organizing materials)

Aiding the Transition to Middle or High School

Chris A. Zeigler Dendy (2000), a leading authority on teens with ADHD and author of several books, suggests the following to teachers or other school personnel to help with the transition to middle or high school:

- Encourage parents to notify the new school about their child and his or her needs.
- Check with the guidance counselor at the new school to find out when student schedules are developed. Parents and the current school should provide input on the fall schedule.
- Develop an IEP or 504 plan for eligible students before they transition to the next school.
- Schedule a student support team (SST) meeting.
- Assign an upper-class mentor to help with the transition.
- Give parents an update on grades after two or three weeks in the new school.

Transition Plans

When IDEA was reauthorized by Congress in 2004, new provisions in transition planning for high school students with IEPs were added in the effort to improve postsecondary results for students with disabilities.

A transition plan is the section of the Individualized Education Program (IEP) that outlines transition goals and services for the student. The transition plan is based on a high school student's individual needs, strengths, skills, and interests. Transition planning is used to identify and develop goals which need to be accomplished during the current school year to assist the student in meeting his or her post–high school goals. (Stanberry, n.d., p. 1)

By the time a student is sixteen years old (although it may occur sooner), plans for transition services are required under IDEA 2004 to become part of the IEP. The IEP team looks at what the student intends to do after high school—perhaps get a higher education or enter the work world. Transition plans address such needs as preparation for college entrance examinations, consideration of career choices, development of extracurricular interests, and job training possibilities (Rief & Stern, 2010).

Transition planning and services include the following new requirements:

- Appropriate, measurable postsecondary goals based on age-appropriate transition assessments related to training, education, employment, and, when appropriate, independent living skills
- Goals that reflect the student's strengths, preferences, and interests (not just the student's deficits)
- A process designed to be results oriented and to focus on improving the academic and functional achievement of the student so as to facilitate movement from school to post-school activities
- A statement of the transition services needed to help the student reach those goals, which includes courses of study

Tips for Parents

- When your child is transitioning from elementary to middle school or from middle to high school, it helps to have a dry run before school starts to walk around the campus, see where the classes are located, and practice quickly opening and closing his or her combination lock.

- Be aware that your ADHD teen may be of driving age but is developmentally less mature. Drivers with ADHD have more speeding citations and accidents in which they were at fault than other drivers. I recommend that you establish firm guidelines and an agreement between you and your son or daughter regarding your driving expectations once they get their license. A driving contract to help enforce rules, encourage responsibility, and keep everyone safe may be helpful, such as the one *ADDitude* magazine shares as an example (see the link in the Section 1.9 references at the end of Part 1).

- Consider hiring a tutor, learning specialist, or ADHD coach to help your son or daughter keep up with school assignments and improve academic and executive skills. This can be a very helpful support for your teen and alleviates some of your burden. Adolescents typically resent parental micromanagement, which becomes the source of conflict between teens and their parents. Having someone else involved in keeping your child on track and following through with school assignments can help foster not only your child's school success but also your relationship.

- "Parents play an important role in preparing their child for, and guiding them through, the middle school transition. Relatively simple steps such as establishing a homework management plan, monitoring friendship patterns and facilitating positive social interactions can make a big difference in the development process" (Evans, Serpell, & White, 2005, p. 31).

- Kids with ADHD need a lot of reminders from parents, but the way those reminders are given can make a difference in how they are accepted by the preteen or teen. Guare, Dawson, and Guare (2013) recommend that you avoid nagging and send your teens reminders that are more indirect, such as a note, voicemail, or text message.

- "If your child has a 504 Plan, maintaining that plan throughout high school is a critical element in keeping your high school student with ADHD academically on track" (Lepre, 2008, p. 46). Lepre also recommends that parents not only meet with the teen's teachers early in the year but also meet and develop a working relationship with the guidance counselor, who is the "link between the school and your adolescent" (p. 46).

- Parents of an adolescent with ADHD need to be vigilant in monitoring their child's performance in his or her classes and not wait until regular progress reports, by which time the student may be too far behind to get caught up. Teachers may be asked to send more frequent progress reports or to keep parents informed by email or other communication systems throughout the grading period.

- Dendy (2002, p. 17) recommends these actions you can take to influence a successful outcome for your teen: "seeking accommodations at school, fine-tuning medication, using positive parenting practices, providing supervision, avoiding hostile interactions and harsh punishments, avoiding nagging and personal attacks, and last and perhaps most importantly, believing in your child!"

Warning Signs (Red Flags) in Middle School and High School

It bears repeating that detecting a problem in its early stages and beginning intervention as quickly as possible will greatly increase the chances of a better outcome. The following signs (Parker, 1999) may alert parents or teachers to the possibility of a problem warranting investigation. At a minimum, parents should schedule a conference with the teacher. I also recommend a school team meeting with parents. If the student has an IEP or 504 plan, the team (including parents and the student) may need to meet to review the plan and determine whether additional services or interventions are indicated. Watch for the following warning signs:

- Frequent complaints of boredom
- Excessive absenteeism from school, including unauthorized absences from class
- Drop in grades
- Lack of interest in doing homework
- Frequent tardiness
- Talk about dropping out
- Resentment expressed toward teacher(s)
- No books or papers brought to or from school
- Reports from teachers that the student is not doing in-class assignments or completing work
- Disorganization—books and papers not appropriately cared for
- Work done sloppily or incorrectly
- Lack of care about school attitude
- Low self-esteem
- Complaints by teacher(s) of frequent inattention in class
- Hyperactivity
- Hanging out with other students who are doing poorly in school (reported by teacher)
- Lack of comprehension of assignments when trying to do them

Warning Signs of Learning Disabilities in Teens

Because coexisting learning disabilities (LDs) are common in children and teens with ADHD, parents and teachers should be aware of signs of LDs. Some children may have LDs that have gone undetected to this point. Academic performance problems most likely had been attributed to their ADHD. To determine whether or not a student has LDs requires a psychoeducational evaluation. Educational interventions should be provided, addressing the student's individual learning needs.

The following is a list of warning signs of possible LDs in teens (Inland Empire Branch of the International Dyslexia Association, 2003). *Note:*

These would be "red flags" only if they show up as a pattern of behaviors, to a significant degree, and over time.

 Language/Mathematics/Social Studies

- Avoidance of reading and writing
- Tendency to misread information
- Difficulty summarizing information
- Poor reading comprehension
- Difficulty understanding subject area textbooks
- Trouble with open-ended questions
- Continued poor spelling
- Poor grasp of abstract concepts
- Poor skills in writing essays
- Difficulty in learning foreign language
- Poor ability to apply math skills
- Difficulty staying organized
- Trouble with test formats such as multiple choice
- Slow work pace in class and in testing situations
- Poor note-taking skills
- Poor ability to proofread or double-check work

 Social Behavior

- Difficulty accepting criticism
- Difficulty seeking or giving feedback
- Problems negotiating or advocating for himself or herself
- Difficulty resisting peer pressure
- Difficulty understanding another person's perspective

Understanding Their ADHD and Self-Advocacy

Preteens and teens should be educated about ADHD to understand the disorder and ways to better manage the symptoms. If they receive medication, they need to know what medication does and does not do. Learning that so many highly successful people in every walk of life have ADHD and that the disorder does not limit their potential can be very encouraging.

As students with ADHD enter the middle and high school grades, they need to learn to advocate for themselves and how to politely request help when needed. Parents still need to take an active role in monitoring and communicating with teachers, but it is important for students of this age to speak directly with their teachers about their needs and the kinds of supports or accommodations they think will help them learn and perform better in their classrooms. Teachers are generally impressed when students care enough about wanting to do well in their classes that they ask for help when needed.

High school students with ADHD who have IEPs should be actively involved as part of the IEP team in developing their own transition plan to be most meaningful and motivating for them.

The Value of Mentorship

A positive role model or mentor can make a significant impact on a child's life. Often a school employee (teacher or other staff member) will give his or her time to an individual student, and that connection and mentorship can make an enormous difference in the success of that student. Parents are in the position of being able to facilitate finding a role model or mentor outside of school to develop their child's interests and skills as well. Parents can connect their child with friends or relatives with a similar interest, take him or her to visit facilities that relate to the child's interests, or call professionals and ask if they would be willing to give fifteen or thirty minutes to share information about their work or interest. These experiences can lead to ongoing mentoring if both parties are willing to sustain the relationship. The following story illustrates the positive impact of a mentor on the life of one young man.

DAN'S STORY
First Published in 1993, Shared by His Mother

Dan was a child with ADHD. He had a history of physical and emotional distress, which centered around his experiences in school. His behavior was impulsive, and his teachers frequently telephoned home to tell his parents that Dan would not stay in his seat and was disruptive, and that they should try to better control his behavior at school. By fifth grade, Dan had several interventions, including stimulant medication and counseling. Although he achieved fairly well, but not "up to his potential," he had been held back a grade due to emotional immaturity. Dan now had much difficulty with peer relationships. His parents pursued every avenue they could find in their search to help him, but not enough changed.

During sixth grade, Dan learned to cook, an activity that really held his interest. At the beginning of seventh grade, he learned about a restaurant with a sports theme that interested him. He asked if he could see it and eat there sometime. His mother, Marla, promised to take him there as soon as she could. One night, Dan's mother and father unexpectedly ended up at the restaurant. Marla mentioned to the hostess that her thirteen-year-old son really wanted to visit the restaurant. The hostess said that if Dan wanted to visit about 1:00 p.m. on a weekday, she would take him on a tour of the kitchen and he could watch the chef at work. The hostess gave Marla her card.

On their next mutual weekday off, Marla and Dan had lunch at the restaurant. When Marla made reservations, she reminded the hostess of their conversation. Dan not only enjoyed the meal but also met the chef, Peter, and watched him work. Peter told Marla and Dan that he was impressed with Dan's mature behavior and interest. He said that Dan could come back and observe sometime during the summer.

As soon as school ended for summer vacation, Dan called Peter and asked if he could come in to visit. It was a thirty-minute drive from his home to the restaurant, but his parents agreed to transport him. Once each month, Peter allowed Dan to come in. First Dan observed, but gradually Peter allowed him to assume certain tasks. Dan loved it! Peter and the rest of the cooking staff began to include Dan in their exchanges of music and in their friendship.

One day after about four months, Peter asked Marla for a "parent-chef conference." Peter asked whether Dan was really learning anything and whether he liked it. Marla's first thought was that Dan was "messing up," but she told Peter that Dan was baking desserts and showing her "meal presentation" tips. Peter said he was concerned about whether Dan was truly interested. Marla thought he was.

Months went by, and Dan continued to help out. He got A's in cooking, and his organizational skills improved, as did his relationships with others, including his peers. Gradually, as he began to perceive himself as competent in his work at the restaurant, Dan seemed to feel more competent in other areas.

Dan was really excited when Peter told him that he had "graduated" and could come in every other week. After over a year invested, Peter told Dan that he really needed him to help with preparation for Saturday nights. Dan was really "staff" now, and Peter gave him his own staff T-shirt. Soon after that, some of the young staff members asked Dan to go to a concert with them. Dan's confidence swelled.

Dan continues to work at the restaurant. Currently he is working on his driver's training, anxiously awaiting the time he can transport himself to the restaurant more often. Dan plans to graduate from high school in three years instead of the usual four and is taking effective steps toward that goal. When he graduates, he knows he wants to enroll in a four-year college hotel and restaurant management program. He has even selected colleges to apply to. Marla reports that, so far, Dan has maintained the academic credentials that will help ensure his college admission.

No one can be sure what contributed to Dan's personal growth—age, the neurochemical changes of puberty, and the attention Dan received at school and at home probably all helped. What seems pivotal, however, is the attention and skill Dan has gained from Peter. Dan knows what he enjoys and that he can become a competent professional one day. He also knows that Peter cares about him and believes in him. In terms of his education and how he feels about what Peter has taught him, Dan told me the following:

"Peter is such a good communicator. He takes his time and tells me how to do things. He taught me what it means to do 'teamwork.' Peter 'cultures me,' and he has fun when he's mentoring me, too. Peter is my top learning experience!"

Follow-Up to Dan's Story (2015)

Note: I am very grateful to Dan for sharing this follow-up to the original "story" published twenty-two years ago.

Although he was active in debate and speech, Dan opted for postsecondary enrollment for the last two years of high school. He was mostly interested in subjects not offered by his high school, and quite frankly felt that kids his age were not what he considered to be intellectual peers. He really wanted more from his education and used this program to gain freedom from the issues that high school presented.

Dan became heavily involved in the radio station at his college. By the end of his freshman year, he had achieved a director's position within the governing body of the station. In college, he designed his own major in theater production and double majored in fine arts. He graduated with a strong GPA in four years.

After graduation, he worked as an artist in electronic arts and had installations in local galleries. Dan tried his hat at teaching, but felt as though it was not his calling to educate others in an institution.

With a turn of fate, Dan entered the restaurant management industry and eventually managed multimillion-dollar facilities. Ultimately he went back to his true desire to be part of an information technology career. Today he is a software systems architect for one of the largest banks in the United States and is happily married.

Part 1 References

Section 1.1

American Psychiatric Association. (2013). *Diagnostic and statistical manual of mental disorders* (5th ed.). Washington, DC: Author.

American Psychological Association. (2008, February). ADHD: Delay or deviation? *Monitor on Psychology, 39*(2), 12. Print version, retrieved online at http://www.apa.org/monitor/feb08/adhd.aspx

Barkley, R. A. (1998). Attention-deficit hyperactivity disorder: A psychological model of ADHD. *Scientific American,* pp. 66–71. Retrieved from www.sciam.com/1998/0998issuebarkley.html

Barkley, R. A. (2013). *Taking charge of ADHD: The complete, authoritative guide for parents* (3rd ed.). New York, NY: Guilford Press.

Barkley, R., Cook, E., Dulcan, M., Prior, M., Gillberg, C., Halperin, J., . . . Pelham, W., Jr. (2002, January). International consensus statement on ADHD. *Clinical Child and Family Psychology Review, 5*(2), 89–111. Retrieved from http://russellbarkley.org/factsheets/Consensus2002.pdf

Brown, T. E. (2013a). Ten myths about ADHD and why they are wrong. *Attention, 20*(3), 6–9.

Brown, T. E. (2013b). Understanding attention deficit: The new ADHD. Retrieved from http://www.additudemag.com/slideshow/28/slide-1.html

Centers for Disease Control and Prevention. (n.d.). Attention-deficit/hyperactivity disorder: Data and statistics. Retrieved from http://www.cdc.gov/ncbddd/adhd/data.html (reporting findings from *Key Findings: Trends in the Parent-Report of Health Care Provider-Diagnosis and Medication Treatment for ADHD: United States, 2003–2011*)

Centre for ADHD Awareness, Canada. (n.d.). What is attention deficit hyperactivity disorder? Retrieved from http://www.caddac.ca/cms/page.php?67

Goldstein, S. (2007, February). Research briefs: The genetics of AD/HD. *Attention, 14*(1), 37–39.

Goldstein, S. (2009, February). Comorbidity in AD/HD. *Attention, 16*(1), 32–33.

Goldstein, S. (2010, February). AD/HD and autism spectrum disorders. *Attention, 17*(1), 32–34.

Goodman, B. (2010, February). Compulsively impulsive/impulsively compulsive. *Attention, 17*(1), 20–23.

Hinshaw, S. P., Owens, E. B., Zalecki, C., Huggins, S. P., Montenegro-Nevado, A. J., Schrodek, E., & Swanson, E. N. (2012). Prospective follow-up of girls with attention-deficit/hyperactivity disorder into early adulthood: Continuing impairment includes elevated risk for suicide attempts and self-injury. *Journal of Consulting and Clinical Psychology, 80,* 1041–1051.

Kutscher, M. L. (2010). *ADHD: Living without brakes.* Philadelphia, PA: Jessica Kingsley.

Littman, E. (2000, July/August). We understand far too little about girls with ADHD. *ADDvance, 3*(6), 17–21.

Littman, E. (2012, December). The secret lives of girls with ADHD. *Attention, 19*(6), 18–21.

MTA Cooperative Group. (1999). A 14-month randomized clinical trial of treatment strategies for attention deficit hyperactivity disorder. *Archives of General Psychiatry, 56,* 1073–1086.

Nadeau, K. G. (2000a, July/August). Elementary school girls with AD/HD. *Attention, 7*(1), 44–49.

Nadeau, K. G. (2000b, September/October). Middle school girls with AD/HD. *Attention, 7*(2), 61–71.

Nadeau, K. G. (2004a). *High school girls with AD/HD.* ADDvance.com. Retrieved from http://addvance.com/help/women/high_school.html

Nadeau, K. G. (2004b). *Helping your daughter with ADD (ADHD) to feel good about herself.* ADDvance.com. Retrieved from http://addvance.com/help/women/daughter.html

Nadeau, K. G., Littman, E., & Quinn, P. (2015). *Understanding girls with AD/HD, updated and revised: How they feel and why they do what they do.* Silver Spring, MD: Advantage Books.

National Resource Center on AD/HD. (n.d.). The science of ADHD. Retrieved from http://www.chadd.org/Understanding-ADHD/About-ADHD/The-Science-of-ADHD.aspx

National Resource Center on AD/HD. (2015). ADHD and coexisting disorders. Retrieved from http://www.chadd.org/Portals/0/Content/CHADD/NRC/Factsheets/coexisting.pdf

Nigg, J. T. (2006). *What causes ADHD: Understanding what goes wrong and why.* New York, NY: Guilford Press.

Norr, M. (2015, October). Recent brain imaging findings in ADHD. *Attention, 22*(5), 16–19.

Polanczyk, G., de Lima, M. S., Horta, B. L., Biederman, J., & Rohde, L. A. (2007, June). The worldwide prevalence of ADHD: A systematic review and metaregression analysis. *American Journal of Psychiatry, 164,* 942–948.

Quinn, P. O. (2008, December). AD/HD in women and girls. *Attention, 15*(6), 20.

Quinn, P. O. (2009, October). Women and girls with AD/HD. *Attention, 16*(5), 10–11.

Quinn, P. O. (2012). How girls and women can win with ADHD. *ADDitude* magazine webinar. Retrieved from http://www.additudemag.com/RCLP/sub/9796.html

Quinn, P. O., & Nadeau, K. G. (2000, May/June). Understanding preschool girls with AD/HD. *Attention, 6*(5), 42–45.

Quinn, P. O., & Nadeau, K. G. (2004). ADD (ADHD) checklist for girls. ADDvance.com. Retrieved from http://addvance.com/help/women/girl_checklist.html

Shaw, P., Eckstrand, K., Sharp, W., Blumenthal, J., Lerch, J. P., Greenstein, D., . . . Rapoport, J. L. (2007, December 11). Attention-deficit/hyperactivity disorder is characterized by a delay in cortical maturation. *Proceedings of the National Academy of Sciences, 104,* 19663–19664.

Spencer, L. E. (2013, April). Helping students with ADHD and language disability. *Attention, 20*(2), 10–12.

Wolraich, M. L., & DuPaul, G. J. (2010). *ADHD diagnosis and management: A practical guide for the clinic and the classroom.* Baltimore, MD: Paul H. Brookes.

Section 1.2

Barkley, R. (2012). Fact sheet: The important role of executive functioning and self-regulation in ADHD. Retrieved from www.russellbarkley.org/factsheets/ADHD_EF_and_SR.pdf

Center on the Developing Child. (n.d.). Key concepts: Executive functions. Retrieved from http://developingchild.harvard.edu/key_concepts/executive_function/

Dendy, C.A.Z. (2002, February). Five components of executive function. *Attention, 9*(1), 26–31.

Dendy, C.A.Z. (2011). *Teaching teens with ADD, ADHD & executive function deficits* (2nd ed.). Bethesda, MD: Woodbine House.

Diamond, A., Barnett, W. S., Thomas, J., & Munro, S. (2007). Preschool program improves cognitive control. *Science, 318,* 1387–1388. Retrieved from www.ncbi.nlm.nih.gov/pmc/articles/PMC2174918/

Duckworth, A. A., & Seligman, M.E.P. (2005). Self-discipline outdoes IQ in predicting academic performance of adolescents. *Psychological Science, 16,* 939–944.

Kutscher, M. L. (2010). *ADHD: Living without brakes.* Philadelphia, PA: Jessica Kingsley.

Raver, C. C., & Blair, C. (2014). At the crossroads of education and developmental neuroscience: Perspectives on executive function. *Perspectives on Language and Literacy, 40*(2), 27–29.

Silver, L. (2010). Not your father's ADHD. *ADDitude, 10*(3), 47–48.

Tangney, J. P., Baumeister, R. F., & Boone, A. L. (2004). High self-control predicts good adjustment, better grades, and interpersonal success. *Journal of Personality, 72,* 271–324.

Willis, J. (2011, June 13). Understanding how the brain thinks. *Edutopia* blog. Retrieved from www.edutopia.org/blog/understanding-how-the-brain-thinks-judy-willis-md

Section 1.3

American Academy of Pediatrics (AAP). (2011). ADHD: Clinical practice guidelines for the diagnosis, evaluation, and treatment of attention-deficit/hyperactivity disorder in children and adolescents. *Pediatrics, 128,* 1007–1022.

American Psychiatric Association. (1994). *Diagnostic and statistical manual of mental disorders* (4th ed.). Washington, DC: Author.

American Psychiatric Association. (2000). *Diagnostic and statistical manual of mental disorders* (4th ed., text rev.) Washington, DC: Author.

American Psychiatric Association. (2013). *Diagnostic and statistical manual of mental disorders* (5th ed.). Washington, DC: Author.

Section 1.4

Adesman, A. (2003, April). Effective treatment of attention-deficit/hyperactivity disorder: Behavior therapy and medication management. *Primary Psychiatry, 10*(4), 55–60.

American Academy of Pediatrics. (2011). ADHD: Clinical practice guideline for the diagnosis, evaluation, and treatment of attention-deficit/hyperactivity disorder in children and adolescents. *Pediatrics, 128,* 1007–1022.

American Academy of Pediatrics & National Initiative for Children's Healthcare Quality. (2002). *Caring for children with ADHD: A resource toolkit for clinicians.* Chicago, IL: American Academy of Pediatrics.

Barkley, R. A. (2013). *Taking charge of ADHD: The complete, authoritative guide for parents* (3rd ed.). New York, NY: Guilford Press.

Barrow, K. (2008). Facts about fish oil. *ADDitude, 8*(3), 44–45.

Brown, T. E. (2005). *Attention deficit disorder: The unfocused mind in children and adults.* New Haven, CT: Yale University Press.

Goodman, B. (2008). Ask the expert: Chats with L. Eugene Arnold. *Attention, 15*(6), 10–12.

Hudziak, J. J., Albaugh, M. D., Ducharme, S., Karama, S., Spottswood, M., Crehan, E., . . . Botteron, K. N. (2014, November). Cortical thickness maturation and duration of music training: Health-promoting activities shape brain development. *Journal of the American Academy of Child & Adolescent Psychiatry, 53,* 1153–1161.e2.

McGavern, K. (2015, April). Music lessons for kids with ADHD. *Attention, 22*(2), 15–17.

MTA Cooperative Group. (1999). Fourteen-month randomized clinical trial of treatment strategies for attention-deficit hyperactivity disorder. *Archives of General Psychiatry, 56,* 1073–1086.

Ratey, J. J. (2008). The exercise solution. *ADDitude, 8*(4), 36–39.

Rodgers, A. L. (2012). Your child's brain on music. *ADDitude, 12*(4), 47–50.

Special report: Diet matters. (2008). *ADDitude, 9*(2), 41.

Zylowska, L. (2012). *The mindfulness prescription for adult ADHD: An 8-step program for strengthening attention, managing emotions, and achieving your goals.* Boston, MA: Trumpeter Books.

Section 1.5

Kalikow, K. T. (2013). ADHD and the decision to medicate. *Attention, 20*(1), 12–14.

Section 1.6

American Academy of Pediatrics (AAP). (2011). ADHD: Clinical practice guidelines for the diagnosis, evaluation, and treatment of attention-deficit/hyperactivity disorder in children and adolescents. *Pediatrics, 128,* 1007–1022.

Barkley, R. A. (2013a). *Defiant children: A clinician's manual for assessment and parent training* (3rd ed.). New York, NY: Guilford Press.

Barkley, R. A. (2013b). *Taking charge of ADHD: The complete, authoritative guide for parents* (3rd ed.). New York, NY: Guilford Press.

Committee for Children. (2008). *Second step: Social skills for early childhood-grade 8.* Retrieved from www.cfchildren.org/second-step.aspx

Cunningham, C. E. (2005). COPE: Large group, community based, family-centered parent training. In R. A. Barkley (Ed.), *Attention deficit hyperactivity: A handbook for diagnosis and treatment* (pp. 394–412). New York, NY: Guilford Press.

Cunningham, C. E., Bremner, R., Secord, M., & Harrison, R. (2009). *COPE, The Community Parent Education Program: Large group community based workshops for parents of 3 to 18 year olds.* Hamilton, Ontario: COPE Works.

Early intervention: Supporting student success. (2014). *Special Edge: Student Behavior, 27*(3), 3–16.

Knoff, H. M. (n.d.). *The stop and think social skills program for schools* (preK–8). Voyager Sopris. Available at http://www.voyagersopris.com/curriculum/subject/school-climate/stop-think-social-skills-program

McGinnis, E., & Goldstein, A. (1999). *Skillstreaming the elementary school child*. Champaign, IL: Research Press.

Mikami, A. Y. (2011). How you can be a friendship coach for your child with ADHD. *Attention, 18*(1), 16–19.

Pelham, W. E., Jr. (2014, November). CHADD Ask the Expert chat: Behavior management and combined treatment for children with ADHD. Archived webinar available at http://www.chadd.org/training-events/Ask-the-Expert/Ask-the-Expert-Archives.aspx

Teeter, P. A. (2000). *Interventions for ADHD: Treatment in developmental context*. New York, NY: Guilford Press.

Walker, H. M., McConnell, S., Holmes, D., Todis, B., Walker, J., & Golden, N. (1983). *ACCEPTS program curriculum guide: The Walker social skills curriculum*. Austin, TX: PRO-ED.

Wolraich, M. L., & DuPaul, G. J. (2010). *ADHD diagnosis and management: A practical guide for the clinic and the classroom*. Baltimore, MD: Paul H. Brookes.

Section 1.8

American Academy of Pediatrics (AAP). (2011). ADHD: Clinical practice guidelines for the diagnosis, evaluation, and treatment of attention-deficit/hyperactivity disorder in children and adolescents. *Pediatrics, 128,* 1007–1022.

Fetzer, N., & Rief, S. (2002). *Alphabet learning center activities kit*. San Francisco, CA: Jossey-Bass.

Inland Empire Branch of the International Dyslexia Association. (2003, Fall). The warning signs of learning disabilities. *Resource, 18*(2), 8. www.dyslexia-ca.org

Katz, M. (2009a). First step to success: An early intervention for children with symptoms of AD/HD. *Attention, 16*(4) 8–9.

Katz, M. (2009b). Tools of the mind: Helping children develop self-regulation. *Attention, 16*(3), 6–7.

Katz, M. (2013). Interventions at the point of performance: The power of play. *Attention, 20*(5), 6–7.

LD basics: Common signs of learning disabilities. (n.d.). LD Online. Retrieved from http://www.ldonline.org/ldbasics/signs

Mahone, E. M. (2012, November). CHADD Ask the Expert chat: ADHD in preschool children. Archived webinar available at https://www.youtube.com/watch?v=1QClbDippZY and http://www.chadd.org/ATEPDFs/ATE_EncoreADHDInPreschoolChildren.pdf

National Center on Birth Defects and Developmental Disabilities, Centers for Disease Control and Prevention. (2014a). Important milestones: Your child at three years. Retrieved from http://www.cdc.gov/ncbddd/actearly/milestones/milestones-3yr.html

National Center on Birth Defects and Developmental Disabilities, Centers for Disease Control and Prevention. (2014b). Important milestones: Your child at four years. Retrieved from http://www.cdc.gov/ncbddd/actearly/milestones/milestones-4yr.html

National Center on Birth Defects and Developmental Disabilities, Centers for Disease Control and Prevention. (2014c). Important milestones: Your child at five years. Retrieved from http://www.cdc.gov/ncbddd/actearly/milestones/milestones-5yr.html

National Institute of Mental Health. (2006, October). Preschoolers with ADHD improve with low doses of medication. Retrieved from www.nimh.nih.gov/news/science-news/2006/preschoolers-with-adhd-improve-with-low-doses-of-medication.shtml

National Joint Committee on Learning Disabilities. (n.d.). Learning disabilities and young children: Identification and intervention. Retrieved from http://www.ldonline.org/article/Learning_Disabilities_and_Young_Children%3A_Identification_and_Intervention

Riddle, M. A., Yershova, K., Lazzaretto, D., Paykina, D., Yenokyan, G., Greenhill, L., . . . Posner, K. (2012, December). The preschool attention-deficit/hyperactivity disorder treatment study (PATS) 6-year follow-up. *Journal of the American Academy of Child & Adolescent Psychiatry*. Retrieved from http://www.ncbi.nlm.nih.gov/pmc/articles/PMC3660093/

Rief, S. (2001). *Ready, start, school: Nurturing and guiding your child through preschool and kindergarten.* Paramus, NJ: Prentice-Hall.

Rief, S., & Stern, J. M. (2010). *The dyslexia checklist: A practical reference for parents and teachers.* San Francisco, CA: Jossey-Bass.

Schusteff, A. (2007). Preschoolers and ADHD. *ADDitude, 7*(3), 49–51.

Teeter, P. A. (1998). *Interventions for AD/HD: Treatment in developmental context.* New York, NY: Guilford Press.

Wolraich, M. L. (2007). Preschoolers and AD/HD. *Attention, 14*(3), 9–10.

Section 1.9

Dendy, C.A.Z. (2000). Teaching teens with ADD and ADHD. Bethesda, MD: Woodbine House.

Dendy, C.A.Z. (2002, June). Finding the joy: Parenting teenagers with AD/HD. *Attention, 8*(6), 14–19.

Driving contract. *ADDitude.* Retrieved from www.additudemag.com/adhd-web/article/579.html

Evans, S. W., Serpell, Z., & White, C. (2005). The transition to middle school: Preparing for challenge and success. *Attention, 12*(3), 29–31.

Guare, R., Dawson, P., & Guare, C. (2013). Get your teen ready for life. *ADDitude, 15*(4), 26–29. Excerpted from their book, *Smart but scattered teens* (2013). New York, NY: Guilford Press.

Inland Empire Branch of the International Dyslexia Association (2003, Fall). *Warning symptoms of adolescence and adulthood. Resource, 18*(2), 11. Riverside, CA: Inland Empire Branch of the International Dyslexia Association.

Lepre, S. (2008). Ten steps to academic success. *Attention, 15*(4), 46–47.

Parker, H. (1999). *Put yourself in their shoes: Understanding teenagers with ADHD.* Plantation, FL: Specialty Press.

Rief, S., & Stern, J. M. (2010). *The dyslexia checklist: A practical reference for parents and teachers.* San Francisco, CA: Jossey-Bass.

Stanberry, K. (n.d.). Transition planning for students with IEPs. Retrieved from http://www.greatschools.org/special-education/health/873-transition-planning-for-students-with-ieps.gs

Part 1 Additional Sources and Resources

Abramowitz, A. (2005, August). Classroom interventions for AD/HD. *Attention,* pp. 27–30.

Adesman, A. (n.d.). ADHD medication guide. North Shore-Long Island Jewish Health System. Retrieved from http://adhdmedicationguide.com/

ADHD Partnership, Fairfax County Public Schools, VA. (2008). Powerpoint: Executive function deficits. Free download retrieved from http://adhdpartnership.com/

Alternative therapies—Diet dos; The right stuff. (2010). *ADDitude, 11*(2), 43–44.

American Academy of Child & Adolescent Psychiatry. (n.d.). Frequently asked questions. ADHD Resource Center. Retrieved from http://www.aacap.org/AACAP/Families_and_Youth /Resource_Centers/ADHD_Resource_Center/Home.aspx

Behavior therapy. (n.d.). ADHD and You. Retrieved from www.adhdandyou.com/adhd-caregiver /behavior-therapy.aspx

Barkley, R. A. (n.d.). How ADHD affects EF in adults and kids. *ADDitude* magazine webinar. Retrieved at http://www.additudemag.com/RCLP/sub/11118.html

Barkley, R. A. (2005). *ADHD and the nature of self-control.* New York, NY: Guilford Press.

Barkley, R. A. (2011, January 20). CHADD Ask the Expert chat: The importance of executive function in understanding and managing ADHD. Archived webinar available at http://chadd .org/training-events/Ask-the-Expert/Ask-the-Expert-Archives.aspx

Barkley, R. A. (2012). *Executive functions: What they are, how they work and why they evolved.* New York, NY: Guilford Press.

Barkley, R. A. (2013). *Taking charge of ADHD: The complete, authoritative guide for parents* (3rd ed.). New York, NY: Guilford Press.

Barkley, R. A. (2013). Understanding and improving your ADHD child's behavior. *ADDitude* magazine webinar. Podcast and transcript retrieved from www.additudemag.com/RCLP/sub /10265.html

Barkley, R. A. (2014). Sluggish cognitive tempo (concentration deficit disorder): Current status, future directions, and a plea to change the name. *Journal of Abnormal Child Psychology, 42,* 117–125.

Barkley, R. A., Robin, A. L., & Benton, C. M. (2013). *Your defiant teen: Ten steps to resolve conflict and rebuild your relationship* (2nd ed.). New York, NY: Guilford Press.

Brown, T. E. (2000). *Attention deficit disorders and co-morbidities in children, adolescents, and adults.* Washington, DC: American Psychiatric Press.

Brown, T. E. (2009, February). AD/HD and co-occurring conditions. *Attention, 16*(1), 10–15.

Brown, T. E. (2013). *A new understanding of ADHD in children and adults: Executive function impairments.* New York, NY: Routledge.

Barrow, K. (2013). The mind-body connection. *ADDitude, 14*(2), 51.

Behavior therapy. (n.d.). ADHD and You. Retrieved from www.adhdandyou.com/adhd-caregiver /behavior-therapy.aspx

Bertin, M. (2011). Mindfulness and managing ADHD. *Attention, 18*(3), 16–17.

Bertin, M. (2012). ADHD goes to school. Huff Post Parents blog. *Huffington Post.* Retrieved from www.huffingtonpost.com/mark-bertin-md/adhd_b_1517445.html

Breathing lessons: Meditative powers. (2010). *ADDitude, 11*(2), 41–42.

Brown, T. E. (2005). *Attention deficit disorder: The unfocused mind in children and adults.* New Haven, CT: Yale University Press.

Brown, T. E. (2008). Executive functions: Describing six aspects of a complex syndrome. *Attention, 15*(1), 12–17.

Brown, T. E. (2013). How our understanding of ADHD is changing. *ADDitude* magazine webinar. Retrieved from http://www.additudemag.com/RCLP/sub/10159.html

Brown, T. E. (2014). *Smart but stuck: Emotions in teens and adults with ADHD*. San Francisco, CA: Jossey-Bass.

Carpenter, D. (2007). The diagnostic puzzle. *ADDitude, 7*(3), 32–35.

Centers for Disease Control and Prevention. (n.d.). ADHD treatment. Retrieved from www.cdc.gov/ncbddd/adhd/treatment.html

Centers for Disease Control and Prevention. (n.d.). Attention-deficit/hyperactivity disorder: Symptoms and diagnosis. Retrieved from www.cdc.gov/ncbddd/adhd/diagnosis.html

Centers for Disease Control and Prevention. (n.d.). Diagnosing ADHD in children. Retrieved from www.cdc.gov/ncbddd/adhd/diagnosis.html

Cohen Harper, J. (2013). *Little flower yoga for kids: A yoga and mindfulness program to help your child improve attention and emotional balance*. Oakland, CA: New Harbinger.

Cooper-Kahn, J., & Dietzel, L. (2008). *Late, lost, and unprepared: A parent's guide to helping children with executive functioning*. Bethesda, MD: Woodbine House.

Dawson, P. (2013). Coaching: A versatile strategy for addressing executive skill weaknesses. *Attention, 20*(6), 22–25.

Dawson, P., & Guare, R. (2009). *Smart but scattered*. New York, NY: Guilford Press.

Dawson, P., & Guare, R. (2010). *Executive skills in children and adolescents: A practical guide to assessment and intervention* (2nd ed.). New York, NY: Guilford Press.

Dawson, P., & Guare, R. (2013). *Coaching students with executive skills deficits*. New York, NY: Guilford Press.

Dendy, C.A.Z., & Zeigler, A. (2015). *A bird's-eye view of life with ADHD and EFD . . . Ten years later: Advice from young survivors* (3rd ed.). Cedar Bluff, AL: Cherish the Children.

DeRuvo, S. L. (2009). *Strategies for teaching adolescents with ADHD: Effective classroom techniques across the content areas*. San Francisco, CA: Jossey-Bass.

Dodson, W. (n.d.). ADHD medications explained. Retrieved from www.additudemag.com/adhd/article/9875.html

Drugs, supplements, and herbal information. (n.d.). Medline Plus. National Institutes of Health, National Library of Medicine. Retrieved from www.nlm.nih.gov/medlineplus/druginformation.html

DuPaul, G. (2015, March). CHADD Ask the Expert chat: When preschoolers have ADHD. Archived webinar available at http://www.chadd.org/training-events/Ask-the-Expert/Ask-the-Expert-Archives.aspx

DuPaul, G., & Kern, L. (2011). *Young children with ADHD: Early identification and intervention*. Washington, DC: American Psychological Association.

Elliott, G. R., & Kelly, K. (2007). AD/HD medications: An overview. *Attention, 14*(4), 18–21.

Ellison, K. (2013). Is neurofeedback for you? *ADDitude, 14*(2), 46–48.

Executive function fact sheet: What is executive function? (n.d.). National Center for Learning Disabilities (NCLD) Retrieved from www.ncld.org/types-learning-disabilities/executive-function-disorders/what-is-executive-function

Flynn, L. (2013). *Yoga for children: 200+ yoga poses, breathing exercises, and meditations for healthier, happier, more resilient children*. Avon, MA: Adams Media.

Fowler, M. (2001). *Maybe you know my teen*. New York, NY: Broadway Books.

Gilbert, P. (n.d.). More attention, less deficit: Brain training. *ADDitude*. Retrieved from www.additudemag.com/adhd/article/10076.html

Giler, J. Z. (2000). *Socially ADDept: A manual for parents of children with ADHD and / or learning disabilities*. Santa Barbara, CA: CES.

Giler, J. Z. (2011). *Socially ADDept: Teaching social skills to children with ADHD, LD, and Asperger's*. San Francisco, CA: Jossey-Bass.

Goldberg, L. (2013). *Yoga therapy for children with autism and special needs*. New York, NY: Norton.

Goldstein, S. (2008). Educators as environmental engineers: Psychosocial interventions for AD/HD in schools. *Attention, 15*(4), 44–45.

Goldstein, S., & Brooks, R. B. (2007). *Understanding and managing children's classroom behavior* (2nd ed.). Hoboken, NJ: Wiley.

Goodman, B. (2008). Everything you ever wanted to know about ADHD coaching (but were too busy to ask): Ask the Expert interview with Nancy Ratey. *Attention, 15*(5), 10–13.

Goodman, B. (2010). Five popular approaches to treating ADHD. *Attention, 17*(3), 14–15.

Guare, R., & Dawson, P. (2013). *Smart but scattered teens: The executive skills program for helping teens reach their potential.* New York, NY: Guilford Press.

Hallowell, N. (2013). Fight back with food. *ADDitude, 14*(2), 44–45.

Holingsworth, P. C. (2015, June). Preschoolers and ADHD: Behavioral treatments first. *Attention, 22*(3), 10–15.

Horowitz, S. H. (n.d.). What's the relationship between ADHD and executive function? National Center for Learning Disabilities. Retrieved from www.ncld.org/types-learning-disabilities/executive-function-disorders/relationship-adhd-attention-deficit

Hughes, R. (2011). Research briefs: Artificial food dyes and ADHD. *Attention, 18*(3), 12–14.

Jackson, M. (n.d.). Treat ADHD symptoms with brain training. Retrieved from http://www.additudemag.com/adhd/article/5539.html

Jones, C. B. (1991). *Sourcebook for children with attention deficit disorder: A management guide for early childhood professionals and parents.* Tucson, AZ: Communications Skill Builders.

Kaiser Greenland, S. (2010). *The mindful child.* New York, NY: Atria Books. Retrieved from www.susankaisergreenland.com/book.html

Katz, M. (2008). Promising practices. Brainology: Using lessons from basic neuroscience. *Attention, 15*(5), 8–9.

Katz, M. (2012). Mindfulness and adult ADHD. *Attention, 19*(3), 7–8.

Katz, M. (2014). Executive function: What does it mean? Why is it important? How can we help? *The Special Edge: Student Behavior, 27*(3), 8–10.

Kaufman, C. (2010). *Executive function in the classroom.* Baltimore, MD: Paul H. Brookes.

Lara, M. (2012). The exercise prescription for ADHD. *Attention, 19*(3), 22–25.

Lewis-Palmer, T. (2007). Embedding social skills instruction throughout the day. Retrieved from www.pbis.org/common/pbisresources/presentations/palmer0RPBS20307.ppt#1

Lougy, R., DeRuvo, S., & Rosenthal, D. (2007). *Teaching young children with ADHD.* Thousand Oaks, CA: Corwin Press.

Low, K. (2010, December 8). The benefits of ADHD coaching: Coaching improves executive functioning for college students with ADHD. About.com. Retrieved from http://add.about.com/od/treatmentoptions/a/The-Benefits-Of-Adhd-Coaching.htm

Mahone, E. M., Crocetti, D., Ranta, M. E., Gaddis, A., Cataldo, M. Slifer, K. K., . . . Mostofsky, S. H. (2011). A preliminary neuroimaging study of preschool children with ADHD. *Clinical Neuropsychologist, 25,* 1009–1028.

Mauro, T. (2013). Executive function. About.com. Retrieved from http://specialchildren.about.com/od/behaviorissues/g/executive.htm

McCarthy, L. F. (n.d.). Behavior therapy for ADHD children: More carrot, less stick. *ADDitude.* Retrieved from www.additudemag.com/adhd/article/3577.html

McCarthy, L. F. (n.d.). What you need to know about ADHD coaching. *ADDitude.* Retrieved from www.additudemag.com/adhd/article/4002.html

McCarthy, L. F. (2007). Top 10 questions about meds . . . answered. *ADDitude, 7*(3), 36–38.

McGinnis, E., & Goldstein, A. (1997). *Skillstreaming the adolescent: New strategies and perspectives for teaching prosocial skills.* Champaign, IL: Research Press.

Meltzer, L. (2010). *Promoting executive function in the classroom.* New York, NY: Guilford Press.

Michaels, P. V. (n.d.). Alternative ADHD treatment: Neurofeedback. *ADDitude.* Retrieved from www.additudemag.com/adhd/article/3330.html

Michaels, P. V. (2008). Special report on neurofeedback: Train the brain. *ADDitude, 8*(3), 42–43.

Moyes, R. A. (2014). *Executive function "dysfunction": Strategies for educators and parents.* London, UK: Jessica Kingsley.

Nadeau, K. G. (1998). *Help 4 ADD @ high school.* Silver Spring, MD: Advantage Books.

Nadeau, K. G., & Dixon, E. B. (2004). *Learning to slow down and pay attention: A book for kids about ADHD* (3rd ed.). Washington, DC: Magination Press.

National Association of School Psychologists (NASP). (2002). Fact sheet on social skills: Promoting positive behavior, academic success, and school safety. Retrieved from www.nasponline .org/resources/factsheets/socialskills_fs.aspx

National Center on Birth Defects and Developmental Disabilities, Centers for Disease Control and Prevention. (2014). Special education services for preschoolers with disabilities. http:// www.parentcenterhub.org/repository/preschoolers/

National Center on Birth Defects and Developmental Disabilities, Centers for Disease Control and Prevention. (2015). If you're concerned. Retrieved from http://www.cdc.gov/ncbddd /actearly/concerned.html

National Resource Center on AD/HD. (n.d.). Complementary and other interventions. Retrieved from http://www.chadd.org/Understanding-ADHD/About-ADHD/Treatment-of-ADHD /Complementary-and-Other-Interventions.aspx

National Resource Center on AD/HD. (n.d.). Preschoolers and ADHD. Retrieved from http://www .chadd.org/portals/0/content/chadd/nrc/factsheets/preschoolers.pdf

National Resource Center on AD/HD. (n.d.). Psychosocial treatments. Retrieved from http:// www.chadd.org/Understanding-ADHD/For-Parents-Caregivers/Treatment-Overview /Psychosocial-Treatments.aspx

National Resource Center on AD/HD. (n.d.). Treatment overview. Retrieved from http://help4adhd .org/Understanding-ADHD/For-Parents-Caregivers/Treatment-Overview.aspx

National Resource Center on AD/HD. (2014). ADHD awareness month: ADHD and the *DSM-5*. Retrieved from www.adhdawarenessmonth.org/wp-content/uploads/ADHD-and-the-DSM-5 -Fact-Sheet1.pdf

Oregon Developmental Disabilities Coalition. (n.d.). *Executive functioning: Skills, deficits, and strategies*. Retrieved from http://oregonddcoalition.org

Park, J. H., Alber-Morgan, S. R., & Fleming, C. (2011). Collaborating with parents to implement behavioral interventions for children with challenging behaviors. *Teaching Exceptional Children, 43*(3), 22–30.

Quinn, P. O. (2009). *Attention, girls! A guide to learn all about your AD/HD*. Washington, DC: Magination Press. (For ages 8–13)

Quinn, P. O. (2013, June). Successfully launching your teen or young adult with ADHD into the world. *Attention, 20*(3), 10–14.

Quinn, P. O., & Stern, J. M. (2009). *Putting on the brakes activity book for kids with ADD or ADHD* (2nd ed.). Washington, DC: Magination Press.

Rabiner, D. (n.d.). Behavioral treatment for ADHD/ADD: A general overview. Retrieved from http://helpforadd.com/add-behavioral-treatment

Rabiner, D. (2013, June). New diagnostic criteria for ADHD: Subtle but important changes. *Attention Research Update*. Retrieved from www.helpforadd.com/2013/june.htm

Rabiner, D. (2014, April). Strong new support for neurofeedback treatment for ADHD. *Attention Research Update*. Retrieved from www.helpforadd.com/2014/april.htm

Ratey, J. J., with Hagerman, E. (2008). *Spark: The revolutionary new science of exercise and the brain*. New York, NY: Little, Brown.

Ratey, N. (2008). Complete guide to ADHD coaching. *ADDitude*. Retrieved from www .additudemad.com/adhd/article/3619.html

Reimers, C., & Brunger, B. (1999). *ADHD in the young child: Driven to redirection*. Plantation, FL: Specialty Press.

Rief, S. (2008). *The ADD/ADHD checklist: A practical reference for parents and teachers* (2nd ed.). San Francisco, CA: Jossey-Bass.

Rief, S. (2015). *The ADHD book of lists: A practical guide for helping children and teens with attention deficit disorders* (2nd ed.). San Francisco, CA: Jossey-Bass.

Rief, S. (2016). *Executive function: Skill-building and support strategies for the elementary classroom*. [Six-page laminated guide]. Port Chester, NY: National Professional Resources. (Available at www.sandrarief.com or www.nprinc.com)

Rief, S. (2016). *Executive function: Skill-building and support strategies for grades 6–12.* [6-page laminated guide]. Port Chester, NY: National Professional Resources. (Available at www.sandrarief.com or www.nprinc.com)

Robin, A. L., & Barkley, R. A. (1999). *ADHD in adolescents: Diagnosis and treatment.* New York, NY: Guilford Press.

Rodriguez, D. (2014). Medications to treat ADHD. *Everyday Health.* Retrieved from www.everydayhealth.com/adhd/adhd-drugs.aspx

Semrud-Clikeman, M., & Teeter Ellison, P. A. (2009). *Child neuropsychology: Assessment and interventions for neurodevelopmental disorders* (2nd ed.). New York, NY: Springer.

Severson, H., Feil, E., Stiller, B., Kavanaugh, K., Golly, A., & Walker, H. (n.d.). First steps to success. Voyager Sopris Learning. Retrieved from www.voyagersopris.com/curriculum/subject/school-climate/first-step-to-success

Sheridan, S. M. (1995). *The tough kid social skills book.* Longmont, CO: Sopris West.

Silver, L. (2011). ADHD treatment. *ADDitude, 11*(4), 44–46.

Sleeper-Triplett, J. (2013). Is ADHD coaching right for my teen? *Attention, 20*(6), 26–29.

Special report on working memory: Programmed for success. (2008). *ADDitude, 8*(3), 46.

Tannock, R. (2014). The other ADHD. *ADDitude, 14*(4), 42–43.

Tools of the Mind. (n.d.). What is self-regulation? Retrieved from www.toolsofthemind.org/philosophy/self-regulation/

Understanding ADHD. (n.d.). Health Central. Retrieved from www.healthcentral.com/adhd/understanding-adhd-000030_4.145_2.html

Walker, B. (2004). *The girls' guide to AD/HD.* Bethesda, MD: Woodbine House. (For teenage girls)

Wendt, M. (2011). Linking fitness and academic readiness. *Attention, 18*(3), 28–29.

Wilens, T. E. (2008). *Straight talk about psychiatric medications for kids* (3rd ed.). New York, NY: Guilford Press.

Wilens, T. E. (2014, January). CHADD Ask the Expert chat: The role of medication in managing children's ADHD symptoms. Archived webinar available at https://www.youtube.com/watch?v=e6otz9LQEGE&feature=share&list=UUtIdw4TxJHT8XUlPBvYZD7A

Websites

ADDitude magazine, www.additudemag.com. See also the free webinars presented by experts on a variety of topics with audio and slides, accessible online at http://www.additudemag.com/webinars/

American Academy of Child & Adolescent Psychiatry, www.aacap.org

American Academy of Pediatrics, www.aap.org

Barkley, R. A. See Dr. Barkley's ADHD information sheets and other resources at his website: http://www.russellbarkley.org/

Brown, T. E. See Dr. Brown's information and resources at his website: www.drthomasebrown.com/

CHADD's National Resource Center on ADHD hosts monthly online webcasts (chats) with leading experts in the field of ADHD on a variety of topics. These webcasts are free, and anyone can participate. For upcoming webcasts, see http://www.chadd.org/Training-Events/Ask-the-Expert.aspx#sthash.wJaIPpFA.dpuf; to watch and listen to recordings of previous webinars, see http://www.chadd.org/training-events/Ask-the-Expert/Ask-the-Expert-Archives.aspx

Children and Adults with Attention-Deficit/Hyperactivity Disorder (CHADD) (www.chadd.org) and the National Resource Center on AD/HD (www.help4adhd.org/), a program of CHADD, provide the most reliable information on ADHD diagnosis, treatment, and multiple other topics that are addressed in this part of the book. See the links on these two websites, and information provided specifically at http://chadd.org/Understanding-ADHD/About-ADHD.aspx and at http://www.chadd.org/Portals/0/Content/CHADD/NRC/Factsheets/aboutADHD.pdf

Goldstein, S. See several articles on a variety of ADHD-related topics at Dr. Sam Goldstein's website: http://samgoldstein.com/cms/index.php/articles/

Preschool Learning Foundations, www.cde.ca.gov/sp/cd/re/documents/preschoolf.pdf

Technical Assistance Center on Social Emotional Intervention for Young Children, www.challengingbehavior.org

Managing the Challenge
of ADHD Behaviors

Section 2.1: Proactive Classroom Management

Section 2.2: Preventing Behavior Problems during Transitions and Less Structured Times

Section 2.3: Class (Group) Behavior Management and Incentive Systems

Section 2.4: Individualized Behavior Supports and Interventions

Section 2.5: Strategies to Increase Listening, Following Directions, and Compliance

Section 2.6: Managing Challenging Behavior: Strategies for Teachers and Parents

Section 2.7: School-Based Social Skills Interventions

2.1

Proactive Classroom Management

Students with ADHD are in particular need of teachers who possess effective classroom management skills and establish a well-structured classroom. These are teachers who spend the majority of their time being proactive—with a focus on problem prevention.

Effective classroom management, of course, goes hand in hand with good teaching and instruction. Behavior problems are minimized when teachers provide engaging instruction and motivating learning activities.

The key to effective classroom management is building positive relationships and rapport with students and making a personal connection. Students typically want to cooperate and please adults whom they like, trust, and respect. Some ways for teachers to build this positive relationship are through

- Modeling respectful language, tone of voice, and body language
- Greeting and welcoming students with a smile every day
- Communicating an enjoyment of and appreciation for the class
- Maintaining high expectations and supporting students in achieving those expectations
- Finding time to make personal connections with students

- Being sensitive, empathetic, and responsive to students' needs
- Maintaining a sense of humor
- Making learning activities interesting and fun
- Providing requests, redirection, and corrective feedback in a way that respects students' feelings and dignity
- Avoiding lecturing, criticism, or embarrassment of students (addressing issues in private when possible, not in front of peers)

Classroom Management Tips

The following are the key components and strategies for effective classroom management and creating a positive, productive learning environment.

Create a Climate for Success

Establish a classroom environment that

- Is structured and well organized (for example, there should be a clear schedule, rules and behavioral guidelines, and careful planning of seating and physical space)
- Is calm and predictable
- Has clearly defined, taught, and practiced procedures that become automatic routines of classroom operation

- Focuses on the use of positive reinforcement for appropriate behavior
- Backs up behavioral limits with fair corrective consequences that are enforced predictably and consistently
- Is respectful and mutually supportive
- Is warm, welcoming, and inclusive
- Builds a sense of community, teamwork, and interdependence
- Is flexible enough to accommodate individual needs of students
- Has high academic and behavioral expectations
- Builds on students' skills of self-management (while supporting those who struggle in this area)
- Is safe (emotionally as well as physically); students are not fearful of making a mistake or looking or sounding foolish and, consequently, are willing to take the risk of participating

Establish Classroom Rules (Behavioral Standards)

The following are effective practices:

- Limit the number of rules/behavioral standards to a few comprehensive ones.
- Explain the rationale for the chosen rules.
- Have students discuss, provide input, and agree on the classroom rules to give more ownership and buy-in.

- Clearly and positively state the behaviors you want (rather than "Don't . . ."), such as "Keep hands, feet, and objects to yourself" and "Be on time and prepared for class."
- Define concretely what the behaviors should "look like" and "sound like."
- Discuss, model, and practice those expectations.
- Role-play the desired behaviors. This can be done by demonstrating "nonexamples" as well, to help teach the appropriate behaviors.
- Post rules in words or pictures, and refer to them frequently.
- Remind students of rules and behavioral expectations before the start of activities and ask individual students to repeat them.
- Clearly communicate your rules and expectations in writing to parents as well as students.
- Reward students for rule-following behavior with praise and other positive reinforcement.

Many schools have character education programs or building-wide standards for prosocial behavior that are taught and promoted throughout the entire school. It is recommended that classroom rules correlate with the schoolwide rules or values being taught. For example, one New York City school uses STARS (below) schoolwide.

This teacher's classroom rules (that students sign as a contract) complement and reinforce the schoolwide STARS values and expectations.

STARS

Safety first

Teamwork

Always Respectful

Ready to learn

Sharing and caring

We agree to

1. Practice safety.
2. Be respectful of others.
3. Follow directions.
4. Take responsibility for our learning.

Teach Procedures and Routines

Smooth classroom management is dependent on the teaching of very specific and consistent procedures and routines. Teachers need to think through and decide on their precise expectations for all classroom procedures throughout the day.

Plan procedures for the start of the school day or class period (from entering class and conducting the morning routine) all the way through dismissal at the end of class or day. This includes such things as what students are expected to do when they finish work early, need to go to the restroom, have a question during independent seatwork, don't have a sharpened pencil or other needed materials, need a drink of water, have homework or papers to turn in, need to line up to leave the classroom, are moving to different learning centers or stations, and so forth.

All procedures and routines must be clear, consistent, explicitly taught, and practiced until they become automatic. Teaching procedures and routines is like teaching other behavioral expectations—using modeling, role playing, and frequent practice with feedback, then monitoring, reviewing, and reteaching as needed.

Use Auditory and Visual Cues and Prompts

Once taught, procedures and routines are best prompted through auditory and visual cues and reminders. Use auditory cues such as timers, chimes, or other noisemakers to signal the start of routines (cleanup, line-up), or songs, chants, or rhymes during the length of time for the procedure or routine. Provide visual cues such as a projected digital countdown timer set for the allotted time for the procedure, or a picture that graphically shows the procedure or routine, such as the poster below of what students need to do before dismissal at the end of the period or day.

- Establish visual and auditory signals for getting students to stop what they are doing

End of Day

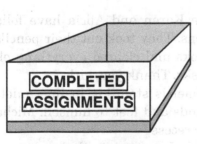

Work turned in

Papers in notebook

All homework recorded in planner

Pack all needed books and supplies

and give you their attention. For example, you could flash the lights, use chimes or other simple instrument, call out a signal word or phrase that students are trained to respond to, or start a clapping pattern such as AABBB that students join on hearing until you stop clapping and speak.

- Use different sounds and noisemakers to signal transitions or specific procedural expectations, such as moving from students' seats to sitting on the carpet area or lining up to leave the classroom.
- Use visual timers, such as Time Timer (www.timetimer.com) or the many different online timers at www.online-stopwatch.com /classroom-timers, which can be projected in the classroom.
- Use pictures or icons of behavioral expectations and point to or tap on picture prompts as a reminder—for example, to raise a hand to speak, or to stay seated and on-task. You can also use an actual photo that you have taken of the student engaged in the appropriate behavior as the visual reminder of expected behavior.
- Teach and use nonverbal signals for communicating either with individual students or the whole class. For example, use hand signs or gestures for such messages as "Please don't interrupt," "Wait your turn," "Make a good choice," "Get back on task."
- Set up a private signal with a student to use for warning or redirecting discreetly, such as a prearranged silly word to say quietly to the student, or a nonverbal signal such as tugging on your ear once you make eye contact with that student. A hand signal, such as two thumbs up, may indicate to the student that he or she can get up and move to another part of the room or outside the door.
- Use color cues such as volume control or noise meter charts. At different times of the day or during certain instructional periods, the teacher clips a clothespin on the chart indicating the noise level permissible at that time—for example, on red (no voice), yellow (partner voice), green (group voice), blue (whole-class sharing voice). Teachers can also remind students verbally, "We are in the yellow zone now."

There are many variations of these volume control charts. Some use numbered levels: 0 = no talking, no sound; 1 = whisper; 2 = only people near you can hear you; 3 = entire class can hear you; 4 = outside voice. For more examples, see www.pinterest.com /sandrarief/class-behavior-management/.

- Many students respond better to visual cues and prompts as opposed to verbal reminders and directions.

Positively Reinforce (Reward) Desired Behavior

Provide Positive Attention and Social Rewards

One of the most effective strategies for motivating and rewarding desired student behaviors is the use of "social reinforcers" provided by the teacher, other school personnel, and classmates. There is no substitute for a teacher's attention to students engaged in appropriate behaviors ("catching them being good"), and reinforcing those behaviors through recognition, acknowledgment, and praise that is specific, descriptive, and sincere. Here are some examples:

"I see Karen and Alicia have followed directions. They took out their pencils and math books and cleared everything else off their desks. Thank you, girls."

"Michael is standing in line quietly with his hands and feet to himself. Michael is ready for recess."

"James, I appreciate that you remembered to raise your hand and wait until I called on you."

"Nick, I see the effort you put into that assignment. Well done."

Additional positive reinforcement can follow praise—for example, "Anna, I noticed how well you followed group rules and were cooperative with your teammates. You earned your team three extra points today." Earning points for a team or group also raises the student's social status with his or her peers.

It is common for students with ADHD to receive many reprimands and much criticism and negative feedback throughout the day. This can be very demoralizing and damaging to their self-esteem. These children need a much heavier dose of positive feedback and recognition for what they are doing right.

Remind yourself to focus your attention on students when they are engaged in appropriate behavior rather than when caught in a rule violation. Make every effort to give at least four times more positive attention and feedback than corrective feedback—particularly to students with ADHD.

Many older students would be humiliated if teachers praised them openly in front of peers. However, they still need and appreciate the positive feedback. Provide positive attention and recognition through thumbs-up signs, pats on the back, smiles, or other nonverbal acknowledgment. If verbal praise is embarrassing to students, provide positive feedback through notes and quiet statements before or after class. Try using a sticky note pad to jot down comments to students, and place them on their desks while circulating throughout the room. More social rewards teachers can provide include

- Positive phone calls or electronic messages directly to the student
- Positive notes, phone calls, electronic messages to parents
- Earning a class privilege of social status (for example, team captain, class messenger)
- Choice of seating for the period, day, or week (near friends, in teacher's desk or chair)
- Being awarded "Star of the Day" or "Student of the Week"
- An object symbolizing success, such as a trophy or stuffed animal, placed on the student's desk for the day

In addition to the teacher's recognition, having classmates provide positive attention and recognition to their peers, such as by giving each other compliments, fist bumps, high fives, applause, or "silent cheers," is a very powerful social reinforcer.

Use Activity Rewards and Privileges

Positive behavior is typically best rewarded in the classroom by enabling students to earn time and the opportunity to participate in activities they enjoy, as well as to earn certain privileges. Teachers often use the contingency: "When you finish . . . you'll get to do . . ." "First, you need to . . . Then you may . . ." "When the class has . . ., we will get to . . ."

Teachers need to know their students and elicit their input to identify what activities would be rewarding to them. Inventory and brainstorm with the class to create a menu of possible privileges and fun activities, such as the following:

- Playing a game, studying, or working on an activity with a friend
- Being first in line for dismissal at lunch, recess, or the end of the day
- Early dismissal of one to two minutes for lunch, recess, or passing to the next class
- Lunch in the class with the teacher and other students who earn the privilege (usually biweekly or monthly); those students bring their own lunch, but the teacher supplies juice or a dessert, such as popsicles
- Earning time in class to catch up on work with teacher or peer assistance if needed
- Extra time or access to the gym, library or media center, music room, or playground
- Various class jobs or responsibilities (being ball monitor, sharpening pencils, taking care of the class pet, being the assistant to the teacher or other staff member, operating audiovisual equipment, taking attendance)
- Use of special materials and tools, such as art supplies, craft materials, electronic equipment, or certain sports equipment not generally available
- Selecting a book to be read to the class
- Being given a special seat, chair, or desk for the day or choice of where to sit for the period or day
- Listening to music of choice
- Reading the morning announcements
- Playing a special game of choice in class, at recess, or during PE

- Having an ice cream, popcorn, or pizza party for the class or group of students who have achieved a certain goal
- Getting awarded a "no homework" pass for the evening, a "good for removing two or three items from an assignment" coupon, "one late assignment accepted as on time" coupon, or "good for removing one bad grade from the daily recorded assignments" coupon
- Earned time for a movement break (dancing to a music video, playing an outdoor game)
- Free or earned time (individual or class) for activities of choice, such as games, listening to music, drawing, cartooning, yoga or dance, working on special projects, or accessing learning or interest centers
- Decorating a bulletin board or a corner of the room
- Sharing a joke in class
- Leading a class game
- Permission to chew gum in class

Games played as a full class, in team competitions, in small groups, or with partners are among the very best classroom incentives. Using a game format for practicing and reinforcing academic skills is a great way to motivate students and make learning fun. Jeopardy, math card or dice games, and Whole Brain Teaching's Mind Soccer (www.wholebrainteaching.com) are great examples of possible games. For a book of over one hundred games used in Whole Brain Teaching (WBT) K–12 classrooms, see Biffle (2015).

Use Your Proximity and Movement

- Circulate and move around the room frequently.
- Use your physical movement, proximity, and positioning for managing disruptive students. Seat them closer to you or in a location that you can reach quickly and easily to be able to make eye contact and provide discreet cues and warnings, such as placing a hand on shoulder, pointing to or placing a visual reminder on their desk, or whispering a reminder or directive to the student.

- Walk or stand near students prone to misbehaving.
- Create a floor plan for desks and other furniture that enables easy access to all students, and paths for walking by and among students without obstruction.

Accommodate Students' Need to Move

- Alternate frequently between seatwork and other activities that allow for movement.
- Assign tasks that will give movement opportunities to students in need of a break, such as passing out papers, cleaning the board, or running an errand to the office.
- Build in brain breaks, particularly after sustained work periods or after students have been seated a lengthy period of time. Have students stand up and stretch, do some jumping jacks, jog or dance near their desks, follow the moves of a brain break video on YouTube, or engage in another brief physical activity for a short amount of time. See several resources, video clips, and ideas for classroom brain breaks at www.pinterest.com /sandrarief/brain-breaks-classroom-games/.
- Students with ADHD particularly need to have the chance during the day to release their energy and engage in physical activity. Avoid using loss of recess time as a consequence for misbehavior or incomplete work.

Environmental Supports and Accommodations in the Classroom

Environmental considerations are essential for classroom management and accommodating individual learning styles.

Student Seating

Seating arrangement is important in any classroom. Many teachers prefer seating arrangements with desks in clusters (four to eight students per group and facing each other) to facilitate cooperative work. This is generally not the ideal arrangement for students with ADHD. More optimal desk formations for students who struggle with attention and productivity may be

- U-shaped/horseshoes
- E-shaped
- Straight rows
- Staggered rows (for example, groups of four students per row in the center and slanted groups of two students per row on the peripheries)

For a variety of classroom seating arrangement options, see http://classroomdeskarrangement.com.

Students with ADHD are usually best seated in these ways:

- Close to the center of instruction
- Surrounded by positive role models and well-focused, on-task students
- Within teacher cueing and prompting distance
- With their desks positioned so that the teacher can easily make eye contact with them and be able to communicate and redirect discreetly
- Away from high-traffic areas and distracters, such as noisy heaters or air conditioners, learning centers, doors, windows, and pencil sharpeners

For students with ADHD, offering alternatives to sitting and working in a hard desk chair often increases productivity and is a reasonable accommodation. For example, consider the following:

- Allow the student to work on the carpet, a beanbag chair, or other location if more comfortable and productive than at a desk, with papers attached to a clipboard.
- Establish some standing work stations: a high table or podium, an easel, or other surface at which a student can do work standing up rather than seated. Place these in the back of the room where they will not obstruct other students' vision.
- Consider assigning two desks to a student with ADHD, with the option of doing his or her work at desk A or desk B. This allows for

the need to get up and move locations, but within boundaries.

- Try seat cushions such as the Disc O'Sit or the Move 'N Sit Cushion, which accommodate a child's need for squirming and wiggling in the chair. Your school's occupational therapist has access to such tools or may provide suggestions. You might also buy inexpensive inflatable beach balls and blow them up partially as an alternative seat cushion.
- Experiment with other kinds of seats, such as a round therapeutic ball, a T-stool (such as the Stabili-T-Stool by Abilitations), the Kids Kore Wobble Chair, or Teen Kore Active Chair.
- See several examples of organized, structured classroom environments and alternative seats and tools beneficial for students with ADHD at www.pinterest.com/sandrarief /class-organization-time-mgmt/ and https: //www.pinterest.com/sandrarief/add-adhd -for-teachers/.

Space, Materials, and Minimizing Environmental Distractions

- Students with ADHD are often spilling into or intruding in others' space. Designate physical boundaries within which the student is to stay. For example, use a strip of colored duct tape on the carpet, floor, or tables. The student is asked to not move his or her desk, chair, or body past the line.
- Reduce clutter and visual distractions, such as unnecessary writing on the board or objects hanging from the ceiling over students' heads.
- Establish rules and procedures for movement within the classroom (such as when it is OK to get up, get a drink, or sharpen pencils) to reduce distractions.
- Permit students to use earplugs or headsets to block out noise during seatwork, test taking, or other appropriate times of the day.
- Purchase or construct privacy boards to place on tables during test taking or at other times to block out visual distractions and

limit the visual field. You can construct desk-size, collapsible privacy boards with three pieces of heavy chipboard and duct tape.

Using Music

Music in the classroom can be used for several purposes. Certain kinds of music may help with focus and concentration: for some students, music acts as a filter for other environmental noises and helps block out auditory distractions. Soothing, quiet music after recess, physical education, and lunch can calm a group of students; playing a lively, upbeat tune in the afternoon when students are feeling sluggish can energize the class. Music can also be used to add structure and time limits during transitions (for example, to clean up and be finished by the end of the song).

Note: See online bonus sections "Music for Relaxation, Transitions, Energizing, and Visualization" for suggested musical selections and "Healthy, Fun, and Therapeutic Ways to Help Manage ADHD Symptoms" for music benefits at this link: www.wiley.com/go/adhdreach.

Other Important Strategies and Tips

- Model respectful language, tone of voice, and body language.
- Position yourself at the door and greet students as they enter the room. Begin instruction promptly.
- Minimize instructional lag time—when students are unoccupied and waiting to find out what they are expected to do next.
- Post the schedule and refer to it frequently. Inform students in advance whenever possible if changes in the schedule will occur. A desk copy of a student's individual schedule is helpful, particularly if the student receives special education and related services.
- Students with ADHD are often penalized for their difficulties with work production by missing out on PE, art, music, media, and other "specials" when they have not completed their class work. Avoid doing this when possible. Find ways to provide more

support and assistance to help them get caught up with their work.
- Smile, laugh, and communicate through your daily interactions that you sincerely care about and expect the best from all of your students and would never give up on any of them.
- For more ideas and strategies for classroom management, see www.pinterest.com /sandrarief/class-behavior-management.

Common Triggers or Antecedents to Misbehavior

The best proactive behavior management involves anticipating potential problems and taking steps to avoid them. Certain conditions, times of day, settings, activities, events, and performance demands can be triggers of students' misbehavior. By becoming aware of common triggers (also referred to as antecedents) to problematic behaviors, teachers can make adjustments to prevent or significantly reduce many behavior problems from occurring.

Some of the antecedents to misbehavior are

A. Environmentally Based
   — Uncomfortable conditions (too noisy, crowded, hot, or cold)
   — Settings (hallways, cafeteria, playground)
   — Lack of structure, organization, predictability, interesting materials, clear schedule, visual supports
B. Physically Based
   — When the child is ill or physically uncomfortable (overly tired, hungry, thirsty)
   — Medication related: medication is wearing off; a change of prescription or dosage, or too high or low a dosage
   — Extended inactivity, restlessness
C. Related to Specific Activity or Event
   — Certain classes or subjects (math, science, reading, PE)
   — Change of routine or schedule without warning
   — Large group discussions
   — Losing a game
   — Taking an exam
   — Seatwork

— Cooperative learning groups and sharing of materials
— Assemblies
— Tasks perceived as boring, lengthy, or frustrating
D. Related to a Performance/Skill Demand
— To remain seated
— To read independently
— To write a paragraph
— To wait quietly and patiently (to speak; for his or her turn in a game)
— To hurry and complete a task
— To refrain from talking
— To refrain from touching things
E. Related to a Specific Time
— First class period of the day
— Before or after lunch
— Transition times of day (changing between subjects or activities)
— After recess
— After school (late afternoon)
— A particular day of the week (for example, Mondays, Fridays)
F. Related to a Specific Person (in the Presence or Absence of . . .)
— Administrator(s)
— A particular teacher or staff member
— Peers (a particular classmate/peer, or group of students)
— Parent(s)
G. Other
— When given no choices or options
— When embarrassed in front of peers
— When having difficulty communicating
— When given no assistance or access to help on difficult tasks
— When teased or bullied

When students misbehave, it helps to understand that there are motivators to behavior—functions, goals, or needs that are being met by demonstrating those undesirable behaviors. Often the child is not consciously aware or deliberately behaving in a way that meets those functions. When able to determine which of the student's needs are being fulfilled as a result of the misbehavior, the teacher can make changes to reduce that inappropriate behavior from occurring. The main functions or goals of student behavior that is disruptive or challenging in the classroom are

- To obtain something (attention, power, access to something fun, rewarding, or stimulating)
- To avoid or escape something (failure, fear, embarrassment, effort)

Address Student Misbehavior

Effective proactive behavior management requires a focus on establishing the structure and climate for success, effectively teaching behavioral expectations, and motivating students to cooperate through the abundance of positive reinforcements available in the classroom. However, students need to know that behavioral expectations will be enforced through both positive and negative or corrective consequences. Here are some tips for addressing inappropriate behavior in the classroom:

- Choose to ignore minor inappropriate behavior that is not intentional. Not every behavior warrants teacher intervention. This is particularly important for students with ADHD.
- Back up behavioral limits with fair and reasonable consequences for misbehavior.
- Handle inappropriate behavior as simply and promptly as possible.
- Deliver consequences using as few words as possible and in a calm, matter-of-fact voice. Act without lecturing or scolding. Discussions about behavior can occur later, and privately when possible.
- Prior to a negative consequence (punishment), teachers can provide nonverbal warnings or cues, such as a hand signal to stop an unwanted behavior, or give a verbal reminder, such as
  — "Steve, remember to raise your hand, please."
  — "Anna, the rule is . . . That's a warning."
  — "Alex, where are you supposed to be right now?"
  — "Jared, next time ask permission before you . . ."

- Provide visual cues of expected behaviors, such as tapping on a picture prompt at the child's desk of a student seated appropriately and busy working.
- Prior to implementing a negative consequence, issue a direct command: "Susan, get busy doing problems 1 to 10 now"; "Brianna, I need you in your seat and facing forward."
- After a student has received clear warnings, infractions of the rules need to result in a minor penalty of some type. Some teachers have an actual hierarchy of consequences they follow. Others may choose an appropriate consequence, considering first the situation, student, and other specific circumstances. The key is that students know that the teacher means business and will enforce some kind of consequence.
- Teachers who follow through consistently can often manage quite well by just asking a student, "Which do you prefer . . . paying me back the time you are wasting after school, or getting busy now? It's your choice."

There are a number of corrective consequences or punishments that teachers can use, such as the following:

- Being the last person to line up or be dismissed
- Losing time from participation in a desired activity
- Being briefly delayed (a minute or two of having to wait before participating in a desired activity or dismissal)
- Restriction or loss of privilege or desired materials for a period of time
- Playground restriction from certain games or areas
- Assignment of an undesirable task or chore
- Filling out a think-about-it (problem-solving) sheet or behavioral improvement form, recording behavioral infractions in a log or notebook (and debriefing in a student-teacher conference later)

- Being "fined" or losing points or tokens of some kind
- Owing time (for taking away time from instruction); this usually involves one to a few minutes paid back after class or school, sometimes longer (detention period)
- Restitution or fixing the problem: if the student makes a mess, he has the responsibility of cleaning it up; if the student was disrespectful, she must apologize verbally or in writing
- Time-out
- Teacher-student conference
- Parent contact (phone call, email, note home, conference)

There are various forms of time-out or time away from class participation:

- Having his or her head down at desk (could involve counting to a certain number)
- Being moved a few feet away from the group temporarily—for example, to sit in a chair rather than on the rug during circle time, but still within view of the group
- Time-out in the classroom, away from the view of other students and without the opportunity for positive reinforcement
- Time-out in a neighboring buddy class that has been arranged to exchange students for this purpose
- Time-out in another school location that has supervision. *Note:* Teachers need to be aware that time-out in other locations may actually be rewarding to the student and not serve the intended purpose of punishment. Being sent out of the classroom can be rewarding if the function of the student's misbehavior is to avoid the effort of an assigned task, escape the environment, or seek stimulation or attention.

Parent Tips: Behavior Management at Home

- Establish a few clear and reasonable, nonnegotiable rules that are enforced consistently.
- Remind your child of expectations through gentle warnings: "The rule is . . ."; "Next time . . ."; "Remember to . . ."
- Use "do" statements rather than "don't" statements. (Say "Walk in the house" rather than "Don't run in the house.")
- Set up routines (for morning, mealtime, homework, bedtime) and adhere to them as closely as possible.
- Provide the supports to enable your child to follow through with chores and responsibilities (for example, reminders or help getting started). Remember that forgetfulness, procrastination, and disorganization are part of ADHD and your child's executive function impairment.
- Use auditory and visual cues (such as timers and visual schedules) to minimize your need to repeat directions and nag your child to start or stop something.
- Make it a goal to pay attention to your child when engaged in appropriate behavior at least four times more frequently than when you need to respond to misbehavior. This is not easy to do if you have a behaviorally challenging child. Misbehavior tends to be on our radar, and it takes a conscious effort to train ourselves to shift our focus.
- Be specific in acknowledging and praising: "I really appreciate how you cleaned up without being reminded"; "I noticed how well you were sharing and taking turns when you played with Bobby"; "You are making such great progress. I can tell you've really been practicing."
- Children with ADHD require more external motivation than other children because their internal controls are less mature. As they also have trouble delaying gratification, provide frequent and immediate rewards (such as tokens).
- Token economy systems are effective for children with ADHD and worth learning how to implement in the home. These systems involve rewarding the child with tokens of some kind (poker chips or points) for demonstrating positive behaviors, such as being ready on time, feeding his or her pet or performing other chores and responsibilities, and remembering to bring home all materials for homework.
- Create a menu of rewards with your child, including material things (toy, book, ice cream) and privileges or activities (screen time, playing a game, special outing) the child values. Include small-ticket items and some bigger ones. Assign a point value or price for each item on the list. The child can purchase rewards with the tokens earned.
- With a token economy system, the child can also be fined (lose tokens) for targeted behaviors (each incident of fighting with a sibling, talking back). It is very important in such a system to ensure that the child is earning far more tokens or points than he or she is losing, or it simply will not work.

INTERVIEW WITH BRAD
Thirty-four Years Old

Brad, a chaplain in the US Navy, received a diagnosis of ADHD and dyslexia at twenty-eight.

Who helped you and made a difference?

"My mother was very supportive. She played an important role in my decision-making process. My mother would let me run things by her—like an article or things I was planning to do. She helped by acting like a filter, so I wouldn't make a lot of the mistakes that would come back and bite me.

"When I was diagnosed, I worked with a specialist for three years. She was excellent. She helped me improve my socialization skills and communication. With dyslexia, it's all tied together. The inconsistency in how you process language filters down on many levels. My mind skips from A to B to G to D to F. It was clear to me what I meant to say, but not necessarily to the listener. She helped me with my writing. I would run past her some of the writing assignments I was working on, and she would help me see when it wasn't linked together . . . it didn't flow. Through her help I developed an 'internal clock.'"

Tell me how you improved socially.

"I had no problems meeting people and getting dates. But after two or three dates, that was it. I knew when the dates were successful and the girl was interested, and I would ask to get together again. But I wanted to know then the date and time of the next date. It wasn't an issue of insecurity, but I was seeking clarification. Everything in my world was black and white. There was no gray area. One of the ways the specialist helped me was to deal with the gray area. I realized it was OK to ask a girl if I could give her a call later . . . no pressure."

How do you remember ADHD affecting you when growing up?

"Teachers attributed my problems to laziness or inattention to detail, even though I spent hours doing my work. I spent so many more hours than anyone else did. I always wondered why I didn't get an A. I would fall asleep during class. At school I would sit ten minutes and be ready to get up and move somewhere else. I always blurted things out in class and couldn't wait to talk. All the kids did that to an extent, but I was 'big time.' I didn't interact well socially. I had friends . . . I did the things everyone else did, only at the wrong time. Others got away with it, but I didn't. They knew when and when not to do something. I didn't realize there was a time and place for everything. I was doing things that were appropriate for kids maybe a few years younger.

"When we would get together and visit family, there were only two things I would talk about— the navy and rabbinical school. Anything else . . . I was a wallflower. Looking back I can see that there were thirty people there and several separate conversations going on at the same time. I couldn't focus or follow any of them. By the time I got involved in a conversation, I was behind everyone else."

How has your life changed since you received your diagnosis?

"Once I found out, I set my own agenda. You can say, 'Look. I can do this work, but I'll have to have extra time. Maybe I need to have an extra semester or year.' I had no problem with spending an extra year in rabbinical school—my ego was not on the line. Once I knew, I was able to ask questions . . . I wanted to find out everything. I started Ritalin at twenty-eight. It improved my ability to concentrate tremendously. I was able to sit down in front of the computer and write a paper. I was able to take notes in class and interact much more effectively. I didn't fall asleep in class. I only took (take) 25 mg. a day, which isn't much, but it has really helped my ADD. Some of my grades went from C's to A's, which is very gratifying when you're in an academic environment."

Preventing Behavior Problems during Transitions and Less Structured Times

Students with ADHD have the greatest behavioral difficulties in the classroom during transition times of the day (changes of activity), as well as in settings outside the classroom that have less structure and supervision, such as the playground, cafeteria, hallways, and bathrooms. Here are some ways to assist students during these more challenging times of the school day.

Classroom Transitions

- Establish procedures and routines for entry into the classroom and starting the school day or class period efficiently and calmly.
- Be prepared before school or the class period begins with the opening activity and prepared materials.
- Clearly teach, model, and have students repeatedly practice transition procedures. This includes such activities as quickly and quietly moving from their desks to the carpet or other central area, putting away and taking out materials, lining up, and moving in and out of their cooperative groups.
- Communicate clearly when activities will begin and when they will end, and give specific instructions about how students are to switch to the next activity.
- Train students to respond to specific auditory signals (a musical sound or novel noise,

a clap pattern, a word or phrase) or visual signals (hand signals, flashing lights, or a color cue).
- Give students a signal a few minutes prior to the end of an activity so that they are alerted to finish what they are working on and prepare for directions for the next activity. You may also want to provide incremental warnings, such as a ten-minute, five-minute, and then a two- or one-minute warning.
- Use songs or chants for transitions such as cleaning up and lining up (in primary grades).
- When an activity ends, obtain all students' attention and give clear directions for transitioning to the new task, which includes their gathering materials needed for the next activity and your telling students where and how they will move if going to a different location. Then signal to begin.
- Closely monitor and provide feedback during and after transitions.
- Create a playlist of recorded songs to use during certain procedures and transitions. You can use songs of various lengths (two or three minutes) depending on how long you expect it to take for students to perform that procedure or transition. Use a specific song or part of a song during transitions to motivate

and cue students as to what they need to do and how much time they have to do it.

Set the timer or play the song and reward students for a quick, quiet transition. If they are ready for the next activity when the timer goes off or the song ends, praise and reinforce. Rewards can be given to the whole class (with, say, marbles in a jar, moves on a class chart, or class points earned) or to successful tables or teams of students or individuals, using tickets, points, or other tokens.

- Use visual timers for alerting students as to how much time they have remaining. Some recommended visual timers are Time Timer (www.timetimer.com), Time Tracker (www.learningresources.com), and the many online timers that can be projected on the board with Internet connection, such as those from www.online-stopwatch.com.
- Provide direct teacher guidance and prompting to students who need more assistance.
- Reward smooth transitions. Many teachers use individual or table points to reward students who are ready for the next activity. The reward is typically something simple like being the first row or table to line up for recess, lunch, or dismissal. Another whole-class technique is to place a circle on the board. Prior to making the transition (such as cleaning up materials), the teacher signals the students, tells them that he or she will count to a certain number, and then proceeds to count. If everyone in the class is ready by the time the teacher finishes counting, the teacher places a checkmark in the circle. If the whole class is not ready, the teacher says, "Oh well, maybe next time." If the class earns a specified number of checks in the circle by the end of the week, there is a class reward.
- Build in stretch breaks and brief exercise between activities, particularly after those that require a lot of sitting or intense work and effort.
- Be organized in advance with prepared materials for the next activity.

Transitions from Out-of-Classroom Activities to the Classroom

- Meet your students after lunch, PE, recess, and other activities outside of the classroom and walk them quietly back to the classroom.
- Provide and structure clear expectations for classroom entry procedures.
- Greet students at the door as they enter the classroom, and direct them to the assigned task to begin immediately.
- Set a goal for the class—for example, that everyone enters class after lunch or recess and is quiet and ready to work by a certain time. On days when they meet that goal, the class is rewarded with a token, class point, or chart move.
- Use relaxation and imagery activities or exercises for calming after recess, lunch, and PE. Playing slow-tempo, quiet music and assigning a silent, calm activity such as journaling or reading to students at these times are also effective.
- Establish clear procedures and expectations for when students are permitted to leave the classroom for any reason, such as to go to the bathroom, bring something to the office, or retrieve an item from their locker.

Out-of-Classroom School Settings

- It is important to have schoolwide rules and behavioral expectations for all out-of-classroom settings (assemblies, cafeteria, playground, bus line, and office) and activities (passing in hallways, moving up and down stairwells, and so on).
- Explicitly teach, model, and provide plenty of practice of behavioral expectations and procedures in all school environments. Positive Behavioral Interventions and Supports (PBIS) schools do an outstanding job of teaching and reinforcing behavioral expectations to all students in all school settings. See the PBIS website (www.pbis.org) for recommended schoolwide practices to prevent behavior problems.
- All staff members should be calmly and consistently reinforcing schoolwide rules

and behavioral expectations through positive and negative consequences. Schoolwide incentives and reinforcers (for example, "caught-being-good tickets" redeemable for school prizes) are helpful in teaching and motivating appropriate behaviors outside of the classroom.

- Some students may require special contracts or some type of individualized behavior chart or form with incentives for appropriate behavior on the playground, in the cafeteria, or in other such settings or times of the day.
- For students who have behavioral difficulty on the bus, arrange an individual contract or monitoring form including the bus behavior on a daily report card (with the cooperative efforts of the school, bus driver, and parent).
- Assign a buddy or peer helper to assist students who have self-management difficulties during transitions to out-of-classroom settings or activities.
- Provide more equipment and choices of activities (including supervised games) during recess to avoid boredom and keep all students engaged.
- It is helpful to have organized clubs and choices for students before and after school and during the break before and after lunch.

- Increase supervision in all environments outside of the classroom: the playground, cafeteria, bathrooms, hallways, stairwells during passing periods, lunch, recess, and school arrival and dismissal. For example, station teachers at the end of hallways between periods.
- Schools should identify and positively target those students in need of extra support, assistance, and careful monitoring outside of the classroom, such as by walking with the student during passing periods.
- Consider allowing certain students to transition a minute or so before or after the rest of the group or at some alternate time.
- For students who don't return to class promptly, use of a timer with incentives for "beating the clock" may help.
- One of the biggest transitions students face is the move from one grade level to the next, particularly the changes from elementary to middle school and from middle school to high school. It is very helpful to prepare students, especially those with ADHD, by visiting the new school, meeting with counselors and teachers, practicing the locker combination, receiving the schedule of classes in advance, and practicing the walk from class to class.

Parent Tips: Preventing Behavior Problems Outside the Home

- Anticipate and prepare for potential problems.
- Give your child advance notice before leaving the house. Avoid catching him or her off guard and provide enough time for getting ready. Talk about what to expect.
- Before going into public places (stores, doctor's office, restaurants, church or temple, movie theaters) or visiting other people's homes:
  — Talk to your child about behavioral expectations.
  — State the rules simply.
  — Have your child repeat the rules back to you.
  — Give written directions if appropriate.
- Establish rewards that your child will be able to receive if he or she behaves appropriately and follows the rules. Remind your child of the contingency: "If you . . ., you will be able to earn . . ."

- A token economy system can be very useful for behavior management in situations away from home. Let your child know that he or she will earn *x* number of tokens or points as an incentive for demonstrating self-control and cooperative behavior when you are out together, and that inappropriate behavior will result in the loss of tokens or points.
- Try not to put your child in situations that are too taxing of his or her self-control and attention span. Avoid places that you know will be too stimulating or where supervising and managing your child's behavior will be difficult.
- If your child is on medication, schedule activities to coincide with the optimal effects of the medication when possible.
- Let your child know the negative consequences if he or she behaves inappropriately. Be prepared to enforce them. Mean what you say!
- Supervise. Supervise. Supervise. For example, when taking your child to someone else's home, remain aware of where your child is and what he or she is doing—ready to redirect or intervene if necessary.
- Be prepared with a bag of tricks. Do not leave the house without being equipped. Bring toys, games, books, tablet or other electronic devices with headsets or earbuds, a pad of paper and colored pencils, and so forth that can occupy your child and keep him or her entertained. Keep the bag of tricks replenished to maintain novelty and interest.
- If your hyperactive or impulsive child will be expected to sit quietly (such as in church or a movie theater), provide a quiet fidget toy, such as a stress ball to squeeze or a piece of Wikki Stix (a piece of twine with a nontoxic wax covering, available at www.wikkistix.com)—or something else to keep his or her hands busy.
- See Dr. Russell A. Barkley's book *Taking Charge of ADHD* (2013) for excellent advice on this topic and with clear steps detailing what to do before, during, and after behavior problems occur in public places.

2.3

Class (Group) Behavior Management and Incentive Systems

Effective behavior management involves having systems and methods in place to motivate students to comply with rules and behavioral expectations. There are many approaches: some systems use strictly positive reinforcement; others are based primarily on rewarding appropriate behavior but also incorporate some type of penalty (response cost) for targeted misbehaviors.

Teachers typically need to change their systems from time to time when effectiveness wears off, or at least tweak the system and add new incentives to keep students motivated. Any system implemented needs to be one that teachers find easy to use and manage. The better the whole-class incentive system works, the less teachers will find they need to devise individualized behavior programs for students with ADHD and others with behavioral challenges.

Positive-Only Group Reinforcement Systems

Praise and Positive Attention

Students are encouraged and cued by the teacher to praise themselves by giving themselves a pat on the back, standing up and taking a bow, or other means. Most effective is when positive attention and recognition are given by peers to each other; for example, the teacher can prompt classmates to give high fives or fist bumps to the student being recognized, or the class can give the student a silent cheer or round of applause (clapping index fingers together in a circular motion).

Table or Team Points

Points are given for specific behaviors—for example, cooperation and teamwork, staying on task, turning in all assignments, cleaning up the area, or transitioning by the allotted time. Table points may be used noncompetitively or competitively. For the noncompetitive method, a table or team is rewarded whenever that table or team reaches a goal, such as having earned a certain number of points or completing their group behavior chart. They don't compete against other tables or teams.

The more commonly used technique is competitive. Points are awarded to tables or teams demonstrating the target behaviors. "Table 4, good job of cooperating and helping your teammates. You just earned a point." At the end of the day or week, the table or team with the most points earns the reward or privilege (or the top two tables win the reward).

Daily or Weekly Target Goals

Another strategy that many teachers use effectively is to identify a behavior in class that is in need of improvement (being out of seat without permission, talking or calling out without raising hand, not turning in homework). The one behavior that is selected is the target for improvement by the whole class. That behavior is monitored daily and calculated precisely. If the students achieve the goal, there is a reward for the class. For example, the goal may be fewer than ten occasions of anyone blurting out or talking without permission during math class, or 90 percent of homework turned in on time for the week, or four out of five days with a smooth morning routine with everyone in his or her seat and prepared by the time the bell rings. Whatever the goal is, it should be clear and reasonable, and achievable if students are motivated to do their best to comply. It should target an existing problematic behavior, with a focus on reducing (most likely not eliminating) that behavior.

Tokens in a Jar

Teachers (usually in primary-grade classrooms) catch students engaged in appropriate behaviors and call attention to the positive behavior (of an individual student, group of students, or something the whole class did well). Then the teacher reinforces the positive behavior by putting a marble (or other small object) in a jar or other container. When the container is filled, the whole class earns a reward (for example, a popcorn party, playing a favorite game, or doing some other special activity).

Chart Moves

A particular goal (or two) is set—for example, all students are in their seats with materials ready by the morning bell, or no observed incidents of a particular problematic behavior occurring in a certain time frame (such as in the morning or after lunch). Each time the class meets that goal, a move is made on the chart, such as connecting to the next dot (on a dot-to-dot chart) or moving a Velcroed object to the next space, as in the racetrack chart below.

Raffles or Lotteries

Students earn tickets of some kind for positive behaviors. When passed out to individual students, they are accompanied with praise for the specific behavior being rewarded. Students write their names on the back of the card or tear off the corresponding number on a raffle ticket, which is placed in the container for a drawing. Those

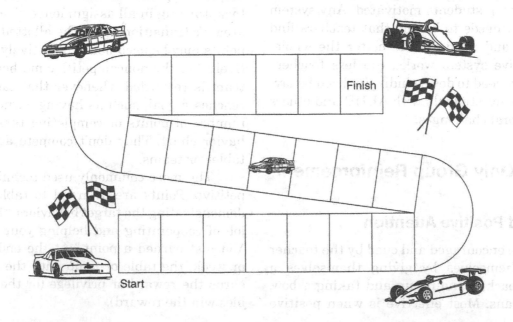

students whose card or ticket is drawn during the raffle are provided with the reward for themselves or their team.

Individual Stamp Cards

Each student has an index card attached to his or her desk. The teacher awards a stamp (as a point) on the card for cooperative, respectful, on-task behavior. This can be for individual behavior and whole-class positive behaviors. At the end of the week, students who have acquired a designated number of stamps receive the reward, which is typically participation in a desired activity.

One variation of this method is shared by Angela Watson, who uses a bead system instead of a stamp card. Each student has a pipe cleaner attached to the desk, and the tokens Angela passes out to students are beads to place on the pipe cleaner. When beads are counted on Fridays, the reward of best choices of activities or centers goes to those students with the most beads, and students with fewer beads have more restricted choices. See http://thecornerstoneforteachers.com /free-resources/behavior-management/bead -system.

Unsolicited Compliment Rewards

With this system, any time the class receives an unsolicited compliment, those compliments are tallied up, and a certain number of tallies earn the class a reward. This is done in many different ways. It typically involves use of a chart that is filled in (for example, a sticker on the chart, a box to color in, a marker to move, a link on a chain) for every compliment the class receives that comes without being solicited. These compliments may come from a visitor, administrator, or anyone who enters the room and praises the class. They can also come from any positive report from a substitute teacher or other staff member for in-class or out-of-class behavior.

A variation is to establish a system in which students are encouraged to be looking for things they appreciate about their classmates. When they observe something about a peer that they want to positively acknowledge, thank, recognize, or praise, they fill out a premade form (of which the teacher has a large supply). It can be something simple like "I really appreciate the way you . . ." or "I thought it was so nice when you . . ."

First, model and talk about what kinds of things should be written on positive notes. For example, "I thought it was so nice when you helped Amanda clean up her work area." The class can decide on a means of distributing these forms and tallying up the number given during the day or week.

Again, the class can be working for a target number of positive notes written and received that when reached will earn the whole class a reward. In the process, it also builds relationships and a positive climate in the classroom.

Note: *If using a system like this, it is critical that all students receive positive comments from peers, not just more popular classmates. It is very important to be inclusive of everyone.*

Lottery Grid, 100 Chart, or Class Bingo Board

Draw a large grid on a board with letters going across on one axis and numbers along the other. On popsicle sticks (tongue depressors) write coordinates for all of the grid spaces (A1, B2, and so on). Students are rewarded for good behavior at the teacher's discretion by getting to pull a stick from a container without seeing the coordinates written on it. Then that place on the grid is marked. When a row is completed (as in Bingo) horizontally, vertically, or diagonally, the class earns a reward. This can also be done using a 100 chart, with numbers 1 to 100 on individual cards or sticks to be drawn.

A variation is for the teacher to make tally marks on the board to reinforce positive behaviors. For every *x* number of tally marks earned by the class, a number stick is drawn, and that space is colored in or covered on the Bingo board or lottery grid.

Mystery Motivator

There are various means of motivating students through their love of a mystery or surprise. One example is to have a secret reward written on a slip of paper and sealed in a "mystery" envelope. When the class meets a certain behavioral goal to a criterion level, such as 90 percent homework turned in during the week, they earn the reward designated in the mystery envelope.

Another example is to have six mystery envelopes with slips of paper inside. When the class earns a certain number of points or reaches a certain goal, someone is called up to roll a die. Whichever number comes up is the number of the envelope to be opened that identifies the class reward.

***

Note: There are several variations of all of these techniques. A good source for seeing how different teachers have adapted the methods can be found at www.pinterest.com/sandrarief/class-behavior -management/.

Reinforcement Systems That Also May Involve Fines or Deductions

Token Economy System

Students have the chance to earn tokens of some kind, such as points, tickets, poker chips, or class money. These tokens are redeemable at a later time for a variety of prizes or privileges. Teacher and students together develop a menu of rewards with corresponding price values attached. Rewards may include small school supplies, snacks, and other items or privileges that students at that grade level value, such as use of certain materials or equipment, or free homework assignment coupons. Students can spend their earned tokens, points, or class money at designated times when there are class auctions or when the "class store" is open. They may spend all or just part of their earnings at this time (for example, buying a small prize now, and saving the rest of their tokens toward a larger, more expensive reward later).

Token economy systems can be used strictly for positive reinforcement (earning tokens). These token systems can also include a "response cost" described in the next section. This means being penalized or fined (losing points or class money). For example, class money or points can also be deducted for misbehaviors. Students would earn a certain amount for everyday expected behaviors (attendance, being to class on time, turning in homework) as well as for any other positive behaviors the teacher wants to reinforce. They may also be fined and lose points or class money for undesired behaviors.

Note: If using a token economy system in this way, it is very important that teachers award students (particularly those with ADHD) generously and frequently for positive behaviors and be careful not to overly fine. If students don't have a chance to accumulate positive points, the system will result in frustration, loss of motivation, and failure of this program to shape students' behavior. Some children have strong emotional reactions to having their earned points or tokens taken away. In these cases, a positive-only system is best.

Group Response Cost

Response-cost techniques are another means of improving and shaping behavior. Instead of giving tokens or points for demonstrating appropriate behaviors, students work to keep the tokens or points that they are given up front, which they can lose for specified misbehaviors.

There are many variations of response-cost systems. The key is that students are working to keep what they have already been given, which can be a bigger motivator for some children. For example, at the beginning of the week, the teacher may give x number of minutes free time or special activity time to the class to be used at the end of week. Specific misbehaviors that occur throughout the week will result in thirty-second losses of time from the free minutes given. The number of remaining minutes is awarded on Friday. *Note:* It is very important to provide just the amount of reward time earned and not go over or under.

Another example is for the teacher to list numbers—for example, 10 to 1—on the board, and for every occurrence of the target misbehavior the class is working to improve (for example, being out of one's seat without permission), a number is erased—beginning with 10, then 9, and so forth. If they still have any numbers remaining at the end of class period or day, the class earns a privilege; if they lose them all, there is a loss of privilege or other consequence.

Good Behavior Game

This class game is a research-validated approach for decreasing disruptive behaviors in the classroom. Basically, the steps involve the following:

- The class is divided into two or three heterogeneous teams, with team numbers listed on the board. Students are taught clearly that

when the Good Behavior Game (GBG) is played, the teacher will be closely monitoring for disruptive behavior; the teacher also defines those specific behaviors (for example, being out of one's seat without permission, talking without permission).

- During game time, a timer is set, and any incident of disruptive behavior by any student that occurs during that time period results in a check mark recorded under the name of the team on which that student belongs. At the end of the game's time frame, any team with fewer than x number of check marks (typically four or fewer) earns a small reward.
- Initially the game is played for periods of ten minutes a few times a week, and rewards are tangible and immediate. Gradually the time frame is extended, and reward times are provided at the end of the day or week.
- It is recommended to schedule the GBG for no more than a total of one to two hours during the day.

The PAX Good Behavior Game (http://paxis .org) evolved from the original GBG. It is included in the US National Registry of Evidence-Based Programs and Practices (www.nrepp.samhsa .gov). The teacher first implements numerous evidence-based positive and proactive strategies in the classroom (referred to as "kernels") before introducing the game. Students clearly know the classroom expectations.

With the PAX GBG, unwanted behaviors are referred to as "spleems." During the time periods that the PAX GBG is played, the teacher identifies and announces each spleem that occurred. Teams at the end of game time with three or fewer spleems earn the reward of a brief, fun activity (such as a minute of dancing around or throwing wadded-up paper balls at each other).

Electronic Feedback Point System— Class Dojo

Class Dojo (www.classdojo.com) is a popular free app for behavior management in the classroom. The program enables teachers to track behavior and provide immediate reinforcement (feedback points) to individual students, groups, or the whole class electronically in real time. This is done with one click via the teacher's smartphone, iPad, laptop, or other device. Class Dojo can run on an interactive whiteboard, a computer connected to a projector, or even just a smartphone, tablet, or other device with Internet connection. The teacher can provide on-the-spot positive points for certain behaviors: participating, staying on task, helping others, persistence, teamwork, or working hard. Feedback points can also be provided for negative behaviors: bullying, being off task, disrespect, no homework, talking out of turn, and being unprepared.

Students choose or are each assigned an avatar as the visual for their name, which is displayed on the interactive whiteboard. When the teacher clicks on the student's name for the positive or negative behavior observed, the plus or minus point and the behavior for which the point was given is projected and entered next to the student's avatar, along with a beep sound. Thus students receive instant auditory and visual feedback, along with reinforcement.

Many teachers find this to be an effective behavior management system. It has, however, raised controversy and concerns because of the public nature of the tallying, as all students' scores are displayed for everyone to see.

Scoreboards, T-Charts, Teacher-Student Points

- Make a T-chart on the board, labeled in the two columns with something positive and negative. For example, smiley face–frowny face, Way to Go!–Oops! or On Target–Off Target.

  At his or her discretion, the teacher places tally marks or points in each column based on students' appropriate and inappropriate behaviors. Points or tallies can be given throughout a class period, the whole day, or in certain time frames, such as before recess or after lunch until dismissal.

If there are more points or tally marks in the positive column at the end of the time frame, the class earns a small reward (such as a short class game, minutes toward free time, or a slight reduction in homework assigned). If there are more points in the negative column, either a small, minor consequence is provided or the reward is not earned.

- Whole Brain Teaching's Scoreboard method uses this technique in a very well designed, motivating way that is simple, flexible, and entertaining, and involves different levels used throughout the course of the school year. The following are some of the highlights of the Whole Brain Teaching (WBT) Scoreboard system:
  — A scoreboard T-chart with smiley and frowny faces for positive and negative behaviors. Points or tallies are given in each column for one of the WBT class rules—for example, "keeping the scorekeeper [teacher] happy."
  — According to the WBT method, there should never be more than three points difference in the columns at all times in order to maintain students' motivation. See the WBT website (www.wholebrainteaching .com/) and Biffle (2013) for more information on how this system is implemented with added levels of motivation throughout the year.

- Another variation of this method is teacher-student points. It works the same way, with the teacher putting tally marks in the Student column when they are on task and following rules. When students are off task, loud, or not following directions, tally marks are placed in the Teacher column. At the end of the day or class period, whichever side has more points earns five minutes. If students win, they get to put the five minutes toward Friday afternoon's choice time. If the teacher has more points, he or she uses the five minutes for more instructional time. See Downeast Teach Blogspot (2013) in the Section 2.3 references for more on this technique.

What to Do about Students Whose Behavior Interferes with Group Success

When teachers implement class incentive systems, they need to face the challenge of how to address individual students whose behaviors tend to ruin their team's chance of earning a reward. A team with a student who has ADHD may be less likely to want that student in their group.

One way to help with this issue is to provide the opportunity for individual students to be a class (or group) hero. A student with ADHD, for example, who has an individual behavior program can earn the class or his or her team the reward of points, advancement on a chart, or something else by meeting his or her own particular goals. Thus the ADHD child's efforts and success in his or her own (individual) behavior program contributes to the rewarding of the group.

Sometimes it may be necessary to group a student with just one partner rather than a few classmates as a team.

Another strategy (but one that should only be used cautiously) is to group students together who have an "I don't care about this" attitude and who may deliberately sabotage the system for others.

By grouping these students together, their behaviors can't hurt the efforts of the rest of the class, just their own. See Whole Brain Teaching's Level 5 of the Scoreboard method (www.wholebrainteaching.com/) regarding this strategy.

Points to Keep in Mind

- The best incentives in a classroom are generally those involving activity reinforcers (rewards). Students are motivated throughout the day to earn time and opportunity to participate in desired activities.
- Students with ADHD are often, unfortunately, penalized for their difficulties with work production—missing out on rewarding activities in order to complete unfinished assignments. If this is happening, provide more support and accommodations to help them get caught up with their work.
- There are numerous classroom games and physical activities that are brief, fun, and motivating. For examples of brief classroom games that can be used as rewards, see those at https://www.pinterest.com/sandrarief/brain-breaks-classroom-games/.

Individualized Behavior Supports and Interventions

Students with ADHD require far closer monitoring, a higher rate and frequency of feedback, and more powerful incentives to modify their behavior than do most children or teens. So, in addition to classroom (group) behavior management incentive systems, students with ADHD often need teachers and parents to implement some kind of individualized behavioral program or intervention as well. These programs are typically

- Tailored to address one or no more than a few specific, observable behaviors
- Tied to a reward or choice of rewards that is meaningful to that individual student—a powerful enough incentive to motivate behavioral change
- Implemented consistently for a period of time, reviewed frequently, and revised as needed

Target Behaviors

Target behaviors selected for intervention might include variations of the following:

- Staying on-task, working productively (for example, resists distractions and stays focused, starts seatwork right away, uses class time effectively, finishes or almost finishes assignments, shows good effort on tasks)

- Cooperating and interacting appropriately with others (for example, uses appropriate language, refrains from fighting or arguing, gets along with peers, respects adults, works with classmates, solves problems peacefully)
- Following directions (for example, follows teacher instructions, obeys class rules, follows playground rules, complies with adult requests without arguing)
- Showing preparedness, readiness to work, and time management and organization skills (for example, brings all needed materials, turns in homework, arrives on time, is ready to work)
- Being in the proper location (for example, stays in seat, participates and stays with group, remains in assigned area)
- Controlling impulsive verbal responses (for example, waits for his or her turn without interrupting, refrains from blurting, raises his or her hand to speak)

Individualized Interventions

There are several types of individualized interventions to help improve a student's behavior and school success, such as the following.

Goal Sheets

- The child or teen identifies one goal to work on for the day or week, such as "organize my desk or locker," "no fights," "get caught up with my incomplete math assignments."
- The goal sheet includes the student's name, the date, and a single goal, such as "My goal that I will work on is _____."
- The student also plans the specific steps he or she will take to reach the goal. For example, "Some steps I will take to reach my goal are _____" or "This is my plan for reaching my goal: _____."
- The teacher, counselor, other adult, or older peer mentor meets briefly in the morning or beginning of the week with the student to discuss the goal and offer encouragement. At the end of the day or week, they meet again, and the student is rewarded if successful.

- Goal sheets may indicate the reward to be received—for example, "If I am successful, I will earn . . ." They may also include a statement of what the adult or peer buddy will do to support the student in achieving the goal.
- The goal sheet is signed by the student and sometimes the adult or older peer mentor.

Contingency Contracts

- This is a written agreement among the teacher, student, and parent (or other parties). The contract includes a clear description of the behavior(s) that the student agrees to perform—for example, "I, _____, agree to do the following: _____." The contract specifies what the reward will be if the student fulfills his or her end of the agreement successfully, and the date the contract ends.
- Some contracts include the criteria for successful performance, such as "at least x days a week" or "with x percent accuracy." Contracts may also include a penalty clause that indicates not only the reward but also what

---

STUDENT GOAL SHEET

My goal for the day/week is:

_____

_____

_____

This is my plan for reaching my goal:

1_____

2_____

3_____

My reward for meeting the goal:

_____

_____

Student Name_____ Date _____

STUDENT CONTRACT

I, _____, agree to do the following:
(Include criteria/standard for successful performance.)

_____

_____

If I fulfill my part of this contract, I will receive the following reward(s):

_____

_____

This contract is in effect from (date) _____ to (date) _____ .

It will be reviewed (daily__ weekly__ other_____).

Signed:

_____   _____   _____
  Student   **Teacher**   **Parent**

the consequences will be for failing to meet the terms of the agreement.

- A date for reviewing the contract is set, and all parties sign the contract to show their agreement with the terms.
- There are several free behavior contracts online. See Intervention Central (www.interventioncentral.org), Free-Behavior Contracts (www.freebehaviorcontracts.com), and Kid Pointz (www.kidpointz.com/behavior-tools/behavior-contracts).

Token Economy and Token Programs

Token programs use secondary reinforcers, or tokens, to provide students with immediate reinforcement for appropriate behavior. When the student earns a designated number of tokens, he or she can exchange them for a primary reinforcement (such as a treat, small toy, or valued privilege or activity).

> Thus, the tokens provide a reinforcement bridge during the time gap between the occurrence of the appropriate behavior and the provision of the primary reward. In this way, tokens may be used to provide students with ADHD the frequent and immediate reinforcement needed to sustain effort on low-interest tasks. (Illes, 2002, p. 92)

Token systems or programs are very effective at home and school. The tokens themselves, which are awarded easily and immediately in the form of points, poker chips, stickers, class money, punches on a card, and so forth, are later redeemed for various privileges or rewards. Children with ADHD have significant difficulty delaying gratification. The immediate reward of the token helps students with ADHD maintain motivation in working toward the goal.

As with other behavioral programs, it is important that token programs focus on improving no more than a few clearly defined target behaviors and that expectations for improvement be realistic and achievable for that individual student. The program needs to be implemented consistently, and the rewards selected (or the choice of rewards from a menu) must be valuable to the child or teen in order to serve as an incentive for behavioral change.

Daily Report Cards (DRCs)

Sometimes called daily behavior forms or reports, home-school notes, or other similar names, a daily report card (DRC) is a research-validated intervention for children and teens with ADHD. DRCs are excellent tools for tracking school performance and motivating a student to improve specific behaviors that are interfering with his or her success. They are highly effective for communicating between home and school and monitoring a child's daily performance.

DRCs can be powerful motivators for students when parents and teachers are willing and able to consistently follow through with positive reinforcement for the student's successful performance on the DRC goals. Any means of forging a partnership between home and school and working together on improving specific behavioral goals is very beneficial for students with ADHD.

How DRCs Work

Basically, DRCs involve selecting and clearly defining one or a few target behaviors or goals to be the focus for improvement. The teacher is responsible for observing and rating daily how the student performed on each target behavior and sending home the DRC at the end of the day.

Parents are responsible for asking to see the DRC every day and reinforcing school behavior and performance at home. "Good days" in school (as indicated by meeting the criteria of the DRC) earn the student designated rewards or privileges at home that evening. A good week (for example, at least three out of five good days initially and then increasing to four) may also earn the child or teen extra privileges on the weekend.

Using this system, parents will provide the consequences at home based on the student's school performance as indicated on the DRC. Rewards at home are provided on days the DRC goal was met, such as TV or other screen time, a favorite snack, or other privilege. A negative consequence (loss of screen time or phone privileges, no dessert, or other mild punishment) may be provided on days the child or teen was not successful. It is important that any reward

_____'S DAILY REPORT

Date_____

	stays seated		*on task*		*follows directions*	
Times or Subjects	No more than __ warning(s)		No more than __ warning(s)		No more than __warning(s)	
	+	-	+	-	+	-
	+	-	+	-	+	-
	+	-	+	-	+	-
	+	-	+	-	+	-
	+	-	+	-	+	-
	+	-	+	-	+	-
	+	-	+	-	+	-
	+	-	+	-	+	-
	+	-	+	-	+	-
	+	-	+	-	+	-
	+	-	+	-	+	-

My goal is to earn at least ___ pluses (+) by the end of the day (or ___% of the day showing great behavior and effort).

If I meet my goal, I will earn a reward/privilege of:

Teacher signature

Parent/guardian signature

Daily Behavior Report for _____

	Stays in Assigned Place	Uses Class Time Effectively	Respectful to Adults & Classmates
Morning	☺ Keep trying	☺ Keep trying	☺ Keep trying
Recess			☺ Keep trying
Afternoon	☺ Keep trying	☺ Keep trying	☺ Keep trying
Specials	☺ Keep trying	☺ Keep trying	☺ Keep trying

Notes:

Daily Behavior Report for _____

	Stays in Assigned Place	Uses Class Time Effectively	Respectful to Adults & Classmates
Morning	☺ Keep trying	☺ Keep trying	☺ Keep trying
Recess			☺ Keep trying
Afternoon	☺ Keep trying	☺ Keep trying	☺ Keep trying
Specials	☺ Keep trying	☺ Keep trying	☺ Keep trying

Notes:

MY BEHAVIOR REPORT

Name: _____ Teacher: _____ Week of: _____

BEHAVIOR	MONDAY			TUESDAY			WEDNESDAY			THURSDAY			FRIDAY		
	Before recess	After recess	After lunch	Before recess	After recess	After lunch	Before recess	After recess	After lunch	Before recess	After recess	After lunch	Before recess	After recess	After lunch
I followed the rules and my teacher's directions.															
I did my work.															

Parent signature _____

_____smileys per day earns _____

_____smileys per week earns

_____
Yes, I did! 😊

***

that is reserved for successful days at school be provided only on the days the child earned it. It is the child's or teen's responsibility to bring the DRC home every day after school. To increase this likelihood, parents may want to provide a mild punishment (such as loss of points) for not doing so.

Another option for implementing this system is to tie it to a token economy. Linda Pfiffner (Barkley, 2013) describes how this would work. Parents give or deduct tokens such as poker chips based on the ratings on the daily report. For example, if the DRC rating is on a scale of 1 to 5, every rating of 1 (the highest score) earns the child five poker chips; a rating of 2 earns three chips; a 3 rating earns the child just one chip. Then the child loses chips for ratings of poor and very poor performance. For example, there would be a five-chip loss for each 5 rating on the DRC.

DRCs can involve school rewards as well as home rewards. For example, a small school reward such as a sticker or computer time can be given to the child at school on a good day. For a good week, the student can earn a special reward at school on Fridays.

If the family is not able to follow through with monitoring and reinforcement on a consistent and daily basis, it is best to do so at school. If the DRC is likely to get lost coming to and from school daily, then perhaps just a card that simply indicates "yes–no" or "met goal–didn't meet goal" can be sent home, or the teacher can notify the parents via a daily email, text, or phone message, and the actual DRC remains at school. In this case, the school needs to be responsible for providing the daily reward when the student was successful, but parents should be asked to reward the child on the weekend if it was a good week. This is manageable in almost all homes.

DAILY REPORT

STUDENT NAME_____ DATE_____

Teachers: Please write Y (yes) or N (no) by each behavior at end of class, and sign/initial. You may also write comments.

1st Period   Comments & Signature/Initials
_____ ON TIME TO CLASS
_____ HOMEWORK TURNED IN
_____ USED CLASS TIME PRODUCTIVELY
_____ FOLLOWED CLASS RULES (no more than 2 warnings)

2nd Period   Comments & Signature/Initials
_____ ON TIME TO CLASS
_____ HOMEWORK TURNED IN
_____ USED CLASS TIME PRODUCTIVELY
_____ FOLLOWED CLASS RULES (no more than 2 warnings)

3rd Period   Comments & Signature/Initials
_____ ON TIME TO CLASS
_____ HOMEWORK TURNED IN
_____ USED CLASS TIME PRODUCTIVELY
_____ FOLLOWED CLASS RULES (no more than 2 warnings)

4th Period   Comments & Signature/Initials
_____ ON TIME TO CLASS
_____ HOMEWORK TURNED IN
_____ USED CLASS TIME PRODUCTIVELY
_____ FOLLOWED CLASS RULES (no more than 2 warnings)

5th Period   Comments & Signature/Initials
_____ ON TIME TO CLASS
_____ HOMEWORK TURNED IN
_____ USED CLASS TIME PRODUCTIVELY
_____ FOLLOWED CLASS RULES (no more than 2 warnings)

6th Period   Comments & Signature/Initials
_____ ON TIME TO CLASS
_____ HOMEWORK TURNED IN
_____ USED CLASS TIME PRODUCTIVELY
_____ FOLLOWED CLASS RULES (no more than 2 warnings)

7th Period   Comments & Signature/Initials
_____ ON TIME TO CLASS
_____ HOMEWORK TURNED IN
_____ USED CLASS TIME PRODUCTIVELY
_____ FOLLOWED CLASS RULES (no more than 2 warnings)

Total number of yeses received today _____.

A minimum of ___ Yeses are required in order to earn agreed-upon reward/privilege.

A successful day of meeting the goal will result in:

Student Signature_____

DAILY/WEEKLY REPORT CARD

Name: _____   **Week of:**_____   **Daily Goal:** _____Points (total for day)

Period	MONDAY		TUESDAY		WEDNESDAY		THURSDAY		FRIDAY	
	Conduct	Classwork	Conduct	Classwork	Conduct	Classwork	Conduct	Classwork	Conduct	Classwork
1										
2										
3										
4										
5										
6										
7										
Total Points →										
Any teacher comments										
	Parent's Signature		Parent's Signature		Parent's Signature		Parent's Signature		Parent's Signature	

CONDUCT: - *Was respectful to adults and classmates*   - *Raised hand to speak (didn't blurt or interrupt)*
                   - *Followed teacher directions*   - *Stayed in assigned place (received permission to leave seat)*
CLASSWORK: - *Participated in lessons & activities*   - *Came to class prepared (with homework and materials)*
                   - *Started on assignments right away*   - *Stayed on task with little redirection*

Teacher Directions: Please enter a conduct score (0-4 points) and a classwork score (0-4 points) at the end of the class period. Base your score on how many of the four specific conduct/classwork behaviors the student demonstrated in your class that day.

Reward/Privilege earned for meeting daily goal: _____

Reward/Privilege earned for a successful week (A minimum of __days of meeting the daily goal): _____

Parents, please sign nightly and have your son or daughter return the form to school each day. It is your child's responsibility to bring the form from class to class and to bring this report to and from school daily.

Daily Monitoring Report

Student's Name_____   Date_____

Time/subject	Had needed materials yes=1 no=0 1 0	Stayed in assigned place yes=1 no=0 1 0	Showed good effort yes=1 no=0 1 0	Raised hand to speak yes=1 no=0 1 0	Followed rules and directions Rate 4-0 (see key below)	points
						/8
						/8
						/8
						/8
						/8
						/8
						/8
						Total /56 ____%

Key: 4- Great job!, 3-Good – tried hard, 2-OK/Most of the time, 1- Had difficulty and needed lots of redirection, 0-Very uncooperative

Daily goal (number of points or %):_____

	Teacher comments:
_____	
Parent/Guardian signature	Parent/Guardian comments

***

Designing the DRC

There are many variations of DRCs. Some forms or charts are designed to be just daily; others have sections for recording each day of the week. DRCs involve the following components:

- Selecting the few goals to be achieved and then defining those goals precisely.
- Collecting data on how frequently the selected behaviors occur to determine a baseline before setting a realistic goal for improvement (which is generally about 25 percent improvement from the current performance initially).
- Setting criteria for success that are reasonable and achievable (for example, at least five smileys out of nine, at least 70 percent

of possible points). The criteria for success are raised gradually.

- Making a chart with time frames broken down by periods of the day, subject areas, or whatever other intervals fit the student's daily schedule and are reasonable for the teacher to monitor consistently.
- Putting a few designated target behaviors on the other axis of the chart.
- Be clear when defining with the child the target behaviors and what you will be evaluating. For example, "on task" might be defined as "no more than x number of warnings or redirections during that time interval," "worked all or most of the time frame without bothering others," or "completed at least 80 percent of the assignment."

- Marking at the end of each time frame: a simple yes or no, plus or minus sign, thumbs up–thumbs down sign, smiley-frowny face, or other such symbol, or circling the number of points (0, 1, 2, 3) earned according to the specific criteria.
- Tallying the student's points at the end of the day to determine the net number of pluses (yeses, smiles) earned that day, and the student's overall performance. (Did the student meet the criteria for success?)
- Informing parents of daily performance (preferably by having the student bring home the DRC each day after school).
- Providing rewards accordingly (at home, school, or both), based on the student's performance on the DRC.

Note: It is important that reinforcement be provided consistently and as promised. A well-coordinated system between home and school is the most effective.

There are different options for rewarding students with a DRC. One option is to provide the reward contingent on the student's successfully achieving a goal for the day or week, such as having earned *x* number of points or smiley faces or a percentage of the points possible. If tied to a token economy as previously described, each rating number would be rewarded at home in tokens given or deducted.

Another option is to use a leveled provision of rewards for daily or weekly report cards. If the child earns, for example, 50–74 percent of the possible plus marks (or yes marks), he or she may choose one item from the reward menu. For scores of 75–89 percent, the child earns a choice of two items from the menu; and 90–100 percent positive marks earn the child a choice of three items from the menu.

See the website of the Center for Children & Families, University of Buffalo, State University of New York (http://wings.buffalo.edu/psychology/adhd) and its ADHD resources at http://ccf.buffalo.edu/resources_downloads.php. The latter site provides excellent information on setting up, implementing, and troubleshooting DRCs for parents and teachers.

See Jim Wright's free guide and apps for creating behavior report cards at www.interventioncental.org.

See the reproducible DRCs in the appendix (A.1 through A.5) that can be used for students of different ages. Some are geared for elementary school students, others for students in middle and high school. The charts and DRCs are also available online at www.wiley.com/go/adhdreach and can be customized before printing.

One New York City middle school teacher also has her students who are on DRCs complete an entry in a daily log that includes the following information: name, date, total points earned and rating for that score (excellent, good, average, poor), as well as a short reflection about their behavioral performance. This is an example of a student log entry: "32 points—good. When kids talked to me, I did not talk back. I focused on my work. I am going to keep trying to be quiet when I'm supposed to and get good or excellent scores on my chart."

Check-In Check-Out (CICO)

Positive Behavioral Interventions and Supports (PBIS; www.pbis.org) uses a targeted behavioral intervention called "check-in check-out" (CICO). The program involves having individual students in need of a daily point card to check in with a designated adult at the start of the school day to retrieve their card.

The CICO form is like a DRC, with a few target behaviors listed on one axis of the form and the subjects or class periods throughout the day listed on the other axis. All students on the program receive the same CICO form and behaviors being evaluated. These are the school rules or schoolwide behavioral expectations—for example, be safe (keep hands, feet, and objects to self), be respectful (use kind words and actions), and be your personal best (follow directions, working in class).

At the end of each time interval, the teacher provides specific feedback and circles the number of points received for each of the behaviors (for example, 2 = excellent! 1= good, and 0 = not yet). The goal or criterion for success is also specified on the form, which is the number of points or the percentage of points received out of the total possible. Rewards are provided for students achieving the goal (meeting the criteria for success).

CICO is basically the same as using a DRC. What makes the CICO program unique is that it is a schoolwide intervention for all students in need of such a targeted intervention program. At the end of the school day, all students in the CICO program leave class a few minutes early to go to the designated adult in the school with their CICO forms for check-out. The adult reviews the CICO form with the student briefly, provides encouragement, and records the score. Then the report or other home report is completed and sent home for a parent's signature. The teachers receive data on their individual students' performance (in graph form). Signed forms are returned to the CICO staff member the next day on checking in.

Several examples of CICO forms used in PBIS schools can be found at www.pbis.org and PBIS state network websites.

Direct Behavior Ratings

See www.directbehaviorratings.org or University of Connecticut's www.dbr.education.uconn.edu for excellent tools and information on using direct behavior ratings (DBRs). Similar to DRCs, DBRs are excellent and efficient for teachers, parents, and others to use for purposes of assessment, communication, monitoring behavior, and targeting intervention, as well as a means for students to self-monitor their own behavior.

Other Behavior Charts and Monitoring Forms

There are many other behavior forms and charts that can be used for school and home behaviors. Behavior charts for preschool and elementary-age children may include sticker charts or ones on which the child gets to color a square or advance forward with a move on the chart when earned. There are also dot-to-dot charts, such as this butterfly chart.

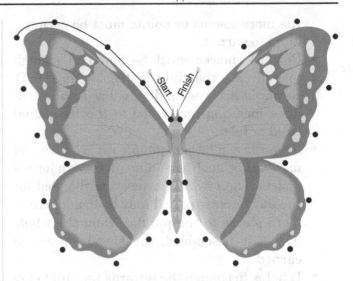

A wealth of free downloadable behavioral charts for parents and teachers can be found online. See, for example, Chart Jungle (www.chartjungle.com), Kid Pointz (www.kidpointz.com), and Free Printable Behavior Charts.com (www.freeprintablebehaviorcharts.com). In addition to the charts and forms found in this book, there are several in *The ADHD Book of Lists* (2nd ed.) (Rief, 2015) and that are downloadable at this link: www.wiley.com/go/adhdbol2 (password: 37754).

For All Positive Incentive Programs

- Focus on improving no more than a few clearly defined target behaviors.
- Expectations for improvement must be realistic and achievable for the individual child.
- Provide reinforcement consistently and as promised. A well-coordinated system between home and school is the most effective.
- Ensure that the child experiences success when beginning these behavioral programs. It is much better to start off with very easy to accomplish goals than to set the bar too high and have the child fail.
- Design a reward menu together with the child and include some tangible items, activities, and special privileges for which the child would be motivated to work. A price or value is attached to each item on the menu. The more desirable and bigger the reward,

the more tokens or points must be accumulated to earn it.

- Reward choices must be powerful enough to motivate the child or teen with ADHD. Rewards are very individualized and must have meaning and value to the individual child or teen.
- Rewards can be very simple yet creative and motivating, such as adding pieces to a jigsaw puzzle. The reward for meeting the goal for the day or class period may be to add one or more pieces to the puzzle. When the whole puzzle is assembled, the bigger reward is earned.
- It helps to change the rewards the child may choose from in order to maintain interest in the program. Add new options to the reward menu from time to time.
- For school rewards, any daily reward when earned needs to be something simple and easy for a teacher to provide, such as a sticker or a few minutes' time for a preferred activity. For weekly rewards, typically the teacher, counselor, or other adult provides on Fridays the reward for students who met their behavioral goal for the week.

Other Individualized Behavioral Interventions

Response Costs

Similar to other reinforcement strategies, a response-cost system offers reward contingent on the child's behavior. However, unlike other reward programs, response cost focuses on the inappropriate rather than the appropriate behavior. Thus it provides the ADHD child with a reward for reducing the frequency of an inappropriate behavior rather than for performing a specific appropriate behavior (Illes, 2002).

Response costs (penalties) are used all the time in daily life to discourage undesirable behavior, such as parking tickets, fines for traffic violations, and yardage fines in football games assessed against the offending team for infractions (Walker, 1997).

Token economies often use a combination of giving the child tokens such as plastic chips, class currency, or points for desired behaviors (positive reinforcement) and response costs (being fined and losing tokens) for specific misbehaviors. If a token program is being used that is a combination of positive reinforcement and response cost, there must be far more opportunities for points or tokens to be earned than to be taken away; otherwise the child will likely become discouraged and give up. The response cost must never become punitive. The student should never lose all his or her points for one infraction or ever be allowed to accumulate negative points.

A response-cost system in the classroom may involve giving the child up front a certain number of tokens; the amount is determined by measuring roughly how often the inappropriate behavior typically occurs during certain time frames. To reduce the inappropriate targeted behavior, the number of tokens given up front should be fewer (but not drastically so) than the baseline number of times the behavior typically occurs. The teacher clearly explains to the student which behavior(s) will result in loss of a token (for example, talking back, being out of seat, hitting). A token is removed or point deducted consistently for each incident of the targeted misbehavior.

The student is rewarded if any tokens remain at the end of the time period. The immediate reward is often a secondary reinforcer—something like a star, sticker, a move on his or her behavior chart, or a certain number of points that are being saved up. When the chart is completed or a certain number of points have been accumulated, the student will then receive the primary reinforcer—the desired object, activity, or privilege that he or she had been working to earn.

Response-cost methods for the whole classroom are described in Section 2.3, and more on this topic is found in Section 2.6. Some individualized approaches include techniques such as the examples shown in the following box:

Mia is a second grader who has difficulty staying with the group during instruction. The teacher discreetly arranges with Mia the following: "I'm going to put three squares on the corner of the board. Each time you get up and move away from the table, I will erase a square. At the end of the period, I will give you a sticker on your chart if there are still any squares left on the board. When you have ten stickers, you will earn . . ."

Kevin has four Velcroed dots attached to his desk, which he loses one by one for disruptive or uncooperative behavior (which is clearly defined to him). If there is one dot remaining at the end of the day (or half-day, or shorter interval), he earns a small individual reward. He may also get to be a class "hero" by earning the class a marble in their jar toward a class party. If Kevin is motivated by this technique, the criteria for success can then be raised (for example, two of the four dots must be remaining).

Samantha blurts and talks out at least ten times during math class, which interferes with instruction. The teacher sets an initial goal of 30 percent reduction in blurting (which is gradually increased) by giving her eight tokens at the beginning of class (chips in a cup, circles on a card taped to her desk, or something else). For every incident of blurting or talking when she is not supposed to, one of the tokens is removed. If at the end of the math period Samantha has one of the eight tokens still remaining (meaning she hasn't talked out more than seven times), she earns a small reward. The criterion for success is gradually raised (for example, to 50 percent reduction, then higher).

When implemented correctly and not overused, response-cost programs in the classroom or at home are generally effective disciplinary techniques for children and teens with ADHD. However, some children are so emotionally reactive or fragile that any loss of earned points or tokens will result in a meltdown, in which case, such a system may not be the best approach.

Self-Monitoring

Self-monitoring is an important self-regulation intervention. Using a self-monitoring strategy, the child or teen pays more attention to his or her own behavior. This self-awareness often leads to improved performance. Rafferty (2010) and McConnell (1999) recommend the following steps for setting up a self-monitoring program for a student:

1. Define the target behavior—for example, "worked without bothering others," "on task," "completed my assignment," or "stayed in my seat."
2. Collect baseline data—typically through frequency count or time sampling procedures.
3. Determine if it is an appropriate behavior to target for self-monitoring. Appropriate behaviors include those that occur frequently and that the student knows how to and is able to control yet has difficulty performing.
4. Schedule a conference with the student.
5. Design procedures and all materials.
6. Teach the student how to use the self-monitoring procedures and provide opportunities to rehearse, practice, model, and review procedures taught.
7. Implement the self-monitoring strategy while providing the student with frequent encouragement and feedback.
8. Monitor student progress.
9. Follow up. Gradually fade use of the self-monitoring procedure as the student gains competence in demonstrating the target behavior, and reinstitute if the behavior reoccurs.

Common Self-Monitoring Techniques

• The student is given a sheet or card for self-monitoring with spaces for recording whether he or she was or was not performing the target behavior (for example, "I am on task") when signaled to do so. During an activity, such as working on a writing or math assignment, the student is given some auditory signal or cue to record either a plus sign or minus sign or other mark, such as smiley-frowny or yes-no, to indicate whether or not he or she was on task at that time. The tone can be a timer or some electronic device set to emit a tone either randomly or at set time intervals (every *x* number of minutes).

- If an individual student is using this technique and the beep or tone that goes off may be distracting to the rest of the class, the student may wear a headset or earbuds. If the whole class or a group is using this self-monitoring strategy, whenever the recorded sound or timer is heard, all students record on their individual sheets.
- Rather than auditory cues, other means can be used to signal when the student is to self-evaluate his or her performance. For example, the student can use a vibrating watch set at time intervals (see WatchMinder.com) or his or her cell phone set on vibration.
- Graphs are frequently used for self-monitoring certain goals, such as the number of problems completed correctly or pages read per day.

SELF-MONITORING FORM

Name: _____ Period: _____ Date: _____

Whenever you hear the signal*, check √ yourself:	YES	NO
"I was focused and on-task."		
Mark the YES or NO box in the columns on the right. Continue doing your work and mark "yes" or "no" each time you hear the sound.		

*Note to teachers or parents
Set a digital timer to make a sound at short regular or random intervals while your child/student is doing independent work (class work or homework).

Teacher Signature _____ (if used at school)

- Another self-monitoring technique involves the student evaluating his or her performance using a rating form (usually 0–4) for one or more behaviors (similar to a DRC). The teacher does the same. At the end of the day, the teacher's rating is compared to the student's. This technique in and of itself is a helpful reality check for many students that may bring about improved performance. An incentive may be added by rewarding the student when his or her rating matches the teacher's or is very close. See the "Self-Monitoring Behavior Log" (A.5) in the appendix for this technique.
- The Bull's Eye Game, which is part of Whole Brain Teaching, uses the following self-monitoring strategy, which Biffle describes in his book *Whole Brain Teaching for Challenging Kids* (2013) and on his website (www.wholebrainteaching.com). The technique basically involves drawing a bull's-eye target with five rings numbered 0 to 5, with the smallest inside circle numbered 5. The teacher and student agree to a target behavioral goal (such as following the teacher's directions or raising his or her hand for permission to speak). Then the behavioral goal is modeled and rehearsed. The teacher and student take turns role-modeling both the appropriate and inappropriate behavior until the behavioral goal is clearly understood. Then the game is explained: Several times a day, the teacher and student will meet briefly to evaluate the student's performance. The teacher will write down the score (5 being a perfect bull's-eye), but not show it to the student. The student then tells the teacher what he or she thinks was the teacher's written score and the reason why. If the teacher's and student's scores match, the student earns two points; if off by only one, then he or she earns one point. If there was more than a two-point difference, the student doesn't earn any points. At the end of the day, the student uses earned points to buy stickers; the size and quality of the sticker depends on the number of points earned.

Social Stories

This is a common intervention for children with autism spectrum disorder, but it is effective for those with ADHD as well. It involves using or creating a simple story that explicitly describes a situation or skill in simple words or pictures. It describes the steps of performing whatever it is that the child will be expected to do or how to behave in a certain event, environment, or activity that is problematic for that student (eating in the cafeteria, walking in the hallways, or behaving appropriately in an assembly, for example). The social story is reviewed with the student before he or she performs that activity or enters into the environment or situation that is problematic. Carol Gray developed this technique. See her website (www.thegraycenter.org) and other resources.

Understanding the ABCs of Behavior

Two fundamental principles of behavior are that (1) challenging behavior occurs within the context of a child's interaction with his or her environment, and (2) challenging behavior is meaningful, has a purpose, and serves a function for the child. Changing the inappropriate behavior of a child requires educators first to identify, and second to change, relevant aspects of the environment that may contribute to the problem—for example, instructional, curricular, or classroom variables (Ryan, Halsey, & Matthews, 2003).

Behavior is always something that can be observed and measured—for example, the number of times a child was out of his or her seat or how many times a student blurted out in class (during a certain time frame), the length of time it took to get started on or to complete an in-class assignment, and so forth. In the ABCs of behavior, *B stands for the behavior* itself—what the child is actually doing that can be observed and measured objectively.

Prior to any behavior occurring, there are *antecedents (A)* to that behavior. As was discussed in Section 2.1, the antecedents are typically the events or conditions that trigger the misbehavior. Teachers can prevent or minimize many undesired student behaviors by making adjustments to those antecedents—for example, making changes to the environment (changing seating, adding more structure or visual supports), to the instruction (providing more direct assistance, reducing the amount of time required to remain quiet by incorporating more partner-talk opportunities during the lesson, modifying tasks and assignments), and so forth.

Following the misbehavior is some kind of *consequence (C)*. The consequence may be either rewarding or punishing to the child, depending on the individual's needs and motivations. What could be perceived by the teacher as a punishing consequence (for example, being sent out of the classroom) could actually be a reward for a student who seeks to escape a task or enjoys the attention or stimulation received out of the classroom setting. Any time a problematic behavior repeatedly occurs, something is reinforcing or maintaining that behavior.

As noted earlier, the underlying function of much student misbehavior is either to get or obtain something (tangible item, attention, control, sensory stimulation) or to avoid or escape something (assigned tasks, activities, embarrassment, discomfort, or negative emotions). Once the underlying motivation or function of a child's behavior is identified, that motivation may be used to determine the most logical and powerful behavioral consequences. Teaching replacement (more acceptable) behaviors and providing strategies and opportunities to get their underlying needs met in more appropriate ways can then be part of the intervention. Students will change their behavior when they see that a different response will more effectively result in a desired outcome.

Note: *When the child is demonstrating the unacceptable behavior to meet a functional need, it is often an automatic response and not something that is done consciously and deliberately.*

Functional Behavioral Assessments (FBAs) and Behavioral Intervention Plans (BIPs)

School districts should conduct functional behavioral assessments (FBAs) and write behavioral intervention plans (BIPs) for students in special education whose behavioral problems are impairing their school success. FBAs and BIPs are required under federal law IDEA to be part of the IEP when behavior is an issue to the degree that disciplinary actions involving a change of placement are being taken. FBAs and BIPs are very beneficial for any student with persistent behavioral challenges and concerns, and may be part of a prereferral process or support for any student exhibiting problem behavior.

What Is an FBA?

Functional behavioral assessment (FBA) is a problem-solving process of determining why a student engages in challenging behavior, the conditions and settings under which a behavior usually occurs, and the probable consequences that are maintaining the behavior. The FBA process uses a variety of techniques and strategies to identify the circumstances and consequences of the student's problem behavior(s), patterns, and probable causes.

The FBA process involves gathering and analyzing information from multiple sources and methods—for example, interviews, informant rating scales, direct observations, and review of the student's records (educational, medical, disciplinary). A variety of school staff (administrators, counselor, teachers) may provide this information and input for the FBA. The IEP team, particularly the school psychologist or other behavior specialist for the school district, analyze the behavioral information from the various sources. The assessment examines and documents the antecedents that preceded the problem behaviors, and consequences or reactions that occurred following the misbehavior. Using this information, the team forms hypotheses or "informed guesses" about the function of the behavior, which guide the team in developing the behavioral intervention plan (BIP).

As noted earlier, when a problematic behavior occurs repeatedly, something is reinforcing or sustaining that behavior. In other words, the consequences (for example, classmates' laughter and attention, being sent out of the classroom) are actually meeting a function or need of that student (such as a need for attention or for escaping an unpleasant task). If the student's needs (functions of behavior) can be met in other, more positive ways, then the inappropriate behavior can be reduced. This includes teaching appropriate alternative skills and behaviors that replace the problem behavior but serve the same function for the student. For example, if the team determines that a student is seeking attention by acting out, it can develop a plan that includes teaching the student more appropriate ways to gain attention.

FBAs involve gathering data and identifying:

- Setting events (lack of sleep, forgetting to take medication, disruption of routine, change of foster homes) or anything that makes the problem behavior or situation worse
- Triggering antecedents (specific situations, events, performance or activity demands, times, certain people) that precede and are likely to set off the occurrence of the problem behavior
- A clear description of the problem behavior, as well as how often it occurs and how long it lasts (frequency, intensity, duration)
- When and where the behavior is most likely and least likely to occur
- The consequences that immediately follow the behavior and may be maintaining the problem behavior (what usually happens after the behavior and the responses of peers and adults to the behavior)
- A desirable or acceptable alternative to the problem behavior

Based on the ABC information derived from the assessment, a hypothesis statement or best guess about the function of the undesirable behavior (or the basic need that is being met by the problem behavior) is identified. What does the student get/obtain or escape/avoid by that behavior? What is the payoff for that behavior? The team can then make a prediction about how the problem behavior can be reduced and design a set of strategies for doing so.

The following are two case examples of hypotheses based on the ABCs determined from an FBA.

Amanda

Antecedents: During independent reading time of the day.

Behavior(s): Amanda is likely to be out of her seat, wandering, and talking to students who are trying to do their reading (disturbing them); knocks her book off the table (deliberately)

Consequence(s): Teacher is frequently near Amanda's desk redirecting or reprimanding; classmates complain she is bothering them. Sent out of room to counselor.

Hypothesis Statement: Amanda is likely engaging in the above behaviors in order to protest and escape a frustrating task demand (independent reading), and to seek attention.

Joel

Antecedents: During cooperative group assignments (with three or four peers in the group).

Behavior(s): Joel is likely to leave the group or engage in behaviors such as making negative comments to peers, grabbing or hoarding materials.

Consequence(s): Group partners let Joel be in charge of the materials. Sometimes the teacher removes Joel from the group to sit and work by himself for not cooperating, but often he is not held accountable to do the group assignment.

Hypothesis Statement: Joel is likely engaging in the above behaviors in order to escape from the effort of the task or escape the group situation, to obtain power and control in the group situation, and perhaps to obtain attention.

What Is a BIP?

After conducting the FBA, the school team uses that information to develop a detailed behavioral intervention plan (BIP) for the student. The BIP specifies what behaviors are being targeted for change and how that will be carried out.

According to Rankin et al. (2002), the BIP should include the following:

- Defining the target behavior(s) and the function that the behavior(s) serve for the student

- Antecedent/setting event strategies—altering in some way any of the antecedent conditions that tend to trigger the problem behavior (for example, environmental, curricular, instructional factors)
- Identifying the replacement behaviors the team wants the child to exhibit (the behavioral goals and objectives stated on the IEP)
- Teaching any needed alternative skills (for example, social skills, conflict resolution, or anger management techniques)

- Skill building and reinforcement strategies (for example, use of specific behavioral programs or strategies such as those described throughout this section) and identifying reinforcers (rewards) that would be motivating and appropriate for this student
- Reduction strategies—identifying appropriate corrective consequences (punishments) for this specific student that take into account the functions of his or her behavior
- Any additional accommodations or modifications to the student's program that would provide more positive ways of getting his or her needs met

As one of the leading special education law experts, attorney Matt Cohen (2009, p. 185) points out:

In developing behavioral intervention strategies, it is critical to recognize that many students may lack the emotional, behavioral, or social skill that is necessary to display the desired behavior. The student may require training or assistance in developing the skill, whether through provision of specified skills training, counseling, modeling of behavior, participation in groups with other students to role play or practice the behavior, and/or ongoing constructive feedback and support from staff.

section

2.5

Strategies to Increase Listening, Following Directions, and Compliance

It is frustrating for teachers and parents when children don't listen and follow directions (a common issue for those with ADHD). Adults may assume that the child or teen is deliberately ignoring them and being deliberately noncompliant, when this is often not the case. Sometimes, a student's not following the adult's directions is due to faulty communication when the adult is giving those directions, such as being too vague or giving a string of multiple directions that the child didn't fully process or promptly forgot.

Not readily following adult directions is also often a result of students' ADHD and their difficulties with executive function–related skills:

- Stopping, disengaging from activities that they are in the middle of (especially something fun that they enjoy doing), and shifting gears to do something else
- Remembering what to do (because of working memory weaknesses)
- Getting started (initiating tasks)
- Performing and following through without prompting and cueing

Strategies and Tips for Teachers

Attention First

- Employ an attention-getting strategy—for example, using auditory signals, such as various sound makers, and using verbal and visual cues which indicate that students are to stop immediately whatever they are doing and give you their attention.
- Do not talk over students' voices. Wait until it is quiet and you have students' attention before giving instructions.
- If necessary, physically cue certain students for their focus prior to giving directions, such as by placing your hand on their shoulder or touching their arm.
- Be sure to face students when you talk.

Clear Directions and Communication

- Give concise, clear verbal directions. Avoid unnecessary talk.
- Write assignments and directions on the board in a consistent spot and leave them there for reference.

- Model what to do by showing the class and walking through the steps.
- Provide multisensory instructions—visual cues and graphics along with simple verbal explanations.
- Let students know that they are not to start the task until signaled to do so (usually with the word "Go!" or "Begin!"). Michael Linsin (2009) of Smart Classroom Management recommends a silent pause for a moment before giving the "Go" signal.
- Establish following directions as a class rule; clearly define, teach, and repeatedly practice this rule. Whole Brain Teaching's class rule 1 is "Follow directions quickly!" See the many techniques Whole Brain Teaching (www.wholebrainteaching.com; Biffle, 2013) uses for teaching and reinforcing this important rule. One example: after every direction (which is always single and short) is given by the teacher, at a teacher cue "Teach!" students are trained to reply "OK!" and turn to their neighbor or partner to repeat what the teacher said.
- Avoid multistep instructions. Whenever possible, provide one instruction at a time or at most two.
- If you do use multistep directions, always clearly delineate the steps and sequence (1, 2, 3) of the directions in writing or pictures that are posted in a highly visible location.
- Break down tasks into smaller steps, simplifying directions for each phase of the task or assignment. Model each step explicitly.

- Check for understanding of directions by having individual students volunteer to repeat or rephrase your directions to the whole class.
- Describe the behavior you want started, and be specific—for example, "Desks cleared except for paper and a pencil" or "Please open books to page 21."
- Use partners and pair-shares for clarification of directions: "Tell your partner what we are going to be doing on page 247."
- Read written directions to the class and have students highlight, circle, or underline key words in the directions.

Feedback, Follow-Through, and Motivation

- Give praise and positive feedback when students are following directions or making a good attempt to do so.
- Follow up after you give directions. Monitor that students have followed your directions, and praise them for doing so. "I see table 3 is ready. They all have their reading logs, pencils, and books on the table, and are ready to begin. Nice job, table 3." You may also provide points or other reinforcement for following directions quickly.
- Check in on students with ADHD to make sure they have begun the task correctly.

Parent Tips: Getting Your Child to Listen and Follow Your Directions

- First, get your child's attention directly before giving directions. This means face-to-face and direct eye contact, not just calling out what you expect your child to do.
- Physically cue your child prior to giving directions, if needed; for example, gently turn your child's face to look at you.
- Do not attempt to give directions to your child if you are competing with the distractions of TV or video games, or when he or she is using an iPad or other electronic device. Pause or turn those devices off first.

- Keep verbal directions clear, brief, and to the point. Eliminate unnecessary talking and elaboration. State what you want with as few words as possible—for example, "Please come to the table now."
- Check for understanding of directions. Have your child repeat or rephrase what you asked him or her to do.
- Show your child what you want him or her to do. Model and walk through the steps.
- Use a chart of tasks or chores depicting the steps or sequence of what your child is expected to do. With young children, for example, make a morning routine chart showing pictures of (1) clothing, (2) cereal bowl, (3) a hairbrush and toothbrush. A clothespin is attached to the side of the chart, which your child moves down to the next picture when completing each task or step in the routine.
- Avoid multistep directions. Giving one direction at a time is better.
- If multistep directions are needed, provide a visual reference such as a checklist or card depicting the steps (1, 2, 3) in pictures or words.
- Write down the task you want done (in words or pictures) and give that written direction or task card to your child. It serves as an easy reference and reduces the potential for conflict that arises from telling your child to do things he or she prefers not to do. For example, chore cards (setting or clearing the table or feeding the family pet) can be made that depict in words or pictures the steps for that chore.
- Be sure to give immediate praise when your child follows directions. "Thank you for being cooperative." "I really appreciate how you listened and quickly did what I asked you to do. Great job!"
- Consider providing additional rewards (such as points or tokens) as well.
- Use more "do" rather than "don't" directives, such as "Put your bottom on the chair" rather than "Stop standing on the chair" or "Hang up your wet towel, please" instead of "Don't leave your wet towel on the ground."
- Do not use vague language that is open to interpretation and lacks enough precise information, such as "Clean your room." Be specific. Define your expectations for a clean room, such as (1) put all dirty clothes in hamper; (2) make bed; (3) put toys away in storage bins.
- Try turning chores and tasks into more pleasant experiences by making a game of them. Beat-the-clock challenges can be motivating, such as "Let's see if you can finish picking up your toys before the timer goes off [or put the blocks back in the basket by the time I count to ten or get dressed by the end of the song]. Ready . . . Set . . . Go!"

Increasing Compliance

Compliance is a completion of a specific request or following previously taught rules. By around eight years old, most children comply with 60 to 80 percent of requests given by adults. A compliance rate of less than 60 percent indicates a problem with either ability (including attention or understanding) or motivation (Robinson, 2000).

It is recommended to keep direct commands (demands) to a minimum. Be sure that any commands you issue are ones you are prepared to enforce. When giving a direct command, follow the same strategies described in the previous paragraphs for communicating what you ask the child to do in a way that increases likelihood that he or she will listen and follow your directions—for example, providing clear commands with precise (not vague) information, and using more "start" rather than "stop" commands.

In addition, experts also recommend the following:

- Use a calm, firm, matter-of-fact tone of voice, one that conveys that you mean business and will follow through.

- Once you give a command, do not repeat, continue to talk, add on new directions, or intervene in any manner without waiting five to ten seconds (or longer depending on the situation) to give the child the chance to comply without interruption.

- If the child complies at this point, praise or thank him or her for listening. If the child does not begin to comply, firmly but calmly state the directive or command again. This time say the child's name followed by the words "you need to . . ." This is called a *precision command*. For example, "Justin, you need to get in your pajamas now." "Susan and Dana, you need to turn around and stop talking."

- If the child still does not comply with the precision command, provide a mild negative consequence, such as loss of some desired activity time or other privilege, brief time-out, or loss of some points or tokens.

- Riley (1997) recommends giving a child a longer time to respond (two minutes). If the child doesn't obey, he suggests calmly saying, "I'm now asking you a second time to . . . Do you understand what I'm asking you to do, and what the consequences are if you don't? Please make a smart decision."

- Increase compliance and cooperation by problem-solving together with the child and collaborating on solutions. See Ross Greene's Collaborative Problem Solving (CPS) model, which is described in his books listed in the references for this section (Greene 2014, 2015).

Oppositional Defiant Disorder and ADHD

Be aware that although many times a child's noncompliance is not willful, oppositional defiant disorder (ODD) does commonly coexist with ADHD. In fact, approximately 40 to 60 percent of children with ADHD have or develop ODD. These children and teens exhibit challenging behaviors (far more than is typical) that are very difficult for parents and teachers to deal with, such as actively defying, ignoring, and refusing to comply with adult requests or rules, and being argumentative. Some experts believe that ODD behaviors are related to poor impulse control and self-regulation skills, difficulty managing frustrations and emotions, and other lagging skills and unsolved problems.

It is important for children with symptoms of ADHD and ODD to receive a diagnosis and to receive therapy for both disorders—the sooner the better. This may include such interventions as medication, parent training in effective behavior management and communication strategies, collaborative problem solving (CPS) and family therapy, and school-based behavioral and academic strategies and programs.

Teachers and parents need to be armed with positive and proactive behavioral techniques and with strategies and guidance in how to defuse conflict, communicate effectively, and avoid getting pulled into power struggles. See Section 2.6 on managing challenging behavior, including oppositional and argumentative behavior, as well as many resources listed in the Part 2 Additional Sources and Resources to help in this regard.

2.6

Managing Challenging Behavior: Strategies for Teachers and Parents

Strategies for Addressing Impulsive and Hyperactive Behaviors

Impulsivity and hyperactivity cause many problems for children and teens with ADHD—often resulting in disruptive behaviors in the classroom and other places that get them into trouble. It is important to remember that these behaviors are not willful, but stem from their brain-based self-regulation difficulties.

Management Tips

- Be explicit about your expectations and remind the student about positive and negative consequences.
- Prioritize your focus—looking for positive behavior to acknowledge, praise, and otherwise reinforce.
- Be tolerant and willing to ignore some minor behaviors (such as pencil tapping and other noises) that are basically annoying and irritating. But clearly deal with those behaviors that interfere with learning in the classroom and any behaviors that are a matter of safety and infringement on the rights of others.
- Review and rehearse behavioral expectations right before entering into activities or situations in which self-control is required. For example, remind the student of appropriate hallway behavior while standing in line waiting to be dismissed to the next class, or review what the rules (and consequences) are right before going to the auditorium for an assembly.
- Provide visual cues—such as a small picture card taped to the student's desk of a stop sign, a raised hand, or a child sitting appropriately in a chair—that you can point to or tap on as a quiet cue, or place a sticky note reminder on the student's desk.
- Use private signals (a gesture, hand signal, cue word) to discreetly remind the student of expectations and encourage him or her to stop and make a good choice.
- Anticipate problems and situations that are challenges for those with poor impulse control. Plan ahead and use proactive strategies to avoid problems in these situations.
- When possible, start the day with some morning exercise.
- Increase supervision and monitoring of the student's behavior in activities and situations requiring self-control.
- Use a verbal signal to stop, such as "Brakes!" "Please . . . Freeze!" or a silly or nonsense word of some kind.
- Teach, model, and practice thoughtful (not impulsive) decision making—for example,

talking things through, identifying and weighing pros and cons, choosing a good option.

- Use strategies to curb interrupting, such as a specific hand signal indicating "wait to speak" or "wait your turn," as well as teaching the child to observe when others are talking and to listen for the break or silence after someone talks as the signal that it is his or her turn to speak.

Feedback and Reinforcement

- Notice the child when he or she is demonstrating self-control. Acknowledge the appropriate behavior and give praise: "Thank you for waiting quietly and patiently." "That was great self-control—not hitting your little brother when he pushed you. I'm proud of you!" A tangible reward, such as points earned or other tokens, or class or home privileges, can also be earned.
- Set up behavior charts and token systems—and award points, stickers, or other tokens for demonstrating self-control. These tokens are later redeemable for tangible rewards and privileges that are motivating to the individual child.
- There are a number of positive-only reinforcement systems that may be best for some children. In these systems, the child either earns the token for the appropriate behavior or does not. When a certain number of tokens have been earned or the spaces on a behavior chart are filled, the reward (prize or privilege) is provided.
- If implemented well, a token economy system involving a combination of positive reinforcement (earning of tokens) and response cost (the penalty of being fined or losing tokens) can be very effective for children with ADHD. This strategy will work only if the opportunity for earning tokens outweighs the loss of tokens so that the child won't be discouraged and lose motivation. As pointed out earlier, some children can't handle the loss of any tokens earned and would respond better to a different approach.

- Response-cost systems can be beneficial for children with poor inhibition. See Section 2.3.

Self-Regulation Strategies and Supports

- Teach and practice self-regulation strategies, such as deep breathing, counting to ten before responding, and using self-talk such as "I'm calm and in control" or "I can handle this."
- Teach and practice a self-control strategy that encourages stopping and thinking before acting. For example, use visual cues such as a stoplight poster:
  — *Red*—**S**TOP and take a deep breath
  — *Yellow*—**T**HINK. What are my **O**PTIONS and possible consequences?
  — *Green*—**P**ROCEED. Make a good choice and go with it.
    There are several variations of this strategy and the wording for the stoplight colors and STOP acronym.
- Provide fidget toys, such as a pencil with something attached on top that can be manipulated, a stress ball, piece of clay or Play-Doh, or other object.
- Play games that help children practice self-control, such as Red Light, Green Light; Freeze or Statues; Simon Says; and others that require the child to inhibit impulses.

More Tips for Teachers in Managing Hyperactive and Impulsive Behavior

- Use instructional methods that provide for frequent opportunities to talk, such as think-pair-shares.
- Teach a few classroom rules and give students so much rehearsal and practice hearing and stating the rules that they can recite by memory each one automatically when prompted to do so.
- Seat the ADHD student next to and pair for activities with classmates who are good behavioral models and tend to be patient and supportive.
- Provide lots of movement opportunities (stretching, brief exercise, and brain breaks

between tasks or activities) and design lessons that involve active learning.

- Increase the distance between desks when possible and avoid seating arrangements that are challenging for students with poor self-control.

- Be tolerant of the student's need to move (squirm, fidget with things, tap pencils). These behaviors may be annoying but don't warrant a punishment. Use tools to accommodate this need and find strategies to help minimize the disruptions; for example, encourage the student to tap the pencil on his leg or a soft pad, provide an inflatable seat cushion or round therapeutic ball with wiggle room, or allow the student to work in the back of the room while standing.

- Use a voice volume scale (for example, 0 = silence; 4 = outside voice) and indicate on a "voice-o-meter" chart the noise level permissible during different activities. This can also include movement level, such as that the red zone means absolutely no talking or getting out of one's seat without permission (such as would be used during test taking).

- Avoid loss of recess as a consequence for misbehavior. Find alternatives or, if needed, limit recess choices of activity. Instead of sitting out recess on a bench, the student can be directed to walk or jog back and forth from one end of the playground to another for x amount of minutes or x number of times before playing.

- Teach, practice, provide visual cues for, and have all adults in the building reinforce the same clear rules and expectations for all school settings (hallways, cafeteria, playground, bus stop, office). See examples of how this is implemented in PBIS schools (www.pbis .org) and at www.pinterest.com/sandrarief /pbis-schoolwide-positive-behavior-support/.

- Use questioning strategies during whole-group activities that build in think time before responding, such as having students jot down their best-guess answer and then calling on volunteers; make a habit of waiting (at least five to ten seconds) to call on students after posing a question; or have students first turn to their neighbor and share before a large-group share.

- Consider using a clear visual sign for when students are not allowed to interrupt you, such as wearing a hat or big colorful necklace while working with small groups in guided reading instruction. In addition, provide clear guidelines on what students may do or to whom they may go if they have questions during that time.

- Set up behavioral charts or contracts specifically focused on one to three behaviors that you want the student to improve (for example, raising hand to speak, staying in seat, completing assignments). Determine the baseline behavior: How frequently does the student typically disrupt by blurting or talking without permission? How long can he or she generally stay seated? What percentage of work assigned is typically done and turned in? Set your goals for gradual and reasonable improvement so that the student can achieve the goal if motivated to try his or her best.

- Teach the student to self-monitor during a class period or for part of the day one of his or her problem behaviors, such as blurting out, interrupting, or being out of his or her seat without permission. The student is responsible for making tally marks on an index card each time you need to remind, redirect, or reprimand him or her for that behavior. Have the student record his or her total at the end of the day or period and set a goal together with you or another adult for improvement.

- Provide clear expectations for working in groups and a specific list of group rules (stay with your group, participate, be on task, be respectful of others, and the like).

- For cooperative group activities, pass out four or five poker chips to each student in the group. The rule is that students are to place one of their chips in the center of the table when they want a turn to talk. Using this technique during group work helps minimize the tendency for some students to

- monopolize the discussion or to talk without listening to others.
- Have students repeat or restate directions in their own words before beginning tasks and assignments.

- Use "what" questions when redirecting, such as "What are you supposed to be doing right now?" "What would be a good choice right now?"

Parent Tips: More Strategies for Managing Your Child's Hyperactive-Impulsive Behavior

- Use timers for setting limits, such as how much longer the child has to play before picking up his or her toys, or how long he or she gets to watch TV or have other screen time before needing to come to the table for dinner. This reduces nagging and arguments.
- Teach your child strategies for what to do when you are on the phone or otherwise engaged and cannot be interrupted, such as jotting down what he or she needs to say so that he or she won't forget or using a quiet signal to get your attention.
- Prepare for times your child needs to wait quietly (driving on errands, going to appointments). Keep a bag of quiet, motivating toys or items of interest in your car with which your child can keep busy when going places, as well as books and electronic devices with headsets.
- Make sure your child gets exercise after school and preferably outdoor play time.
- Indoor exercise equipment (treadmill, exercise bike, trampoline, mounted mini basketball hoop) is also helpful to have in your home, especially if your children are limited in their outdoor play time.
- Set up a safe area somewhere in your home where more rambunctious behavior is allowed; also make it clear which areas are off limits.
- Teach your child polite words to use if he or she needs to interrupt, such as "Excuse me, may I ask you something?" or "I'm sorry for interrupting, but . . ."
- Notice, acknowledge, praise, and reward your child frequently for demonstrating appropriate behavior and self-control.

Strategies for Emotional Regulation and Control

Children and teens with ADHD commonly have a low frustration tolerance and are prone to anger and outbursts because of their neurological immaturity and delayed development of emotional control. There are many preventive measures and strategies to support these self-regulation difficulties and to help avoid and manage escalation of emotions from spinning out of control.

Prevention Strategies for Teachers

- Be aware of the triggers or antecedents that cause the student to become frustrated,

agitated, and upset so that you can make whatever adjustments or accommodations are needed to alleviate those feelings and prevent escalation.
- Frustration and anxiety can often be eliminated or significantly reduced by adjusting the task demand (shortening the assignment, giving more time to complete the task, or providing peer or teacher assistance) and modifying the environment (such as by providing seating options). Avoid situations or conditions that make the student anxious and can provoke emotional reactions.
- Provide the calm, structured, predictable, organized, respectful, and supportive environment that all students need

(particularly those with ADHD), as described in Section 2.1.

- Alert the student about changes in routine and provide warnings and preparation for transitions.
- Take steps to prevent the student from becoming overstimulated, and employ calming techniques in the classroom.
- Offer choices, such as where the student will do his or her work or which part of an assignment to do first.
- Competition can trigger anxiety and fear of failure, which in turn can lead to anger and meltdowns. Use more strategies that encourage students to compete against their own best efforts and work on beating their own records.
- Help the student recognize his or her own physical signs of getting upset (tensed muscles, tight jaw, clenched fists, feeling flushed or hot) and the need to request a break to calm down.
- In order to be able to prompt or cue students to use effective strategies for managing their emotions, the strategies first need to be taught and practiced. Teach and model positive strategies for anger management, calming, and stress reduction (such as visualization, deep breathing, counting slowly, and "self-talk"). It also helps to train the student in peer mediation, conflict resolution, social skills, and problem solving, as well as to provide support and strategies for dealing with disappointments and frustration.
- If we want students to use their words when angry, give them suggested statements and specific language they might use to express their feelings.
- Teach positive self-talk to repeat to themselves (aloud softly or silently) when they feel frustrated or upset, such as "I can deal with this"; "This is going to be OK. I can do it"; "I need to chill out"; "I am calm and in control."
- Affirm and acknowledge the child's or teen's feelings: "I understand why that would make you angry"; "I can see you are upset [or frustrated]."

- Alert the school administrator, nurse, or counselor if the student arrives at school angry or exhibiting behaviors that clearly predict that he or she will need intervention early. A chance to talk with the counselor or other adult before school or to have someone from the school staff follow the child into class and stay there a while until he or she is settled down may help.
- Problem-solving strategies are among the most important things we can teach our students. Teach problem solving and practice the skills in every possible situation and opportunity that arises. There are excellent programs and methods that educators can use for teaching problem solving, such as *I Can Problem Solve* by Myrna Shure (1992), and collaborative problem solving (CBS) strategies that Ross Greene describes in his books (Greene, 2014, 2015). Restorative justice programs are also becoming more widely implemented in schools, which focus on problem-solving practices using mediation and agreement rather than punishment, and empowering students to solve problems on their own in peer-mediated small groups.
- Consider using a self-regulation curriculum for helping students with poor emotional control, such as these:
  - Zones of Regulation (www.zonesofregulation.com) by Kuypers (2011), which uses a traffic-light analogy
  - *Hunter and His Amazing Remote Control* by Copeland (1998), which uses a remote-control analogy
  - The Alert Program (www.alertprogram.com) by Williams and Shellenberger (1996), which uses an engine analogy
  - *The Incredible Five-Point Scale* by Buron and Curtis (2012)

It is often helpful to provide a place that a student can access briefly as a preventive (not punitive) measure before behaviors escalate to a higher level. This might be a designated location outside of the room, such as the nurse's or counselor's office, that the student may go to when needed. Elementary classrooms may be designed with an area that students can use specifically for this purpose. To that end, keep the following points in mind:

- Consider creating a calming area in the room that is equipped, for example, with such items as a fish tank or lava lamp, stuffed animal, soothing music to listen to with headsets, stress ball, pillows, or perhaps a rocking chair.
- Such an area is designed as a take-a-break or cool-down spot. Some teachers give these areas such names as *Hawaii* or *Tahiti*, or some other name that the class agrees is a pleasant, relaxing reference. Such an area is also sometimes referred to as *Alaska*—and going to Alaska means being able to chill out.
- Students can be taught to go directly to this spot when they feel they need to or are directed or prompted to visit the cool- or calm-down area for a short amount of time when feeling agitated or angry ("Would you like to go to Hawaii for a few minutes?").
- Establish a prearranged signal with the student to request use of this area discreetly.

Note: This is not the same as a time-out, which is a negative, corrective consequence that must be time away from anything rewarding.

More Teacher Strategies to Aid Calming and Avoid Escalation

When a student is showing signs that he or she is beginning to lose control, intervene at once by doing the following:

- Provide a cue or prompt, such as standing near the student, placing a gentle hand on his or her shoulder, or pointing to a picture card of steps to take to calm down.
- Use a prearranged private signal—a word, gesture, or visual prompt of some kind—as a reminder to settle down.
- Divert the child's attention if possible.

- Give the student an alternative task or independent activity to do for a while, such as an easy worksheet or coloring.
- Redirect to a different location, situation, or activity. For example, the student can be asked to run an errand, bring a note to a neighboring class or the office, pass out materials, sort papers, or sharpen a can of pencils. The student can also be redirected to the designated cool-down location.
- Provide the student time and a means to regroup, regain control, and avoid the escalation of behaviors.
- Use statements of empathy, understanding, reassurance, and concern.
- When the student is agitated or angry, encourage him or her to express his or her feelings through drawing or writing.
- Breathing slowly is calming. Encourage the student to take a deep breath and hold (for about three to five seconds), then slowly release. Have the student repeat a few or several times. Ask the student to breathe together with you or someone else.
- Signal the student or direct him or her to go to the calm-down area (Hawaii, Tahiti, Alaska) if there is such an area in the classroom, or send the student from the room with a pass to a designated location for a certain amount of time to relax and calm down.
- When you see warning signs of agitation or frustration, assign a task to the student that would involve something physical—for example, carrying heavy boxes, stacking chairs, or, if someone can supervise, running a lap or quickly going up and down the stairs a few times.
- Call for a quick brain break time with the whole class. Play one of the YouTube songs that include dance motions. This may change the emotional state of the student without his or her being singled out as needing it.

Note: If the calming strategies don't work and the student escalates into a full meltdown, follow the school's protocol for dealing with such situations.

Parent Tips: Prevention Strategies for Frustration, Anger, and Melt-Downs

- Know your child's triggers—the situations and conditions that typically lead to frustration, anxiety, overstimulation, and anger. Then take steps to remove or minimize these triggers—for example:
  — Shorten tasks or break them into a series of manageable steps.
  — Provide more support with chores, homework, or other tedious tasks.
  — Avoid situations in which your child is expected to sit quietly for any length of time or otherwise tax his or her limits of self-control.
  — Prepare your child for changes of routine.
- When your child is showing signs of becoming overly stimulated, frustrated, or upset, intervene at once—for example, by doing the following:
  — Signal him or her to calm down with a prearranged gesture or cue word.
  — Try to divert your child's attention and redirect him or her to something else (watch a TV show, listen to music, shoot baskets, take the dog for a walk).
  — Change the expectations, setting, or activity.
  — Cue your child to start using one of the self-calming strategies that he or she has been taught and has practiced. Coach your child through using the technique ("OK. Breathe slowly with me . . .").
  — Offer your child assistance and direct support.
- Speak softly and slowly. Position yourself at the same level as your child when talking to him or her. (Sit down if your child is seated.)
- Affirm and acknowledge your child's feelings: "I understand that would make you mad"; "I can see why you would be disappointed."
- Show that you recognize what your child wanted or his or her intent: "You were hoping . . ." "You were expecting . . . and . . ."
- Be empathetic, understanding, and reassuring.
- Use strategies involving an image your child can visualize. Novotni (2009) suggests asking your child to imagine that there is a candle painted on his or her palm and blowing out the imaginary flame as a calming technique. She also recommends asking the child to hold an imaginary remote control and press the buttons to lower the emotions. Copeland's *Hunter and His Amazing Remote Control* (1998) uses the remote-control analogy with buttons for channel changer, pause, fast forward, slow motion, coach, zapper, and way to go! You can say, for example, "Hit your pause [or slow motion] button," then have your child employ one of the calming strategies, such as breathing or counting backward.
- You may want to use a visual like a thermometer or scale showing levels of emotion and ask your child how he or she is feeling according to the scale or thermometer. For example, an anger or frustration thermometer on a 1–5 or 1–10 scale, with low numbers and a cool color (blue or green) for "I'm calm, happy, all is well" moving up to the highest levels (orange, then red) for intense feelings and "ready to explode."
- Offer your child choices: "Would you rather . . . or . . .?" "What would be better for you . . . or . . .?"
- Have your child do something involving movement and physical activity when you see warning signs of frustration or agitation. Exercise is a positive mood changer. Get your child outside to play a game or do something active.

- Discussing the behavior or issue with your child while doing something physical together (talking while walking or shooting baskets, for example) can be helpful.
- Have a basket or box ready at home or the car filled with fidget toys or small items your child can play with when he or she is beginning to get restless or agitated.
- Teach your child the following:
  — How to recognize his or her physical signs of getting angry (tight jaw and other muscles, clenched fists, feeling hot or flushed, knot in stomach) and steps to calm down when feeling these signs.
  — To use words to express his or her feelings. Your child may lack the language and need you to teach some appropriate words or phrases to use when angry.
  — Positive self-talk statements to repeat, such as "I am calm and in control" or "I can handle this."
- Discuss potential disappointments in advance and ways to deal with them.
- Problem-solve. This is a critical skill that requires a lot of practice: identifying the problem, brainstorming possible solutions, identifying and evaluating the pros and cons of the possible solutions, choosing one of the best options, reviewing its effectiveness, and trying another if it does not work. Greene's collaborative problem solving (CPS) approach is widely used with success. It has been found helpful in reducing children's rage and explosive episodes. See www.ccps.info and Lives in the Balance (www.livesinthebalance.org) for more information, as well as Greene's books (2014, 2015) listed in the Section 2.6 references at the end of Part 2.

Dealing with Argumentative and Oppositional Behavior

As noted earlier, many children and teens with ADHD (at least 40 percent) also have oppositional defiant disorder (ODD). Argumentative, oppositional, and defiant behavior is very difficult for parents and teachers to deal with, and imposes a great strain on the child-adult relationship. The following tips are recommended to help defuse conflict and avoid getting pulled into a power struggle:

- Communicate in ways that are most likely to improve a child's listening and compliance, as described in Section 2.5.
- Make a conscious effort to pay attention to, compliment, and reinforce the child when he or she is being cooperative.
- Also be prepared to follow through and enforce negative consequences (for example, time-out, loss of privilege, or other response cost) when the disrespectful or defiant behavior warrants taking action.

- Children and teens with ADHD seek stimulation. An emotional response is very stimulating. You do not want your highly charged response to be rewarding and, therefore, to reinforce the misbehavior. Also be aware that children with ODD seek power and control. If the child knows how to push your buttons and you "lose it"—responding with an emotional reaction—the child will have effectively gained power and control over you.
- Take whatever steps you need to first gain your composure before responding when provoked, such as taking a few deep breaths and cueing yourself to calm down. Relax your body and facial muscles. Watch your body language (crossed arms, hands on hips, finger pointing). Speak slowly, softly, respectfully, and in a matter-of-fact manner.
- Communicate your confidence in the child's ability to make good choices and your hope that he or she will choose to cooperate.
- Do not feel compelled to give an immediate response in dealing with situations until you

are in a calm, thinking state. You might say, "I'm upset right now and need time to collect my thoughts. I'll get back to you." Then walk away.

- Realize that you cannot control anyone's behavior but your own: how you interact and your attitude, body language, tone and volume of voice, strategies, and consistency and follow-through.
- Use charts, schedules, and timers—creating less room for argument and getting drawn into a power struggle when you need the child to start or stop activities.
- Disengage from power struggles. Remember that you cannot be forced into an argument or power struggle. You enter into one only if you choose to do so. (It takes two.) Say calmly, for example, "I am not willing to argue about this now. I will be free to discuss it later if you wish" (and give a specific time, such as after dinner, after class, during lunch period).
- Avoid nagging, scolding, lecturing, sarcasm, or threatening.
- Set up signals and cues to serve as warnings and private communication, giving the child the opportunity to save face in front of others.
- Avoid "why" questions—for example, "Why did you do that?"
- Use "what" questions—for example, "What are you supposed to be doing right now?" "What do you want?" "What is your plan to solve the problem?" "What can I do to help you?" "What would you like to see happen?" "What are you risking by doing that?"
- Use "when . . . then" contingencies ("When you put away your toys, then you can go outside and play") rather than "If you don't . . . you won't . . ." statements ("If you don't pick up your toys, you can't go outside and play").
- Send "I messages": "I feel . . . when you . . . because . . ." or "I want [or need] you to . . ."
- Use words that tend to deescalate a conflict, such as "I wonder . . . ?" "What if . . . ?" "Maybe . . . ?"
- Seek the child's ideas or solutions to problems.

- Use the broken record technique: respond by repeating your directions with the same words in a calm, neutral voice. Use the words *however* and *nevertheless*—for example, "I understand you are feeling . . . However . . ." or "That may be . . . Nevertheless . . ."
- Other effective words to defuse power struggles include "and" statements, such as "I know you don't want to . . ., *and* what was our agreement?" and *regardless*—"Yes, I know you think it is unfair; regardless . . ."
- Do not take the behavior personally. Think "Q-TIP": **q**uit **t**aking **it** **p**ersonally.
- Avoid giving many direct demands or commands. Only do so when necessary.
- Avoid an audience when interacting with the child when there is a conflict.
- Do not try to rationalize, defend yourself, or convince the child or teen that you are right when he or she is trying to engage you in conflict. It is better to stop talking and walk away.
- Provide lots of opportunities for the child or teen to make choices and take on leadership responsibilities and other means of having some power (the biggest motivator for many children and teens with oppositional behavior).
- Let go of your own anger and keep a disability perspective in mind. Remember that this child's behaviors are generally more a result of lagging skills and neurological immaturity than intended to deliberately push your buttons and make you angry.
- The tougher the child or teen, the greater your efforts must be to find ways to build and strengthen a positive, mutually respectful relationship.
- Take time to actively listen to the child or teen: be attentive and listen carefully without interjecting your opinions. Ask a lot of open, reflective, and clarifying questions, rephrasing and restating what was said.
- Provide a two- or three-choice option: "I can't make you . . . But your choices are either . . . or . . ." (or choices of A, B, or C).
- It is OK to call for a break. Go to a different location or do something away from each

other for a while to calm down and have a chance to think.

- Taylor (2007) suggests scheduling pit stops when things get tense. This is just a private conversation in a quiet area where nobody will interrupt. Discuss, problem-solve, and negotiate win-win solutions after you both have had time to cool down.

- Show the child that you are listening to his or her point of view—for example, "I never thought of it that way before. Let me think about that."

- See the listing at the end of Part 2 of excellent problem-solving resources by Ross Greene and Myrna Shure, and Russell Barkley's books on parenting children with ADHD and on challenging behaviors.

- Use Whole Brain Teaching's strategy of "the agreement bridge" (www.wholebrainteaching .com), which was inspired by the work of Ross Greene.

- Use individualized behavior programs such as daily report cards (described in Section 2.4) with goals related to cooperation.

Other Things to Keep in Mind

- Dealing effectively with children's challenging behavior takes *flexibility,* a *sense of humor,* and a good deal of *tolerance* on your part.

- IDEA provides protections for students with disabilities so that they are not unfairly disciplined when misbehavior stems from the disability itself. This safeguard is particularly important for students with ADHD, whose behavior frequently results in disciplinary action (such as school suspension). It is important to know about "manifestation determination reviews" and other aspects of the law—particularly before school districts impose a change of placement (removing a student from school). See Section 6.4.

- If a student with ADHD has significant behavioral problems, speak to your school psychologist, special education teacher, or other IEP team member about a functional behavioral assessment (FBA) and behavioral intervention plan (BIP).

- Many children and teens with ADHD have coexisting medical or mental health conditions (for example, ODD, depression, anxiety disorder, sleep disorders) that intensify and exacerbate their behavioral difficulties and further impair their functioning. It is important for these other disorders and conditions to be diagnosed and treated in addition to the ADHD.

School-Based Social Skills Interventions

Children and teens with ADHD frequently have difficulties developing positive relationships with peers. Many have a hard time establishing and maintaining friendships. Social challenges can result in a lot of negative outcomes and low self-esteem, as well as be a source of sadness, pain, and frustration, not just for the child, but for the entire family.

ADHD-Related Difficulties

Some common struggles in children and teens with ADHD that negatively affect their interactions and social acceptance are

- Poor self-control and inhibition—causing difficulties with taking turns, sharing, saying something impulsively that is hurtful or inappropriate
- Poor social problem-solving skills and over-reactivity—being easily provoked to fighting, arguing, name-calling, and inappropriate means of resolving conflicts
- Poor self-awareness and underdeveloped sense of the future—being unaware of their behaviors and how they affect others, and

not considering the consequences of their actions
- Difficulty controlling or regulating their emotions, noise level, and activity level
- Poor communication skills (for example, listening to others, refraining from interrupting others)

In addition, children and teens with ADHD often miss important verbal and nonverbal cues that may alert them to regulate their emotional reactions and to modify their behaviors when things are not going well in social interchanges (Teeter Ellison & Goldstein, 2002).

According to Wallace (2000), individuals with the predominantly inattentive presentation of ADHD (and children with coexisting learning disabilities) may have social problems that are different from those who are impulsive and hyperactive. They tend to be unsure, anxious, initially withdrawn in social situations, and reluctant to take social risks. They may misinterpret tone of voice or nonverbal language, believing others are being more critical than they really are, and may lack the language skills to keep up verbally—remaining quiet or making inappropriate or out-of-context comments.

Skill Deficits versus Performance Deficits

Social skills problems can result from a skill deficit, meaning that the child lacks the skill; that is, he or she does not know what to do and needs to learn the appropriate skills to become socially competent. Social challenges can also have nothing to do with a lack of skills. According to leading ADHD authority Dr. Russell Barkley (2014), children with ADHD typically do not have a skill deficit but rather a *performance deficit*. They know what they are supposed to do and how to do it, but fail to apply or perform the needed skill with consistency or at an acceptable level.

For those children who do not yet know the appropriate social skills, they need to be taught age-appropriate social behavior, and social skills training can be beneficial. For those with performance deficits, they need prompting, cueing, and reminding about the appropriate behavior and consequences, and positive reinforcement of their use of good social skills in activities and environments where they have problems (for example, during recess, at the bus stop, in the cafeteria, and when playing competitive games with other children). Zumpfe and Landau (2002) suggest that those with social performance deficits should be trained to develop control strategies (for example, anger management training) so that they can better apply what they already know.

The Impact on Children and Families

An important study and national survey called IMPACT (Investigating the Mindset of Parents about ADHD and Children Today), conducted by New York University Child Study Clinic (2000), revealed some of the impact of having ADHD on the life of the child and the whole family. According to the survey results,

- Seventy-two percent of parents of children with ADHD report that their child has trouble getting along with siblings or other family members (compared to 53 percent of parents of children without ADHD).

- Nearly one-quarter say their child has problems that limit their participation in after-school activities (compared to only 7 percent of parents of children without ADHD).

David Rabiner (2015) shared the results of one study reporting that over 80 percent of children with ADHD experience negative peer relationships and that many have no mutual friendships.

Susan Sheridan (1995) explains that in any classroom, students can be classified into one of four groups:

1. Popular students—those who are highly rated or named frequently as those with whom others would like to play.
2. Neglected students—not many classmates report them as those with whom they would like to play, and not many report them as those with whom they would not like to play.
3. Controversial students—several students say they would like to play with them, but several say they would not like to play with them.
4. Rejected students—not named by many of their classmates as those with whom they would like to play, and named by many as those with whom they would not like to play.

Using sociometric methods of data collection (classmates identified peers they would and would not like to work and play with), research has repeatedly shown that, unfortunately, many children with ADHD are the most rejected among their classmates (Zumpfe & Landau, 2002).

As discussed in Section 1.4 on multimodal treatments and Section 1.6 on behavioral therapy and other psychosocial interventions, social skills problems for children with ADHD are best addressed on several fronts: with interventions and supports provided at school by teachers and other school staff; interventions and supports provided by parents; and direct child interventions, such as receiving social skills training and participation in a summer treatment program for youth with ADHD. School-based interventions are the focus of this section.

DECKER FORREST

Classroom Interventions

Every day, teachers informally model and teach students positive social behaviors. When teachers set behavioral standards and enforce expectations for respectful, cooperative behavior, most students learn and practice social skills daily. Teachers infuse social skills training into daily instruction when they explicitly model, coach, prompt, monitor, and positively reinforce such skills as sharing and taking turns, listening without interrupting, participating in conversations without dominating them, giving and accepting compliments, disagreeing and expressing opinions appropriately, and employing general manners of using respectful and polite verbal and body language.

Within the classroom, there is no better place and structure for teaching and practicing appropriate social skills than in the context of cooperative learning groups. Research has proven cooperative learning to be effective not only in increasing student learning but also in developing positive and supportive relationships, student acceptance, and the ability to see other points of view. (See "Peer-Mediated Instruction and Intervention" in Section 3.2.)

Having at least one friend at school is very important. Research suggests that having a best friend may have a protective effect on children with difficulties in peer relations as they develop through childhood and into adolescence (Hoza, 2007; Hoza, Mrug, Pelham, Greiner, & Gnagy, 2001; Mrug, Hoza, & Gerdes, 2001; Rabiner, 2015). Teachers and other school staff may need to facilitate the fostering of friendships for students with ADHD and others who tend to be socially isolated or rejected.

Teacher Tips

- Help children weak in social skills by carefully pairing them with positive role models and assigning them to groups who will be tolerant and supportive.

- Look for compatible peers, and create opportunities for them to interact and engage in fun activities together.
- Specific social behaviors can be the target for improvement in designing daily report cards (DRCs) and goal cards for individual students.
- Take photos of groups or individuals engaged in cooperative, friendly, and prosocial behavior and use them as visual cues and reminders.
- Reward students for demonstrating good sportsmanship at recess and physical education classes.

Schoolwide Programs and Interventions

Many schoolwide interventions can be employed to increase the social functioning and interpersonal relationships of students. Among them are conflict resolution, peer mediation, peer tutoring, and antibullying programs. Schoolwide programs, such as PBIS, that teach and reinforce positive, prosocial behavior in all school settings are also proven to be highly effective.

Schoolwide Positive Behavior Supports (SWPBS) and Positive Behavior Intervention & Supports (PBIS)

Schools across the nation have recognized the importance of SWPBS and are now implementing

it—a continuum of schoolwide positive behavior supports for all students, which Sugai, Simonsen, and Horner (2008) describe as

> a data-driven, team-based framework or approach for establishing a continuum of effective behavioral practices and systems that (a) prevents the development or worsening of problem behavior and (b) encourages the teaching and reinforcement of prosocial expectations and behavior across all environments for all students by all staff. (p. 5)

The PBIS (Positive Behavioral Interventions and Supports) model is proven to increase students' behavioral and social skills as well as academic performance—with numerous benefits to the entire school community. For students with ADHD, attending a school that is committed to implementing PBIS structures and strategies is an ideal intervention for addressing their behavioral and social needs and providing the necessary level of support.

The PBIS schoolwide model involves a clear set of positive expectations and behaviors, with procedures for teaching those expected behaviors, a continuum of procedures for encouraging expected behavior and for discouraging inappropriate behavior, and ongoing monitoring and evaluation (Lewis-Palmer, 2007).

PBIS, like Response to Intervention (RTI), is a three-tiered model that offers tier 1 (school- and classroom-wide primary prevention strategies), tier 2 (secondary prevention and supports for targeted groups and at-risk students), and tier 3 (specialized, individualized interventions for students with high needs and levels of risk). Social skills instruction is part of the intervention at all levels.

Tier 1 support involves explicit modeling, teaching, and practicing of social skills, with all staff involved in prompting, cueing, and reinforcing skills throughout the school in every setting and in a variety of ways that increase student motivation. Lessons and interventions that take place in the classroom are for the whole class or some groups.

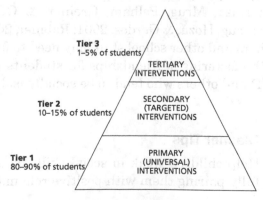

SCHOOLWIDE POSITIVE BEHAVIOR SUPPORTS (SWPBS)

Tier 3
1–5% of students
TERTIARY INTERVENTIONS

Tier 2
10–15% of students
SECONDARY (TARGETED) INTERVENTIONS

Tier 1
80–90% of students
PRIMARY (UNIVERSAL) INTERVENTIONS

Tier 2 intervention is more targeted, offering social skills lessons and interventions for groups and individual students. Tier 2 interventions typically focus on intensifying the supports provided in tier 1 (by increasing structure, providing more intensive social skills instruction, and delivering more frequent reinforcement).

Tier 3 provides more intensive, highly individualized and customized interventions and supports for those students with behavioral and social challenges not responding sufficiently to intervention at the tier 1 and 2 levels. Students needing intervention at the tier 3 level should have an individualized functional behavioral assessment (FBA), followed by the development of an individualized behavioral intervention plan (BIP).

See the national website of OSEP Technical Assistance Center on Positive Behavioral Interventions and Supports (www.pbis.org) for developing a comprehensive schoolwide system and a model that is successfully being used in schools throughout the United States. More information is also found through PBIS state networks at www.pbisnetworks.org and links to individual states. See additional PBIS resources and links in Part 2 Additional Sources and Resources, including https://www.pinterest.com/sandrarief/pbis-schoolwide-positive-behavior-support/.

Social Skills Programs and Materials

Some schools provide social skills training through cognitive-behavioral curricula. Systematic lessons and units are taught by the classroom teacher to the whole class, or by another staff member, such as the school counselor. Social skills training can be taught to the whole class or to small groups of students as an intervention in sessions outside of the classroom (for example, in the counselor's office).

In any context or format that social skills are taught, do the following:

- Explain the need or rationale for learning the skill and define the skill clearly. This can be done through discussion and reinforced by visual displays, such as posters and photos.
- Demonstrate appropriate and inappropriate skills through positive and negative examples.

- Have students role-play and rehearse the appropriate skill with adult and peer feedback.
- Ask students to look for and observe the skill being displayed in different settings.
- Provide many opportunities to practice the skill in authentic, real-world activities, and encourage students to self-monitor their use of the targeted skill.

There are evidence-based commercial social skills curricula available, such as *ACCEPTS: The Walker Social Skills Curriculum* (Walker et al., 1983), *Stop and Think Social Skills Program* (Knoff, n.d.), *Skillstreaming the Elementary School Child* (McGinnis & Goldstein, 1999), the Incredible Years (www.incredibleyears.com/programs/), *Second Step* (Committee for Children, 2008), Superheroes Social Skills: A Multimedia Program (https://pacificnwpublish.com/products/).

According to Knoff (n.d.), the Stop and Think Social Skills Program, as part of a comprehensive discipline, behavior management, and school safety system, has been proven effective in decreasing student discipline referrals and improving students' prosocial interactions, among other positive effects. The major components of this program involve (1) teaching the steps of the desired social skill, (2) modeling the steps and social skill language or script, (3) role-playing the steps and language with students using real-life situations, (4) providing performance feedback on how accurately the students are using the skill language or script and demonstrating the new skill, and (5) applying or transferring the skill throughout the day in different settings and situations. For all social skills taught, the steps involve:

Stop and think! Students are taught to take time to calm down and think about what to do.

Good choice or bad choice? Students learn to think about the likely rewards or consequences of their actions.

What are your choices or steps? Students learn sequences of skills or decisions in order to successfully demonstrate a specific social skill.

Just do it! Students actually carry out their plan, implement the social skill, and evaluate whether or not it has worked.

Good job! Students learn to reinforce themselves for successfully using the social skill and responding to a situation or request.

See recommendations of the National Association of School Psychologists (2002) for school social skills interventions and evidence-based curricula; see also the Part 2 Additional Sources and Resources.

Social-Emotional Learning Programs

Many schools are implementing social-emotional learning (SEL) programs, which can be used alone or in conjunction with PBIS or other schoolwide programming.

> Through the efforts of individual prevention scientists and practitioners, such as those who founded the Collaborative for Academic, Social and Emotional Learning [www.casel.org], SEL has matured and expanded to the point where it is beginning to make a significant difference in our schools and communities. (Merrell & Gueldner, 2010, p. xii)

The Collaborative for Academic, Social, and Emotional Learning (n.d.) has identified five SEL competencies:

Self-awareness. The ability to accurately recognize one's thoughts, emotions, strengths, and limitations.

Self-management. The ability to self-regulate one's thoughts, emotions, and behaviors effectively in different situations. It includes controlling impulses, self-motivation, and goal-directed behavior.

Social awareness. The ability to take the perspective of and empathize with others from diverse cultures and backgrounds, and to understand social norms for behavior.

Relationship skills. The ability to establish and maintain healthy and rewarding relationships with diverse individuals and groups.

Responsible decision making. The ability to make constructive and respectful choices about personal behavior and social interactions.

There are some research-based SEL commercial programs, such as *Strong Kids Curricula* (Merrell et al. 2007), *I Can Problem Solve* (Shure, 1992), *Raising Healthy Children* (Social Development Research Group, n.d.), the Incredible Years (www.incredibleyears.com), and *Promoting Alternative Thinking Strategies*—PATHS (Kusche, n.d.).

There are also other schoolwide research-supported intervention programs that incorporate the elements of SEL, PBIS, and other strategies to create a safe, positive school environment and strengthen students' interpersonal, behavioral, and academic skills. One such schoolwide program is PeaceBuilders (http://www.peacebuilders.com), which teaches the following values in multiple ways, enabling them to become infused throughout the entire school and community culture: (1) Praise People, (2) Give Up Put-Downs, (3) Seek Wise People, (4) Notice Hurts, (5) Right Wrongs, and (6) Help Others.

Goal-Setting Tips

Teachers and other adults need to help children set concrete, achievable social goals to work on. Goals should include the "who, what, when, and where" and be as specific as possible. The following are some examples (Cohen, 2000; Sheridan, 1995):

- *Goal:* Kyla will say hello (what) to Pam (whom) tomorrow at lunch (when) in the cafeteria (where).
- *Goal:* Jack will start a conversation (what) with a child (whom) in school (where) at least three times in one week (when).
- *Goal*: I will ask Sarah (who) to play with me (what) at recess (where) tomorrow (when).

The Social Skill Lesson Plan and Report Form shown on pages 160–163 are adapted and used with permission from *Cooperation in the Classroom* (Johnson, Johnson, & Holubec, 1998).

Lunchtime . . . Trouble Time

Lunchtime is mostly trouble time
For an ADHD kid
It's a welcome break to a boring routine
(and prime time to flip teacher lids!)
This diversion gives time for some mingling
But to the teacher a job must be done
Thirty kids through the line in five minutes
But the hyper kid thinks "time for fun"!
Every dessert in the case he handles,
Every cookie his fingers must touch
At the end of the line teacher wrinkles her nose
Barks "You just get into trouble too much!"
He carelessly strolls to the table
Spilling most of the food on his tray
When he asks "Can I sit down beside you?"
His friends say "I don't think you may."
So he sits at the end of the table, alone.
His dessert he wolfs down first
He drinks a whole carton of milk in one gulp
To drown his unquenchable thirst.
Next comes an enticing challenge
The hot dog lying there on his plate . . .
1–2–3 chops of karate it takes
To sentence predictable fate.
Now he's stuck at the table of outcasts
Where the crew is always the same,
This table is watched by the Eyes of a Hawk
So no one can wrongly cast blame.
Sighing, he accepts his usual sentence,
It's the same as his classroom fate—
You see, lunchtime is not the only time
The ADHD kid can't seem to relate.

Karen Easter, 1995

Social Skill Lesson Plan

What social skills are you going to teach?

_____

_____

_____

_____

Step 1: How are you going to communicate the need for social skills?

_____ Utilize room displays, posters, bulletin boards, and so forth.

_____ Tell students why the skills are needed.

_____ Jigsaw materials on the need for the skills.

_____ Have groups work on a cooperative lesson and then ask students to brainstorm what skills are needed to help the group function effectively.

_____ Give bonus points or a separate grade for the competent use of the skills.

_____ Other(s):_____

Step 2: How are you going to define the skill?

Phrases:

_____

_____

_____

Behaviors:

_____

_____

_____

How will you explain and model each social skill?

_____ Demonstrate the skill, explaining each step of engaging in the skill, and then redemonstrate the skill.

_____ Use a video to demonstrate and explain the skill.

_____ Ask each group to plan role-play demonstrations of the skill to present to the entire class.

_____ Other(s): _____

Adapted from *Cooperation in the Classroom* by Johnson, Johnson, and Holubec, 1998, and used with permission. Edina, MN: Cooperative Learning Institute. See authors' eighth edition (2008) of this book and others at http://www.co-operation .org/books-and-materials/

Social Skill Lesson Plan, contd.

Step 3: How will you ensure that students practice the skill?

_____ Assign specific roles to group members, ensuring practice of the skills.
_____ Announce that you will observe for the skills.
_____ Have specific practice sessions involving nonacademic tasks.
_____ Other(s): _____

Step 4: How will you ensure that students receive feedback and process their skill use?

Teacher monitoring: How will you monitor students' use of the skill and give feedback?

_____ Formally observe with a social skills observation sheet, focusing on each learning group an equal amount of time (30 minutes, six groups; each group is observed for 5 minutes) and counting how many times each student uses the targeted skill and other needed behaviors.
_____ Informally observe each group: give verbal or written feedback on how well members are working together and using the targeted skill.
_____ Other(s): _____

Teacher intervening: How will you prompt groups to use the skill?

_____ Noticeably give positive feedback to a group using the skill to remind surrounding groups to use it.
_____ Supplement positive feedback with a tangible reward to students or groups using the skill.
_____ Give a "secret note" to a group member asking him or her to use the skill; praise the whole group when the group member uses it.
_____ Other(s): _____

Student observers:

_____ Have one student in each group tally each time a member uses the skill while he or she continues to participate in the group work.
_____ Teach students to observe using a social skills observation sheet. Students take turns sitting outside the group and observing members' use of the skill.
_____ Provide time for the student observers to give group members feedback.

Adapted from *Cooperation in the Classroom* by Johnson, Johnson, and Holubec, 1998, and used with permission. Edina, MN: Cooperative Learning Institute. See authors' eighth edition (2008) of this book and others at http://www.co-operation .org/books-and-materials/

Social Skill Lesson Plan, contd.

Processing: Students need to reflect on their skill use so they can congratulate themselves for improvement as well as devise ways to continuously progress. How will you have students reflect on their use of the skill?

_____ Ask them to analyze the feedback from you (the teacher), student observers, and their own memories.

_____ Provide questions to help the groups engage in reflective thinking: "How well did you use the skill?" "How well did each group member use the skill?" "What are some things that helped you use the skill?" "What are some things that helped group members use the skill?"

_____ Help the students plan for continuous improvement with such questions as "What are two things you did today to help your group?" "What do you plan to do differently next time to help your group work better?" "What did you learn about being a good group member?"

Step 5: How will you ensure that students persevere in practicing the skill until it becomes natural?

Daily:

_____ Remind them that you will be listening for their use of the skill.

_____ Give feedback on what you heard.

_____ Have them process their use of the skill.

Periodically:

_____ Discuss with the class the stages of learning a skill (awkward, phony, mechanical, and automatic).

_____ Have students or groups rate their level of use and chart progress.

_____ Give a class reward if students use their skill a preset number of times.

_____ Have the principal, an aide, a parent, or another teacher observe and give feedback on how frequently the skill is being used.

_____ Tutor or coach target students on the use of the skill.

_____ Have students think of places outside of the class to use the skill; have them do so and report on how it went and what they noticed.

When most students have reached the automatic stage, plan to teach them another skill!

Adapted from *Cooperation in the Classroom* by Johnson, Johnson, and Holubec, 1998, and used with permission. Edina, MN: Cooperative Learning Institute. See authors' eighth edition (2008) of this book and others at http://www.co-operation .org/books-and-materials/

Report Form: Social Skills

Student: _____ *Date:* _____ *Grade:* _____

N = Needs Improvement *P = Making Progress* *S = Satisfactory* *E = Excellent*

Shows Cooperative Attitude (Forming Skills)
___ Moves into Group Quietly
___ Stays with Group; No Wandering
___ Uses Quiet Voice in Group Work
___ Takes Turns
___ Uses Others' Names
___ Respects Rights of Others
___ Positive about Working in Group
___ Is Willing to Help Others
___ Follows Directions
___ Shows Courtesy toward Others

Facilitates Understanding (Formulating Skills)
___ Summarizes, Integrates
___ Seeks Accuracy
___ Relates New Learning to Old
___ Helps Group Recall Knowledge
___ Checks for Understanding
___ Makes Covert Reasoning Overt

Leadership (Functioning Skills)
___ Gives Direction to Group's Work
___ Contributes Ideas, Opinions
___ Requests Others' Ideas, Opinions
___ Summarizes, Integrates
___ Encourages Others' Participation
___ Supports; Gives Recognition, Praise
___ Paraphrases
___ Facilitates Communication
___ Relieves Tension
___ Clarifies Goals

Intellectual Challenge (Fermenting Skills)
___ Differentiates Members' Ideas
___ Integrates Members' Ideas
___ Asks for Rationale, Justification
___ Extends Others' Reasoning
___ Probes; Asks Complex Questions
___ Criticizes Ideas, Not People

Adapted from *Cooperation in the Classroom* by Johnson, Johnson, and Holubec, 1998, and used with permission. Edina, MN: Cooperative Learning Institute. See authors' eighth edition (2008) of this book and others at http://www.co-operation.org/books-and-materials/

Part 2 References

Section 2.1
Biffle, C. (2015). *122 amazing games*. Whole Brain Teaching. CreateSpace Independent Publishing Platform.

Section 2.2
Barkley, R. A. (2013). *Taking charge of ADHD: The complete, authoritative guide for parents* (3rd. ed.). New York, NY: Guilford Press.

Section 2.3
Biffle, C. (2013). *Whole brain teaching for challenging kids*. San Bernardino, CA: Whole Brain Teaching. Retrieved from www.wholebrainteaching.com

Downeast Teach Blogspot. (2013, February 21). The simplest classroom management system ever. Retrieved from http://downeastteach.blogspot.com/2013_02_01_archive.html

Section 2.4
Barkley, R. A. (2013). *Taking charge of ADHD: The complete, authoritative guide for parents* (3rd. ed.). New York, NY: Guilford Press.

Cohen, M. (2009). *A guide to special education advocacy: What parents, clinicians and advocates need to know*. London, UK: Jessica Kingsley.

Illes, T. (2002). *Positive parenting practices for attention deficit disorder*. Salt Lake City, UT: Jordan School District.

McConnell, M. E. (1999). Self-monitoring, cueing, recording, and managing: Teaching students to manage their own behavior. *TEACHING Exceptional Children, 33*(2), 14–21.

Rafferty, L. A. (2010). Step-by-step: Teaching students to self-monitor. *TEACHING Exceptional Children, 43*(2), 50–58.

Rankin, B., Dungan, S., Allison, R., Ikeda, M., Rahn, A., & Beener, T. (2002, March). A problem-solving approach to functional behavioral assessment. NASP *Communique, 30*(6). Retrieved from www.nasponline.org/publications/cq306probsolve.html (This URL may no longer be active.)

Rief, S. (2015). *The ADHD book of lists: A practical guide for helping children and teens with attention deficit disorders* (2nd ed.). San Francisco, CA: Jossey-Bass.

Ryan, A., Halsey, H., & Matthews, W. (2003). Using functional assessment to promote desirable student behavior in schools. *Teaching Exceptional Children, 35*(5), 8–15.

Walker, H. M. (1997). *The acting out child—Coping with classroom disruption* (2nd ed.). Longmont, CO: Sopris West.

Section 2.5
Biffle, C. (2013). *Whole brain teaching for challenging kids*. San Bernardino, CA: Whole Brain Teaching. Retrieved from www.wholebrainteaching.com

Greene, R. (2010, June). CHADD's Ask the Expert: Parenting "difficult" children: A chat with Ross Greene. *Attention, 17*(3), 10–12.

Greene, R. W. (2014). *Lost at school: Why our kids with behavioral challenges are falling through the cracks and how we can help them* (2nd ed.). New York, NY: Simon & Schuster.

Greene, R. W. (2015). *The explosive child: A new approach for understanding and parenting easily frustrated, chronically inflexible children* (5th ed.). New York, NY: HarperCollins.

Linsin, M. (2009). How to get students to follow directions. Smart Classroom Management. Retrieved from www.smartclassroommanagement.com/2009/12/19/how-to-get-students-to-follow-directions/

Riley, D. A. (1997). *The defiant child: A parent's guide to oppositional defiant disorder.* Lanham, MD: Taylor Trade.

Robinson, K. (2000, July/August). Compliance—It's no mystery. *Attention, 7*(1), 38–43.

Section 2.6

Barkley, R. A. (2013). *Taking charge of ADHD: The complete, authoritative guide for parents* (3rd ed.). New York, NY: Guilford Press.

Barkley, R. A., & Benton, C. M. (2013). *Your defiant child: Eight steps to better behavior* (2nd ed.). New York, NY: Guilford Press.

Barkley, R. A., Robin, A. L., & Benton, C. M. (2013). *Your defiant teen: Ten steps to resolve conflict and rebuild your relationship* (2nd ed.). New York, NY: Guilford Press.

Biffle, C. (2013). *Whole brain teaching for challenging kids.* Retrieved from www.wholebrainteaching .com

Buron, K. D., & Curtis, M. B. (2012). *The incredible 5-point scale: Assisting students in understanding social interactions and controlling their emotional responses* (2nd ed.). Shawnee Mission, KS: AAPC Publishing.

Copeland, L. A. (1998). *Hunter and his amazing remote control: A fun hands-on way to teach self-control to ADD/ADHD children.* Chapin, SC: YouthLight.

Greene, R. W. (2014). *Lost at school: Why our kids with behavioral challenges are falling through the cracks and how we can help them* (2nd ed.). New York, NY: Simon & Schuster.

Greene, R. W. (2015). *The explosive child: A new approach for understanding and parenting easily frustrated, chronically inflexible children* (5th ed.). New York, NY: HarperCollins.

Katz, M. (2006). Promising practices: Preventing explosive behavior in children. *Attention, 13*(5), 14.

Katz, M. (2012). Promising practices: The zones of regulation: A curriculum designed to foster self-regulation and emotional control. *Attention, 19*(5), 7–8.

Kuypers, L. (2011). *The zones of regulation: A curriculum designed to foster self-regulation and emotional control.* San Jose, CA: Social Thinking Publishing. Retrieved from www .zonesofregulation.com

Novotni, M. (2009, Spring). 7 quick fixes for ADHD meltdowns. *ADDitude.* Retrieved from www .additudemag.com/adhd/article/5762.html

Shure, M. B. (1992). *I can problem solve: An interpersonal cognitive problem-solving program.* Champaign, IL: Research Press.

Taylor, J. K. (2007). Discipline without regret. *ADDitude, 8*(2), 27–28.

Williams, M. S., & Shellenberger, S. (1996). *How does your engine run: Leader's guide to the alert program.* Albuquerque, NM: Therapy Works. Retrieved from www.alertprogram.com

Section 2.7

Barkley, R. A. (2014). *Attention deficit hyperactivity disorder: A handbook for diagnosis and treatment* (4th ed.). New York, NY: Guilford Press.

Collaborative for Academic, Social, and Emotional Learning (CASEL). (n.d.). *Social and emotional learning core competencies.* Retrieved from http://www.casel.org/social-and-emotional-learning /core-competencies

Committee for Children. (2008). *Second step: Social skills for early childhood-grade 8.* Retrieved from www.cfchildren.org/second-step.aspx

Cohen, C. (2000). *Raise your child's social IQ.* Silver Spring, MD: Advantage Books.

Hoza, B. (2007). Peer functioning in children with ADHD. *Journal of Pediatric Psychology, 32,* 655–663.

Hoza, B., Mrug, S., Pelham, W. E., Jr., Greiner, A. R., & Gnagy, E. M. (2001). A friendship intervention for children with attention-deficit/hyperactivity disorder: Preliminary findings. *Journal of Attention Disorders, 6,* 87–98.

Johnson, D., Johnson, R., & Holubec, E. (1998). *Cooperation in the classroom* (7th ed.). Edina, MN: Cooperative Learning Institute. Updated 2008 edition available at http://www.co-operation .org/books-and-materials/

Knoff, H. M. (n.d.). *The stop and think social skills program for schools* (preK–8). Available through Voyager Sopris at http://www.voyagersopris.com/curriculum/subject/school-climate /stop-think-social-skills-program

Kusche, C. A. (n.d). *Paths Curriculum (Promoting Alternative Thinking Strategies)*. Channing-Bete Company, http://www.pathstraining.com/main/ and http://www.channing-bete.com /prevention-programs/paths/paths.html

Lewis-Palmer, T. (2007). Embedding social skills instruction throughout the day. Retrieved from www.pbis.org/common/pbisresources/presentations/palmer0RPBS20307.ppt#1

Merrell, K. W., Carrizales-Engelmann, D., Feuerborn, L., Gueldner, B., Tran, O., & Walker, H. (2007). *Strong kids curricula* (programs from kindergarten through high school). Baltimore, MD: Paul H. Brookes.

Merrell, K. W., & Gueldner, B. (2010). *Social and emotional learning in the classroom: Promoting mental health and academic success*. New York, NY: Guilford Press.

McGinnis, E., & Goldstein, A. (1999). *Skillstreaming the elementary school child*. Champaign, IL: Research Press.

Mrug, S., Hoza, B., & Gerdes, A. C. (2001). Children with attention-deficit/hyperactivity disorder: Peer relationships and peer-oriented interventions. In D. W. Nangle & C. A. Erdley (Eds.), *The role of friendship in psychological adjustment: New directions for child and adolescent development* (pp. 51–77). San Francisco, CA: Jossey-Bass.

National Association of School Psychologists (NASP). (2002). Fact sheet on social skills: Promoting positive behavior, academic success, and school safety. Retrieved from www.nasponline .org/resources/factsheets/socialskills_fs.aspx

New York University Child Study Clinic. (2000). *I.M.P.A.C.T. survey and study: Investigating the mindset of parents about AD/HD and children today*. New York, NY: NYU Child Study. www .AboutOurKids.org

Rabiner, D. (2015, June). Helping teens with ADHD develop friends. Attention Research Update. Retrieved from http://helpforadd.com

Sheridan, S. M. (1995). *The tough kid social skills book*. Longmont, CO: Sopris West.

Shure, M. B. (1992). *I can problem solve: An interpersonal cognitive problem-solving program*. Champaign, IL: Research Press.

Social Development Research Group (SDRG) University of Washington. (n.d.). *Raising healthy children*. Seattle: University of Washington.

Sugai, G., Simonsen, B., & Horner, R. H. (2008, July/August). Schoolwide positive behavior supports: A continuum of positive behavior supports for all students. *Teaching Exceptional Children, 40*(6), 5.

Teeter Ellison, P. A., & Goldstein, S. (2002, April). Poor self-control and how it impacts relationships. *Attention, 8*(5), 19–23.

Walker, H. M., McConnell, S., Holmes, D., Todis, B., Walker, J., & Golden, N. (1983). *ACCEPTS program curriculum guide: The Walker social skills curriculum*. Austin, TX: PRO-ED.

Wallace, I. (2000). *You and your ADD child*. Sydney, Australia: HarperCollins.

Zumpfe, H., & Landau, S. (2002, April). Peer problems. *Attention, 8*(5), 32–35.

Part 2 Additional Sources and Resources

Adams, M. (2002). Solutions to oppositional defiant disorder. *Attention, 8*(6), 28–33.

Barkley, R. A. (1996). Using a daily school-behavior report card. *ADHD Report, 4*(6), 1–14.

Brady, C. (2005). Helping your little tyrant avoid outbursts. *ADDitude, 6*(2), 56–57.

Buck, G. H., Polloway, E. A., Kirkpatrick, M. A., Patton, J. R., & McConnell Fad, K. (2000). Developing behavioral intervention plans: A sequential approach. LD Online. Retrieved from www.ldonline.org/article/6031.

Catalano, R. F., Mazza, J. J., Harachi, T. W., Abbott, R. D., Haggerty, K. P., & Fleming, C. B. (2003). Raising healthy children through enhancing social development in elementary school: Results after 1.5 years. *Journal of School Psychology, 41*(2), 143–164.

Center for Effective Collaboration and Practice. FBA problem behavior. Retrieved from http://cecp.air.org/fba/problembehavior/main.htm

Children and Adults with Attention Deficit/Hyperactivity Disorder (CHADD). See articles and links related to behavioral and social skills interventions for children with ADHD at http://www.chadd.org/Understanding-ADHD/For-Parents-Caregivers/Treatment-Overview/Psychosocial-Treatments.aspx

CHADD. (2003, October). One-on-one with William E. Pelham, Jr. *Attention, 10*(2), 33–37.

Chafouleas, S. M., Riley-Tillman, T. C., & Christ, T. J. (2009). Direct behavior rating (DBR): An emerging method for assessing social behavior within a tiered intervention system. *Assessment for Effective Intervention, 34*, 201–213.

Chafouleas, S. M., Riley-Tillman, C. T., & Jaffery, R. (2011). DBR: An overview. University of Connecticut. www.directbehaviorratings.org

Choi, J. (2012, June 19). The busy box: How to teach productive waiting. Retrieved from http://adhdmomma.com/2012/06/the-busy-box-how-to-teach-productive-waiting.html

Clark, L. (2013). *SOS: Help for parents* (3rd ed.). Bowling Green, KY: SOS Programs & Parents Press.

Collaborative for Academic, Social, and Emotional Learning (CASEL). (n.d.). What is social and emotional learning? Retrieved at http://www.casel.org/social-and-emotional-learning/

Committee for Children. (2008). *Second step: Social skills for early childhood-grade 8.* Retrieved from www.cfchildren.org/second-step.aspx. Each grade level of this evidence-based classroom program features developmentally appropriate ways to teach core social-emotional skills such as empathy, emotion management, and problem solving, as well as self-regulation and executive function skills.

Crone, D. A., Hawken, L. S., & Horner, R. H. (2010). *Responding to problem behavior in schools: The behavior education program* (2nd ed.). New York, NY: Guilford Press.

Cunningham, C. E., Bremner, R., & Secord-Gilbert, M. (2000). *The Community Parent Education Program (COPE Program): A school-based family systems oriented course for parents of children with disruptive behavior disorders.* Hamilton, Ontario: McMaster University and Chedoke-McMaster Hospitals.

Dalporto, D. (n.d.). Restorative justice: A different approach to discipline. Retrieved from http://www.weareteachers.com/blogs/post/2015/04/03/restorative-justice-a-different-approach-to-discipline

Davis, M. (2015, October). Restorative justice: Resources for schools. Retrieved from http://www.edutopia.org/blog/restorative-justice-resources-matt-davis

Dendy, C.A.Z., Durheim, M., & Teeter-Ellison, A. (Eds.). (2006). *CHADD educator's manual on AD/HD* (2nd ed.). Lanham, MD: CHADD.

Diamond, S. (2011). *Social rules for kids: The top 100 social rules kids need to succeed*. Shawnee Mission, KS: AAPC Publishing.

DuPaul, G. J., & Stoner, G. (2003). *ADHD in the schools* (2nd ed.). New York, NY: Guilford Press.

Fabiano, G. A., Vujnovic, R. K., Pelham, W. E., Waschbusch, D. A., Massetti, G. M., Pariseau, M. E., . . . Volker, M. (2010). Enhancing the effectiveness of special education programming for children with attention deficit hyperactivity disorder using a daily report card. *School Psychology Review, 39*(2), 219–239.

Fad, K. S., Ross, M., & Boston, J. (1995). We're better together: using cooperative learning to teach social skills to young children. *Teaching Exceptional Children, 27*(4), 28–34.

Fairbanks, S., Simonsen, B., & Sugai, G. (2008, July/August). Classwide secondary and tertiary tier practices and systems. *Teaching Exceptional Children, 40*(6), 44–52.

Flippin, R. (n.d.). Parenting your child with oppositional defiant disorder. *ADDitude*. Retrieved from http://www.additudemag.com/adhd/article/879-2.html

Flippin, R. (2005). Making peace with your defiant child. *ADDitude, 5*(6), 41–43.

Forehand, R., & McMahon, R. (1981). *Helping the noncompliant child*. New York, NY: Guilford Press.

Frankel, F. (2010). *Friends forever: How parents can help their kids make and keep good friends*. San Francisco, CA: Jossey-Bass.

Giler, J. (2011). *Socially ADDept: Teaching social skills to children with ADHD, LD, and Asperger's*. San Francisco, CA: Jossey-Bass.

Goldstein, A., Sprafkin, R. P., Gershaw, N. J., & Klein, P. (1980). *Skillstreaming the adolescent—A structured learning approach to teaching prosocial skills*. Champaign, IL: Research Press.

Goldstein, S., & Brooks, R. (2007). *Understanding and managing children's classroom behavior* (2nd ed.). Hoboken, NJ: Wiley.

Gray, C. (n.d.). Social stories. Retrieved from www.thegraycenter.org/social-stories

Grey Olltwit Educational Software. (n.d.). Social stories. www.greyolltwit.com/social-stories-2.html

Harris, K. R., Friedlander, B. D., Saddler, B., Frizzelle, R., & Graham, S. (2005). Self-monitoring of attention versus self-monitoring of academic performance: Effects among students with ADHD in the general education classroom. *Journal of Special Education, 39,* 145–156.

Horner, R., Sugai, G., Todd, A., Dickey, C. R., Anderson, C., & Scott, T. (n.d.). Check-in check-out: A targeted intervention. Retrieved from www.pbis.org/common/pbisresources/presentations/05BEPCICO.ppt#13

Johnson, D. W., & Johnson, F. (2009). *Joining together: Group theory and group skills* (10th ed.). Boston, MA: Allyn & Bacon.

Katz, M. (2004). Promising practices: The good behavior game. *Attention, 11*(2), 12–13.

Knoff, H. M. (n.d.). *The stop and think social skills program for schools* (preK–8). Available through Voyager Sopris at http://www.voyagersopris.com/curriculum/subject/school-climate/stop-think-social-skills-program

Koplewicz, H. S. (2002, April). Managing social skills all day, every day. *Attention, 8*(5), 25–31.

Kusche, C. A. (n.d). *Paths Curriculum (Promoting Alternative Thinking Strategies)*. Channing-Bete Company, http://www.pathstraining.com/main/ and http://www.channing-bete.com/prevention-programs/paths/paths.html

Linsin, M. (2014). A fun way to get your students to follow directions. *Smart Classroom Management*. Retrieved from www.smartclassroommanagement.com/2014/01/18/a-fun-way-to-get-your-students-to-follow-directions/

Mackenzie, R. J. (1998). *Setting limits: How to raise responsible, independent children by providing clear boundaries* (Rev. and expanded 2nd ed.). New York, NY: Random House.

Mackenzie, R. J., & Stanzione, L. (2010). *Setting limits in the classroom: A complete guide to effective classroom management with a school-wide discipline plan* (3rd ed.). New York, NY: Random House.

Martin, K. (2013). How to stay calm when your child acts up: Strategies for the difficult child. *ADDitude* magazine webinar. Retrieved from www.additudemag.com/webinars

McGinnis, E., & Goldstein, A. (1997). *Skillstreaming the adolescent: New strategies and perspectives for teaching prosocial skills.* Champaign, IL: Research Press.

McGinnis, E., & Goldstein, A. (1999). *Skillstreaming the elementary school child.* Champaign, IL: Research Press.

McGinnis, G., & Goldstein, A. (1990*). Skillstreaming in early childhood—Teaching prosocial skills to the preschool and kindergarten child.* Champaign, IL: Research Press.

McIntyre, T. (2014). Functional behavioral assessment (FBA). Retrieved from www.behavioradvisor.com/FBA.html

Merrell, K. W., Carrizales-Engelmann, D., Feuerborn, L., Gueldner, B., Tran, O., & Walker, H. (2007). *Strong kids curricula* (programs from kindergarten through high school). Baltimore, MD: Paul H. Brookes.

Merrell, K. W., & Gueldner, B. A. (2010). *Social and emotional learning in the classroom: Promoting mental health and academic success.* New York, NY: Guilford Practical Interventions in the Schools.

Mikami, A. Y. (2011). How you can be a friendship coach for your child with ADHD. *Attention, 18*(1), 16–19.

Morris, R. (2007). *Eight great ideas: Simple ways to transform your teaching.* San Diego, CA: New Management. www.newmanagement.com

Morris, R. (2013). *New management handbook: Creating a happier, more productive classroom.* San Diego, CA: New Management. www.newmanagement.com

National Resource Center on AD/HD. (n.d.). Social skills interventions. Retrieved from http://www.chadd.org/Understanding-ADHD/For-Parents-Caregivers/Treatment-Overview/Psychosocial-Treatments/Social-Skills-Interventions.aspx

Nelson, J. (2011). *Positive discipline: The classic guide to helping children develop self-discipline, responsibility, cooperation, and problem-solving skills* (revised and updated ed.). New York, NY: Ballantine Books.

The ODD-ADHD link in children. (n.d). *ADDitude.* Retrieved from http://www.additudemag.com/adhd-web/article/4646.html

O'Neill, R. E., Horner, R. H., Albin, R. W., Storey, K., Sprague, J. R., & Newton, J. S. (1997). *Functional assessment of problem behavior: A practical assessment guide.* Pacific Grove, CA: Brooks/Cole.

Otten, K., & Tuttle, J. (2010). *How to reach and teach children with challenging behavior (K–8): Practical, ready-to-use interventions that work.* San Francisco, CA: Jossey-Bass.

Parker, H. (2002). *Problem solver guide for students with ADHD.* Plantation, FL: Specialty Press.

PeaceBuilders Creating Safe, Positive Learning Environments. PeaceBuilders program. Long Beach, CA: Peace Partners. www.peacebuilders.com

Peterson, K. S. (2012). *Activities for building character and social-emotional learning* (Safe and Caring Schools). There are separate books of activities for grades preK through high school. Golden Valley, MN: Free Spirit.

Pfiffner, L. (2011). *All about ADHD: The complete, practical guide for classroom teachers* (2nd ed.). New York, NY: Scholastic Teaching Resources.

Phelan, T. W. (2010). *1-2-3 magic: Effective discipline for children* (4th ed., pp. 2–12). Chicago, IL: ParentMagic.

Rabiner, D. (2014, January). An innovative approach for helping "explosive and inflexible children." *Attention Research Update.* Retrieved from http://cpsconnection.com

Rhode, G., Jenson, W. R., & Reavis, H. K. (1995). *The tough kid book.* Longmont, CO: Sopris West.

Rief, S. (2008). *The ADD / ADHD checklist: A practical reference for parents and teachers* (2nd ed.). San Francisco, CA: Jossey-Bass.

Rief, S. (2015). *The ADHD book of lists: A practical guide for helping children and teens with attention deficit disorders* (2nd ed.). San Francisco, CA: Jossey-Bass.

Rief, S., & Heimburge, J. A. (2006). *How to reach and teach all children in the inclusive classroom* (2nd ed.). San Francisco, CA: Jossey-Bass.

Riley, D. A. (1997). *The defiant child: A parent's guide to oppositional defiant disorder.* Lanham, MD: Taylor Trade.

Robinson, K. (2000, July/August). Compliance—It's no mystery. *Attention, 7*(1), 38–43.

Rosenthal-Malek, A. (1997, January/February). Stop and think! Using metacognitive strategies to teach students social skills. *Teaching Exceptional Children, 29*(3), 29–31.

Shure, M. B. (1992). *I can problem solve: An interpersonal cognitive problem-solving program.* Champaign, IL: Research Press.

Shure, M. B. (2011). *Thinking parent, thinking child: How to turn your most challenging everyday problems into solutions.* Champaign, IL: Research Press.

Shure, M. B., & DiGeronimo, T. F. (1996). *Raising a thinking child: Helping your young child to resolve everyday conflicts and get along with others.* New York, NY: Gallery Books.

Shure, M. B., & Israeloff, R. (2001). *Raising a thinking preteen: The "I can problem solve" program for 8- to 12-year-olds.* New York, NY: Holt Paperbacks.

Simonsen, B., Sugai, G., & Negron, M. (2008, July/August). Schoolwide positive behavior supports: Primary systems and practices. *Teaching Exceptional Children, 40*(6), 32–42.

Smith, C. A. (1993). *The peaceful classroom: 162 easy activities to teach preschoolers compassion and cooperation.* Beltsville, MD: Gryphon House, Inc.

Social Development Research Group (SDRG) University of Washington. (n.d.). *Raising healthy children.* Seattle: University of Washington.

Sugai, G., Horner, R. H., & Gresham, F. (2002). Behaviorally effective school environments. In M. Shinn, H. Walker, & G. Stoner (Eds.), *Interventions for achievement and behavior problems II: Preventive and remedial approaches* (pp. 315–350). Bethesda, MD: National Association of School Psychologists.

Taylor, J. F. (2011). *From defiance to cooperation.* New York, NY: Random House.

Taylor, J. K. (2007). Discipline without regret. *ADDitude, 8*(2), 27–28.

Walker, H. M., McConnell, S., Holmes, D., Todis, B., Walker, J., & Golden, N. (1983). *ACCEPTS program curriculum guide: The Walker social skills curriculum.* Austin, TX: PRO-ED.

Walker, H. M., & Walker, J. E. (1991). *Coping with noncompliance in the classroom.* Austin, TX: PRO-ED.

Wright, D. B. (2009). Using daily report cards: General principles. Handouts from behavior /discipline trainings. Retrieved from http://www.pent.ca.gov/pos/cl/str/dailyreportcards.pdf

Wright, J. (n.d). Classroom behavior report card resource book. Intervention Central (www .interventioncentral.org) and Jim Wright Online (www.jimwrightonline.com/pdfdocs/tbrc /tbrcmanual.pdf)

Websites

ADDitude magazine, http://www.additudemag.com/resource-center/adhd-parenting-skills.html and http://www.additudemag.com/resource-center/adhd-parenting-discipline-behavior.html

Association for Positive Behavior Support, www.apbs.org

Blueprints for Healthy Youth Development, www.blueprintsprograms.com, provides a registry of evidence-based positive youth development programs designed to promote the health and well-being of children and teens.

Evidence-Based Programs on the Good Behavior Game, http://evidencebasedprograms.org/1366.2 /good-behavior-game

The Incredible Years, www.incredibleyears.com/programs/, for reducing challenging behaviors in children and increasing their social-emotional learning and self-control skills.

Intervention Central, www.interventioncentral.org, the website of Jim Wright, has many free resources including free apps for behavioral interventions, such as the behavior rating scales, report card maker and the behavior intervention planner.

Intervention Central, www.interventioncentral.org/behavioral-interventions/schoolwide-classroom mgmt/good-behavior-game

OSEP Technical Assistance Center on Positive Behavioral Interventions and Supports; for information and resources, see www.pbis.org

Pax Good Behavior Game, http://goodbehaviorgame.org/

PBIS World, with links to numerous FBA and BIP forms, tools, and other great resources, http:// www.pbisworld.com/tier-2/behavior-intervention-plan-bip/

Pinterest boards of Sandra Rief on: class and behavior management at www.pinterest.com /sandrarief/class-behavior-management/; positive parenting at https://www.pinterest.com /sandrarief/parenting/; brain breaks and classroom games at https://www.pinterest.com /sandrarief/brain-breaks-classroom-games/; self-regulation at https://www.pinterest.com /sandrarief/self-regulation/; PBIS at https://www.pinterest.com/sandrarief/pbis-schoolwide -positive-behavior-support/; and several ideas for the individualized management and support of children with ADHD for parents and teachers at https://www.pinterest.com/sandrarief/add -adhd-for-teachers/ and https://www.pinterest.com/sandrarief/add-adhd-for-parents/

Positive Behavioral Interventions and Supports (PBIS), Technical Assistance Center of the US Department of Education's Office of Special Education Programs (OSEP), www.pbis.org

Instructional, Learning, and Executive Function Strategies

Section 3.1: Attention!! Strategies for Engaging, Maintaining, and Regulating Students' Attention

Section 3.2: Research-Based Instructional Approaches and Interventions

Section 3.3: Organization and Time Management

Section 3.4: The Homework Challenge: Strategies and Tips for Parents and Teachers

Section 3.5: Learning Strategies and Study Skills

Section 3.6: Memory Strategies and Supports

3.1

Attention!! Strategies for Engaging, Maintaining, and Regulating Students' Attention

Being able to capture and hold students' interest and attention is not always easy. Keeping a student with ADHD focused and engaged is a monumental challenge to teachers, and one that requires experimenting with a variety of approaches.

Getting and Focusing Students' Attention

Before beginning instruction, teachers need to obtain students' attention and direct their focus to the task at hand. The following are classroom strategies and techniques to do so.

Auditory Techniques

- Signal through the use of music: chimes, rainstick, xylophone, a bar or chord on a keyboard, or a few seconds of a recorded song.
- There are various toys and other noisemakers that make a novel sound that could be a fun auditory signal. Beepers, timers, and ring tones may also be used.
- Use a clap pattern. You clap a particular pattern (for example, two slow and three fast claps), and students repeat the clap pattern back to you.

- Use a clear verbal signal ("Popsicles . . . Freeze!" or "Everybody. . . Ready. . ." or "1, 2, 3, eyes on me").
- Use your voice to get attention, making use of effective pauses and tone variation; whispering also works.
- Use a call-and-response technique: call out a word or phrase, and students respond by repeating the word or phrase or with a specific set response word or phrase. See Whole Brain Teaching's "Class . . . Yes!" technique and variations for getting students' attention (www.wholebrainteaching.com).

Visual Techniques

- Use flashing the lights or raising your hand, for example, to signal the students to raise their hands and stop talking until everyone is silent and attentive.
- Teach specific hand signals such as American Sign Language to signal students. See free downloadable posters and examples for the classroom on Rick Morris's website (www.newmanagement.com).
- Use pictures and other graphics, gestures, manipulatives, and other interesting visuals to engage students' attention and interest. If using a projector such as a document

camera, project on the screen some novel object or image to grab students' attention.

- Use a dowel or other pointer to point to written material you want students to focus on.
- Use visual timers such as Time Timer (www.timetimer.com), Time Tracker (www.learningresources.com), online visual timers such as those found at Online-Stopwatch (www.online-stopwatch.com/classroom-timers), or one of the visual timer apps such as Stoplight Clock.
- Cover or remove visual distractions. Erase unnecessary information from the board, and remove visual clutter.
- Eye contact is important. Students should be facing you when you are speaking, especially when you are giving instructions. Position all students so that they can see the board, screen, or chart. Always allow students to readjust their seating and signal you if their visibility is blocked. Teach students who are seated with desks in clusters and not facing you how to turn their chairs and bodies around quickly and quietly when signaled to do so.
- Try using a flashlight or laser pointer. Turn off the lights and get students to focus by illuminating objects or words with the laser or flashlight.
- Color is highly effective in getting attention. Use colored pens and bold colors to write or frame important information. Use colored highlighting pens or tape and colored sticky notes. Write, circle, or underline keywords in color (particularly when giving directions).

The Tech Advantage

In today's classrooms, we have the benefit of modern technology to capture students' attention and increase their participation. Document cameras, interactive whiteboards, tablets, Chromebooks, and other constantly emerging and evolving multimedia tools, online programs and software, and apps are highly motivating and engaging—greatly enhancing our ability to reach and teach all learners.

Different models of instruction—such as blended learning (described in Section 3.2), a combination of online and face-to-face instruction—can also be beneficial for students with ADHD. Blended learning, for example, provides students significant time and opportunity to work at their own pace on digital programs and in small-group instruction with their teacher. Such instructional formats can be advantageous for getting students' attention and keeping them focused and on-task.

Arousing Students' Curiosity and Anticipation

- Ask an interesting, speculative question; show a picture; tell a little story; or read a related poem or passage to generate discussion and interest in the upcoming lesson.
- Add a bit of mystery by bringing in one or more objects relevant to the upcoming lesson—hidden in a box, bag, or pillowcase, or draped with a cloth—that you later reveal. This is a wonderful way to generate predictions and can lead to excellent discussions or writing activities.

Liven It Up

- Try playfulness, silliness, humor, props, and a bit of theatrics to get attention and pique interest.
- Use storytelling, real-life examples, and anecdotes, particularly personal ones—for example, narrating something that happened to you as a child.
- Be an animated, enthusiastic presenter. Model excitement about the upcoming lesson.

Make It Personal

- When giving examples, use students' names or other people they know (only in a positive way and not to embarrass the student). Make the examples interesting and relevant to them.
- Activate students' prior knowledge and draw on their past experiences.

Organize Student Thinking

- Provide an overview of the major points the students will be studying and the relationship of those points to prior learning.
- Explain the lesson's purpose and importance. Identify the objectives, content standards being addressed, and ultimate goals or outcomes to be achieved by the end of the session or unit.
- Deploy graphic organizers (there are numerous kinds) as tools to focus attention as well as help students organize and comprehend ideas and information.
- Prior to presenting information, post a few key points for students to be attentive to, listen for, and think about during the lesson, or provide partial notes to structure thinking and cue what to listen for.

Maintaining Students' Attention through Active Participation

Keeping or sustaining students' attention requires active, not passive learning. It also requires that teachers weave a variety of formats and activities throughout the lesson. Within a fifty-minute period of time, for example, the lesson may be formatted to include a mix of (1) whole-group instruction and end-of-lesson closure (with engaging ways for students to respond and participate); (2) predominantly small-group and partner structures for maximum involvement in learning activities; and (3) some time to work on a particular task independently.

General Tips for Keeping Students Engaged

- Provide instruction that is relevant and meaningful.
- Design lessons to incorporate novelty, variety, and fun.
- Present at a lively pace and with enthusiasm.
- Move around in the classroom, maintaining your visibility and providing individual assistance (clarification, cueing and prompting, redirection) and feedback as needed.

- Use high-interest materials and teach to students' varied learning styles and strengths.
- Write keywords or pictures on the board or projector while presenting.
- Use technology and multimedia to enhance instruction—for example, interactive whiteboards; animated slide shows; video streaming of relevant, interesting content; and motivating software and apps.
- Illustrate throughout your presentation, even if you lack the skill or talent to draw well. Drawings do not have to be sophisticated or accurate. In fact, generally the sillier they are, the better, and stick figures are fine. Your efforts to illustrate vocabulary, concepts, and so forth not only focus students' attention but also help them retain information.
- Incorporate demonstrations, role playing, hands-on activities, anecdotes and storytelling, and multimedia presentations into your teaching whenever possible.
- Build in several movement opportunities during the lesson.
- Reduce lag time by being prepared.
- Monitor and vary your rate, volume, and tone of voice.
- Have students write down brief notes or illustrate key points during instruction.
- Endeavor to greatly increase student responses by having them say and do something with the information being taught throughout the lesson. This can be done, for example, through frequent pair-shares. "Turn to your partner and summarize [or paraphrase or share] your understanding," or "With your partner, clarify any questions you still have about what we just discussed."
- Supplement verbal presentations with visuals, graphics, and demonstrations.
- Use a variety of graphic organizers and techniques, such as webbing, graphing, clustering, mapping, and outlining.
- Increase the amount of your modeling, guided practice, and immediate feedback to students.
- Use study guides, partial outlines, or other graphic tools to accompany verbal

presentations. While you are presenting a lesson or giving a lecture, students fill in the missing words based on what you are saying or writing on the board or overhead. Jotting down a few words or filling in missing information in a guided format is helpful in maintaining attention.

- Create an environment where students feel safe to risk participation and make mistakes.
- Employ cooperative learning formats (partners or small groups); they are highly effective in keeping students engaged and participating during lessons. Follow the proper structure for cooperative learning groups in regard to assignment of roles, individual accountability, and other matters. This is not just group work. Many students with ADHD do not function well in groups without clearly defined structure and expectations. See Section 3.2 on cooperative learning.
- Use motivating apps, games, and programs for specific skill building and practice that provide for frequent feedback and self-correction.
- Differentiate instruction to keep students motivated and engaged. Offer students a choice of activities, projects, and assignments, and options in how they demonstrate their learning—oral or written reports, demonstrations, or creative designs, for example.
- Differentiate instruction through use of learning centers, flexible grouping, interest groups, independent projects and study, and a variety of other instructional strategies, structures, and accommodations. See Section 3.2 for more on differentiated instruction.

Questioning Techniques to Increase Student Engagement and Response Opportunities

Teachers who succeed most often in engaging students and holding their attention are those who are skilled in the art of questioning. They know how to design instruction and provide numerous opportunities for student response, accountability, and active participation, with everyone having a voice that is heard and respected.

- Format lessons to include a variety of questioning techniques that involve whole-class, small-group, partner, and individual responses.
- Build "wait time" into your questioning so that students have the time to process the question and formulate their thoughts before responding. Provide a minimum of five seconds.
- Before asking for a verbal response to a question, have all students jot down their best-guess answer. Then call for volunteers to verbally answer the question.
- Provide extra guidance, scaffolding, and support to students as needed during the questioning process. Common Core questioning, with its focus on deep critical thinking, elaboration of ideas, and being able to explain one's reasoning and support with evidence, is challenging for many students.
- Structure the lesson so that it includes the opportunity to work in pairs or small groups for maximum student involvement and attention. Use alternatives to simply calling on students one at a time. Instead, have students respond by telling their partner, writing down or drawing their response, and so forth.
- Use questioning strategies that encourage student success—for example, employing probing techniques, providing clues, and asking students if they would like more time to think about the question. Tell students you will come back to them in a little while if they need more time, and do so.
- Expand on students' partial answers: "Tell me more." "How did you arrive at that answer?"
- Pose a question, ask for volunteers, and wait until there are several hands raised or thumbs up before calling on individual students to respond. Acknowledge those students by making eye contact and giving them a head nod or other gesture while waiting for more students to be ready with an answer.

- Give all students an equal opportunity to respond to questions and be heard. Make use of a set of individual student cards or popsicle sticks with the names of each student written on them. Draw a card from the deck or pull a stick from the can to call on students randomly and fairly. Draw names from the discard pile as well or use two sets of class cards that you pull from. That way, students who have already been called on must remain attentive, because they know their name may be drawn again. There are also randomizing apps for calling on students following the same method, such as Kid Pick, Teachers Pick, Stick Pick, and Random Student Selector.
- For novelty, mix up the ways you call on students—for example, "Everyone wearing earrings, please stand up . . . this question is for you," "Everyone who has fewer than six letters in his or her last name . . .," or "Anyone who has a birthday in January, February, or March may respond to this question." Students from that group may answer or have the option to pass.

It is important for teachers to incorporate many techniques that enable students to have frequent response opportunities throughout instruction. Following are some suggestions for whole-group (full-class), small-group, and partner responses that require active involvement of students.

Whole-Group and Unison Responses

- *Choral and unison responses.* Have students recite poems or share reading of short passages or lines from the text chorally (in unison). Singing songs or chants, and reviewing material (such as irregular and sight words or math facts) with whole-class responses to flash cards are examples of choral responses. Unison responses to questions for which there is just one correct and short answer (typically called out after the teacher gives a signal) can be interspersed throughout instruction to activate students. For example,

"Is that a simile or metaphor?" "Class . . . proper or improper fraction?"
- *Hand signals for whole-group responses.* Unison responses can also be obtained by having students use various hand signals—for example, thumbs up–thumbs down or open hand–closed hand responses from students indicating "yes-no," "I agree–I disagree," or any other "either-or" response.
- *Write-on tools* (other than paper and pencil). Most students (particularly those with ADHD or learning disabilities who often resist paper-and-pencil work) are more motivated to use alternatives such as colored pens and markers on individual dry-erase boards. These can be used in any content area for short-answer responses and enable the teacher to quickly assess students' understanding.
- *Electronic devices and digital response tools.* Whole-group responses can be made via apps such as I Response (http://iresponse app.com), iClicker (www1.iclicker.com), and Poll Everywhere (www.polleverywhere.com /classroom-response-system). These are all useful for formative assessments.
- *Premade response cards.* Elicit unison responses through premade response cards— for example, (1) a small set of cards with a single-hole punch, which are held together by a metal ring; (2) four or five cards that are held together by a brass fastener and opened up like a fan; or (3) a single card made of card stock or construction paper that is divided into sections (halves, thirds, or quarters), preprinted with a choice of answers in each section of the card. Each student indicates his or her answer by placing a clothespin on

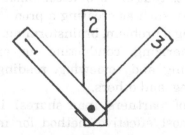

the box of the card containing that choice or by holding up his or her answer choice on the ringed card set. When the teacher poses the question and provides a signal ("Ready . . . show"), students select their answer and hold up their response card so that the teacher can see. Premade response cards are very useful at any grade level or content area to integrate into whole-class questioning strategies. The following are examples of some uses for premade response cards:

— The vowel sound heard in different words (a, e, i, o, u choices)

— The part of speech of a particular word within a sentence (for example, noun, verb, adjective, adverb)

— The math process needed to solve a problem (add, subtract, multiply, divide)

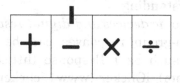

— Final punctuation mark needed (period, question mark, exclamation point)

— Social studies terms or concepts (legislative, executive, judicial branches of government)

— Literary term that a given example demonstrates (alliteration, idiom, personification)

— Multiple choice (a, b, c, d)

Small-Group and Partner Responses

- Much of classroom instruction involves small groups of students working together. Small-group active responses take place in any cooperative learning group structure. There are countless activities, learning tasks, and projects that are best accomplished in small groups, such as creating a product together, solving a problem, brainstorming, analyzing, summarizing, conducting an experiment, studying and reviewing, reading and discussing, and others.

- Use of partners (pair-shares) is perhaps the most effective method for maximizing

student engagement. Students turn to their partner for short interactions: predicting, clarifying directions, summarizing information, drilling and practicing (vocabulary, spelling words, math facts), combining ideas and resources for a joint project, taking turns reading aloud or questioning and discussing a reading passage together, listening to and providing feedback on each other's writing, working out math problems together, checking that their partner has correctly recorded homework assignments in his or her daily planner, and numerous other tasks.

- Partner activities are an excellent format for keeping students with ADHD engaged and productive. When these students are partnered with well-focused, tolerant, and cooperative classmates, there is also less likelihood of behavioral or social problems than in a whole or small group.

- Partner responses can be structured informally (turn to your neighbor) or with teachers more carefully assigning partners. Partners can be numbered 1s and 2s or A's and B's so that the teacher can assign different partner tasks. For example, "A's, tell your partner your prediction for the next page" (Archer, 1997).

- Try building in some opportunities for "standing partner" activities—enabling students to get out of their seats to work and share with their partner while standing rather than sitting.

Here are some more examples of partner-structured activities:

- "Pair up with your neighbor and share your ideas about . . ."

- "Turn to your partner [or neighbor] and . . ." After giving partners a chance to respond, ask for volunteers to share with the whole class: "Who would be willing to share what you or your partner thought about . . . ?"

- "Turn to your partner [or the person across from you or behind you], and discuss . . . for a few minutes" or "Write down with your partner all the things you can think of that . . ."

- "Help each other figure out how to do this . . ."
- "Try answering your partner's three selected questions about this reading material."

Keeping Students On-Task During Seatwork

Students with ADHD often have significant difficulty remaining focused and productive during independent seatwork activities because of inattention, distractibility, and poor impulse control. Weaknesses in working memory and self-monitoring also interfere with successful completion of independent class assignments. The following strategies are beneficial for all students, but are particularly important for those with ADHD:

- Provide sufficient guided practice before having students work independently on seatwork activities.
- Be aware that if the student was not paying attention when you taught something necessary for understanding the seatwork assignment, he or she won't be able to do the work without being retaught or getting assistance.
- Check for clarity. Make sure your directions are clear and that students understand them before beginning their seatwork.
- Give students a manageable amount of work that they are capable of doing independently.
- Make sure necessary supplies are available so that students can work during independent time without excuses. Have extra (but less desirable) materials available for unprepared students. For example, rather than providing new pencils, have a can of old pencils or golf pencils they may borrow from.
- Have students keep a small plastic pencil sharpener at their desk, eliminating the excuse for students to get up and sharpen their pencil when they should be seated and working.
- Send students to their seats with a written task card or checklist of things to do. Instruct them to cross out or make a check mark as they complete each task.

- Be sure that the independent seatwork assigned is developmentally appropriate and within the student's capability of doing it successfully without assistance. Nevertheless, provide access to peer or adult assistance as needed.
- Assign study buddies or partners for clarification purposes during seatwork. When part of the class has a seatwork assignment to do while you are working with other students (say, during a guided reading group), set the expectation that students who have a question during seatwork must first ask their partner or classmates in their table group. Only if no one in the group can answer the question may the teacher be interrupted. Some teachers also assign one or more "experts" of the day for students to go to in need of help.
- Scan the classroom frequently, praising students specifically whom you observe to be on task. All students need this positive reinforcement, and it also serves as a reminder to students who tend to have difficulty in this area.
- Monitor students with ADHD frequently during seatwork time. Ask them periodically to show you what they have accomplished. Redirect them when they are off task.
- Prepare a signal for the student to use from his or her desk to indicate that he or she needs help. One method is to provide a red card to prop up or a red plastic cup or other object that can be placed on the desk when the student needs to signal for assistance. When scanning the room, you can spot the red cup or card to see who needs help.
- Give other fail-proof work that the student can do in the meantime if he or she is stumped on an assignment and needs to wait for your attention or assistance.
- Try using a timer and beat-the-clock system to motivate completion of a reasonable amount of work for students with ADHD. Set short time intervals for each timing. For example, if it is a twenty-minute seatwork period, provide for two ten-minute timings or four five-minute timings with mini-goals

set in advance (how much work must be completed during that time frame). Reward on-task behavior and students' having met the work completion goal during that time interval.

- Accommodate the need for quiet, less distracting work areas during independent work through the use of study carrels, privacy boards, and an optional seat or table away from the student's regular assigned desk.

- Permit the use of headphones or earplugs or other tools during seatwork as an accommodation for students who are easily distracted by sounds in the classroom environment.

- Help students with ADHD get started on assignments, supporting and monitoring as needed. Once they do get started, they are often able to do the work independently.

- Read the first paragraph or page together or watch as the student solves the first few math problems. Then let the student continue independently.

- Provide examples of problems or other references at students' desks to help with the assigned task.

- Block or mask some pages of assigned seatwork by covering up part of the page or folding the page under so that smaller amounts are visible at one time. Alternatively, you can cut worksheet assignments in half or into smaller segments and pass out one part at a time. Blocking parts of worksheets or cutting work into segments may help reduce the frustration a student feels on seeing a paper that appears lengthy and overwhelming.

Teacher Tips for Helping Inattentive, Distractible Students

Environmental Factors and Accommodations

- Provide preferential seating: up front, within your cueing distance, near well-focused classmates, and away from as many distractions as possible, such as doors, windows, and high-traffic areas of the room.

- Provide options for a less distracting work area through the use of study carrels, office areas, partitions, and privacy boards. These should not be used if they are viewed by the students in the class as punitive measures or as accommodations only for students with special needs.

- Be aware of and reduce environmental distractions, such as unnecessary writing on the board, clutter on tables, squeaky table and chair legs, and buzzing fluorescent lights.

- Allow the use of earphones or earplugs for distractible students at certain times of the day—for example, during seatwork time. Keep a few sets available for students to access as well as requiring their use when listening to the audio of any device in the classroom.

Management Factors and Accommodations

- Increase visual, auditory, and physical prompts to gain attention and help refocus inattentive, distractible students:
  - Place hand on the student's shoulder, arm, or back.

Raise hand.
Don't call out.

Stay seated.

Keep on-task.

— Use private, prearranged visual signals after making eye contact with the student (for example, when you point to and tap your chin, you mean, "Watch my face and pay attention").

— Attach a cue card to the student's desk showing pictures depicting behavioral expectations (such as raise your hand, stay seated, and keep on task). When the student needs a reminder, point to or tap on the card, prompting him or her to demonstrate the appropriate behaviors.

• Increase proximity—standing near or sitting close by distractible students.

• Use eye contact, your movement, and voice modulation to get and maintain students' attention.

• Clear students' desks of distracters, allowing on the desk only essential items for the current task.

• Provide students with access to a fidget toy—something to hold or manipulate while seated and listening, as long as it stays in their hands and is not bothering others. For students with ADHD, fidgeting is a means of self-regulating, and can help in their ability to pay attention. Examples of fidget items

are a small squishy ball, Silly Putty, a piece of Wikki Stix (www.wikkistix.com), or a key chain with a little object on it that the child can attach to his or her belt loop as a discreet fidget tool. Companies that sell sensory toys and other resources to occupational therapists are good sources of such products. A few of these companies are www.childthera pytoys.com, www.sensorycomfort.com, www .theraproducts.com, and www.headsupnow .com.

• Provide lots of movement and brain breaks to reenergize and facilitate focus.

• Monitor closely and provide students with frequent check-ins and reinforcement for on-task behavior.

• Recognize and call positive attention to on-task, focused students: "Thank you, Nick, for having your book open to the right page and following along"; "See how nicely Sarah is sitting up and looking at the board."

• Include paying attention and being on task as target behaviors on individual student contracts, behavior charts, or daily and weekly report cards.

• Establish mini work production goals that are reasonable and realistic for the student.

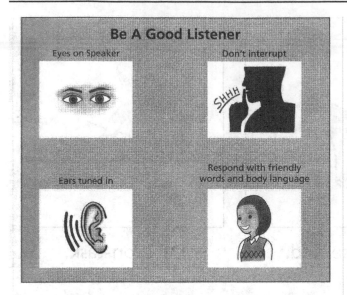

For example, "Complete the first two rows of the math problems with at least 80 percent accuracy by the end of the period" or "Write three complete sentences before the timer goes off." Reward the student when he or she meets the goal.

Instructional Factors and Accommodations

- Add color to increase focus on work, such as a colored poster board under the student's work on the desk or a strip of colored plastic overlay on the page.
- Provide note-taking assistance. Give an advance copy of your outline or provide a copy of another student's class notes from your lessons. This should be a supplement, with the student still taking some of his or her own notes. Jotting things down while listening can be a helpful strategy for staying focused and attentive. However, students who have difficulty listening and writing quickly

at the same time often struggle with note taking and fail to listen well or record the important information presented. They would benefit from having either a partial outline to fill in during lectures or a copy later of someone else's notes that are more fleshed out, readable, and useful for studying.

- For students who have difficulty staying focused during silent reading, consider using a "whisper phone" made from curved PVC pipe or the Toobaloo by Learning Loft (http://www.learning-loft.com/). This kind of plastic, curved, tubular tool can be very helpful. The student is able to read aloud in a soft whisper while holding the device like a phone. Because of its hollow shape, the student is able to hear his or her voice loud and clear without disturbing others. See an illustration of a whisper phone in Section 4.2.
- Physical strategies may help students raise their level of alertness and help them pay better attention in class. Teach students SLANT, developed by the University of Kansas Center for Research on Learning:

  Sit up straight
  Lean forward (writing position)
  Activate your thinking
  Note important points
  Track the speaker (keep your eyes on the person doing the informing)

  Here is another variation (Graser, 1992):
  1. Change posture.
  2. Sit up straight in the chair.
  3. Put both feet on the floor.
  4. Raise head off shoulders.
  5. Take a quick, deep breath to get a burst of oxygen.
  6. Track and observe closely the speaker's facial expressions and gestures.
  7. Move in closer to the speaker if possible.

Parent Tips: Helping Your Inattentive, Distractible Child

- Structure and organize your child's environment and minimize distractions in order to increase your child's focus and productivity (particularly during homework time).

- ADHD medication is a research-validated intervention that has been proven effective in helping children with ADHD improve attention, focus, and on-task behavior.
- Provide visual reminders, such as a checklist, chart, or sticky notes, listing in words or pictures your child's responsibilities and routines (for example, morning routine, chores, bedtime routine). Post these in strategic locations.
- Some people need it to be very quiet in order to focus, but for many people with ADHD, trying to concentrate in silence is more distracting and difficult. If your child prefers music, experiment with having him or her listen to the radio or recorded music of different kinds. Familiar songs the child hears on the radio and to which he or she knows the lyrics may be better for some and aid focus. Others will have greater focus listening to instrumental classical music or a recording of sounds of nature. Experiment with headsets (to either block out noise if your child needs it quiet or for listening to music while working if he or she is more productive doing so). Use this link to see the online bonus section on music selections for home and school that you may want to try: www.wiley.com/go/adhdreach
- Some children work best when they are isolated (alone in their bedroom or other location); others need to have people around and work better in a more central location, such as the kitchen. It helps them stay alert. Again, experiment with different homework areas in the house to find the best location for your child's focus and productivity.
- Martial arts such as tae kwon do and tai chi help in building concentration and focus as well as in practicing self-control.
- Chewing gum or eating something crunchy may help your child stay alert and better able to focus.
- Strengthen attention skills through card and board games, chess, and puzzles.
- Read aloud to your child and engage in discussion and questioning about the book. This is another excellent way to strengthen attention as well as build your child's vocabulary and reading comprehension skills.
- Attention and focus are strengthened when your child practices skills through a variety of activities (reading, learning to play an instrument, sports).
- Fidgeting helps many people with ADHD activate their brains when in a state of understimulation. They literally need to fidget to focus. There is an excellent book by this title (Rotz & Wright, 2005) with useful information and strategies. Provide your child with a fidget toy (Koosh ball, pencil with an object attached at the top, some kind of bracelet, or other object that can be quietly and discreetly touched and manipulated) to help him or her better focus.
- Try using a timer when your child is working with mini-goals for what to complete before the timer goes off. Reward him or her for meeting those goals. Your child may better focus and stay on task if you can motivate him or her to beat the clock.
- Provide controlled breaks during homework. Schedule breaks either after working a certain amount of time (for example, after every x number of minutes of work production) or after completing each assignment. Breaks between tasks should be short—for example, dancing to one or two songs, shooting baskets for five minutes, playing with a pet, text-messaging friends, or eating a snack.
- Parents may want to explore some of the technologies and brain-training programs that are designed to help improve attention, focus, and other cognitive skills, such as Cogmed (www.cogmed.com), an online working memory and attention training program, and Play Attention (www.playattention.com), a program based on neurofeedback. There are various apps for helping with attention, focus, and work production. Learning Works for Kids

(www.learningworksforkids.com) provides a review of several apps and online programs that it has evaluated and rated for children and teens with ADHD.

- There are also some sensory integration programs that may be of interest, such as the Alert Program (www.alertprogram.com), Brain Gym (www.braingym.com), and Learning Breakthrough (www.learningbreakthrough.com).

Self-Monitoring Attention (Self-Regulatory Techniques)

It is very helpful for students with ADHD to employ self-monitoring strategies to become more aware of their behaviors. As mentioned in Section 2.4, one such strategy is having the student(s) do seatwork while playing an audio recording that has been prerecorded with intermittent beeps, a ring of a bell, or other auditory signal. Children are trained to record on an index card or paper divided into two columns whether they were on-task and paying attention or not whenever they hear the auditory signal. Students mark in one of the two columns either +/– or yes/no at each signal. Then the student is expected to immediately get back to work (Parker, 2000).

Teach students to self-monitor work production and to set individual short-term goals for improvement—for example, "I am going to write at least three more sentences by the time this work period is over" or "I will read to page 121 by the time the timer goes off." If he or she meets the mini-goal, the student self-rewards in some way (for example, giving himself or herself a star on a self-monitoring card).The following "shiny light bulb" strategy was developed by Terri Hiltel, a speech-language pathologist in California, and is shared with her permission from the second edition of this book. She has found this unique technique to be very effective in increasing her students' awareness and ability to self-regulate their attention level. Terri uses the analogy of a light bulb that can be dark or unlit, dim (25

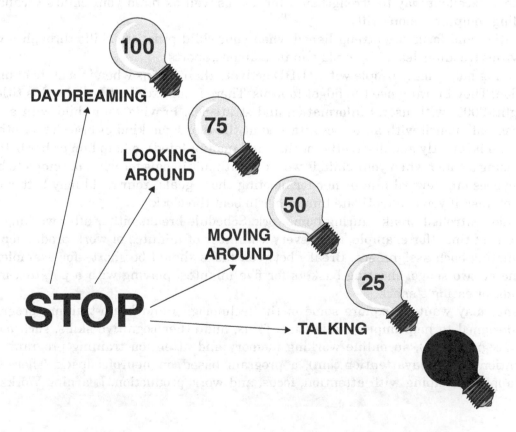

100 DAYDREAMING

75 LOOKING AROUND

50 MOVING AROUND

25 TALKING

STOP

watts), semibright (50 watts), brighter (75 watts), and very bright (100 watts) to relate to the degree of attention. Students learn to equate the visual of a dark, unlit light bulb with being off-task and inattentive, and a bright, shiny light bulb (at 100 watts) with being at full attention. Students are taught to stop, self-check, and correct four behaviors that will enable them to pull themselves from a state of inattention back to attention. The four behaviors are

1. Stop talking—and the bulb is lit at 25 watts.
2. Stop talking and moving around—and the bulb is lit at 50 watts.
3. Stop talking, moving around, and looking around—and the bulb is lit at 75 watts.
4. Stop talking, moving and looking around, and daydreaming—and the bulb is shiny bright at 100 watts.

Students learn that "shiny light bulbs" enable them to learn best, and the technique is taught in either small- or large-group instruction. For example, working in collaboration with classroom teachers, Terri teaches full classes of elementary- through secondary-level students different lessons (which she refers to as "communication labs"). During the labs, each of the stops (the four listed behaviors) are discussed and role-played in various situations, and then students color in their individual light bulbs (from faint yellow for the 25-watt bulb to the brightest shade of yellow for the 100-watt) or color one-quarter of the 25-watt bulb in yellow marker or pencil, half of the 50-watt bulb, three-quarters of the 75-watt bulb, and all of the 100-watt bulb.

Students are taught to use the expression "shiny light bulb" as a reminder if they see another student off-task. Students with attention difficulties are given a small copy of the five light bulbs (as shown) to keep on their desks in the classroom or other instructional settings, such as the speech therapy or resource room. If they break a stop rule, the teacher uses the visual prompt of touching or tapping on the black light bulb, which is a cue to check and self-correct their four stop behaviors. It saves the need for verbal redirection.

I NEED TO FOCUS MY ATTENTION!!!

"SHINY LIGHT BULBS HELP ME LEARN."

I HAVE TO <u>STOP</u>...

- **TALKING**
- **MOVING AROUND**
- **LOOKING AROUND**
- **DAYDREAMING**

Terri introduces the light-bulb strategy in the first communication lab. The first lab includes the following:

1. Introduction—Students are told the daily target, which is to learn the STOPS so that they can be 100-watt learners.
2. Sound Off—Students learn and practice the language, "shiny light bulbs—!!!" and the four associated STOP behaviors in order of their "wattage" (stop talking, stop moving around, stop looking around, stop daydreaming).
3. Role Play—Students then are given an opportunity to act out "positive and negative" situations through role-plays: (a) two people talking at the same time; (b) too much moving; (c) too much looking around; (d) too much daydreaming.
4. Wrap Up—Students orally interact in discussion about what "communication discovery" they made during this lab. For example, "Today I learned that to be an effective listener and learner, I need to use shiny light bulb behavior."
5. Conclusion—The communication challenge is discussed.

In the second communication lab, students review and practice the strategy, as follows:

1. Introduction—Students are told the daily target, which is a brief review of the

behaviors needed to be focused, 100-watt learners.

2. Sound Off—Students practice asking, "What are the four STOPS?" and responding to the question by telling each other the four STOP behaviors.

3. Role Play—Different role-play situations are acted out, incorporating how to employ the shiny light bulb strategy.

4. Wrap Up—Students orally interact in discussion about the communication discovery they made during this lab.

5. Conclusion—The communication challenge is discussed: Terri challenges students to check their attention five times during the day.

At the completion of these labs or lessons, once the rationale for and specifics of the strategy are clear to students, the strategy continues to be practiced and reinforced (by teachers, peers, and parents). The self-regulation technique can be employed when the student is prompted or reminded by someone else or when the child or teen prompts himself or herself to activate the light bulb and make it shine at 100 watts.

Research-Based Instructional Approaches and Interventions

This section describes instructional structures, models, frameworks, and approaches for reaching and teaching *all* students—including those with varying learning challenges. Most have been proven effective (or, if not yet proven, are showing promise) in enabling diverse learners to access the curriculum, optimize learning and engagement, and accommodate individual learning needs. It is important for educators to be aware of these approaches for designing and delivering curriculum and instruction.

Universal Design for Learning (UDL)

Universal Design for Learning (UDL) is a research-based educational framework first defined by researchers at the Center for Applied Special Technology (CAST) in the 1990s. It is a framework for creating curriculum from the outset designed to remove barriers and provide all learners with various ways of acquiring information and knowledge, and multiple means of student engagement, representation, action, and expression.

CAST (n.d.) describes UDL as an approach to curriculum that minimizes barriers and maximizes learning for all students. It does so by using three UDL principles to create flexible paths to learning so that each student can progress: (1) provide multiple means of representation (showing the information in different ways and multiple formats); (2) provide multiple means of action and expression (allowing students to approach learning tasks and demonstrate what they know in different ways); and (3) provide multiple means of engagement (offering options that fuel students' interests to engage and motivate them). CAST also explains that UDL provides a blueprint for creating instructional goals, methods, materials, and assessments that work for everyone through flexible approaches that can be customized and adjusted for individual needs.

UDL adapts and applies the ideas and concepts associated with universal design in architecture. The overarching idea of universal design is that buildings and tools should be accessible to everyone—those with and those without disabilities. For example, curb cuts allow people who use wheelchairs to move freely and independently from sidewalks to streets or parking lots. At the same time, they benefit people who use strollers, shopping carts, scooters, and skateboards. (IRIS Center for Training Enhancements, 2009)

The aim of UDL is to create curricula that are flexible enough to challenge the most gifted students, students struggling below grade level, and everyone in between. It does this by providing students with alternative ways to explore content, using multiple approaches at various levels of complexity. Because flexibility is built into the curriculum and the environment, UDL helps each student to participate and succeed even when a teacher is less familiar with the individual needs of each student. (Casper & Leuichovius, 2005)

See UDL information and tools from CAST at www.cast.org, the National Center on Universal Design for Learning at www.udlcenter.org, the National Center on Accessible Educational Materials at http://aem.cast.org, and other resources on this topic listed in the Part 3 Additional Sources and Resources.

Differentiated Instruction

To address the learning differences of all students and maximize their performance and achievement, teachers need to differentiate instruction in the classroom. As with UDL, differentiated instruction is based on the understanding that every learner is unique and that curriculum and instruction need to be designed with this understanding in mind. *One size does not fit all.* By differentiating instruction, teachers can effectively reach and teach the full range of learners and abilities in the classroom—high, low, and everything in between. Differentiated instruction is very beneficial for students who have learning challenges, as it means setting important goals of understanding, then figuring out how to build scaffolding leading to success in meeting those goals—not just diluting the goals.

Carol Ann Tomlinson (2001), one of the key educational leaders in differentiated instruction who speaks and writes extensively about this topic, describes these elements of differentiated instruction:

Proactive. Teachers plan a variety of ways to get at and express learning, and plan them to be robust enough to address the range of learner needs.

More qualitative than quantitative. Teachers adjust the nature of the assignment, not necessarily its length or quantity.

Student centered. Learning experiences are engaging, relevant, and interesting.

Rooted in assessment. Throughout the unit of study, teachers assess students' developing readiness levels, interests, and modes of learning in a variety of ways—and adjust instruction accordingly.

According to Tomlinson (2000), "Curriculum tells us *what* to teach. Differentiation tells us *how* to teach the same standard to a range of learners by employing a variety of teaching and learning modes" (p. 6).

We can differentiate content, presentation and instructional strategies, activities, performance tasks, and assessment tools (Chapman, 2000). Differentiated instruction typically involves multiple approaches and adaptations in the areas of content (what students learn), process (the ways students learn and how the content is taught), and product (how students present or demonstrate their learning).

Content can be differentiated by complexity based on readiness level. For example, the class may be studying long division, but students who are more advanced may be solving problems with two- and three-digit divisors, while others are solving problems with single-digit divisors (Pettig, 2000). When teachers differentiate by readiness level, they can do so through varied scaffolding, tiered tasks or products, small-group instruction, varied texts or supplementary materials based on reading level, homework options, and negotiated criteria for quality (Tomlinson, 2001).

There are numerous ways a teacher can go about differentiating the content of the lesson, learning tasks, activities, the lesson presentation, materials used, and student products. The following are some strategies that incorporate differentiated instruction:

- Multiple and flexible groupings of students (for example, whole class, small groups, partners, individualized)
- Materials, tasks, and activities that span the developmental skill and ability range of students—for example, providing tiered

assignments that vary the level of difficulty, the process, or the product

- Giving students choices about topics of study, ways of learning, and modes of expression
- Varying the pacing and degrees of supports for individual students
- Providing academic and instructional scaffolds and accommodations based on students' individual needs
- Offering students choices of where, how, and with whom they work
- Lessons, assignments, and assessments that take into account and tap into students' individual learning preferences, strengths, and interests
- Implementing inclusive teaching practices and strength-based approaches to reach and teach all students, such as using multisensory instruction and addressing learning style differences and multiple intelligences in the classroom

A Word about Multisensory Instruction, Learning Style Preferences, and Multiple Intelligences

Multisensory instruction refers to a way of teaching that presents information with some combination of visual, auditory, and tactile-kinesthetic input. The lesson presentation may include visuals—for example, graphic organizers, maps, charts, flash cards, handouts, videos, illustrations, modeling, and showing in pictures and words. Auditory techniques may be used: presentations involving lecture; discussion; use of stories, music, and audio materials; and teachers can provide opportunities for students to study and share verbally—for example, via pair-shares, oral reports, and study groups. Lessons that use tactile-kinesthetic strategies may incorporate hands-on activities, manipulatives, movement, and active learning opportunities (acting things out and role playing, lab experiments, student use of technology, and learning games).

Students differ in the way they approach learning—the way they most comfortably and efficiently do so. This is often referred to as their individual *learning style*. Learning styles may incorporate a number of factors, such as preferences for how a person is taught and how he or she likes to receive new information, the learning environment a person prefers or that is best suited to his or her needs, where and how the person studies best, and so forth. There are various learning styles inventories and questionnaires that may be of interest to teachers, parents, and students, such as the interview questions provided later in this section.

Dr. Howard Gardner's theory of *multiple intelligences* has made a significant impact since the 1980s in the field of education and on inclusive teaching practices. This theory identified first seven (Gardner, 1983), then eight intellectual capacities—each with its own distinctive mode of thinking and corresponding styles of learning: *linguistic* (word smarts—the person is adept in verbal and language skills); *logical-mathematical* (number smarts—the person is skilled at manipulating numbers, problem solving, and analytical reasoning); *musical* (the person is able to appreciate, recognize, and be attuned to rhythm, melody, pitch, and tone); *spatial* (art smarts—the person is skilled at visualizing, perceiving, and recreating aspects of the spatial world); *bodily-kinesthetic* (the person is adept in physical activities and executing goal-oriented movements with his or her body); *interpersonal* (people smarts—the person is attuned to others' feelings, moods, desires, and motivations); *intrapersonal* (self-smarts—the person is able to recognize and pursue his or her own interests and goals and use self-knowledge to guide actions and make decisions); and *naturalist* (nature smarts).

Special education teachers have long been aware that to reach and teach their students with disabilities, they need to use multisensory instruction, build on their students' strengths, and be sensitive and attuned to their individual learning differences and needs. Fortunately, general education has come to understand this as well—embracing the need for differentiated instruction for all students (which is particularly beneficial for those with learning challenges in the general education classroom).

Explanation to Students Regarding Differentiation

It is helpful for students to understand that we all learn differently and that there is no right or wrong way to learn. Teaching students why you will be differentiating instruction in your classroom is very beneficial. Doing so also addresses the "fairness" issue that some children and parents have a problem with when teachers do something different (such as make accommodations) for individual students that the rest of the class does not receive.

Differentiated instruction addresses the fact that fairness is not treating everyone the same but means giving every student what he or she needs to have an equal chance to achieve success. So teachers may want to communicate from the beginning of the school year something like the following: "Each of us has our own unique way of learning and needs different things or kinds of help and support in order to do our best at school. I promise to do my best to give each of you what you need to be successful in this class, and it won't be the same thing for each of you. It's just like the way we won't all be reading the same book in class or might not all be working on the same project or assignment."

Note: The books How to Reach and Teach All Children in the Inclusive Classroom *(Rief & Heimburge, 2006) and* How to Reach and Teach All Children through Balanced Literacy *(Rief & Heimburge, 2007) have several differentiated lessons and learning activities designed for and used successfully with students in grades 3–8.*

Student Learning Style/Interest Interview

When teachers are trying to learn more about their students' learning style preferences, interests, and motivators, one of the best ways to find out is to ask them. The following are some sample questions you may wish to ask students in one-on-one interviews. It is very rewarding to find the time to meet with students individually, talk with them, and get their input as to how they learn best and what they enjoy doing in and out of school. Also, students typically appreciate their teacher's attention and interest in learning more about them as unique individuals.

Various learning style inventories and assessments are available. They can provide helpful insight as to how one learns best. This is useful for teachers wishing to address individual learning differences and for the child or teen in his or her efforts to identify the most effective study skills and learning strategies. I developed the following interview questions, which were published in previous editions of this book.

1. Think back over the past few years of school. Whose class did you feel most comfortable in? Tell me a little about your favorite classes—ones you felt successful in. What did you particularly like about those classes or teachers?

2. What are some of the best school projects you remember doing? Is there any project you did or activity that you participated in that you are especially proud of?

3. Do you prefer working in a classroom that is warmer or cooler in temperature?

4. When you are trying to concentrate in class or read silently, do you need the room to be completely quiet? Do you mind some amount of noise and activity during these times when you are trying to concentrate, study, or read silently? Do you think it would help to use earphones or earplugs to block the noise? Would it help to have some music in the background, or would it distract you?

Note: *More questions may be asked regarding music preferences/dislikes.*

5. I want you to imagine that you can set up the perfect classroom any way you want. Think about it and tell me or draw for me how you would like the classroom to be arranged. Would you like the tables or desks in rows? In clusters? Tell me or show me where you would choose to sit in order to learn best in this room. Where would you want the teacher to be standing when giving instructions?

6. Do you like to do school projects alone, or would you prefer to work with others?

7. When you have to study for a test, do you prefer to study alone? With a friend? In a small group? With a parent or teacher helping you?

8. In your classroom, if you had a study carrel (private office area or partition) available, would you choose to do your seatwork in it if some other students in your class were also using them?

9. When do you feel you are able to do your best work and concentrate best? In the morning before recess? After recess but before lunch? After lunch in the afternoon?

10. Do you usually get hungry and start wishing you could have a snack during the school day? What time of day do you usually start feeling hungry?

11. If your teacher assigned a big project, giving you choices of how to do it, would you prefer to
   a. Make an oral presentation in front of the class?
   b. Make an audio recording?
   c. Act it out/use drama?
   d. Build something (for example, from clay or wood)?
   e. Draw something?
   f. Write something/type it (or have someone else type it)?

12. Do you think you are good at building things? Taking things apart and putting them back together?

13. Do you like listening to stories?

14. Are you good at learning words to songs?

15. Do you like to read? Write stories? Do math? Do science experiments? Do art projects? Sing? Dance? Play an instrument? Play sports? Which ones? Use the computer?

16. What school subjects and activities do you usually do best in? What do you like about those subjects/activities?

17. What are the subjects/activities that you usually have the hardest time doing at school? What don't you like about those subjects/activities?

18. What kind of school assignments do you dread or hate having to do?

19. Tell me what you think you are really good at. What do you think you are not so good at?

20. Do you ever feel you cannot concentrate in class and have problems paying attention? What kinds of things distract you?

21. How is it easier for you to learn: when someone explains something carefully to you or when someone shows you?

22. If you have to give directions to somewhere or instructions for how to do something, is it easier for you to explain and tell that person, or is it easier for you to draw a map or write it down?

23. When do you concentrate best and prefer to do your homework: Do it soon after you get home from school? Have a break (play first) after getting home from school, but do it before dinner? Do it after dinner?

24. What are your favorite things to do at home?

25. If you had a chance, what would you love to learn to do? For example, if you could take special lessons or have someone work with you to teach you, what would you really want to learn how to do?

26. At home, where do you usually do your homework? If you had your choice, in what place in the house would you like to do your homework and study?

27. Pretend that your parents would build you or buy whatever you needed in your home for a good study space. What would it look like, and what would you have in it?

28. Do you like to be alone or with someone else around when studying/doing homework? Do you need it to be really quiet? Do you like having some music or background noise when studying?

29. At school (in this classroom) name five people you prefer to work with in partner activities. Don't name your best friends; give me names of students with whom you can productively get work done well.

30. If you were to work toward earning a special privilege, activity, or other reward at school, name some things you would like to be able to earn.

31. What do you think is important for your teacher to know about you?

32. If you were promised a trip to Hawaii with your family and also $1,000 for spending money only if you got an A on a very difficult test (for example, a unit test covering four chapters, with lots of information and stuff to memorize and learn):

    a. How would you want your teacher to teach it to you?

    b. Exactly what would you like your teacher to do in class so that you can learn the information?

    c. How would you go about learning and remembering all the information you were taught?

    d. How would you need to study at home?

    e. What kind of help would you want your parents to give you?

    f. Do you want to study alone? With someone? Tell me as much as you can.

Note: I recommend that you select just some of the listed questions for the interview (not all of them), and that you conduct the interview via audio recording, direct notes, or a combination of both.

Response to Intervention (RTI)

For over a decade, many school districts throughout the United States have been implementing (at various stages) a Response to Intervention (RTI) model in their efforts to better reach and teach students in need of support and catch them early. RTI is

- A schoolwide process that provides systematic, research-based instruction and a tiered continuum of intervention to struggling learners

- A single, integrated system of instruction and intervention aimed at improving educational outcomes for all students and guided by data on student outcomes from frequent progress-monitoring measures
- The practice of providing high-quality instruction and research-based interventions matched to students' needs, using individual students' response to those interventions to make a range of educational decisions—including some that are part of the process of determining whether a student qualifies for special education under the specific learning disabilities category
- An approach intended to eliminate a wait-to-fail situation before struggling students are provided the help they need to succeed in school
- Included in federal special education law, IDEA 2004, as part of the effort to direct schools to address students' problems earlier, before a referral to special education is needed
- A framework for structuring early intervening services (EIS) under IDEA 2004 that offers an alternative to the traditional model of requiring a discrepancy between IQ and achievement as a means of identifying students with learning disabilities who qualify for special education
- A process intended to enable more students to have their needs adequately met in general education, which would in turn reduce the number of students requiring special education

Essential Components of RTI

- High-quality, research-based instruction for all students, differentiated to match their learning needs
- Universal screening of all students early in the school year and repeated during the year to identify students at risk for academic or behavioral failure
- Implementation of scientifically proven interventions to address students' learning problems

- Administration of interventions by highly qualified personnel, delivered with fidelity (in accordance with the programs' instructions and protocol)
- Multiple, increasingly intense tiers of intervention
- Continuous monitoring of students' performance and response to interventions
- Educational decisions about individual students based on solid assessment data and monitoring of student progress
- Parental involvement and team-based decision making in regard to a student's educational needs

The Three-Tiered Model of Intervention

The Positive Behavioral Interventions and Supports (PBIS) model described in Section 2.7 and the Response to Intervention (RTI) model are basically the same three-tiered system for schools to provide the appropriate level of supports and interventions—based on solid data and progress monitoring—for school success. Whereas PBIS addresses students' behavioral and social-emotional needs, RTI focuses on addressing students' academic and instructional needs. Both RTI and PBIS or Schoolwide Positive Behavior Supports (SWPBS) provide a tiered system (generally three tiers), represented as a pyramid as shown on page 198, with increasingly more intensive levels of support and intervention provided to students, depending on their needs.

The RTI and PBIS/SWPBS model shows three tiers: tier 1 (primary or universal), which represents the level of supports and interventions needed by approximately 80 to 90 percent of students; tier 2 (secondary or targeted) level of interventions, which is what is needed for approximately 10 to 15 percent of students; and tier 3 (tertiary or intensive) interventions, which is what approximately 1 to 5 percent of students will require.

Tier 1: Primary (Universal) Intervention

Tier 1 focuses on taking a proactive approach, aiming to prevent problems by identifying at-risk

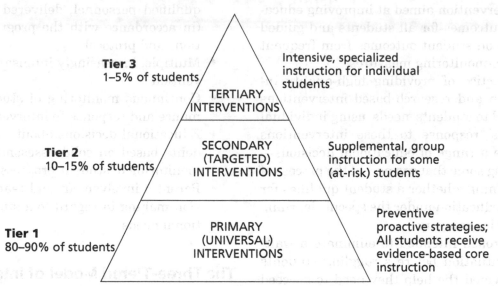

RESPONSE TO INTERVENTION (RTI)

Tier 3
1–5% of students

TERTIARY INTERVENTIONS

Intensive, specialized instruction for individual students

Tier 2
10–15% of students

SECONDARY (TARGETED) INTERVENTIONS

Supplemental, group instruction for some (at-risk) students

Tier 1
80–90% of students

PRIMARY (UNIVERSAL) INTERVENTIONS

Preventive proactive strategies; All students receive evidence-based core instruction

students and catching students in need of support before they fail. At this tier, primary or universal interventions are provided by the classroom teacher, which involves high-quality, research-based instruction in the core curriculum. Differentiated instruction is ideal at this tier for enabling all students to access the curriculum, addressing students' learning differences, and providing universal intervention. Screening, regular assessment, progress monitoring, and group interventions are provided for all students. Students identified as struggling with the curriculum or being at risk should receive additional instruction and teacher support within the general education classroom (for example, an additional reading group, or skill instruction in areas of weakness), during which progress is closely monitored and data collected, to determine the need for tier 2 intervention.

Tier 2: Secondary (Targeted) Intervention

Tier 2 involves more intense, targeted interventions to strengthen the skills of students who do not responding adequately with tier 1 support. Research-based interventions and programs are provided *in addition* to core instruction in the general curriculum, usually in small groups. This supplemental instruction does not replace the classroom curriculum, and it can take place outside of the classroom. Tier 2 interventions are applied for a limited time (generally no more than ten weeks), during which students' progress is frequently monitored in order to gauge the effectiveness of the intervention and determine whether tier 2 intervention is no longer needed, continued tier 2 intervention should be provided, or tier 3 intervention is needed.

Tier 3: Tertiary (Intensive) Intervention

In tier 3, intensive, individualized interventions target the skill deficits of students who do not adequately respond to intervention in tiers 1 and 2. Students at tier 3 receive the most minutes of instruction, delivered by teachers who are well trained to implement the intensive intervention programs.

Tier 3 is the stage at which children are considered for special education. In some school districts, tier 3 is where referral for special education and evaluation takes place. (Documented evidence of lack of response to intervention at tiers 1 and 2 is a component of the evaluation.) For students who are found to be eligible for special education, tier 3 intervention would include special education services. In other districts, a more intensive, individualized tier 3 intervention is provided within general education, generally delivered by reading specialists or other specialists. Referral and evaluation for special education follow if the student does not make adequate progress. In these districts, special education is tier 4.

A Word about RTI and the Individuals with Disabilities Education Act (IDEA)

When the Individuals with Disabilities Education Act (IDEA) was reauthorized in 2004, it changed the way that school districts are permitted to evaluate and identify students with learning disabilities. It is important to note that students with ADHD who have coexisting learning disabilities may qualify for special education if they meet the eligibility criteria under the specific learning disability (SLD) category or the other health impaired (OHI) category.

Traditionally, a formula that quantified the discrepancy between a student's IQ and his or her achievement was used to determine whether a student had a learning disability and qualified for special education under the SLD category. There had been problems with the IQ-achievement discrepancy formula and concerns about requiring its use in the diagnosis of learning disabilities and determination of eligibility for special education. Many people felt strongly that the discrepancy formula was not a reliable means of diagnosing a learning disability and was also resulting in too many students having to wait to fail before they were able to qualify for needed services.

IDEA 2004 changed this. It enabled schools to use RTI (the student's response or lack thereof to interventions) as part of the evaluation process in determining whether a student has specific learning disabilities and is eligible for special education. According to IDEA 2004, a student who consistently performs below state-approved grade-level standards on scientifically validated interventions and who fails to respond successfully to additional supports and interventions of increasing intensity may be determined to have a learning disability.

The law stresses the need to use instructional practices in general education that are supported by research and that focus on prevention of problems. Early intervening services (EIS) are to be provided to help students who are not yet identified as eligible for special education but who require additional academic or behavioral support. IDEA 2004 allows school districts to use up to 15 percent of their federal special education funds for EIS for students in need of academic or behavioral support and intervention who have not yet been identified as needing special education. RTI is a perfect vehicle for providing these EIS.

Note: On January 21, 2011, the US Department of Education, Office of Special Education Programs (OSEP), issued a memorandum to states telling them that schools cannot use the RTI process to delay or deny an evaluation (Cortiella & Hertog, 2012). The law specifies that a referral for special education and a comprehensive evaluation may be made at any time. If a disability is suspected, regardless of the tier, parents and teachers or other school personnel may refer the student for a special education evaluation. See more on this topic in Section 6.4.

Peer-Mediated Instruction and Intervention

Peer-mediated instruction involves students taking an instructional role with classmates. Classwide peer tutoring and cooperative learning are two research-validated peer-mediated structures and approaches proven to be both effective in enhancing academic engagement and skill acquisition and beneficial in promoting positive peer interactions.

Classwide Peer Tutoring

Classwide peer tutoring programs involve student dyads (paired by the teacher) being taught how to tutor one another so that each tutee receives one-on-one instruction and feedback for half of the time period. After each tutee completes the assigned tasks and earns points for his or her progress, the students switch roles. The point earnings of the dyads are posted in the classroom. Because the students are rewarded as a pair, the tutor is as invested in the exercise as the tutee.

Classwide tutoring may also involve dividing the classroom into small, heterogeneous learning groups. Teams should consist of at least one high-performing student, one average-performing student, and one low-performing student or student with a disability. Thus, while there is heterogeneity within groups, groups are similar across the class, allowing the teacher to capitalize on the groups' complementary knowledge to achieve higher-level, collaborative objectives (Ashman & Gillies, 2013). The teacher explains to students that each team as a whole is responsible for helping all teammates learn the content from previous instruction. Team members should be given opportunities to work together to solve problems or understand material, with each having the chance to be the designated "tutor" of the group (Bell & Carter, 2013).

The Peer Assisted Learning Strategies (PALS) programs for reading and math, developed by researchers Douglas and Lynn Fuchs at Vanderbilt University, are classwide peer tutoring programs being used successfully in many schools. For more information on this topic, see Part 3 Additional Sources and Resources.

Cooperative Learning

Cooperative learning is another peer-mediated approach whose efficacy has been validated by decades of research. All teachers should be trained in best practices for implementing cooperative learning in the classroom. Teachers may mistakenly believe they are using cooperative learning when they simply have students working together in groups. This is not cooperative learning. In fact, students (particularly those with ADHD) often have difficulty learning and functioning productively during unstructured group work. Cooperative learning is a well-structured group format, designed to include specific elements that yield many benefits (academic and social).

Dr. Roger T. Johnson and Dr. David W. Johnson—researchers, professors at the University of Minnesota, and codirectors of the Cooperative Learning Institute (http://www.co-operation .org)—are international authorities on cooperative learning, whose works have influenced instruction in the classroom for over thirty years. They explain that all learning situations can be

structured so that students either compete with each other ("I swim, you sink; I sink, you swim"), ignore each other and work independently ("We are each in this alone"), or work cooperatively ("We sink or swim together").

With *individualization*, there is no correlation among goal attainments. Students work by themselves to accomplish learning goals unrelated to those of other individuals. With *competition*, there is a negative correlation among goal attainments. Individuals work against each other to achieve a goal only one or a few can attain. Through *cooperation*, there is a positive correlation among goal attainments. Individuals in the group work together to achieve shared goals and maximize their own and one another's learning. Cooperative learning is supported by a vast amount of research as the most beneficial structure in the classroom. Much of the information presented here about cooperative learning, and used with permission since the first edition of this book, is summarized from the works of Johnson, Johnson, and Holubec (1990, 2008).

According to Johnson and Johnson (n.d.), there are different types of cooperative learning: (1) formal, consisting of students working together for between one class period and several weeks, to achieve shared learning goals and complete jointly specific tasks and assignments; (2) informal, consisting of having students work together to achieve a joint learning goal in temporary, ad hoc groups that last from a few minutes to one class period; and (3) cooperative base groups, which are long-term, heterogeneous cooperative learning groups with stable membership.

The Five Elements of Cooperative Learning

Johnson, Johnson, and Holubec (1990, 2008) discuss the following five elements of cooperative learning:

1. *Positive interdependence.* This is the most important element—when group members perceive that they need each other to complete the task and cannot succeed unless everyone in the group is successful. To structure positive interdependence, the teacher must

establish and include mutual goals, joint rewards, shared resources, and assigned roles.

2. *Individual and group accountability.* In addition to the group needing to achieve its goals, each member of the group must be accountable for contributing his or her share of the work. The teacher must assess the performance of each individual in the group and give the results to the individual and the group. There are various ways to provide for individual accountability that may include giving each group member an individual exam, observing and recording the frequency of each member's contribution, and randomly calling on one member to answer questions or present his or her group's work to the teacher or the whole class.

3. *Promotive interaction.* This kind of interaction among group members (which preferably takes place face-to-face), occurs as individuals in the group encourage and facilitate each other's efforts to achieve. Team members promote each other's productivity by helping, sharing, and encouraging one another's efforts to produce and learn. This facilitates the building of personal commitment to one another, as well as to their mutual goals.

4. *Interpersonal and small-group skills.* Students do not come to school with all the social skills they need to collaborate effectively. The teacher must teach teamwork skills as purposefully and precisely as he or she teaches academic skills.

5. *Group processing.* Group members need to discuss how well they are achieving their goals and maintaining effective working relationships. The teacher gives time and procedures for students to evaluate how well their group is functioning. For example, after each session, the teacher has groups answer these questions: "What did we do well in working together today? What could we do even better tomorrow?" In addition, the teacher monitors groups, providing feedback on how well they are working together.

Structuring to Achieve Positive Interdependence

As a teacher, you need to help students understand that they achieve their goals only if all members of the group also attain their goals. You can do this by using any of the following structures and techniques from Johnson, Johnson, and Holubec (1990, 2008):

- Structure positive goal interdependence. For example: "You are responsible for learning the assigned material and making sure that all other members of your group learn the assigned material."

- Require one answer from the group. Randomly select or collect only one product that is signed by all (meaning that all contributed and can explain and defend). This single product represents the group for evaluation.

- Establish a mastery level required for each member and reward for success. For example, the group goal is for every member to demonstrate 90 percent mastery (or other criterion) on a particular test. The group is rewarded with extra points if all members attain the goal: "If all members of your group score at least 90 percent [or x percent], each of you will receive five bonus points [or other reward]."

- The goal is for the overall group score to reach the criterion specified. Each member's individual scores are added to make a total group score. The total group score must reach a specified criterion for success.

- Build positive interdependence through regular celebrations of group efforts and success.

- Build interdependence by establishing a division of labor—through different roles necessary to the group dynamics and/or through different student responsibilities (for example, each member being responsible for parts of the task). *Note:* See book club roles as examples of division of labor in the appendix (A.9).

- Provide resources that must be shared (division of materials), which also helps build positive interdependence.

Teaching Social Skills through Cooperative Learning

Section 2.7 addresses the social challenges and difficulties with interpersonal relationships that are common among children and teens with ADHD, explaining that some children have social skill deficits, meaning that they have not learned how to perform a specific social skill. However, typically children with ADHD do not have a skill deficit, but a performance deficit. They know what they are supposed to do, but fail to perform the skill when needed. Whether a child is deficient in social skill awareness or in social skill application, it is vital for him or her to learn and practice these skills in order to use them appropriately in daily life. There is no better place or structure for teaching and practicing appropriate social skills than through the context of working in groups together with classmates in real learning situations.

There are different ways to teach what working cooperatively "looks like" and "sounds like." The behaviors must be stated very explicitly. One way is to develop a T-chart together with the students. A specific social skill is selected (for example, reaching agreement). Then behaviors describing what reaching agreement might look like are listed—for example, heads together, smiling, shaking hands, thumbs up. Similarly, behaviors are listed under what reaching agreement might sound like: "Good idea." "How do you feel about that?" "What do you think?" (Johnson, Johnson, & Holubec, 1990).

Another technique is for students to brainstorm the behaviors for the specific social skill and then create a rubric of observable behaviors demonstrating that skill. Groups can refer to the rubric and score themselves on the criteria after the cooperative activity.

In the context of each cooperative group lesson, incorporate one or more social skills or collaborative skills to teach and practice (along with the instructional and academic tasks). Teach the skill by explaining the need for the skill and its importance in students' daily lives. Together with students, brainstorm what the skill would look like and sound like to an observer. Model, demonstrate, and role-play examples (and nonexamples). As students are working, circulate around the room, recording observations of groups' implementation of the targeted social skills. As students are working, positively reinforce prosocial skills; and at the end of the lesson, provide feedback—sharing your observations. In addition, have students self-evaluate their group's performance on the targeted skill(s).

Note: See the Social Skill Lesson Plan, provided at the end of Section 2.7, for use in any cooperative learning situation.

More on Cooperative Learning Principles and Strategies

The Kagans are other national authorities on cooperative learning, who have created numerous strategies and resources to help teachers implement this instructional format in the classroom. Their acronym for what they see as the four basic principles of cooperative learning is PIES: **p**ositive interdependence, **i**ndividual accountability, **e**qual participation, **s**imultaneous interaction. They have developed a variety of structures and formats for teachers to use that ensure that all students within the group are active and equal participants. Tasks are structured to promote simultaneous interactions rather than sequential participation (one student at a time), significantly increasing each student's response opportunities and participation.

The Kagans have developed a number of structures teachers can choose to implement in cooperative groups to ensure that the principles of cooperative learning are being addressed in each lesson. For example, one strategy the Kagans recommend that equalizes participation during a team open-ended discussion is "Talking Chips." It involves providing each member of the group a certain number of plastic chips. Any student on the team can begin the discussion by placing his or her chip in the center of the team's desk and keeping his or her hand on the chip while speaking. When finished, the chip is left in the center of the desk. Other team members do the same when they wish to speak. Teammates continue in this fashion while sharing their ideas (Kagan &

Kagan, 2009; Kagan, Kagan, & Kagan, 2015). This is an excellent strategy to use with students who have ADHD, as it helps them regulate their impulsive talking and provides structured practice in how to take turns appropriately.

Cooperative Learning and Students with ADHD

Without proper structure and management, many students have difficulty working cooperatively. Students with ADHD tend to struggle the most in such group situations. Teachers need to take particular care in planning for students who have difficulty inhibiting their behavior and attending to task so that these students will be successful academically and socially within the cooperative learning situation. When possible, students with ADHD should be placed in groups with peers who are supportive and tolerant and are positive role models. If the cooperative learning assignment provides for students with ADHD to assume a role of responsibility in the group and to contribute to the assigned task in ways that draw on their strengths and interests, most are motivated and can function well in the cooperative group format. Students with ADHD will likely need more monitoring, prompting (for example, through visual cues and gentle reminders), and rewards.

There are wonderful resources available on the "how-to's" of implementing cooperative learning in the classroom (such as those found in the Section 3.2 references). Cooperative learning is particularly beneficial for students with ADHD because it offers many opportunities to respond, increased peer interaction in a structured format, and practice of social skills in an authentic setting and context.

See "Social Skill Lesson Plan" and "Report Form: Social Skills" in Section 2.7, which are adapted from *Cooperation in the Classroom* (Johnson, Johnson, & Holubec, 1990) and used with their permission. Information and tools adapted from Rief and Heimburge (2007) for implementing book clubs that are designed for student accountability, cooperation, and success can be found in Section 4.3, as well as in the appendix and online at www.wiley.com/go/adhdreach.

Blended Learning

Blended learning, although in its early days and not as yet proven, is showing great promise as being an effective model for delivering instruction that reaches and teaches all learners. K–12 blended learning is described as follows:

Definitions

- Blended learning is a teaching model that combines in-person instruction and education technology that enables personalized learning and competency-based progression (Learning Accelerator, 2015).
- It is "a formal education program in which a student learns: at least in part through online learning, with some element of student control over time, place, path, and/or pace; at least in part in a supervised brick-and-mortar location away from home; and the modalities along each student's learning path within a course or subject are connected to provide an integrated learning experience" (Christensen Institute, n.d.).
- It's a mix or hybrid of computer (or digital) lessons and traditional face-to-face learning every day.

Benefits

- When structured and implemented well, blended learning can be a powerful means of differentiating instruction and keeping students engaged and motivated as they work to achieve their academic goals.
- The online or software (digital) programs students use personalize their learning—addressing individual learning preferences and challenging them as they learn at their own pace to master the content or skill. The technology provides students with immediate or frequent feedback on their performance, and provides real-time data for teachers to be able to monitor individual progress and inform instructional needs.
- "Blended learning offers defined opportunities and spaces for teachers to work with small groups of students to address learning

goals (individualization), enhance or extend the curriculum (rigor), or spend time analyzing student data (monitoring). By offering differentiated experiences in both online and in-person contexts, blended learning allows teachers to further focus on individual students as learners and access multiple data points to measure student growth" (Arney, 2015, p. 2).

Models of Blended Learning

There are different models of blended learning and variations within the model in terms of how it is structured and implemented. Two primary models are used in schools (elementary through high school): rotation and flex.

Rotation models are most common at the elementary level. In rotation models, students transition from face-to-face instruction to online learning in classroom centers or a computer lab. This model includes station rotations, lab rotations, flipped classrooms, and individual rotations (Bailey, Schneider, & Vander Ark, 2013).

An elementary grade rotation for English Language Arts (ELA) or math may involve students within a classroom or lab rotating across differentiated learning stations on a fixed schedule or at the teacher's discretion. Stations often include (1) small-group instruction by the teacher, (2) collaborative or independent practice, and (3) self-directed, online activities.

An example of rotations, shared by Aspire Public Schools (2013), is as follows: During a ninety-minute ELA instructional block, students in small, differentiated groups rotate across learning stations at thirty-minute intervals. Group 1 engages in guided reading with teacher; members of group 2 read to themselves or listen to a digitized book; group 3 works with the computer program.

More common at the secondary level, *flex* models feature one-to-one technology access, instructional delivery primarily online, and competency-based progressions. Learning online is often augmented by small-group instruction, projects, and individual tutoring (Duty et al., 2015).

The Technology

For a significant part of the day or subject area (sometimes one-third of the time), schools implementing blended learning have students working on a computer, iPad, Chromebook, or other device using software or online programs. There are a number of adaptive software and online programs that schools are using at this time as part of the instructional program or as an intervention, such as Achieve 3000 (www.achieve3000.com) i-Ready (www.curriculumassociates.com), Dreambox Learning (www.dreambox.com), Read 180 (http://www.scholastic.com/read180), and Wowzers (http://www.wowzers.com).

Designing Interventions for Struggling Learners: Key Instructional Components

As noted throughout this book, many students with ADHD also have coexisting learning disabilities, such as dyslexia, and need targeted, more intensive academic intervention through RTI, special education, or other means. The key elements of instructional design for such intervention programs, based on an abundance of research, generally have the following characteristics (Rief & Stern, 2010; Vaughn Gross Center for Reading and Language Arts, 2010):

- *Direct and explicit.* Each skill, rule, and strategy is taught clearly and directly, without assuming that the student has even the most basic foundational skills or background knowledge.
  - Introduce and focus on one new skill or strategy at a time.
  - Introduce, practice, and review skills using specific procedures.
  - Provide explicit teacher modeling using demonstrations, graphics, manipulatives, think-alouds, and other multisensory tools and techniques.
  - Have students practice using one skill or strategy multiple times before combining with other skills or strategies.

— Provide a high degree of guided practice, frequently checking for students' understanding and giving immediate corrective feedback.

- *Systematic and structured.* Students are taught a systematic scope and sequence of skills, starting at a beginning level to ensure mastery of foundational skills and filling in of holes in a student's repertoire of skills.
  — Complex tasks are broken down into simpler, more manageable ones.
  — Skills and tasks are taught step-by-step.
  — Each lesson gradually builds on previously taught skills or concepts.
  — Students are moved along at an appropriate individual pace.
  — Supports and scaffolding are provided as needed for success.

— The scaffolds or supports are gradually reduced or eliminated as the student gains proficiency.

- *Multisensory.* Multimodal techniques are used to tap into individual learning strengths, strengthen connections, and make learning more memorable.
- *Targeted and intensive* (as described in RTI). Intensifying instruction usually involves increasing the amount of instructional time for teaching and practicing the skills, or decreasing the number of students in the intervention group.
- *Frequently monitored for progress.* Using reliable, valid measures of student progress, teachers adjust instruction accordingly.

INTERVIEW WITH AMY
Seventeen Years Old, California

Amy received a diagnosis of ADHD (inattentive type) and learning disabilities at a young age.

Tell me about your favorite teachers in school.

"My best teacher was in second grade. She expected so much of you, and she made learning fun. She wasn't mean, but she was firm. She gave me individual time, had me come up to the board, and really talked to me. When I had trouble concentrating, she had me sit at a table with walls around it, but it wasn't a punishment. It was just so I could work without distractions. It was a very supportive classroom.

"My history teacher last year was very understanding. You were supposed to read a whole chapter at a time and, at the end of each section, answer the questions. I worked really hard, but couldn't get it done in time. Then I told my teacher that I have a learning disability. I am dyslexic. He gave me all the time I needed. I was never frustrated or nervous in his class."

How about your worst classes?

"In tenth grade, my math class was so difficult for me. I would raise my hand for ten minutes and the teacher always ignored me. He would walk right by me and never listen to me or help."

What is your advice to teachers?

"Teachers should be understanding of the student's needs. If the kid says, 'I just need a little more time on this,' the teacher should say, 'OK. Would you like more time tomorrow? Do you want to take it home or do it in the Learning Center?' Sometimes teachers are so difficult, you just want to cry. You get so frustrated!"

INTERVIEW WITH BRITA
Thirty-seven Years Old, California

Brita received a diagnosis of learning disabilities and ADHD (predominantly inattentive) as an adult.

What are your memories of elementary school?

"My family was one of avid readers. I grew up surrounded by books. I loved to be around books, but I couldn't read them. I remember how much I loved hearing my teacher read *Charlotte's Web* to the class in third grade. Hearing the stories was so powerful. My biggest frustration was not being able to get further in my reading."

Tell me how your attention difficulties affected you in school.

"One of the pitfalls with ADD is that I would have my good days and my bad days. I never knew when the trap door would open and I'd lose my train of thought. For example, in class I would want to ask a question. I would raise my hand and repeat in my head over and over the question I wanted to ask, so I wouldn't forget. In the meantime, I would miss everything in between the waiting and getting called on. I lost a lot, and it was very frustrating. I spent hours on homework. Reading and writing were very difficult for me."

What about junior high and high school?

"One of my survival skills was being 'Miss Goody Two Shoes.' I wasn't popular, but that didn't matter much to me. Friends came second to my wanting to do well. Teachers always liked me. I would always tune in to what the instructors wanted and do what I could to please them.

"I had some very good teachers. A lot of my trauma was self-inflicted. I used to have teachers so fooled. I fooled everybody, but in fooling people (for example, hiding that I couldn't read), I thought I was cheating. In speaking with a lot of other adults who have learning disabilities, many of us felt that we were cheating by not doing what was expected of us the traditional way. We might have squeaked through the system, but we had to find our own methods. Most of us knew when we were very young that something was wrong, but we didn't know what.

"In junior high I remember being the last to get started. I would sit down to write something, but I just couldn't get started. I would get so frustrated, and my anxiety level would go up and up, making it worse. I often felt that my body and I were separate. My body was next to me. My brain and body weren't coordinated with each other."

How did you cope with your difficulties?

"I had trouble coping. In fact, I went through periods of serious depression. I saw psychiatrists when I lived back East. No one ever figured out that I couldn't read. I have learned how to accommodate myself. In class I sit up front, close to the teacher, and do as much one-to-one with the teacher as possible. In college I never missed a single class. I am a very disorganized person, but I have an office that I am responsible for organizing. I can do this successfully by setting up visual cues for myself. I set things up in neat little boxes and color-code them all. I use electronic tools to help me compensate, and I take advantage of Recordings for the Blind and Dyslexic [now called Learning Ally, www.learingally.org], which provides audiobooks and texts for individuals with reading disabilities. If I can't reach the top shelf, I can with a ladder. So what if you need aids to compensate! I can do a lot of things that others can't do. I'm very creative. I'm learning to pat myself on the back now, so I don't go back into that black hole I was in for thirty years."

3.3

Organization and Time Management

Most people with ADHD are challenged in their daily lives (from a mild to severe degree) with weaknesses in organization, time management, and study habits. It is common for students with ADHD to be unprepared for class (for example, frequently losing or misplacing papers, leaving needed books and materials and completed homework at home). They are often late. Poor time awareness and time management typically cause students to have incomplete work and

fail to meet important deadlines and due dates. This is a direct result of their executive function deficits.

Regardless of how bright and capable a student may be, missing or late assignments and poorly organized work affect his or her grades and academic achievement. It is important to recognize that for students with ADHD, this is not laziness, apathy, or lack of caring about their work but a manifestation of their disorder. Rather than admonishing them for their weak executive skills, parents and teachers must work to provide the needed supports, structure, and teaching and practice of organization and time management. Students with ADHD need to be taught effective strategies and encouraged to use methods that will work for them.

Children and teens with ADHD often exhibit these problematic behaviors that are caused by disorganization and poor ability to judge and manage time:

- Has a messy desk, work area, locker, backpack, notebook, bedroom
- Cannot find, forgets to bring, or frequently loses important things (books, materials, assignments, personal belongings)
- Exhibits poor management of long-term projects and assignments (research projects, book reports)
- Is poor at scheduling and pacing
- Lacks foresight and planning
- Has difficulty prioritizing activities and things that need to be done
- Is poor at accurately estimating how long a task will take and allotting sufficient time to complete it
- Is not prepared with needed materials
- Has difficulty remembering and keeping track of assignments
- Is oblivious to deadlines and due dates
- Is slow to get started and initiate tasks; procrastinates
- Exhibits poor judgment of how much time is needed to accomplish tasks or arrive somewhere on time (factoring in the extra time for traveling and unforeseen interferences)
- Lacks awareness of time passing

- Is frequently late (to class, activities, appointments)

What Teachers Can Do to Help with Organization

Fortunately, any efforts to create and maintain an organized classroom and to directly teach organizational skills benefit *all* students, not just those with ADHD.

Organize Student Work Spaces and Materials

- Require the use of a three-ring binder or notebook starting in third grade (fourth grade at the latest).
- Students in kindergarten through second grade should use a pocket folder for carrying their papers daily.
- Require all students to carry a backpack and to bring the notebook, binder, or pocket folder to and from school in their backpack every day. Starting at an early age with this expectation builds the habit by training both students and their parents to consistently use these organizational tools daily.
- Require the use of colored subject dividers and a pencil pouch for the notebook to include a few sharpened pencils with erasers, a plastic pencil sharpener, and other small supplies and essentials. A flat plastic three-hole punch that can be inserted in the rings of the notebook is also recommended.
- Teach students how to keep their papers organized by placing them in the appropriate subject section of their notebooks.
- Require the use of a monthly assignment calendar or planner or a daily or weekly assignment sheet to be kept at the front of the notebook at all times. Whichever is used (calendar, student planner, or assignment sheet), it should be three-hole punched for storage in the notebook. Students should use it consistently for recording all classroom assignments, and the teacher should model and monitor its use.

- Students should have a consistent location in their notebook for storing homework assignments (or work to do and work to turn in). There are a variety of ways to do this; for example:
  — Use colored pocket folders (single pocket or double) that are three-hole punched and inserted in the notebook. For example, a red pocket folder can be labeled "Homework" and contain all homework; a different colored folder may be for graded and returned papers or anything to leave at home.
  — Use large laminated envelopes that are three-hole punched and inserted into the notebook for homework, assorted project papers, and so forth.
- Encourage students to keep a supply of notebook paper handy in a consistent location in their binder.
- Provide handouts that are always three-hole punched in advance.
- Give students a clipboard for anchoring loose papers or when they are working in a beanbag chair or other location.
- Consider attaching a pencil to the child's desk (with either string or Velcro).
- Provide bins, cans, boxes, buckets, trays, baskets, and other containers for storing materials and supplies and having them easily accessible at desks and tables or nearby when needed.
- To help students keep papers stored appropriately in the notebook, provide adhesive hole reinforcers for ripped-out papers and plastic sleeves for papers that you do not want to three-hole punch.
- Some students have difficulty managing the three-ring notebook system and may do better using an accordion folder. Students who are using the accordion folder should color-code and label the tabs of each section or pocket of the folder: the subjects (preferably labeled sequentially according to the daily schedule), homework to do, papers to turn in, and a place for storing the planner, for example.

- Limit the amount of materials or clutter on the student's desk or work area.
- Some students do better with a large envelope attached to the side of the desk for their papers or a tote bag on back of the chair for their books. This enables them to keep materials near them and accessible without needing to place them in a desk. A basket or box on the floor or shelf is another alternative to keeping things on or in their desk.
- Organize the classroom with clearly labeled shelves, files, and bins so that you and the students know precisely where things belong and can easily locate (and replace) them.
- Provide a work-in-progress folder for incomplete work and do not allow students to place incomplete work in their desk.

Use Visual Reminders and Memory Cues

- Use visual cues for showing expected materials, daily routines, and schedules to organize for the day.
- Encourage students to use sticky notes for reminders to themselves. Have them stick the notes on book covers, their lockers and planners, and other useful places.

- Provide or help students create a laminated checklist for their binder, desk, or locker, itemizing the materials they should have in that location.
- Use color strategically for help in organizing:
  — Color-coordinate by subject area to make locating subject materials quick and easy. For example, the science text is covered in yellow paper or has a yellow adhesive dot on the binding, the science notebook or lab book or folder is yellow, the schedule with the science class period and room number is highlighted in yellow, and so is the tab or divider for science in the three-ring notebook or accordion folder.
  — Use one specific colored box, tray, or folder for students to place completed assignments they are turning in and another colored box, tray, or folder for unfinished work.
  — Prepare important notices and handouts on colored paper, preferably color-coded for certain categories—for example, weekly or monthly newsletters in blue and spelling lists in pink.
  — Use brightly colored paper for project assignments, providing details and due dates. Give the student two copies: one for the notebook and one to be posted at home.

Monitor, Support, and Motivate

- Schedule a periodic desk and notebook organization time (end of day, once a week, or bimonthly). Time should be provided for cleaning out unnecessary papers and items from students' desks and filing papers in the proper sections of their notebooks. Students with ADHD may need assistance from table partners, a well-organized classmate, or an adult.
- Cleaning up student work areas should be part of the daily routine between activities. You can offer incentives for quick cleanups (finishing the job before a timer goes off or a song ends): allowing students to earn table

points or the class to earn a minute or two toward a preferred activity at the end of the week.

- Have random desk and notebook organization spot checks. Positively reinforce passing inspection of notebook and work space checks with prizes, certificates, and privileges such as "no homework tonight" passes. See the Notebook Check form in the appendix (A.6).
- Provide bonus points for improved organization and reward your disorganized students who are able, on request, to quickly locate a certain book or paper in their desk or notebook.
- Provide peer or adult assistance to help disorganized students organize desks, backpacks, and binders. It helps, for example, to have another organized student or adult supervise as desk contents are dumped into a shopping bag and brought to another area with a larger table space to work on. Recycle unnecessary papers, apply adhesive hole reinforcers to ripped-out papers, refile papers in the appropriate section of the notebook, and throw away trash.
- Arrange for peer or adult assistance in locker organization and suggest to parents that they provide their child with some locker organization tools and accessories, such as shelves, magnetic hooks, and a mini whiteboard and dry-erase pens for reminder notes.
- At the end of the day, make sure that students with ADHD have necessary books or materials in their backpack to take home.
- Use the buddy system (partners A and B) to monitor each other for organization. For example, when giving instructions on where items need to be put away or papers filed, partners check with each other to make sure that the task is done properly.
- Provide in-school help and adult assistance as needed for putting together projects, such as display boards for a research project. For example, many students with ADHD impulsively glue papers to display boards without first planning for the amount of space

they have. Help with the little extras that make projects look much better, such as nice lettering on the computer, cutting papers straight with a paper cutter rather than scissors, and organizing prior to mounting objects.

Provide Organizational Assistance in Planning and Thinking

- Provide study guides to help students organize their thinking about key topics of the lesson.
- Model the use of graphic organizers, and guide students through the use of all organizers that aid comprehension as well as the planning and organizing of ideas before writing: sequence charts, story maps, webs, and flowcharts, for example.
- Provide framed outlines for filling in missing words and phrases during instruction.
- Help students organize their ideas (prewriting, planning) with the many strategies and techniques suggested in Section 4.4.

More Organizational Tips

- Encourage students to organize materials when they arrive at class each day and before dismissal at the end of the period or school day.

- Provide models for how to organize papers (for example, a sample paper with proper headings, margins, and spacing).
- Provide models of well-organized projects.
- Require that materials and supplies be labeled with students' names or numbers.
- Help individual students create a list of materials or items they need to remember to bring to class on the different days of the week, as per their schedule.
- Keep spare supplies available so that students waste no time searching or asking around to borrow from classmates. Consider "charging" students (for example, they must pay you from their class money or tokens) or fining them in some way (points) for not being prepared and needing to borrow supplies.
- Allow for natural consequences of not having materials. Do not positively reinforce students who are unprepared by giving them new, desirable materials and supplies. Instead, let students borrow only your less desirable materials. For example, many teachers keep a box of golf pencils and old pencils and erasers for this purpose.
- Many teachers have provided ideas for organizing the classroom environment and student materials on Pinterest. See many wonderful examples at www.pinterest.com /sandrarief/class-organization-time-mgmt/.

Parent Tips: Helping Your Child with Organization

Support your child with being organized at school and home with these strategies and tips.

Supplies and Materials

- Provide your child with a backpack and notebook or binder according to the teacher's specifications.
- A backpack that has an outside pocket or mesh for holding a water bottle, and separate zipper compartments for textbooks, notebooks, and small supplies is recommended.
- Provide other organizational tools, supplies, and materials requested by the teacher.
- Inventory with your child which school supplies need to be replaced or replenished.
- Provide a spelling dictionary or list of common and frequently misspelled words, a multiplication chart, and any other useful reference materials for your child's notebook.

- Use a specific bag for organizing and keeping each of your child's extracurricular activity supplies. Provide a laminated list or place the list inside a transparent plastic sleeve that itemizes what needs to be inside the bag (for example, equipment, shoes, uniform, or notebooks).
- Provide materials to organize your child's locker at school (for example, shelves, magnetic hooks, and other accessories).

Your Child's Room and Work Area

- Help your child clear out desk drawers and shelves of work, projects, and papers that were from different school years. Together, decide on what you would like to keep and store out of the way (in colored boxes, portfolios, or large plastic zipped bags) in order to make room for current papers and projects.
- Provide your child with a corkboard and pins or a magnetic board and magnets to hang up important papers.
- Use trays and bins for storing supplies and materials so as to remove some of the clutter from your child's desktop.
- Provide the necessary storage space for organizing your child's room efficiently: shelves, closet space, bins, trays, drawers.
- Label shelves and storage bins. Clear storage bins are often preferable.
- Use fun, creative ways to keep your child's (and family's) belongings organized and easy to locate. See examples of organized children's rooms and homework areas as well as tips and creative home organization ideas from Pinterest users at www.pinterest.com/sandrarief /home-organization-homework-areas/.

Visual Reminders and Memory Cues

- Dry-erase boards are helpful to hang in a central location of the home for all messages and notes to family members. In addition, hang one in your child's room for important reminders and messages.
- Write notes and reminders on colored sticky notes and place on mirrors, doors, and other places your child is likely to see them throughout the house and elsewhere.
- Encourage your child to write himself or herself notes and leave them on the pillow, by the backpack, by car keys, and so forth.
- Use electronic reminders and organizers.
- Create a checklist of items your child needs to take to school. Have your child check off each item in the evening or morning as it is packed, to include homework, textbooks, binder, lunch, forms to be returned, and so forth. You may want to have a laminated checklist placed inside your child's backpack and sports or dance bags, or a small one to attach to the bag like a luggage tag, listing materials needed and things to remember.
- Use color strategically:
  — Provide a file with color-coded folders in which your child can keep papers stored categorically.
  — Color-coordinate by subject area as described earlier for teachers.
  — Color-code entries on a calendar according to category: school related, sports, and social activities, for example.
- Take photos to use as cues or reminders for how your child's room or work area should be straightened up and organized, or provide a visual checklist your child can follow.

More Organizational Tips

- Take the time to help your child clean and organize his or her backpack, notebook, desk, and room. Help with sorting, filing, and discarding. Some families schedule a daily or weekly time for doing so, such as Saturday mornings or Sunday evenings.
- Assist your child with cleaning and organizing by at least starting the job together or giving clear reminders for how to carry out the tasks, such as with a simple task card or checklist.
- Offer a reward or incentive for straightening and organizing materials, putting away belongings, and so forth.
- If using a token economy system or other behavioral incentive program at home, give points or tokens for meeting an organizational or clean-up goal.
- Label your child's materials and possessions with his or her name.
- Take digital pictures of school projects and scan and save important documents of your child's work each semester or school year for safekeeping. You may want to consider taking digital pictures of your child's arts-and-crafts projects, favorite writing samples, and so forth and printing an album every year or so as a keepsake (for example, through Shutterfly or Costco). This will allow you to have a valuable reminder of your child's accomplishments without having to keep and store all of the paper products. It also makes a great gift for grandparents!
- To avoid early-morning rush and stress, have your child get as much as possible organized and ready for school the night before; for example, set out the next day's outfit, prepare lunch, and load everything into the backpack. Have your child shower or bathe in the evening.
- Every night, have your child place his or her loaded backpack in the same spot by the door from which he or she leaves for school each morning.
- Check your child's backpack and school folders every day (before and after school if possible).
- If organization and time management are areas of weakness for you as well as your child, consider hiring an ADHD coach.
- According to Kutscher and Moran (2009), people use three basic organizing styles: visual, spatial-cozy, and chronological-sequential. Because everyone's brain organizes and recalls information differently, the organizational method that works for you may not be the one that works best for your child. I recommend that you learn how a given child best organizes himself or herself and use techniques that fit the child's organizational style.
- See the organizational strategies recommended for teachers, and see Section 3.4 for tips to create an organized homework area with recommended materials and supplies. Section 4.4 shares ways to help your child plan and organize ideas for writing assignments.
  The case studies in Sections 5.1 and 5.2 also share wonderful organizational strategies for children, teens, and adults.

What Teachers Can Do to Help with Time Management

Time Awareness

Any opportunity to practice time estimation is helpful in increasing time awareness. For example, challenge your students to estimate how long it takes to walk to the office and back without running. Make a game out of predicting, timing, and

checking the students' time estimates for various tasks and activities.

Encourage self-monitoring during independent seatwork time by recording the start time on the paper. When the work period is over, have the student record the time, regardless of how much work he or she actually produced. This also serves as helpful documentation of how well the student is able to stay on task and work productively.

Timers, ranging from kitchen and hourglass timers, digital timer devices, and visual timers, are a standard tool in any classroom. Many students with ADHD benefit from the use of visual timers that enable them to more clearly see the passage of time (how much time has elapsed and is remaining before the time period ends). The company Time Timer (www.timetimer.com) has been very popular for over twenty years. Their timers are excellent for helping children of all ages easily recognize the passage of time by showing a red disk that shrinks with the passing of each minute the timer is set for. There are many great online visual timers for projecting in the classroom, such as the animated online timers at Online-Stopwatch (www.online-stopwatch.com /classroom-timers/).

Note: Be aware that some children get very anxious and stressed with timed tasks and "beat the clock" incentives. One teacher shared with me this strategy: Rather than setting the timer in the countdown mode and rewarding the child for completing the task by the time the timer goes off, you reward the child for showing improvement or beating his or her own time. The student simply records how long it took to complete the task and is rewarded if he or she shows improvement.

Assignment Sheets, Student Planners, and Calendars

Many of us cannot consider managing our lives and myriad responsibilities without our planners or calendars or other tools for recording our schedule and what we need to remember to do. The sooner we build the habit and routine in students, the better. The planner or assignment sheet also serves as a powerful means of home-school communication and enables mutual monitoring and reinforcement of school assignments.

Communicate and maintain the clear expectation that all assignments are to be recorded on whatever tool is used in your classroom: a student planner, calendar, or assignment sheet. School success depends on students' maintaining a written record of all assignments to easily refer to and tracking their work toward completion of assignments. For students to build this important study habit, you need to be consistent, make recording assignments a priority, and monitor that students are keeping up.

- Model and walk students through the process of recording assignments by writing down and projecting a copy of a filled-in planner, calendar, or assignment sheet. Allow time at the beginning or end of the subject period or school day to do so.
- Provide extra assistance (from an adult or peer) to students who have difficulty recording assignments.
- Check assignment calendars or planners, as students with ADHD often make careless recording errors, such as entering assignments on the wrong date.
- Assign study buddies so that students can help each other. These partners can be responsible for checking in with each other to make sure assignments are recorded on their planner or calendar. When a student is absent, the buddy can collect all handouts, notices, and assignments for the absent student. Partners should exchange contact information so that they can call, text, or email when the other is absent and communicate about what was missed that day in class.
- Routinely ask table partners or buddies (or groups seated together) to check in with each other and make sure everyone has recorded the information accurately. Some teachers have partners initial each other's planner after doing so.
- Keep a master monthly calendar posted in the classroom, recording special activities

and events that are scheduled and when assignments are due.

- If students are using a daily planner or assignment sheet, also provide them with a single- or double-page monthly calendar for important dates they can see at a glance. Help them record onto the monthly calendar the due dates of projects, tests, class trips, and other important activities and events for the month.
- Check and initial the assignment sheet, calendar, or planner for students who need extra monitoring and ask their parents to do so as well.
- Recommended planners for students with ADHD and learning disabilities are those with plenty of writing space for each day of the week and that are as clean and distraction free as possible. Some student planners provide very little room for recording assignments, which is problematic for many children.

See examples of homework assignment sheets in the appendix (A.7 and A.8).

Schedules

- Post all schedules and refer to them throughout the day.
- Walk through the schedule each day, and point out any changes in the daily or weekly schedule or routine that will be taking place.
- With younger students, use a pictorial schedule depicting the daily routine.
- For students receiving special education or related services, write down their weekly schedule and have copies that they can tape to their desk, place in their notebook, or attach to the inside of their locker door for easy reference.
- Keep each student's special schedule accessible so that you know the days and times that he or she is to be pulled out of class or when service providers are coming to the classroom to work with the student.
- Encourage students and parents to plan a weekly schedule, including an established study and homework schedule.

Long-Term Projects

- Structure long-term assignments (book reports, research projects) by breaking them into smaller, more manageable increments.
- Make sure students have access to needed materials.
- Assign incremental due dates to help structure the timeline toward project completion. For example, assign separate due dates for each stage of the project: getting a topic approved, submitting an outline, listing notes or resources, turning in a first draft, and so forth. Post those due dates and frequently refer to them as reminders.
- Make sure that parents of students with ADHD are aware of the project and due dates. Besides sending home a hard copy of the handout explaining project guidelines, a timeline, and a scoring rubric, consider also calling home or sending an email attachment with the important information. You may want to have parents sign a form to return to school indicating that they are aware of the assignment. Keep project information and reminders posted on your school or class website if you have one.
- Monitor progress by asking to see what the student has accomplished and provide feedback along the way.
- Consider providing some of your parents of students with ADHD advance notice about upcoming projects and reports, enabling them to get a head start, especially with planning and research.

Other Ways Teachers Can Help with Time Management

- Provide students with a course outline or syllabus.
- Teach students how to tell time and read a nondigital clock.
- Teach students how to read calendars and schedules.
- Make sure that all due dates are presented to students both orally and visually, with frequent reminders.

- Use to-do lists, modeling for the class how to write down and cross off accomplished tasks.
- Use a homework tracking sheet such as A.8 in the appendix with students who need close monitoring by parents and teachers to ensure that assignments are being completed on time.
- Allow older students to use their electronic devices (calendars, things-to-do features, productivity apps, vibrating alarms) for time management. For students who prefer to use their electronic device for recording assignments, allow them to do so if it works well for them instead of the paper planner. Apps to check out that may work well for some students are MyHomework and MyStudyLife. Taking a snapshot with their smartphones

- of the assignments written on the board is another option.
- Provide enough time during transitions to put materials away and get organized for the next activity.
- Set timers for transitions. ("You have five minutes to finish working and put away your materials.")
- If tardiness is an issue with a student, try an individual contract to motivate him or her to improve this behavior, or include "on time" as a target behavior on a daily report card (DRC).
- Provide extended time as needed; consider flexibility regarding late work.
- Use frequent praise and positive reinforcement. Reward students for meeting deadlines and finishing assignments on time.

Parents Tips: Helping Your Child with Time Management

Time Awareness

- Practice time estimation with your child. Make a game out of predicting, timing, and checking your child's time estimates for various activities.
- Cue your child with time reminders such as "You have fifteen minutes to get ready before we leave the house" and set the timer.

Tools, Schedules, and Supports

- Watches or alarms can be set to vibrate and cue your child to be on task, be somewhere, call home, or take medication, for example. The WatchMinder (www.watchminder.com) is a vibrating wristwatch that can be set to alert your child silently in class or elsewhere with preprogrammed or personalized messages at fixed times or intervals.
- There are other beneficial electronic devices with timers to help your child remember appointments and curfews, and keep on schedule—for example, My Time Activity Timer (www .mytimeactivitytimer.com).
- Visual timers are very useful. The visual timer, Time Timer (www.timetimer.com), enables your child to see the passing of time—how much time is remaining—with a shrinking red disk. This popular timer is very beneficial for children with ADHD (even very young ones). It is available in different forms (clock, watch, app, computer software).
- There are many time management, productivity, and organizing apps that your teen may find helpful, such as 30/30 and inClass. Learning Works for Kids, www.learningworksforkids .com, and *ADDitude* magazine, www.additudemag.com, are good sources for recommended time management apps and tools.
- Help your child schedule the evening and estimate how long each homework assignment or other activity should take.

- Developing the habit of using a personal planner or agenda is essential. Your child should be expected to record assignments in a planner, calendar, agenda, or assignment log of some sort by the mid- to upper-elementary grades.
- Expect your child to record assignments, and monitor that this is being done. Ask to see your son's or daughter's assignment calendars, sheets, and planners every day. See the teacher for help in ensuring that assignments are recorded. Your child may need direct assistance from a classmate or the teacher to be sure assignments are recorded.
- Post a large calendar or wall chart in a central location of the home for scheduling family activities and events. Encourage everyone to refer to it daily. Each family member could have his or her own color of pen for recording on the calendar.
- Help transfer important extracurricular activities and scheduling to your child's personal calendar or planner.
- Help your child create a weekly schedule. For older children, a recommended time management strategy is to take a few days to track and record how they spend their time over the course of twenty-four hours. After a few days, your child should have better awareness of how much time is typically spent on routine activities: meals, sleeping, grooming, walking to class, screen time (watching television or the computer), texting or talking on the phone, recreational and social activities, and study and homework time.
- In addition to a master family calendar, provide your child with a desk calendar that serves as an overview of important dates, activities, and events.

Managing Routines and Schedules

- Try to keep bedtime and wake-up time as consistent as possible, with predictable routines for getting ready in the morning and at night. Clear reminders of the routine (for example, through the use of a checklist of sequential tasks to complete) reduce the nagging, rushing around, and negative interactions at these times of the day.
- Checklists are great tools for time management and staying on schedule. Each task that is completed on the list or chart is crossed off.
- Combine checklists and routines with a positive reinforcement system. If your child has all items completed and checked off by a certain time, he or she earns extra points or tokens as a reward.
- Help your child establish a routine for extracurricular activities as well. Include scheduled time for practice and gathering needed items (with the aid of a checklist) for that extracurricular activity.
- Help your child get in the habit of checking his or her planner and calendar a few times a day.
- Try not to overschedule your child, particularly during the school week.

Long-Term Projects

- Your assistance with time management and structuring of long-term school assignments such as book reports and science and research projects is critical to your child's success. Build in plenty of time. When scheduling, allow for unforeseen glitches and delays.
- Help your child break down longer assignments into smaller, manageable chunks with deadlines marked on the calendar for completing incremental steps of the project.
- Pay close attention to due dates and post the project requirements. Together with your child, record on a master calendar the due date of the final project, and plan when to do the steps

along the way (for example, going to the library, gathering resources). Monitor timelines and help your child with pacing.

- Ask the teacher for feedback and help in monitoring that your child is on track with the project. Do not assume that your child is working on projects at school, even if he or she is given some time in class to do so.
- Large and long-term projects can easily become overwhelming and discouraging for your child (and you, too). Your son or daughter will need your assistance, as well as help at school, with pacing, tracking, and monitoring timelines toward project completion.
- See more strategies for keeping on top of long-term projects and homework assignments in Section 3.4.

3.4

The Homework Challenge: Strategies and Tips for Parents and Teachers

In families of children and teens with ADHD, tears and battles over homework are common and chronic problems. The frustration, conflict, and stress surrounding daily homework issues can be very intense—placing an enormous strain on the parent-child relationship. Students with ADHD typically have major issues with homework production, which requires organization, time management, and other executive skills. Failure to remember the assignment and bring home the needed books and other materials, for example, is directly related to working memory weaknesses.

In regard to homework production, teachers need to be aware that it often takes students with ADHD considerably longer than average to complete the work, and factor that in when giving homework assignments. What teachers anticipate should take fifteen to twenty minutes to finish often takes a child with ADHD well over an hour—even with parental supervision and direct assistance.

Homework is particularly a challenge because of the child's fatigue and frustration at the end of the day. Without the provision of home structures and supports (and often some medication), it is unlikely that the child will be able to accomplish much work by the end of the day or evening. As pointed out earlier, these difficulties are related to these children's underdeveloped

executive functions, and punishment for weak skills caused by their neurobiological disorder is not the solution.

Homework is a complex series of subtasks that must be completed in a sequential order. In order to complete a homework assignment, the student must (1) know what the assignment is, (2) record it, (3) bring the required materials home, (4) do the homework, (5) return the homework to his or her backpack or book bag, (6) bring it to school, and (7) remember to turn it in.

According to my friend the late Dr. Terry Illes, an exceptional school psychologist and ADHD expert, children with ADHD have a difficult time maintaining their focus and motivation as they proceed from one subtask to another. They are easily sidetracked and may forget to perform one of the subtasks or simply give up because the process appears to require too much effort. He also explained that because children with ADHD are unconcerned with future consequences, often the only motivation to perform the homework is to get their teachers or parents off their backs, which is a reason why students with ADHD commonly complete their assignments but then fail to turn them in. Although adults see the failure to get credit for work completed as being a ridiculous waste of effort, it makes more sense if we understand that receiving credit for the completed homework was not the motivation for completing it. From the ADHD child's point of view, once the homework is completed, the nagging stops and playtime resumes; the homework process becomes irrelevant and is forgotten (Illes, 2002).

In addition to the strategies and tips to help build organization and time management skills and to help children compensate for weaknesses in these areas, described in Section 3.3, there are many ways for parents and teachers to provide support in the homework process.

Homework Tips for Parents

Create the Work Environment

- Make sure your child has a quiet, organized work space for homework, preferably a homework location where it is easy for you to supervise and monitor work production. See the many wonderful and creative examples of homework desks, stations, and locations in homes posted by Pinterest users at https://www.pinterest.com/sandrarief /home-organization-homework-areas/
- Limit distractions (unnecessary noise, activity, and phone calls) in your home during homework hours. Turn off the TV.
- Experiment with playing music softly while your child is doing homework. Music may help block other auditory distractions in the environment. Certain kinds of music also stimulate the brain and can be helpful for studying. Try various types of classical and instrumental music and other selections of your child's choice that may make studying more pleasant and increase productivity. For music selections that may be helpful, see the bonus section found online at this link: www .wiley.com/go/adhdreach

Develop a Homework Routine and Schedule

- Together with your child, establish a specific time and place for homework. In order to develop a homework habit, your child needs to adhere to a homework schedule as closely and consistently as possible.
- Consider a variety of factors when scheduling for homework: extracurricular activities, medication effects at that time, mealtimes and bedtimes, other chores and responsibilities, your availability to supervise and monitor, and your child's individual preferences and learning styles.
- Some children prefer starting homework shortly after they come home from school. Others need time to play and relax first, and then start homework later. However, they should not wait until the evening to get started.
- Provide healthy snacks and build in study breaks during homework time.
- Encourage and help your child to get in the habit of putting all books, notebooks, signed notes, and other necessary materials inside his or her backpack before bedtime.
- Place the backpack in a consistent location (for example, by the front door) so that your child cannot miss seeing or tripping over it when leaving the house in the morning.

Organize Homework Supplies

You can help your child reduce time spent searching the house for homework supplies and materials. This is a frustrating waste of precious minutes that also causes a major break in productivity, unnecessarily pulling your child off task. A homework supply kit can help. The kit can be stored in anything portable—preferably a lightweight container with a lid. With this system, it does not matter where your son or daughter chooses to study. The necessary supplies can accompany your child anywhere.

These are some recommended supplies to store in the kit or otherwise keep in the homework area (depending on the age of your child):

- Plenty of paper
- Paper clips
- Sharpened pencils with erasers
- Single-hole punch
- Pencil sharpener

- Three-hole punch
- Ruler
- Dictionary
- Crayons
- Thesaurus
- Paper hole reinforcers
- Spell-checker
- Glue stick
- Self-stick notepads
- Colored pencils
- Highlighter pens
- Colored pens and markers (thick and thin points)
- Index cards
- Stapler with box of staples
- Calculator
- Clipboard

Note: If your child has a tablet, smartphone, or other electronic device available for homework, you can exclude the dictionary, spell-checker, and thesaurus from the supply kit.

Prepare and Structure

- Expect your child to have all assignments recorded. Request the teacher's help in making sure all assignments are recorded daily. Perhaps the teacher can initial or sign your child's planner or assignment sheet each day; or you can use another system, such as having your child use his or her cellphone or other electronic device to take a picture of the assignments written on the board (if school policy permits), or record an audio message to himself or herself listing the homework and materials needed.
- Emphasize to your child the importance of not leaving school without double-checking the assignment sheet, planner, or calendar and making sure all necessary books and materials for doing the homework are in the backpack. This expectation can be reinforced by a reward for doing so (for example, earning points or privilege such as TV time) and mild punishment (loss of points or privilege) for not doing so.

- Have your child take the phone numbers of a few responsible classmates to call or text if there are questions about school work. Many schools help in this regard with homework hotlines, recording daily assignments on teachers' voice mail, or classroom websites where teachers post assignments online.
- Help your child look over all homework assignments for the evening and organize the needed materials before beginning.
- If your child frequently forgets to bring textbooks home, ask if you can borrow another set for home. If not, consider purchasing one if you are able.
- Assist your child in dividing assignments into smaller segments that are more manageable and less overwhelming. Long-term assignments such as reports and projects particularly need to be structured into a series of shorter steps in order for your child to complete them on time. Help do so and then be vigilant in monitoring and supporting your child through the process.

Help during Homework

- The amount of direct assistance required during homework will depend on the complexity of the assignment, the task demands (such as the amount of writing required), and the needs of your child.
- Assist your child in getting started on assignments, perhaps by reading the directions together, highlighting the key words in the directions, doing the first few items together, observing as your child does the next problem or item independently, and offering feedback and help if needed. Then get up and leave.
- Monitor and give feedback without doing all the work together. You want your child to attempt as much as possible independently.
- Even with younger children, try to get your child started and then check and give feedback on small segments of his or her independent work (for example, after every few problems or one row completed). Being

available to support and assist as needed is wonderful, but try not to get in the habit of having your child rely on your overseeing every minute.

- As tempting as it may be, even when homework time is dragging on, do not do the work for your child.

- Have your child work a certain amount of time and then stop. Do not force him or her to spend an excessive and inappropriate amount of time on homework. If you feel that your child worked enough for one night, write a note to the teacher and attach it to the homework.

- If your child struggles in writing, he or she may dictate as you write and record the responses. These accommodations to help bypass writing difficulties are reasonable for children with ADHD. Speak to the teacher.

- It is not your responsibility to correct all of your child's errors on homework or make him or her complete and turn in a perfect paper.

- As homework supervisor and coach, praise your child for getting to work, being on task, and showing effort. Give extra praise for accomplishment and progress.

Increase Motivation and Work Production

- Use a timer to challenge your child to stay on task, and reward work completed with relative accuracy during that time frame. A beat-the-clock system is often effective in motivating children to complete a task. Tell your child that you will come back to check his or her progress on homework when the timer rings.

- Older children can be encouraged to set a timer for a reasonable amount of time for focused work (twenty to thirty minutes), take a brief reward break when the timer goes off, then reset and work in this mode until homework is completed.

- Ask to see what your child has accomplished after a certain amount of time or to show you when a particular assignment is done.

Praise and reward work on completion. Help your child in setting up mini-goals for work completion (for example, read a specified number of pages, finish writing one paragraph, complete a row of problems). When your child has met the goal, reward him or her with a break and perhaps points or tokens or other reinforcers.

- Remind your child to do homework and offer incentives: "When you finish your homework, you can do . . ."

- Allow your child a break between homework assignments. In fact, your child can reward himself or herself with a snack and a break for play or exercise, or with access to his or her phone or electronic device after completing each assignment or two.

- You can work out a contract for a larger incentive or reinforcer as part of a plan to motivate your child to persist and follow through with homework—for example, "If you have no missing or late homework assignments this next week, you will earn . . ."

- Avoid nagging and threatening. Instead use incentives to support and motivate your child through the difficult task of doing homework.

- Enforce consequences (such as loss of points on a token economy or behavior modification system) when your child fails to bring home needed assignments or materials to do the homework.

- Withhold privileges (for example, no TV or other screen time or access to the phone) until a reasonable amount of homework has been accomplished.

- Encourage your child and praise his or her efforts on homework.

- Check into productivity apps and software that may help your distractible child get homework done faster—particularly if he or she gets easily sidetracked by the phone, social media, and distracting apps and websites. *ADDitude* magazine ("Success at School," 2015), recommends these three apps: Forest (http://www.forestapp.cc), Rescue Time (www.rescuetime.com), and Self Control (http://selfcontrolapp.com).

Communicate with Teachers about Homework Issues

- Let the teacher know if the homework is too confusing or difficult for your child to do (or for you to understand what is expected, given the directions).
- If homework is a frequent cause of battles, tears, and frustration in your home, seek help. Make an appointment with the teacher to discuss the homework problems and request reasonable modifications and adjustments in homework assignments.
- Communicate with the teacher and try to come to an agreement about daily homework expectations. Remind the teacher that children with ADHD often take at least two to three times longer to complete the same amount of work as their peers and that some of the homework demands exceed your child's capacity without enormous stress.
- Let the teacher know your child's frustration and tolerance level in the evening. The teacher needs to be aware of the amount of time it takes your child to complete tasks and what efforts you are making to help at home.
- Ask for progress notes or use of a daily or weekly report card or tracking sheets that keep you apprised of how your child is doing. For example, see the Daily Report and the Homework Tracking Sheet in the appendix (A.3 and A.8).

Other Ways to Help

- If your child is on medication during the school day but cannot get through the homework once the medication effects wear off, consult with your doctor. Many children with ADHD are more successful with homework when given a small dose of medication in the late afternoon or switching to a prescription with a long-acting formula.
- Many students with ADHD need homework accommodations written into a 504 plan or IEP.
- Supervise your child in placing completed work in his or her homework folder and

backpack. You may want to arrange with the teacher a system of collecting your child's homework immediately on his or her arrival at school or emailing homework to the teacher to ensure that your child turns in the work and receives credit for doing so.

- Help your child study for tests and use effective learning strategies. Use memory strategies to increase recall and retention of material. Practice and study using a variety of multisensory formats and memory techniques. See Section 3.6 for more on this topic.
- If your child struggles with reading, math, or writing, see academic strategies and supports found in Part 4.
- Many parents find it very difficult to help their own child with homework. If that is the case, find someone who can. Consider hiring a tutor. Often a junior or senior high school student or college student is ideal, depending on the needs and age of your child. Every community has a variety of tutorial services available. Of course, check references.
- Phone calls, electronic messages, and social media can easily pull your child off task and interfere with staying on schedule. If your child has a cellphone, consider removing it from the room or otherwise restrict access if possible during homework time; have your child return calls and messages or check social media during breaks.
- Have your child write start times and stop times on homework assignments for better awareness of how long it takes to do work; this is also good information to share with the teacher.
- For more ideas, check out Homework Planet www.homeworkplanet.com and other resources listed at the end of Part 3.

Homework Tips for Teachers

It is important for teachers to be sensitive and responsive to parents who are reporting great frustration surrounding homework. Be willing to make some adjustments so that students with ADHD spend a reasonable, not excessive, amount of time doing their homework. For example, shorten the assignment or reduce the amount of writing required. Ask yourself, "What is the goal?" "What do I want the students to learn from the assignment?" "Can they get the concepts without having to do all the writing?" "Can they practice the skills in an easier, more motivating format?" "Can they practice the skills doing fewer problems?"

Many teachers have a practice of sending home unfinished class work. Avoid this if possible. Of course, some in-class assignments will need to be completed at home, but try to find alternatives for your students with ADHD. Consider that students with ADHD who receive medication during the school day to help them focus and stay on task are often not receiving medication benefits after school or in the evening hours. It is unreasonable to expect parents to be able to get their child to complete in-class assignments that you were not able to get the child to complete during a full day of school (especially in addition to their other homework assignments). Provide the necessary accommodations, modifications, and supports so that in-school work is in-school work and homework is homework.

Communicate Clearly

- Read homework instructions aloud. Make sure you have explained the assignments carefully and clarified students' questions.
- If your school has homework hotlines or you use online sites for sharing information and communicating with parents and students, use them regularly. Keep information to parents and students regarding assignments up-to-date.
- Ask parents to let you know if their child is spending too much time on homework or expressing significant frustration or lack of understanding. Agree on time limits so that a child has needed free time every evening.
- Communicate regularly with parents of students who are falling behind in homework. Do not wait until the student is so far behind in completing work that catching up is almost impossible. Notify parents in some way (phone, text, email, daily or weekly monitoring form). See the Weekly Progress Report

shown here, as well as forms A.3, A.4, A.7, and A.8 in the appendix.

- When you assign a long-term major project or report, consider calling the parents of some students. Just because you have talked about the assignment a lot in class and provided written information does not mean the parents know a thing about it. You may call to ask parents to check the notebook for the written information about the project, or volunteer to send another copy to post at home. A heads-up phone call, text, or email to parents about the assignment and letting parents know you are available for support and assistance as needed are appreciated and can make a big difference in how the student does the assignment.
- Communicate with other teachers in your team. Students who have several teachers are often assigned a number of tests, large projects, and reading assignments all at the same time from their different classes. Be sensitive to scheduling. Stagger due dates and coordinate whenever possible with other teachers to avoid the heavy stress of having everything be due at the same time.

Provide Monitoring and Support

- Before students leave at the end of the day, supervise those who tend to be forgetful. Make sure they have their materials, books, and assignments recorded and in their backpacks.
- Assign a study buddy (or two) to your students with ADHD. Study buddies are responsible, willing classmates whom they can contact in the evening regarding homework questions or to find out what they missed on days they were absent.
- One of the most important things you can do to help all students (and their parents) keep on top of homework, tests, and long-term projects is to require use of an assignment sheet, calendar, or planner. Then guide, walk through, and monitor the recording of assignments. If this is a daily expectation and routine, everyone in the class will benefit.

WEEKLY PROGRESS REPORT

STUDENT'S NAME _____ ROOM NUMBER _____ WEEK STARTING _____

WORK HABITS

_____ WORKED HARD TO COMPLETE ASSIGNMENTS – GREAT JOB!

_____ PARTICIPATED & USED TIME EFFECTIVELY MOST OF WEEK

_____ WORK COMPLETION SO-SO THIS WEEK

_____ POOR WORK COMPLETION (CLASS AND/OR HOMEWORK)

_____ PARENT/TEACHER CONFERENCE NEEDED

CITIZENSHIP

_____ EXCELLENT BEHAVIOR – TRIED HARD MOST OF THE WEEK

_____ ACCEPTABLE BEHAVIOR MOST OF THE WEEK

_____ BEHAVIOR SO-SO THIS WEEK (SOME DIFFICULTIES)

_____ BEHAVIORAL PROBLEMS – DIFFICULT WEEK

_____ PARENT/TEACHER CONFERENCE NEEDED

MISSING ASSIGNMENTS LISTED ON BACK THAT MUST BE DONE

TEACHER COMMENTS:

_____ _____
TEACHER'S SIGNATURE   DATE

PARENT COMMENTS:

_____ _____
PARENT'S SIGNATURE   DATE

- Check and initial students' assignment calendar, sheet, or planner every day if needed.
- Have parents initial the assignment planner, calendar, or sheet daily. Designate a place for parents and teacher to write notes to each other—an excellent system for communication between home and school.
- Establish a system for directly collecting homework from your students with ADHD. Even when they have spent hours on homework assignments, it is very common for students with ADHD to forget to turn them in and get credit for the work they did.
- Work with your school about the possibility of having supervised study halls, homework labs or clubs, tutorials, and other assistance available for students who need it. For many students, being able to begin homework at school with support is very helpful.
- Be sure to collect homework and give some feedback when you return it. It is frustrating to students and parents to spend a lot of time on homework that the teacher never bothers to collect.
- Allow the student to email homework to you to avoid lost assignments, a common problem of students with ADHD.
- For long-term projects or large tests, provide students with a written timeline or checklist of intermediate deadlines to encourage appropriate pacing of the work. Allow students to turn in long-term assignments in parts as they are completed.

Increase Motivation

- Try to make the homework assignments more interesting. One way to add interest and increase motivation to work on homework is to build in the component of student choice. For example, you can tell students to select three of the five questions to answer or choose one of the three topics offered.
- Include some homework that incorporates an element of play or fun, such as a learning game to reinforce or practice a skill.

- Allow students to create products other than written ones (for example, a poster, song, or multimedia presentation) in order to show understanding of a concept.
- Write a goal for improvement in homework performance together with the student (and the parent if possible). If, for example, the child turns in fewer than 50 percent of homework assignments during the typical week, the initial goal might be to turn in 70 percent of weekly assignments, gradually raising the goal or performance standard to 80 percent and then 90 percent as the student achieves success. Write the goal into a contract or daily report card with rewards for achieving the goal.
- See www.homeworkopoly.com for a tool and method to motivate students to turn in their homework.

Keep Things in Perspective

- It is critical for students with ADHD to participate in extracurricular activities. They need every opportunity to develop areas of strength and interest (sports, dance, arts, music) that will be their source of self-esteem and motivation. These nonacademic, after-school activities are important to their development, and the child or teen should have the time to participate.
- Keep in mind that some of your students with ADHD may work with tutors or counselors and participate in programs outside of school to boost skills. Factor that in as well when assigning homework to these students.
- Be flexible and willing to make adjustments in the homework load, differentiating homework assignments and making accommodations as needed. Remind parents that you do not expect to see perfectly done homework with no errors. Homework is a tool for seeing what students can do independently. It is not the parent's job to make sure that everything is correct.
- Be flexible on giving credit for work that is turned in late, and accept homework that is dictated by a student to a parent scribe.

More Tips

- Remember that homework should be a time for reviewing and practicing what students have been taught in class. Do not give assignments involving new information that parents are expected to teach their children.
- Homework should never be busywork. Make the homework relevant and purposeful so that the time spent on it is helpful in reinforcing skills or concepts you have taught.
- Never add on homework as a punishment or negative consequence for misbehavior at school.
- Avoid unnecessary copying, recopying, or expectations for high standards of neatness for students with ADHD.
- Visually post homework assignments as well as explain them. Write the assignments in a consistent location of the classroom (corner of the board or on a chart stand, for example).
- If you have extra copies of textbooks to loan parents, do so for students who are forgetful and frequently leave the books they need at home or school.
- Do not excessively penalize students with ADHD for late or incomplete homework assignments. If a negative consequence is necessary, a point deduction is reasonable; a zero grade is not.
- See differentiated homework assignments and student project choices in reading, writing, and math found in the Rief and Heimburge books (2006, 2007) listed at the end of Part 3, and a selection of possible book club project choices (Book Club Culminating Activities, A.10) in the appendix.
- See online resources to communicate with parents and students and support with homework, such as Homework Now, http://www.homeworknow.com, and Your Homework, http://www.yourhomework.com, and other resources listed at the end of Part 3.

section
3.5

Learning Strategies and Study Skills

Children and teens with ADHD generally are deficient in their awareness and application of skills necessary for learning strategically and studying efficiently. All students, but particularly those with ADHD and learning disabilities, will benefit from instruction and practice in learning and study skill strategies for school success.

What Are Learning Strategies?

Learning strategies are

- Efficient, effective, and organized steps or procedures used when learning, remembering, or performing (Sousa, 2011)
- Thoughts or activities that assist in enhancing learning outcomes

Chamot and O'Malley (1994) describe learning strategies as encompassing the following types or categories:

- *Metacognitive knowledge.* Understanding one's own mental processes and approach to learning, the nature of the learning task, and the strategies that should be effective
- *Metacognitive strategies.* Planning for learning, monitoring one's own comprehension and production, and evaluating how well one has achieved a learning objective

- *Cognitive strategies.* Manipulating the material to be learned mentally (as in making images or elaborating) or physically (as in grouping items to be learned or taking notes)

Metacognition and Metacognitive Strategies

What do we mean by "metacognition" and "metacognitive strategies"?

Definitions

- Metacognition is "thinking about thinking" and involves consciously overseeing whether you are on the right track or need to make changes in your thinking or approaches.
- Metacognition refers to an awareness and control over one's own thinking processes. Effective thinkers constantly monitor their own thinking—frequently checking, reassessing, and setting goals—and engage in metacognition to know how and when to apply a variety of problem-solving strategies (Gregory & Parry, 2006; McTighe, 1990).
- Metacognitive strategies are self-regulatory; they help students become aware of learning as a process and of what actions will facilitate that process.

Metacognition involves these skills:

- Previewing and planning for how to go about learning or studying the material, or previewing main ideas or concepts of a text
- Organizational planning: figuring out in advance and planning when, where, and how to study or accomplish the learning task; getting ready; and setting goals
- Planning and ordering the steps necessary to complete a task
- Monitoring one's progress on those steps and one's own attention, production, and comprehension
- Self-assessing how well one has accomplished a learning task, and self-evaluating how well goals were met and what learning took place
- Making connections ("This reminds me of . . .") or recording what one is thinking, picturing, visualizing, or wondering; wants to explore further; has questions about; and so forth
- Reflecting on what one has learned

Metacognitive Questions

Students with ADHD typically lack self-awareness of what is working and not working for them and adjusting what they are doing accordingly to accomplish their goals. They need to actively think about such questions as "How do I learn?" "How can I learn better?" "What plan will I follow?" "How well am I doing?"

After teacher modeling of how to do so, encourage students to ask themselves the following metacognitive questions (Hennessy, 2003; Hennessy & Soper, 2003):

Self-Direction

What is my goal?
What do I need to do?
What will I need?
How will I do this?
How much time will I need?

Self-Monitoring/Self-Correction

How am I doing?
Do I need other information/resources?
Do I need more support?

Self-Evaluation

How did I do?
Did I finish on time?

Gregory and Parry (2006) describe additional reflective questions that students can use to engage in metacognition for problem solving:

- What am I being asked to do or find out?
- What information have I been given?
- What strategies have I used in similar situations?
- Who or what could help me with this?
- What has to be done by when?
- How well does the solution conform to the criteria?
- What helped me in this process? What hindered me?

Metacognitive Strategies

The following are a few examples of metacognitive strategies.

Journal Responses

There are a variety of ways to use journals to engage students in thinking, questioning, and making associations during their reading, and responding and reflecting after their reading. The following are two examples:

Double-entry journal. Students divide the paper into two columns. They take notes in the left column, citing anything they find of particular interest (for example, a quote, description, or metaphor) along with the page number. In the right-hand column, students comment and record personal thoughts, interpretations, connections, and questions triggered by that section of the text.

Metacognitive journal/learning log. Students divide the page into two columns. The left column is labeled What I Learned; the right is labeled How I Learned This. This format assists students in thinking about and analyzing their own learning process. The right-hand column can state other things, as well—for example: How This Affects Me or Why This Was Difficult [or Easy] for Me. The key is for students to reflect on and analyze their own learning.

Reading Logs

Students can write their feelings, associations, connections, and questions in response to their reading. They may be given specific prompts to guide what they record in their logs—for example: "What did you learn?" "How did this make you feel?" "How did this relate to any of your own life experiences?" "What did you like/dislike about the author's style of writing?"

Think-Aloud

This involves externalizing and making overt one's thinking process—demonstrating what efficient thinking sounds like when one is trying to solve a problem or comprehend something. Students have a model of what it might sound like to internally grapple with a text when reading for better understanding. A think-aloud in reading involves these steps:

- The teacher reads to students while they follow along in their books.
- While reading, the teacher models aloud the process of interacting with the text (for example, making predictions, describing what he or she visualizes, working through problems to figure out unknown vocabulary, and making connections).
- The teacher models how to self-monitor his or her own comprehension by stopping periodically and asking, "Is this making sense to me?"
- Students can then practice some of these strategies with partners.

****

Other examples of metacognitive strategies are "close reading" strategies involving annotated note taking while reading, use of prewriting checklists in the planning stage before written composition, and explaining one's thought processes (verbally or in writing) for solving a math word problem.

See numerous metacognitive strategies for reading, writing, and math in Part 4 of this book.

Cognitive Learning Strategies

Definition

Cognitive strategy instruction is an explicit instructional method that is well researched and uses a highly interactive, sequenced approach consisting of guided instruction and practice leading to internalization of the strategic routine and independent performance of the task over time (Krawec & Montague, 2012).

Cognitive Strategies

The following are examples of some cognitive strategies (Chamot & O'Malley, 1994):

Resourcing: using reference materials, such as dictionaries, encyclopedias, textbooks

Grouping/classifying: organizing words, terminology, quantities, or concepts according to their attributes

Note taking: writing down key words and concepts in abbreviated verbal, graphic, or numerical form

Elaboration of prior knowledge: relating new to known information and making personal connections

Summarizing: making a mental, oral, or written summary of information gained from listening or reading

Deduction/induction: applying or figuring out rules to understand a concept or complete a learning task

Imagery: using mental or real pictures to learn new information or solve a problem

Auditory representation: mentally replaying a word, phrase, or piece of information

Making inferences: using information in the text to guess meanings of new items or predict upcoming information

Cognitive strategies are often expressed as acronyms, mnemonic (memory) devices for students to better recall the steps of the strategy, which are explicitly taught and practiced. Mnemonics and other memory strategies and techniques are discussed in Section 3.6. The following are examples of some common cognitive learning strategies.

SQ3R

This strategy increases comprehension and retention of textbook material (expository or informational) and involves the following steps:

1. **S**urvey. Briefly look through the reading assignment at the titles, chapter headings, illustrations, charts, and graphs. Skim through the assignment and read the chapter summary or end-of-chapter questions.
2. **Q**uestion. Turn the headings and subheadings of the text into questions. For example: *Producing Antibodies* can become "How do our bodies produce antibodies?" *Organic Motor Fuels* can become "What are the different organic motor fuels?"
3. **R**ead. Read to find the answers to the questions you developed. Identify the main ideas and jot down any questions, notes, or unknown vocabulary.
4. **R**ecite. At the end of each chapter section, state the gist of what was read. *Note:* Restating or summarizing into an audio recorder is often very effective.
5. **R**eview. Check recall of important information from the reading. To that end, create a study guide of some kind.

SQ4R

This is the same as SQ3R but includes an additional step beginning with the *r* sound: *write*. The SQ4R procedure is **s**urvey, **q**uestion, **r**ead, **r**ecite, **wr**ite, and **r**eview. After making a brief verbal summary of what the reading passage is about, the student writes the answers to the questions (in step 2) and then reviews.

RCRC

This study strategy involves the following steps (Archer & Gleason, 1989):

- **R**ead a little bit of material. Read it more than once.

- **C**over the material with your hand.
- **R**ecite. Tell yourself what you have read.
- **C**heck. Lift your hand and check. If you forgot something important, begin again.

POW + TREE

The Self-Regulated Strategy Development Approach (SRSD), pioneered and researched by Harris and Graham (1992), University of Kansas, has developed numerous learning strategies that are widely used. Harris, Graham, Mason, and Friedlander (2008) created these steps for writing persuasive essays. The POW and TREE go together. This and several other SRSD strategies are described on the IRIS Center website of Vanderbilt University. (See http://iris.peabody.vanderbilt .edu/module/pow and http://iris.peabody.vanderbilt .edu/module/srs.)

POW

- **P**ick an idea or opinion.
- **O**rganize and generate notes and ideas for each part of the TREE.
- **W**rite and say more.

TREE

- **T**opic sentence. Formulate a topic sentence that expresses an opinion.
- **R**easons (give at least three) to support the topic sentence.
- **E**xplanation. Explain your reason.
- **E**nding. Formulate a statement to summarize the topic sentence.

RAP

The Strategies Instructional Approach developed by researchers at the University of Kansas for Research on Learning (Schumaker et al., 1981) provide a number of research-validated cognitive learning strategies. The RAP strategy (Schumaker, Denton, & Deshler, 1984) for paraphrasing involves the following steps:

- **R**ead the paragraph.
- **A**sk yourself to identify the main idea and two supporting details.

- **P**araphrase or put the main ideas and details into one's own words.

SCORER

SCORER is a test-taking strategy that assists students in carefully and systematically completing test items (Hoover & Patton, 1995; Polloway, Patton, & Serna, 2001):

- **S**chedule time effectively.
- **C**lue words identified.
- **O**mit difficult items until end.
- **R**ead carefully.
- **E**stimate answers requiring calculations.
- **R**eview work and responses.

S2TOP and CHECK

James Madison University's Special Education Program developed a wonderful, user-friendly website called Learning Toolbox (http://coe.jmu.edu/LearningToolbox), designed to be responsive to the specific needs of students with learning disabilities and ADHD. It contains over sixty unique learning strategies in the form of acronyms, categorized under the topics of organization, test taking, study skills, note taking, reading, writing, math, and advanced thinking. S2TOP and CHECK are two examples of Learning Toolbox strategies.

S2TOP is a study skills strategy to help stay focused when studying:

- **S**et a timer.
- **S**ee if you are off-task.
- **T**ouch the circle (and make a tally mark inside the circle when you notice that you have drifted off the task). *Note:* The student first draws a circle on a piece of paper, sticky note, or index card for noting the tally marks.
- **O**rganize your thoughts.
- **P**roceed again.

CHECK is a study skills strategy to help start studying:

- **C**hange environments (to one free from distractions).
- **H**ave all equipment nearby.

- Establish rewards for yourself.
- Create a checklist of tasks to be done.
- Keep a "worry pad" (if ideas popping into your head are distracting you).

Other Ideas

Chamot and O'Malley (1994) recommend that learning and study strategies be taught explicitly by

- Modeling how one uses the strategy with a specific academic task by thinking aloud as you work through the task (for example, reading a text or writing a paragraph)
- Giving the strategy a name and referring to it consistently by that name
- Explaining to students how the strategy will help them learn the material
- Describing when, how, and for what kinds of tasks they can use the strategy
- Providing many opportunities for practice of the strategy

The University of Nebraska-Lincoln's website on cognitive strategy instruction shares a number of cognitive strategies for reading, writing, math, note taking, test taking, and other study skills; lesson plans; and other information for implementation (http://cehs.unl.edu/csi). James Madison University's Learning Toolbox (http://coe.jmu.edu/learningtoolbox/site_map.html, mentioned earlier) is another online source of cognitive strategies that are beneficial for students with ADHD. There are numerous other cognitive learning and study strategies, many of which are interspersed throughout the academic sections of this book.

More Learning and Study Strategies

The following are some additional study and learning strategies.

Note Taking

Writing down key words and concepts while listening to an oral presentation or reading text material is a very important learning strategy and study skill. Note taking is, however, a difficult skill for many students (particularly those with ADHD and learning disabilities). It requires the ability to determine and summarize what is most important while actively listening or reading, and writing the information in an abbreviated format or through simple illustrations. Note taking during lectures is particularly challenging, as it requires simultaneous processing (listening and recording/writing) and speed of processing and output. This is why note-taking supports and accommodations are very common for students with ADHD and with learning disabilities in IEPs and 504 accommodation plans.

Students need a lot of guided practice in learning how to identify and write down major ideas and key information in a useful format so that they can later read and use their notes as a tool for studying. There are a variety of note-taking techniques. One common and traditional method involves dividing the page into two sections (split-page notes) with a vertical line about one-third the width of the paper down the page. In the right column (the one with more space), the student writes down the information in short phrases from the lecture, video, book, or other source; later, the student uses the other column to list main ideas and concepts from the notes, or questions, applications, reactions, or other mental responses.

Good note taking requires learning how to use abbreviations and symbols. Students should also highlight key vocabulary and points when looking over and reviewing their notes, and review their notes within twenty-four hours (preferably within three hours) after the lecture. During this time, they reread and fill in key terms, making additions, corrections, and so on.

Nancy Fetzer, my friend with whom I have had the pleasure of coauthoring one book and coproducing two educational videos, is one of the most dynamic and creative teachers and models of the use of exemplary, research-based teaching techniques I have ever known. Click on her website at www.nancyfetzer.com to see Nancy's online demonstrations of her dynamic "Lecture Notes" instructional strategies.

The four-part scaffolded lecture note strategy that Nancy demonstrates authentically in the classroom uses powerful and highly engaging techniques for frontloading information for expository writing across the curriculum. The video clips (2011) show a lesson for taking notes using a simple, easy-to-use structure (simple illustrations, symbols, dropboxes), and practicing reading the notes multiple times for retention and recall of the information. Nancy demonstrates exemplary instructional practices that enable all students in the class to learn the information, express and explain the content using grade-level or above grade-level academic vocabulary and language, and then use their notes to independently write a well-crafted summary quickly and efficiently about the topic:

- Physical motions (gestures), which are a memory cue and actively engage all students in the classroom
- Use of nonlinguistic representations (simple icons) for note taking
- Teacher-guided rehearsal of information (whole group) and frequent opportunities for students to practice in their table groups
- Teacher clarification of the meaning of content vocabulary words
- Effective questioning techniques and behavior management strategies
- Guiding students with clues so they can grasp or discover the "big idea"
- Frequent stopping throughout the lesson to rehearse and read the lecture note information (using gestures) to enhance memory and recall
- Modeling how to refer to the big idea so that the supporting details remain focused and on topic

In the lesson demonstrated for Lecture Notes, for example, when Nancy lectures about the four regions of California, she holds up one of her arms in an *L* position—making a right angle with that arm to represent California. Holding the arm up, she makes a mountain peak by touching fingers of both hands together (as the gesture representing mountains), then touches or swoops along the outside of the arm from top to bottom to represent the Pacific Ocean, which is the "coastal region." She explains that the Central Valley is farmland where much of the crops are grown. She represents this physically by telling students to make a muscle and touch the bicep muscle of that arm. For the fourth region (desert) at the southern part of the state (by the armpit), she gestures by waving the other hand under the armpit of the L arm—fanning because of the heat of the desert.

These physical gestures and associations are memory pegs. The information gets transferred to long-term memory as they are frequently repeated throughout the lesson (teacher and students making the gestures as they verbalize about the four regions). Students copy the teacher-written notes from the board, which at this point are simply a crude outline of California and the numeral 4 (representing the four regions) next to it. Then she draws a ragged line at the top of the simple figure for California (representing mountain peaks), a sun or cactus at the bottom of the illustration (representing the desert), corn or other vegetable in the center (indicating Central Valley), and a wavy line along the outer edge (coastal) of the illustration. As Nancy presents more information, she expands the notes following the same method.

I highly recommend that you view the videos and see Nancy in action using her Lecture Note strategies and techniques.

Graphic Organizers

These are described in Part 4, which comprises the academic sections of this book. Part 4 discusses, for example,

- Using advance organizers and study guides to help organize thinking about key topics of the lesson
- Using sequence charts, story maps, sentence maps, webs, clusters, flow charts, and Venn

diagrams to aid in comprehension of material, planning for writing about a topic, and so forth
- Providing framed outlines for filling in missing words and phrases during instruction

Resource Materials

Students need to learn research skills (grade-level appropriate, of course) for locating information and using reference materials. There are prerequisite skills to using many resource materials, such as understanding alphabetical order and the use of guide words, being able to read and understand the legend of a map, and knowing how to read a variety of graphs and diagrams. Upper-grade students need to be taught research skills—how to access information and cite appropriately.

Review Games

Races at the board for solving problems or answering questions, Jeopardy, Around the World, and Whole Brain Teaching's Mind Soccer (www.wholebrainteaching.com) are examples of some of the many kinds of games that students can play in the classroom to review and practice any content information. Parents may also use or invent games to help motivate their child to practice and review skills or academic content, such as spelling words, math facts, and vocabulary. For example, parents can adapt card games (such as War for math facts) or make a Memory or Concentration game. In the latter games, pairs of cards are placed face down on the floor or table top; the child needs to look for and find matches to turn face up. For example, one card of a pair can show an illustration of perpendicular lines, and the other card would have the word "perpendicular" written on it.

Note: *See the discussion of memory strategies (Section 3.6) and other sections in Parts 3 and 4 for more techniques and supports to strengthen learning and study skills.*

INTERVIEW WITH SUSAN
Thirty-eight Years Old, California

Susan has a BA in occupational therapy and an MA in rehabilitation. She is a rehab counselor who was identified as an adult as having learning disabilities and ADHD.

What is your advice to teachers?

"Help students be aware of their strengths. If we just go after the 'sore teeth,' people give up and leave school. If they work through their strengths, interests, and learning styles, students will be motivated to learn the skills they need and will forget about their 'sore teeth.' Set up an environment that will make them reach out and interact with other people."

What has helped you get through school successfully?

"I've learned to identify my learning style and to compensate for my weaknesses. I am a weak auditory processor. [*Note:* Susan requested a face-to-face interview rather than one conducted over the phone.] I am a strong kinesthetic learner. I take walks a lot. That is how I get my best ideas. When I get bogged down on a project, I go walking and am able to get the whole concept. Then I can move forward. I allow my kinesthetic abilities to help me. For example, my statistics class was extremely difficult for me. I recorded lectures and would listen to them a few times at home, but it didn't help much. Then I started walking around the lake while I listened to the lectures. This helped me considerably. I now take frequent breaks, move around a lot, and balance my activities. I don't make myself sit at a desk."

section

3.6

Memory Strategies and Supports

Children and teens with ADHD experience many of their most significant academic and functional difficulties as a result of working memory (WM) weaknesses.

Definitions and Descriptions of Working Memory

There are various descriptions, definitions, and metaphors for working memory:

- WM has been described as our mental work space, a place to hold information online, so to speak, long enough to manipulate it in order to solve a problem or complete a task (Katz, 2011).
- WM has also been described as our brain's sticky note (Alloway, 2010) or cognitive desktop (Kaufman, 2010), which allows a person to temporarily hold and manipulate information while engaging in other cognitive tasks.
- WM is holding in mind what you are doing: the goal that you hope to attain and the means that you intend to use to get there (Barkley, 2013).
- WM is an active and limited-capacity memory system that acquires information from short- or long-term memory, sensory input,

and automatic memory, and then holds the information for a short time while a task is being performed (Baddeley, 2006; Meltzer, 2010).

- WM can be understood as an internal scratch pad. It provides us with a place to store information that we will need to use for the next step of a task, but that we do not need to store beyond that time. For those with weak WM, it is as if their scratch pads are much smaller than expected, so that they cannot hold as much information in mind as others do. Further, the lettering on the scratch pad seems to be written in disappearing ink, so the words or images fade more quickly than for others (Cooper-Kahn & Dietzel, 2008).
- WM provides a mental jotting pad that is used to store important information in the course of our everyday lives for short amounts of time—for seconds or minutes at most (Gathercole & Alloway, 2008).

According to Barkley (2013), WM comes in two forms that we use for holding things in mind to guide us over time to our goals:

Verbal. This type of WM uses words—for example, talking to ourselves in our mind's voice as we go about our day, writing notes to ourselves, and reciting rules to ourselves.

Nonverbal. This type of WM is largely composed of imagery. We use visual images of our past to guide us, similar to a car's GPS when driving.

Nonverbal (visual-spatial) working memory uses a kind of visual sketchpad. It allows you to envision something and to keep it in your mind's eye. Verbal (auditory) working memory taps into the sound or phonological system (Alloway, 2010; Baddeley, 2006; Meltzer, 2010).

Working Memory Deficits and ADHD

Students with ADHD lag behind their peers significantly in their development of WM and other executive functions. Their WM ability may be a few years behind that of most of their classmates. WM weaknesses are directly related to academic difficulties. A key challenge for students with ADHD is that school work places a heavy demand on WM, often overloading their limited WM capacity. This can result in a host of academic and learning problems. Most common academic problems for students with ADHD are in the areas of reading comprehension, mathematical problem solving, and written composition. These are complex skills requiring high WM demands—being able to hold and mentally juggle large amounts of information throughout the process.

WM weaknesses also affect other areas of functioning, besides learning and academic. For many children with ADHD, their impaired ability to hold events and information in mind (such as rules, past experiences, and consequences) to guide their actions interferes with their behavioral and social success.

Impairments of WM are not exclusive to children and teens with ADHD. Memory weaknesses, for example, also are associated with learning disabilities such as dyslexia. Many children with ADHD with coexisting dyslexia struggle with word identification, reading fluency, and spelling, which also involve WM skills.

Difficulties Associated with Poor Working Memory

Students with poor WM

- Have difficulty following multistep directions
- Lose track of steps taken or where they are in a process
- Often cannot remember instructions for what to do next and may appear noncompliant (but actually forgot what to do)
- Forget to do assigned tasks, chores, and other responsibilities
- Forget to record assignments and bring required materials to and from school
- Forget steps in a process (of academic tasks and classroom procedures)
- Forget to do parts of assignments (incomplete work)
- Forget to turn in homework (even when it is completed)
- Possess poor reading comprehension skills, such as pulling out the main idea, summarizing, making inferences
- Frequently need to reread because of forgetting the information
- Struggle with the whole process of written language (for example, having trouble remembering and expressing ideas effectively in well-organized sentences, paragraphs, and essays; giving incomplete or off-target responses to writing prompts)
- Make numerous errors in writing mechanics (forgetting to use punctuation marks or capitalization)
- Make numerous errors in math computation (having difficulty remembering steps of long division or other algorithms)
- Have poor mental math skills and ability to solve word problems
- Have poor note-taking skills
- Forget what they want to say (and may blurt out or interrupt so as not to lose that thought)
- Frequently misplace and lose items and belongings

Supports and Accommodations for Memory Weaknesses

The primary intervention for supporting individuals with WM weaknesses is to minimize WM demands. Teachers and parents need to be aware of how we present information, give directions, and expect children to perform tasks—making appropriate adjustments to avoid overloading their WM capacity.

Because their internal cognitive space for remembering things is limited (significantly more so than other children or teens their age), use strategies that externalize the information for them. This means placing verbal and visual reminders directly in their immediate environment where they need to use that information. Doing so frees up some of the space needed from their cognitive desktop (WM) in order to more efficiently carry out the expected task or behavior. Support students with poor WM by doing the following:

- Give clear, simple, step-by-step directions.
- After directions are given, have the child repeat the directions to you or someone else, such as a peer partner.
- Provide all directions in verbal and written forms.
- Provide lots of visual and auditory cues and prompts.
- See Sections 3.3 and 3.4 for strategies and supports that teachers and parents can provide to help children and teens with memory weaknesses function better in the areas of organization, time management, and homework.
- Supply and use sticky notes for reminders—place them in strategic locations.
- Use color to highlight important information.
- Provide checklists, task cards, reminders of expectations, and written directions for independent work activities.
- Post and provide visual references to schedules, class and group rules, steps of procedures and routines, and task expectations. Give individual copies as well.

- Model and encourage use of to-do lists and schedules. Prompt children to refer to their list and schedule for what to do next.
- Directly teach, provide time and assistance, and motivate students to use their calendar or planner for recording all assignments, activities, and important events. Getting in the habit of recording information such as assignments and due dates and referring to the planner or calendar consistently are a must for individuals with WM weaknesses.
- Use technology tools to compensate for memory weaknesses, such as recording information and programming reminders on personal electronic devices, using vibrating alarms, and using aids such as spell-checkers and calculators.
- Present information and have students practice it through multiple modalities so that memory is built through multiple pathways. To better remember: read it, type it, say it, write it, hear it, feel it, taste it, smell it, and use some kind of gesture or movement together with it. Any combination using more than one of the senses makes for stronger learning and better recall.
- Look for ways to help students visualize the ideas and information being taught. Images are much more memorable than words. Provide graphic cues. Illustrate while teaching and have students draw illustrations or symbols of some kind to help them remember information.
- Help students recognize and find patterns in what they are trying to remember—for example, identifying letter patterns in words to make spelling easier and noting number patterns on a 1–100 chart or grid.
- Link any new learning to prior knowledge. If we don't connect or process information in some meaningful way, the brain will not store that information.
- Use semantic maps and other graphic organizers for helping students see how information is connected and giving a visual framework that aids memory.

- Provide partial outlines to accompany verbal presentations so as to minimize the amount of note taking required. It is less taxing on WM to take notes when some of the information is already provided in written form.
- Provide frequent practice and review of material and skills, taught in a variety of formats so that different neural networks are activated, which aids memory.
- Give students frequent opportunities to practice and rehearse what they are learning with partners or within cooperative groups. The more they talk about it, the better they remember it.
- Adapt tests to accommodate memory weaknesses, such as by providing word banks for fill-in-the-blank tests.
- Avoid timed tests. Give extra time for recalling and responding.
- Use strategies that minimize the need for students to wait a long time to respond to a question or share what is on their mind— for example, by making frequent use of pair-shares during instruction. Also, provide sticky notes for jotting down thoughts they don't want to lose while waiting to be called on to speak.
- Provide memory aids in literacy, such as anchor charts for reading comprehension and written language, and lists (posted or individual copies) of high-frequency words, commonly misspelled words, examples of different parts of speech and figurative language, synonyms for overly used vocabulary words, and phonics and spelling rules.
- Provide memory aids in math, such as posted or individual copies of multiplication tables, examples of algorithms, and steps for mathematical problem solving; math anchor charts; number lines; and manipulatives.
- Use active reading strategies that involve doing something immediately after reading short amounts of material.
- Allow use of a multiplication grid and calculator during mathematical problem solving.
- Break down all assignments and tasks into a series of shorter parts and steps.

- Give enough practice and rehearsal of procedures so that they become routine. Behaviors that are automatic no longer require use of much WM space.
- Present information in small chunks and have students use it right away. For example, after a few minutes of mini-lecture on a topic, students then work with their partners or small groups, responding in some way to the information.
- Consider the services of an ADHD coach or an educational therapist to help students with WM difficulties keep on target.
- Explore the various technology (apps and tools) to aid in keeping track of things and alleviating some of the burden on memory, some of which were shared in Section 3.3.

Cognitive Working Memory Training (CWMT) Programs

For over a decade, various cognitive (brain) training programs have been developed—designed to improve WM and other cognitive functions. Cogmed (www.cogmed.com) is a well-known cognitive WM training program used by many clinicians and with commercial versions for home and school use. There are also other programs that use video games and interactive exercises that are for improving some cognitive skills, including attention and memory. Activate (c8sciences.com), Play Attention (playattention.com), and Fit Brains (fitbrains.com) are a few.

There have been mixed reviews of the benefit of CWMT in ADHD treatment. According to Schultz and Cook (2014, p. 30), "brain-training research is in its infancy and the results are as yet inconsistent and inconclusive." Rabiner (2014) reviewed some of the newest research on WM training at this time, concluding, "If one's treatment goal is to enhance WM, CWMT may have real value. If the goal is to bring ADHD symptoms under control, however, these findings indicate that for most children with ADHD, CWMT would not currently be considered a reasonable substitute for medication and/or behavior therapy."

Mnemonics

Mnemonics are memory devices or aids that help us remember information by associating it with something familiar. Mnemonics include acronyms, acrostics, keywords, pegwords, and more. Teach children to create first-letter mnemonics (acronyms and acrostics) to help them remember steps in a process or procedure, sequences, or other information.

Examples of Acronyms

- HOMES (the Great Lakes): Huron, Ontario, Michigan, Erie, and Superior
- ROY G. BIV (the seven colors in the spectrum of the rainbow): red, orange, yellow, green, blue, indigo, violet
- SCUBA: self-contained underwater breathing apparatus
- RICE (for how to treat a sprain): rest, ice, compress, elevate

Examples of Acrostics

- **D**ead **M**onsters **S**mell **B**ad (the steps for long division): divide, multiply, subtract, bring down
- **E**very **G**ood **B**oy **D**oes **F**ine (the sequence of lines in the treble clef): E, G, B, D, F
- **P**lease **E**xcuse **M**y **D**ear **A**unt **S**ally (the order for solving algebraic equations): parentheses, exponents, multiplication, division, addition, subtraction. This is also remembered by the acronym PEMDAS.

Many cognitive learning strategies use acronyms and acrostics; examples can be found throughout this book. There are several academic, organization, and study strategies found at the website of James Madison University's Learning Toolbox (http://coe.jmu.edu/learningtoolbox).

Keyword Mnemonics

When students are learning new vocabulary words and their meanings, try using the keyword technique: pair the new word with a similar-sounding word that can be visualized. For example, to learn the word *felons,* which sounds like *melons*

and means "criminals," visualize some melons in prison clothing marching to jail.

Mastropieri and Scruggs (1991) describe three steps in the use of the keyword mnemonic method:

1. Students reconstruct the term to be learned into an acoustically similar, familiar, and easily pictured concrete term.
2. They select a keyword that relates to the new information in an interactive picture, image, or sentence.
3. Students retrieve the appropriate response by thinking of the keyword, recalling the interactive picture and what is happening in the picture, and then stating the information.

For example, to help students remember that a barrister is a lawyer, students create a keyword for the unfamiliar word *barrister.* Then they create a picture of that keyword and definition interacting together—for example, a picture of a bear that is acting as a lawyer in a courtroom, standing in front of a jury (Kleinheksel & Summy, 2003; Mastropieri & Scruggs, 1991).

See Vocabulary Cartoons (www.vocabulary cartoons.com) for books and resources that teach vocabulary words by using this technique of linking word associations that rhyme with visual associations in the form of humorous cartoons. The keyword mnemonic is very helpful in learning vocabulary words in foreign languages as well.

Pegword Mnemonics

To help learn and remember math facts, using pegwords is a helpful mnemonic device. Associate each number from zero to nine with what is called a *pegword*—a rhyming or similar-sounding word that can be visualized concretely (for example, two-shoe, three-tree, four-door, six-sticks), and then make an association for the numbers you are trying to memorize. For example, to learn $6 \times 4 = 24$ or $4 \times 6 = 24$, one can visualize a door (4) with a pile of sticks (6) in front of it, and think: "Every day (24 hours), someone leaves a pile of sticks in front of my door." See the programs Memory Joggers (www.memoryjoggers.com) and Times Tables the Fun Way (www.citycreek.com), which use this technique; this technique is also explained further later in this section.

Use mnemonics for learning and remembering the spelling of tricky words, such as these (Suid, 1981):

Attendance: **At ten** we'll take attendance for the **dance**.

Enormous: A th**ous**and p**ou**nds is an enorm**ous** am**ou**nt.

Rhythm: **R**hythm **h**as **y**our **t**wo **h**ips **m**oving.

For remembering that there is the letter *r* after *b* in *February,* teach the child: "Fe**br**uary is a cold month . . . brrr"; to remember which spelling to use (*principle* or *principal*), the mnemonic of "The princi**pal** is my pal" is helpful.

Creating mnemonics that involve a memorable association or visualization is useful in learning and recalling lots of information, such as state and national capitals. For example, to remember that Springfield is the capital of Illinois, a student might think, "I can't spring out of bed when I'm ill." To remember that Amsterdam is the capital of the Netherlands, a student might think of hamsters running around in Never-Never Land.

Music and Rhyme

Many of us have been amazed at how very young children with limited speaking vocabularies quickly learn the lyrics to lengthy songs. Songs and rhymes are powerful vehicles for learning and remembering information. They are how most of us learned the sequence of the alphabet (ABC song) and the months of the year. As adults, we may still rely on the melody to which we learned the order of US presidents and months of the year to recall the sequence.

- Encourage children to create their own verses with information they want to learn and remember, using familiar melodies such as "Row, Row, Row Your Boat" or "Twinkle, Twinkle, Little Star." This method facilitates memorization and makes learning more fun.

- Sing a list of names, a to-do list, or other items to the melody of a well-known simple song, such as "Happy Birthday to You."
- Use rhymes to help students remember rules (for example, "i before e except after c").
- Raps, rhymes, jingles, and songs help in learning lots of information (for example, steps in a cycle or process, phonics and spelling patterns, the sequence of US presidents, multiplication tables). Some resources that teach through this method can be found on these websites:
  — Songs for Learning (http://songsforlearning.com/)
  — Musically Aligned (www.musicallyaligned.com)
  — Songs for Teaching (www.songsforteaching.com/index.html)
- Many learning songs and videos are found on YouTube, such as the several phonics songs at (www.pinterest.com/sandrarief/phonics-decoding-fluency).

Other Memory Strategies and Tips

- Memory is strengthened by creating meaningful links and associations. Find ways for information that is related to go together, such as by grouping the information into categories.
- Create silly stories that link information (such as a lengthy sequence of items to remember) by associating each item you want to recall with an image or action in the story. Your stories should use vivid imagery, color, and action and be as absurd and exaggerated as possible, which makes them more memorable.
- Chunk information that needs to be remembered into small bites. Long series of numbers, such as Social Security numbers and phone numbers, are chunked for that reason.
- Emotional memory is very strong. When you can evoke an emotion while teaching something, it sticks. Storytelling is a powerful teaching tool because stories evoke emotions in the listener. When something is humorous,

it also evokes emotions that make learning fun and more likely to be remembered.

- To help lock new information into long-term memory, have students do something interactive or reflective with the new learning; for example, talk about it, jot down notes, write an entry in a learning log or journal, draw something related, or fill out a graphic organizer.
- Play memory games, such as these:

    I'm Going on a Trip. One person says, "I'm going on a trip, and in my suitcase, I'm packing a ____." The second person repeats that line and the item the previous person said in correct sequence, then adds a new item at the end of the list. The next person does the same, adding another item. This game gives children practice with attention, memory, and sequencing skills.

    Concentration. Place an array of paired cards facing down and spread out on a table or the floor. When it is each player's turn, he or she turns up any two of the cards, looking for matches. If that player finds a match, he or she takes it; if not, the player turns the cards back over. This game is good for practicing visual memory skills. This can also be done as a study technique. For example, one of the cards in each pair can be a question, and the other is the answer; or you can pair states and their capitals, uppercase and lowercase letters, vocabulary words with their meanings, or the same word in English and Spanish or another language.

- There are a number of games that can be played at home and school, such as those suggested by Teacher Support Force (www.teacher-support-force.com/memory activities.html) and at websites such as Kids Memory (www.kidsmemory.com/) and Play Kids Games (http://www.playkidsgames.com/memoryGames.htm). Learning Works for Kids, https://learningworksforkids.com, is a good source of recommended apps and online games for children and teens with

ADHD. See links to games for enhancing WM skills (such as GeoDash Wild Animal Adventure by National Geographic for Kids) that they suggest.

- Use frequent repetition, practice, and review.
- After instruction, have students list all they remember, in whatever order, as fast as they can.
- Have students review during the last five minutes of the lesson and during the first five minutes of the next lesson.

Multimodal and Memory Techniques for Learning Multiplication Tables

Although there is no longer the need to memorize much information in today's world of technology, students still do need to memorize some things in order to use that information quickly and efficiently when problem solving, reading, or writing. Multiplication tables and words that are irregular in their spelling (not written as they sound), for example, are best memorized. Fluency (being fast and accurate) with basic math facts is important, and by the end of third grade, students are expected to have memorized multiplication facts.

The following is an example of how to teach multiplication facts and multiples of a number (in this example, 4) using a multisensory approach and a variety of techniques, including mnemonics. A combination of some of these strategies and methods are useful in learning and remembering multiplication tables.

Auditory

Teach multiplication tables through music. There are various CDs, MP3s, and apps that use songs for teaching multiplication facts, such as Best Multiplication Songs Ever (Corey Green), Multiplication Rock (Songs of Higher Learning), and Kidwize Multiplication Songs (Kidzup). Multi Rap HD by Rock N'Learn comprises ten separate multiplication iPad apps. Each one has a music video devoted to a times table and a skip-counting video.

Visual and Tactile

Flash Cards

- Use flash cards that students make and color. Triangular flash cards are often best because the same cards can also be used to practice the division fact. For example, there will be a set of triangular flash cards for each of the multiples of four. The numeral 4 will be written on one point of the triangle, and for each of the flash cards, 0 to 9 is written on one of the other points. The product for each is written on the third point. Students practice by covering with their hand each of the points of the triangle while reciting, for example: "4 × 3 = 12; 3 × 4 = 12; 12 ÷ 3 = 4; 12 ÷ 4 = 3."

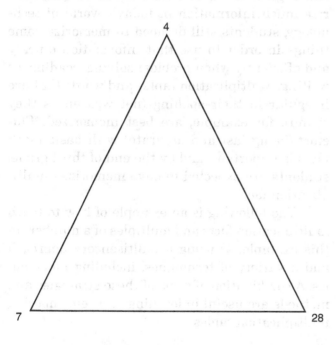

- Make tactile flash cards to trace with the finger. This can be done by writing the math facts in any material that is textured when dry (puff paint, or glue with colored sand or salt sprinkled on top).

Grids and Arrays

- Use graph paper and make grids for each of the multiples of four. Students can write the product in the center of each of the rectangles, as shown in the next column.

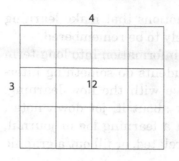

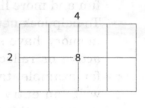

- Have students make a variety of multiplication arrays using tangible objects like dry cereal, beads, or candy. See http://tonyastreatsforteachers.blogspot.com/2012/10/multiplication-table-project-and.html for creating a class array chart.
- Use a number chart or matrix of the numerals 1–100 and have students count by fours—coloring in each box that is a multiple of four. Seeing the visual pattern that is formed on the matrix helps many students who learn best visually and spatially.

Manipulatives

- Have students use interlocking plastic cubes that are combined into groups of four, using a different color for each group. As they stack ten groups of four, have students count by fours. This can be done the same way with plastic links or other objects.

Patterns

- The following is another method that is fun for spatial and visually oriented children. Draw a circle and space the numerals 0 through 9 along its circumference (as shown on page 245). This is a base 10 circle clock. Write a 4 in the center of the circle. Have students write out the multiples of four in sequence (4, 8, 12, 16, 20, 24, 28, 32, 36, 40). Have them begin by putting their pencils on the numeral 4 (4 × 1) on the circle. Draw a straight line from the 4 to the 8 (the next multiple in sequence). From the 8, students draw a straight line to the 2 (which represents 12), and from the 2 to the 6 (which stands for 16), then to the 0 (which represents 20), and continue the pattern. From

0 back to 4 (representing 24), then to 8 (28), to the 2 (32), the 6 (36), and 0 (40). The same digits (4, 8, 2, 6, 0) will be repeated over and over as students continue the sequence (24, 28, 32, 36, 40, 44, 48, and so on). Students love to make these designs. Each of the multiples makes its own unique pattern and design.

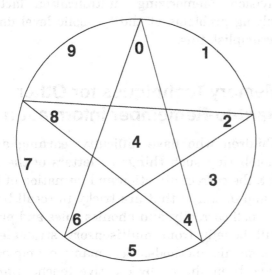

- Give students a blank multiplication chart (matrix of × 0 through × 9 horizontally and × 0 through × 9 vertically). Have them fill in the facts they know and look for patterns and shortcuts. Completing the row of times 0s, times 1s, times 5s, and times 10s is easy, and these can quickly be eliminated from the list of multiplication facts that must be memorized. Once students know and are fluent in multiples of 0 through 5 and are able to recognize and recall the commutative property of multiplication (for example, 3 × 7 = 21, so 7 × 3 = 21), it significantly reduces the stress that there are so many facts to learn. Actually, there will be only nine more facts left to memorize (6 × 6, 6 × 7, 6 × 8, 6 × 9, 7 × 7, 7 × 8, 7 × 9, 8 × 8, 8 × 9).

Writing and Typing

- Have children practice each multiple by filling in the sequence with missing numbers: 4, 8, __, 16, ___, 24, ___, 3_, 36, 40 or typing the sequence several times in different colors.

Tech Games and Programs

- There are several online programs and apps for practicing multiplication tables. Splash Math, Squeebles Times Tables 2, and Tower Math are three of the many apps available.

Other Games and Practice

- Dice games: Play games by rolling a die and multiplying the number on the die by four. Because students can only practice up to 4 × 6 with the use of one die, the same technique can be used by spinning a spinner that has numerals that go higher. An alternative is to have students first roll two dice of the same color together and add the numbers (for example, 6 + 3 = 9), then multiply that sum by 4 (or whatever math fact is being practiced). For a full review and practice of multiplication facts, after adding together the two dice of the same color, they can roll a third die of a different color and multiply those two numbers.

Verbal

It is critical, of course, that students understand the concept of multiplication. They should have many opportunities to make up their own word problems to share with the class. One way to do this is to have students brainstorm as a class and generate a class chart that lists "things that come in fours." From this list (which might include wheels on a wagon, quarts in a gallon, quarters in a dollar, legs on a horse, and suits in a deck of cards), students then make up problems for their classmates to solve. See more on word problems and problem solving in Section 4.6.

Mnemonic (Memory) Devices

Another excellent technique for learning math facts and aiding memorization is by learning a fact through association with a cartoon and story. A few programs mentioned earlier in this section teach math facts this way. One is called Times Tables the Fun Way (www.citycreek.com). An example of one of the facts is a picture of a teen in a vehicle driving up a steep hill. On the door is the fact "4 × 4." The teen is saying, "16! At Last!" The picture has the caption: "Remember: When it's 4 × 4, the fours become a 4 by 4 (4 × 4), and you have to be 16 to drive it."

Another program with a similar method of teaching multiplication facts through associations is called Memory Joggers. The Memory Joggers system (http://memoryjoggers.com) uses numbers and words that rhyme or are shape related in order to stimulate memorization. Each number has a corresponding visual object. For example: 1 sounds like *gum*; it sticks to another number and becomes that number. 2 rhymes with *shoe*. Shoes come in twos (pairs). 8 is Nate the snowman, shaped like the numeral 8 with two circles for the snowman's head and body. 9 is Nina (sounds like "nine-a") the porcupine, and the numeral 9 is embedded in the figure of the porcupine. The program has little stories and associations for each of the multiplication facts to make them memorable.

Semple Math (http://semplemath.com) is another program that incorporates a network of mnemonic cues (images, songs, rhymes, stories, associations) and multisensory methods for teaching math to students with learning difficulties.

Finger tricks and clever mnemonics for learning some of the multiplication tables (multiples of six through nine) are found on YouTube videos including some of the links at https://www.pinterest.com/sandrarief/math-strategies-activities/. *Note:* This Pinterest board has many multiplication activities including games, visuals, arrays, songs, and more.

Conceptual

There are hundreds of hands-on games and activities that can help students understand multiplication at the conceptual level. Students need to see the relationship between multiplication and addition (repeated addition of numbers), and the inverse relationship between multiplication and division. Memorizing multiplication facts and solving problems at the symbolic level does not accomplish this.

Memory Techniques for Other Hard-to-Remember Information

Children who have difficulty learning and remembering such things as letters of the alphabet, the correct direction and formation of letters *b* and *d*, words that are tricky to recall by sight or spell correctly, and phonics rules and patterns will benefit from multisensory strategies and mnemonic methods. See many examples that have been shared by creative teachers and are posted at my Pinterest boards, including these:

https://www.pinterest.com/sandrarief/b-d-tricks-strategies/

https://www.pinterest.com/sandrarief/sight-words/

https://www.pinterest.com/sandrarief/alphabet-letter-sounds/

https://www.pinterest.com/sandrarief/phonics-decoding-fluency/

Part 3 References

Section 3.1

Archer, A. (1997). *Beginning reading: A strategic start.* Santa Rosa, CA: The Sonoma County Office of Special Education and SELPA.

Graser, N. S. (1992). *125 ways to be a better listener.* East Moline, IL: LinguSystems.

Parker, H. (2000). *Listen, look and think—A self-regulation program for children.* Plantation, FL: Impact Publications.

Rotz, R., & Wright, S. (2005). *Fidget to focus.* New York, NY: iUniverse.

Section 3.2

Arney, L. (2015). *Go blended! A handbook for blending technology in schools.* San Francisco, CA: Jossey-Bass.

Ashman, A. F., & Gillies, R. M. (2013). Collaborative learning for diverse learners. *The International Handbook for Collaborative Learning,* 297–313.

Aspire Public Schools. (n.d.). *Blended learning 101: Handbook.* Retrieved from http://www.blend mylearning.com/wp-content/uploads/et_temp/aspire-blended-learning-handbook-2013.pdf

Bailey, J., Schneider, C., & Vander Ark, T. (2013). Navigating the digital shift: Implementation strategies for blended and online learning. Retrieved from http://digitallearningnow.com/site /uploads/2014/05/DLN-ebook-PDF

Bell, L., & Carter, E. W. (2013, May). Peer-mediated support strategies. Retrieved from http://vkc .mc.vanderbilt.edu/ci3t/wp-content/uploads/2013/05/Peer-MediatedStrategies.pdf

Casper, B., & Leuichovius, D. (2005). Universal design for learning and the transition to a more challenging academic curriculum: Making it in middle school and beyond. Retrieved from National Center on Secondary Education and Transition (NCSET) at http://www.ncset.org /publications/viewdesc.asp?id=2165

CAST. (n.d.). About universal design for learning: UDL at a glance (video). Retrieved at http:// www.cast.org/our-work/about-udl.html#.VZVx9aVFCUk

Chapman, C. (2000). *Sail into differentiated instruction.* Thomson, GA: Creative Learning Connection.

Christensen Institute. (n.d.). What is blended learning? Retrieved from http://www.christensen institute.org/blended-learning

Cortiella, C., & Hertog, A. (2012). Parent rights in the era of RTI. Retrieved from http://www.ncld .org/wp-content/uploads/2014/11/NCLD_parent_rights_era_of_rti.pdf

Duty, L., Ellis, S., Martin, N., Mohammed, S., Owens, D., Rabbitt, B., . . . Wolfe, J. (2015). Blended learning implementation guide 3.0. Digital Learning Now Smart Series. Retrieved from http:// digitallearningnow.com/site/uploads/2013/09/BLIG-3.0-FINAL.pdf

Gardner, H. (1983). *Frames of mind: The theory of multiple intelligences.* New York, NY: Basic Books.

IRIS Center for Training Enhancements. (2009). Universal design for learning: Creating a learning environment that challenges and engages all students. Retrieved from http://iris.peabody .vanderbilt.edu/udl/

Johnson, D. W., & Johnson, R. T. (n.d.). Introduction to cooperative learning: An overview of cooperative learning. Retrieved from http://www.co-operation.org/home/introduction -to-cooperative-learning

Johnson, D. W., Johnson, R. T., & Holubec, E. (1990). *Cooperation in the classroom* (7th ed.). Edina, MN: Interaction Book Company.

Johnson, D. W., Johnson, R. T., & Holubec, E. (2008). *Cooperation in the classroom* (8th ed.). Edina, MN: Interaction Book Company.

Kagan, S., & Kagan, M. (2009). *Kagan cooperative learning.* San Clemente, CA: Kagan Publishing.

Kagan, S., Kagan, M., & Kagan, L. (2015). *59 Kagan structures: Proven engagement strategies.* San Clemente, CA: Kagan Publishing.

Learning Accelerator. (2015, May). Blended learning research clearinghouse 1.0. Retrieved from http://learningaccelerator.org/blended-learning

Pettig, K. L. (2000, September). On the road to differentiated practice. *Educational Leadership, 58*(1), 14–18.

Rief, S., & Heimburge, J. A. (2006). *How to reach and teach all children in the inclusive classroom* (2nd ed.). San Francisco, CA: Jossey-Bass.

Rief, S., & Heimburge, J. A. (2007). *How to reach and teach all children through balanced literacy: User-friendly strategies, tools, activities, and ready-to-use materials.* San Francisco, CA: Jossey-Bass.

Rief, S., & Stern, J. M. (2010). *The dyslexia checklist: A practical reference for parents and teachers.* San Francisco, CA: Jossey-Bass.

Tomlinson, C. A. (2000). Reconcilable differences: Standards-based teaching and differentiation. *Educational Leadership, 58*(1), 6–11.

Tomlinson, C. A. (2001). *How to differentiate instruction in mixed-ability classrooms* (2nd ed.). Alexandria, VA: Association for Supervision and Curriculum Development.

Vaughn Gross Center for Reading and Language Arts. (2010). Response to intervention: Intervention handouts. University of Texas System/Texas Education Agency. Retrieved from www.centeroninstruction.org/files/3_Handouts.pdf

Section 3.3

Kutscher, M. L., & Moran, M. (2009). *Organizing the disorganized child: Simple strategies to succeed in school.* New York, NY: Harper Studio.

Section 3.4

Illes, T. (2002). *Positive parenting practices for attention deficit disorder.* Salt Lake City, UT: Jordan School District.

Rief, S., & Heimburge, J. A. (2006). *How to reach and teach all children in the inclusive classroom* (2nd ed.). San Francisco, CA: Jossey-Bass.

Rief, S., & Heimburge, J. A. (2007). *How to reach and teach all children through balanced literacy.* San Francisco, CA: Jossey-Bass.

Success at school: Homework: 3 apps to get homework done faster. (2015). *ADDitude, 16*(1), 50–51.

Section 3.5

Archer, A., & Gleason, M. (1989). *Skills for school success.* North Billerica, MA: Curriculum Associates.

Chamot, A., & O'Malley, J. (1994). *The CALLA handbook: Implementing cognitive academic language learning.* Reading, MA: Addison-Wesley.

Gregory, G. H., & Parry, T. (2006). *Designing brain-compatible learning* (3rd ed.). Thousand Oaks, CA: Corwin Press.

Harris, K., Graham, S., Mason, L., & Friedlander, B. (2008). *Powerful writing strategies for all students.* Baltimore, MD: Paul H. Brookes.

Harris, K. R., & Graham, S. (1992). Self-regulated strategy development: A part of the writing process. In M. Pressley, K. R. Harris, & J. Guthrie (Eds.), *Promoting academic competence and literacy in school* (pp. 277–309). New York, NY: Academic Press.

Hennessy, N. (2003, Winter). Homework hints for parents. *Perspectives, 29*(1), 32–35.

Hennessy, N., & Soper, S. (2003, November 12–15). *Exercising executive function for efficient learning.* Conference session at 54th Annual Conference of the International Dyslexia Association, San Diego, California.

Hoover, J., & Patton, J. (1995). *Teaching students with learning problems to use study skills: A teacher's guide* (pp. 107–109). Austin, TX: PRO-ED.

Krawec, J., & Montague, J. (2012). *Current practice alerts: A focus on cognitive strategy, 19.* Division for Learning Disabilities and the Division for Research. Retrieved from http://s3 .amazonaws.com/cmi-teaching-ld/alerts/21/uploaded_files/original_Alert19.pdf?1331403099

McTighe, J. (1990). *Better thinking and learning.* Baltimore: Maryland State Department of Education.

Polloway, E. A., Patton, J. R., & Serna, L. (2001). *Strategies for teaching learners with special needs* (7th ed.). Upper Saddle River, NJ: Merrill/Prentice-Hall.

Schumaker, J. B., Denton, P., & Deshler, D. D. (1984). *The paraphrasing strategy.* Lawrence: University of Kansas.

Schumaker, J. B., Deshler, D. D., Nolan, S., Clark, F. L., Alley, G. R., & Warner, M. M. (1981). *Error monitoring: A learning strategy for improving academic performance of LD adolescents* (Research Report No. 32). Lawrence: University of Kansas, Institute for Research on Learning Disabilities.

Sousa, D. A. (2011). *How the brain learns* (4th ed.). Thousand Oaks, CA: Corwin Press.

Section 3.6

Alloway, T. P. (2010). *Improving working memory: Supporting students' learning.* Thousand Oaks, CA: Sage.

Baddeley, A. (2006). Working memory: An overview. In S. Pickering (Ed.), *Working memory and education* (pp. 3–26). Boston, MA: Academic Press.

Barkley, R. A. (2013, February). Understanding and improving your child's behavior. *ADDitude* magazine's ADHD Expert Webinar and Podcast series. Webinar archive available at http:// www.additudemag.com/RCLP/sub/10265.html

Cooper-Kahn, J., & Dietzel, L. (2008). *Late, lost, and unprepared: A parent's guide to helping children with executive functioning.* Bethesda, MD: Woodbine House.

Gathercole, S., & Alloway, T. P. (2008). *Working memory and learning: A practical guide for teachers.* Thousand Oaks, CA: Sage.

Katz, M. (2011). Classroom strategies for improving working memory. *Attention, 18*(1), 6–9.

Kaufman, C. (2010). *Executive function in the classroom.* Baltimore, MD: Paul H. Brookes.

Kleinheksel, K., & Summy, S. (2003, November/December). Enhancing student learning and social behavior through mnemonic strategies. *Teaching Exceptional Children, 36*(2), 30–35.

Mastropieri, M. A., & Scruggs, T. E. (1991). *Teaching students ways to remember: Strategies for learning mnemonically.* Cambridge, MA: Brookline Books.

Meltzer, L. (2010). *Promoting executive function in the classroom.* New York, NY: Guilford Press.

Rabiner, D. (2014, March). New research casts doubt on working memory training for ADHD. *Attention Research Update.* Retrieved from www.helpforadd.com/2014/march.htm

Schultz, J., & Cook, P. (2014). Brain fitness programs: Buy? Or buyer beware? *Attention, 21*(5), 28–31.

Suid, M. (1981). *Demonic mnemonics.* Torrance, CA: Fearon Teacher Aids.

Part 3 Additional Sources and Resources

ADDitude magazine (www.additudemag.com). See recommendations for organization and time management devices for children, teens, and adults with ADHD, such as: Timers for ADHD children: ADDitude readers—and their attention deficit children—put three timers to the test. (n.d.) *ADDitude*. Retrieved from www.additudemag.com/adhd/article/6653.2.html

Alloway, T. P. (2015, February). ADHD and working memory. *Attention, 22*(1), 14–17.

Archer, A. L., & Hughes, C. A. (2010). *Explicit instruction: Effective and efficient teaching (What works for special needs learners)*. New York, NY: Guilford Press.

Arney, L. (2012). *Go blended! A handbook for blending technology in schools*. San Francisco, CA: Jossey-Bass.

Ashman, A. F., & Gillies, R. M. (2013). Collaborative learning for diverse learners. In Hmelo-Silver, C. E., Chinn, C. A., Chan, C., & O'Donnell, A. M. (Eds.), *International Handbook of Collaborative Learning* (pp. 297–313). New York, NY: Routledge.

Bell, L., & Carter, E. W. (2013, May). Peer-mediated support strategies. Retrieved from http://vkc .mc.vanderbilt.edu/ci3t/wp-content/uploads/2013/05/Peer-MediatedStrategies.pdf

Bos, C. S., & Vaughn, S. (1994). *Strategies for teaching students with learning and behavior problems*. Boston, MA: Allyn & Bacon.

Carter, C. R. (2011). *Organize your ADD/ADHD child: A practical guide for parents*. London, UK: Jessica Kingsley.

Carter, E. W. (2008). *Peer buddy programs for successful secondary school inclusion*. Baltimore, MD: Paul H. Brookes.

Carter, E. W., Cushing, L. S., & Kennedy, C. H. (2009). *Peer support strategies: Improving all students' social lives and learning*. Baltimore, MD: Paul H. Brookes.

Center on Instruction. Online free self-paced course: Intensive interventions for students struggling in reading and mathematics (http://centeroninstruction.org/online-course-intensive -interventions-for-students-struggling-in-reading-and-mathematics)

Dawson, P., & Guare, R. (2011). *Smart but scattered: The revolutionary "executive skills" approach to helping kids reach their potential*. New York, NY: Guilford Press.

Dendy, C.A.Z. (2011). *Teaching teens with ADD, ADHD & executive function deficits* (2nd ed.). Bethesda, MD: Woodbine House.

Drapeau, P. (2004). *Differentiated instruction: Making it work*. New York, NY: Scholastic Teaching Resources.

Ellis, E. (1991). *SLANT: A starter strategy for participation*. Lawrence, KS: Edge Enterprises.

Feber, J. (2013). *Student engagement is FUNdamental: Building a learning community with hands-on activities*. North Mankato, MN: Maupin House.

Fetzer, N. (2011). Lecture notes strategy [four-part video, free online]. Retrieved at www .nancyfetzer.com

Fox, J., & Hoffman, W. (2011). *The differentiated instruction book of lists*. San Francisco, CA: Jossey-Bass.

Frazier, N., Mehle, D., & Davidson, J. (2013). *Activators: Classroom strategies for engaging middle and high school students*. Cambridge, MA: Engaging Schools (formally Educators for Social Responsibility).

Gallagher, R., Abikoff, H. B., & Spira, E. G. (2014). *Organizational skills training for children with ADHD: An empirically supported treatment*. New York, NY: Guilford Press.

Gardner, H. (2008). *Multiple intelligences: New horizons in theory and practice*. New York, NY: Basic Books.

Gardner, H., & Blythe, T. (1990). A school for all intelligences. *Educational Leadership, 47,* 33–37.

Goldberg, D., with Zwiebel, J. (2005). *The organized student: Teaching children the skills for success in school and beyond.* New York, NY: Fireside.

Grauvogel-MacAleese, A. N., & Wallace, M. D. (2010). Use of peer-mediated intervention in children with attention deficit hyperactivity disorder. *Journal of Applied Behavior Analysis, 43,* 547–551.

Harmin, M. (2007). *Inspiring active learning: A complete handbook for today's teachers* (2nd expanded ed.). Alexandria, VA: Association for Supervision and Curriculum Development.

Harris, B. (2010). *Battling boredom: 99 strategies to spark student engagement.* New York, NY: Routledge.

Harris, K. I., Pretti-Frontczak, K., & Brown, T. (2009, March). *Peer-mediated intervention: An effective inclusive strategy for all young children.* National Association for the Education of Young Children. Retrieved at www.pakeys.org/uploadedContent/Docs/Higher%20Ed/2011%20 Conference/P%20Harris-Kathleen%20Building%20A%20Learning%20Community%20 Handouts.pdf

Hennessy, N. (2003, Winter). Homework hints for parents. *Perspectives 29*(1), 32–35.

Heward, W., Gardner, R., Cavanaugh, R., Courson, F., Grossi, T., & Barbetta, P. (1996, Winter). Everyone participates in this class. *Teaching Exceptional Children, 28*(2), 4–9.

Himmele, P., & Himmele, W. (2011). *Total participation techniques: Making every student an active learner.* Alexandria, VA: Association for Supervision and Curriculum Development.

Hughes, C., & Jigsaw Classroom, at http://www.jigsaw.org/. This is the website of Elliot Aronson, developer of the Jigsaw cooperative learning technique.

IRIS Center. (n.d.). PALS: A reading strategy for grades K–1. Module outline. Retrieved from the IRIS Center Peabody College Vanderbilt University at http://iris.peabody.vanderbilt.edu /palsk1/palsK1_01.html

Jensen, E. (2005). *Teaching with the brain in mind* (rev. 2nd ed.). Alexandria, VA: Association for Supervision and Curriculum Development.

Jenson, W. R., Bowen, J., Clark, E., Block, H., Gabrielson, T., Hood, J., . . . Radley, K. (n.d.). *Superheroes social skills: A multimedia program.* Eugene, OR: Pacific Northwest Publishing.

Johnson, D. W. (2009). *Reaching out: Individual effectiveness and self-actualization* (10th ed.). Boston, MA: Allyn & Bacon.

Juarez, B., Parks, S., & Black, H. (2000). *Learning on purpose: A self-management approach to study skills.* Pacific Grove, CA: Critical Thinking Books and Software.

Kagan Online, http://www.kaganonline.com/free_articles/research_and_rationale/

Kardamis, L. (2014, May). Seven review games that won't waste your time. Retrieved from Teach4the Heart at http://teach4theheart.com/2014/05/15/7-review-games-that-wont-waste-your-time

Klatz, M. B. (2006). Response to intervention (RTI): A primer for parents. National Association for School Psychologists. Retrieved from www.nasponline.org/resources/factsheets/rtiprimer.aspx

Kulman, R. (2013, November) *Five ways to boost working memory and improve math skills.* Retrieved at https://learningworksforkids.com/2013/11/5-ways-working-memory-improves-math-skills/

Kulman, R. (2015). Brain training: 10 programs to check out. *ADDitude, 16*(1), 37–38.

Kulman, R. (2015, January). *Five more ways to improve math and working memory.* Retrieved at https://learningworksforkids.com/2015/01/5-ways-improve-math-working-memory/

Learning Works for Kids. 10 apps to improve ADHD attention span, memory, and time management. Retrieved from https://learningworksforkids.com/2014/10/apps-to-improve-adhd -attention-span-memory-and-time-management/

Livingston, J. A. (1997). Metacognition: An overview. Graduate School of Education, State University of New York at Buffalo. Retrieved from http://gse.buffalo.edu/fas/shuell/cep564 /metacog.htm

Martín, J. L. (n.d.). Legal implications of response to intervention and special education identification. RTI Action Network. Retrieved from www.rtinetwork.org/learn/ld/legal -implications-of-response-to-intervention-and-special-education-identification

Marzano, R. J., Pickering, D. J., & Heflebower, T (2010). *The highly engaged classroom.* Centennial, CO: Marzano Research Laboratory.

McMaster, K. L., Fuchs, D., & Fuchs, L. S. (2006). Research on peer-assisted learning strategies: The promise and limitations of peer-mediated instruction. *Reading & Writing Quarterly, 22*, 5–25.

Meyer, A., Rose, D. H., & Gordon, D. (2014). *Universal design for learning: Theory and practice.* Wakefield, MA: CAST Professional Publishing.

Murray, C. S., Coleman, M. A., Vaughn, S., Wanzek, J., & Roberts, G. (2012). *Designing and delivering intensive interventions: A teacher's toolkit.* Portsmouth, NH: RMC Research Corporation, Center on Instruction. Retrieved from www.centeroninstruction.org /designing-and-delivering-intensive-interventions-a-teachers-toolkit

Nunley, K., http://help4teachers.com/. See Dr. Kathie Nunley's website for numerous resources and sample layered (or tiered) curriculum units across grades and subjects.

PALS (reading and math peer-assisted learning strategies) programs. Vanderbilt Kennedy Center for Research on Human Development. Retrieved from http://kc.vanderbilt.edu/pals

Power, T. J., & Karustis, J. L. (2001). *Homework success for children with ADHD: A family-school intervention program.* New York, NY: Guilford Press.

Ratey, N. A. (2008). *The disorganized mind: Coaching your ADHD brain to take control of your time, tasks, and talents.* New York, NY: St. Martin's Griffin.

Rief, S. (2008). *The ADD/ADHD checklist: A practical reference for parents and teachers* (2nd ed.). San Francisco, CA: Jossey-Bass.

Rief, S. (2015). *The ADHD book of lists: A practical guide for helping children and teens with attention deficit disorders* (2nd ed.). San Francisco, CA: Jossey-Bass.

Rief, S. (2016). *Executive function: Skill-building and support strategies for the elementary classroom* [6-page laminated guide]. Naples, FL: Dude Publishing (an imprint of National Professional Resources).

Rief, S. (2016). *Executive function: Skill-building and support strategies for grades 6–12* [6-page laminated guide]. Naples, FL: Dude Publishing (an imprint of National Professional Resources).

Rutherford, P. (2012). *Active learning and engagement strategies: Teaching and learning in the 21st century.* Alexandria, VA: Just ASK Publications & Professional Development.

Sousa, D. A. (2011). *How the brain learns* (4th ed.). Thousand Oaks, CA: Corwin Press.

Staker, H. (2011). The rise of K–12 blended learning: Profiles of emerging models. Retrieved from http://www.innosightinstitute.org/innosight/wp-content/uploads/2011/05/The-Rise-of-K–12 -Blended-Learning.pdf

Stuart, A. What is working memory and why does it matter? Retrieved from www.ncld.org /types-learning-disabilities/executive-function-disorders/what-is-working-memory-why-does -matter/

Texas Education Agency. (2014). *The dyslexia handbook: Procedures concerning dyslexia and related disorders.* Retrieved from Vaughn Gross Center for Reading and Language Arts http:// www.region10.org/r10website/assets/File/DHBwithouttabs10214.pdf

Tomlinson, C. A. (n.d.). What is differentiated instruction? Retrieved from www.readingrockets .org/article/263

Tomlinson, C. A. (2014). *A differentiated approach to the Common Core: How do I help a broad range of learners succeed with a challenging curriculum?* Alexandria, VA: Association for Supervision and Curriculum Development.

Tomlinson, C. A. (2014). *The differentiated classroom: Responding to the needs of all learners* (2nd ed.). Alexandria, VA: Association for Supervision and Curriculum Development.

Tomlinson, C. A., & Moon, T. R. (2013). *Assessment and student success in a differentiated classroom.* Alexandria, VA: Association for Supervision and Curriculum Development.

Tucker, C. R. (2012). *Blended learning in grades 4–12: Leveraging the power of technology to create student-centered classrooms.* Thousand Oaks, CA: Corwin.

Universal Design (from University of Washington). (2012). Academic accommodations for students with learning disabilities. Washington DO-IT. Retrieved from www.washington.edu/doit /Brochures/Academics/accomm_ld.html

Vander Ark, K. (2013, September). 125 top blogs on blended learning. Retrieved from http://gettingsmart.com/2013/09/120-top-articles-on-blended-learning/

Vanderbilt University. (2013, May). Peer-mediated support strategies. Retrieved from http://vkc.mc.vanderbilt.edu/ci3t/wp-content/uploads/2013/05/Peer-MediatedStrategies.pdf

Vaughn Gross Center for Reading and Language Arts. (2010). Response to intervention: Intervention handouts. University of Texas System/Texas Education Agency. Retrieved from www.centeroninstruction.org/files/3_Handouts.pdf

Wallace, M. D. (2010). Use of peer-mediated intervention in children with attention deficit hyperactivity disorder. *Journal of Applied Behavior Analysis, 43,* 547–551.

Warger, C. (2001, March). Five homework strategies for teaching students with disabilities. Retrieved from www.ldonline.org/ld_indepth/teaching_techniques/five_homework_strategies.htl

Wolfe, P. (2010). *Brain matters: Translating research into classroom practice* (2nd ed.). Alexandria, VA: Association for Supervision and Curriculum Development.

Zentall, S., & Goldstein, S. (1998). *Seven steps to homework success: A family guide to solving homework problems.* Plantation, FL: Specialty Press.

Websites

American Institutes for Research: Access Center, http://www.k8accesscenter.org/training_resources

Blended Learning Now, www.blendedlearningnow.com

BJ Pinchbeck's Homework Helper, http://bjpinchbeck.com/

Center for Applied Special Technology (CAST), www.cast.org

Center on Instruction, www.centeroninstruction.org

Center on Response to Intervention at American Institutes for Research, www.rti4success.org/

Digital Learning Now, www.digitallearningnow.com

Homework Now, http://www.homeworknow.com/

Homework Planet, http://homeworkplanet.com

Homework Spot, http://www.homeworkspot.com/

Homeworkopoly game, http://teachnet.com/manage/classroom-decor/get-work-done-by-playing-homeworkopoly/

Infoplease Homework Center, http://www.infoplease.com/homework/

IRIS Center Peabody College Vanderbilt University, http://iris.peabody.vanderbilt.edu/

Learning Toolbox, James Madison University Special Education Program's website of learning strategies designed for middle and secondary students with ADHD and LDs, http://coe.jmu.edu/learningtoolbox

National Center on Accessible Instructional Materials, http://aem.cast.org/

National Center on Universal Design for Learning, www.udlcenter.org

Pinterest. See many organization and time management tools and ideas from Pinterest users at www.pinterest.com/sandrarief/class-organization-time-mgmt/ and www.pinterest.com/sandrarief/time-management/

Pinterest links on PBIS, www.pinterest.com/sandrarief/pbis-schoolwide-positive-behavior-support/

Pinterest links on RTI, www.pinterest.com/sandrarief/response-to-intervention-rti/

Positive Behavioral Interventions and Supports. US Department of Education's Office of Special Education Programs (OSEP) Technical Assistance Center on PBIS, www.pbis.org

Ref Desk Homework Helper, http://www.refdesk.com/homework.html

RTI Action Network, www.rtinetwork.org

RTI Central, www.rtictrl.org

RTI Classification Tool and Resource Locator (RTI CTRL), www.rtictrl.org

Vaughn Gross Center for Reading and Language Arts and Meadows Center for Preventing Educational Risk. See the Meadows Center's materials library at http://www.meadowscenter.org/library/

part
4

Strategies and Supports for Reading, Writing, and Math

Section 4.1: Common Reading and Writing Difficulties

Section 4.2: Decoding, Fluency, and Vocabulary

Section 4.3: Reading Comprehension

Section 4.4: Writing: Strategies, Supports, and Accommodations

Section 4.5: Spelling and Handwriting

Section 4.6: Mathematics

Common Reading and Writing Difficulties

The Reading Process: What Good Readers Do

Reading is a complex process with the goal of acquiring meaning from the printed word. Good readers are adept at the following:

- Decoding and recognizing words at a rate that enables them to read with fluency and automaticity

- Using all cueing systems (semantic, syntactic, and graphophonic) to figure out unfamiliar words or language
- Understanding and figuring out challenging vocabulary and word meanings
- Knowing how to read for specific purposes
- Using whatever background or prior knowledge they have about the subject to make inferences and derive meaning from what they are reading

DECKER FORREST

- Making connections as they read to other material previously read, to their own life and experiences, and to other information and concepts they know ("This reminds me of . . .")
- Reflecting as they read
- Using effective metacognitive strategies to think about what they are reading and self-monitoring their comprehension and understanding using self-correcting (fix-up) strategies when they realize they are not getting meaning or making sense of what is being read
- Constantly thinking ahead, predicting, and either confirming or changing their predictions as they read
- Self-monitoring the amount of attention and effort required when reading; being aware of which parts can be read quickly by skimming and scanning and which parts require close attention, concentration, and perhaps rereading a few times for better recall and comprehension
- Understanding the organization and structure of different types of text (literary and expository)
  — Understanding story structure and the organization of literary text (characters, setting, problem, action, resolution to problem)
  — Understanding the structures or schemas for various kinds of expository (nonfiction) text and how to use text features and organizational and graphic aids (such as the glossary, index, table of contents, charts, graphs, headings and subheadings, graphs and diagrams) to aid comprehension
- Visualizing when they are reading (scenes, characters) and making mental images
- Distinguishing main ideas and important information from details and less important information in the text
- Critically evaluating what they are reading in whatever format it is presented (printed or digital)
- Engaging in many kinds of thinking processes while reading (such as questioning, analyzing, synthesizing, interpreting, evaluating, and reflecting)
- Focusing on the main content rather than extraneous information
- Recognizing and understanding text structures, such as cause-and-effect, problem-and-solution, and compare-and-contrast relationships
- Making inferences (reading between the lines) based on clues in the text using schema—what they already know, connections they have made, and the process of predicting and confirming
- Finding evidence in the text to support their opinions
- Knowing which strategies to use for various reading tasks and types of material
- Being able to flexibly apply and monitor a variety of effective strategies in the process of actively reading for meaning

In addition, good readers do the following:

- Self-select books of personal interest and find pleasure in reading books and other choice reading materials
- Read from a variety of fiction and nonfiction genres (such as historical fiction, biographies, fables, memoirs) and critically evaluate what they are reading in whatever format it is presented (printed or digital)

Coexisting Learning Disabilities

- Roughly 25 to 50 percent of children with ADHD also have specific learning disabilities, and reading disorders are the most common.
- According to Barkley (2013), up to 35 percent of school-age children with ADHD are likely to have a reading disorder.
- Learning disabilities are neurobiologically based problems with processing information that affect one or more processes of input (taking in), integration (organizing, sequencing, remembering), and output (expression) of the information.
- The most common of the learning disabilities is *dyslexia,* which refers to a language-based learning disability in basic reading skills

and spelling. The problems of children with dyslexia most commonly stem from difficulty in processing speech sounds within words (phonological awareness) and making the connection between sounds and the written symbols—letters and patterns of letter combinations (graphemes) that represent sounds in words.

Definition of Dyslexia

The International Dyslexia Association (2013) defines dyslexia as a specific learning disability that is neurobiological in origin. It is characterized by difficulties with accurate and/or fluent word recognition and by poor spelling and decoding abilities. These difficulties typically result from a deficit in the phonological component of language that is often unexpected in relation to other cognitive abilities and the provision of effective classroom instruction. Secondary consequences may include problems in reading comprehension and reduced reading experience that can impede growth of vocabulary and background knowledge (p. 3).

Some signs of dyslexia (Rief & Stern, 2010) include the following:

- Poor phonemic awareness and phonological processing (noticing, thinking about, and working with or manipulating the individual sounds in words). Difficulties may include rhyming; identifying the beginning, middle, and ending sounds in words they hear; and recognizing, blending, and separating individual sounds within words.
- Difficulty learning the alphabet and letter-sound correspondence.
- Poor decoding skills—the ability to learn and apply phonics skills and sound out individual words.
- Poor reading fluency—very slow, labored, and choppy; difficulty reading aloud with ease, speed, and expression.
- Many inaccuracies (adding or deleting letters, sounds, or syllables from words, skipping words or lines of text when reading).
- Sequencing errors (reading words with sounds out of order, such as "aminal" instead of "animal"; missequencing letters or

syllables in a word when spelling, such as "gril" for "girl"; or confusing the order of events when summarizing a story or trying to recall the beginning, middle, and end).
- Difficulty recognizing and remembering common sight words, such as *said, from,* and *they*; may approach these as new words each time they are seen.
- Poor reading comprehension.
- Difficulty remembering what was read.
- Very poor spelling and difficulty learning spelling strategies.

If a child is exhibiting signs of dyslexia, it is important that he or she be evaluated and receive the research-validated interventions that are known to be most effective in building deficient reading skills. See the Part 4 Additional Sources and Resources for more information on dyslexia and learning disabilities.

Instruction for Students with Dyslexia

Students with reading disabilities who struggle with word recognition and decoding need intensive, systematic instruction in language skills. Most research-validated programs for teaching decoding skills and the recommended intervention programs for children with dyslexia, whether provided at school or privately, use curriculum that is based on Orton-Gillingham methodology. The instructional approach of these programs is as follows:

Direct and explicit. Each skill, rule of language, and strategy for reading and spelling words must be taught clearly and directly, without assuming that the student has even the most basic foundational skills or background knowledge of the English written language.

Systematic and structured. Students with dyslexia typically have gaps in their understanding of how the English written language system works. They need to be taught a systematic scope and sequence (coverage and organization) of skills, starting at a beginning level to ensure mastery of foundational skills and to fill in holes in a student's repertoire of skills.

Cumulative. Each lesson and skill taught is cumulative—gradually building on previously taught skills or concepts as students are moved along step-by-step, at an appropriate individual pace.

Multisensory. Regardless of the program used, teaching children with dyslexia requires the use of multisensory techniques, which make learning more memorable. Students with dyslexia usually learn best when instruction incorporates some combination of auditory, visual, and tactile-kinesthetic input.

In addition, students with dyslexia need a greater intensity of instruction than is needed for students without learning problems:

- Sufficient time provided for direct skill and strategy instruction
- Numerous practice opportunities with immediate corrective feedback and reinforcement
- Instruction provided either one-on-one or in small groups of students of the same skill level
- Ongoing assessment and careful monitoring of progress

Note: See the International Dyslexia Association (IDA) Knowledge and Practice Standards at http://eida.org/knowledge-and-practices—defining what all teachers of reading need to know and be able to do to teach all students to read proficiently.

Tips for Parents: If You Suspect Your Child Has a Reading Disability

- As is true of ADHD, dyslexia is a brain-based disorder. Both disorders commonly coexist. The treatment for dyslexia is instructional—providing reading training by a trained professional using a multisensory structured language program with the appropriate degree of intensity to achieve results. We know the research-based instructional approaches that actually retrain the brain and strengthen the neural connections involved in reading—helping dyslexics learn to read and spell.
- If your child has signs and symptoms of dyslexia, do not wait to see if your child improves with time and maturity. Waiting to intervene does not benefit a child.
- Early identification and intervention (that is, when a child is in preschool through second grade) are most effective in preventing reading problems. Research shows that with appropriate early intervention, most children who are at-risk readers can overcome many of their difficulties and increase their reading skills to an average level.
- Regardless of your child's age, diagnosing a reading disability and intervention are very important and are never too late. However, remediation is more difficult as a person gets older and must be more intensive in order to overcome years of reading failure.
- Discuss concerns with your child's teacher. Ask the teacher or the principal, special education teacher, reading specialist, school psychologist, or speech-language therapist about screening or assessment for dyslexia and reading disabilities. Be relentless if the school district is suggesting a wait-and-see approach.
- Some states have enacted dyslexia laws, and school districts have protocols for specifically screening and evaluating students who are at risk of or show signs of dyslexia. Students identified as having dyslexia are provided specialized interventions by qualified professionals, using research-based dyslexia instructional programs and best practices. Check if your school district has dyslexia screening and intervention.
- Become familiar with the information in Part 6 on educational rights and laws as well as with the system or structure that may be in place at your child's school for providing and monitoring targeted intervention programs for students in need.

- In general, intervention programs for children with dyslexia use a multisensory-structured language approach, what is often referred to as Orton-Gillingham-based programs. A few of these programs include Barton Reading and Spelling System (www.bartonreading.com), Orton-Gillingham (www.orton-gillingham.com), Project Read Language Circle (www.project-read.com), Wilson Fundations (www.fundations.com), Wilson Reading (www.wilsonlanguage.com), Slingerland (www.slingerland.org), and Sounds in Syllables (http://www.mlti-nm.com/sounds-in-syllables.html).

Common Reading Errors and Weaknesses in Students with ADHD

Many individuals with ADHD do not have coexisting dyslexia or a reading disorder per se. They may have strong reading aptitude and read high-level text fluently, yet often do have some reading challenges (errors, inconsistencies, and spotty comprehension) that are directly related to their ADHD and executive function impairments.

Research shows that reading comprehension is strongly dependent on the quality of students' self-directed cognitive abilities—his or her executive functions (Gaskin, Satlow, & Pressley, 2007; Kaufman, 2010).

Inattention-Related Reading Errors and Difficulties

- Students can be drawn off task while reading and therefore miss words and important details.
- People cannot remember what has been read if they haven't paid attention to what they were reading—affecting recall and comprehension of the text.
- Maintaining attention and focusing on what they are reading, particularly when reading silently or if there are distractions in the environment, can be a challenge for students with ADHD.
- When students' attention drifts, so do their eyes from the page, and they lose their place when reading.
- Inattention may cause students to not notice and omit parts of a word, the whole word, or even whole lines of text when reading.
- Students may have trouble paying attention to stories and other texts that are read out loud in class. When one person is reading orally, students with ADHD commonly have a hard time following along with the rest of the class. They are frequently on the wrong page of the book and especially struggle to follow if the reader lacks fluency and expression.
- "[Students] may be unable to sustain attention with sufficient consistency to learn letter names and/or letter-sound correspondences, resulting in an incomplete or erratic knowledge of phonics, even though the language processing skills are otherwise intact" (Kaufman, 2010, p. 98). They may also not notice all the parts of the word they are reading (such as word endings) and omit words or parts of words.

Impulsivity-Related Reading Errors and Difficulties

- Children with ADHD may tend to guess at unfamiliar words without taking the time to decode them (even though they have strong decoding skills) or to read words by looking at only part of the word, resulting in inaccuracies.
- Impulsive students may respond to teacher questions about the reading material too quickly—before fully thinking about the question and forming a thoughtful answer.

Working Memory–Related Errors and Difficulties

- Working memory (WM) plays a very significant role in reading, and limited WM capacity can cause problems with decoding accurately, reading with fluency, recall, and comprehension of the text.

- Reading multisyllable words requires keeping part of the word (one syllable) in mind while decoding or sounding out the next syllable. Some decoding difficulties may result from WM issues (Kaufman, 2010; Levine, 1998).
- Children who can read fluently in an automatic manner are freed from having to devote much WM to the decoding process. Those who are slow, laborious readers use so much WM to decode the words that they have little WM capacity left for the act of comprehension (Kaufman, 2010; Samuels, 2006).
- Students with poor WM often forget the content of what they have read from one paragraph or page to the next. People with ADHD frequently need to reread the material numerous times for it to sink in.
- Poor WM results in limited recall of the reading material. This affects the ability to summarize, retell accurately, and respond to reading comprehension questions.
- Kaufman (2010, p. 103) shares Dr. Mel Levine's analogy (2002): WM is the cognitive stewpot in which new information is mixed with prior knowledge to allow comprehension to occur. Some students have small or "leaky" WM systems that are unable to contain the various bits and pieces of information needed for comprehension to occur.

Metacognition-Related Errors and Difficulties

- This refers to a person's ability to think about his or her own thinking, learning, and understanding. Reading comprehension requires the ability to self-monitor while reading—to be aware of and know when the text is making sense or not.
- Students with ADHD often read passively and superficially, going through the motions but not fully engaged and actively thinking about what they are reading.
- When noticing that what they have read does not make sense, good readers then apply fix-up strategies in order to repair their comprehension and gain meaning from the text. Children with ADHD often do not do so.

- Poor metacognition affects the ability to read critically and deeply—to derive the most meaning from the text.

Other Executive Function–Related Difficulties

- Students with ADHD may have difficulty with initiation—or getting started on and keeping up the level of effort and motivation necessary to complete reading assignments (particularly material that is dry, lengthy, and tedious to read).
- Cognitive flexibility may be an issue, causing students to have difficulty using flexible strategies—for example, to decode unfamiliar words—or applying strategies to aid their reading comprehension.
- When reading, students may not be using their internal language and self-talk to be actively engaged in the text—for example, by asking themselves such questions as these:
  — "What is the main idea?"
  — "What is the author trying to say in this paragraph?"
  — "What does this remind me of?" (making connections, reflecting as they read)
  — "What do I predict is going to happen next?"

Processing Speed–Related Errors and Difficulties

Some children and teens with ADHD (particularly those with the inattentive presentation) and learning disabilities often have slower processing speed. This has nothing to do with intelligence. It is not that someone with this problem is a "slow learner" but that he or she processes information at a slower speed, which may cause difficulties with the following:

- Automatic word recognition and reading fluency
- Keeping up with the pace of instruction
- Responding quickly to teacher questions and following along in class discussions
- Word retrieval—pulling up from memory the precise words one wants to use when speaking or writing

turning prewriting plans into a viable first draft. Some children are also immobilized when ideas don't flow or they don't know how to spell a certain word.

Revise Once an initial draft is completed, good writers understand that a number of changes will be needed before a writing project is in its final form. Revising requires the ability to self-monitor one's work, reread it carefully, and identify ways to improve it (flow and sequence, language usage, clarity, and other aspects). These are difficult tasks for children and teens with ADHD or learning disabilities. When writing is a struggle and a first draft has finally been produced, these students often resist making revisions and want to submit their initial draft.

Edit Editing is the proofreading stage of writing. Noticing and identifying grammatical, spelling, and mechanical (capitalization and punctuation) errors and then fixing them are tedious tasks requiring attention to detail and close self-monitoring. It is unrealistic to expect students with ADHD or learning disabilities to edit their work without help (such as adult or peer editing or use of assistive technology).

Publish The last stage of the writing process is completing and sharing the final product. When a student feels proud of a piece of writing and shares it, this part of the process is rewarding.

Steps of the Writing Process and Potential Problems

Prewrite This very important step of the writing process is when planning and organization take place—before beginning the actual writing. This initial stage is where students with ADHD often get stuck; many of them have difficulty analyzing the task, brainstorming and gathering ideas and information, deciding what to write about and narrowing down a topic, and organizing and sequencing ideas and information.

Draft Writing a draft involves turning ideas from the planning stage into written sentences, adding details, and elaborating. This is the composition stage, which can be very difficult for students with ADHD and learning disabilities. For these writers, weaknesses in WM and retrieval, language usage, and self-monitoring (or metacognitive awareness), and slow processing or production speed can impair their efficiency in

Why Writing Is a Struggle

Written language is the most common area of academic weakness in children and teens with ADHD because the process is complex and places a very high demand on executive functions. These students are often verbal and knowledgeable, but struggle to show what they know on paper, and for many students with ADHD or learning disabilities (LDs), the act of writing is tedious, overwhelming, and aversive.

Producing a writing assignment requires the integration and often simultaneous use of numerous skills and brain processes, many of which are areas of significant weakness for them, including the following.

Planning and Organization

Prewriting steps are where students with ADHD often have the most difficulty:

- Focusing and taking the time to first think carefully about what one wants to communicate, and planning and mapping out what and how to write it before actually beginning to write
- Organizing one's thoughts, prioritizing ideas, and thinking through components needed (beginning, middle, and end; main ideas and supporting details)
- Awareness and knowledge of the specific organizational structure for different types of writing (for example, persuasive essays, response to literature, narrative account)
- Organizational preparation for the task (materials, resources)

Attention and Inhibition

Self-management issues frequently interfere with writing effectively:

- Resisting distractions, staying focused, and sustaining attention through the difficult task of written composition
- Attention to and awareness of all the components of the writing task assigned
- Focus and attention to details to avoid errors in spelling, capitalization, and punctuation
- Self-control—waiting . . . not jumping in and writing before hearing all of the instructions, analyzing the writing prompt, or taking the time to plan before beginning

Working Memory and Retrieval

WM is necessary in order to hold on to and juggle the many different thoughts the writer wants to express while manipulating those ideas and transcribing simultaneously onto paper. Writing involves these skills:

- Holding on to the big ideas as well as the supporting details while constructing a written piece
- Remembering the goal and purpose of the writing assignment, the structure of the writing genre, and the intended audience
- Keeping in mind the language choices and mechanics (vocabulary, grammar, sentence structure, spelling, punctuation) and sequencing of ideas while recording ideas in written format
- Maintaining focus on the train of thought so that the flow of the writing will not veer off course

The process of writing also requires the retrieval of information from long-term memory, such as facts and experiences and other prior knowledge, and recall of vocabulary words, spelling, rules of grammar, and mechanics (capitalization and punctuation).

Shifting and Cognitive Flexibility

Writing requires being able to constantly shift back and forth between the big picture (major themes) and the relevant details to meet the demands of the writing task (Meltzer, 2010). As writers are constructing and transcribing what they want to communicate, they flexibly make revisions as they write (such as changing wording and moving ideas around).

Self-Monitoring

Fluent writing and successful completion of writing assignments require the following self-monitoring skills:

- Awareness of the writing assignment requirements, how much time one has for completing the assignment, what resources or information needs to be obtained for doing so, and other such information
- Keeping the intended audience in mind and writing to that audience with a clear purpose

- Following and referring back to the specific structure of the writing genre to make sure that the parts of the organizational structure (for example, for a five-paragraph essay) are all included
- Knowing how to read one's own work critically in order to make revisions and develop ideas
- Checking one's work to see that teacher expectations and performance standards are being met

Speed of Written Output and Production

Some students with ADHD rush through writing assignments, producing illegible work with many careless errors. Others with ADHD write excruciatingly slowly. Although they know the answers and can verbally express their thoughts and ideas articulately, they are unable to put more than a few words or sentences down on paper. Needless to say, this is extremely frustrating. Part of the problem with speed of output may be due to the following issues:

- Impulsivity
- Difficulty sustaining attention to task
- Difficulty maintaining the mental energy required in written expression
- Graphomotor dysfunction
- Slow processing speed
- Just wanting to be done with a very tedious and difficult task

Language

Writing requires the ability to do the following:

- Express thoughts in a logical, fluid, and coherent manner
- Use the most precise vocabulary and word knowledge to express oneself and communicate to the reader effectively

- Use figurative language (such as similes and metaphors) and descriptive, colorful vocabulary to make the piece of writing more interesting
- Use proper grammar and sentence structure

Graphomotor Skills

Many children with ADHD or LDs have impairments in graphomotor skills (and have *dysgraphia*), which affect the physical task of writing (handwriting) and organization of print on the page. They often have trouble with the following:

- Writing neatly on or within the given lines
- Spacing and organizing their writing on the page
- Copying from the board or book onto paper
- Using fine motor skills, causing the act of handwriting to be very inefficient, fatiguing, and frustrating; it can affect, for example, pencil grip, pressure exerted, and legibility
- Executing print or cursive or typing with precision or speed

Spelling

Children with ADHD may be poor spellers because of inattention to visual detail and not noticing and therefore not being able to recall the letters, sequence, or visual patterns within words. WM difficulties affect spelling—keeping in mind the letter sounds and sequence for the word while getting it down on paper. Impulsivity and inattention also make these children more prone to careless spelling errors. Children and teens with coexisting dyslexia have more significant spelling errors as a result of difficulties with phonemic awareness and phonological processing.

4.2

Decoding, Fluency, and Vocabulary

As explained in Section 4.1, many children with ADHD also have the coexisting learning disability *dyslexia,* characterized by poor ability to read and spell words. These children struggle with word recognition and the ability to use phonics and other skills to decode or figure out unfamiliar words. Because they read slowly and laboriously, their reading fluency (speed, flow, and accuracy) is affected and therefore impairs their reading comprehension.

However, not all children who have poor word recognition and decoding skills and lack fluency have dyslexia. These students may have had minimal phonics and word analysis instruction and simply may not have been taught these skills and strategies sufficiently. Also, children with ADHD who do not have dyslexia may be weak in these skills because of issues related to inattention and poor WM capacity.

In order to become fluent readers, children must first become skilled at recognizing and decoding the printed word. They need a large enough bank of words that they can read at an automatic level without having to sound them out (for example, high-frequency words and irregular or sight words such as *said, their,* and *they*), so that they don't overly tax their WM capacity.

These students also need direct, explicit instruction (and early intervention whenever possible) in how to break the code in reading, which involves learning and proficiency in these skills:

- Alphabet knowledge
- Letter-sound association for all consonants, vowels (long and short *a, e, i, o, u*), consonant blends (for example, *cl, br, st*), consonant digraphs (*ch, sh, th*), vowel digraphs and dipthongs (such as *oa, ea, ai, oi, ou*), and vowel patterns (final *e, r*-controlled)
- Rapid blending of isolated sounds into words
- Recognition of rhyming sound families or visual patterns in words such as *rock/stock/flock* or *right/might/flight/bright.* These are called word families or onsets and rimes. *Note:* Onsets are the letters before the vowel (*r, st, fl*). Rimes are the vowel and following letters in single-syllable words (*-ock* and *-ight*).
- Structural analysis of words—awareness of word parts such as root words, prefixes, and suffixes that carry meaning
- Knowledge of syllable types and strategies for decoding multisyllabic words
- To decode the text correctly, children need to be taught strategies and cueing systems to use as they read.

Semantic cues: determining if the word makes sense in the context of what is being read and being able to self-correct (substitute a different word if it does not make sense)

Syntactic cues: determining if the word sounds right grammatically and being able to self-correct (substitute a different word that grammatically fits in the context of what is being read)

Graphophonic cues: using recognition of the printed letters (graphemes) and their corresponding sounds (phonemes) to figure out unfamiliar words

Word Recognition and Decoding

Most children learn best to read and spell when provided with explicit, systematic phonics instruction. This is a key instructional intervention for children with dyslexia. Kaufman (2010) explains how this type of instruction is also important for children with executive function weaknesses:

> Word identification strategies that emphasize systematic, explicit teaching methods and that keep returning to specific skills until they are clearly mastered are far more likely to produce lasting skill development in children with executive function challenge because they make clear what is being taught and include lots of guided repetition. (p. 105)

There are programs for teaching letter-sound associations that are multisensory and use various mnemonic strategies to make the learning more memorable and permanent (such as incorporating a kinesthetic body movement associated with the letter sound or calling attention to how the sound is formed in the mouth). Some programs that use such techniques are Zoo-Phonics (www.zoo-phonics.com), Lindamood-Bell (www.lindamoodbell.com), and *Alphabet Learning Center Activities Kit* (Fetzer & Rief, 2002).

Decoding and Word Recognition Strategies

- Explicitly teach strategies for decoding words, such as breaking multisyllable words apart according to syllable types (closed, open, final *e*, vowel team, *r*-controlled, diphthong, consonant *-le*), and explicitly teach prefixes and suffixes and rapid recognition of these important word parts.

- Teach strategies for pulling apart words, stretching out sounds (particularly vowel sounds), and substituting the alternate sounds that vowels or vowel combinations can make when one doesn't work. For example, in sounding out the word *health,* the *ea* can make the long *e* sound as in *sea* or the short *e* sound as in *set*. If the child reads the word with the long *e* sound and figures out that it is not a recognized word, he or she should then try the other vowel sound (short *e*).

- Sight words can be taught and practiced using a variety of multisensory strategies, color to highlight and call attention to certain letters within the word, and game formats to motivate practice and repetition. These are all beneficial techniques for helping lock these words into memory for automatic retrieval when reading or spelling them.

- Word Sorts is another popular instructional technique for studying words and focusing on elements that are the same or different. This involves sorting words into two or three categories according to features of the word— for example, sounds within the word (sorting into long *a*, short *a*, *ch / sh*, *er / ir / ur*, *ou / oi*) or different word endings (*-sion / -tion*).

Note: My books Alphabet Learning Center Activities Kit *(Fetzer & Rief, 2002) and* The Dyslexia Checklist *(Rief & Stern, 2010) contain several strategies and motivating activities for teaching and practicing alphabet and letter-sound association, sight words, phonics, and decoding skills. Also see the numerous strategies posted on my Pinterest boards under the categories of phonological and phonemic awareness (https:// www .pinterest.com / sandrarief / phonological-phonemic-awareness /), alphabet and letter sounds (https:// www.pinterest.com / sandrarief / alphabet-letter -sounds /), sight words (https:// www.pinterest .com / sandrarief / sight-words /), phonics, decoding, and fluency (https:// www.pinterest.com / sandrarief / phonics-decoding-fluency /), b-d tricks and strategies (https://www.pinterest.com/sandrarief/b-d -tricks-strategies/), and spelling and word attack (https://www.pinterest.com/sandrarief/spelling -word-work/).*

There are several websites with great activities for learning and practicing phonics, sight words, word recognition, and spelling, such as FunFonix (www.funfonix.com), ABC Teach (www.abcteach .com), Fuel the Brain (www.fuelthebrain.com), Fun-Brain (www.funbrain.com), Internet4Classrooms (www.internet4classrooms.com), Starfall (www.star fall.com), and Turtle Diary (www.turtlediary.com).

Fluency

Reading fluency is the ability to recognize words and read with ease, speed, accuracy, and expression. Because fluent readers do not need to put forth a lot of mental energy trying to figure out the words on the page, they are free to focus their attention on comprehension, and find reading far more enjoyable and rewarding than it is for readers who labor to read word by word (Allington, 2006; Armbruster, Lehr, & Osborn, 2001).

Factors That Contribute to Fluency

Accuracy. Being able to decode or recognize words correctly. Building phonics skills, word attack skills, and sight recognition of high-frequency and irregular words is necessary to improve reading accuracy.

Rate. Being able to read individual words and connected text quickly. Reading speed (rate) increases with practice and rereading. Rate is measured by the number of words correct per minute or length of time needed to complete a passage.

Automaticity. Accurate, effortless, and rapid word recognition—not having to put mental effort into identifying words. Automaticity requires rapid decoding of unfamiliar words and recognizing a high number of familiar words by sight. Practice and memory play a significant part in automaticity.

Prosody. Being able to read with good expression that sounds like speech (appropriate pitch, tone, phrasing, stress or emphasis, pacing, and rhythm). Prosody, which plays an important part in comprehension of text, is developed through listening to good reading models and practice.

Vocabulary. Word knowledge. Knowing the meaning of a word makes that word easier and quicker to read. Vocabulary development increases fluency by improving recognition of words in print.

Processing speed. How quickly one processes information—for example, on seeing written words, how quickly one can convert those symbols into speech (whether one is reading silently or aloud).

Reading volume. How much one reads. The more children read, the greater their exposure to words will be, facilitating vocabulary acquisition and word recognition. Struggling readers read less because it is not pleasurable; therefore, they often get less exposure to words and less practice than their grade-level peers.

Correct practice. Repeated use of reading skills. Fluency is developed through many opportunities to practice skills correctly, which means reading aloud to an adult or skilled reader who can provide corrective feedback as needed.

Fluency-Building Strategies

Research shows that fluency can be developed through a variety of techniques, particularly through repeated monitored oral reading.

Student-adult reading. The adult reads aloud first, providing a model of fluent reading. The student then rereads the same passage, with adult assistance and coaching as needed. For example, if the student gets stuck on a word, the adult reads the word and the child repeats it. The student rereads the passage a few times until he or she reads it fluently with ease and expression.

Partner reading or buddy reading. Partner reading can be done in various ways. One way is to pair a stronger reader with a less fluent reader. The stronger reader first reads the page or passage aloud, pointing to the words while the partner follows along. Then the less fluent reader rereads the same passage while the stronger partner assists and coaches (gently correcting errors, after which the partner rereads the passage). In another variation, partners at the same reading level are paired in order to reread a passage or story a few times in different formats:

- Alternating paragraphs or pages
- Having first one partner read the whole passage, then the other
- Having one partner read for a few minutes, then switching
- Reading in unison while one points under the words

Choral reading. This technique involves reading text aloud in unison after it is first modeled for fluent oral reading. Everyone looks at the text as it is read. There are different ways of doing choral reading in the classroom: using individual copies for rereading aloud together or providing large-size text that students can see from where they are seated. This is usually done by projecting text on a screen (for example, via a document camera), using a big book, or writing the words of a poem, song, or passage in large print on the board or chart paper.

- The teacher models and reads the text with fluency while sweeping a finger or marker under the words in phrases—not word by word—to match the flow of speech.

- The material is reread; this time, students join in for choral rereading of all or parts of the text a few times.
- For fun, teachers can divide sections of the text to be read by different groups (for example, boys and girls, left side of room and right side of room).

Echo reading. The teacher reads aloud a short section of text (a single sentence, a paragraph, or a verse of a poem). Immediately, the students echo what was just read while the teacher points to or sweeps under the words. Echo reading can be done with a whole group or an individual student. Poetry and song lyrics work well for fluency practice.

Recording-assisted reading. A student reads along with an audio recording of a passage or book that has been recorded by a fluent reader. After hearing it read several times, the student reads along with the recording and practices until he or she can read the text fluently. Some recorded books may not be appropriate for fluency practice because they may have too many unfamiliar words or concepts.

Software and online programs. Students use a program such as Read Naturally (www.readnaturally.com), which combines teacher modeling, repeated reading, assessment, and progress monitoring on the computer.

Additional Fluency Strategies

Readers theater. Many theater scripts are excellent for fluency practice. Students practice reading their assigned parts from the script in order to perform for classmates or other audiences.

Practicing in order to perform. In addition to readers theater, many other performance opportunities—for example, puppet shows, plays, choral concerts, or poetry parties—can provide a means of getting struggling readers to practice fluency by rehearsing in preparation for performance.

Cross-age buddy reading. Older students often have younger reading buddies. Reading a book with good expression provides fluency practice in preparation for reading that book to their younger buddies.

Timed repeated reading and charting. Students read a short passage for one minute. The teacher determines the words correct per minute (reading rate) on that passage, and the student charts or graphs the score. This procedure continues with repeated readings until the student reaches the target reading.

Note: See my books How to Reach and Teach All Children through Balanced Literacy *(Rief & Heimburge, 2007) and* The Dyslexia Checklist *(Rief & Stern, 2010) for additional strategies and activities for strengthening reading fluency. Also see these online resources for fluency building: Giggle Poetry (www.gigglepoetry.com), Poetry 4 Kids: Ken Nesbitt's Children's Poetry Playground (www.poetry4kids.com), and Teaching Heart (www.teachingheart.net/readerstheater.htm).*

Remediation Challenge

For older students with reading disabilities, fluency is probably the most difficult area to remediate because of the cumulative effect of years of minimal practice in reading words correctly.

Lack of correct practice results in a huge deficiency in the number of words that the reader can recognize instantly by sight and a much slower reading rate than grade-level peers.

Some fluency-building programs include Jamestown Timed Reading (www.glecoe.com), Quick Reads (www.quickreads.org), Read Naturally (www.readnaturally.com), and the Fluency Formula Program (www.scholastic.com).

Explore the tool BeeLine Reader (www.BeeLineReader.com) to aid easier, faster reading on computers, tablets, and smartphones. This technology applies an eye-guiding color gradient to text that helps guide the reader's eyes from the end of one line to the beginning of the next, which significantly reduces the chance of accidentally skipping or repeating lines. By making line transitions easier and more natural, BeeLine Reader enables the reader to transition more quickly from line to line—increasing reading speed, particularly on mobile devices.

Tips for Oral Reading in the Classroom

Oral reading in the classroom is necessary, but can be problematic. To discuss a text, it is of course important that all students have read the material. However, round-robin reading, with the students taking individual turns reading aloud to the class, is generally not the most effective strategy, especially for students with reading disabilities or attention difficulties.

Students who have reading difficulty have a hard time following along and staying on track. They may also become so fearful of being embarrassed by their poor reading skills that they spend the whole period in anxiety, trying to predict what will be their portion to read and practicing ahead. Therefore, they are not listening or following along.

Have students first read silently before the class or group reads orally. Students (particularly older ones) who are uncomfortable reading orally should never be forced to read out loud to the class. They should be able to volunteer when they wish to read in front of the class. Buddy reading or reading in small groups is a much safer, preferable way for students to practice their oral reading.

Tips for Independent Reading

Independent reading is also critical for building fluency, but the book must be at an appropriate level to read without support. One method of quickly determining if a book is at a child's appropriate independent level is the Five-Finger Check described in the Parent Tips box later in the section. Another method is "one in twenty." Select a passage from a child's chosen book to read orally. If the child makes fewer than one error in twenty words, the reading material is at his or her independent level.

Note: Many children with ADHD have a hard time maintaining their focus and paying attention to the words they are reading silently. Hearing the words (softly saying the words aloud to themselves) may help them attend to or better process what they are reading. Permit them to take their book to a quiet corner and read to themselves aloud. Another strategy is to provide a curved, hollow plastic device that the child holds to his or her ear like a telephone receiver while softly whispering the words into the other end. The device (sometimes referred to as a whisper phone) channels the voice directly to the child's ear to provide the auditory input without disturbing others. One such commercial product is Toobaloo, available through www.superduperinc.com. The device can also be constructed by fitting together two PVC elbow pipes.

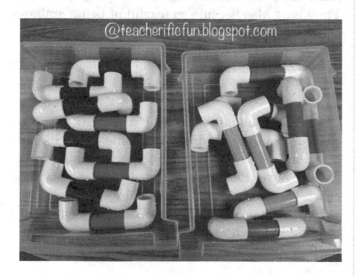

Vocabulary

Although many students with ADHD and LDs have a strong oral vocabulary, their poor reading skills impede their recognition and acquisition of the hundreds of new words that their classmates who are skilled readers learn through reading. Students who read a lot are exposed to complex, sophisticated words through their reading and have a stronger vocabulary than minimal readers.

Students with ADHD and LDs may also have a weaker vocabulary than their peers because of poor retrieval of words from memory, which restricts word usage when speaking and writing, as well as underlying language difficulties impeding comprehension of figures of speech and nuances of language (such as metaphors, idioms, puns, and words with multiple meanings).

Strategies for Vocabulary Development and Working with Words

Directly teaching words. Define words for students using simple explanations and synonyms. If possible, use antonyms (opposites) as well. For example, tell students, "The word *emaciated* means really skinny—extremely thin, often from starving. It's the opposite of fat or plump." Give examples and nonexamples: "The starving kitten was weak and emaciated when they found it." "Might a child living in poverty who is undernourished be emaciated?" "Do these people look emaciated?" (Show pictures of average and heavy people.) Have students generate their own examples of the word in a sentence or with a picture.

Context clues. Reading a word in the context of the rest of the sentence and surrounding sentences is an important strategy for figuring out the meaning of unknown words. Have students read a word (or listen to it being read) in the context of the surrounding sentences and try to guess the meaning.

Semantic webs. These are visual displays or graphic organizers for helping students learn vocabulary and understand word relationships. Write a specific vocabulary word in the center of the page. Then have students record other words, phrases, characteristics, properties, or examples relating to that word around the page, radiating from the center vocabulary word (like a spider web).

Multiple meanings. Provide practice in working with words with multiple meanings.

Teach word roots. Many English words have Greek, Latin, or Anglo-Saxon roots. For example, *phon* is the Greek root that means "sound." From that root, many words can be derived—such as *telephone* and *phonics*. Recognizing words with the same root is helpful in understanding word meanings.

Word lists or anchor charts. Post lists of words, adding to them throughout the year as new words are encountered. Topics for these lists might include the following:

- Character traits—for example, *inquisitive, stubborn, compassionate*
- Feelings—for example, *suspicious, optimistic, discouraged*
- Alternatives to overused words such as *said, went,* or *nice*—for example, some alternatives to *said* include *stated, responded,* and *announced*

Definitions. Teach dictionary skills. Model and provide practice in looking up words in dictionaries, glossaries, and thesauri.

Make it visual, make it memorable. Make illustrations, use symbols to represent ideas, label, color, highlight, or use graphic organizers to help students remember words and their associations with other words or ideas.

Games and word play. Games that build vocabulary and make learning about words fun can be made or purchased. Choose games carefully or make adaptations as needed (extended or no time limits, providing assistance in reading words on the game card).

- Crossword puzzles are excellent for building word knowledge.
- Play commercial games that enhance vocabulary and language skills, such as Password, Jeopardy, One-Minute Wonders, Outburst, and Pictionary.

Mapping unknown words. Provide activities that require students to map information for a new word. Have them write the word and sentence in which it is found in the text; record its definition, synonyms for the word, and an example or illustration; and write a sentence using the word.

Figurative language. Teach these elements through a variety of activities:

- Share idioms such as "He saw the handwriting on the wall." Explain the difference between literal and figurative meaning.
- Find examples of metaphors to chart and illustrate. Examples: "The man is a rock." "That is a half-baked idea."

Precision with words. Teach students how valuable it is to use just the right words to convey meaning most precisely. Provide activities in which students work in groups or partners to arrange an array of words along a continuum—for example, words that describe moving from here to there: *ambled . . . strolled . . . walked . . . jogged . . . dashed.*

Preview text and frontload. Point out, explain, and define important or difficult vocabulary that students will encounter in the text prior to having them read it.

Note: See my books (Rief & Heimburge, 2007; Rief & Stern, 2010) for several other recommended strategies for vocabulary development, as well as many activities across grade levels, posted at www .pinterest.com/sandrarief/vocabulary/language. Also see www.vocabulary.com and www.funbrain .com/words.html for online vocabulary games and activities as well as Picture Dictionary (www .pdictionary.com) and http://thesaurus.com.

Points to Keep in Mind

A number of students have difficulty with the language and vocabulary of books at their grade level. However, all children should have the opportunity to hear and discuss literature and expository text that is interesting, motivating, and at a challenging level. Although the vocabulary may be difficult, a nonproficient reader can participate equally in reading of grade-level material through shared reading, read-alouds, teacher-guided reading, listening to recorded text, and the host of reading comprehension strategies in which students collaboratively read the text.

According to Dr. Louisa Moats (2001), normally progressing students can read most of the words in their listening vocabulary by fourth or fifth grade. From then on, they learn new vocabulary—primarily by reading—at the rate of several thousand new words per year. Many poor readers must overcome a huge vocabulary deficit before they will be able to read successfully beyond the fifth-grade level.

Parent Tips: Reading Strategies

- Try to read to and with your child every day. It is very beneficial to read to your child even if he or she is a proficient reader. Doing so enables your child to enjoy books of interest with you that are at a higher reading level than he or she can read independently. Exposing your child to good literature and the various writing styles of several different authors does wonders for developing language and vocabulary, building comprehension skills, and providing a model for your child of good writing.

- For independent reading, it is very important that your child find just-right books, which means books that he or she can read without a struggle (with about 95 percent accuracy). The general rule of thumb for determining if a book is too hard or just right is no more than five words on the page that are too difficult for the child to read or understand.

- Try the Five-Finger Check method—hold up one finger for each word your child doesn't know or cannot pronounce on the page, and if fewer than five fingers go up, the book is the appropriate level for independent reading. Encourage your child to read with these easy-to-read books independently. Doing so builds confidence as well as reading fluency skills. These are the kinds of books that can be read and reread aloud (to you, younger siblings, or anyone who will listen).

- It is also fun to practice oral reading by reading into a recording device. Children tend to enjoy doing this and playing their recordings back.

- Read the same book together with your child. You can do shared reading in a number of ways—for example, you read the pages on the left and your child reads the pages on the right, or switch off between paragraphs. You can also read small parts together in unison, with you running your finger under the words as you and your child read those lines aloud together.

- When listening to your son or daughter read, do not stop to correct or make your child sound out every single word. You can just tell him or her most of the unknown words to keep the reading moving along. For some words, you can coach your child in using different cueing strategies. For example, when approaching a tricky word that your child cannot figure out, prompt to pass over that word and read to the end of the sentence. Then see if your child can go back and figure out the unfamiliar word. Ask such questions as the following:
  — "Does that make sense?"
  — "Did that sound right to you?"
  — "What other word beginning with that sound would make sense here?"
  — "Does that look like another word you know?"
  — "Let's look at the first part of the word and try sounding that out." (Break the word into syllables and sound out part by part.)
  — "Are there any little words in that big word that you know?"

- Distractible children often lose their place easily while reading, so provide a bookmark to help keep their place. You might also block the page partially by placing an index card or a piece of cardboard or paper over part of the page. You may also want to try a boxed frame around a piece of colored transparent plastic to place on the book while reading.
- Play games and do activities that strengthen your child's phonological and phonemic awareness, alphabet skills and knowledge of letter-sound correspondence, sight word recognition, and phonics skills. Many such activities can be found in the resources and websites shared earlier.
- See Learning Ally (www.LearningAlly.org) and Bookshare (www.bookshare.org). Both organizations offer wonderful services and resources for students with reading disabilities. Membership provides your child unlimited access to books, textbooks, and other material in audio format. For some, membership is free. Definitely check their websites for more information if your child has dyslexia and is a struggling reader.

Reading Comprehension

Comprehension—getting meaning from text—is the purpose of reading. It requires the reader to actively process the text, self-monitor for understanding, and know how and when to apply various meaning-making strategies when something doesn't make sense. Key strategies for readers with ADHD are those that keep them actively engaged throughout the reading process— thinking about, questioning, and responding to the reading material in order to maintain their attention and to comprehend and recall what they have read.

All students in today's classrooms with Common Core State Standards (CCSS) are required to interact with and read complex texts carefully and deeply for meaning. They also must support their opinions and responses to reading comprehension questions by going back and finding evidence from the text. Students spend time working together and need to analyze and discuss more and explain their thinking verbally and in writing. This is not an easy task for those with attention and executive function weaknesses. The CCSS emphasize critical thinking skills, and students need to demonstrate their use of the skills that proficient reading and comprehension of text involve.

Proficient readers (McGregor, 2007; Pearson, Roehler, Doe, & Duffy, 1992) do the following:

- Use schema (make connections, retrieve and activate prior knowledge)
- Infer (draw conclusions, make predictions and form interpretations)
- Question (generate questions before, during, and after reading)
- Determine importance (sift out relevant and useful information)
- Visualize (create mental images)
- Synthesize (continually change their thinking in response to text)

A number of strategies are helpful and effective prior to reading, during reading, and after completing the reading assignment to aid with recall and comprehension of the text.

Strategies throughout the Reading Process

Before-Reading Strategies

Prereading strategies are important for activating the reader's prior knowledge about the topic, building connections and comprehension of the text, and generating interest and motivation to read the material.

- Prior to reading, relate the story or reading material to the students' experiences and background knowledge through discussions, brainstorming, and charting prior knowledge ("What do we already know about . . .?").

- Set the stage and establish the purpose for what they are about to read—for example, "As you read, think about what you would do if . . ."

- Ask students to make predictions prior to reading.

- Generate interest and increase students' background knowledge and frame of reference before reading by using concrete objects and audiovisuals related to the topic of study, such as maps, music, photos, and videos.

- Provide time to preview the text (look at the cover, illustrations, chapter titles, headings, diagrams, and other text features)—taking a guided walk through the book to see how the author organized and presented the information and to anticipate what the reading selection will be about *before* reading the material. Another way to preview is to have the students listen to passages read aloud first before independently studying and rereading.

- To activate prior knowledge, you can ask students to write down everything they know about the topic in their learning log or to brainstorm as a group and record in the first column of a KWL chart (see the "KWL" section later in this discussion).

- Discuss selected vocabulary that may be challenging in the text.

- Using advance organizers, anticipation guides, and other prereading strategies and tools, link prior knowledge to new concepts and information that will be studied.

During-Reading Strategies

Students need to be taught information about different kinds of text and strategies to apply while reading to aid comprehension. They need to learn (through teacher modeling and guided practice) how to interact with the text while reading, through such strategies as questioning, visualizing, annotating, and jotting down thoughts. They also need to be able to identify the author's

purpose and audience, text structures for literary and expository text, and how to use clues the author provides and other information to infer and draw conclusions. See the "More Key Comprehension Strategies" and "Other Reading Comprehension Strategies" sections later for more details on some of these strategies.

- Teach students how to paraphrase a paragraph or section, putting into his or her own words the main idea and significant details. Have students do so with a partner. Stating one's paraphrase into a recording device is a helpful technique for independent reading.

- Teach the student how to find and pay attention to the introductory and summary paragraphs, how to find the subject and main ideas, and how to sift out the key facts and important details.

- Teach clustering, webbing, and mapping to pull out the main idea and supporting details from the text.

- Teach students how to use the glossary, table of contents, index, charts, graphs, diagrams, time lines, and maps, and to pay attention to italicized and boldface print, headings and subheadings, and other text features to get meaning from informational text.

- Give a few stopping points at strategic locations throughout the text for readers to interact with the material in some manner: to stop and question, react to, discuss, summarize, predict, clarify, or record. This can be done independently or through Turn and Talks with a partner or table group.

- Provide thinking stems for reading responses, such as: "I predict _____ because _____." "I disagree with _____ because _____." "This reminds me of _____."

- Provide a pad of sticky notes to annotate the text. Encourage students to jot down notes, connections made, reactions to what they have read, unfamiliar words to clarify, and questions, and to place the sticky notes by the relevant passage in the text.

- Have students use specific coded symbols as they are reading and placing sticky notes in the text. The code may be, for example, a question mark (for confusing parts or questions), an exclamation point (for exciting or surprising parts, "aha" moments), a star or asterisk (to indicate something important or a favorite part), a check mark (for "I understand"), a heart (for a feeling or emotional reaction that part evokes), T-T (for text-to-text) and T-S (text-to-self) connections, and so forth.

- Have students annotate or make marks directly on printed articles (circling unfamiliar vocabulary, underlining words or phrases, and writing thoughts in the margins)—which is a key strategy in close reading.

- Teach story mapping: identifying the setting (time and place), characters, conflicts and problems, action and events, climax, and resolution of conflicts.

- Help children learn to self-monitor their own comprehension by asking themselves questions while reading: "What is the problem or conflict?" "What might the character do to resolve the problem?" "Why did she say that?" "What was the main point the author is trying to make in this section?" "Did I understand this?" "What were the steps for this procedure?" "What part does not make sense?" Questioning and self-questioning keep readers actively thinking about and processing the material.

- Teach and model strategies for resolving difficulties when comprehension breaks down: slowing the pace, going back and rereading, reading ahead to see if their questions are clarified later, talking with someone about their confusion, or jotting down questions to check later.

- Provide study guides to aid in looking for key information in the text.

- To help students who have difficulty staying on task, focused, and motivated while reading silently, try the following:
  — Set mini-goals in pacing their reading. Have the child read to a certain point in the text or for a predetermined amount of time. After reading to that point, the child is rewarded with a brief break.

  — Allow the child to subvocalize—say the words aloud softly while reading to himself or herself or use a whisper phone device (described in Section 4.2). This auditory feedback can assist with focus and attention to the reading material.

- Use any of the instructional strategies involving collaborative reading and analysis of the material, such as reciprocal teaching, GIST (described later), book clubs, and buddy or partner reading. Learning and recall are greatly enhanced by the act of talking about the text. See "Other Reading Comprehension Strategies" for some of these strategies. More are described in my other published books.

- Read Works (www.readworks.org)—a nonprofit presented by leading researchers and teachers in research-based reading comprehension instruction—provides free informational articles (grades K–12) with question sets on a wide variety of topics as well as literary passages.

After-Reading Strategies

These strategies involve the reader in deeper thinking and exploration of the reading material.

- After reading the text, students use their new insights and understanding to complete filling out the charts and graphic organizers (such as KWL charts and learning logs) that they partially filled out during the prereading and during-reading stages.

- Have deep discussions about the concepts or events in the text or in character analysis.

- Make connections through related writing activities.

- Do further extension activities related to the theme and content of the reading to apply the learning.

- Have students respond to questions—justifying their answers and defending their thinking through examples and evidence from the text.

Many of the strategies used during reading are also continued or completed after the reading.

The Importance of Teacher Modeling of Strategic Reading

Fisher, Frey, and Lapp (2008) identified four areas teachers need to be explicitly modeling to students—showing their thinking processes for reading strategically: *comprehension* (cognitive processes such as visualizing, predicting, summarizing, and questioning to make sense of the text), *word solving* (using context clues, word parts, and resources to determine the meaning of unknown words), *text structures* (figuring out the way in which the author structured the text—narrative or expository, as well as structures including cause-effect, sequence, and problem-solution), and *text features* (visual and graphic tools that are added to the text to aid understanding).

Fisher and Frey (2015) later revised what they recommend teachers need to be modeling to include additional factors addressing the increased complexity of text. Deep, critical thinking and analysis of text are required in all content areas and disciplines. Modeling these skills is important for different types of texts. With historical text, for example, the reader needs to consider the document in historical context (where and when it was written and what was happening at the time), examine the source (who produced the document), and use that information to analyze the viewpoint and reliability of the document.

Teachers need to take the time to model their thinking aloud as they grapple with reading and understanding text. More is discussed about this among the metacognitive strategies described in Section 3.5.

Graphic Organizers

The following graphic organizers are useful for increasing comprehension and recall of text:

- *Framed outlines*. Students are given copies of a teacher-prepared outline that contains missing information for them to fill in during and after the reading.
- *Storyboards*. Students divide a board or piece of paper into sections and draw or write story events in sequence in each box or frame.
- *Story maps*. This graphic includes essential elements of a story (setting, characters, time, place, problem or conflict, actions or happenings, and resolution).
- *Story frames*. These are sentence starters to fill in that provide a skeleton of the story or chapter. For example: "The setting of this chapter takes place in _____. The character faced a problem when _____. First he _____. Next, _____. Then _____. I predict in the next chapter _____."
- *Time lines*. These are used to help the student visualize chronological text and the sequence of events.
- *Plot charts*. Students fill in the following information that cycles through the plot of a story: Somebody (list the character) . . . wanted (goal) . . . but (what happened or interfered with the character achieving his or her goal) . . . and so (what happened next) . . .
- *Prediction charts*. These charts are modified as students read the story. Students make initial predictions based on the title and illustrations. As they read, they stop and predict what will happen next. They continue questioning, predicting, and recording. Make clear to students that predictions are best guesses based on the information they know at the time and that good readers are constantly predicting when they are reading.
- *Venn diagrams*. Two overlapping circles are used to display differences and similarities between characters, books, settings, topics, or events.
- *Comparison charts*. Much like a Venn diagram, this chart compares and contrasts two or more items, events, concepts, characters, and themes.
- *Flowcharts*. A flowchart organizes a series of items or thoughts in logical order.
- *Webs, cluster maps, and semantic maps*. Students place a central concept or main idea in the center of related subtopics, and further details extend from each of the subtopic areas. These are used to categorize or identify related information.

- *5W charts.* After reading an article or excerpt from a text, students identify the 5W elements (Who? What? When? Where? Why?) and record that information on the chart.
- *Character webs.* Students put the character's name in the center of the web with traits and descriptions stemming from the center.

Where the Red Fern Grows

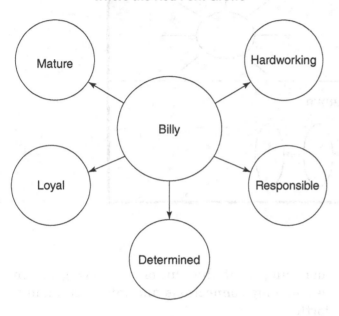

Note: There are numerous other graphic organizers for main idea and supporting detail, cause and effect, sequence, classification matrices, and so forth. See the many online graphic organizers, many of them free, such as those found at www .edhelper.com and www.graphic.org.

More Key Comprehension Strategies

Summarizing

Summarizing is one of the most important reading comprehension skills. Sometimes the main idea is explicit and easy to find; other times it is implied or embedded in the passage. Use techniques that require students to summarize what they have read at various stopping points throughout the text. For example, students can summarize at the end of a passage with a one-sentence statement to tell to their partner or write down the main event

or two key points on a sticky note at the end of a passage or section of text.

Narrative Text Structure

Explicitly teach story grammar or story mapping so that students understand the structure of the narrative (literary) text. This includes setting (time and place), characters, problems or conflicts, sequence of major events (rising actions), climax, and the resolution of conflicts or problem solution. Younger students generally focus on the main characters, setting, and story structure—beginning, middle, and end.

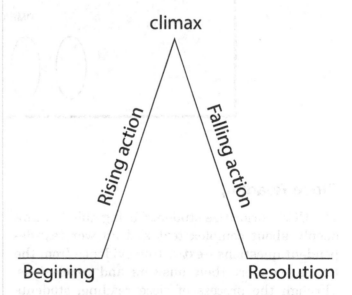

Expository or Informational Text Structure

Teach students how to identify the main ideas and supporting details (facts, statistics, examples) in the text. Students learn that informational text uses the structures of *description* (providing details or characteristics of a topic); *order and sequence* (outlining chronological events or steps in which events occur, as in a procedure); *compare and contrast* (showing similarities and differences between people, places, things, or events); *problem and solution* (information is given about a problem, and at least one solution is presented or the issue is solved); and *cause and effect* (a description of a cause or reason for why something happens and the effect that follows the cause).

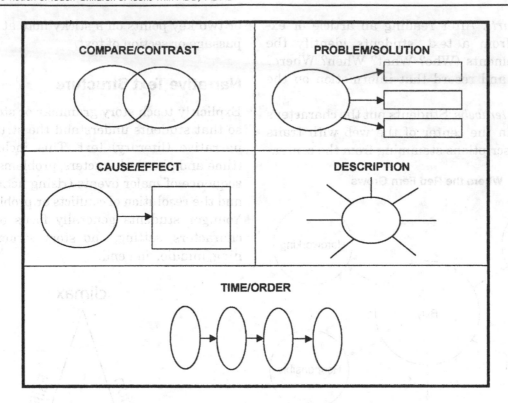

Close Reading

The CCSS prioritize students' being able to think deeply about complex text and answer text-dependent questions—extracting evidence from the text to support their answers and conclusions. Through the process of close reading, students learn to do so.

According to Fisher (2014), close reading is

a careful and purposeful rereading of a text . . . an encounter with the text where students really focus on what the author had to say, what the author's purpose was, what the words mean, and what the structure of the text tells us.

It is an approach for uncovering multiple layers of meaning (Boyles, 2012). The strategy involves rereading the text or portions of it a few times for specific purposes. The first read is to get the gist (Lynette, 2014). In the second read, the reader digs a little deeper. Students may explore some elements, such as the organizational structure or the author's word choices and language used. A third read goes deeper—critically

analyzing what the author was trying to convey, making connections and inferences, and so forth.

Close reading is a very interactive process that may involve a variety of strategies, such as discussion with partners or groups; circling unfamiliar words; highlighting important information; and jotting down thoughts, questions, reactions, and connections on sticky notes or in the margins. Close readers are actively observing, questioning, and interacting with the text as they dig deep for clues to figure out what the author is really trying to say and gathering evidence to respond to text-dependent questions.

During close reading, students are often annotating their text with sticky notes or directly writing on the pages to keep track of their thoughts. The act of annotating while reading ensures active engagement and use of metacognition, which is very important for all readers—and particularly for those with ADHD. Using different colors for coding specific information is also helpful. For example, all questions, wonderings, or confusing parts can be coded in yellow highlighter pen or sticky note.

Close reading lessons, according to Fisher and Frey (2015), rely on students' ability to analyze texts at increasingly complex levels, a skill they have learned by participating in modeling and practice. Nancy Boyles (2012) suggests four basic questions students should ask themselves in close reading: What is the author telling me here? Are there any hard or important words? What does the author want me to understand? How does the author play with language to add to meaning?

Other Reading Comprehension Strategies

Anticipation Guide

This is a series of teacher-generated statements about a topic given to students *before* they read, intended to activate students' prior knowledge and build curiosity. Students individually respond to the statements (with true-false or agree-disagree responses) before reading about that topic. Typically, they are asked to discuss their choices briefly with partners or small groups prior to reading the passage. After reading the text material, they discuss whether their beliefs have changed.

Directed Reading-Thinking Activity (DRTA)

With this DRTA strategy (Stauffer, 1969), the teacher guides students in active reading to make predictions about a passage or story. Then the passage is read (orally or silently), and at predetermined points, the teacher asks students to summarize the reading, confirm or revise their predictions, and give reasons for their decisions with evidence located and cited from the text. After a certain number of passages or pages read, the process starts again.

Imagery and Visualization

This is a technique that aids comprehension by having students create mental pictures of what they are reading. Students are encouraged to create an image or "movie" in their mind as they read. This skill can be taught through guided questioning that elicits from students vivid, detailed pictures as they move through the passage. Examples of guiding questions: "What do you see?" "What colors?" "Where is he sitting?" "How does it feel?" *Note:* A good resource for teaching this skill is *Visualizing and Verbalizing for Language Comprehension and Thinking* (Bell, 2007).

KWL (and Variations)

KWL is a strategy (Ogle, 1986) used prior to, during, and after reading. It employs a chart divided into three columns:

- The first column (K) indicates what is already *known* about the subject or topic. This step activates students' prior knowledge. Ideas are recorded during a class brainstorm.
- The middle column (W) is what the students *want* to learn or find out about the subject. This column sets the purpose for reading—to find the answers to those questions.
- The third column (L) is filled in as new information is *learned* from the reading or other teaching. This column is for recording "what we learned."

KWL Plus is the same as KWL, except that it adds mapping and summarizing to the original KWL strategy. These two tasks incorporate the powerful tools of restructuring text and rewriting to help students process information (Ong, 2000). Students map the information listed on the chart and organize it graphically under categories of topics. Finally, students write a summary based on that graphic organization of ideas.

Another variation is **KWHL,** adding H (**h**ow) to the strategy chart: "How do I find out?" "How will we find the answers to our questions?" and so on. Silvia Rosenthal Tolisano's blog (2011) describes expansion of the strategy to **KWHLAQ**: What do I **k**now? What do I **w**ant to know? **H**ow do I find out? What have I **l**earned? What **a**ction will I take? What new **q**uestions do we have?

GIST

GIST stands for **g**enerating **i**nteraction between **s**chemata and **t**ext (Swanson & DeLaPaz, 1998).

This is a strategy used for comprehending informational text and determining the gist of the reading material:

1. In cooperative groups, students read sections silently.
2. When done reading a short section, the members of the group work together to write a one-sentence summary.
3. All group members then record that summary sentence.
4. Students continue in this fashion, reading a segment, stopping at logical points, jointly deciding on a summary sentence, and then recording on their own papers.
5. Those papers can then serve as a study guide for the reading material.

PASS

This reading comprehension strategy by Deshler, Ellis, and Lenz (1996) is a four-step process (**p**review, **a**sk, **s**ummarize, **s**ynthesize). Sousa (2001) describes the steps of this strategy. The teacher guides the students through the four steps.

1. Preview, review, and predict
   — Preview by reading the heading and one or two sentences.
   — Review what you already know about this topic.
   — Predict what you think the text or story will be about.
2. Ask and answer questions
   — Ask content-focused questions (Who? What? Why? Where? How does this relate to what I already know?)
   — Ask monitoring questions (Does this make sense? How is this different from what I thought it was going to be about?
   — Ask problem-solving questions (Do I need to reread part of it? Can I visualize the information? Does it have too many unknown words?)
3. Summarize
   — Explain what the short passage you read was all about.

4. Synthesize
   — Explain how the short passage fits in with the whole passage.
   — Explain how what you learned fits in with what you knew.

Reciprocal Teaching

This approach, originally developed by Palincsar and Brown (1984, 1985), is one of the best-researched strategies available to teachers (Marzano, Pickering, & Pollock, 2001). It involves students working together in cooperative groups taking turns designing and asking questions and leading the group in the process of discussing and working through small portions of the text for comprehension purposes. Research has found that good readers spontaneously use strategies of predicting, questioning, clarifying, and summarizing, which lead to understanding. Poor readers do not self-monitor or use these strategies.

In a reciprocal teaching format, the group is led through the process of reading a short section and

1. *Questioning* about the content read to identify important information in the passage.
2. *Summarizing.* Questions to help with summarizing may be asked, such as "What is this paragraph mostly about? What would be a good title for this passage?"
3. *Clarifying* anything confusing in the reading. Clarifying questions might include "Has anyone heard this expression before? What do you think it means? Can anyone explain this?"
4. *Predicting* what will happen in the next portion of the reading.

The students proceed in this format, taking turns in the leader role as they read the next portions of the text.

Question-Answer Relationships (QAR)

Students are taught different classifications of questions: (1) right there, (2) think and search, and (3) on your own (Raphael, 1982):

- The answers to right-there questions are stated directly in the text and simply require literal comprehension.

- The answers to think-and-search questions are not as explicit and easy to locate, but are found somewhere within the text. Answering these questions requires interpretive or inferential comprehension and reading between the lines. Finding the main idea of a passage is an example of inferential comprehension.
- On-your-own questions are more abstract, and the answers cannot be found in the text. These questions require reading beyond the lines and involve higher-order thinking skills, such as analyzing, evaluating, and creative thinking. Examples include comparing and contrasting or answering such questions as "What do you think caused . . . to happen?" "What other solution can you think of for that problem?"

Journal Entries

Use reflective journals, metacognitive journals, and double-entry journals, described in Section 3.5.

Literature Logs

Have students record their personal reflections, summaries, and predictions.

Retelling

Review the literature students have read through storytelling, summarizing, time lines, quick writes, quick draws, audio recordings, pocket charts with colored sentence strips, plot charts, or any of the graphic organizers.

Hot Seat

A student volunteer, representing a particular character from the story, is put on the hot seat. Students ask him or her questions that must be answered in the way the character would answer them.

Readers Theater

Work on scripting a piece of literature into dialogue, then read it aloud dramatically.

* * *

Note: See the websites with motivating content and activities that can boost reading comprehension listed in the Parent Tips box later in this section, as well as numerous practical ideas and creative reading comprehension strategies for elementary through high school shared by teachers on Pinterest at www.pinterest.com/sandrarief /reading-comprehension/.

To view a dynamic video of highly creative and engaging instructional strategies being demonstrated authentically in a classroom, view the Response to Literature lesson on Nancy Fetzer's website at www.nancyfetzer.com. See students summarizing a story, forming an opinion about its theme, then backing up their judgments with evidence from the text.

Classroom Book Clubs

Note: The following section and book club forms and activities found in the appendix (with additional bonus pages online) are taken directly or adapted from *How to Reach and Teach All Children through Balanced Literacy* (Rief & Heimburge, 2007).

What Is a Classroom Book Club?

A book club (also referred to as Literature Circles) is an instructional format or strategy in which small groups of students talk and think about a common book as they are reading. During and after reading a section of the book, the students prepare formally or informally for discussion. Some book clubs assign roles or responsibilities in a more formal manner, whereas others follow a natural flow of conversation with more informal planning. Students prepare for discussion by taking notes, writing journal entries, drawing illustrations, and reflecting on the book before the meeting of the group. The children have regular meetings where they discuss the portion of the book pages read and then come to consensus as to how many pages should be read for the next meeting. At the end of the book, the club members prepare a culmination activity as a way of sharing highlights of the book with the rest of their classmates. After the extension activity, students select new reading and move into a new cycle.

Note: The term club *gives members a sense of belonging, and belonging invites socialization and interaction. It connotes the sense that we are part of something important, and therefore, "book clubs" is my term of choice (mine and coauthor Julie Heimburge).*

The Benefits of Book Clubs

There are many advantages to starting up book clubs in the classroom. First, children seem to read *more* when they are independent of the teacher. Because they are making choices by themselves, having input into what they want to read, and pursuing their own reading interests, they enjoy reading more. The added element is the conversation that ensues, giving students the ability to bounce ideas off of each other and to question and wonder about the characters, plot, and setting in fiction, or the events and information from nonfiction books.

Another benefit is that students work harder when they are pacing themselves, while assuming responsibility for scheduling and accountability. Because they are making their own decisions about how much they read as a group, oftentimes they do not allow lax behavior—they like having a self-selected schedule of the number of pages to read and when the book has to be finished.

Book clubs teach students how to work together and how to be independent of the teacher. This collaboration gives them a feeling of responsibility and success—they are guiding their own reading behaviors that they have put in place.

Most students do not like to let their peers down, so they do what is expected of them. When the group agrees on an assignment, each member has to do his or her part. It might mean that everyone is pushed a little bit more than normal, and there is a feeling of urgency to finish the assignment. There is real camaraderie that develops. Students who are falling behind are encouraged and motivated by their teammates. Often, they are assisted in finishing their part.

Because book clubs are child oriented and child driven, students share responsibility for their learning and are actively engaged in purposeful and relevant learning. They begin to take risks, experiment with their independence, and feel successful when they receive positive feedback. Book clubs are filled with learning possibilities.

Book clubs meet CCSS English Language Arts (ELA) Literacy Speaking and Listening Standards. For example:

- Engage effectively in a range of collaborative discussions (one-on-one, in groups, and teacher-led) with diverse partners on grade-level topics and texts, building on others' ideas and expressing their own clearly.
- Come to discussions prepared, having read or studied required material; explicitly draw on that preparation and other information known about the topic to explore ideas under discussion.
- Follow agreed-upon rules for discussions and carry out assigned roles.
- Pose and respond to specific questions to clarify or follow up on information, and make comments that contribute to the discussion and link to (elaborate on) the remarks of others.
- Review the key ideas expressed and explain their own ideas and understanding in light of the discussion.
- Identify the reasons and evidence a speaker provides to support particular points.

See online bonus content provided from the book club chapter of *How to Reach and Teach All Children through Balanced Literacy* (Rief & Heimburge, 2007) by going to the following link: www.wiley.com/go/adhdreach. These materials (created by Julie Heimburge) share detailed information on how to structure and implement book clubs in the classroom, and include tools for doing so.

Book Club Etiquette

(Rules to guide your conversations and behavior)

Everyone must:

- Participate in the conversation.
- Show evidence of reading and thinking with sticky notes.
- Sit at the same level and close together.
- Stay focused on reading talk—not social talk.
- Have your own book.
- Stay with your own group for the entire discussion time. Discussion between groups is not appropriate.
- Be a polite listener.
- Use an inside voice so other groups can hear each other.
- Come to consensus about what the next assignment will be.

Book Club Folders

Every member of the club should have a notebook in which to keep his or her book club activities and responses to literature pieces. A notebook with two pockets works well, one side for book club management information and one side for a response journal and a good supply of sticky notes. As the group progresses to the culminating activity, the students will want to keep their work-in-progress notes.

Students can keep the following sheets inside the folder. Two of these forms are in the appendix; and, other than the first form, which you can create, all are downloadable:

- Book Club Reading Schedule. Create a form or page to be kept up front and visible, on which students record the name of the book they are reading and the names of the group members in their book club, dates, and the page numbers next to each date that they agree to read (from page . . . to page . . .).
- Book Club Roles (A.9 in the appendix).
- Book Club Culminating Activities (A.10 in the appendix).
- Additional forms (Book Club Daily Evaluation, Book Club Discussion Notes, Book Club Planning Sheet, and Questions to Keep Your Book Club Conversation Going) are online at this link: www.wiley.com/go/adhdreach

Parent Tips: Strengthen Comprehension and Motivate Your Child to Read

There are many ways to help your child strengthen reading comprehension skills and become a more proficient, motivated reader.

- Read to and with your child; discuss the book together.
- Help your child break down lengthy reading assignments (such as reading a chapter book and writing a book report). Encourage your child to read a few pages a day or a certain number of chapters per week so that the task isn't so overwhelming or left to the last minute to complete. It is important to review and talk about what has already been read to keep the previous pages fresh in your child's mind.
- Photocopy a chapter or unit from your child's textbook to make it easier to study the text. Encourage your child to highlight key information and take notes directly on those photocopied pages. For example, important vocabulary and definitions can be highlighted in one color (yellow), the main ideas can be highlighted another color (orange), and so forth.
- Encourage your child to summarize after reading sections or pages of a book (for example, verbally to you or aloud into a recording device).
- Use some of the before-, during-, and after-reading strategies from this section to keep your child actively engaged in the reading process and to build reading comprehension skills.
- Try having your child use some of the metacognitive and cognitive learning strategies described in Section 3.5, such as think-alouds, SQ3R, or the RCRC strategy, while reading.

Motivate Your Struggling or Reluctant Reader

- Find the right books that will capture your child's interest. Before heading to the library or bookstore, check some of the many lists of award-winning books, such as Children's Choice, Caldecott Medal, and Newbery Award winners, and numerous compiled lists of best books for children of all ages and reading levels. See www.pinterest.com/sandrarief/books-for-kids/ for some such lists.
- Take advantage of all the audiobooks that are available for listening pleasure. Try listening to an audiobook as a family—for example, during a long car ride. Explore your public library and

the following resources: Audible (www.audible.com), Audio Bookshelf (www.audiobookshelf .com), Tumble Books (www.tumblebooks.com), Tales2Go (www.tales2go.com), and Story Place (www.storyplace.org).

- There are several alternatives to reading just books. Your child may be motivated to read other forms of material, such as joke and riddle books, comic books, poetry, recipes, sheet music with lyrics of favorite songs, closed-caption TV shows, lyrics of favorite songs on YouTube videos or sheet music, reference books with color pictures and short reading passages, directions or manuals for a new game or project, and magazines (for example, *Ranger Rick, Cricket,* or *Kids Discover*).

- There are many apps and online interactive websites for kids that have fun, motivating activities. For example, *Sports Illustrated for Kids* (www.sikids.com) has activities that may be a great way to get a sports-loving reluctant reader to read. Other online resources for sparking interest in reading nonfiction include *Animal Discovery* (http://animaldiscovery.com), *Arkive* (www.arkive.org), *Discovery Education* (www.discoveryeducation.com), *Inner Body* (www .innerbody.com), *National Geographic for Kids* (http://kids.nationalgeographic.com/kids), *ReadWorks* (www.readworks.org), and *NASA* (www.nasa.gov/audience/forkids/kidsclub/flash /index.html).

- Use incentives for home reading. Create a chart of some type, placing a sticker on the chart for each book read; or have your child record the number of pages he or she reads and provide a reward when he or she reaches a goal of a certain number of pages read.

INTERVIEW WITH JOHN
Twenty-three Years Old, University Senior, Colorado

John received an ADHD diagnosis as an adult.

Tell me what you remember as being difficult for you in elementary school.

"From first grade I felt that I was one of the 'dumb kids.' Teachers always said that I had the ability, but just didn't apply myself. I remember in sixth grade that for a school project I worked very hard and built a solar house all on my own. I didn't have any help from my parents. I knew what I wanted to do, but I didn't have the tools to get it all together. I got a poor grade on the project because it didn't look like I spent much time on it. My teacher said, 'You could have done better than that!'

"In elementary school, storytelling time was difficult for me. I fell asleep. My teacher would ask all the time, 'John, do you feel all right?' because I couldn't listen to her stories. She didn't understand . . . I had to sleep to stay quiet.

"In one of my grades, one of the kids in the 'top' group did a project on optical illusions. I remember thinking how her project didn't look like much . . . I know I could have done a better job. But because I was in the lower group, I never had a chance to do all the special projects."

What do you wish could have happened when you were younger?

"If I could go back now, I would like to relearn how to learn. If only there had been teachers who tried to find out what my problem was. For a long time I could hardly read a story. I had to keep rereading it because I was 'off somewhere else' and not paying attention to what I was reading. I would read a sentence over and over again, and read it out loud, and still not have any idea what I read."

What about junior high (middle school)?

"Most of the problems I had in school were disciplinary, especially in junior high. I started ditching class because algebra was so difficult for me."

What is your advice to teachers?

"The most important thing is to be there for the kids. Those kids who have problems early and are identified are the ones who can be helped!"

section
4.4

Writing: Strategies, Supports, and Accommodations

As described in Section 4.1, written language is the most common area of academic weakness in children and teens with ADHD. Many struggle with the writing process and its multiple skill components, which are complex and place high demands on WM and other executive functions.

Prewriting, Planning, and Organizing

Prewriting is a critical stage of the writing process involving the generation, planning, and organization of ideas and deciding what and how to express ideas before beginning to write. This is a significant challenge for children and teens with ADHD. The prewriting techniques listed here are designed to stimulate ideas, topic selection, and effective planning and also provide much-needed structure, organization, and motivation to write.

Prewriting Techniques in the Classroom

Brainstorming. Sessions are no more than three to five minutes and focused. Given a general theme or topic, students call out whatever comes to mind related to that topic while someone records all responses from the class.

Quick writes. Students have a few minutes to write down everything that they can think

of related to a given topic, which can be single words or phrases or simple pictures or symbols to represent ideas. Model the same uninterrupted writing or drawing on a topic of your choice to demonstrate the process to students.

Writing topic folders. Students maintain a folder, card file, or notebook of possible ideas for writing topics. These might include hobbies, places visited, jobs they have done, personal interests, colorful and interesting people they know, pets, special field trips or activities, observations, wonderings, and so forth. The writing folder can also be in the form of a personal collage. Students can use words and pictures cut out of magazines and travel brochures or printed from online sources that they find interesting and that may spark an idea for future writing. The collage folder should be laminated when finished.

Capturing ideas electronically. There are a number of apps for capturing, sorting, and storing ideas—for example, Popplet, Springpad, and Evernote. Gathering and organizing ideas and topics of interest visually can also be done on Pinterest.

Telling personal stories. In small groups or with partners, students tell personal stories in response to prompts—for example, "Tell about a time you or someone you knew got lost." After sharing in their groups, students fill out graphic organizers or outlines of their story.

Writing prompts. Provide a stimulus, such as a story, quote, picture, news article, video, or song, to prompt writing.

Sample topic sentences. For students who continue to struggle to find ideas, providing a choice of topic sentences or a story starter (a sentence or two to introduce a topic) might be helpful.

Looking at reference books. Students can browse many kinds of books in order to gather ideas for writing topics (for example, mysteries of nature, music, sports, fashion).

Verbalizing ideas into a recording device. Some students benefit from talking into a digital recorder and then transcribing their ideas.

Sharing exemplary and at-standard pieces of writing. To help students generate ideas of their own as well as understand the structure of a particular genre, read them some good examples. Read aloud (and project on an overhead or document camera) some pieces of student writing and then discuss them.

Talking them through. Help students who are stuck in picking a topic by sharing ideas aloud, jotting the ideas down for them, and helping them narrow down and choose.

Modeled writing. Model the process of brainstorming, organizing, and recording ideas.

Frames. Provide frames to help struggling writers get started and guide them in planning. Example: "I remember my first day of _____ when I was ___ years old. I felt _____."

Explicitly taught strategies. Explicitly teach students strategies for analyzing the writing prompt or assignment, thinking and gathering ideas, and planning and organizing prior to allowing students to start writing.

Once students have selected the topic, model the process of jotting down main ideas and related details in some format that can then be manipulated easily—moving ideas around and organizing them.

- A helpful technique is to have the student write main ideas and supporting details on separate index cards, sticky notes, or sentence strips. This makes it easier to spread out and group, organize, and sequence those thoughts and ideas. Color-coding related ideas and information is also helpful.
- Capturing ideas (words, phrases, pictures) on a Word document or on the student's electronic devices and moving them around and organizing that way are also very helpful in the planning and prewriting stage.
- Sandler (2005) recommends that in the prewriting stage, students can use their learning style preference for representing and organizing ideas. Visual learners, for example, can draw pictures to represent main and secondary points to move around on the table. Kinesthetic learners who think best by feeling things can use pieces of a game board to represent each of their ideas to move around, and auditory learners can dictate ideas into a digital recorder, download data into a computer, and move ideas around.

Using Planning Forms and Visual Organizers

Graphic organizers are among the most effective ways to help writers generate their ideas as well as formulate and organize their thoughts. The following are some examples of graphic organizers;

others, such as compare-contrast charts, are described in Sections 3.5 and 4.3.

Clustering Write the main idea in a box or rectangle in the center of the page and surround the main idea box with bubbles containing the supporting ideas.

Mind mapping This is a visual showing a central idea (in the center of the graphic) with related ideas and subtopics stemming from it with connecting branches. This technique is also called *webbing,* and the graphic is called a *web*.

Story maps These are used in planning the critical elements to be included when writing a story: setting, characters, problem, action, and resolution.

Other idea development tools and resources See the excellent resources and tips for teaching idea development at Writing Fix (http://writingfix.com/6_traits/idea_development.htm), a website sponsored by Nevada educators Corbett and Dena Harrison and the Northern Nevada Writing Project.

There are many websites with free downloadable graphic organizers, such as Houghton Mifflin's Education Place (http://www.eduplace.com/graphicorganizer/) and Ed Helper (http://edhelper.com/teachers/General_graphic_organizers.htm). The linear organizers—those that provide the specific step-by-step structure (for example, the introduction, three main ideas and supporting details, and a conclusion)—are often the most beneficial.

Apps and Software

There are a variety of apps and software for creating mind maps and other visual organizers to aid in the prewriting process. Two recommended programs that are easy and motivating for even young children to use are Inspiration and Kidspiration (www.inspiration.com). Inspiration also has an outlining feature built in. Categories listed in the graphic web format are automatically placed in outline form with the press of a button. Older students may find these programs useful for mind mapping or just capturing ideas quickly: Mindjet OneNote, Mindomo, X Mind, Evernote, MindNode, MyStudyBar, Popplet, Mindjet MindManager, and FreeMind.

The free program Mendeley (www.mendeley.com) may also be useful for older students to support in researching and making citations. Mendeley enables students to make their own fully searchable library in seconds, cite as they write, and read and annotate PDFs on any device.

Thinking and Questioning

Provide a prewriting checklist that lists specific questions students need to ask themselves at this stage of the writing process. These help the writer think through, plan, and organize prior to drafting. Such questioning can be done independently, but it is also recommended that students engage in this questioning process with someone else (a peer or partner or with a parent or teacher) and during guided writing, as talking through their ideas during the planning stage is very helpful.

When creating a prewriting checklist, teachers may want to select a few questions, such as these:

- Who is my target audience?
- What is my purpose for this writing: to persuade, inform, entertain, or something else?
- What do I already know about this topic?
- Can I write enough about my selected topic?
- What is my message?
- Where will I gather enough interesting information about my topic?
- Which writing genre am I going to use?
- In what style or voice will I write?
- What are some words, ideas, or phrases related to my topic?

Prewriting checklists may be divided into specific questions for the beginning, middle, and end of the piece of writing.

Beginning (Opening)

- How will I introduce the subject or topic?
- What kind of hook can I use in the introduction to capture the audience's attention and interest?
- What will be the main idea about my subject?

Middle (Body)

- What interesting details and examples might I use?
- What will be my flow and sequence of ideas?
- Can I support my points with sufficient evidence?

Ending (Conclusion)

- What would be an interesting, snappy, or exciting ending?
- How will I wrap up my ideas and convey my message to readers?

Mnemonic Strategies

There are a few cognitive strategies in the form of acronyms that help students remember prewrite steps:

- **PLEASE** (Meltzer, 2010; Welch, 1992): **P**ick a topic. **L**ist your ideas about the topic. **E**valuate your list. **A**ctivate the paragraph with a topic sentence. **S**upply supporting sentences. **E**valuate your list.
- **BOTEC**—This is a prewrite strategy originally found in Essay Express (Research ILD & FableVision, 2005) and adapted by Kaufman (2010): **B**rainstorming, **O**rganizing (or **O**rdering), **T**opic (or **T**hesis), **E**vidence (or **E**xamples), **C**onclusion
- The **POW + TREE** prewrite strategies by Karen Harris and Steve Graham (Graham & Harris, 1989; Harris & Graham, 2005) are explained in Section 3.5.

Other Instructional Techniques in the Prewriting Stage

See Nancy Fetzer's website (www.nancyfetzer .com) for demonstrations of exemplary instructional techniques in a whole-class setting that include modeling aloud the thinking process, use of graphic organizers to structure thinking and planning, mnemonic strategies (total physical response and gestures; acronyms to remember steps and writing components), oral rehearsal of what students plan to say prior to writing, and other research-based and engaging techniques.

My appreciation to Beth Black, English department chairperson at Piedmont High School, for sharing some of her instructional strategies and scaffolds that have been particularly beneficial for her students with ADHD:

Example: High School Prewrite Strategies

I like to have students brainstorm several ideas before they move into the writing process. Besides using brainstorming, they also do quick writes using guided questions for students to choose from. For the book *Of Mice and Men* by John Steinbeck, I used quick writes this year with success. After we finished reading the final pages together as a class, I gave the students a sheet of paper, broken up into four segments. In each segment, I put a number (1, 2, 3, 4). Right away, I asked the students to write their reaction to the ending of the text in box 1. I then timed them for two minutes as they did so. The expectation for this exercise is that students write whatever comes to mind for two minutes. It can range from one thought to as many as they can fit in two minutes, but the goal is to get something on paper. Next, I ask the students a higher-level question. For example: "Do you think John Steinbeck believes George will have a better life?" Students write their responses to the question in box 2. Again, the same timing and expectations are in place. For the third and fourth boxes, I give the students a list of guided questions that they can ponder to fill in boxes 3 and 4. We read all the questions out loud and then they are allowed to write on each for three minutes.

At the end of this exercise, we take a break from writing and get into groups to discuss their ideas. Here is where students can add new thoughts, change their minds, or just listen to others. Once they have written on their own and talked with others, they are ready to start organizing one of the thoughts for an essay. It is at this time that I give them their choice as to how they want to organize their essay. My students are pretty savvy in that they have identified, at this point in the year, an organizational tool that works for them. I have blank graphic organizers ready for them, and they take the type (concept map, webbing, or compare/contrast) that they know will help them get started. After this, we set deadlines for the parts of the essay and begin crafting.

The strength of this system benefits students with ADHD and LD because they get to think and write at their own pace, get input from others, and control the organizational tool they wish to use. I agree that self-monitoring is a difficult concept for my freshmen ADHD and LD students, but these small steps really help put them in charge of their direction. This system also lets me see, by breaking writing down into parts, where is their biggest block. I had one student this year who just needed the beginning stage with timed idea generating, and then was able to take off in his writing. I had another student who struggled in the idea section. For her, even if she got two of the four blocks filled in, she felt successful and knew she could move forward.

Parent Tips: Help Your Child with Prewriting

- Look through family albums together and reminisce about people and events. Talk about happenings in your child's life (humorous incidents, places visited, milestones) that your son or daughter may not remember. Share family stories and discuss current events.
- Ask leading questions that encourage your child to open up and share his or her feelings, fears, dreams, aspirations, or likes and dislikes.
- Provide books, reference materials, and access to the library, the Internet, and other resources.
- Read through the writing prompt or directions with your child to make sure he or she knows the expectations.

- Talk about the writing assignment with your child; this will help him or her organize thoughts and clarify his or her thinking before getting started on the actual writing.
- Encourage your child to keep a journal or digital file for jotting down thoughts or questions he or she is pondering; observations; things that have happened to him or her that caused embarrassment, fear, joy, or other strong feelings; reactions to events in the news; and connections he or she has made between movies seen, books read, music heard, and his or her own life. These are all possible topics for future essays, personal narratives, and other writing assignments.
- For research projects, help your child find and choose a topic that is not too broad or too narrow to write about and begin the research process as early as possible.
- When your child is researching a topic, remind him or her of the importance of writing down the source so that he or she can later cite it. If your child is cutting and pasting from the Internet, show him or her how to always copy the URL as well.
- Help your child get started early in deciding on and narrowing down the topic and gathering resources.
- Explore the writing software and apps listed earlier under "Apps and Software."

Strategies for Building Skills in Written Expression

Written expression is the most common academic area of difficulty among students with ADHD. Several brain processes and skills are involved and used simultaneously (for example, language, attention, memory, sequencing, organization, planning, self-monitoring, and critical thinking) when composing a written piece of work.

Students are expected to meet grade-level standards in several writing formats and genres, such as persuasive essays, personal narratives, summaries, and reports, and teachers have the challenge of differentiating instruction to writers of varying levels. The teaching of writing requires knowing how to scaffold the instruction and provide the necessary structures and supports to students who need more help in the writing process. Even students with significant writing difficulties are able to meet writing standards when they receive explicit teaching, modeling, and guided practice of writing skills and strategies.

Instructional Approaches

Teach the craft of writing and composing by using some of these approaches:

Modeled writing Demonstrate the use of strategies, enabling students to witness the thinking and self-questioning processes that are used while composing. Speak aloud what you are thinking (metacognition) while creating a draft of some piece of writing— for example, a beginning paragraph with an interesting lead. Project your writing on a screen so that students can follow the process.

Explicit instruction in paragraph construction Good writers need to be proficient in constructing various types of paragraphs (such as procedural, descriptive, compare and contrast, how-to, and narrative).

Student examples To provide examples for the class, have student volunteers share parts of what they are writing. Student sharing in front of the whole class should be done only by volunteers (unless the work is in its final form).

Guided writing Work with students in groups that are differentiated in various ways, such as by skill level or degree of assistance needed, topic chosen, or stage of the writing process. Some students in the class may be writing a single cohesive paragraph, others composing multiple paragraphs.

Sensory descriptions Teach students through modeling by sharing descriptive examples from literature, helping the reader feel, hear, see, taste, and smell through words.

Sentence starters Provide a list of sentence starters that students can use to help them remember to include important points, such as evidence and support for their statements in their writing (for example, "This was demonstrated when . . .").

Topic sentences Help students who have difficulty getting started by providing a list of possible sentence starters or topic sentences.

Frames Provide writing frames for scaffolding or support. Example: "The author, _____ (insert name), wrote a/an _____ (insert genre) titled _____ (title), which took place_____ (where and when)."

Genre structures Explicitly teach, model, and illustrate the structure and format for each genre used—for example, informational reports with a topic, main ideas (usually three), supporting details, and a conclusion; or a summary structure that includes an introduction, body, and conclusion.

Rubrics Provide rubrics (scoring guides) with all writing assignments. Rubrics explain the performance standards for the assignment and what is expected for such elements as content, organization, mechanics, or neatness in order to meet or exceed grade-level standards. Rubrics are particularly helpful for students with writing difficulties and their parents, teachers, and tutors because they explain exactly what is expected in the assignment and describe the criteria for proficiency. Rubrics typically use a 1–4 or 1–5 scale (for example, 1 = novice, 2 = apprentice, 3 = practitioner, 4 = expert). See the example of a five-paragraph persuasive essay rubric in the appendix (A.11).

Teachers can create their own rubric that is specific to an assignment or use generic ones for a specific genre. Rubrics can also be found on the Internet—for example, at www.rubistar.4teachers.org.

Instructional programs There are some excellent commercial programs that employ a structured approach using multisensory tools to explicitly teach students written composition skills. Such programs scaffold learning through step-by-step approaches, graphic organizers, color coding, and other means in order to enhance the craft of writing. Some recommended resources are Empowering Writers by Mariconda and Auray (www.empoweringwriters.com) and Step Up to Writing by Maureen Auman (www.voyagersopris.com).

Teaching Sentence Structure and Expanded Word Choices

- Teach sentence structure and build sentence-writing skills. Children need to understand that all complete sentences have (1) a subject (a noun: a person, place, or thing) that tells who or what is doing something and (2) a predicate (a verb or prepositional phrases) that tells about the subject.
- Teach children to write interesting, expanded sentences. Start with a simple sentence (for example, "The puppy cried."). Have them dress it up by adding or substituting descriptive adjectives and adverbs, more powerful verbs, and prepositional phrases (When? Where? How? Why?) Example: "The frightened puppy whimpered and whined

as it hid, shaking, under the sofa during the thunderstorm."

- Teach students to use descriptive language that will enhance their writing style. Generate class and individual lists of descriptive and figurative language found in literature or poetry:
  - *Metaphors* (comparisons such as "The room is an oven" or "His temper is an unpredictable thunderstorm")
  - *Similes* (comparisons using the word *like* or *as,* such as "helpless as a newborn baby")
  - *Onomatopoeia* (words that echo sounds, such as *sizzle, crack,* and *pop*)
- Post lists and provide desk or notebook copies for reference of transition or linking words and phrases:
  - Words that signal sequence: *first of all, furthermore, later*
  - Words that signal comparison and contrast of two or more things: *nevertheless, conversely*
  - Words that signal cause and effect: *consequently, as a result*
  - Words that indicate an author's point of view: *I suggest, I believe*

See many examples of such lists at www.pinterest.com/sandrarief/vocabularylanguage.

Teaching Students to Compose a Draft

- Help students with writing by teaching them to prepare effectively. When students write their initial draft, they should be guided by a graphic organizer or planning sheet filled out at the prewriting stage. They should already know their audience, genre structure, topic, point of view, and sequence (for a narrative piece) or main idea and supporting details (for an informational piece).
- Have students write their rough drafts in pencil or erasable pen if writing by hand.
- Allow and encourage students to draft electronically (on a computer, laptop, Chromebook, netbook, or other word processor) when developmentally appropriate.

- If students are typing drafts, show them how to save each successive draft with a new date or draft number and how to back up their work. Handwritten drafts should also always be dated.
- Provide a scribe for students who have trouble getting their thoughts written down.
- Encourage students not to worry about spelling or mechanics at this stage of initial drafting—as long as they can read their own work.
- Students with ADHD sometimes get stuck on the introductory paragraph and may do better if, after the initial planning, they write some of the other paragraphs first. They can work on an introductory paragraph and conclusion later.
- When assigning an essay, particularly in response to questions or a prompt, ensure that students understand what they are being asked and what they need to address in their essay. First, carefully read, discuss, and analyze the prompt or question.
- See online supports such as Essay Information (http://essayinfo.com/essays), which provides explicit instructions and information for writing different types of essays, such as paragraph, argumentative, persuasive, response, comparison, and narrative.
- For several strategies and activities for writing composition across grade levels, see Rief and Heimburge (2007) and www.pinterest.com/sandrarief/writing-strategies-activities.

Teaching Self-Monitoring

Written expression requires considerable self-monitoring. Writers should put themselves in the place of their potential readers and keep asking themselves such questions as "Does this make sense?" "Is this clear?" "Do my ideas flow logically?" and "Am I using the best choice of words?"

- Provide students with a checklist of self-monitoring questions to use as a guide while composing—for example, "What kind of hook can I use to capture the reader's attention?"
- Teach students to use learning strategies such as OSWALD (from James Madison

University's Learning Toolbox at http://coe.jmu.edu/learningtoolbox/oswald.html), which provides steps to follow in composing an essay:

— **O**utline the major points and details that you want to include in your paper.

— **S**ay the outline aloud. Read the outline over to see the relationship between ideas. As you read the outline, think of the main ideas that are most important to your paper.

— **W**rite an introduction, a paragraph introducing your paper. Include the main ideas that you chose when you read the outline aloud.

— **A**dd connecting ideas. Write sentences to connect ideas from one paragraph to another. Think of words that help show the relationship between ideas (for example, *therefore, after*).

— **L**ook over the connections. Reread your paper, starting with the introduction. Make sure that each paragraph is connected to the introduction and to the other paragraphs.

— **D**raft the conclusion. Guided by your introduction and the ideas presented in the body of your paper, write an ending that wraps up the ideas.

Apps and Software

- Text-to-speech software, such as Read & Write GOLD and Kurzweil 3000, read aloud the words on a page. This can be helpful for writers who work on their drafts electronically. The student can listen via the text-to-speech program to what he or she has written so far—identifying where revisions are needed.

- Speech recognition software and apps, such as Dragon Dictation, Dragon Naturally Speaking, and Write:Outloud, can be useful when students struggle to write down or type ideas. (Be forewarned, however, that depending on the voice recognition software, what one dictates does not always translate into those words being correctly written electronically on the page.)

- DraftBuilder (www.donjohnston) is a program designed to help students with writing challenges in the prewriting and composition stages.

Thanks again to Beth Black, English department chairperson at Piedmont High School, for sharing the exemplary instructional strategies and supports she employs for her students' research project.

High School Research Project (I Search)

In my freshmen English class, all students complete a nine-week-long research project called I Search. As you can imagine, this project creates anxiety for my students with ADHD and executive functioning problems. I have developed the following strategies to assist them:

All students bring a three-ring binder to class at the start of the project. During the introduction to the project, students receive a packet with a breakdown and explanation of each component of the research project. The first page is a schedule with due dates for each component; it goes in their binder as the opening page for easy reference. This page must be signed by a parent, indicating that they are aware of this major project and all of the incremental due dates. It is recommended that families copy the page and keep it posted at home.

I also have students create a "Questions" page that they place next in the folder. This page is for writing down their questions that pop up during the project. I use these questions at the start of each class as a check-in. I remind students that we all need a place to keep questions as they arise throughout the day.

Students are given support (for example, time in class to explore and discuss ideas) in finding a research topic. As they begin the project, I explicitly model steps and strategies on a research topic of my own. This past year my topic was examining US policies regarding vaccinations. I modeled the steps of brainstorming and listing questions related to my topic of interest—sharing my graphic organizer and several of the questions that I wrote down. Students work in class on their own topic doing the same, then sharing out their best question that they recorded with classmates.

The next step involves reading from various sources about their topic and taking notes. First, I model doing so using the LCD projector and a sheet for recording information that serves as a guide. I explicitly demonstrate to the class—reading and taking notes from sources related to my topic using the organizer sheet. The goal of this exercise is to show how to read and cite the source, record direct quotes, and paraphrase notes of other information on the organizer page. I begin with an article that I found, using one of the school databases, and read it aloud. One example I modeled was reading and note taking from an *LA Times* newspaper article about the measles outbreak at Disneyland. Another day I modeled reading, citing, and recording information about measles complications found on the website of the Centers for Disease Control and Prevention (CDC). *Note:* The organizer sheet used for note taking has space for recording the following: Source, Type, Info, Direct Quotes, Paraphrase, My Own Thoughts.

During this process, I read aloud, stopping to color-highlight key parts that I find interesting, and explain to the students why I think it matters (my own metacognition). I then read further and ask students to find key parts for me. As they come up with suggestions, both in groups and individually, we discuss the importance of the information and how I should record that information on my organizer—going through each part together.

Then I have students begin researching on their own topics. Students have space on their note-taking sheet/form that has a line for the source citation, type of source (magazine, newspaper, website), direct quotes, paraphrase of other information, and jotting down their own thoughts about the topic. They are given twenty minutes to work on this, during which time I circulate through the classroom helping students who need individual assistance and feedback. After students have completed the twenty minutes, they are accountable for their research by having to share out with a partner their best research finding during that given time frame.

Students are given time in class every day to work on this project. We always work in fifteen- to twenty-minute time increments only. I have the students set their own goal as to how much they want to accomplish in that time frame and then allow them time to research. For example, I will ask them to decide how many sources they want to examine or how many pages of notes they think they can accomplish in the time. This strategy helps students realistically set the pace that they need in order to accomplish the entire research task (both in class and at home).

What I found is that use of the organizer sheet/form works to help students gather information without them worrying about where it is going to go in the paper. Later (and with supports as needed), students work on taking their research findings and grouping them by category in order to help them organize their research essay. Students have shared with me that they felt that they gained more knowledge of their topics overall and are better prepared to write more interesting papers by using this method and tools.

Students turn in each project part and essay separately according to the schedule, receiving clear feedback on each along the way. I notify parents immediately if students fail to turn in any component, in order to identify any problems right away and help the student get back on track for the long term.

Parent Tips: Help Your Child in the Drafting and Composing Stage

- Consider purchase of writing tools (hardware, software, and apps) that your child will be motivated to use that have functions to make the various stages of the writing process easier. See the later discussion of writing accommodations and assistive technology.
- If your child is writing by hand in the drafting stage, encourage him or her to do so on every other line to enable easier revision for future drafts.
- Go over the writing assignment with your child, breaking it down into smaller parts to focus on.
- Refer to the planning sheets or graphic organizers for the assignment that should have been prepared in the prewriting or planning stage, while having your child talk with you about what he or she plans to write first.
- After reviewing the planning sheet and talking about it, help your child get started on the actual writing. For some, this means just being available to answer questions or being a sounding board for your child as he or she begins the task. For others, it may involve your child dictating and you writing down or typing what he or she says.
- Support and monitor in regard to time management issues that interfere with your child's success on long-term projects (such as research papers). Set mini-goals and deadlines for completing parts (for example, number of sentences or paragraphs written, or research and notes taken from various sources). Use of a log for tracking time spent on daily work on a long-range project is helpful, such as the research log (A.12) in the appendix.
- Offer suggestions or ask questions to help your child flesh out the details or make the writing more logical and coherent if needed.
- Help your child understand that initial drafts are not the final product but a work in progress.
- Ask your child to read the draft to you and be sure to date and save it.

Strategies for Revising and Editing

For children and teens with ADHD, this stage of the writing process (revising, proofreading, and making corrections) is the one that generally meets with the most resistance.

Revising written work involves adding or deleting information, resequencing the order of sentences and paragraphs, and choosing words that better communicate one's meaning. Revision requires self-monitoring and critically evaluating one's own work, as well as the motivation to put forth the effort in rewriting subsequent drafts. This is very difficult and tedious for students with ADHD or learning disabilities. For many, once they have struggled to complete the first draft, they consider their written work as done.

Editing involves proofreading for errors in grammar, mechanics, and spelling and then polishing the final product. Students with ADHD are typically very weak in editing skills because editing requires focused attention to details and close self-monitoring. It is unrealistic to expect that they will be able to adequately proofread for their own errors and fix them without direct help, such as teacher, parent, or peer editing or assistive technology supports.

Strategies for Helping Students with Revision

- Encourage students to write rough drafts on every other line of the paper to make it easier to revise and edit.
- Allow students to compose on a computer, laptop, netbook, or other tablet with a word processing app, or a Chromebook using Google Docs. Composing on an electronic device with word processing capabilities is ideal for revising subsequent drafts more easily and for organization and management of written work. Being able to write from anywhere (such as can be done using Google Docs and storage of work in the cloud) is very beneficial.
- Model and demonstrate the steps for revising—one step at a time.

- Provide checklists to help students self-monitor during the revision process. Select some (not all) of the following questions in creating a list appropriate to the developmental level of the child:
  — Does my introduction capture the attention of my readers?
  — Did I develop my ideas logically?
  — Have I given enough information?
  — Does everything make sense?
  — Did I stick to my topic?
  — Have I presented my ideas clearly and in the right order?
  — Have I given details and examples for each main idea?
  — Do I need to insert, move around, or delete any ideas?
  — Have I used interesting descriptive words?
  — Do my paragraphs have a beginning, middle, and end?
  — Have I replaced overused words?
  — Did I write an interesting, powerful conclusion?
- Have students read their drafts to a peer in order to obtain feedback. The partner listens, asks questions, indicates when more information is needed, and makes other suggestions. Parents can also provide feedback to help their child learn to make appropriate revisions. Information can be inserted with carets (^) or on sticky notes next to where it will be added.
- When a student is revising a composition, suggest that he or she address one aspect of the writing at a time. For example, a student could focus first on clarity, flow, and sequence, then read and revise for sentence variety and descriptive language, and next for overused words.
- Teach the skill of combining sentences and encourage this technique when students are revising. Example: "The day was hot and sunny. The girls ate ice cream cones. They played and rode their bikes." These three sentences can be combined: "The girls ate ice cream cones, played, and rode their bikes on the hot, sunny day."

- During the revision process, have students identify sentences that can be improved. Encourage them to find boring, simple sentences and embellish them.
- When listening to a child read an initial draft, provide positive feedback by describing something you like about the piece, acknowledging the student's growth in a specific skill, or recognizing the student's effort. Ask probing questions when something is unclear and more information is needed.
- If revising is overwhelming for the student, consider providing a scribe. Let children dictate the changes they want to make and have the scribe record those changes on the paper.
- Teach the revision mnemonic of **ARMS**: **A**dd sentences, details, examples, and descriptive words. **R**emove unneeded words and sentences. **M**ove the placement of words, phrases, sentences, or paragraphs. **S**ubstitute words or sentences for others (for example, more powerful verbs).
- Encourage the use of word prediction, spell-checking, and grammar-checking tools and features while word processing. These are very helpful supports for writers— particularly in the revision and editing stages.

Strategies for Helping Students with Editing

- Provide direct instruction and guided practice in the proper use of mechanics (punctuation and capitalization).
- Have students use peer editing as well as adult assistance. A peer or adult partner can point out run-on or incomplete sentences, missing or incorrect capitalization or punctuation, and misspelled words.
- Teach students how to use editing tools and options (thesaurus, spell-checker, cut and paste) on word processing programs or apps.
- Even though self-editing is hard, encourage it by having students read aloud their

work and identify what doesn't look or sound right.
- When self-editing, have students circle (or code) words that they think are misspelled. Later, with assistance as needed, they can go back and check the spelling.
- There are many spell-check and grammar-check apps, software, and online programs that are very helpful in the editing process. Ghotit (www.ghotit.com), for example, is one such program designed especially for people with dyslexia. Besides those built into word processing programs, there are various editing apps, such as Hemingway and Proofread Text Editor, and spell-check apps available. Talking handheld spell-checkers, such as Children's Talking Dictionary and Spell Corrector by Franklin Electronics, are helpful as well.
- Teach editing symbols (insert, delete, capitalize, new paragraph). Provide reference charts that show those symbols.
- After modeling how to jointly edit a piece of writing for the whole class, have students work with partners to check each other's work.
- Have students use colored pencils as they edit for one thing at a time. For example, have them check each sentence and underline the final punctuation in red, capital letters in blue.
- Provide an editing checklist to help students proofread their own work for capitalization, sentence structure, and mechanical errors. Following is a list of possible questions to include in a proofreading checklist:
  — Did I use complete sentences?
  — Did I begin all sentences with capital letters?
  — Did I end sentences with a final punctuation mark (., ?, !)?
  — Have I capitalized all proper nouns?
  — Have I checked spelling?
  — Have I indented my paragraphs?
  — Are verb tenses consistent?
  — Are there run-on sentences?
  — Is my paper neat and organized?

Mnemonic Proofreading Strategies

Strategies that incorporate mnemonic techniques to remember steps of a strategy and apply them independently are powerful for students with ADHD and learning disabilities. Here are four learning strategies for revision and editing:

- **COPS** is an error-monitoring strategy (Schumaker et al., 1981). A writer reads through his or her work four times, each time checking the writing for one of the four components in the following list and correcting errors.

    Capitalize. Have I capitalized the first word of each sentence and all proper nouns?
    Overall. How is the overall appearance (spacing, indentation, neatness)?
    Punctuation. Have I put in commas, semicolons, and end punctuation?
    Spelling. Have I spelled the words correctly?

- **SCOPE** is a learning strategy for proofreading from Learning Toolbox at James Madison University (http://coe.jmu.edu/learningtoolbox). The student reads the paper five times, each time looking for a different type of error.

    Spelling. Reread your paper for misspelled words. Use a spelling checker. Try writing misspelled words in different ways to see if one looks right. Use a dictionary to find correct spellings.
    Capitalization. Reread your paper to make sure all words are correctly capitalized.
    Order of words. Read your paper aloud. Point to each word as you say it to make sure that no words have been omitted, added, or mixed up.
    Punctuation. Reread your paper to check for correct punctuation.
    Express complete thoughts. Reread each sentence aloud to make sure that sentences are grammatically correct. (Each sentence should have a complete thought, there should be no run-on sentences, and all parts of the sentence should agree.) The sentences should sound right.

- **SPORTS** (Meltzer et al., 2006) is an acronym for editing written work for these elements:

    Sentence structure
    Punctuation
    Organization
    Repetition
    Tenses
    Spelling

- Sandler (2005) recommends that in the editing process, students read their work aloud and ask themselves these three Cs:

    Clear (Are my points clear and understandable?)
    Concise (Am I wordy or repetitive?)
    Clean (Are there grammar, spelling, or typo errors to clean up?)

Other Tips for Teachers

- Conduct teacher-student writing conferences in which students respond to their own writing. ("My best sentence is _____." "A simile or metaphor I used was _____.") The student reflects on his or her own work. Student and teacher share what they like about the writing.
- Have students evaluate where they have improved and skills to target for continued improvement. ("My writing has improved in _____ [sentence structure, paragraphing, organization, punctuation, spelling]. I plan to work on _____.")
- Provide a rubric with all writing assignments. Show models of work that is at standard and that exceeds the standard.
- Teach students who are drafting on a computer how to find overused words that they

might want to replace. With the control-F function, they can type in the word and quickly find it throughout the document so that it can be replaced.

- Use the Track Changes and Comment features in Microsoft Word. Another reader (parent, teacher, peer) can make comments and note suggested changes in the file of a draft that a student has written on a computer.

Strategies to Bypass and Accommodate Writing Difficulties

Note: In addition to the information presented in this section, see Part 4 Additional Sources and Resources for more information on technological supports.

Tips for Teachers

- It commonly takes students with ADHD significantly longer than others their age or grade to produce written work. An assignment that takes most students twenty minutes or so to complete may take hours for a child or teen with ADHD. Keep that in mind when giving written assignments and homework to these students and when sending home incomplete work.
- Assign reasonable amounts of homework.
- Make adjustments in order to accept modified homework that requires reduced amounts of writing. Discuss the adjustments ahead of time with students and parents.
- When writing in class is required, allow students to take extra time as needed, particularly on essay questions for written assessments.
- Substitute nonwritten, hands-on assignments and oral presentations for written assignments.
- Give students options that do not require writing but may involve investigating, building, drawing, simulating, telling, demonstrating, and so on.
- Reduce the need to copy from the board or book. Provide photocopies of notes or share

notes digitally with students. Another option is to let students access notes via the interactive whiteboard or take snapshots from the board or book on their smartphone or other personal devices to download later.

- Enlarge the space for doing written work on math papers, tests, and worksheets.
- Stress the accuracy and quality of writing, not the volume.
- Permit students to dictate responses and have someone else (an adult, classmate, or cross-age tutor) be a scribe and write down what the student says.
- Allow oral responses for assignments and tests when appropriate.
- Follow written exams with an oral exam and average the two grades for students who may know the correct answers but cannot show their understanding adequately on a written exam.
- Allow students to print, use cursive handwriting, or type when appropriate—whichever is easiest, quickest, and most legible.
- Provide in-class time to get started on assignments.
- Provide note-taking assistance. Assign students who need assistance a buddy with whom to share and compare notes. Encourage students to take their own notes, but allow them to supplement their own notes with more detailed, organized copies from the note taker.
- Provide partial outlines or frames in which the student fills in the missing information while listening to lectures.
- Provide tools such as highlighting tape, paper with wide and narrow lines, various types of pens and pencils, and different shapes of pencil grips.
- Allow the student to use audio recorders instead of writing for summarizing learning, responding to questions, planning and recording ideas, and instructions.
- Teach keyboarding and word processing skills or suggest that students learn to type by using software, an app, or an online program at home.

- Help the student get started writing by talking or prompting through the first few sentences or so, or have him or her dictate while an adult writes the first few sentences.
- On writing assignments, grade content and mechanics separately.
- Provide graphic organizers or other structural aids for written assignments.
- If a child struggles to hold a pencil, have him or her try a pencil grip to make it easier. Pencil grips in different shapes, materials, and designs are available.
- Have students try a mechanical pencil if they frequently break pencil points from applying too much pressure.
- Set realistic, mutually agreed-on expectations for neatness.
- If a student's paper frequently slides around, attach it to a clipboard.
- Post your expectations for how assignments should appear (for example, writing on one side of the paper only, drafts written double spaced, math papers completed with two or three line spaces between problems).
- Provide visual cues such as starting dots and numbered arrows in order to support correct letter formation (direction and sequence of strokes).

Assistive Technology

Many writing difficulties can be alleviated significantly with assistive technology, which is now affordable and accessible. An assistive technology device is any item, piece of equipment, or product system used to increase, maintain, or improve the functional capabilities of individuals with a disability.

- Students with ADHD who qualify for assistive technology under IDEA or Section 504 have that fact documented in their IEP or 504 accommodation plan. This includes the tools and the training in their use. Assistive technology equipment or services designated in their plan are provided by the school district.

- Allow the use of electronic spell-checkers, dictionaries, thesauri, and other electronic tools if helpful.
- Use quality programs that are designed with features to support the writing process, such as the many mentioned earlier throughout this section.
- Provide or allow the use of a computer, tablet, netbook, Chromebook, or other portable device with word processing capability (such as NEO or Fusion).
- Some software programs are designed specifically for people with reading and writing disabilities. They have features such as speech recognition, word prediction, text-to-speech, and audible spell-check. A few of the companies that carry such software are TextHelp, Kurzweil Educational Systems, BrightEye Technology, Quillsoft, and Don Johnston.

Word Processing

The use of word processing has revolutionized the way we write, freeing us from the task of handwriting and enabling us to easily save drafts of work, revise by cutting and pasting, edit with tools such as spell-check and grammar-check, and produce easy-to-read copies.

Knowing that it is relatively easy to revise, reorganize, replace vocabulary, and correct spelling and grammar enables writers to focus on the content and produce better writing. Learning how to use word processing with proficiency needs to be a priority for students with writing disabilities.

Typing and Keyboarding Software, Online Programs, and Apps

To get the most out of word processing, learning how to type quickly and accurately is very beneficial. Even though today's students are commonly very proficient with messaging and typing on their electronic devices, learning proper keyboarding skills and being able to type without looking at a keyboard are still beneficial.

Some software and online programs as well as apps for learning or practicing keyboarding and typing include the following:

- Typing Instructor Deluxe or Typing Instructor for Kids Platinum (Individual Software)
- Type to Learn (Sunburst)
- Disney's Adventures in Typing with Timon & Pumba (Disney Interactive)
- Read Write and Type (Talking Fingers)
- JumpStart Typing (Knowledge Adventure)
- Mavis Beacon Teaches Typing (The Learning Company)
- Look and Learn Keyboard Typing System and iColorType (KeyWrite)
- UltraKey (Bytes of Learning, Inc.)
- Dance Mat Typing (BBC UK Schools)
- Burning Fingers (itunesapple.com)

Word Predictors and Spelling Checkers

- Word predictors analyze words as they are typed and try to predict the words that the user is most likely to want. As the writer types a letter of the alphabet, the program offers a list of the most common words beginning with that letter. If the first letter does not bring up the right word, more choices are offered when a second letter is typed. Some programs speak the words from the list out loud to help the writer select the desired word. WordQ and Co:Writer are two such programs.
- Spelling checkers are very helpful for writers with spelling difficulties. Many software or online programs that are designed for struggling readers and writers have word prediction and spell-checking functions with an audio component (Co:Writer, Write:OutLoud, Read & Write GOLD, WordQ, and SpeakQ). The word choices are read aloud from the computer to make it easier for the user to identify the appropriate word.
- Ghotit Context Spellchecker Service (www .ghotit.com) is a set of services designed specifically for dyslexic children and adults or others with significant spelling disabilities whose spelling and typing errors are too far from the correct spelling of the word or too out of context to benefit from regular spelling checkers.

Speech-to-Text Software

Speech recognition technology, such as Dragon Naturally Speaking (by Nuance), enables users to dictate and have their oral language automatically converted into print. Speech-to-text technology can be very beneficial for those who struggle to get their ideas down in writing or who need to type and find doing so slow and tedious. It can be very useful in the writing process, but it does have its glitches.

Harris (2014) points out that the skill of dictation is not as easy as it seems. Students must organize what they are going to say before they speak it and then need to edit what they have dictated, which is not an easy task for children or teens with ADHD. Sometimes there are many errors that need to be corrected because the program does not recognize or misinterprets what the speaker has dictated, which is frustrating for the user.

As voice-recognition technology continues to improve, this may be the most efficient way for struggling writers to independently express what they want to say in writing.

Text-to-Speech Software

Text-to-speech software enables the user to see the print (digitized text) highlighted as they hear it being read aloud. Some examples of text-to-speech software include Read & Write GOLD, ClaroRead Plus, Kurzweil 3000, Write:OutLoud and Read:OutLoud, and ReadPlease. Programs with these text-to-speech features can be very helpful for individuals with ADHD or learning disabilities, particularly during the revision and editing stages of writing.

section
4.5

Spelling and Handwriting

In addition to the writing process difficulties so common in ADHD, many children and teens with ADHD (particularly those with coexisting learning disabilities) also have illegible written work due to poor spelling and/or handwriting. Inaccurate spelling and messy, hard-to-read work can have a negative impact on the way a written product is judged.

Helping Children with Spelling Difficulties

Students with ADHD and learning disabilities often struggle with spelling, due to a variety of brain-based weaknesses. Fortunately, there are many strategies and supports that teachers and parents can provide to boost students' spelling proficiency.

Spelling Challenges

- Accurate spelling requires good phonological processing and phonics skills, which are areas of significant weakness for students with dyslexia. Because ADHD and dyslexia are common coexisting disorders, many children and teens with ADHD have these phonological and language-based processing difficulties, which make spelling a struggle.

- Poor spellers have trouble remembering the letters in words because they have trouble noticing, remembering, and recalling the features of language that those letters represent. Most commonly, poor spellers have weaknesses in underlying language skills, including the ability to analyze and remember the individual sounds (phonemes) in the words, the syllables, and the meaningful parts (morphemes) of longer words, such as *sub-*, *-pect*, or *-able* (International Dyslexia Association, 2011).

- Individuals with ADHD who do not have coexisting dyslexia may have spelling difficulties related to inattention (not noticing features of the word), impulsivity (writing the word without thinking through each of the letters or checking to see if it looks accurate), and weaknesses in WM (inability to hold the word in mind while sounding out and recording it).

- Spelling taxes a child's memory (WM and long-term memory) and is complicated by the ease or difficulty with which the child writes the letters legibly and in the proper order (International Dyslexia Association, 2009).

- When students are weak spellers, their written work suffers. Instead of using words they may not know how to spell, they may limit the vocabulary they use, reducing the quality and quantity of their writing.

- When students struggle with spelling, they have less mental energy to focus on what they want to say and how to organize their thoughts when writing.
- Students with spelling disabilities need to have effective instruction to learn to spell, and accommodations and modifications to help them compensate for their weaknesses.

Spelling Instruction

To become competent spellers, all students must master a sequence of skills and progress through developmental stages of spelling, which take longer and require more intensive instruction for students with dyslexia.

A systematic, sequential approach is the most effective form of spelling instruction for most students, but is a necessity for those with dyslexia. Effective spelling instruction encompasses the following characteristics:

Multisensory. Students learn by seeing, hearing, saying, and writing the words.

Sequential and incremental. Instruction moves in order from simple concepts and skills to more complex ones.

Cumulative. Students are engaged in ongoing review of previous concepts and words.

Individualized. Instruction is customized because students vary in their spelling acquisition skills and level of performance.

Explicit. Students are taught specific spelling rules rather than being expected to figure out spelling patterns on their own.

Teachers should consider the following instructional tips that strengthen students' spelling skills and proficiency:

- To guide instruction, use developmental spelling inventories and assessment tools to determine the extent of a student's spelling knowledge as well as missing skills.
- Provide systematic phonics training to students who are deficient in this skill and are poor spellers. The majority of words in the English language are phonetically regular and can be decoded and spelled correctly with phonetic knowledge and the application of phonetic strategies.
- Explicitly teach letter-sound correspondences; letter patterns from simple to the more complex; the six basic English syllable types; spelling rules, such as when to double consonants; and meaningful word parts (prefixes and suffixes). Although there are exceptions and irregular words in the English language, the English spelling system is not unpredictable. Even students with severe spelling disabilities can become much more competent spellers when they are explicitly and directly taught these spelling patterns, rules, and phonics skills.
- Teach students about word origins. Many English words are derived from other languages (such as Latin, Greek, French, Old English), resulting in letter combinations that may be unfamiliar to students. Learning about the origin of words is also helpful in improving skills in reading, vocabulary, and spelling.
- Introduce words on the board or projector. Ask students as a class to look at the configuration or shape of the word. Have them also look for little words within the word and any mnemonic clues that would be helpful in remembering how to spell the word. Write the word in syllables in different colored pens. Discuss its meaning and use it in context.
- Teach students to look for patterns in words by using phonograms, word families, and onsets and rimes. Color-highlight patterns within the words.
- Use word sorts to provide opportunities for students to discover common patterns. For example, students would place *stopping, sitting,* and *cutting* in one column (doubling the consonant before adding *-ing*), while *reading, playing,* and *sorting* would go in another

column. Have students state the spelling rules for each column.

- Post, in a highly visible location, the high-frequency irregular words that students are expected to spell correctly in their written work. In addition, you can provide student desk or notebook copies for reference.
- Maintain a word wall in the classroom that includes content-area words, high-frequency words, and other words deemed important listed under each letter of the alphabet.
- Use mnemonics whenever possible to help students remember and learn memory strategies to apply in the future.
  — Examples: *friend*: I am a friEND to the END; *church*: You are (U/R) in church.
  — Create pictures using words (For example, write *look* with the *o*'s drawn as eyes; write *clown* and then draw a funny hat on top.)
- Use choral and unison techniques for practicing the spelling of nonphonetic words. Practice irregular nonphonetic words with creative techniques to help in recall. For example, make up a chant, clap out the letters in the words, spell the words using American Sign Language, or use voice inflection to help call attention to certain letters (for example, emphasizing the tricky letters in a louder voice).
- Post an example of a picture association for different phonograms for student reference—for example, a picture of an eagle for *ea*, a picture of a house for *ou*, and a train or snail for *ai*.
- Provide many peer tutoring and partner spelling opportunities, such as quizzing and practicing together in fun ways.
- Have several resources readily available for student access, such as dictionaries, electronic spell-checkers, and lists of commonly used words.
- Teach the "look, say, write" method of practice: "Look at the word and trace it with your finger or your pencil. Say the word. Spell it out loud while you copy it. Now, write the word without looking. Check it against the one you traced. Did you write it correctly? If

you made a mistake, fix it now, and think of a way to remember the correct spelling."

- Modify spelling lists for students with spelling disabilities, as needed.
- Make up word skeletons. Example: ___ ___ s ___ r ___ ___ e ___ t for the word *instrument*. The child fills in the missing letters.
- Have the student make a set of flash cards and study each of the words with a partner or parent. The child then puts aside the cards of the words that he or she missed and restudies them.
- There are irregular, high-frequency words that are best to learn a few at a time; have students practice writing them frequently in multisensory ways.

Motivating, Multisensory Techniques to Practice Spelling

Children with ADHD need fun, novel ways to be motivated to practice spelling words. Experiment with having them try the following.

Using Fun Materials and Tactile Strategies

- Dip a clean paintbrush in water and write words on the tabletop, wall, or sidewalk.
- Write words in the air using a stiff arm and large muscle movements while sounding the words out (sky writing).
- Use the rainbow technique of tracing over each word at least three different times in different colors (pencils, crayons, chalk, or markers). Then, without looking, write the word from memory.
- Write words in a flat tray or box of colored sand or salt using one or two fingers.
- Write words in glue or liquid starch on pieces of cardboard. Then sprinkle any powdery material, glitter, yarn, beans, macaroni, sequins, or other material to create textured, three-dimensional spelling words. (Substances such as sand, salt, and glitter are good to use for students who benefit from tracing the words with their fingers. *Note:* The act of tracing with fingers on a texture

helps make a sensory imprint on the brain that increases memory and retention.)

- Write words in a sandbox with a stick.
- Write on a dry-erase board the words your teacher dictates.
- Pair with another student (or with parent) and write words on each other's back with a finger, with the receiver identifying the word by feel.
- While sitting on the carpet, practice writing the words directly on the carpet with two fingers using large muscle movements.
- Finger-paint words using shaving cream on desks or tabletops. Or use pudding, whipped cream, or frosting on waxed paper or paper plates.
- Type each of the words in a variety of fonts, colors, and sizes.
- Write the words using alphabet manipulatives and tactile letters. Examples are magnetic letters, sponge letters, alphabet stamps, alphabet cereal, letter tiles, and linking letter cubes.
- Practice writing words with a glitter pen, a neon gel pen on black paper, or other special pen.
- Use a flashlight in a darkened room or laser pen to "write" the words on a wall.
- Write words forming the letters with clay or Wikki Stix (www.wikkistix.com).

Using Song and Movement

- Pair movement while spelling words aloud: clapping to each letter, bouncing a ball, using a yo-yo, jumping rope, or jumping on a trampoline are some of the many possibilities.
- Tap out the sounds or syllables in words using a pencil on a desk or your fingertips on the desk or your other arm; or spell words while tapping with one hand down the other arm, from shoulder to hand.
- Chant the spelling of words that are irregular and hard to sound out phonetically.
- Use kinesthetic cues for letters and sounds and act out those motions or refer to those cues when segmenting words to spell. (Various programs for teaching letter and sound

associations include body movements as a kinesthetic cue for each sound or calling attention to the mouth and tongue positions and how sounds are formed and feel.) Sing spelling words to common tunes or melodies.

- Spell words standing up for consonant letters and sitting down for vowels.
- Trace words with a pencil while spelling the word. Then trace with an eraser. Get up and do a brief physical activity, such as five jumping jacks. Now write the word and check it for accuracy.

Using Color and Visual Highlighting

- Color-code tricky letters (silent letters) in hard-to-spell words.
- Write the words by syllables in different colors.
- Write silent letters (ghost letters) using a white pen.
- After taking a pretest, color the known part of a word (correctly spelled letters) in one color. By the time the word is spelled correctly with further trials, the whole word should be written in color.
- Write all the vowels of the word in red.
- Color-code key elements and features of the word (for example, prefixes and suffixes, final *e*).
- Write out each of the words. Circle the silent letters and underline the vowels.
- Underline misspelled letters or trouble spots in words.

Other Techniques for Spelling

In addition to the activities listed, students can use games and apps for learning and practicing spelling—phonetic spellings and sight word spellings. A few examples are Mystery Word Town—Sight Word Spelling, PBS Kids spelling games (http://pbskids.org/games/spelling), board games such as Boggle and Scrabble, and suggestions from these websites: http://topnotchteaching.com/lesson-ideas/35-spelling-games/ and http://www.theschoolrun.com/best-word-games-for-children.

For many creative strategies for helping children become better spellers, check these Pinterest boards:

www.pinterest.com/sandrarief/spelling-word-work/

www.pinterest.com/sandrarief/phonics-decoding-fluency

www.pinterest.com/sandrarief/sight-words/

Also see the Part 4 Additional Sources and Resources for more on spelling instruction for students with spelling disabilities, including my books.

Additional Spelling Tips

- When grading written work of students with spelling disabilities, teachers should be reasonable in penalizing for spelling errors (minimal if any point deduction or grade reduction).
- If a child is a very poor speller, a structured phonics-based program using a systematic, multisensory approach (such as those described in Section 4.2) is most beneficial in building the skills needed to decode and spell the majority of words in the English language. That should be the primary intervention and focus of spelling instruction. Practice in learning and remembering the spelling of "sight" words (those that cannot be sounded out or spelled phonetically) is also important, and there are numerous fun ways for doing so (as described in the preceding lists).
- Spelling tools and word processing features, such as spell-checkers, word prediction, and text-to-speech functions can be a significant help for poor spellers. See Section 4.4 under the heading "Strategies to Bypass and Accommodate Writing Difficulties" for more on this topic and recommended programs.

Improving Handwriting and Legibility of Written Work

Struggles with handwriting and written organization interfere with production and being able to show what you know. Paper-and-pencil tasks are a source of great frustration for many children with ADHD. When the physical act of writing is so tedious and the results of these efforts are messy and illegible, it is no wonder that children with ADHD often hate to write and resist doing so.

If you observe a child struggling with the physical task of writing (correct letter formation, pencil grip, speed, and legibility), share concerns with school staff and consider consulting with an occupational therapist. An evaluation and perhaps services from an occupational therapist or other specialist may be needed. Accommodations and supports, such as use of assistive technology to compensate for or alleviate some of the writing struggle, are also generally necessary.

Dysgraphia and Other Handwriting Struggles

Many children with ADHD also have the coexisting learning disability referred to as *dysgraphia*—a disability in handwriting. Children with dysgraphia may have difficulty with orthographic coding, which is the ability to store written words in WM while the letters in the words are analyzed (in order to spell them). They may also have difficulty with planning the sequential finger movements to form the letters when handwriting (International Dyslexia Association, 2012).

Signs of dysgraphia include the following (Jones, 2003; National Center for Learning Disabilities, 2014):

- Inconsistencies: mixtures of print and cursive and/or capital and lowercase; irregular sizes, shapes, or slants of letters
- Unfinished words or letters, omitted words
- Words inconsistently positioned on the page with respect to lines and margins
- Cramped or unusual grip, especially holding the writing instrument very close to the paper or holding the thumb over two fingers and writing from the wrist
- Strange wrist, body, or paper position
- Talking to self while writing or carefully watching the hand that is writing

- Inability to write or draw in a line or within margins
- Slow or labored copying or writing even if it is neat and legible
- Content that does not reflect the student's other language skills
- Inefficient speed in copying
- Poor fluency of letter formation
- Fatigue while writing
- Lack of automatic letter formation

Some children may also be developmentally delayed in their fine motor skills (the small muscle movements required in writing). The following are some observable behaviors of children with fine motor difficulties (Landy & Burridge, 2000):

- Poor grasp, leading to poor form and fluency, and frequent discomfort when writing
- Difficulty controlling speed of movements, leading to excessive speed and resultant untidy work or to incomplete work due to overly slow movements
- Difficulty with precision grip and inaccurate release, and therefore problems with games that involve placement of pieces (for example, dominoes)
- Difficulty with spatial relations, leading to difficulties with design and copying
- Tearing paper or breaking pencils due to force-control difficulties
- Difficulty with learning to dress and undress (tying shoes, buttoning, zipping)
- Clumsiness and frustration: spills food, drops objects, breaks objects
- Frustration and/or resistant behavior toward manipulative and graphic tasks
- Excessive muscular tension when performing fine motor tasks

Handwriting Tips and Strategies

Because more emphasis has come to be placed on communicating in writing with technology, less has been placed on teaching and learning handwriting. This is reflected in the CCSS. Standards for legible manuscript writing are included for kindergarten and grade 1, but beyond that,

individual states are given the option of including handwriting in the curriculum at higher grades. Several states have done so ("Handwriting and the Common Core State Standards," 2012), but not all.

Research supports the benefits of teaching and learning handwriting skills, besides the obvious. According to Bounds (2010), MRI studies show that the practice of writing by hand helps with learning letters and shapes, can improve idea composition and expression, and may aid the development of fine motor skills.

The following are some strategies and programs for teaching and improving handwriting:

- Group letters by similarity of formation (for example, *l/t/i*; *a/c/d*; *v/w*) when teaching and practicing how to write them.
- After he or she has first traced over letters, have the child write a few independently and then circle his or her best effort.
- Provide visual cues such as a starting dot and numbered arrows as a guide for the correct letter formation (direction and sequence of strokes).
- There are pencil grips of different shapes, materials, and designs that can make it easier if a child struggles to hold and manipulate a pencil. Experiment with different kinds. See www.therapro.com, www.therapyshoppe.com, and other companies that carry such products.
- Try self-drying clay around the pencil to mold to the size and shape of the child's fingers and grip.
- Try mechanical pencils for students who frequently break their pencil points from applying too much pressure. Although mechanical pencil points can also break easily, at least the student doesn't need to sharpen his or her pencil frequently throughout the day—pulling the student off task.
- Share how studies have proven that teachers tend to give students the benefit of the doubt and grade higher if their papers are neat rather than sloppy or hard to read.
- Provide sufficient time to write in order to avoid time pressure.

- Set realistic, mutually agreed-on expectations for neatness.
- Some children find it easier to write using narrow-ruled paper; others do better using paper with wider-ruled lines.
- Teach placing an index finger between words (finger spacing) to help children who run their words together without spacing.
- If the students is using a pen, provide one with erasable ink.
- Remind the child to anchor his or her paper with the nonwriting hand or arm to keep it from moving while writing.
- If the student paper is frequently sliding around, try attaching the paper to a clipboard.
- Provide a strip or chart of alphabet letters (manuscript or cursive) on the student's desk for reference. Draw directional arrows on the letters the child finds confusing and difficult to write.

Handwriting Programs and Apps

- One highly recommended program for teaching print and cursive to children, especially those with writing difficulties, is Handwriting Without Tears, developed by the occupational therapist Jan Olsen (www .hwtears.com). The program uses multisensory techniques and mnemonic cues for helping children learn proper letter formation; it also structures the sequence of letters introduced by clusters. For example, cursive o, w, b, and v are taught together as the "tow-truck letters" because of their special high endings.
- Another recommended handwriting program is Living Letters, developed by Cindy Pahr (www.educlime.com). This program uses multisensory techniques, associative stories, special colored writing paper (sky, grass, earth), magnetic tracer sets, and other unique and motivating tools.
- The CASL Handwriting Program (Graham & Harris, 1999) is one that has been research validated as successful for children with disabilities.

- There are several apps that teach and provide motivating practice in letter formation, such as Touch and Write (by Fizzbrain), LetterSchool (by Letter School), ABC Cursive Writing (by Deep Pocket Series), iCanWrite (by Fiendsoft), iWriteWords (by gdiplus), Writing Wizard (by L'Escapadou), and Wet-Dry-Try Suite (part of the Handwriting Without Tears program). Touch and Write, for example, is a fun app in which children practice writing (print or cursive) using several different writing textures (such as shaving cream and grape jelly) on a variety of paper options.

Tactile-Kinesthetic Techniques to Motivate Practice

- Make a gel bag by placing some hair gel in a plastic bag with a zipper lock. With a permanent marker, write each letter for practice on the outside of the bag. While tracing the letter, the child feels the interesting texture of the gel inside the bag, especially when the gel or ooze bag has been refrigerated.
- Color-code the strokes of a letter on the outside of the gel bag. The first phase of the stroke can be one color and the second phase can be another color. Arrows can be drawn indicating the directions of the letter formation as well.
- Practice correct letter formation by having the student trace with his or her finger letters written with directionality arrows on a variety of textures (for example, puff paint, which is a fabric paint with a 3-D effect when it dries, or sandpaper). Have the child also practice writing the letters with two fingers in a colored salt or sand tray or on the carpet. The sensory input through the fingers helps in recalling the letter formation.
- Provide guided practice by modeling letter formation in large movements, talking through the steps while writing the letter in color.
- Write letters in the air with large muscle movements while giving a verbal prompt. Holding the child's wrist, write in large

strokes in the air while talking through the strokes. For example, for the letter *B,* give the following instruction: "Start at the top. Straight line down. Back to the top. Sideways smile. Another sideways smile." Then repeat without guiding the child's hand, but observe that the formation is correct.

- When teaching the correct relative size of letters and their formations, it is helpful to give a concrete reference for the top, middle, and bottom line. Introduce the graphic of a person with a head line, belt line, and foot line. For example, instruct the child to write the letter *h* without lifting his or her pencil off the page, using these references: "Start at the head line and go straight down to the foot line. Now trace back up to the belt line and make a hump and go back down to rest on the foot line." *Note:* Other graphics and references and special paper, such as those used in the Living Letters program (sky-grass-earth), can be used instead.

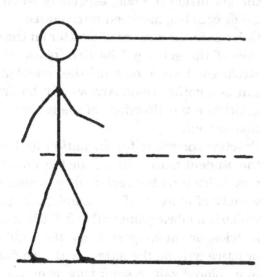

- To view several motivating strategies for teaching, practicing, and enhancing handwriting and fine motor skills, see the many posted at www.pinterest.com/sandrarief /handwriting-fine-motor-skills/. For ideas to help with letter formation of commonly confused letters *b* and *d,* see www.pinterest .com/sandrarief/b-d-tricks-strategies/.

Additional Tips

- Provide a lot of practice at home and school when children are learning how to print or write in cursive. Observe carefully as the child practices and intervene immediately when you notice errors in letter formation. Gently correct if you observe the child making the strokes incorrectly (for example, bottom-to-top rather than top-to-bottom or circles formed clockwise rather than counterclockwise).
- Teachers can provide parents with a model of how the letters are being taught in class and any verbal prompts, so that there is consistency between home and school in teaching handwriting.
- Provide prompts for correct letter formation and directionality by placing a green dot indicating the starting point for the stroke and arrows showing the direction to write the strokes of the letters.
- Provide frequent practice and corrective feedback using short trace-and-copy activities.
- Allow students for whom cursive is a struggle to print.
- Encourage appropriate sitting, posture, and anchoring of paper when writing.
- Add variety for motivational purposes, using different sizes, shapes, textures, and colors of paper and assorted writing instruments. Also have students write on individual chalkboards with colored chalk or dry-erase boards with colored pens.
- Provide a slant board for better wrist position. You can make one by covering an old three-ring notebook completely with contact paper. The child then places his or her paper on the slant board when writing.
- Teach and post your expectations—for example, writing on one side of the paper only, drafts written double spaced, math papers completed with two or three line spaces between problems, heading on upper-right section of paper.
- Post and provide individual copies of handwriting checklists for students to self-monitor

their own written work for legibility. This list could contain questions (depending on age and developmental level and grade-level standards):

— Are my letters resting on the line?
— Do tall letters reach the top line, and do short letters reach the middle line?
— Do I have space between words?
— Are my letters the right size (not too small, not too large)?
— Am I writing within the lines?

— Are my words in lowercase unless there is supposed to be a capital?
— Am I consistent in my letters: all print or all cursive, not mixed?
— Have I stayed within the margins of the paper?

• See Section 4.4 under "Strategies to Bypass and Accommodate Writing Difficulties" for tips to help compensate for handwriting difficulties, including technology tools such as typing and keyboarding programs.

section
4.6

Mathematics

Math Difficulties Associated with ADHD and Learning Disabilities

- Although many students with ADHD and learning disabilities (LDs) have strong mathematical aptitude and excel in math, many others have significant weaknesses and struggle with math computation and problem solving. Mathematics involves multiple cognitive processes and brain functions, some of which may be areas of weakness for students with ADHD or LDs.
- Math difficulties may be because of ADHD symptoms and executive function–related weaknesses such as inattention, poor organization and planning, working memory weakness, and difficulty self-monitoring. Others may result from an LD and weaknesses in, for example, sequential processing or visual-spatial-motor skills.
- Approximately 25 percent of students with ADHD have a specific math disability (Aro, 2014; DeRuvo, 2009; Mayes & Calhoun, 2006). A learning disability in mathematics is called *dyscalculia*.

Attention Weaknesses

Problems with attention result in numerous careless errors and inconsistent performance. Attention weaknesses may affect the following:

- Noticing operational signs in math problems (for example, being aware that the plus sign has changed to a minus sign, and needing to switch from adding to subtracting)
- Noticing other details (for example, decimal points, dollar signs, and other symbols)
- Checking one's work, finding errors in computation, and self-correcting
- Keeping one's place while working on a math problem
- Being able to sustain the focus necessary to complete the problems with accuracy

Memory Weaknesses

Working memory (WM) is heavily taxed in math computation and problem solving—having to hold multiple pieces of information in mind during the process. Rapid retrieval of information from long-term memory is also involved.

Memory weaknesses may affect the following:

- The learning and acquisition of basic math facts
- Being able to recall math facts and retrieve those facts quickly and automatically
- Computing multistep problems (being forgetful of sequence and having difficulty recalling where he or she is in the process)
- Recalling rules, procedures, algorithms, teacher instruction, and directions

Other Executive Skill Weaknesses

Executive function weaknesses involving planning, organizing, inhibition, cognitive flexibility, and self-monitoring may affect the following:

- Planning and organizing strategies and steps for solving a problem
- Previewing the problem, thinking ahead, and planning before beginning

- Being aware that something is not working or making sense (for example, the answer is not close to the estimate) and shifting or readjusting to try another strategy
- Time awareness in pacing and working the problems given
- Self-monitoring one's performance, persevering when strategies need to be changed or calculations need to be reworked, checking for errors and self-correcting
- Being able to hold on to information in order to do "mental math"

Sequencing Weaknesses

Sequential processing difficulties may cause problems with

- Being able to do algebra and other step-by-step equations involving following an order of operations

- Executing any multistep procedure
- Skip-counting or counting by multiples of a number (3, 6, 9, 12, 15, . . .; 4, 8, 12, 16, . . .)
- Recognizing and following patterns

Visual-Motor, Fine Motor, and Spatial-Organization Weaknesses

Visual-motor, fine motor, and spatial-organization weaknesses may affect the following:

- Copying problems from the board or book onto paper
- Aligning numbers, decimal points, and so forth accurately on paper
- Writing and computing within the amount of given space on the page, spacing between problems, and leaving enough room to compute and record answers
- Using correct directionality when computing math problems (for example, knowing which column to start with and which direction to move when regrouping)
- Recognizing and not confusing similar-looking symbols and sequences (such as + and × signs, 6 and 9, geometric shapes, 18 and 81, 203 and 302)
- Speed of writing down problems and answers—the student is either too fast and illegible or too slow and cannot keep up or complete assignments and tests

These difficulties result in numerous errors and the need for frequent erasing and correction, causing the student much frustration.

Language Weaknesses

Linguistic or language weaknesses may affect the following:

- Understanding and relating to the numerous abstract terms in math
- Difficulty with processing the language of mathematics
- Solving word problems (interpreting and understanding what is being asked, separating relevant from irrelevant information provided)

- Following directions
- Explaining coherently one's reasoning and problem solutions (an emphasis in today's classrooms)

Written Expression Weaknesses

Writing is infused in all curricular areas, and students are expected to communicate (in writing as well as verbally) how they solved a math problem—describing their thinking and reasoning and explaining the approach they took. So students who are strong with numbers and mathematical problem solving but struggle in written expression may do poorly in math class as a result of language and writing difficulties.

Mathematics: Standards and Student Expectations

Mathematics instruction and curriculum have been changing and evolving in the United States, especially in the past two decades; and expectations for students are more challenging in today's K–12 classrooms than they were for most of us when we were in those grades. The following goals and standards (NCTM and CCSS) are the expectations for US students, and they guide mathematics instruction.

National Council of Teachers of Mathematics (NCTM) Standards

The NCTM standards (National Council of Teachers of Mathematics [NCTM], 2000) emphasize the need to prepare all students for algebra beginning in kindergarten and progressing through each grade. Gagnon and Maccini (2001) summarize these standards, based on five basic goals for students:

1. Learning to value mathematics
2. Becoming confident in their ability to do mathematics
3. Becoming mathematical problem solvers
4. Learning to communicate mathematically
5. Learning to reason mathematically

The NCTM Principles and Standards involve a framework of six general principles, five content standards, and five process standards for achieving these goals:

Six General Principles for School Mathematics (NCTM, 2000; NCTM, n.d.)

1. *Equity.* Excellence in mathematics education requires equity—high expectations and strong support for all students. It demands that reasonable and appropriate accommodations be made and appropriately challenging content be included to promote access and attainment for all students.
2. *Curriculum.* Curriculum is more than a collection of activities; it must be coherent, focused on important mathematics and well articulated across the grades.
3. *Teaching.* Effective mathematics teaching requires understanding what students know and need to learn and then challenging and supporting them to learn it well.
4. *Learning.* Students must learn mathematics with understanding, actively building new knowledge from experience and previous knowledge. By aligning factual knowledge and procedural proficiency with conceptual knowledge, students can become effective learners.
5. *Assessment.* Assessment should support the learning of important mathematics and furnish useful information to both teachers and students.
6. *Technology.* Technology is essential in teaching and enhances students' learning of mathematics. It can help support investigation by students in every area of mathematics and allow them to focus on decision making, reflection, reasoning, and problem solving.

Five Content Standards or "Strands" Addressed in the NCTM Standards

These content strands extend across four grade bands (preK–2, 3–5, 6–8, 9–12) and have different value or weight within each band.

1. Number and operations
2. Algebra
3. Geometry
4. Measurement
5. Data analysis and probability

Five Process Standards (NCTM, 2000; NCTM, n.d.)

1. *Problem solving*—emphasizes the use of problem-solving contexts to help students build their mathematical knowledge. Frequent opportunities for students to formulate, grapple with, and solve complex problems and reflect on their thinking are necessary in order to apply and adapt the strategies they develop to other problems and contexts.
2. *Reasoning-and-proof*—involves logical thinking during problem solving, developing mathematical ideas, and considering whether an answer makes sense. By exploring phenomena, using mathematical conjectures, and justifying their thinking and solution process, students should see and expect that mathematics makes sense.
3. *Communication*—involves talking about, describing, explaining, and writing about mathematics in a clear and organized manner, as well as listening to others' ideas about mathematics.
4. *Connections*—refers to relating mathematical ideas to other mathematical ideas, curricular areas, and real-world situations.
5. *Representation*—refers to representing math ideas and concepts through a variety of ways. Some examples include charts, graphs, diagrams, pictures, tables, models, manipulatives, and symbols (letters, numbers, variables, equations).

Note: See the full publication Principles and Standards for School Mathematics *(2000), published by NCTM, available at www.nctm.org, and a summary at http://www.nctm.org/up loadedFiles/Standards_and_Positions/PSSM _ExecutiveSummary.pdf.*

Common Core State Standards (CCSS)

In June 2010, the National Governors Association Center for Best Practices (NGA Center) and the Council of Chief State School Officers (CCSSO) released the final Common Core State Standards (CCSS), which lay out what students should know and be able to do by each grade. The CCSS focus on developing the problem-solving, critical thinking, and analytical skills students will need to be successful.

Part of the CCSS are the Standards for Mathematical Practice, which guide instruction and curriculum across grade levels:

- CCSS.Math.Practice.MP1: Make sense of problems and persevere in solving them.
- CCSS.Math.Practice.MP2: Reason abstractly and quantitatively.
- CCSS.Math.Practice.MP3: Construct viable arguments and critique the reasoning of others.
- CCSS.Math.Practice.MP4: Model with mathematics.
- CCSS.Math.Practice.MP5: Use appropriate tools strategically.
- CCSS.Math.Practice.MP6: Attend to precision.
- CCSS.Math.Practice.MP7: Look for and make use of structure.
- CCSS.Math.Practice.MP8: Look for an express regularity in repeated reasoning.

See http://www.corestandards.org/Math/Practice/ for more details.

Key Shifts in Mathematics Instruction

The CCSS emphasize the following shifts in mathematics education (Common Core State Standards Initiative, n.d.)

1. *Greater focus on fewer topics*—rather than covering multiple topics, teachers are to focus deeply on specific topics:
   — In grades K–2: Concepts, skills, and problem solving related to addition and subtraction
   — In grades 3–5: Concepts, skills, and problem solving related to multiplication and division of whole numbers and fractions

   — In grade 6: Ratios and proportional relationships, and early algebraic expressions and equations
   — In grade 7: Ratios and proportional relationships, and arithmetic of rational numbers
   — In grade 8: Linear algebra and linear functions
2. *Coherence:* linking topics and thinking across grades. Learning is carefully connected across grades so that students can build new understanding onto foundations built in previous years. Each standard is not a new event but an extension of previous learning.
3. *Rigor:* pursue conceptual understanding, procedural skills and fluency, and application with equal intensity
   — *Conceptual understanding.* The standards call for conceptual understanding of key concepts.
   — *Procedural skills and fluency.* The standards call for speed and accuracy in calculation.
   — *Application.* The standards call for students to use math in situations that require mathematical knowledge.

Today, 20 percent of all jobs across the country require a high level of knowledge in a STEM field. (*Note:* STEM refers to **s**cience, **t**echnology, **e**ngineering, and **m**athematics.) Experts predict that these fields will be among the country's highest-growth industries in the years to come (Marchitello & Brown, 2015). The CCSS are intended to help students achieve the level of knowledge they will need for success in STEM and to compete globally for jobs in these industries.

The Challenge for Students with ADHD

The standards place high executive skill demands on all students, and for those with ADHD, they can be a particular challenge. As just described, students are expected to attend to and focus deeply on the mathematical processes they are using; communicate about their thought processes/metacognition (listening to classmates share their ideas, and explaining coherently to others their own thinking and reasoning, both verbally and in writing); solve problems flexibly and problem-solve from different perspectives (cognitive flexibility); and self-monitor and determine whether the strategies they are using and the results they are getting make sense, taking the time to rework problems and make adjustments accordingly. They also must gain fluency in mathematical procedures and are expected to calculate quickly and accurately. These are all difficult expectations and tasks for children and teens with ADHD and executive function impairments.

Mathematics Instruction

Researchers have determined that certain components of effective instruction positively influence the mathematical performance of students with learning and behavioral disabilities (Maccini, McNaughton, & Ruhl, 1999). These include

1. Teaching prerequisite skills, definitions, and strategies
2. Providing direct instruction in problem representation and problem solution
3. Providing direct instruction in self-monitoring procedures
4. Using organizers
5. Incorporating manipulatives
6. Teaching conceptual knowledge

There are many strategies and supports that teachers can employ in the classroom to help students acquire math skills and proficiency. Here are some recommended problem-solving and computation strategies that apply across grade levels (as developmentally appropriate, of course).

Word Problems

- Explicitly teach and model a number of strategies for solving word problems and provide many opportunities for guided and independent practice. Strategies include the following:
  — Read the problem out loud.
  — Read the problem at least twice before beginning.
  — Restate the problem in one's own words.
  — Identify wanted, given, and needed information.
  — Look for and highlight significant clue words (for example, *altogether, how much more, faster than, part of*).
  — Draw pictures, diagrams, graphs, and sketches representing the problem.
  — Cross out unnecessary, irrelevant information.
  — Circle, underline, or highlight the numbers that are important.
  — Write the kind of answer needed (for example, miles per hour, degrees, dollars and cents).
  — Use objects/manipulatives.
  — Construct a chart or table.
  — Make an organized list.
  — Act it out.
  — Look for a pattern.
  — Make a model.
  — Divide the problem into parts, working on one part at a time.
  — Work backwards.
  — Eliminate possibilities.
  — Guess (estimate) and check.
- Make up word problems using students' names, situations, and interests.
- Post charts or other visual references for various problem-solving strategies.
- Provide many opportunities for students to make up their own word problems to share with the class, and figure out the solutions as a group whenever possible within the context of classroom activities. For example, when planning a class party or field trip, the students can work in teams deciding how many cars and drivers are needed, how many dozens of cookies are to be baked, and so forth.
- Teach important math vocabulary and key words that indicate the process or strategy needed—for example: *doubled, tripled, product, times* (indicating multiplication); *more than, less than, fewer, difference, what's left? what's missing? larger than/ faster than/ smaller than, average, quotient, equal parts, divisible by, sharing* (indicating division).

- Explore websites ideal for teachers of mathematics, such as Inquiry Maths, http://www.inquirymaths.com; Desmos, https://www.desmos.com/; Galileo, http://galileo.org/; Illuminations, https://illuminations.nctm.org; and Khan Academy, https://www.khanacademy.org.

Bassarear (2001) suggests the following four steps for solving problems:

1. **Understanding the problem**
   - Do you understand what the problem is asking for?
   - Can you state the problem in your own words—that is, paraphrase the problem?
   - Have you used all the given information?
   - Can you solve a part of the problem?
2. **Devising a plan**
   - For example, guess, check, and revise, keeping track of "guesses" with a table; make an estimate; look for patterns; look to see whether the problem is similar to one already solved.
3. **Carrying out the plan**
   - Are you keeping the problem meaningful, or are you just "groping and hoping"?
   - On each step, ask what the numbers mean. Label your work.
   - Are you bogged down? Do you need to try another strategy?
4. **Looking back**
   - Does your answer make sense? Is the answer reasonable? Is the answer close to your estimate if you made one?
   - Does your answer work when you check it with the given information?
   - Can you use a different method to solve the problem?

Gojak (2011) shares these four principles in problem solving:

1. **Understand the problem.** Help students do so by focusing on such questions as: What do I want to find out? What do I know? Do I need more information? If so, what additional information do I need? What am I looking for to reach a solution?
2. **Devise a plan.**
3. **Carry out the plan.**
4. **Look back.** At this stage, students dig deeper by taking the time to ask themselves questions, such as: Does my solution make sense? Is my solution reasonable? Does my solution fit all of the conditions of the problem?

Use mnemonics as a learning strategy to recall math processes or procedures. For example: **RIDE** (from the website of the Special Education Department of James Madison University, www.coe.jmu.edu/learningtoolbox):

Read the problem correctly.
Identify the relevant information.
Determine the operations and unit for expressing the answer.
Enter the correct numbers and calculate, then check.

Another is **STAR** (Maccini & Hughes, 2000; Maccini & Ruhl, 2000):

Search the word problem (read the problem carefully; write down knowns/facts).
Translate the words into an equation in picture form.
Answer the problem.
Review the solution (reread the problem; check the reasonableness of the answer).

Instructional Formats and Routines

Humphreys and Parker (2015) recommend use of a routine they call Number Talks, during which students reason mentally with numbers. The routine takes about fifteen minutes. With students' pencils put away and their fists positioned on their chests, the teacher puts a problem on the board or document camera—usually written horizontally in order to discourage the use of rote procedures. The teacher watches as students solve the problem mentally and raise a thumb when they are ready. When most thumbs are up, the teacher asks for volunteers to share what they think the answer is, recording the answers students give. Then the teacher asks, "Who has a strategy he or she is willing to share?" "Is anyone willing to convince us that your answer makes sense by telling us what you did?"

During the Number Talk routine, the teacher uses several other kinds of questions as well, to help students recognize that there are often many ways to solve a problem and to encourage and develop students' flexible thinking, understanding of number sense, and ability to clearly communicate their thought and reasoning processes. For example:

- How did you keep track mentally of what you did?
- Did anyone use the same strategy but break the number up differently?
- Who figured this out a different way?

Muschla, Muschla, and Muschla-Berry (2013) recommend five- to ten-minute "math starter" activities. Students solve problems and provide written explanations of their work in a math starter notebook, and discuss and share their problem-solving strategies in cooperative groups.

Cooperative learning structures—partner or group formats—work well in the classroom for any kind of problem solving. The Kagans (2000) describe examples of partner and small-group (team) structures for working on math problems in class.

- *Partners.* Working in pairs, one student works a problem while the other coaches. Roles are reversed. Then, after a couple of problems are completed, partners pair up with another set of pairs and compare answers.
- *Groups or teams.* Teams of four work a problem together and check one another's understanding on one or more problems. Then the team breaks into two pairs who continue to work together to solve the next couple of problems. Students then continue independently working similar problems and comparing answers with each other.

Instructional Tips

- Work problems on the board or document camera using color to make the steps and processes visually clear.
- Always build in time during the lesson for students to share how they solved the problem, and emphasize that there are a variety of ways, not just one method, to solve them.
- Try graphing on a regular basis at all grade levels (bar graphs, picture graphs, Venn diagrams, circle graphs, line graphs). Graphing is a way to present and organize data so that relationships in the data are seen easily. In order to interpret and use graphs as a problem-solving tool, students need to make their own first.
- Teach how to first estimate and then evaluate the answer to determine whether it is reasonable or not.
- Show how to reason whether an answer should be larger or smaller than the numbers given.
- Analyze the problems that students miss to determine where their understanding breaks down. Then teach those targeted skills.
- Explicitly teach, illustrate, and maintain a word wall or anchor chart of grade-level math vocabulary—particularly any words in math that cause confusion for students.
- Use money (pennies, dimes, dollars) to teach place value.
- Encourage keeping a file or notebook section of specific math skills, concepts, rules, and algorithms taught, along with specific examples of each on a card for reference.
- List and number the steps of multistep problems and algorithms. Post them or give students a desk copy for reference.
- Provide frequent checks for accuracy and immediate feedback whenever possible. This reduces the frustration of having to erase and fix a number of problems done incorrectly. Set a certain number of problems to complete (for example, one row only or three to four problems) and then check students before they are permitted to continue. Student

partners can also compare answers after working every few problems on their own. If they don't agree on any of the answers after reworking the problem together, those students can then ask other classmates or the teacher for help.

- Use individual dry-erase boards. Have students compute one step of a problem at a time, asking them to hold up their boards on your signal after each step.
- Compensate for memory difficulties and help students increase recall of math facts and procedures through techniques such as those described in Section 3.6 that include a variety of mnemonics and multisensory techniques for learning multiplication tables.
- Go over homework assignments the next day, allowing students to comfortably ask questions and work any problems that they did not understand together as a class.
- Encourage students to use calculators to check their work.

More Math Strategies, Supports, and Accommodations

Make the Abstract More Concrete

- Provide many kinds of manipulatives to help students visualize and work out math problems. Cubes, chips, tiles, counters, beans, base-ten blocks, and number lines are some of the many possibilities.
- Introduce mathematical concepts with demonstrations using real-life examples and motivating situations. For example, cut a sandwich into five equal parts to share in a small group (1/5 per student), or first count the total and then equally divide a bag of candy among a number of students (32 pieces divided by 5 kids = 6 each with 2 left over).
- When teaching multiplication, relate things that come in sets of a certain number (for example, fours—quarters in a dollar, legs on a dog; fives—fingers on a hand, days in a school week).

Increase Students' Motivation

- Play team math games in class.
- Let students choose one or two problems that they get to cross out or eliminate from their math homework assignment.
- As students are working on their assignments in class, reward a few (or all) who are on task by having them roll a die. Whatever number comes up on the die is the number of *fewer* math problems the student is required to do that night for the homework assignment.
- Make it relevant. Provide many opportunities for using math in the context of real-life situations—for example, using money, balancing a checkbook, determining mileage on a fantasy road trip, comparison shopping, and paying for a meal (including tax and tip). See Rief and Heimburge (2006) for more than eighty such math activities that are appropriate for students in grades 3–8.
- Use electronic games for drill and practice of math skills. These programs have the benefit of being adjusted for speed and level of difficulty. They also provide immediate feedback and are fun, nonthreatening, and motivating for children.
- There are many sources of engaging, motivating online games and programs, such as FunBrain.com, Math-Play.com, CoolMath 4Kids.com, Fuel the Brain.com, Math Cats .com, Mr.Nussbaum.com, IXL.com, Math letics.com, AAAmath.com, Webmath.com, and others (as well as apps and software programs).
- There are numerous math ideas shared by creative teachers for grades K–12 found on Pinterest, such as those at www.pinterest .com/sandrarief/math-strategies-activities/.

Compensate for Spatial Organization and Graphomotor Difficulties

- Encourage students to write and solve their computation problems on graph paper rather than notebook paper. Experiment with graph paper of varying square/grid sizes.

- Turn notebook paper sideways (with lines running vertically rather than horizontally). This makes it much easier for students to keep numbers aligned in columns, reducing careless errors.

	⭘				⭘			⭘	
1	6	3	2	0					
−	1	5	9	6					

- Reduce the requirement of copying problems from the board or book by photocopying the page or writing out the problems on paper for certain students.
- Provide a large work space on tests. If necessary, rewrite test items on other paper, with lots of room for computation.
- Provide lots of space on the page between problems and at bottom of the page.

Increase Focus and Attention

- Color-highlight or underline key words and vocabulary in word problems (for example, shared, doubled, product, average, larger, slower, difference, altogether, equal parts).
- Color-highlight processing signs for students who are inattentive to change in operational signs on a page. For example, color addition signs yellow, subtraction signs pink, and so forth.
- Color-highlight place value. For example, given the number 16,432,781, write the hundreds (781) in green, the thousands (432) in orange, and the millions (16) in blue.
- Reduce the number of problems on a page.
- Cut up a page of problems into strips or rows, and give to students one at a time.

- Have the student block part of the page while working on problems, or fold the paper under to reveal just one or two rows at a time.
- Allow the student to softly say steps of the problem out loud to keep attention focused.
- Allow the child to stand up and stretch or take a break of some kind after a certain number of problems are completed and checked for accuracy.

Increase the Amount of Practice and Review

- Frequently review previously learned skills.
- Have review problems prepared on cards (three to five per card); students choose a card to complete. Or make sets of practice and review problems (a few per page) with answers on the back for independent practice.
- Use electronic games for drill and practice of math skills. These programs can generally be adjusted for speed and level of difficulty. They provide immediate feedback and are fun, nonthreatening, and motivating to students. Also, they tend to hold the interest of students with ADHD, as the stimuli are constantly changing.
- Pair students to practice skills taught and to quiz each other.
- Motivate the practicing of skills through the use of games, and suggest that parents do the same. Many board games (for example, Uno and Battleship) and card games are excellent for building math skills (for example, counting, logic, probability, strategic thinking).

Use Self-Monitoring and Metacognitive Strategies

- Help students self-monitor their attention to task when working (as described in Section 3.1), or their work production and accuracy (for example, number of problems completed correctly).
- Model how to first read problems (particularly word problems) and plan a strategy for solving them before beginning the work.

- Teach how to estimate and determine the reasonableness of an answer.
- Use all of the strategies described earlier in this section that require students to share verbally or in writing how they approached and solved a problem.
- Have students keep journals of their thinking, reasoning, questions, and understanding of math concepts. Encourage PYBOP: "Put your brains on paper." Also have students write their understanding of mathematical concepts before and after the unit is taught.
- Model talking out loud while thinking and reasoning about a mathematical problem. Encourage students to do the same—externalize their thinking and verbalize while solving problems. Listen to students as they think out loud, and correct gaps in their comprehension when possible at this point.
- Have students keep track of their own scores on math quizzes, graph or otherwise record their own progress, and share their own learning goals.

Provide Other Accommodations

- Allow extra time on math tests so that students are not rushed and make careless errors.
- Grade by number of correct problems over the number assigned (which could be different for students receiving modified homework or class work).
- Reduce the number of problems assigned (half-page, evens only, odds only).

Parent Tips: Strengthen Your Child's Math Skills

- Practice functional math skills (measurement, time concepts, counting money and making change) as much as possible at home. These are critical skills that teachers often do not have enough time to teach until mastery. Include your child in such activities as cooking, baking, constructing, sewing, gardening, making home improvements, and estimating how much items to purchase at a store will cost before checking out at the cashier. These are great ways to teach and reinforce functional math skills and are fun to do together.
- Motivate the practice of skills through the use of games. Although there are many electronic math games that children can play by themselves, they do not compare to the benefits derived from the face-to-face interaction of playing board, card, and dice games together as a family. Many board games and card games, such as Battleship, Mastermind, Othello, chess, dominoes, Uno, Crazy 8s, Rummy, and War, are great for sharpening a host of skills (for example, counting, arithmetic, problem solving, logic, sequencing, spatial relationships, mental math, probability, and strategic thinking) while having fun.
- Build in mathematical problem-solving activities whenever possible. While waiting for appointments, standing in line, driving in the car, and other opportune times, pose math questions and challenges for your child to figure out (preferably mentally). For example, when in line to purchase tickets at the movie theater or prior to going to the theater, ask such questions as: "For this movie, an adult ticket costs $9.50 and a child's ticket is $7.00. How much will our three tickets cost? If we want to also buy two small popcorns to share, what's our total cost going to be with tickets and popcorn?"
- See "Fun Ways to Boost Your Child's Math Skills This Summer and Beyond" for numerous math games and puzzles, real-life math applications, and online math resources at http://www.sandrarief.com/fun-ways-to-boost-your-childs-math-skills-this-summer-and-beyond/.
- For suggested math apps, see Learning Works for Kids (www.learningworksforkids.com).

Connecting Math to Writing and Literature

The following are possible math journal starters:

- Today I learned about [or how to] . . .
- The most important ideas I learned today are . . .
- I am still confused by . . .
- Next time I . . ., I plan to . . .
- I discovered that . . .
- The mathematical rule for this problem is . . .
- The way I remember (how to) . . . in my head is . . .
- The tricky part of this problem is . . .
- The thing you have to remember with this kind of problem is . . .
- The steps I used to solve this problem were . . .
- I could use this type of problem solving when . . .
- I was frustrated with this problem because . . .

The following are some examples of literature books that involve mathematical concepts and can be integrated into math instruction:

- *A Million Fish . . . More or Less,* by Patricia C. McKissack, illustrated by Dena Schutzer (New York: Dragonfly Books, 1992)
- *A Remainder of One,* by Elinor J. Pinczes, illustrated by Bonnie MacKain (New York: Houghton Mifflin, 1995)
- *Anno's Magic Seeds,* by Mitsumasa Anno (New York: Philomel Books, 1995)
- *Anno's Mysterious Multiplying Jar,* by Mitsumasa Anno (New York: Penguin Putnam Books for Young Readers; reprint ed., 1999)
- *Cubes, Cones, Cylinders, and Spheres,* by Tana Hoban (New York: HarperCollins, 2000)
- *If You Made a Million,* by David Schwartz (New York: Mulberry Paperback Books, 1989)
- *Inchworm and a Half,* by Elinor Pinczes, illustrated by Randall Enos (New York: Houghton Mifflin, 2001)

- *Math Appeal: Mind-Stretching Math Riddles,* by Greg Tang, illustrated by Harry Briggs (New York: Scholastic Press, 2003)
- *Math Attack,* by Joan Horton, illustrated by Kyrsten Brooker (New York: Farrar, Straus & Giroux, 2009)
- *Math Curse,* by Jon Scieszka and Lane Smith (New York: Viking/Penguin, 1995)
- *Multiplying Menace: The Revenge of Rumpelstiltskin,* by Pam Calvert, illustrated by Wayne Geehan (Watertown, MA: Charlesbridge, 2006)
- *One Grain of Rice: A Mathematical Folktale,* by Demi (New York: Scholastic Press, 1997)
- *Sadako and the Thousand Paper Cranes,* by Eleanor Coerr (New York: Dell Yearling, 1993)
- *Sir Cumference and the Dragon of Pi,* by Jon Scieszka and Lane Smith (Watertown, MA: Charlesbridge, 1999)
- *Sir Cumference and the Knights of the Round Table,* by Jon Scieszka and Lane Smith (Watertown, MA: Charlesbridge, 1997)
- *Sir Cumference and the Great Knight of Angleland,* by Jon Scieszka and Lane Smith (Watertown, MA: Charlesbridge, 2001)
- *The Best of Times: Math Strategies That Multiply,* by Greg Tang, illustrated by Harry Briggs (New York: Scholastic, 2003)
- *The Doorbell Rang,* by Pat Hutchins (New York: Greenwillow Books, 1986)
- *The Grapes of Wrath: Mind-Stretching Math Riddles,* by Greg Tang, illustrated by Harry Briggs (New York: Scholastic Paperbacks; reprint ed., 2004)
- *The King's Chessboard,* by David Birch, illustrated by Devis Grebu (New York: Puffin Books; reprint ed., 1993)
- *The King's Commissioners,* by Aileen Friedman, illustrated by Susan Guevara (Portsmouth, NH: Heinemann, 1994)
- *The Lion's Share: A Tale of Halving Cake and Eating It, Too,* by Matthew McElligott (New York: Walker, 2009)
- *The Number Devil: A Mathematical Adventure,* by Hans Magnus Enzenberger (New York: Holt, 1997)

- *The Patchwork Quilt,* by Valerie Flournoy (New York: Dial Books, 1985)
- *The Rabbit Problem,* by Emily Gravett (New York: Simon & Schuster Books for Young Readers, 2010)

See these links for more math-related literature books:

http://teachers.redclay.k12.de.us/pamela.waters/math/literature.htm

http://teacher.scholastic.com/products/dothemath/math-reads/books-topics.htm

http://www.the-best-childrens-books.org/math-for-kids.html

Part 4 References

Section 4.1

Barkley, R. A. (2013). *Taking charge of ADHD: The complete, authoritative guide for parents* (3rd ed.). New York, NY: Guilford Press.

Gaskin, L.W., Satlow, E., & Pressley, M. (2007). Executive control of reading comprehension in elementary school. In L. Meltzer (Ed.), *Executive function in education: From theory to practice* (pp. 194–215). New York, NY: Guilford Press.

International Dyslexia Association. (2013). *Dyslexia in the classroom: What every teacher needs to know.* Baltimore, MD: Author.

Kaufman, C. (2010). *Executive function in the classroom.* Baltimore, MD: Paul H. Brookes.

Levine, M. (1998). *Developmental variation and learning disorders.* Cambridge, MA: Educational Publishing Services.

Levine, M. (2002). *A mind at a time.* New York, NY: Simon & Schuster.

Meltzer, L. (2010). *Promoting executive function in the classroom.* New York, NY: Guilford Press.

Rief, S., & Stern, J. M. (2010). *The dyslexia checklist: A practical reference for parents and teachers.* San Francisco, CA: Jossey-Bass.

Samuels, S. J. (2006). Reading fluency: Its past, present, and future. In T. Rasinski, C. Blachowicz, & K. Lems (Eds.), *Fluency instruction: Research-based best practices* (pp. 7–20). New York, NY: Guilford Press.

Section 4.2

Allington, R. (2006). *What really matters for struggling readers: Designing research-based programs* (2nd ed.). Boston, MA: Pearson Education.

Ambruster, B. B., Lehr, F., & Osborn, J. (2001, September). Put reading first: The research building blocks for teaching children to read. National Institute for Literacy. Retrieved from www.nifl.gov/parthershipforreading/publications/reading_first1.html

Fetzer, N., & Rief, S. (2002). *Alphabet learning center activities kit.* San Francisco, CA: Jossey-Bass. Book and holders and fasties alphabet charts available at www.sandrarief.com.

Kaufman, C. (2010). *Executive function in the classroom.* Baltimore, MD: Paul H. Brookes.

Moats, L. (2001). When older kids can't read. *Educational Leadership, 58*, 6.

Rief, S., & Heimburge, J. A. (2007). *How to reach and teach all children through balanced literacy: User-friendly strategies, tools, activities, and ready-to-use materials.* San Francisco, CA: Jossey-Bass.

Rief, S., & Stern, J. M. (2010). *The dyslexia checklist: A practical reference for parents and teachers.* San Francisco, CA: Jossey-Bass.

Section 4.3

Bell, N. (2007). *Visualizing and verbalizing: For language comprehension and thinking* (2nd ed.). Avila Beach, CA: Gander.

Boyles, N. (2012). Closing in on close reading. *Educational Leadership, 70*(4), 36–41. Retrieved from www.ascd.org/publications/educational-leadership/dec12/vol70/num04/Closing-in-on-Close-Reading.aspx

Deshler, D., Ellis, E., & Lenz, B. (1996). *Teaching adolescents with learning disabilities: Strategies and methods.* Denver, CO: Love Publishing.

Fisher, D. (2014). Close reading and the CCSS, part 1. Retrieved from www.mhecommoncoretoolbox.com/close-reading-and-the-ccss-part-1.html

Fisher, D., & Frey, N. (2015). Teacher modeling using complex informational texts. *Reading Teacher, 69*(1), 63–69. doi:10.1002/trtr.1372. Retrieved from http://onlinelibrary.wiley.com/doi/10.1002/trtr.1372/full

Fisher, D., Frey, N., & Lapp, D. (2008). Shared readings: Modeling comprehension, vocabulary, text structures, and text features for older readers. *Reading Teacher, 61,* 548–557.

Lynette, R. (2014). Close reading freebie. Teachers Pay Teachers. Retrieved from https://www .teacherspayteachers.com/Product/Close-Reading-Freebie-1226669

Marzano, R., Pickering, D., & Pollock, J. (2001). *Classroom instruction that works: Research-based strategies for increasing student achievement.* Alexandria, VA: Association for Supervision and Curriculum Development.

McGregor, T. (2007). *Comprehension connections: Bridges to strategic reading.* Portsmouth, NH: Heinemann.

Ogle, D. M. (1986). K-W-L: A teaching model that develops active reading of expository text. *Reading Teacher, 39,* 564–570.

Ong, F. (Ed.). (2000). *Strategic teaching and learning: Standards-based instruction to promote content literacy in grades four through twelve.* Sacramento: California Department of Education.

Palincsar, A. S., & Brown, A. L. (1984). Reciprocal teaching of comprehension fostering and comprehension monitoring activities. *Cognition and Instruction, 1*(2), 117–175.

Palincsar, A. S., & Brown, A. L. (1985). Reciprocal teaching: Activities to promote reading with your mind. In T. L. Harris & E. J. Cooper (Eds.), *Reading, thinking, and concept development: Strategies for the classroom* (pp. 147—160). New York, NY: The College Board.

Pearson, P. D., Roehler, L. R., Dole, J. A., & Duffy, G. G. (1992). Developing expertise in reading comprehension. In J. Samuels and A. Farstrup (Eds.), *What research has to say about reading instruction* (pp. 145–199). Newark, DE: International Reading Association.

Raphael, T. (1982). Questioning-answering strategies for children. *Reading Teacher, 37,* 377–382.

Rief, S., & Heimburge, J. A. (2007). *How to reach and teach all children through balanced literacy: User-friendly strategies, tools, activities, and ready-to-use materials.* San Francisco, CA: Jossey-Bass.

Rosenthal Tolisano, S. (2011, July 21). Upgrade your KWL chart to the 21st century. Retrieved from http://langwitches.org/blog/2011/07/21/upgrade-your-kwl-chart-to-the-21st-century/

Sousa, D. (2001). *How the special needs brain learns.* Thousand Oaks, CA: Corwin Press.

Stauffer, R. G. (1969). *Directing reading maturity as a cognitive process.* New York, NY: Harper & Row.

Swanson, P. N., & DeLaPaz, S. (1998). Teaching effective comprehension strategies to students with learning and reading disabilities. *Intervention in School and Clinic, 33,* 209–218.

Section 4.4

Graham, S., & Harris, K. R. (1989). Improving learning disabled students' skills at composing essays: Self-instructional strategy training. *Exceptional Children, 56,* 201–214.

Harris, K. R., & Graham, S. (2005). *Writing better: Effective strategies for teaching students with learning difficulties.* Baltimore, MD: Paul H. Brookes.

Harris, Z. (2014). To write or to type? *Attention, 21*(2), 18–21.

Kaufman, C. (2010). *Executive function in the classroom.* Baltimore, MD: Paul H. Brookes.

Meltzer, L. (2010). *Promoting executive function in the classroom.* New York, NY: Guilford Press.

Meltzer, L. J., Roditi, B. N., Steinberg, J. L., Rafter Biddle, K., Taber, S. E., Boyle Caron, K., & Kniffin, L. (2006). *Strategies for success: Classroom teaching techniques for students with learning problems* (2nd ed.). Austin, TX: PRO-ED.

ResearchILD & Fable Vision. (2005). Essay express: Strategies for successful essay writing [Computer software]. Boston, MA: Fable Vision.

Rief, S., & Heimburge, J. A. (2007). *How to reach and teach all children through balanced literacy: User-friendly strategies, tools, activities, and ready-to-use materials.* San Francisco, CA: Jossey-Bass.

Sandler, M. (2005). Personal best: Term paper time. *ADDitude, 6*(2), 47–48.

Schumaker, J. B., Deshler, D. D., Nolan, S., Clark, F. L., Alley, G. R., & Warner, M. M. (1981). *Error monitoring: A learning strategy for improving academic performance of LD adolescents* (Research Report No. 32). Lawrence: University of Kansas, Institute for Research on Learning Disabilities.

Welch, M. (1992). The PLEASE strategy: A metacognitive learning strategy for improving the paragraph writing of students with mild disabilities. *Learning Disability Quarterly, 15,* 119–128.

Section 4.5

Bounds, G. (2010, October 5). How handwriting trains the brain: Forming letters is key to learning, memory, ideas. *Wall Street Journal.* Retrieved from http://online.wsj.com/article/SB10001 4240527487046315045755319327549225 18.html

Graham, S., & Harris, K. R. (1999). CASL Handwriting Program. Retrieved from http://peabody .vanderbilt.edu/docs/pdf/sped/CASL%20Handwriting%20Program.pdf

Handwriting and the Common Core State Standards. (2012, January 12). Universal Publishing blog. Retrieved from www.upub.net/Handwriting-and-the-Common-Core-State-Standards -News.html

International Dyslexia Association. (2009). Testing and evaluation. Retrieved from http://eida .org/testing-and-evaluation/

International Dyslexia Association. (2011). Spelling. Retrieved from http://eida.org/spelling/

International Dyslexia Association. (2012). Just the facts: Understanding dysgraphia. Retrieved from www.interdys.org/ewebeditpro5/upload/UnderstandingDysgraphiaFactSheet3.14.12.pdf

Jones, S. (2003). Accommodations for students with handwriting problems. *The Resource, 18*(1), 6–12.

Landy, J., & Burridge, K. (2000). *Fine motor skills and handwriting activities for young children.* Paramus, NJ: Center for Applied Research in Education.

National Center for Learning Disabilities (NCLD). (2014). What is dysgraphia? Retrieved from http://ncld.org/types-learning-disabilities/dysgraphia/what-is-dysgraphia

Section 4.6

Aro, L. (2014). When things don't add up. *ADDitude, 14*(4), 51–53.

Bassarear, T. (2001). *Mathematics for elementary school teachers: Explorations* (2nd ed.). Boston, MA: Houghton Mifflin.

Common Core State Standards Initiative. (n.d.). *Key shifts in mathematics.* Retrieved from http:// www.corestandards.org/other-resources/key-shifts-in-mathematics/

DeRuvo, S. L. (2009). *Strategies for teaching adolescents with ADHD (grades 6–12).* San Francisco, CA: Jossey-Bass.

Gagnon, J. C., & Maccini, P. (2001, September/October). Preparing students with disabilities for algebra. *Teaching Exceptional Children, 34*(1), 8–15.

Gojak, L. (2011). *What's your math problem? Getting to the heart of teaching problem solving.* Huntington Beach, CA: Shell Education.

Humphreys, C., & Parker, R. (2015). *Making number talks matter: Developing mathematical practices and deepening understanding.* Portland, ME: Stenhouse. Also retrieved from http:// www.stenhouse.com/emags/0998/index.html

Kagan, S., Kagan, M., & Kagan, L. (2000). *Reaching standards through cooperative learning in mathematics.* Port Chester, NY: National Professional Resources.

Maccini, P., & Hughes, C. A. (2000). Effects of a problem-solving strategy on introductory algebra performance of secondary students with learning disabilities. *Learning Disabilities Research & Practice, 15*(1), 10–21.

Maccini, P., McNaughton, D., & Ruhl, K. (1999). Algebra instruction for students with learning disabilities: Implications from a research review. *Learning Disability Quarterly, 22,* 113–126.

Maccini, P., & Ruhl, K. L. (2000). Effects of a graduated instructional sequence on the algebraic subtraction of integers by secondary students with learning disabilities. *Education and Treatment of Children, 23,* 465–489.

Marchitello, M., & Brown, C. (2015, August). Math matters: How the common core will help the United States bring up its grade on mathematics education. Retrieved from https://www .americanprogress.org/issues/education/report/2015/08/13/119239/math-matters/

Mayes, S. D., & Calhoun, S. I. (2006). Frequency of reading, math and writing difficulties in children with clinical disorders. *Learning and Individual Differences, 16,* 145–157.

Muschla, J., Muschla, G. R., & Muschla-Berry, E. (2013). *Math starters: 5- to 10-minute activities aligned with the common core math standards, grades 6–12* (2nd ed.). San Francisco, CA: Jossey-Bass.

National Council of Teachers of Mathematics. (n.d.). Principles and standards for school mathematics. Retrieved from http://www.nctm.org/uploadedFiles/Standards_and_Positions/PSSM _ExecutiveSummary.pdf

National Council of Teachers of Mathematics. (2000). *Principles and standards for school mathematics.* Reston, VA: Author.

National Governors Association Center for Best Practices & Council of Chief State School Officers. (2010). *Common core state standards for mathematics.* Washington, DC: Authors. Retrieved from http://corestandards.org/the-standards/mathematics

Rief, S., & Heimburge, J. A. (2006). *How to reach and teach all children in the inclusive classroom: Practical strategies, lessons, and activities* (2nd ed.). San Francisco, CA: Jossey-Bass.

Part 4 Additional Sources and Resources

Allington, R. L. (2011). *What really matters for struggling readers: Designing research-based programs* (3rd ed.). Boston, MA: Pearson.

Allington, R. L., & Cunningham, P. M. (2007). *Schools that work: Where all children read and write* (3rd ed.). Boston, MA: Pearson.

Atwell, N. (1987). *In the middle: Writing, reading, and learning with adolescents.* Portsmouth, NH: Heinemann.

Auman, M. (2008). *Step up to writing.* Dallas, TX: Voyager Sopris Learning.

Beck, I. L. (2006). *Making sense of phonics: The how's and why's.* New York, NY: Guilford Press.

Bell, N. (2007). *Visualizing and verbalizing for language comprehension and thinking* (2nd ed.). Avila Beach, CA: Gander.

Berninger, V. W., Vaughn, K., Abbot, R. D., Brooks, A., Begay, K., Curtin, G., Byrd, K., & Graham, S. (2000). Language-based spelling instruction: Teaching children to make multiple connections between spoken and written words. *Learning Disability Quarterly, 23,* 117–135.

Blake, K. (2000). Two common reading problems experienced by many AD/HD adults. *Attention, 6*(5), 30–36.

Boehler, J. (2014). Fluency without fear: Research evidence on the best ways to learn math facts. Retrieved from http://youtubedorg/teachers/wp-content/uploads/2014/10/Fluencywithoutfear .pdf

Boyles, N. (2013). Closing in on close reading. *Educational Leadership, 70*(4), 36–41.

Burke, B. (n.d.). A close look at close reading: Scaffolding students with complex texts. Retrieved from http://nieonline.com/tbtimes/downloads/CCSS_reading.pdf

Carreker, S. (2011). Teaching spelling. In J. R. Birsh (Ed.), *Multisensory teaching of basic language skills* (3rd ed., pp. 251–291). Baltimore, MD: Paul H. Brookes.

Daniels, H. (1994). *Literature circles: Voice and choice in the student-centered classroom.* Markham, Ontario: Pembroke.

Duff, F., & Clarke, P. (2011). Practitioner review: Reading disorders: What are the effective interventions and how should they be implemented and evaluated? *Journal of Child Psychology and Psychiatry, 52*(1), 3–12.

Duffy, F. (n.d.). The write tools for ADHD students. *ADDitude.* Retrieved at http://www .additudemag.com/adhd/article/9365.html

ERIC/OSEP. (2002, Winter). Strengthening the second "R": Helping students with disabilities prepare well-written compositions. *Research Connections in Special Education,* no. 10.

Fetzer, N. (2013). Nancy Fetzer's writing curriculum. Murrieta, CA: Nancy Fetzer's Literacy Connections. (For grades K–1, 2–3, and 4–6)

Fisher, D., & Frey, N. (2014). Scaffolded reading instruction of content-area texts. *Reading Teacher, 67,* 347–351.

Fisher, D., Frey, N., & Lapp, D. (2011). Coaching middle-level teachers to think aloud improves comprehension instruction and student reading achievement. *Teacher Educator, 46,* 231–243.

Francis, E. (2013). *Teach your child the multiplication tables, fast, fun & easy: With dazzling patterns, grids and tricks!* (2nd ed.). Irvine, CA: TeaCHildMath.

Graham, S. (2005). *Writing better: Effective strategies for teaching students with learning difficulties.* Baltimore, MD: Paul H. Brookes.

Graham, S., & Harris, K. R. (2006). Preventing writing difficulties: Providing additional handwriting and spelling instruction to at-risk children in first grade. *Teaching Exceptional Children, 38,* 64–66.

Graham, S., Harris, K. R., & Fink Chorzempa, B. (2003). Extra spelling instruction: Improving spelling, writing and reading right from the start. *Teaching Exceptional Children, 35,* 66–68.

Graham, S., MacArthur, C. A., & Fitzgerald, J. (Ed.). (2013). *Best practices in writing instruction* (2nd ed.). New York, NY: Guilford Press.

Guadagni, B. (n.d.).Writing made easy: Tech tools to the rescue. Retrieved at http://www.additudemag.com/adhdblogs/35/10928.html

Harris, K. R., & Graham, S. (1996). *Making the writing process work: Strategies for composition and self-regulation.* Cambridge, MA: Brookline.

Harris, K. R., Graham, S., & Mason, L. H. (2002). POW plus TREE equals powerful opinion essays: Improving writing in the early grades. *CASLNews, 6,* 1–4.

Harris, K. R., Graham, S., Mason, L. H., Friedlander, B., & Reid, R. (2007). *Powerful writing strategies for all students.* Baltimore, MD: Paul H. Brookes.

Harris, Z. (2014). To write or to type? *Attention, 21*(2), 18–21.

Harvey, S., & Goudvis, A. (2000). *Strategies that work: Teaching comprehension to enhance understanding.* Portland, ME: Stenhouse.

Hatton, D., & Hatton, K. (n.d.).Apps for students with dysgraphia and writing difficulties. National Center for Learning Disabilities (NCLD). Retrieved from www.ncld.org/students-disabilities/assistive-technology-education/apps-students-ld-dysgraphia-writing-difficulties

Henry, M. K. (2010). *Unlocking literacy: Effective decoding and spelling instruction* (2nd ed.). Baltimore, MD: Paul H. Brookes.

International Dyslexia Association. (2008, March). Just the facts: Definition of dyslexia. Retrieved from www.interdys.org/ewebeditpro5/upload/Definition.pdf

International Dyslexia Association. (2013). *Dyslexia in the classroom: What every teacher needs to know.* Baltimore, MD: Author.

Israel, S. E., Block, C. C., Bauserman, K. L., & Kinnucan-Welsch, K. (2005). *Metacognition in literacy learning: Theory, assessment, instruction, and professional development.* Mahwah, NJ: Lawrence Erlbaum.

James Madison University Special Education Program. (n.d.). Learning toolbox strategies. Retrieved from http://coe.jmu.edu/LearningToolbox/writing.html

Jitendra, A. (2002, March/April). Teaching students math problem solving through graphic representations. *Teaching Exceptional Children, 34*(4), 34–38.

Kazemi, E., & Hintz, A. (2014). *Intentional talk: How to structure and lead productive mathematical discussions.* Portland, ME: Stenhouse.

Lapp, D., Flood, J., & Farnan, N. (2004). *Content area reading and learning.* Mahwah, NJ: Routledge.

Levine, M. (1998). *Developmental variation and learning disorders.* Cambridge, MA: Educational Publishing Services.

Lovett, M. W., Lacerenza, L., Steinbach, K. A., & De Palma, M. (2014). Development and evaluation of a research-based intervention program for children and adolescents with reading disabilities. *Interventions to Improve Reading Skills, 40*(3), 21–29.

Luckey Frog Learning. (2014, March). Teaching kids to go back in the text when answering comprehension questions. Retrieved from http://www.luckeyfroglearning.com/2014/03/teaching-kids-to-go-back-in-text-when.html

Lyon, G. R. (1999). *The NICHD research program in reading development, reading disorders and reading instruction: A summary of research findings. Keys to successful learning: A national summit on research in learning disabilities.* [Monograph]. New York, NY: National Center for Learning Disabilities.

Mariconda, B., & Auray, D. P. (2005). *The comprehensive expository writing guide: All the skills you need to teach good writing* (2nd ed.). Trumbull, CT: Empowering Writers.

Mather, N., Wendling, B. J., & Roberts, R. (2009). *Writing assessment and instruction for students with learning disabilities* (2nd ed.). San Francisco, CA: Jossey-Bass.

McCutchen, D. (2006). Cognitive factors in the development of children's writing. In C. A. MacArthur, S. Graham, & J. Fitzgerald (Eds.), *Handbook of writing research* (pp. 115–130). New York, NY: Guilford Press.

Misunderstood Minds. (n.d.). Difficulty with mathematics. WGBH Educational Foundation. Retrieved from www.pbs.org/wgbh/misunderstoodminds/mathdiffs.html

Misunderstood Minds. (2002). Math strategies. WGBH Educational Foundation. Retrieved from www.pbs.org/wgbh/misunderstoodminds/mathstrats.html

Misunderstood Minds. (2002). Writing. WGBH Educational Foundation. Retrieved from www.pbs.org/wgbh/misunderstoodminds/writing.html

Moats, L. C. (2001). When older kids can't read. *Educational Leadership, 58,* 6.

Moats, L. C. (2010). *Speech to print: Language essentials for teachers* (2nd ed.). Baltimore, MD: Paul H. Brookes.

Multisensory structured language programs: Content and principles of instruction. (n.d.). LD Online. Retrieved from www.ldonline.org/article/6332/

National Institute of Child Health and Human Development (NICHD). (2000). *Report of the National Reading Panel: Teaching children to read; An evidence-based assessment of the scientific literature on reading and its implications for reading instruction: Reports of the subgroups* (NIH Publication No. 00-4754). Washington, DC: US Government Printing Office.

Nicholls, C. J. (2001, October 17–21). *The link between AD/HD and learning disabilities in mathematics.* CHADD 13th annual conference, Anaheim, California.

Polloway, E. A., Patton, J. R., Serna, L., & Bailey, J. W. (2012). *Strategies for teaching learners with special needs* (10th ed.). Upper Saddle River, NJ: Pearson.

Phillips, C., Rust, M., Persaud, L., Jacobs, B., & Satterfield, B. (2015). Assistive technology solutions for writing. Retrieved from http://www.gatfl.gatech.edu/tflwiki/images/c/c5/2015_EASI_Webinar_-_AT_for_Writing.pdf

Raskind, M., & Stanberry, K. (2009). The best software and gadgets for ADHD students. Retrieved from http://www.additudemag.com/adhd/article/6585.html

Reading Rockets. (n.d.). Spelling and word study. Retrieved from http://www.readingrockets.org/research/spelling-and-word-study

Reutzel, D. R. (2015). Early literacy research: Findings primary-grade teachers will want to know. *Reading Teacher, 69*(1), 14–24. doi:10.1002/trtr.1387. Retrieved from http://onlinelibrary.wiley.com/doi/10.1002/trtr.1387/full

Richards, R. (2005). *When writing's a problem: Understanding dysgraphia and helpful hints for reluctant writers* (4th ed.). Riverside, CA: RET Center Press.

Richards, R., & Richards, E. (2008). *Eli, the boy who hated to write* (2nd ed.). Riverside, CA: RET Center Press.

Rief, S. (2001). *Ready . . . start . . . school: Nurturing and guiding your child through preschool and kindergarten.* Upper Saddle River, NJ: Prentice Hall.

Rief, S. (2013). Fun and free interactive online math games. Retrieved from www.sandrarief.com/2013/06/28/fun-interactive-online-math-games

Rief, S. (2015). *The ADHD book of lists: A practical guide for helping children and teens with attention deficit disorders* (2nd ed.). San Francisco, CA: Jossey-Bass.

Rief, S., & Heimburge, J. A. (2007). *How to reach and teach all children through balanced literacy: User-friendly strategies, tools, activities, and ready-to-use materials.* San Francisco, CA: Jossey-Bass.

Rief, S., & Stern, J. M. (2010). *The dyslexia checklist: A practical reference for parents and teachers.* San Francisco, CA: Jossey-Bass.

Rodriguez, J., & Rodriguez, D. (2013). *Times tables the fun way: A picture method of learning the multiplication facts* (3rd ed.). Minneapolis, MN: City Creek Press.

Samuels, S. J. (2006). Reading fluency: Its past, present, and future. In T. Rasinski, C. Blachowicz, & K. Lems (Eds.), *Fluency instruction: Research-based best practices* (pp. 7–20). New York, NY: Guilford Press.

Semple, J. L. (n.d.). *Semple math: A complete basic skills mathematics program.* Attleboro Falls, MA: Semple Math. Retrieved from www.semplemath.com/

Spear-Swerling, L. (2006). The importance of teaching handwriting. LD Online. Retrieved from www.ldonline.org/spearswerling/The_Importance_of_Teaching_Handwriting

Sunderhaft, K. (n.d.). The organized school paper. Retrieved from http://www.additudemag.com/adhd/article/803.html

Texas Education Agency. (2014, July). Dyslexia handbook: Procedures concerning dyslexia and related disorders. Retrieved from www4.esc13.net/uploads/dyslexia/docs/TEA_Dyslexia_Handbook_08_04_14_Final_1.pdf

Tompkins, G. E. (2011). *Teaching writing: Balancing process and product* (6th ed.). Boston, MA: Pearson.

Vacca, H. L., Vacca, R. T., Grove, M. K., Burkey, L., Lenhart, L. A., & Keon, C. (2003). *Reading and learning to read* (5th ed.). Boston, MA: Allyn & Bacon.

Van de Walle, J., & Lovin, L. H. (2006). *Teaching student-centered mathematics, grades 5–8*. Boston, MA: Allyn & Bacon.

Yates, D. (n.d.). *Memory joggers.* Irvine, CA: Memory Joggers.

Websites

Common Core State Standards Initiative, http://www.corestandards.org/

Council for Exceptional Children, www.cec.sped.org

Dyslexia Reading Well, www.dyslexia-reading-well.com

Education World, www.educationworld.com/a_curr/archives/mnemonics.shtml, links to several math mneumonics

Fetzer, N., www.nancyfetzer.com. Click on Nancy's authentic video demonstrations of her instruction using very creative and engaging techniques with students summarizing a story, forming an opinion about its theme, then backing up their judgments with evidence from the text.

Florida Center for Reading Research, www.fcrr.org

International Dyslexia Association (IDA), www.interdys.org

LD Online, www.ldonline.org, learning dsabilities information and resources

Learning Disabilities Association of America (LDA), www.ldanatl.org

Math Fundamentals Problem of the Week, http://mathforum.org/funpow

Math Giraffe, http://www.mathgiraffe.com/blog/5-websites-that-will-revolutionize-your-math-teaching

National Center for Learning Disabilities (NCLD), www.ncld.org

National Council of Teachers of Mathematics (NCTM), www.nctm.org

PBS Learning Media, www.pbslearningmedia.org/collection/i-3-math (video series), for grades 4–8 math

Project WRITE, www.kc.vanderbilt.edu/projectwrite

Reading A-Z, www.readinga-z.com

Reading Rockets, www.readingrockets.org

ReadWriteThink, www.readwritethink.org

Rief Pinterest boards, https://www.pinterest.com/sandrarief/, for numerous practical strategies and fun activities for teachers and parents in phonemic and phonological awareness, phonics, spelling, decoding and fluency, sight words, vocabulary, reading comprehension, writing, math, and more

The Writing Center at the University of North Carolina at Chapel Hill, http://writingcenter.unc.edu, and its video demos at www.youtube.com/user/UNCWritingCenter

part
5

Personal Stories and Case Studies

Section 5.1: A Parent's Story . . . What Every Teacher, Clinician, and Parent of a Child with ADHD Needs to Hear

Section 5.2: Student Case Studies and Interventions

A Parent's Story . . . What Every Teacher, Clinician, and Parent of a Child with ADHD Needs to Hear

A very special parent whom I had the pleasure of meeting and befriending years ago when speaking at an ADHD conference has shared her family's very personal and powerful story in this section. I believe that this story—originally written and published in the 2005 edition of this book when Vincent was a seventeen-year-old high school senior—is a "must-read" for educators, clinicians, and parents of children with ADHD. In the case study she wrote for the book, Diana A-G, Vincent's extraordinary, wonderful mother, generously and poignantly shared her son's health, developmental, and educational history; school intervention plans; and other multimodal treatments he received over the years. At the end of Vincent's case study, his sister, Victoria, was briefly introduced to us as well.

Vincent's compelling story illustrates the reality of how difficult it is to find what works for any given child. It takes a great deal of caring, commitment, and effort on the part of all parties (parents, educators, and clinicians) to figure out and do what it takes for a child with ADHD to be successful. The various interventions and treatments that are needed at different times during the child's life will change. Readers will note how Vincent's parents steadfastly helped their son by assuming the important role of "team managers" in their son's care, and being vigilant in addressing his needs—making every effort to pursue an accurate diagnosis, obtain proper intervention, and communicate and collaborate effectively with the school and clinicians.

A decade later, I am so grateful that Vincent and Victoria, both adults now, agreed to allow Diana to write a follow-up on their educational experiences that transpired since. I am certain that readers will find this follow-up, titled "Everything Ripples: The Education of Vincent and Victoria," to be fascinating, insightful, and inspiring. There is much to be learned from Diana's wisdom and articulate telling of her family's story.

Note: Names and identifying information have been changed to protect the family's anonymity, but Diana welcomes correspondence from interested readers. If you wish to contact her, send your email through my website, www.sandrarief.com, and it will be forwarded directly to her.

Vincent (Seventeen Years Old, High School Senior)

Medical History

Vincent is the older of two children in our family, the result of a planned pregnancy with appropriate prenatal care. He was born full-term, and his weight was within normal limits. As an infant, Vincent received all appropriate medical care and timely immunizations. He suffered from ear infections and upper respiratory infections during infancy, and was treated with numerous rounds of oral antibiotics until P.E. tubes were surgically inserted at age eighteen months, after which his health improved. Sinus infections, allergies, and strep infections were identified and treated in early childhood and the primary grades, with less frequent episodes of upper respiratory problems continuing into adolescence. Irritable bowel syndrome was identified, and treatment with antispasmodic medication followed an acute episode when Vincent was about nine years of age. Gastroesophogeal reflux was identified in about the seventh grade. Allergies persisted, and Vincent continues to take daily medications to prevent and treat them. Vision and hearing have been tested regularly, and no problems have been identified in those areas. Vincent's academic and behavioral progress is described in the social/educational narrative here.

Social/Educational History (Narrative)

Vincent's behavioral issues were noted first with feeding problems, jaundice, and tremors in early infancy. He began to be able to feed well within a few days; he responded well to phototherapy, and the jaundice resolved. A pediatric neurologist who saw Vincent at two months of age stated that the tremors might be what was called "twilight tremors," noted when a baby is waking up, and otherwise, Vincent appeared to be functioning within normal limits. At about eighteen months of age, Vincent began experiencing what is referred to as "night terrors," a sort of "gear-shift problem" in the brain that typically occurs when the child is making the transition from one phase of sleep to another (for example, from deep sleep to lighter sleep phases that include more motoric activity). These night terrors went away before Vincent was three years of age.

Vincent achieved all developmental milestones, including toilet learning, within normal limits. He did not tantrum at a rate above what would be expected for his age, but he was observed to have great difficulty calming down once he was upset. It was observed that if he could not calm himself within about five minutes, he was unlikely to be able to do so even an hour later without parental intervention, such as holding or rocking. Vincent was observed to have a vocabulary that was within normal limits (that is, he was not observed to be precocious in any way), although visitors frequently commented on the clarity of his articulation. Other than his night terrors and difficulty with calming down, he appeared to be a "regular kid," but "quirky." That is, if one only considered developmental milestones . . .

Some of Vincent's "quirks" included a tendency to avoid eye contact with people, a resistance to being touched, a tendency not to smile much, a tendency to resist changes in his routine or his environment, and overreaction to emotions like joy or anger. (For example, if he got "really happy," he'd become so "silly" that he'd hurt himself or others, and he appeared not to be able to calm himself down; in fact, it almost appeared that he had to cry to get calmed down.) These quirks became much more pronounced as he got older, and these behaviors became more "discrepant" from his peers' behavior. For example, we could do a lot of "prevention work" to ensure that Vincent would not become overaroused, but the avoidance of eye contact began to be labeled as "attitude" and "disrespect" by his teachers and grandparents and perceived as "aloofness," "coldness," or "haughtiness" by peers.

Another behavior noted at the time was that Vincent was extremely "picky" about the texture of his clothing. He would "chafe" at materials that seemed to "itch" him, and would refuse to wear (or would take off, as soon as he was able) clothing that contained tags, "bumpy" seams, or even button-plackets. Certain socks, for example, or polo shirts that had a few buttons on the chest, would irritate him to the point of distraction. Nowadays, some professionals would suggest that Vincent was suffering from what is referred to as a sensory processing disorder or sensory integration disorder, but information of that type was not readily available at that time. At this time, such disorders are still considered speculative, and there is a need for more scientific study of these behaviors.

When Vincent was two, a caregiver remarked that Vincent was particularly "selfish" and "grabby" in his Mother's Day Out program. We replied that it was our understanding that it was developmentally appropriate for children not to "share" until about age three, and that a more reasonable expectation was that a two-year-old could "take turns" (the developmental precursor to sharing). However, at ages three, four, and five, Vincent was observed across many settings, such as church, school, home, and in public, to have continued difficulty with taking turns, much less sharing. Behaviorally, he appeared to have increasing problems with impulsive grabbing, pushing, "bossing," following directions, accepting changes in routine, and hyperactivity. The older he became, the more apparent the social discrepancy between Vincent and his peers became.

Vincent was fortunate to have a remarkable preschool teacher (Ms. JH), who, in addition to staying in excellent communication with us, documented examples of the behaviors that would help our family as we sought diagnostic help in later years. This teacher communicated in meaningful ways to Vincent that he was a valuable human being, and she employed some noteworthy teaching strategies:

Modeling the desired behavior. Each day, Ms. JH gathered the children and then simply and briefly outlined what was going to happen that day. For example, if they were going to be spreading peanut butter on crackers in an "interest center," she demonstrated the proper use of the knife and how to avoid spreading germs, and so forth. This type of modeling not only helped Vincent adjust to changes but also helped him (and all the children, for that matter) know what behavior was expected and how to behave well.

Music. Another particularly effective strategy was her use of song to aid in gaining the children's attention and in easing transitions from one activity to another. While her songs were not typical ones for most classrooms, it was amazing to see how the rhythm of a song like "Johnny Be Good" (made popular by Chuck Berry) could result in the rhythmic picking up of blocks.

Although Vincent's response to the following behavioral interventions was not specifically assessed at preschool, he was observed at home to respond well to

"Broken record" and "rehearsal." We had to "give ourselves permission" to repeat behavior rules over and over and over, like a broken record. This was rather difficult, at first, as we had grown up with the idea that you should not have to repeat rules that a child of normal intelligence should already know. It became apparent that Vincent did know the rules, but he exhibited great difficulty "retrieving" them on demand. In other words, he knew the rule; he just wasn't using the rule to help govern his behavior. The "broken record" or "rehearsal" approach seemed to help him, especially before the event occurred. For example, we would rehearse "The blocks stay in your hand." If he got excited and threw a block, he was calmly told the rule again (broken record) as an appropriate consequence was applied. In this case, we put away the blocks and tried again on another day.

"When/then" statements (also known as Grandma's Rule). "When you finish your dinner, then you get dessert." Not only did this help with motivation, it helped with making the transition to the next activity.

Enjoyable challenges. He enjoyed a race with himself (not competing with others), such as racing an egg timer to complete a task.

Obstacle course. Vincent also responded well to "obstacle course," a game that we played to help him learn to keep multistep commands in his head. We would start with one step and then increase the number of steps in the command as he became successful with remembering what he was supposed to do. He enjoyed this game immensely, and while we don't have much evidence to prove it, we believe that it helped him with remembering classroom routines (such as "Take off your coat, hang it up, go to your desk, sit down, and get out your pencil"), and much later, when remembering rules to complex math problems.

Novelty and complexity. This strategy sounds strange, but Vincent always acted like he was trying to "feed his brain." That is, he was "hungry" for stimulation. While he'd settle for "good" stimulation or "bad" stimulation (like getting in trouble), he behaved best and "stayed focused" longest when his brain was "fed" with a moderate amount of novelty and complexity. We found that if a situation was too familiar ("boring") or too simple (like copying easy words on paper while sitting in a chair), he'd lose interest and behave poorly. On the other hand, if the situation was too novel or too complex (like playing an unfamiliar game with lots of rules), he'd become overwhelmed and quit. However, we could spark his interest and he could maintain appropriate amounts of attention when the task was given "just a twist" of novelty. For example, he did better copying when he did it in sand, on special-shaped paper, standing up at an easel, or other ways like that. Or instead of copying the word, he'd write a word, widely spaced, in the middle of a sheet of paper and then he'd trace around each letter with a series of colored pencils, so that when completed, it looked like a rainbow. It was kind of like the old story of the three bears: not too hot, not too cold, but just right. Of course, because Vincent seemed to need more novelty than other children, we often felt as though he was riding on one of those "people-mover" conveyor belts at the airport and we were running alongside him, placing new challenges just in front of him. We had to "keep our running shoes on" with him, but his love of learning made it all worthwhile. It was fun!

Simplifying tasks. If a task was too complex, as just mentioned, Vincent seemed overwhelmed. Vincent responded best to performing complex tasks, such as cleaning up his room, when the task was broken into smaller interesting parts, such as attribute recognition: "Find all the things with wheels" or "Pick up all the blocks that are long."

Social scripts. Another type of rehearsal that we called "script rehearsal" was used frequently. He responded fairly well to rehearsal of "scripts" for social situations; for example, we would practice saying "No, thank you" to an offer of asparagus, instead of "Gross, those are slimy!" Please note, however, that we are still working on that.

In kindergarten, Vincent "touched everything" and was constantly "fiddling." He was in an educational setting that promoted the idea that a child was "self-regulating" and would learn certain things as he became ready to learn them. Later we realized that he was one of a subgroup of children who don't self-regulate very easily and for whom certain educational aspects were not going to be mastered by "readiness" alone. For example, Vincent avoided any tasks that involved writing, but he did not avoid all fine motor tasks. Vincent was exceptionally good at puzzles and linking blocks like Legos. Therefore, his writing problems were considered to be "developmental." His teacher described him as "bright, but immature," and recommended that he repeat kindergarten. While we agreed with his very kind teacher, who had actually described him accurately, we chose not to accept that recommendation, for the reason that he seemed "bored," and we were concerned that he would be even more bored the following year.

Instead of repeating kindergarten, Vincent was enrolled in a "developmental" first-grade class, which in retrospect was not a good decision for our particular child. He continued to feel bored, and he continued to be labeled "immature." We pursued additional testing in the second half of that year, as Vincent seemed "miserable." It was determined that he was functioning intellectually just fine. His fine motor skills were technically OK; in other words, he passed developmental and psychoeducational testing. It was noted that Vincent was not reading yet, at age seven, but it was considered to be a "developmental problem," and "time" was offered as the only intervention. In response to our increasing awareness that something was interfering with Vincent's ability to function well, and our expressed concerns about possible ADHD, his developmental first-grade teacher exclaimed, "If Vincent has ADHD, then every other child in my class has ADHD!" We continued to seek information and support for an increasingly unhappy but intelligent child. [See Section 1.8, ADHD in Preschool and Kindergarten.]

Diagnosis, Part I

A diagnosis of ADHD was made by a neurologist in the summer between developmental first grade and first grade, and Vincent was prescribed stimulant medication. We could tell on the first day of the medication trial that Vincent was helped by the medication. It was a tremendous relief. We now had a "name" for what was troubling Vincent, and we could get some help for him. When Vincent calmed down, it seemed like our whole family calmed down. However, that was not the end of our story, and, unfortunately, we did not live happily ever after with the aid of modern pharmacology.

Behavioral challenges continued, in spite of a reduction in the symptoms of hyperactivity, distractibility, and fluctuating attention. Eye contact problems and social skills problems persisted. Academically, Vincent seemed to improve dramatically, especially in his reading skills, but he demonstrated significant problems with handwriting, spelling, punctuation, and grammar.

About that time, we joined CHADD (www .chadd.org), a national support group for children and adults with ADHD and related disorders. We learned that most people with ADHD respond best when they are supported by three things:

- Up-to-date diagnosis/appropriate medical help
- Appropriate educational supports
- Appropriate emotional support/counseling/ therapeutic interventions [See Section 1.4, Multimodal Treatments for ADHD.]

At a CHADD meeting, we heard that appropriate support for a person with ADHD can be compared to a three-legged stool. A three-legged stool cannot stand up if one of the legs is missing. We were

fortunate that we had access to all three of those factors, and we have relied on them in varying degrees over the years.

While it would be untrue, in a strict sense, to say that we valued one of the "legs" more than another, it is absolutely true when we say that we relied on educational supports and interventions more often than the other two supports. This statement becomes logical when one considers that Vincent was in school or doing homework for the majority of his waking hours.

In the section discussing helpful educational supports, we have combined supports that were implemented primarily at school with those that were implemented primarily at home. This is because many of the items were shared at home and at school, or they led from one setting to the other.

First- Through Third-Grade Educational Supports

Positive outlook of teacher. We placed the most difficult-to-define feature of support first in this list because it, by far, has made the most difference for Vincent. After years of partnering with teachers, we can say that those teachers who were able to withhold judgmental behavior and find "something positive" in each child in their classrooms were the teachers who were able to help Vincent find "the positive" in himself. In our case, it wasn't always the kind of positive we'd expect, and in some cases, it was just plain funny. For example, when Vincent was in the second grade, he dictated the caption for a photograph of him showing off a "city" they'd built during a class project. His caption read "I'm good with cardboard!"

We are not saying that a teacher must never get tired or frustrated or dislike a particular child's poor hygiene or always feel happy. That is not realistic; we know that teachers are human beings too. But positive outlook, for us and for Vincent, was communicated as respect for the child as a worthwhile human being, one who has something meaningful to offer the world. For at least one child, "cardboard" is meaningful! Those moments of "positive outlook" have served us as a sort of "booster shot" of self-esteem; they have tided Vincent over many moments of discouragement and doubt.

Facilitation of medication monitoring. While this does not sound like an accommodation, our experience has been that teachers have been critical partners in helping us and his physicians determine the appropriate type, dosage, and timing of Vincent's medication. One morning in first grade, Vincent was accidentally sent to school without having taken his morning medication. His teacher called at about 9:00 a.m., stating, "I don't know what is wrong with Vincent, and he isn't hurting anybody, but he is rolling around on the floor under his desk, giggling." Over the years, we have gained invaluable information from different teachers who were sensitive observers of their students.

Allowing Vincent to stand at his desk or lie down to work when appropriate. We quickly learned that the typical recommendation of positioning the student with ADHD close to the teacher can be difficult to implement if the classroom is set up traditionally, with the teacher at the front of the class and the students in rows of desks. In addition to the likelihood that an average classroom contains more than one student with ADHD, and the difficulty that comes when trying to place all of those students near the teacher, Vincent, being rather tall, would have caused visual disruption to the class if he were allowed to stand. In consulting with the teacher, we learned that he seemed to need to stand or lie down, particularly when working on writing tasks or after fairly long periods of seatwork. So in most cases, the teacher arranged for everyone to have that option, so it "normalized" the process, and it seemed like everyone was happier. We learned, over the course of time, that it was less important for Vincent to be seated close to the teacher than it was for him to be positioned where he could not be a visual distraction to other students, and that contact and encouragement from the teacher

were best facilitated when the teacher moved around the room and provided contact and encouragement to all the students.

Allowing him to hold things or touch things or chew things that did not make noise. While this appeared to be allowing "immature" behavior, and one teacher expressed disgust at the idea, we still advocated that he be allowed to continue this "bad habit." We had found, via home-school communications, that when he wasn't allowed to chew his pencil, he was being more disruptive to the learning environment, such as talking to his neighbor, tapping on his desk, or humming to himself. So in the interest of minimizing classroom disruptions, Vincent was able to hold, touch, or mouth objects as long as they did not make any noise.

Staying by the teacher for transitions. One of the things we learned very quickly with our child was that he tended to have more problems with behavior during the transition from one activity to another or from one place to another (for example, in going to the library or to "specials" like music class). During those times, Vincent did seem to need extra support from the teacher as to what to do with his hands, his feet, or other items, so having him assist the teacher and stay close to her/him was extremely helpful. It became clear to the other students that Vincent was "special," and like a child who experienced mobility problems and required special assistance, they quickly realized and accepted the fact that "fair doesn't always mean equal" and were very gracious about the situation.

Proactive playground and cafeteria supervision. After careful observation, it became clear that behavioral problems tended to happen more often when Vincent was in low-supervision situations. Communication with key individuals at the school resulted in subtle changes in monitoring of those settings so that any emerging problems could be "nipped in the bud."

Providing a "homework" folder. This folder consisted of assignments and notes to come home in one section and things to be completed and returned in the other section. As Vincent got older, a "planner" or "agenda" took its place.

Keeping the backpack by the front door. Our house probably looked a wreck to visitors, but this strategy made all the difference to us. Our efforts to get a child with ADHD up and out the door in the morning resulted in trying out every bit of organizational support that we could find. This really worked for us. After homework time, the backpack went back to the front door.

Parent sitting with him to do homework. While this does not appear to be reasonable or doable for some families, it was critical for us. Early on, Vincent could not stay seated in a chair, much less focus on directions or written assignments.

Providing a designated place, time, and stuff for homework. We stored all necessary/useful items in a portable box, what the author refers to as a "homework survival kit." With a child like ours, we could not afford to have any distractions like getting up to find a stapler or something. If we did, we had to "start over" with the whole process.

We made a real commitment not to answer the phone during this time. This effort was made harder by the negative response of friends, family, and coworkers, but eventually everyone adjusted to this commitment.

Reduced written assignments, especially for rote tasks like copying spelling words. Even with a parent sitting with Vincent, we found that he took about two hours (this is not an exaggeration) to complete what should have been twenty minutes' worth of work. Instead of copying a word three times, he copied it once.

If written assignments were not completed within allotted class time, then allow extra time or send them home. This was a trickier accommodation to pull off in reality than we expected. In one case, Vincent had a teacher who, for whatever reason, thought that giving him extra time to complete an assignment meant "allowing"

him to finish it during recess. To Vincent, and to us, this was perceived as punishment, so we immediately requested that the work be sent home with him. For a child who has significant problems with "production," having work sent home can be an incredible burden on an already stressed family. As a result, we have become stronger advocates of the "quality, not quantity" theory, in which we ask, "If the child can show you what he knows, why would he need to demonstrate it five times over?" We never did completely solve the "within class time" problem, but we tried to balance the reduction of written work with extra time or bringing the work home.

Allowing Vincent to dictate instead of writing, when possible. At this stage, in the primary grades, this was fairly easy to accomplish. We have learned some lovely things about Vincent's creative mind that we'd never have seen if he'd had to write the words himself.

"Earnings" for progress. "Earnings" were things that Vincent would select, with our help, to reward himself for small successes. This was a strictly voluntary process for our son. For example, Vincent might choose to have a sip of his drink for every three spelling words he copied. Or he might get to put an animal cracker into a cup to eat after his homework was finished. He could see the animal crackers pile up (to five or six) and he would be very pleased with his progress. (This process was carefully set up and monitored, and under no circumstances could we take away what he'd earned once he'd earned it, even if his behavior "fell apart" five minutes later. This is a crucial aspect of "earnings," in our opinion, and involves basic respect for the child's efforts. Please see note 1 in "Notes on Section 5.1.")

Fourth and Fifth Grades and Diagnosis, Part II

Academically, Vincent struggled with "production problems"; that is, he was clearly bright, but he was not able to produce quality written work. His teachers appeared to be very frustrated, and the terms "lazy," "smart, but inconsistent in his work," and "undisciplined" began to creep into communications with us. Vincent became increasingly oppositional and discouraged during this period (fourth grade, in particular), both at home and in school.

In the fifth grade, we began seeking further assessment, suspecting learning disabilities, as Vincent's writing skills appeared to be at about a second-grade level (a three-year discrepancy between his grade level and his performance). The assessments in the fifth grade revealed that Vincent was, indeed, struggling with learning disabilities. We pursued an Individualized Education Program (IEP) via the local public schools, and Vincent finished fifth grade with accommodations in place for specific learning disabilities in the area of "written expression."

Sixth through Twelfth Grades

Vincent was accepted into one of our city's magnet schools, which included students from sixth through twelfth grade. We were very fearful of the idea of communicating with eight teachers (even more when we counted the special services faculty and therapists and administrators). However, we discovered a few things that relieved our anxiety tremendously and helped us to ensure that Vincent would not flounder at this level of his education.

First, we discovered that Vincent would have a "case manager" who would serve as an excellent point of contact. In our case, Vincent's case manager was a learning disabilities teacher; but we have since come to believe that a great middle school point of contact could be any teacher or staff member who cares about your child and is willing to serve as an informal liaison between home and school. This could be a librarian, a vice principal, or an administrative assistant—anyone who is a good communicator. In other words, a good point of contact, in our opinion, does not need to be someone in a position of formal authority at the school. Vincent's LD teacher, Ms. B, incidentally, never actually had him in her classroom, as

he was able to be "mainstreamed" in every subject. Ms. B became a mentor to Vincent, a communication facilitator, an advocate for him, and served as a "reality check" for us at home if and when we faced difficulties. She was wonderful.

Second, after making several mistakes in communicating with the faculty in his elementary school and after coming to feel that we had slid into an adversarial role with his teachers in the fourth and fifth grades, we knew we needed to adjust our own communication strategies and come up with a better way of advocating for our child. After some real soul-searching, it became evident that we had been saying something to this effect: "What can you do to help our child learn?" This statement seemed to cause teachers and others to feel defensive and resentful and, more often than not, brought out resistance in teachers rather than the kind of assistance we were seeking. In looking back over some truly awful episodes, we realized that we needed to find nonthreatening ways to advocate for Vincent. So we began to ask teachers, "How can we help you help Vincent to learn?"

This seemingly small change in wording became a critical change of strategy for us, and it helped us reestablish the kind of rapport that we wanted. That is, by asking how we could help the teacher, instead of demanding that the teacher help us, we could all relax and enjoy being united in our concern for Vincent's success in school. "Help for the teacher" was generally interpreted, it appeared, to mean that we respected the difficulty of the teacher's task, that we wanted to support him or her, not drain precious energy or make overwhelming demands. While we were never asked to do anything that was outside of our ability to do, we *were* asked to

- Assist the teacher by providing as much information as we could about Vincent.
- Arrange communication routes that fit the teacher's routine.
- Let the teacher know as soon as possible if it appeared that Vincent was beginning to struggle in or outside of class (including things like sleeping problems).

The third thing that made all the difference for us during middle school (and on) was making sure that we had the most effective IEP that we could. [See Section 6.4, Federal Laws and Educational Rights of Students with ADHD.]

Truthfully, this took more work than we expected, given that we were both working full-time and raising two children and dealing with everyday challenges of life in an ADHD household. We attended workshops offered by our local Parent Training Center to learn about the rules and regulations for the different types of plans for which our child might be eligible. (Each state has at least one office, and they provide support and training for parents at regional sites.) We went to a couple of conferences and fairs that had to do with children with special needs (in fact, it was at one such fair that we found out about all the assistive technology that was available, such as specialized computers), and we talked to other parents to find out what had helped their children. We checked books out of the library or borrowed them from our local chapter of CHADD. We tried to anticipate every resource that would help prevent problems or nip them in the bud. Our goal was that Vincent, who was bright but seemed "allergic" to school and homework and even the social demands of school life, would not just "survive," but maybe even thrive in his new school.

The IEP: Vincent's IEP included the following list of symptoms and the relevant accommodations:

1. Works very slowly, cannot finish assignments and tests during time allotted.
   Accommodations:
   — Provide extended time for classroom assignments and tests.
2. Handwriting problems.
   Accommodations:
   — Provide AlphaSmart word processor (laptop) for keyboarding in class. (Please see note 2 in "Notes on Section 5.1.")
   — Accept typed work in lieu of written work.
   — Occupational therapy X hours per week.
3. Frequent spelling, grammar, punctuation errors

Accommodations:
   — Do not count off for spelling, etc., errors unless specifically being tested on those subjects.
   — Allow Vincent to edit in-class work.
4. Disorganization.
   Accommodations:
   — Teacher to provide written back-up notes and assignments.
   — Structure activities and transitions to prevent confusion.
5. Problems following directions.
   Accommodations:
   — Give Vincent extra time to process directions or requests.
6. Problems maintaining proper behavior.
   Accommodations:
   — Ignore negative vocalizations unless determined to be abusive.
   — Allow extra time for Vincent to attempt to calm himself if upset.
   — If unable to calm within two or three minutes, employ "Safety Net" in which Vincent leaves class and goes to specified school places/personnel. (This included his school librarian; please see note 3 in "Notes on Section 5.1.")
   — Provide positive reinforcement for his efforts.
   — Do not touch Vincent without his permission.
7. Medical problems—for example, irritable bowel syndrome.
   Accommodations:
   — Allow Vincent to discreetly notify teacher and leave class to use restroom as needed.

Discipline

We have already mentioned his LD teacher, but it is vital to add that she was the one who helped us put our ideas for Vincent's IEP into appropriate wording and into measurable terms in order to comply with local, state, and federal guidelines. She helped educate her colleagues about Vincent and his IEP and kept us informed every step of the way. Perhaps most important, after the drafting of Vincent's IEP, she also helped Vincent improve his behavior by being gentle but firm about her expectations for him. She became Vincent's "Number One Safety Net"; he was to go to her class first if he became too upset to remain in the classroom. Incidentally, Vincent only needed to employ his Safety Net a few times in all his years at the school, in large part because of this teacher's care and concern. However, she was not Vincent's only fantastic teacher. And to be blunt, some of the best teacher supports came from the teachers we least suspected.

Avoiding Power Struggles

Vincent's seventh-grade history teacher appeared to be the strictest teacher on earth, and Vincent seemed to "butt heads" with this teacher, Mr. C, on the very first day of school. When we visited with Mr. C, we learned that he expected all his students, when responding to a question, to stand at their desks, look at the teacher, and articulate as clearly as they could. Vincent had difficulty making eye contact with the teacher, but Mr. C, with unbelievable wisdom, chose not to confront Vincent about it. Rather than approaching and looming over Vincent, which would have likely resulted in a "fight or flight" response from Vincent, Mr. C backed up, away from Vincent, so that Vincent had to lift his chin and head to even gaze in the general direction of the teacher. By stepping back, Mr. C could also pretend that he could not hear Vincent; and in order to project his voice better, Vincent had to look up and raise his chin. Mr. C helped Vincent begin to communicate better, first, making it a normal expectation for everyone in the class; second, by thinking through how to obtain the desired behavior; and third, by refraining from a power struggle or the use of shame or intimidation. Mr. C not only had the best-behaved classes in the school, and students who learned to respect each other and respect each other's opinions, but his enthusiasm for history and the self-discipline necessary for scholarship were contagious. We can't say that Vincent quit complaining about doing homework, but he began to express a love of learning that he'd not shared in some time.

Assistive Technology

We had learned about AlphaSmart, a remarkably affordable type of word processor that looks similar to a laptop computer, at a "health fair" for individuals with special needs. AlphaSmart discontinued production in 2013, but there are newer types of assistive technology that share the essential feature of allowing students with disabilities to enter information into them and then recover that information at a later time. (Please see note 2 in "Notes on Section 5.1.") The AlphaSmart was attractive to us because, in addition to its being practically indestructible, it featured (at that time) eight different word processing files that the student could access with the touch of one key. Vincent could have one file for each class. For example, Vincent could open up his English class file at a touch; he could type notes into the file, then bring it home and "dump the data" either to a computer or a printer almost instantaneously. We must admit that when we first asked about it, through Vincent's occupational therapist, she indicated that she did not know what we were talking about. However, we were pleasant but firm about wanting to access this possible resource, and persistent in advocating that the school "go up the ladder" a little bit. We quickly learned that an AlphaSmart could be loaned to us by our school district, along with the simple cable that allowed the data to be "dumped." This was to become a real relief to us, once Vincent started using it. At first, he was concerned about "looking different" from the other students, a valid concern, but when he actually began to use it (out of desperation), he found out that it became a status symbol! All the other students wanted one. Overall, this resource turned out to be even better than we expected. Our only regret was that we had to "educate educators" in order to access it. It was disconcerting to find that we, as parents, knew more about some resources for our child than our child's therapist did. We had been "trained" to believe that professionals in a position of authority were experts and should never be questioned. However, the experience taught us to be patient and to consider that we had strong motivation to seek out resources for our particular child. In the meanwhile, teachers and therapists and other professionals were, out of necessity, focused on groups of children, not on one particular child's needs. We learned the importance of sharing our knowledge politely and the importance of not underestimating our own ability to serve as advocates for our child. As a lovely teacher (who was also the parent of a child with ADHD) once reassured us, "If you don't advocate for your child, who will?"

Note Taker in Math

Vincent had a truly challenging time copying off the board, and the assistive technology that was provided for us could not meet his needs in algebra and geometry classes, as he needed to copy mathematical terms and equations. At our request, his teacher discreetly found a capable student who was willing to take the class notes using carbonless paper (one type is called an NCR form), which can be purchased from printing companies or even copy shops like Kinko's. After the student took notes on this special paper, he kept the original and gave Vincent the copy each day. This accommodation worked remarkably well; the only factor that gave us any concern, initially, was confidentiality. However, his teacher was very thoughtful about it and educated the note-taking student about the importance of privacy. The boys became friends.

Drama

Vincent was only mildly interested in this subject at first, but at the recommendation of his counselor, he enrolled in a drama class. Vincent made good, if sporadic, progress socially and in his maturity, under the tutelage of his drama teacher. Because it was a small drama program, he worked with the same teacher for five years. This could have become a problem, because he entered the class in the sixth grade after a couple of years with teachers whom he felt he could not trust. Given the types of activities that usually take place in a drama class, activities that require the student to feel safe and secure in extending himself or herself and "take risks," Ms. MW certainly had her work cut out for her. As Ms. MW

taught Vincent, she patiently built trust with him, and she balanced her nurturing with appropriate doses of constructive criticism, challenging him to "stretch" to meet higher and higher levels of performance, understanding, behavior, and teamwork. While Vincent experienced some of his most spectacular social failures in her class, and he suffered tremendous personal agony at those times, he also gained important skills. He learned how to "take direction," become more introspective, take responsibility for his behavior, become a real team player, and how to get back up and dust himself off and try again, even when he made (sometimes humiliating) mistakes. As it turned out, five years with the same teacher was probably not enough! He has gone on to work with two other stellar drama teachers, but he will probably always describe his first drama teacher as one of the most powerfully positive influences in his life.

Creativity, Empathy, Care, and Concern in Teaching

Vincent had another excellent teacher, but as with the other teachers we've mentioned, things started out "rocky." His school required a foreign language early on, and each sixth grader took a course that provided an overview of French, Spanish, and Latin. Vincent decided he'd prefer to take Latin in the seventh grade. We were horrified because we knew that Latin was primarily a written language, and Vincent had trouble writing or spelling or forming proper sentences in English, much less in Latin. We tried to discourage him from pursuing what we considered a suicide course, but he, very logically, stated that if he wanted to become a doctor or a scientist someday, he'd be best served by knowing Latin (and Greek) so that he could understand all the terminology. How could we argue with that? Well, as it turned out, Dr. G, the Latin teacher, was probably more concerned than we were. We went to visit with her, and sensing Dr. G's hesitation to work with Vincent, we tried to take things slowly in an attempt to avoid an adversarial relationship. We asked about her approach to teaching the class, which turned out, to our pleasant surprise, to sound quite inviting. Dr. G's use of story, games, and the planned class explorations of cultures and history and architecture sounded wonderful to our ears. She mentioned some of the trips that she and her husband, a well-respected French teacher, took to Europe frequently. As she talked about their experiences in other cultures, she mentioned an expression in France that is loosely interpreted as "being comfortable in one's skin." "That describes Vincent!" we replied. "Only in his case, he has never felt 'comfortable in his own skin.'" From that moment on, she seemed to understand, or at least have empathy for Vincent. Dr. G had a wry sense of humor that Vincent truly enjoyed, and while he was probably never her best student, with creativity on her part, he was able to master it well enough to earn A's and B's in the subject over the subsequent three years. One of our favorite memories of this period in his life is this: At a school open house one year, Dr. G quietly remarked that she was informally using some of the accommodations/supports she'd used with Vincent with another student, with great success. While Vincent's original reason for taking Latin may be long forgotten, we reaped the benefits of a teacher whose love of scholarly endeavors was contagious, and whose care and concern for her students extended well beyond what was required by law.

Medication

We feel strongly that Vincent would not have been able to pay a bit of "attention" to any of his teachers or learned any of the important lessons he needed to learn without taking the stimulant medications he was prescribed. See the next item in the list for an example that convinced us.

Good Communication

In addition to the wonderful Ms. B (Vincent's case manager/LD teacher), we were impressed with communications in general. Vincent's teachers sandwiched their occasional concerns between so many encouraging comments that we gradually lost our sense of "phone phobia" (that fear of answering the telephone that many parents of children with ADHD develop). Anyhow, toward the winter break of sixth grade, Ms. C, Vincent's

English teacher, called, saying that for the previous three weeks, he had failed every quiz and not turned in any assignments. When we questioned Vincent about it, we learned that he had been placing his medication each morning on a little ledge ("lip") under the kitchen table. We discovered precisely fifteen tablets on that ledge! When we assessed the situation with Vincent, he told us that he only wanted to be able to "control himself," since we had been telling him for years that it was his responsibility to control his own behavior. This was a real dilemma, in a tragically funny sort of way, as we attempted to find a balance between the reality that he had a problem in his brain that he could not solve with willpower alone and our stated expectation that he take responsibility for his behavior and that he engage in appropriate self-discipline. After learning that he was "crashing" in his English class, he agreed to begin taking his medication again. Later, he painfully referred to that self-imposed experiment as "The Time of the Very Bad Idea." We prefer to think of that time as an important experience that we'd not have had without good communication with his school.

Behavioral Plan

Vincent's success in school was also supported by a thoughtful behavioral plan. By the time he entered sixth grade, we knew that he'd never been involved in aggression in which he instigated the problem. Rather, he was observed to be highly reactive to other people's aggressive acts. However, we very quickly learned that, in school, it does not matter who "started the trouble": all participants are guilty and must be punished! We already had a good idea of the situations in which he could get into trouble (see notes from his elementary years as well). His IEP included the following plan: If Vincent began to get upset or too frustrated, he would be given a special card, shaped like a regular business card, which he was to place on his desk if he needed to leave the room to employ his "Safety Net." Vincent's "Safety Net" was a series of places he could go to calm himself down. In his case, his number one place was his homeschool liaison, Ms. B's class. His number two place, in case Ms. B was not available, was his history teacher, with whom he had excellent rapport. He had three other steps in his Safety Net, in the event that the first two "steps" were not available. It should be mentioned that while Vincent was in excellent hands, academically, he was attending an inner-city magnet school in a neighborhood very concerned with gang violence and drug/alcohol abuse. As a result, at his school, students were not typically allowed to be unescorted anywhere in the building during class time, so this accommodation was not given lightly.

Naturally, Vincent was expected not to abuse this accommodation by going anywhere except the places he was authorized to go. He was also expected to be the one to monitor his own emotional state and to employ his Safety Net before he got into trouble. This was a big responsibility. As he grew, the "players" in his Safety Net changed a little, but the plan remained unchanged. Over the years, Vincent needed to employ his Safety Net only a few times, and he never needed to employ steps three, four, or five. However, we believe that having that plan in place gave him the sense that he had safe options when his emotions overcame his ability to function in the classroom.

In addition to having problems with calming down if he became frustrated or upset, and problems with his behavior during transition times, we were aware that he seemed to be "hyper-reactive" to being touched. This was particularly evident when he was touched by surprise (such as someone approaching him from behind and laying a hand on his shoulder or poking him) or when someone got too close to him (such as a person approaching him rapidly, "getting in his face," or shaking a finger in his face). Unfortunately, Vincent would usually respond to those behaviors in a reflexive flash. In the case of being touched or bumped from behind, he'd typically whip around with his arm extended, or, if he perceived threat from the front, he'd fling his arms up in a reactive attempt to protect himself. We were afraid that if he responded that way to a teacher or administrator, he could accidentally hit someone and then he'd be accused of assault. In order to prevent those possibilities from becoming horrifying realities, we asked that teachers remain at least three feet away from him and gain his specific

permission before touching him. At the same time, we instructed Vincent to place his hands in his pockets whenever he felt "pressed" by another's physical presence and to take literal steps backward if he could. The hands-in-pockets rule was especially effective with peers, and in one isolated occasion, it saved him from real trouble with an administrator who chose not to comply with the behavioral terms of his IEP. The administrator was held accountable, by the way.

Another behavioral aspect of Vincent's plan was handled beautifully, in our opinion. He had been diagnosed with irritable bowel syndrome, which can include bouts of diarrhea. In order to accommodate for this potentially embarrassing problem, all he had to do was put the same Safety Net card on his desk, and he was able to leave the room to go to the restroom.

Finally, we knew that Vincent had problems with blurting out impulsive statements, which he'd always want to "take back" the moment he'd considered the wisdom of the statement. While we are confident that his medication has helped him become less impulsive, and we can't imagine how many inappropriate things he'd say if he wasn't taking his medication, he still struggles with this problem. So we asked that his teachers ignore impulsive comments (usually groans or sighs about an assignment, or an under-his-breath muttered complaint that it was boring) unless it was directly abusive. That is, if the statement broke a school rule, such as cursing or threatening, then clearly it should not be ignored. Vincent was never to be allowed to break a school rule, but impulsive groans of discontent were not violations of a rule. They were just annoying.

This was potentially a difficult situation in that Vincent's inappropriate comments could, theoretically, disrupt the learning environment for everyone. We carefully reasoned that if the teacher ignored his impulsive comment (which Vincent would instantly retract anyway), then it would be considerably less likely that his comment could ignite a power struggle between Vincent and the teacher. However, if the teacher responded to Vincent's impulsive statement, it would practically be guaranteed to disrupt the learning environment. This line of reasoning was very difficult for some teachers to accept, and a good argument on their behalf was that Vincent's mutterings and "blurtings" could incite other students to behave in the same way. In other words, it could be "contagious."

Our response to this valid concern was that we recognized that most students who had spent any time at all with Vincent would know that he was "special" and would not be likely to emulate him. We also indicated that Vincent would continue to work with his counselor on controlling his impulses and that they could look forward to those behaviors becoming increasingly rare over time. As it turned out, our rationale for obtaining the accommodation that teachers ignore his impulsive statements was accurate, and he never caused or experienced discipline problems with his regular classroom teachers again. Truthfully, though, Vincent's "blurtings" did cause some difficulty for a young student teacher one year. As we'd experienced numerous times at this school, excellent communication between home and school provided us the opportunity to meet with this young teacher and his senior mentor (whom Vincent admired very much). Our good rapport enabled us to learn that Vincent was frustrated by the presence of this student teacher (Mr. H) because he admired the fabulous teaching skills of the mentor-teacher (Ms. CB), and he missed her and the intellectual stimulation of her presence. Through consultation, we were able to find another way for Vincent to work closely with this fabulous mentor-teacher in after-school activities, and we were able to gain Vincent's resolve that he would work even harder to control his impulses in order to support the very able but inexperienced Mr. H's already fragile sense of control in the classroom. The student teacher ended the year with confidence; he earned the admiration of his new colleagues; he became liked and respected by all his new students (Vincent included); and his career as a teacher looks bright.

High Expectations for Success

The mentor-teacher, Ms. CB, who taught history, mentioned earlier, and another mentor-teacher, Ms. TD, who taught English (Vincent's hardest subject by far), provide two examples of individuals

who believed that Vincent could be successful even when he (and we, at times) did not. While not every teacher is recognized for his or her exceptionality (Ms. TD earned State Teacher of the Year when Vincent was in tenth grade), these two teachers, along with a mathematics teacher (Mr. McG) and all the other teachers we've mentioned so far did something that his IEP could never mandate. They held out high expectations for Vincent. They expected him to put forth his very best effort for them. They encouraged him to stretch beyond his "comfort zone" and work hard to show people what he knows. These teachers never allowed him to use his ADHD or his learning disability as an excuse for not doing his best. They helped him see that he was capable of being successful and that his input was as valuable as anyone's. He was asked to submit some of his writing to a poetry contest, he entered a piece of artwork in a national competition, and he tried out for all the school plays. Vincent chaired his high school's Junior-Senior Prom committee because Ms. CB said she believed he could do a fine job. And he did.

Therapeutic Interventions

Earlier, we mentioned the importance of a "three-legged-stool" of support for individuals with ADHD. The counseling/therapeutic "leg" of the three-legged stool, in our opinion, has been another important facet in Vincent's life, but we must admit that not all of the people who have been important in supporting Vincent socially and emotionally were clinicians. We defined therapy as any experience that enabled Vincent to better understand himself and others and that resulted in improved behavior. Therefore, Vincent could experience therapy in a variety of ways, and he did.

As far as clinicians go, we worked with a couple of skilled therapists, both of whom have helped Vincent develop more insight into his behavior and feelings; and they have helped him gain more emotional balance in his life. However, one therapist, in particular (Mr. G), made such a difference for Vincent that we can't imagine what our lives would be like without his caring and sensitive support. He suggested that Vincent consider enrolling in some drama courses or workshops in order to improve his eye contact, increase his ability to pay attention to what people are saying, enhance his understanding of nonverbal social cues (like facial expressions), improve his turn-taking skills, "take direction," and enhance his ability to communicate socially. As a result, Vincent began taking drama classes in the sixth grade. The impact of that suggestion has been remarkable. While Vincent may admit that he still experiences problems with social skills in "unscripted" situations, his acting skills are noteworthy.

Beyond the important few clinicians with whom we have worked, the majority of the people who have been meaningful supports for Vincent have been teachers who mentored Vincent at different points in his school career. But they were not always teachers. As of this writing, in addition to two new drama teachers and a physics teacher in his life, he feels well supported by the mother of a friend who has become like an "aunt." She can "tell it like it is," and Vincent listens "from the heart."

We have also found that supportive people do not need to have been in Vincent's life for very long or involved in an intensive relationship with Vincent. For example, another key support person for Vincent when he was first entering high school was actually a friend of ours who is a clinical psychologist. Vincent has never "seen" this psychologist (Dr. LP) professionally, but she was introduced to him at a family party. At this party, Dr. LP showed him a couple of card games, played with "regular" cards, that contain the added value of helping improve attending, impulse control, the remembering of rules, and the social skills involved in winning and losing. Thus we have found that even brief interactions have resulted in meaningful supports for Vincent. Incidentally, the impact of that experience, not counting the hilarity, resulted in our collaboration with Dr. LP in designing and implementing a Family Game Night in the community, designed to help improve the social skills of school-age children with ADHD. This helpful community-based intervention is still ongoing, years later, and while the name of the project has changed, it all began with Vincent's therapeutic moment at an informal party.

In addition to the informal therapeutic supports already mentioned, Vincent found that volunteering in the community and (to a lesser extent) through church was therapeutic. His volunteer work provided a sense of purpose, of belonging, and of well-being that he'd not necessarily experienced in other ways. We'd tried to get him involved in volunteering through scouts, community events, and so on, but those avenues never "took." We were worried that he'd never "find his niche" in the community, but eventually Vincent found that volunteering on stage or behind the stage was engaging enough for him to "stick with." He spent two summers volunteering with our local Shakespeare in the Park and another summer volunteering at a nearby town's Community Theatre, and he also performed in occasional dramas for our church.

It is important to mention that we are not suggesting that scouts or other leadership-building or service programs are not good for youths with ADHD. We simply want to share the importance of continuing to search for the best "fit" for any one person. What is meaningful to one person may be completely uninspiring to another. Vincent learned that volunteering (or a paid job, for that matter) is not always fun, and we encouraged him not to expect "fun" all the time. Sometimes it was boring, or just plain hard work, but as with most other successful experiences in his life, he found the right combination of novelty and challenge to motivate him, and he had enough fun and gained enough of a sense of mastery and satisfaction to sustain him.

The Saga Continues

As of this writing, Vincent is completing his senior year in high school. He recently starred at his school as Macbeth in Shakespeare's play of the same name. He is smart, talented, funny (when you get to know him), "dead sexy" (as his admirers say), shy (hard to believe when you see him on stage), awkward in unplanned social situations, philosophical, moral, loyal, creative, sensitive, and (at times) his own worst critic. We know he wishes he could have done better in many ways, but we also know that he can also look back on his school years with some satisfaction. His senior class ring has become a very meaningful symbol for him, like a badge of honor, because he had to work so much harder than average to earn it.

Vincent is considering college now. He has begun auditioning for college scholarships and was very encouraged when he was offered a generous theatre scholarship on his first try. However, he is concerned, too. He has to write essays for admission to some of the colleges, even the college to which he was offered a scholarship. Will he be accepted? Will he need accommodations at college? What about the living arrangements and the new social demands?

We share those concerns as well. However, we have seen tremendous development in Vincent's ability to take responsibility for himself and his academic performance, manage his time, and participate appropriately in class. We have witnessed Vincent growing from "getting lost between the kitchen and the bathroom" in the mornings to taking on long-term projects like teaching himself to play guitar or learning complex scripts for a play. We are painfully aware that he will have to work harder than most other people his age to become a successful college student and young adult.

As a gardener might say, we hope that we have "planted seeds" of competence and justice. We hope we have nourished him with balanced amounts of support. We hope we have "pruned" and "weeded" with appropriate discipline so that Vincent will become a functional adult member of society. We hope he will understand that asking for needed help is a sign of strength, not weakness, and that he'll continue to seek out any supports he might require in the future. And we hope that Vincent will be able to show all those who have supported him throughout his school career that their efforts were fruitful.

Also, because a gardener's work is never done, we are not really done either. We failed to mention that Vincent's younger sister, Victoria, was given a diagnosis of ADHD and learning disabilities in the area of written expression when she was in the third grade . . .

> Thanks from the bottom of my heart to Diana for so generously and eloquently sharing this powerful follow-up piece on her family's story, and for the extraordinary lessons and insights she gives us. I am so grateful to Vincent and Victoria for granting their mother permission to write this following section.

Everything Ripples: The Education of Vincent and Victoria

It has been ten years since I shared my son Vincent's educational journey and all-too-briefly introduced his sister, Victoria. As their mom, I must admit that the process of reviewing the educational lessons our family has learned over the past decade feels as if I'm attempting to condense hundreds of little snapshots containing blurry or too-bright or chaotic or dark moments in our lives into just a few "Kodak moments" of wisdom to share.

Vincent and Victoria have traveled different paths toward "telling their story." Happily, as they're both adults now, each has given me permission to translate as many of their educational stories into words as I'm able. I'm grateful to Vincent and Victoria for educating us about those things in life that truly matter.

Everything Ripples

As I look back over the events of past years, I've realized how rootless, disconnected, and drifting our educational experiences would appear without the context in which those events occurred. In order to firmly yet fairly anchor Vincent's and Victoria's experiences with ADHD in our family's educational history, I will offer some of the snapshots I've taken over time. Here's one snapshot from my own early days in education, because, well, everything ripples . . .

When I was in second grade, my teacher often made me take my desk and chair out into the hallway where any and all school personnel would play a role in the following "educational script":

Principal, librarian, secretary, janitor, etc.: *Why are you sitting out here in the hallway?*

Me *(vaguely):* . . . *because I was looking out the window [or] . . . because I wasn't paying attention [or] . . . because I was reading ahead in my book . . .*

Principal, etc. *(frowning, stepping closer to loom over child, pointing finger at child): Shame on you! [or] You should be ashamed!*

In spite of such ritualized shaming/blaming and the lack of awareness of learning disabilities in that era, I was not a disengaged or poor learner. My grades were always above average with the exception of the now-archaic subject called "penmanship." I do recall that in the fourth grade I earned a D in penmanship on my report card, and at the ensuing parent-teacher conference, the teacher stated to my mother that he gave me a D so that I would "work harder" (to write neatly)! Later on, I was dubbed "Space Girl" by a group of boys in high school, and my school counselor indicated that I was not "college material."

Regarding my own learning processes/style, my intellectual self was far from neglected. Both my parents were college educated; my dad earned his degree in industrial arts education, and my mom, a homemaker who'd trained as an American history teacher, passed along her knowledge of history, civics, and culture and her love of learning in remarkably "incidental" ways. For example, everyone in my family loved music of all kinds, and I spent many brief yet meaningful periods of time—while riding in the car or folding laundry—discussing with my mom the meaning and symbolism contained in a wide variety of songs. I smile now, because my mother explained so many words, colloquial expressions, and euphemisms that I developed a real appreciation for regional dialects. I also received a matter-of-factly-delivered and culturally relevant education on such topics as sexuality education, law, parenting education, literacy, psychology, sociology, religion, history, and politics. For instance, my mom shared how character development could be found in all of the arts (including literature) via such archetypes as the hero, the healer, the suffering servant,

the traveling bard, the teacher, and even the fool (often the wisest one!). My mom and I debated such ethical questions as whether a person would be able to retain/preserve his/her own beliefs and values and continue to behave in ethical ways if the leaders in the person's culture were replaced by leadership characterized by bigotry, dehumanization, and the use of propaganda or torture to control others' behavior. We debated whether placing a baby up for adoption was a sign of strength or a sign of weakness (my mom was adopted) . . . all because we listened to and discussed the lyrics to songs we heard!

I'll "polish up" this not-so-pretty snapshot of my own early experiences in formal education with an iconic "caption" in response to my complaint regarding the fact that we were absolutely required to stop and read every single historical marker spied along the many roads we traveled. Momma glared at me and—through her firmly clenched teeth—commanded:

"YOU will have FUN whether you LIKE it or NOT!"

These days, the question posed by members of my own family is

"Are we having FUN yet?"

Yes, my mom's historical legacy ripples on . . .

Handwriting and the Generation Gap?

A couple of decades later, I learned that my problems with handwriting had acquired a diagnostic label (a name): *dysgraphia*. I often joked that I had "terminally ill handwriting," but seriously, *dysgraphia* is typically an unfamiliar term to parents, teachers, and diagnosticians in both the educational and the medical communities. The "generation gap" I'm referring to is the gap created by school personnel when I was in school, who mistakenly believed that my poor handwriting occurred because I was lazy or slovenly or just didn't care. I believe that this pervasive lack of awareness of dysgraphia is due to the term's no longer being specifically named in the fifth edition of the widely used *Diagnostic and Statistical Manual of Mental Disorders* published by the American Psychiatric Association (2013).

As the parent of two children who eventually received diagnoses of a specific learning disability in the form of disorders of written expression (in addition to their diagnoses of ADHD and related issues), I've learned a lot about disorders of written expression. Please note, though, that the diagnosis of a *disorder* does not automatically mean that the person has a *disability*. Here's an example that helped me understand the difference, and I hope it will help you, too:

> A child with *asthma* (a *disorder*) is not necessarily *disabled* by his or her *asthma*.

Having said that, though, I must add that in our own case, my children were given a diagnosis of a *disorder* of written expression, and then each child was determined to qualify for an IEP due to a specific learning *disability* in written expression. Also, it was my understanding that students with neurodevelopmental disorders like ADHD or certain medical disorders may have qualified for an IEP as "other health impaired," or they may have qualified for a civil rights–based 504 plan. I will come back to our options—and choices made—later on.

In my previous narrative, I described the surprise and dismay we felt when we discovered that we actually knew more about disorders of written expression than our school's therapy staff did about adaptive technologies and successful accommodations in the classroom—as well as at home—for students who struggle with the various subtypes of a disorder of written expression. I felt that perhaps what I'd experienced was a communication gap rather than a generation gap—that miscommunications and misunderstandings between home and school often occur due to an unspoken difference in *focus* between parents and educators. You see, parents tend to focus primarily on the education of their own *individual child or children,* while educators are typically focused on the education of *whole groups of children.*

YOU Will Have FUN Whether You LIKE It or NOT!

A snapshot of Victoria's early days in education takes place in the context of her very real family: Victoria was highly observant and appeared to be a natural-born artist; we felt she was an artist from the first time she held a piece of paper in her toddler's fists. Although most children at her stage of development would have used their mouth as their "third hand" and mouthed such flimsy objects, Victoria approached pieces of paper in the same delicate manner with which she'd observed her preschool-age brother so carefully tending our books with paper pages. That is, at least at our house, we described and demonstrated—in great detail—each tiny step involved in the careful turning of each page of a book. We had spontaneously behaved that way with Vincent, beginning with toddler board books constructed of heavy paper, such as *Pat the Bunny* (Kunhardt, 1940/2001) and over time we demonstrated and practiced the skills needed to carefully turn the pages of paper books. Truthfully, I cannot recall a single case in which either of my children damaged the paper found in books. I mention this because Victoria began treasuring paper in all forms—junk mail, stickers and stamps acquired from a number of sources (including the stickers that appeared on fruit), and so on—and by the time she was about thirty months old, she was composing multimedia montages with glee. When Victoria was about three years old, she discovered a scrap of a paper grocery sack lying on the curb; she stopped and picked it up. By the time we got home from the grocery store, she had gently folded the somewhat-triangular scrap into what distinctly appeared to be a tiny bird. It was Victoria's first 3-D sculpture, and I kept that little brown bird at the very top of our bulletin board, where it remained until we moved to another state over ten years later—at which time it became mysteriously misplaced. Perhaps I'll discover it again someday.

Victoria's art developed as she did. A number of her creations were featured in a month-long exhibit at a nearby coffee shop when she was five years old. Another of her works was selected for the permanent collection at our regional children's science and art museum, and by the end of second grade, one of her drawings was selected for the cover of a guide to private schools in our community. When she was nine years old, she indicated an interest in seeing a collection of over seventy Van Gogh paintings that had been loaned to only two museums in the United States while the Van Gogh museum in Amsterdam was being renovated. We journeyed over a thousand miles so that Victoria could see Van Gogh's works, and much to our surprise, having lived with a young artist like Victoria, we learned that she was, by far, the youngest artist attending the exhibit! Spontaneously, the large crowds of adults who'd also come to experience the exhibit created a semicircular space around Victoria so that she could clearly view each Van Gogh painting from any angle she desired. If I had not been so astounded by the care and concern shown for Victoria's experience of Van Gogh by complete strangers, I might have cried grateful tears, but to this day, fifteen years later, all I can remember from the experience of being there with Vincent and Victoria was how many artists and professors of art and art teachers and art lovers came up to us to share how inspiring it felt to witness such a young child with such incredible focus—as evidenced by her spending from fifteen minutes to nearly an hour viewing one painting and then another, and another . . . I was surprised and astounded myself—not only at Victoria's intense focus on Van Gogh's works but by her mental and emotional stamina when it came to experiencing art.

As I stated without qualification when I first introduced her, I've always felt that Victoria was simply born an artist—and I felt in awe of the creative ways in which she noticed details and colors and textures and patterns in the world around her. I often described her unique style of interacting with the world to others by suggesting, *"Maybe Victoria simply wears finer-grained glasses or different-colored lenses than the rest of us."*

In spite of the joy and wonder of Victoria's precocious love of art, I'm obliged to share a contrasting snapshot of life with Victor and Victoria that occurred at about the time that Victoria was completing first grade. Unlike most of her peers, Victoria was not yet reading.

At that time, Vincent was in third grade—he'd attended a developmental first-grade class for a year—so even though he was three full years older than his sister, he was two grades ahead of her when this particular snapshot was taken. We (parents) were becoming quietly concerned about the fact that although Victoria possessed all the developmental building blocks needed for reading, *something* appeared to be interfering with her ability to "put it all together" and master the puzzle of reading. We had had her development, vision, and hearing assessed. No particular problems were identified at that time. Victoria's behavior appeared to be well within normal limits, too.

Far too many well-intentioned helping professionals had advised us over the years, "Don't worry; these things just take time," so we parents were attempting to relax about the fact that Victoria appeared to us to be "stuck in an endless countdown"—but were also concerned that she might never get to the point where she could "launch" as a reader. In addition, we could easily tell that even Victoria—a smiley, easy-going child—was feeling frustrated by the fact that as far as she was concerned, reading was *not* the exhilarating "blast-off" experience all her friends were enjoying.

Meanwhile, we'd already learned that Vincent had ADHD, and it was clear that he truly *needed* an adult sitting with him in order to do his homework. Since we had two adults present, it made sense for us to have one-on-one homework time with each child. Thus, on the particular evening of this snapshot, I was seated at right angles from Vincent at our kitchen table. Vincent needed to complete a worksheet of math problems. My position at the table allowed me to have a clear view of him, with the added ability to use *both* hands to assist with anchoring his paper or, if needed, to bring his arms down by gently pressing down on his shoulders (because children who become overaroused often flail their arms, which in turn increases their state of arousal). Vincent was also armed with one of his favorite "menu items"—a mug of "warm tea with sugar," as he called it. However, per our family rules, he wasn't allowed to drink it all right away, because his mug of sweet tea was actually serving as what our family called "earnings." ("Earnings" was a dynamic process of earning rewards for optimal behavior; once the rewards were earned, they could never ever be taken away. See note 1 in "Notes on Section 5.1.") That evening, we had an agreement with Vincent that after he completed each row of three problems, he "earned" a gulp of his tea.

At the same time, Dad was sitting on the couch in the living room next to Victoria with the goal of reading aloud. I could hear them, but not distinctly—yet I could tell things were not going well for Victoria, partly because I could hear her dad murmuring far too often for my comfort, and in part because I could detect distress in the tone of her voice . . . Vincent was having more trouble focusing than usual, and I could tell that in addition to the likelihood that his stimulant medication was wearing off, he was also bored with the math problems. They were not challenging enough for him—as evidenced by his telling me the correct answer without even a moment's hesitation—and this became a real problem with him later on, because he could and would "see" the correct answer to complicated math problems, and he'd write the answer down while notoriously failing to "show his work"! The sequential steps he employed in his head had become so "automatic" that he found it almost impossible to break his "process" down into the sequence of steps involved. I liken it to an experienced truck driver teaching a novice truck driver by trying to break down each step in shifting gears while also attending to speed and where the truck is situated in space and the other drivers around the truck!

So Vincent and I were slogging along, with me striving to keep him on-task by "narrating" the process verbally and drawing his attention visually to the next problem by masking the other problems with a couple of strips of paper. I was feeling frustrated with his off-task behavior and I was ready to "be done" before we'd even gotten halfway through the page. Victoria suddenly came running into the kitchen with a horrified look on her face; she threw herself into my arms and cried out,

"Momma! I think I've caught A-D-D!"

I replied in my grumpiest Eeyore voice:

"You've caught A-D-D, hunh? Well, great—let's just throw a party!"

Vincent—more than ready to be finished with his homework—called out, with real enthusiasm (and the volume to match):

"Really, Mom? Can we really throw an A-D-D party?"

Their dad was standing in the kitchen doorway by now, looking worriedly at the three of us as if he was afraid to hear what any one of us would say next, and I could see in Dad's eyes the flashing of a "caution light" in my direction, but Vincent's enthusiastic response to my admittedly inappropriate (sarcastic) reaction to Victoria's perfectly logical (yet mistaken) concern re: ADD being contagious—well, logic was not part of the equation as I "charged right off the cliff" and proclaimed to all present:

"Yeah! Let's throw us a big ADD party! We can invite all of our relatives with ADD and our friends with ADD and our teachers with ADD and their families, too!"

Vincent, as if unable to believe his ears, asked me again:

*"**Do you** mean it, Mom?"*

*"**Do you** really **mean it**?"*

"Do you mean I can be who I really am—and nobody will yell at me?"

Are We Having FUN Yet?

It may be difficult to recall that I was actually sharing a snapshot of the educational development of Victoria when one of the most profoundly poignant perceptions of her brother Vincent's young life "emerged from the background" of the image. But frankly, that evening provides a fairly representative picture of the educational environment in which Victoria lived! We are all "works in progress," and in Victoria's case, it was not hard to explain to her that, to my knowledge, ADHD wasn't a "disease," so it was not something she could catch the way she might catch chicken pox or a cold. However, I explained to her, it could be that ADHD was a set of symptoms or characteristics passed down in families the same way that family characteristics like eye color or hair texture could be passed along. We were able to view photos of her grandfather and her brother, who looked remarkably similar, and it appeared to help reassure Victoria that no—she had not "caught" ADHD—but we also let her know that we were taking her concern very seriously and that we would seek help in finding out whether she had ADHD as her brother did.

As it happened, we decided to wait a bit longer (to seek diagnostic testing) in order to monitor her learning process after she entered second grade. We felt quite fortunate when we got to know her second-grade teacher. Ms. P was a masterful teacher who not only understood the concept of individual differences and learning styles but also capably managed the behavioral dynamics of communicating unconditional regard for each student while holding out reasonably high expectations for their behavior and their development in groups. Ms. P's willingness to model and then rehearse with her students the details of behaviors needed for successfully accomplishing the creatively designed variety of tasks she presented (so invitingly) in her classroom made hers one of the most nurturing yet inspiring classrooms I'd ever seen. I must add that a significant influence on my perception of Ms. P's second-grade teaching mastery was the happiness, the excitement, and the sense of accomplishment Victoria exuded throughout that school year. The fact that she was still not reading, even toward the end of second grade, did not appear to bother Victoria as much as it had the previous spring.

However, we parents were growing more concerned regarding the increasing discrepancy between Victoria's excellent development in other aspects of her education and her reading level. The following spring, as she was completing second grade, I arranged for Victoria to participate in developmental and psychoeducational assessments with a couple of skilled professionals, and she was

diagnosed with ADHD. Oddly (to us), while she possessed some of the symptoms of a reading disorder, she was not diagnosed with any known forms of dyslexia . . . but she *was* diagnosed with a disorder of written expression (a big surprise to us), and she also struggled with relatively slow processing speed both physically and mentally. She also exhibited word-finding problems; that is, it took Victoria significantly more time to retrieve and then express words to describe objects or concepts, even though her vocabulary, memory, and nonverbal skills were well above average for her age and grade in school. The accommodation recommended regarding her word-finding problems was to give Victoria extra time to respond to verbal questions, but we found that it was a surprisingly difficult accommodation for some of her subsequent teachers to implement. It appeared to me that those teachers felt that giving Victoria two to three seconds to respond to questions was "too much time"—as if they feared that by allowing her those seconds, their other students would begin "acting out" during the "dead time"! Naturally, Victoria never perceived those seconds as "dead time," and, thankfully, teacher resistance to accommodating Victoria for her word-finding problems became less of a problem when Victoria entered middle and high school.

Back to the issue of the specific learning disability: disorder of written expression, Victoria's handwriting was observed to be remarkably legible, especially compared to the "doctor handwriting" of her mother and brother, and even to her dad's "printed-in-all-capital-letters" that he'd learned in architecture school and uses constantly as an architectural engineer. So it's safe to say that poor Victoria and her brother, Vincent, both got a "double dose" of handwriting problems! In spite of my speculation about the heritability of Victoria's and Vincent's learning disabilities, I want to mention that although her handwriting was considered legible, Victoria produced all written work at the speed of the proverbial turtle, especially when required to copy words from a workbook (near-point copying) or off the board (far-point copying), and she also demonstrated significant problems with written grammar, punctuation, and spelling—all of which are symptoms found in disorders of written expression.

It was determined that she certainly would (and did) benefit from the accommodation of extra time on tests as well as limiting the amount of material she needed to write in the time periods allotted during the school day. I want to add, also, that one of the most frustrating hallmarks of dysgraphia is that "penmanship" practice alone fails to result in any significant increase in an individual's handwriting legibility. In other words, in the case of dysgraphia, *Practice does **not** make perfect!*

Victoria was also prescribed stimulant medication, and whether she was suffering from "microattentional shifts" or some other neurobiological form of "interference," her problems with reading were solved rapidly. Only two months after Victoria was prescribed stimulant medication, her reading proficiency was assessed at the fourth-grade level—that is, two grade levels above her actual grade in school. To this day, though, she still struggles with a very slow reading speed and other subtle decoding/processing problems.

From second grade on, Victoria's academic development appeared to progress steadily, but she failed a screening test for basic physical education in the fourth grade. Further testing of her balance, coordination, and strength revealed a highly significant 50 percent delay in Victoria's gross motor skills (*motor* defined as the brain "driving" or "directing" the bones and muscles). *Gross motor* generally refers to the coordination of the large muscles and bones, balance, and moving one's body through space (as opposed to *fine motor*, which involves the coordination of tiny muscles in the eyes, hands, mouth, and elsewhere in the body).

Her 50 percent delay in gross motor skills roughly translated to: "She's nine years old, but her balance, coordination, and movement skills are—functionally—only at the level expected for a four-and-a-half-year-old!" This was particularly striking/alarming because she'd apparently been performing "within normal limits" up until that time, and no one—not me as her mom, nor her teachers, nor any coaches she'd worked with (she was playing softball at the time)—had seen it coming! It was as if Victoria had subtly and mysteriously "quit developing" in the gross motor area of her life! However, there appeared to be no

medical reasons to explain it, nor were there any environmental factors that could account for it, either . . . In addition, as I'll explain soon, the fact that Victoria was experiencing such a significant delay seemed completely at odds with the typical developmental path expected for children in our culture!

Victoria was determined to be eligible for an IEP, and she received accommodations for her ADHD and learning disabilities, as well as physical therapy to treat her motor delays and occupational therapy for her problems with written expression.

Readiness Is Everything, Except . . .

I will continue Victoria's educational story later, but it is here that I must explain in some detail my objection to the way in which a seemingly benign belief is perpetuated in our culture, and my recommendations will follow. I referred to it with regard to Victoria's reading, but I must clearly state the belief and the problem it poses for any and all persons who care for children and their families:

> *Children will grow and develop at their own rate.*

In spite of well-meaning professionals repeatedly telling us things like "give it time" and "she/he is just a late bloomer" and so on, there are times when such words are not only unhelpful—they may even be overtly harmful!

Generally, a *theory* is a statement describing or explaining the way certain things in this world appear to work or function. Theories are accepted or rejected over time, based on how reliably or effectively they continue to serve as an "explanation." Thus it is important to test careful observations against a "working theory" (a theory being used in real life) to be sure it's really the best explanation for how things work. Theories often need to be "polished," and in some cases, it's best to simply dismiss one theory in favor of a better one. For example, I once asked my mom what she'd been told about me before ADHD was recognized as a neurodevelopmental disorder, and she did not hesitate to tell me that she'd been informed that I was "morally defective." I appreciated her sharing that theoretical perspective because I understood that the "moral defect" theory spread from the late 1800s through the 1960s in the United States (Lange et al., 2010), and may still be believed in some settings.

A *human developmental theory* is one that helps explain why certain significant changes occur over time in our lives (Horowitz, 1987/2014). Please keep in mind that the developmental theory that children will grow and develop at their own rate is *not* a statement of *fact!*

Further, when persons behave as if developmental theory is completely factual, then what was once a fine *working theory* of child development becomes no better than a *myth!* Frankly, it's what I call a *logic error* (a faulty conclusion), and persons transmitting such logic errors may, in turn, cause meaningful harm.

I must add a quirky "disclaimer" here: if my children and I did not have ADHD and related disorders, I might never have noticed the *logic error* contained in such statements as "Don't worry" and "Just give her time"! If it weren't for people like Sandra Rief and her colleagues who've worked diligently for decades striving to understand and assist and "reach and teach" those of us with ADHD, we may never have become able to show people what we know or celebrate our strengths! I feel honored that I'm able to identify the problem in the context of my children and this book—the book that's helped us since about 1994—so that when parents and educators become aware of this too-subtle barrier to ensuring that children get the most appropriate support needed (appropriate in terms of timing, quantity, and quality of support), the barrier may be overcome.

The developmental theory that children will grow and mature/develop at their own pace fails to hold up well when (1) the child's health or functioning is atypical or, for a variety of reasons, (2) their environment's health/functioning/support is impaired/absent. My recommendation is that persons in the educational community, the medical community, and the helping professions *extinguish* potentially harmful statements like the ones mentioned earlier, and focus instead on gathering evidence that actually helps answer this important question:

How much help does this child need—not only to survive but to thrive—as a developing life-long learner?

As much as I've just criticized people who behave as if developmental theory is not a theory but a fact, I do want to celebrate the strengths of developmental theory and the ways in which the theory has led to improvements in teacher education, developmentally appropriate teaching practices, and more inclusive methods for assessing student learning. I'm thankful for the remarkable improvements in the quality of education my children have experienced, yet I'm reminded that both of my children also needed a moderate amount of specialized help in support of their learning and development. Victoria even needed specialized support for her gross motor development—a facet of human development that's widely considered to be "hardwired" and in need of little more than gravity and room to explore in order to "spring forth." I am so keenly reminded of the special developmental needs and challenges faced by my own children and by so very many others that I must ask: *Can we really afford the luxury of just waiting around to see if our children will ever "bloom"?*

Goodness of Fit and Dead Meat

In addition to the questions I posed earlier, I often ask, "What is the *goodness of fit* between *this* environment and *this* child's behavior and development?" We can assess this for children and their environments just as we assess the goodness of fit between our own feet and possible new shoes. I was first introduced to the concept via the research of Stella Chess and Alexander Thomas (1999/2014), a husband-and-wife team of child psychiatrists at New York University. I admired their work in part because they introduced the useful concept of *temperament,* which may help us understand individual differences in personality and see that the interaction between an individual and his or her environment can be assessed in terms of how well a person is supported by a particular environment (*goodness of fit*). I'll share a snapshot of me and my son here: Vincent had developed "short-timer's attitude" regarding living at home while anxiously and excitedly anticipating living in a dorm at college. I felt his frustration at having to comply with our family rules and his excitement at the idea of living (more or less) on his own—and believe me, I was just about as ready for him to move out as he was! Vincent was complaining about something I cannot even recall, but I'd just shouted at him:

"YOU are just LUCKY you live in OUR house! You know WHY? Because you'd be DEAD MEAT if you lived in anyone else's house!"

Apparently there was some merit to my heated (and loud) argument, because it "broke right through" whatever he'd been complaining about. He looked at me in complete surprise, and as soon as he processed the words I'd said, he busted out laughing the biggest belly-laugh—and holding up one finger as he gasped for breath, he laughed, "You got me there, Mom!" and then made his escape just as fast as he could! And there you have an example of the real-life application of the goodness-of-fit model in the home of a family with ADHD. Which brings me back to Victoria and the goodness of fit between her and her environments as she developed.

When Victoria entered the sixth grade, she was able to attend the same magnet school as her older brother, and her IEP was easily transferred to her new school setting. However, when Victoria experienced the reality of changing classes and teachers a number of times each day and she began to try to manage the demands of a changing schedule (from "A-Day" to "B-Day"), she began to express regret at being pulled out of class sessions in order to work with her physical and occupational therapists. Thankfully, she had already developed good rapport with the majority of her teachers, and she demonstrated great study habits and worked diligently toward mastery, so her concerns were not, in my opinion, rooted in reality so much as they were rooted in her empathy for her teachers!

The spring before Victoria entered high school, her dad was laid off when the company he worked for closed down the facility in our state and sent all those jobs to another country. After months of job-hunting, he secured a new job—but it was located three states away. We held a family meeting and decided that we would move as soon as possible so that Vincent and Victoria could meet their fellow students before the summer recess—and (we hoped) ease the transition to Vincent's senior year and Victoria's first year in high school.

In retrospect, I'm not certain that our plan assisted Vincent as much as it helped Victoria adjust to a new school in a new city and state. She made friends easily, and became involved in the art honor society as soon as she became eligible. The only significant crisis we faced was that we were informed almost immediately that their new school would not honor the terms of Vincent's and Victoria's IEPs from our old state. Given that IEPs are actually federally recognized legal documents, I was completely caught off guard by such an absolute refusal to serve my children, and I appealed that decision immediately. We were informed, again, that under no circumstances would our new school district approve/allow an IEP for either of my children, even if we applied for a new one, because our children "were not failing." I was astounded by the gatekeeping demonstrated by the special education representative (a school psychologist, in our case), as evidenced by such statements as "So sue us!"

I investigated in order to confirm our family's rights in our new state, and to summarize: I learned that we certainly had the right to apply for new IEPs, but the local education authority (our new school district) could block them from being approved until my children were failing a grade or two! In other words, because our new school district had not witnessed, firsthand, the significant discrepancy between our students' potential and their achievement—which our old school district had documented quite thoroughly—our new school district could and would and did refuse to serve my children.

I found it impossible to imagine either of my children being able to "show teachers what he/she knows" without the accommodations and therapies they'd received in the past. I began reviewing the research and legal literature to determine whether there were any cases in which the "significant discrepancy between performance and potential" had been successfully challenged. Much to my surprise, I found that one of the landmark court cases that had resulted in a complete reversal of a local education authority's denial to serve a student had actually occurred in the very state to which we had just moved! The only factor that differed between my children's situation and the landmark case was that the court case involved a request for a 504 plan rather than an IEP. It was my understanding that a 504 plan is essentially a civil rights plan, whereas an IEP is a special education plan, and there were some other meaningful differences between them. (Please see note 4 in "Notes on Section 5.1.") I reasoned that, being seriously determined to advocate that my children receive the kind of educational support and accommodations for which they'd already demonstrated a need, I would need to give up the idea of seeking IEPs and instead seek 504 plans for my children. One of the primary compromises we made in doing so was that our children would no longer be able to receive physical or occupational therapy because those were considered "exceptional children's services" and could not be obtained via a 504 plan. I spoke with Victoria about it, and she reminded me that she had disliked missing class (for therapy), so she took the loss of allied health services in stride. Vincent was not receiving any special services beyond a "consult plan" in which his learning disabilities/resource teacher consulted periodically with his classroom teachers to monitor that his accommodations—such as extra time on tests and the ability to leave class to go to the restroom, if needed, as well as his behavioral Safety Net—were continuing to meet his special needs.

However, it was clear to me, even then, that I was simply going to have to grieve the loss of services in the same way that so many parents of children with special needs grieve so many, many losses over time. (Please see note 5 in "Notes on Section 5.1.")

We proposed a 504 plan in which each of the accommodations they'd previously received (via their IEPs at their old school) would again be honored. Although I witnessed a few more barriers willfully placed in our way, the 504 plan and all accommodations requested were indeed approved. In addition to the significant barriers I've already mentioned, I witnessed a few "yes, but" statements from teachers who'd not been appropriately informed of our children's 504 plans, but once we communicated with each of the teachers and reassured them that *we were actually there to help them help all their students learn,* we found that we and almost every teacher at my children's new high school became great partners.

College and Professional Development

After winning the starring role in their new school's production of Shakespeare's *Macbeth* his senior year and auditioning at regional colleges, Vincent was offered theater scholarships at each of the colleges to which he'd applied. At a couple of the colleges, he was invited back to compete for additional scholarship funding (called merit scholarships, which were scholarships based upon a combination of factors, including interviews, grades, community service, and teacher recommendations). For a student who infrequently smiled and relied on "scripts" to negotiate the complex world of social skills, the interviews posed huge challenges, so Vincent rehearsed a wide variety of possible responses to every question we could imagine him being asked. It was a completely nerve-wracking time—and not just for Vincent, mind you! To our incredible relief, he was offered a full-tuition scholarship for four years to attend a small private college about ninety miles away.

One of the remarkable things that accompanied his outstanding scholarship was the fact that the college's student assistance coordinator explained how easy it would be to "roll his 504 plan over" from his old high school to their college.

While there were aspects of college life that were difficult for him to negotiate, Vincent graduated on time with his BS in theater and a minor in dance. "Why dance?" I asked, and while looking sideways at me with his glittering eyes almost closed by his cheeks rising up with his quirky half-smile, Vincent slowly replied, "Well, it's a good way to meet the ladies . . ." I laughed and thought "What a great fit for him—he doesn't need to converse much while dancing!"

Vincent is an instructor in lighting and sound design and entertainment law at the one-and-only community college in our state that offers an associate degree in entertainment technologies. Vincent's strengths as an instructor include a remarkable ability to design and implement lesson plans and student assessment procedures that accommodate a wide variety of student learning styles or special needs. His social skills may still be a bit "rough around the edges" in "unscripted" social situations, but over the past few years, he's developed engaging hands-on activities and projects as well as a reputation of being firm but fair with his students. I will come back to Vincent's teaching style later.

Victoria, three years younger, became an innovative and motivating leader via the National Art Honor Society chapter at her high school, and with hundreds (if not thousands) of extra hours spent studying and completing assignments, Victoria graduated near the top of her class. It had been Victoria's dream—since about the eighth grade—to attend an art conservatory (a specialized type of art college). However, she also honored our request that she apply to some regional liberal arts colleges, because her dad, an engineer, had been laid off again. It was no secret at our house that the amount of scholarships she might be offered would become a crucial factor in selecting where she would attend college. Anxiety reigned.

As it happened, Victoria was accepted to every college and art conservatory to which she'd applied, and the art conservatories did offer what appeared to be great scholarships, on the surface. However, when we compared the scholarship amounts offered to the full cost of attending college, the art conservatories were simply too expensive for our family to afford. Victoria agonized over the college choices she had left, and she delayed making her decision until the very last hour of the last day before the deadline "to declare" which college she'd attend. Her best buddy from high school came over to the house that night, and he sat right next to Victoria on the couch as she sighed and moaned and leaned on him as if her bones were no longer strong enough to hold up her head. Finally, she burst into tears and sobbed:

"I'm just going to have to tell all my teachers and my friends that I wanted to go to art school, but we couldn't afford it—so I had to go to Duke instead!"

Her dad and I were caught so thoroughly by surprise at her words that we could not help but giggle for just a heartbeat—before hanging our heads in shamed silence. There was Victoria, in the throes of despair, sobbing—and her parents just did *what?*

In our own defense, I must claim that her tragic statement struck us as utterly hilarious because Duke University, a private university in North Carolina, accepts only about ten of every hundred student applicants each year—yet our heartbroken Victoria *had to go to Duke instead!?* Alas, it was official: we would never achieve my dream of winning the Hallmark Hall of Fame Parenting Award. Never mind that such an award never even existed—but I could dream, couldn't I? Commence grieving the loss of a dream. Whose dream, you ask? I'm not saying another word.

Well, Victoria lived, in spite of her intense disappointment at being unable to go to a conservatory to study art. She earned her bachelor's degree from Duke in visual studies with a minor in documentary studies and another minor in film.

Immediately following Victoria's graduation, Duke hired Victoria to work full-time with the Wired! Group: Digital Art History and Visual Culture. (According to the group's website, http://www.dukewired.org/about/, "Our practices in digital art history, visual culture, digital humanities, and humanities scholarship transform both teaching and research, as well as providing new methods for communicating knowledge to a broad public.") Victoria worked with the Wired! Group at Duke for three years and then, after she'd been at Duke for a total of seven years, she applied to universities that offered a master of fine arts (MFA) in art and technology. Victoria is currently attending graduate school and working as a graduate teaching assistant at a large public university with a nationally recognized art program. It appears that both my children—ADHD and LDs and all—are not only artists and lifelong learners but also active contributors to the art-and-technology education of others! Who'd have guessed?

Learning Strategies Ripple, Too . . .

I've found it particularly exciting to explore with each of my children the subject of those learning strategies they've found most helpful and useful over time. Vincent and Victoria, who both have strong skills in concept formation and are creative as well—building mental bridges between diverse concepts and disciplines with ease—have each indicated that the learning strategies that continued to help them as they navigated college and began developing their own professional lives have tended to be clustered around knowledge organization and knowledge presentation strategies.

Homework Survival Kits, Grown Up

I must acknowledge with a grateful grin of appreciation a seed that Sandra Rief planted in my mind-garden so many years ago: a seed called the homework kit. We used that strategy with great success, and one of the many benefits of this practical approach was that Victor's and Victoria's homework kits got translated into college-style homework kits. That is, Vincent carried his version of the homework kit in a designated pouch in his backpack when he went to college, and now that he's a college instructor, his homework kit is contained in a special pocket in his briefcase. His kit has expanded to include a couple of special templates for symbolizing various types of lighting fixtures on stage design drawings and a pair of work gloves and a couple of tools used in live sound engineering and lighting design, but all the homework basics are still there. Victoria's kit expanded back in high school to include a couple of art journals/sketchbooks, and key art supplies and small tools, and she experimented with putting everything in a fishing-tackle box that she carried around almost everywhere she went, but it was deemed too bulky after a while. Victoria relocated her kit into a black satchel/briefcase which

had a long and very sturdy strap so that her black bag could (and did) travel with her everywhere she went, because she was either creating art or writing about art almost continuously. She even had friends who tenderly teased her as "the bag lady," as she was practically inseparable from that bag—after all, it contained her most valuable possessions! I can even recall seeing her using it as a pillow when she'd nap on the floor in whichever location she was studying.

Learning Styles and Developing Insight

Vincent and Victoria both learned that college required many more term papers and long-term projects than high school, so the new skills they needed to master had to do with proposal development and project management. They also needed the problem-solving ability to break overwhelmingly large portions of those projects down into more manageable tasks. Further, they both needed to be able to recognize and avoid those approaches that worked beautifully for their peers, but that can become frustrating time-wasters for people with ADHD.

An example of a great idea that can become frustrating for students with ADHD is the creation of lists and outlines. Lists and outlines can be a wonderful learning and organizational tool for people who tend to think in a systematic and logical manner. They are undoubtedly helpful for students with ADHD when the lists or outlines have already been created and are essentially complete—that is, no steps are missing and everything is in the correct order or sequence—or when the lists and outlines can be created by simply following along with the content of a single document or book. However, for students with ADHD who must summarize knowledge from a variety of sources in a timely manner, the creation of lists and outlines may require the insertion of forgotten or out-of-sequence steps and tasks and so many revisions and corrections that the student may become confused and overwhelmed. I had learned an effective strategy for project management and shared it with my children. Victoria, in particular, found it a wonderful supplement to the use of lists and outlines. We both just refer to it as "the sticky-note method." Victoria has employed it for research and term projects, grant proposal development, project management, team-building, lesson planning, and for each of her many art installations (large-scale art projects that may take months of preparation and may require whole teams of people to install).

The sticky-note method does require some funding in order to purchase quantities of sticky notes and a poster board or wall space on which to arrange them. Ideally, you write only one concept/fact/step per sticky note. Then you stick that sticky note on a large surface in any position you'd like. You keep jotting down single thoughts regarding the subject and sticking them onto your desired surface until you feel you have run out of thoughts on the matter. Then you can arrange and rearrange your sticky notes in highly flexible ways: you can cluster all the related sticky notes; you can arrange them in the sequence in which events should occur; you can use them in lesson planning by grouping the sticky notes by topic and then arranging them in a sequential order. If you later learn that you've forgotten to include a step or another piece of information, it's a breeze to create another sticky note and rearrange your collection to include the missing piece of your "puzzle." If it happens that you realize you've listed a step or concept that really needs to be broken down into smaller parts, all you need to do to "fix it" is to jot down the smaller parts on a couple of sticky notes and then move a few notes around to make room for the new one—it's that easy! Victoria added that she still makes lists, and in her case, they are often "microanalytic" (very tiny tasks) and "survival oriented." For example, her lists may include tasks like (1) Drink 2 cups of water. (2) Set up lights and cameras. (3) Calibrate lights in studio. (4) Go pee. (5) Start cameras filming/shooting periodic stills. (6) Step into camera range. (7) Blow orbs of glass. (8) Place glass in cooling space. (9) Place blowpipe in default setting. (10) Stop cameras. (11) Drink 2 cups of water. (12) Do yoga.

Stress and Coping Strategies

Speaking of stress and anxiety experienced when a student must work longer and/or a lot harder than her peers in order to show people what she really knows, Victoria offered a couple of coping strategies that she has found useful:

1. When faced with a large number of tasks she must accomplish, rather than causing herself to feel overwhelmed and discouraged by making an extensive list, or feeling panicky by looking at her whole project-management sticky-note array, she covers those items up and simply limits her to-do sticky note or list to *only* the next step in her process. Victoria reported that this approach motivates her to act because it's doable, and she gets to celebrate the fact that she did take that next step—and she is that much closer to achieving her *next* next step!

2. In the course of Victoria's education and work, she is often required to give timed talks and presentations. Time management and the accurate awareness of time passing can pose real problems for students (and teachers) with ADHD and related disorders. Victoria followed the recommendation of a college mentor and began filming herself giving talks so that she could better assess the amount of content that could be delivered in the time allotted to her. She reported that she tended to prepare too much material for the given time frame, so she's had to learn to determine the most critical pieces of information she wants to communicate. Her biggest challenge came in making tough decisions as to what parts weren't quite as important—and could and should be cut.

3. Regarding her coping strategy for having to "hone" or "prune" information she often feels is equally important, Victoria has developed a little script to repeat to herself as often as needed—and she reports that it's been effective when used with her students, as well. Victoria's script goes something like this:

"You are here to connect with others. This is not the last _____ you will ever do, so you don't have to put in every idea."

4. Victoria is still seeking a coping strategy for one chronic problem: "The pressure of being ADHD and being in academia is mostly the strain of constantly wanting to make complete theories of the universe—and not knowing where to start."

Vincent's Notebooks, Accordion Files, and Color

Vincent's preferred style of learning is "full immersion" and "whole brain," with a slight edge toward auditory learning. When he was younger, while listening to his teachers, he would fiddle with the tiniest objects or explore the texture of something while looking down (generally at the object or texture). Some teachers felt that he could not possibly be paying attention if he was not looking at them, but when challenged to repeat back to the teacher what he or she had just said, Vincent was quite accurate in reporting what he'd heard. He also tended to offer feedback that indicated his comprehension of their words, as well. However, he found it frustrating to have to learn bits and pieces of information without a context in which he could manipulate ideas and conduct his own experiments to test out his predictions regarding outcomes (*hypotheses*, he later learned). He longed for education settings that would allow him to immerse himself in a subject until he'd attained mastery, and then move on to another subject.

Vincent found that the drama program he'd enrolled in (primarily to assist him in developing helpful "social scripts") offered the closest thing to "full immersion" learning that he'd ever experienced. In addition, theater training offered a range of learning opportunities and skill development that allowed for him to strive for mastery on a number of levels while simultaneously offering immense content depth, which allowed him to make continuously exciting discoveries. If my late dad, who'd earned his college degree in industrial arts, had been around to see the goodness of fit between Vincent and his immersion-learning style, he'd have instantly asked me something along the lines of "Why didn't you send that young man to Vo-Tech?"

But "readiness is everything," as the saying goes—and I'm not sure, in retrospect, that there would have been anything offered at our local vocational-technical program that was quite as interesting and success oriented for Vincent as theater training was. However, I'm mentioning the Vo-Tech interests of my late dad because in perhaps prophetic ways, the immersion/mastery/skill-based learning model of the technical community colleges in our state came into sharper focus a decade or so later.

As I'd mentioned earlier, Vincent had earned his high school diploma at a magnet school for the arts, and he earned a full-tuition scholarship to study theater in college. The learning and organizational strategies that worked well for him in college have formed a rather cohesive "team" I can only call "Notebooks, Accordion Files, and Color."

For each class taken (or taught, nowadays), Vincent's shopping list typically includes the following:

- A D-ring binder notebook
- A plastic accordion file of the same hue as the notebook (please note: this type of file has been added since Vincent began teaching at a technical community college)
- A large quantity of transparent three-ring sheet protectors
- Enough file dividers with pockets to allow for separation of each chapter in the textbook for the class; these go into the notebook

Vincent learned in college that he relies heavily on color when organizing his notes for writing papers. He cannot manage a lot of loose papers and file folders, nor does he feel comfortable with filing needed materials away where he can't view them. Thus the creation of his notebook approach. He does well with making outlines in order to organize the material with which he's working—so long as he can do as much of his work as possible on a laptop computer or the equivalent. He uses the same basic strategy for organizing his music compositions and his written lyrics and when creating arrangements for different instruments, as well as for his instructional stage or lighting designs. His accordion files are the same color as the relevant class's notebook, and they are used to store a number of different files needed for his classes, such as copies of his course syllabus, the course grading rubric, quizzes, tests, project instructions, and so on. The notebook for each class he teaches is essentially his way of "filing" older documents; he places them in sheet protectors and adds pocket dividers to contain extra copies of materials if needed.

Vincent's lesson plans are set up in the form of a very long and detailed outline on a computer. Class announcements and reminders are inserted into the lesson plans in such a way that they will appear at the top of the relevant page of lecture notes at the next class session. He tends to print out more of the relevant pages than he feels he'll need, but he finds that the process of amending the lesson plans when needed and then printing out more pages of lessons than he would expect to "get through" in a class period or two is helpful. That is, if his class demonstrates mastery sooner than usual, he's able to forge ahead with new material. In addition, I want to mention that Vincent's lesson plans are filled with stories to illustrate concepts, and he plans (in great detail) a range of class activities and assignments that will allow students to "shine" via their own learning styles/preferred modalities. He offers his students numerous opportunities for immersion learning in the lab (a small "black-box theater" with staging and lighting fixtures that can be arranged quite flexibly), while thoughtfully facilitating activities that support team development as well. Basically, Vincent has developed into an educator—an educator of students who themselves may not have experienced much success in previous school settings—and he's providing for them the kind of immersive learning environment he'd love to have experienced himself. I suspect that Vincent's Vo-Tech-supporting grandfather would grin proudly to himself while silently reading the daily news.

Notes on Section 5.1

Note 1: "Earnings" were implemented only for brief "bursts" of time—usually no more than three weeks—and employed only when a rather new undesired behavior had emerged. The reason for using it only in the case of newly emerged inappropriate behaviors was that the reward system was most effective when used to reinforce (increase the likelihood of) the child's exhibiting desired/appropriate behaviors while simultaneously minimizing/"extinguishing" those recently appearing undesired/inappropriate behaviors. What we were aiming for was essentially a simple "replacement system" of positive behaviors instead of negative behaviors. In other words, we did not waste time on punishing misbehavior—we chose instead to focus on providing tangible and almost immediate external support for those behaviors and skills that we felt Vincent needed to become a successful learner. Please keep in mind that each of the tangible reward options that made up the "Earnings Menu" for Vincent and/or Victoria were selected by the child and approved by the parents. We did that (and updated the menu frequently) because the process of selecting rewards that are (1) motivating/rewarding enough for a child to consciously work toward is a highly-individualized process, and (2) "developmental"—in other words, what appears to be motivating/rewarding to a child at one point in time may not be at all rewarding to him or her just a couple of weeks later.

Note 2: A sample of some recent resources regarding assistive technology for writing (as of October 2015) can be seen at http://www.gatfl .gatech.edu/tflwiki/images/c/c5/2015_EASI_Webi nar_-_AT_for_Writing.pdf.

Note 3: I recognize that my outlook on the development of appropriate teams and teamwork regarding the promotion of positive outcomes for students may be substantially more "inclusive" than others may expect. I mention this because I viewed *all* persons who interacted with my children before, during, and after school as important and valuable members of the education team. I paid close attention to the fact that there were key persons involved in my children's life at school who were all-too-frequently overlooked as team members of importance—I mean bus drivers, janitors, librarians, secretaries, cafeteria staff, security officers, and so on . . . The importance of respectfully acknowledging the relevance of those individuals' roles when building a strong home-school partnership becomes clear when you consider that children with ADHD and related biobehavioral disorders are more likely to "run into trouble"

- During transitions from one type of activity to another
- When moving from one location to another
- During less structured activities at school, such as playing on the playground, riding a school bus, and eating in the cafeteria

Sandra Rief provides a great deal of assistance regarding the need for teachers to carefully define and articulate behavioral expectations for all students during transition times, but there are a number of valid occasions each day when teachers are not in responsible charge of their students. It is not uncommon, though, for school support staff and/or school volunteers to be the adults present in the area during those times. When such individuals are respectfully included as team members and are given

- Appropriate training on the subject of maintaining student confidentiality
- Information regarding the kinds of behaviors that tend to lead to "trouble" in those settings
- The most appropriate "scripts" to use when interacting with all children, but particularly the scripts to use with the target child(ren)
- An outline of the appropriate lines of communication they should use

. . . then their assistance may be invaluable!

Note 4: It is my understanding that a 504 plan refers to a section 504 of the Rehabilitation Act of 1973, a civil rights code which states that students with special needs have a civil right to receive an education equivalent to those of students without disabilities. For more information, see http://www2.ed.gov/about/offices/list/ocr/504faq.html.

Note 5: It has been my experience that parents of children with special needs (regardless of the type or the cause of those special needs) may experience feelings that may be more subtle and difficult to describe or name than the feelings our culture typically associates with "grief and/or loss." In addition, assuming that we can even recognize those peculiar feelings as being those of "grief and loss," the grief experienced by parents of children with special needs appears to occur whenever the parent(s) are faced with the reality that their child has failed to attain developmental and/or behavioral milestones achieved by most other children. Developmental or behavioral milestone failures that may trigger grief experiences for parents/guardians of children with special needs include such tasks as sleeping through the night, smiling, speaking, feeding oneself with a spoon or fork, walking, graduating from diapers to underpants upon mastering "toilet learning," dressing oneself, being invited to another child's party, writing, reading—and so very many other tasks, it's impossible to list them all . . . Therefore—for parents/guardians of children with special needs—feelings of grief and loss occur on such a regular basis that they might be considered chronic. However, *chronic* cannot serve as an accurate descriptor because each time another developmental or behavioral milestone is missed, the pangs of loss are suffered as if they were new.

Student Case Studies and Interventions

Chloe (Seven Years Old, First Grade)

> This student profile and intervention plan was written by T. Cohen, a first-grade teacher, and used with her permission. The student's name and identifying information have been changed. My thanks and appreciation to Ms. Cohen for sharing this with me.

Student Profile

Chloe is a very creative student. She enjoys art, engaging in dramatic play, and is a popular friend in our classroom. Chloe loves books in spite of her trouble with decoding and comprehension. She is an amazing older sister to her toddler at home and shares stories about her every day. Chloe is funny and fun-loving and adds spice to our class. She is a bright girl who has wonderful ideas to share when she is focused on classroom conversations. Recently she was diagnosed with ADHD (inattentive type). Her ADHD symptoms are clearly getting in the way of her learning.

Chloe is struggling in a number of areas and has been falling further behind rather than gaining skills as the year progresses. She has great difficulty paying attention and staying on-task. Even when she has an action plan, she is unable to get her work done in the time allotted and loses focus very easily. I have been in close contact with Chloe's parents since the beginning of the school year and they shared the same concerns. We have been working together to reduce some of the struggle with homework, and getting her more help and support at school. Chloe has been referred for a Student Study Team (SST) meeting, which has been scheduled for later this month. In the meantime, we have been working with her in a number of areas to provide support so she can continue to grow, and will determine next steps of intervention when we meet as a team with parents in a couple weeks.

Current Performance Levels

Reading Level

Using the Teacher's College assessment, Chloe recently read a level F book as an assessment. (Level G is the school district benchmark.) Chloe read the story at a rate of 21 words per minute with 8 errors, which means that the book was too difficult to be at her independent reading level. For reading on her own, level D would be more appropriate. Chloe's phrasing was word-by-word at first, but as she warmed up, she was able to read longer phrases. When I helped her with a new word, she was able to recall that word on subsequent pages. Chloe worked hard to decode unknown words using picture clues as well as context and sounds.

Chloe's knowledge of phonics and recognition of letter-sound combinations is below grade level expectations for this time of the year. She knows most short vowel sounds, digraphs (th, sh, ch, wh), and blends (such as tr, nk, fl). Chloe has difficulty recognizing and decoding words with long vowel sounds (final-e, vowel pairs such as ea, oa, ay), r-controlled (ar, or, er/ir/ur) and other vowel patterns.

Reading comprehension skills are also below grade level. She particularly has difficulty remembering the details and sequence of events in a story.

Writing

Chloe is able to complete a sentence on her own. She rarely completes three to four sentences, which is the benchmark for this time of year for our first graders. Her handwriting is legible but inconsistent. She does not form her letters correctly and makes several letter reversals. She will write her one sentence in the middle of the page, completely ignoring the lines and the edges of the paper. She uses too much space between words and is very inconsistent with capitalization and punctuation.

Work Completion

Chloe is very challenged to get her work done in the time allotted. On class assignments and projects, she spends a lot of time off task, and is rarely able to finish more than half. This is with my direct support and trying to refocus her in class. Her parents share that it is very difficult to get Chloe to do her homework, and it takes her "forever" to get anything done. I have reduced homework requirements for Chloe and we have an arrangement to work for a certain amount of time and then stop when it becomes too stressful.

Behavior

Chloe knows the rules and can tell me what they are, as well as help monitor the class at times on the rug to see if students are showing listening behavior (which is a class job in my room). Still, Chloe is unable to focus on the rug. She looks around, has trouble keeping her body to herself and does not offer her ideas when we are brainstorming or having a discussion because she is not following along. Chloe is a big girl and has muscle tone issues which tend to affect her ability to stay in place and be attentive.

Desired Outcomes for Chloe

- A stronger ability to focus during listening times so she can participate in more classroom discussions and activities
- Increased work completion
- Better fluency in reading
- Writing in a more organized fashion on the page with the ultimate goal of completing more sentences in one sitting

Intervention Plan

1. Increased work output

Like so many students impacted by ADHD, Chloe struggles to get her work done in the time allotted. When I observe her at work time and when our special educator and psychologist have observed her as well, we have come to a number of conclusions.

Chloe needs a quiet place to work away from visual distractions and peers. We have set up a desk where she is able to work well when she needs to that is in a more distraction-free location in the classroom. The desk has a privacy board made from cardboard (so she is able to be in a cubby of sorts and have nothing in front of her but her paper and a pencil). Chloe needs to have frequent check-ins with an adult and to have directions for a project given to her one on one so she can get started right away. Visual aids help her. Providing a sample of the project we are completing is very helpful for her to use as a model so she can get a task done but also so she can complete high quality work. When she looks at a sample she can see all the parts to the whole, which she does not often take in when provided with oral instructions alone.

Having Chloe take responsibility for her use of time is essential in tackling her work output. She uses a timer on her table so she knows how much time she has to accomplish a task. We also use a timer with an alarm because giving her short and frequent breaks really helps her to focus during work times. Before setting the timer I will tell her something like, "You have five minutes. When the timer goes off you can take a stretch break. How many story problems do you think you can complete in five minutes?" We will decide upon a reasonable goal and then I will let her start.

In order to know if the times and new work space are working, I am charting the number of problems she completes during math time to see if this increases over time, as she is more and more able to focus. In addition, we have created a work portfolio where we store copies of her writing and math pages so we can track how much work she is producing over time.

2. Focus and attention during whole group listening times

Because Chloe is a big girl with low muscle tone, she needs support to sit. Having her on the floor with the rest of the children is too hard for her. She struggles to sit up and keep herself from touching others. Having consulted with our school's occupational therapist, she suggested a number of interventions to test. The first is the use of a thick, air-filled bumpy rubber cushion, which will force Chloe to sit up straight and engage her core muscles. This can both help with building her stamina and muscle tone and also with her focus. After watching her response to this (the OT will come observe as well) and tracking how many times she raises her hand to participate, we will be able to evaluate whether this strategy is one to stick with or move on to another. A chair for her circle spot will be the next level of intervention we try. The chair will need to be low enough that she can put her feet on the floor. She will also need training to make sure she is not tipping the chair backwards or forwards. Again, we will monitor her responses and interactions to see if this is helping her focus. Another way to use the chair is to add a physical therapy band tied across the chair legs. This way she can put her feet up on it and push down, thus again increasing her strength and giving her something to do with her body to help her focus and stay on track without classroom conversations. If we are not seeing the desired results, we can move on to the fourth intervention, which is a one-legged stool. Chloe will have to balance herself by keeping her feet firmly on the ground at circle time. This is often a tool used for slightly older children, but because Chloe is tall for her age this might also be a potential support to put into place. We are tracking her progress by monitoring how often she raises her hand to participate in classroom conversations.

3. Increasing Chloe's reading fluency

Chloe's word-by-word reading is impacting her reading comprehension. She is sometimes able to read a phrase with a few words, but mostly she reads each word, stumbling to get to the next one. As a result, the text ends up making little sense. To provide Chloe with extra opportunities to increase her fluency we work with her one-on-one and in small groups. Using repeated reading and echo reading are both strategies that we are using to help her to read longer phrases and sentences—strengthening her fluency and thus her comprehension. Because she is dramatic and fun, choral reading appeals to Chloe as well. She likes to hear her voice in tandem with the whole class and she particularly likes reading expressively when a character has something interesting or funny to say. She loves to listen to stories read by adults and children. I decided to turn this love of listening to books into an opportunity to have her listen to audio recordings of stories. This helps her to hear an ideal model of fluent reading so she can duplicate this as time passes and she gains more skills. Nonfiction passages, such as those in the *Read Naturally* program, are also a good tool for Chloe. She is very interested in nonfiction text, so these passages are motivating for her. We will read one together and then I challenge her to read it a number of times before checking in with me to read aloud. These passages are perfect for timing words per minute (wpm) and for listening for signs of increased fluency; so they double as an instructional strategy and an informal assessment tool.

We are fortunate to have a very skilled reading specialist at our school to work with first graders who are not growing at the rate we would like. She works with Chloe three times a week with a focus on both decoding and fluency. Because the reading specialist works with a group of no larger than five students, she is able to read sentences aloud to Chloe and have Chloe duplicate her pace and cadence. This skilled professional also uses a lot of phonetically-regular (decodable) text. The predictability of these stories helps Chloe to read more quickly and more fluently. She also uses chants, rhymes, and songs to help children get used to reading more smoothly. She uses audio recordings of great role models for reading fluency, and then has children make recordings of their own once they are very fluent with a text. These can be shared with parents and are always a great cause for celebration. The small group setting is also a very good opportunity for Chloe to practice these skills in a place with fewer distractions.

4. Writing with better organization on the page

Throughout the school year I have been working with Chloe to help her organize her writing so it can be read by others. We talk about the purpose of writing being to communicate to an audience, and if she cannot make her work suitable for this, then she is wasting her wonderful ideas that everyone would love to read and experience. Using the *Handwriting Without Tears* program is teaching Chloe more appropriate letter formation and how to use the lines of the paper to write well. She also needs visual aids to see what a page looks like when it is printed on in the appropriate fashion. The special *Handwriting Without Tears* paper uses lines that are matched to the handwriting book, and guide children how to make letters the appropriate size. Chloe uses a journal that is exclusively bound pages of this paper so she can transfer her handwriting practice into real life writing exercises. Having a work sample is always a great support for Chloe and

other students. With assistance, Chloe completed a wonderful work sample that she keeps at her seat. The paper we use has lines but has a white space at each side. I have her use a colored pencil to mark a perpendicular line so she can see where to begin and where to end as she writes. Chloe has recently begun to use this strategy independently, and it really helps.

Also, in speaking with the special education teacher, I realized that while her organization on a page is a struggle, Chloe also hesitates because she is not sure where her writing pieces are headed next. For this reason, I have been doing a verbal prewrite/brainstorm with Chloe and sometimes in a small group. I find this strategy to engender much creativity. Chloe has wonderful ideas that also spark others to be more creative and think outside the box as she does.

In order to monitor her progress in organizing her text on the page, I am saving work samples. This provides the best evidence of her learning. I have noticed positive changes, and the perpendicular lines as well as the work sample reference have been invaluable tools.

Teaming with School Staff

As noted above, we have been pooling our resources to support this able girl! We are fortunate to have a skilled occupational therapist at our school who has provided a great deal of support for Chloe even though she does not have an IEP. Our reading specialist works with Chloe three times weekly, and we meet to evaluate her progress with reading word lists, texts, and comprehension activities. This teacher also teaches whole group phonics lessons using the *Wired for Reading* program. This gives us a common vocabulary and helps us to know what letter patterns are confusing Chloe, so we can add more instruction and practice. I have also consulted with our special education teacher who has helped me with prewriting strategies, questioning techniques, and paper format brainstorms. She has also come in to work with us during writing time. Our school psychologist also comes into our classroom and offers her expertise and advice. She was very helpful in looking at environmental factors impacting Chloe's ability to get work done in a timely fashion. It has been really important to work as a team and glean everyone's expertise to support my students. Additionally, when we meet for the Student Study Team, all of the professionals in the room will already know Chloe. This will help give Chloe's parents confidence in us and help us to efficiently choose next steps for this child. I suspect that we will give her the full set of evaluations and that Chloe will likely qualify for some special education services.

Teaming with Parents

I know how important it is to have positive communication with all parents from the first day of school. Chloe is a child whose reputation preceded her, and for that reason I was sure to look for positives from the first day of school so that I was able to call and email her parents with positive comments. I was very sad when I received a reply from Chloe's parents stating that they had not received one positive comment during her entire kindergarten year. Starting with these positive communications, I have already built a strong relationship with Chloe's family. At our beginning of the year conference, I delicately brought up the issue of focus and distractibility. Her parents expressed that they are aware of these problems, but were reluctant to have their daughter evaluated or diagnosed for fear of being told to medicate her. I was able to let them know that a diagnosis does not mean she has to use medication, but just gives us more information as to what Chloe is struggling with so we can better help. As mentioned above, Chloe's parents did recently have her evaluated, and she was diagnosed with ADHD. I completed a rating scale and shared my observations about Chloe's performance in the classroom that was requested by her doctor during the evaluation process. She is not receiving any medication for treating ADHD at this time.

Chloe's parents have come to me a number of times for help with routines at home, and we have been able to problem-solve together. This has bolstered their confidence in themselves as parents and in me as a teacher. I have also shared some website resources (e.g., www.chadd.org and www

.help4adhd.org) with Chloe's parents. They were thrilled to find this wealth of information. I think they feel far less isolated now that they can see this is a widespread struggle and how many families are experiencing similar challenges. My relationship with Chloe's family has improved her relationship with me in the classroom. She knows how much I care and sees the extra time I spend with her parents. I am more than willing and very happy to do so. The more support I can offer her parents, the greater success Chloe will experience at school.

Anne (Eleven Years Old, Sixth Grade)

This student profile and intervention plan was written (with some adaptations) by Beverly Shorter, a teacher who was part of the middle school's intervention team at the time the case study was written. The student's name and identifying information have been changed. This case study includes a follow-up addendum provided a few months later in the school year (at the end of sixth grade) as well as a recent update almost four years later. The addendum is also provided by Mrs. Shorter, who is currently one of the special education teachers at the high school that Anne is now attending. My thanks and appreciation to Beverly for sharing this student's case study with me.

Student Profile

Anne is a 6th grade middle school student. She is a sweet child who seems to love school and does well socially. Anne's strengths are her joy of learning and love of reading. She is an active student and enjoys sports and everything to do with horses.

School History

Anne was diagnosed with ADHD in 4th grade when it was observed by both teachers and parents that she had impulse control issues, difficulty paying attention and staying focused through task completion, keeping organized, and getting her assignments (class and homework) done without a struggle.

Student records indicate that on all of her assessments (formal and informal), Anne functioned at grade level in reading fluency, reading comprehension, and math skills, but below grade level in written expression. The last DRA reading assessment in 5th grade showed her to be at grade level in reading fluency and reading comprehension. Informal testing was also done in these reading skill areas and they confirmed the DRA results. In the Holt math curriculum assessments she tested at or above grade level, and this was further confirmed in district-wide and state testing. In the district-wide writing assessments she consistently tested at slightly below grade level performance.

During her 5th grade year Anne was brought to the table in the grade-level Response to Intervention (RTI) meetings regarding her deficits in on-task behavior, organization, and writing skills. The grade-level team evaluated her work, charted observations by her teacher, listened to parent input, and discussed interventions that could be tried. Intervention goals were put into place to help her with these particular issues. Written expression deficits were the main concerns academically, and were preventing her from succeeding in the writing process. The team reviewed her writing assignments and assessments to determine the specific areas of weakness.

Interventions were put into place to help with her written expression deficits, which included: direct instruction of prewriting strategies, modeling of well organized writing pieces, use of graphic organizers, and a breakdown of the writing process with due dates for each part clearly stated. Anne's teacher also consistently went over her writing topic with her to make sure she was staying on topic. In addition, the teacher monitored Anne through each part of the writing assignments, and areas of weakness were addressed. With these interventions in place, Anne's writing assessments showed overall improvement. She was still testing at slightly below grade level, but her skills in prewriting, organization and topic focus had greatly improved.

During her 5th grade year many interventions were also put into place to assist Anne in her organization skills. The organizational interventions included: color-coded subject dividers in her notebook, input in a daily and monthly agenda, and organized supplies that were checked and kept refreshed weekly. The teacher and parents went over the agenda daily with Anne, and if all was organized and turned in, they signed off on it. This daily check system greatly improved communication and expectations between home and school. However, when Anne started middle school, as Anne did not have a 504 plan or IEP, many of these interventions that helped her in elementary school went by the wayside.

Present Level of Functioning and Areas of Concern

Even though Anne has had use of a binder since 3rd grade, she is challenged when having to find or file anything in her binder. The start of middle school has exacerbated this issue due to the fact she now has to organize six different subjects and maintain a locker that she can easily access and find what she needs. Homework is often missing, and completed assignments are not making it home for parents to check. Another issue that has come to the forefront since starting middle school is her difficulty with time awareness and management. Anne is consistently tardy to class and has spent an inordinate amount of time in ISS (in-school suspension), due to her tardiness. Anne also has extreme difficulty surmising how much time a given task will take her, and this has affected her ability to complete tasks in a timely fashion and turn in her work on time.

Unfortunately, in the transition to middle school, Anne's challenges and needs were not known until weeks into the first trimester. She was struggling with the expectations of a whole set of six different teachers, without the supports and interventions that helped her in the past.

It was not until the second trimester of the 6th grade year that these deficits became apparent to her teachers. The first sign of trouble was the daily tardy slips she accumulated that led to ISS on almost a weekly basis. This, of course, caused her to miss class learning time which then led to late assignments, missing work, and failing grades on assessments. When a pattern of failing grades became apparent, teachers, administrators, support staff, and special educators met to discuss the issues Anne was having, review her records, previous goals and interventions, and possible steps to support her. The issues brought to the table were: being late to class, disorganization of materials, lost or unfinished homework, and failing grades in her writing assignments. It was at this time that Anne's 5th grade teacher was contacted and records reviewed to get a better understanding of issues and supports that had previously taken place.

At this point, the team agreed to do specific assessments to recheck her levels of performance in reading, writing and math, and scheduled an intervention team meeting with parents. Anne once again DRA tested at grade level in both reading fluency and comprehension, along with grade-level assessments in the Holt math curriculum. However, her writing competencies were still at a lower level than that of same-age peers and seemed to be declining. This may be due to the higher level of expectations and number of classes that require good written expression. Curriculum-based and district-wide writing assessments showed a weakness in prewriting, organization, and completion of the writing assignments. All the deficiencies seemed to stem from her lack of organization and weaknesses in the writing process itself.

Next, we met as a team together with Anne's parents to share concerns, gather more information, and design a plan of intervention. Together we created a plan of strategies and supports to be implemented immediately to help her with organization, time management, prewriting and topic focus writing skills. It was agreed to follow-up in six weeks to go over interventions, goal measurement and communication between home and school—at which time we would determine next steps. As a team we also discussed letting our para-educator staff know what interventions and goals we have set for Anne, so they could be an additional support when in the general education classrooms helping other students. In addition, we talked about Anne's ADHD, and asked parents about any interventions she may have received.

Her parents shared that Anne has never been treated medically for ADHD; they are against the use of medications.

It is very unfortunate that Anne did not get the help and support she needed for the first trimester of the year. Unfortunately, what happens when a student enters middle school, unless they have a 504 plan or an IEP, or if someone doesn't alert the school, many prior issues may remain unknown until they show up on a consistent basis. Of course, Anne's ADHD was noted in her student file, but teachers remained unaware of supports that were previously in place that enabled her to succeed.

Intervention Plan

The following intervention plan was created and put into effect immediately:

Areas of concern:

- Time Awareness and Management
- Organization
- Work Completion
- Written Expression (prewrite and topic focus skills)

The first priority was to support Anne in time management and organization deficits. These skills are required in every aspect of home and school in order to be successful. Teachers and parents were both extremely concerned with the amount of tardy slips she had been receiving which led to in-school suspension. A little investigation was required before interventions could take place. Was she late because she was talking to friends, not being aware of how long it takes to get to the next class, and/or was she having trouble finding the materials she needed from her locker? After some shadowing, it was found that her awareness of time passing and a disorganized locker led to her being late on a regular basis.

Goal: Organization of locker and notebook.
Goal: Organization of homework and long-term assignments
Goal: Arrival to class before the last bell rings

Interventions for Organization and Time Management

- Work with Anne to get her binder and locker organized so that all materials are easy to find.
- Provide a locker organization and supply checklist that she can check over daily to make sure all materials needed are ready and easily available.
- Conduct locker and binder checks once a week to go over checklists and calendars to make sure she remains organized.
- Each period teacher will place a monthly calendar page at the front of each content area that she can write homework and long-term assignments on, and go over them with her at the end of each period.
- Parents will sign off on each calendar on a daily basis so both teachers and parents know that information is getting back and forth. (This also gives parents a way to know what supports she may need at home to finish homework and long-term assignments.)
- Assign a passing buddy that has the same classes that she does to walk with her to her locker and between classes. Having a reliable peer buddy to support her during passing time would be a benefit and provide a good model for appropriate passing etiquette.
- Teachers will keep track of arrival times via the computer attendance for every class, and all late arrivals will be noted.

Measurement of goals:

- Binder and locker calendars and checklists
- Charting on-time arrival to all classes with documented late arrivals

The next priority was to help and support Anne with work completion and written expression deficits. Parents asked for more communication to come home regarding homework and long-term assignments. The class calendars that were implemented in the first interventions will be of great help to both teachers and parents so they know that each is aware of what is coming up and what is due in advance of the due date. The portion on the class calendars that requires parents and teachers to sign it daily ensures that all parties are aware of what is coming up in the near future and that communication is going back and forth on a regular basis. As parents have stated: "There is nothing worse than trying to help your child get an assignment done the day before it is due."

Goal: Management and organization of writing assignments
Goal: On-time homework and class assignment completion
Goal: Communication between school and home on a daily basis

Interventions for Work Completion and Written Expression

- Make available graphic organizers that will help Anne with prewriting and supply different ways to brainstorm ideas.
- During class time, provide opportunities to work with a peer buddy or in small groups.
- Give her a writing example that will be a model of good organization and topic focus for the larger writing assignments.
- Teachers will break down writing assignments into manageable sections with due dates clearly stated on class calendars. Teachers will provide immediate feedback on each portion of writing when it is due.
- Special Ed. staff will provide homework and writing assignment support during Focus period every day to help get her started and stay on task. (This also prepares her for what she needs to get done at home.)
- Also during Focus period, continued support in organizational skills will be provided by going over checklist, calendars and doing binder checks.
- Communicate with parents on a daily basis of what was worked on during Focus period.

This particular middle school has a twenty-minute daily period that they refer to as "Focus period." All general and special education teachers participate in helping students who are struggling in any of their classes at this time. Students who do not need assistance read silently during this period. The school's RTI team assigned Anne to Mrs. Shorter for this daily period as an intervention step.

Measurement of goals:

- Grade improvement on writing assignments and assessments
- Teacher observation during the writing process
- Charting work completion for all classes documenting missing assignments
- Communication from parents on a regular basis

[Mrs. Shorter reported: "In addition, I had a private meeting with parents to talk about any issues that they may be having at home with Anne, and how we (school) could help support them. Parents felt that the strategies we put in place will much improve the struggles they had been having with getting Anne's work done and turned in on time, and greatly improve communication between home and school. I also provided some community resources and organizations (our local CHADD) that may help them to better understand ADHD and get support from other families that are going through the same thing."]

Follow-up (Reported Spring Trimester of Sixth-Grade School Year, Provided by Mrs. Shorter)

The interventions put into place were helping some at the six-week follow-up, but not nearly enough to pull up Anne's failing grades in all classes. Our team recommended special education testing, but parents did not want to pursue a special education evaluation.

As an additional intervention, I was able to place Anne in a peer tutor position in my self-contained special education class. We have a schoolwide program in which students apply to be peer tutors for one period a day to support students in our special education classes. Anne didn't meet the criteria to be a peer tutor, but wanted to become one. We decided to make this exception, mostly to be able to provide her more direct support. During this time, we had Anne do just a little peer tutoring (helping read with students); but for the majority of the period, we helped Anne organize her binder and get caught up on her many past-due assignments. As a result of this intervention, she got caught up on all assignments.

After watching her put so much effort into just getting all of her assignments in on time, it was hard on her (and broke my heart) when she was still getting very low grades, especially in math, because of low testing scores in her classes. At this point, [her] parents agreed to let us test Anne. She has finally been evaluated and qualifies for special education services under Other Health Impaired (OHI) criteria.

I am being moved up to teach high school next year. I can only hope that with continued supports, advocacy and encouragement, and more intensive interventions through special education, it will have a positive impact on Anne and set her up for a successful future.

Follow-up (Tenth-Grade School Year)

Mrs. Shorter shared with me that Anne is now a sophomore at the same high school where she teaches, and continues to receive (since seventh grade) special education services through the Resource program. Although she doesn't work with Anne directly, Mrs. Shorter still checks in with her frequently, monitors her progress, and encourages her.

Mrs. Shorter was delighted to report that Anne is thriving in high school. The advocacy in sixth grade to get her the help she needed has made a huge difference in this student's life. "By educating Anne's parents about her condition and finally getting her tested and entered into the special education program, Anne is succeeding in school. I can't imagine where she would be right now without this intervention."

The high school also has a peer tutoring program. Anne applied to be a peer tutor her freshman year and met full criteria to become one (with qualifying grades and attendance)!

Mrs. Shorter created and was coordinator of the peer tutor program at the middle school when she taught there, and then re-created and is still coordinating the program at the high school. Designed as a way to bring the general education population into her special education program and build a more caring, empathetic community, the program has had a significant impact on the whole school community.

Part 5 References

Section 5.1

American Psychiatric Association. (2013). *Diagnostic and statistical manual of mental disorders* (5th ed.). Arlington, VA: Author.

Chess, S., & Thomas, A. (2014). *Goodness of fit: Clinical applications, from infancy through adult life.* New York, NY: Routledge. (Original work published 1999)

Horowitz, F. D. (2014). *Exploring developmental theories: Toward a structural / behavioral model of development.* New York, NY: Psychology Press. (Original work published 1987)

Kunhardt, D. (2001). *Pat the Bunny.* New York, NY: Penguin Random House. (Original work published 1940)

Lange, K. W., Reichl, S., Lange, K. M., Tucha, L., & Tucha, O. (2010, December). The history of attention deficit hyperactivity disorder. *Attention Dificit Hyperactivity Disorder*, 2(4), 241–255.

6

Collaborative Efforts and School Responsibilities in Helping Students with ADHD

Section 6.1: Teaming for Success: Communication, Collaboration, and Mutual Support

Section 6.2: The Role of the School's Multidisciplinary Team

Section 6.3: School Documentation and Communication with Medical Providers and Others

Section 6.4: Federal Laws and Educational Rights of Students with ADHD

6.1

Teaming for Success: Communication, Collaboration, and Mutual Support

The Necessity of a Team Approach

As ADHD is a chronic disorder that is "managed," not cured, a young person with ADHD will typically need various supports and treatments from a variety of different professionals and service providers throughout childhood and adolescence. Teamwork is required through every phase.

The diagnostic process involves a team:

- Parents provide information about their child (through interviews, rating forms, and questionnaires).
- Teachers and other school personnel provide information regarding the student's symptoms and functioning.
- The multidisciplinary assessment (IEP) team may conduct a school-based evaluation of the student (involving, for example, the special education teacher or other learning specialist, school psychologist, speech-language therapist, school nurse).
- A physician or mental health professional evaluates the child for ADHD.

The treatment plan involves a team:

- School interventions are generally provided by a variety of school professionals and other individuals, who may include general and special education teachers, school

counselors, social workers, psychologists, nurses, speech-language therapists, adapted physical education teachers, occupational therapists, administrators, instructional or management aides/paras, other staff and school mentors, tutors, and volunteers (peer, cross-age, parent, community).
- Medical intervention may be provided by pediatricians, family practitioners, child psychiatrists, neurologists, or other licensed professionals who are able to prescribe medication.
- The child or teen may be involved in other treatments and interventions to address specific needs, among them counseling or behavioral therapy, private academic tutoring, and ADHD coaching.
- It is important for the child or teen to participate in activities that build on his or her interests and strengths and provide an emotional and physical outlet. This may involve the support of athletic coaches, youth group leaders, scout leaders, mentors, or instructors working with the child or teen in extracurricular activities.
- Parent training groups may be provided by various community professionals or other trained facilitators in behavior management and positive discipline strategies.

- A multidisciplinary team of school professionals will be involved in the development and monitoring of supports and intervention for students in need. This may mean the school's SST or RTI team or the IEP team for students being evaluated for or receiving special education and related services. A multidisciplinary team will be involved in any IEP or 504 accommodation plan. If the student is receiving special education, then the school's special education service providers will be involved in the implementation of all aspects of the student's IEP.
- Support groups for parents of children and teens with ADHD, such as CHADD (Children and Adults with Attention Deficit/Hyperactivity Disorder; www.chadd.org), are composed of a number of people in the community, both parents and professionals, who can serve as a resource and support, a very helpful intervention for parents.

Communication among key parties (parents, teachers, and clinicians and other service providers) is necessary for the diagnostic process and for any treatment or intervention provided. Students with ADHD require close monitoring and mutual support between the home and school to be successful.

- Teachers need to keep parents well informed about assignments (particularly upcoming tests and projects), how the student is performing and keeping up with daily work, and behavioral and other issues affecting the student's achievement and success in the classroom.
- Parents need to communicate with teachers regarding any concerns or issues that may be affecting their child's school performance. In addition, they need to stay on top of monitoring to ensure that homework is being done.
- Both parents and teachers need to follow through with any home-school plans (for example, to aid and reinforce behavior, work production, and organization skills).

See an explanation of daily and weekly progress reports and home-school monitoring forms in Section 2.4 and examples of such forms in the appendix. These are excellent tools for parents and teachers to use for communicating between home and school.

Medical and mental health professionals involved in the care of the child or teen must also be monitoring the treatment effects and seeking feedback from home and school in regard to the interventions. If the child has been prescribed a medication in treatment, this requires communication between the teacher(s), parents, and the physician. If there is a school nurse, he or she is often the liaison regarding medication management.

Most students with ADHD will be educated in general education classrooms. Some receive special education services, whereas others do not. Collaboration and consultation among classroom teachers and special educators or other learning specialists regarding effective strategies and accommodations are very helpful, whether or not the student receives special services or instruction.

The child or teen must be included in the team effort. Once students are old enough, they need to learn about ADHD and understand the reason for the treatments and interventions. If they are taking medication, they need to understand what medication does and does not do. Teens need to be involved and take an active role in their treatment plan.

There are excellent books written specifically for children and teens with ADHD. For some suggestions, see lists at these links:

http://add.about.com/od/adhdresources/a/kidbooks.htm
www.addvance.com/bookstore/children.html
www.addwarehouse.com/shopsite_sc/store/html/children.html

The Parents' Role in the Collaborative Team Process

It is the parent who is ultimately the director or case manager of his or her child's ADHD support team. Parents are responsible for assembling the best team of professionals for treating and educating their child, and coordinating and monitoring the efforts of the team. Parents generally need to oversee that parties are communicating as needed and that agreed-on interventions are taking place. Taking on this leadership and overseer role does not come easily for many parents. It involves learning how to become a knowledgeable and competent advocate for their child's needs.

To be an effective advocate, parents must communicate with school staff regarding their son or daughter to a far greater degree than is necessary for most children. The level of involvement with the school significantly increases when one has a child with any disability or special needs.

To best advocate for your child, it is essential to become knowledgeable about ADHD, your child's educational needs, and effective strategies, supports, and interventions. You must educate yourself to understand as much as you can about the disorder and about research-validated treatments for ADHD.

It is very important to be aware of your child's educational rights under the law and how to communicate with school personnel and navigate within the school system to ensure that your child obtains the necessary help for school success. You must also learn to communicate with medical and mental health systems and providers involved in your child's care.

None of this is easy. It is time-consuming and difficult, but no one is more invested in your child's well-being than you, the parent or guardian. Seek help and guidance. There are many resources to assist you. Be confident in your ability, and try not to get discouraged. Parents and guardians who are experienced in advocating for their child with school and health care systems have acquired their skills out of necessity, over time, and do not give up.

All parents are urged to read Section 5.1.

Know Your Child's Educational Rights

- Learn about your child's rights under federal and state laws to a free, appropriate public education; eligibility criteria; procedures; and the protections and provisions for students who qualify under IDEA and Section 504.

- You have a right to request an evaluation of your child's educational needs at no charge to you if there is a known or suspected disability that you feel is affecting your child's school performance and functioning.
- If your child has significant behavioral issues resulting in disciplinary actions such as suspensions or expulsion, be aware of disciplinary rights under the law for students with disabilities.
- If your child qualifies for special education or related services, an IEP will be written with specific goals and objectives to address his or her areas of need. You are an integral part of the team in planning your child's special education program and goals. Be prepared for that IEP meeting in order to give your input and ensure your satisfaction with the goals, objectives, and accommodations designed to address the needs of your child.
- Your child might not need or qualify for special education programs or services, but may be eligible for and benefit from a 504 accommodation plan. If your child receives a 504 plan, be prepared to share the accommodations and supports that you feel are necessary for your child to learn and succeed in school.
- Be aware that if there are conflicts between you and the school district, there are provisions in the laws for due process and other less adversarial ways of resolving those conflicts.
- You have the right to an independent educational evaluation if you disagree with the school district's evaluation.

See Section 6.4 for more on this topic.

Be an Effective Advocate at Team Meetings

Parents can easily feel uncomfortable and emotional at school team meetings (which may involve several members of the school or district staff). It is not easy discussing your child with all of these people, and hearing about your child's difficulties at school or the results of diagnostic testing. Sometimes parents and school personnel disagree about issues and what to do about them. Here are some tips:

- Try to enter such meetings with an open mind, cooperative attitude, and problem-solving approach. Be willing to share your opinions, feelings, observations, suggestions, and any information about your child or the rest of the family that may help with planning and intervention.

- Do not be embarrassed to ask questions and request that any unfamiliar language (educational jargon) be explained. Ask for clarification on anything you do not understand. If you need a more thorough explanation of the test results and recommendations, make sure it is provided.

- Be open to what the other team members have to say, but make sure that your concerns are expressed as well. Speak up if you feel that your point of view has not been heard.

- Take notes during meetings. In addition, it is helpful if you come to meetings prepared with a few notes to yourself regarding items you wish to share, discuss, or ask about.

- It is most helpful if both parents can attend school meetings together. You are welcome to bring someone with you to meetings. For example, if your child is working privately with a tutor, educational therapist, ADHD coach, or other professional, you may want to bring that person to the school to participate in meetings with the school team.

- Prepare for meetings by trying to learn how your child is functioning at school (in classroom and other settings), in what areas your child is struggling (academic, social-emotional, behavioral), and the kinds of supports and accommodations that may be helpful and available.

- At certain meetings, such as IEP meetings, you should receive a copy of any reports or paperwork to which staff members make reference. If you do not, request a copy.

Maintain Records

It is important to maintain good records. These will most likely come in handy at some point and save you time and effort digging them up later when needed.

- Keep a file on your child that includes copies of testing and evaluations, IEPs and 504 plans, report cards each year, health and immunization records, and other important data.

- Include in the file a log of communication with the school and other professionals working with your child, such as dates of doctor appointments and medication logs, summaries of conversations and meetings, notification of disciplinary actions and referrals your child received at school, and interventions promised to be put into effect.

If Requesting an Evaluation from the School District

Parents have a right to have their child's educational needs assessed by the school district. If you wish to have your son or daughter evaluated to determine whether he or she has a disability that qualifies for special education, related services, or accommodations, it is advised that you do the following:

- Speak with the classroom teacher, the special education teacher, other members of the multidisciplinary team, the principal, or the director of special education about pursuing an evaluation.

- Submit to the school a written, dated letter requesting an evaluation, including the reason you are asking for the assessment (for example, your concerns that your child may have a disability interfering with his or her school success). This written request is most important. This will begin the IEP process and timeline. The evaluation will determine whether a student qualifies for special education and related services based on an identified area of disability.

- It is generally recommended to first proceed through the student support team (SST) or Response to Intervention (RTI) team process to initiate and evaluate the effectiveness of prereferral interventions before testing for special education eligibility. However, this is not a requirement. See Section 6.2 on SST and RTI, and sample letters to the school district in Section 6.3.
- Read the paperwork the school provides regarding procedures, the assessment plan, and due process rights under the law. If you have any questions, ask.
- Know that you are a key member of the team in this entire process.

Ensure the Right Care from Doctors and Other Clinicians

When you are seeking a physician or other clinician to evaluate and treat your child, you are looking for someone who exhibits the following qualities:

- Is knowledgeable about what is currently known about ADHD and research-validated treatments
- Has experience and training working with children and families with ADHD
- Is familiar with the surrounding issues and other conditions or disorders that commonly coexist with ADHD
- Adheres to the American Academy of Pediatrics guidelines in diagnosis and treatment of children and teens with ADHD (meeting *DSM*-5 criteria)
- Possesses a firm belief in a multimodal treatment approach
- Is willing to communicate and work together as a team with parents and school personnel

Be assertive in checking the level of expertise of the professionals you seek out. If you are uncomfortable with their treatment approach, express your concerns. If they do not appear committed to a team approach, you will be better off finding someone else.

More Advocacy and Communication Tips for Parents

- Any plan, formal or informal (for example, 504, IEP), can be reviewed at any point during the school year. If you have concerns, you may always request a review of the plan or any services, programs, or special placements. You do not have to wait until an annual review meeting or a quarterly/semester parent-teacher conference. The best is to continuously remain in close communication to monitor progress. If something is not working, it can always be changed.
- Keep in mind what is reasonable when making requests. Take into consideration the challenges for teachers trying to meet the individual needs of a classroom (or five or six classrooms) of students—a few to several of whom may also have various learning, behavioral, or social-emotional difficulties requiring the teacher's extra time, attention, and effort.
- Choose your words carefully and avoid antagonism. Many requests can be framed in such a way that they invite discussion rather than refusal. Your tone and manner can help create a strong, positive relationship or an adversarial one with a school.
- Most teachers want to help their students succeed in their class and are willing to put forth the extra time and effort to do so. This is especially true when they have a positive, friendly relationship with parents and feel respected, appreciated, and supported by them.
- Let teachers know you are interested, available, and accessible and want to do what is needed to help your child. You are asking your child's teachers and school to go the extra mile for your child. Offer your own support and cooperation. Ask for suggestions on how you can best help and ways to work together effectively.
- At the beginning of the school year (within the first few weeks), meet with your child's teachers, share information about your child, and establish the best means of

communication (phone, email, text, communication notes, a journal between home and school, or other method).

- Besides informing teachers early in the year about your child's challenges and needs, be sure to share your child's strengths and interests and some strategies that have been most successful in the past.

- Some parents find it helpful to provide teachers at the beginning of the year with a brief letter or form with written information introducing their child.

- When teachers share their perspective about your child or school situations, try to remain calm and polite even if you disagree or find what teachers say upsetting. After listening carefully, ask specific questions for clarification and then focus the discussion on solutions to problems. Keep discussions constructive and respectful.

- Try to ensure that your son or daughter is coming to school ready to learn: adequately rested; prepared with books, materials, and homework; and having received medication if it is prescribed.

- Often the best way to establish a positive relationship with the school is to be a helpful, involved parent who volunteers time and service to the school. There are countless ways that schools can use the direct or indirect services of parents. All schools seek parent involvement in the classroom or on various school committees, programs, and projects. Become more involved in the school community and get to know staff members.

- Express your appreciation to teachers or other staff members who are making an effort on behalf of your child. It is generally the little things that make a difference in showing your appreciation: a thank-you note, a positive comment or message to the teacher or administrator, a positive email to the teacher with a copy to the principal.

- You might wish to donate a book or other resources and information about ADHD to the teacher or school professional library. Much of the teacher training and public awareness regarding ADHD has been a direct result of parents' strong efforts (individually, as a small group of parents and interested professionals, and through organizations such as CHADD) to educate others about the needs of their children.

- Your child's school success may require the use of tools, such as timers and assignment notebooks, and the purchase of items to be used as rewards for achieving goals in a behavioral plan. These can be expensive for a teacher, so consider offering to purchase such items the teacher needs to help your child.

The Educators' Role in the Collaborative Team Process

To optimize the success of students with ADHD, educators must make every effort to collaborate closely with parents (as well as clinicians and other service providers involved in their care). It is essential for teachers and other school professionals to reach out to parents—welcoming their involvement, building positive rapport, and communicating effectively.

When a student has behavioral challenges, teachers and other school personnel sometimes view the child and his or her family in a negative light or make unfair assumptions. The overt or subtle message received by many parents of children and teens with ADHD is "What are you going to do about your child and his or her inappropriate behavior?" Such a message can sabotage any efforts to build teamwork between home and school. When parents perceive that their child is disliked, misunderstood, or blamed for the disorder (or that their own disciplinary methods and parenting style are being questioned or criticized), an adversarial rather than collaborative, respectful relationship is most likely.

Establish Communication and a Positive Relationship

To build a positive relationship with parents, communicate

- In a manner that is respectful and nonjudgmental

- That you welcome their "partnership"
- Your acknowledgment that they are the "experts" on their son or daughter
- Your sincere interest in understanding their child's needs
- That you value their input and any information or insights they can share with you
- Your willingness to put forth the extra time and effort to help their child be successful

It is much easier to discuss any concerns or issues with parents once you have opened the lines of communication in a positive manner. In order to establish rapport with parents, it is important to recognize and speak about their child's areas of strength and competence. Make every effort to learn about the student, identifying his or her individual strengths, interests, and positive characteristics.

Much closer, frequent, ongoing communication is needed with parents of students with ADHD than is generally necessary with other parents. Determine with parents what system will work best: phone calls, text messages, email, daily or weekly notes, logs, or something else.

Be Proactive

- Call or write notes home communicating positive messages to parents about their child (what you have noticed and appreciate about the student).
- Make yourself easily accessible and let parents know when and how they can best contact you.
- Make every effort to accommodate parents' needs in scheduling parent-teacher conferences, so that you have the chance to meet face-to-face.
- If the student has been diagnosed with ADHD and is taking medication, your observations and feedback about the child's functioning during the school day are very important. If you note positive or negative changes in a student's behavior and performance—for example, increased ability to stay on task and complete work, increased attentiveness, notably better self-control, an

increase or decrease in outbursts and emotional responses, or lethargy—report these observations to parents. Parents need your feedback to share with treating physicians.

- Having observed a change in a child's behavior, positive or negative, you may suspect that the student has been placed on medication, had a change of prescription, or did not take his or her medication. Do not wait for the student's parents to inform you of changes in treatment; they may be waiting to see if you noticed anything different or significant enough to contact them. When observing such changes, communicate with parents—for example, "I noticed that Jared had three really good days so far this week. He has been very focused and completed 90 percent of his work. I'm so pleased," or "I don't know why, but Kelli has been weepy and not wanting to participate in class the past two days. She didn't want to go out for recess either, which is very unusual for her."

When You Have Concerns about a Student

- Make personal contact and explain to parents what you are concerned about. Again, try to always indicate something positive as well.
- Describe how the child is functioning (academically, behaviorally, socially).
- State your observations objectively without labeling the behavior or the child as, for example, "lazy," "unmotivated," or "apathetic."
- Communicate your sincere interest in doing everything possible to help the student do well in school.
- Ask parents whether they notice any of the difficulties you have described or if previous teachers have ever communicated these concerns in the past.
- Let the parents know what specific strategies and interventions you are currently using or that you plan to implement to address the areas of concern.
- Ask parents about strategies that have been effective in the past, what they have found to be helpful at home, and their suggestions.

- Really take the time to listen to what parents have to say, and communicate your respect for their opinions, feelings, and goals for their child.

Give Teachers the Supports and Training They Need

It is by no means an easy job to be an effective teacher and address the numerous and diverse needs of students in the classroom. There are high demands and expectations on teachers to be accountable for student achievement, yet there are often shrinking resources and support available to do so. Parents and administrators must keep in mind that teachers frequently have several students in a classroom or whom they teach throughout the day who need extra assistance, support, and attention, including those with

- ADHD, learning disabilities, and other neurobiological, developmental, or behavioral disorders
- Limited English proficiency (English language learners)
- Social, emotional, and behavioral problems due to trauma, instability, or situations in their personal lives

The following are some of the supports that teachers need in order to address the needs of students with ADHD (and all students in the classroom).

Training and Professional Development

Teachers need training and professional development opportunities

- To understand ADHD and strategies and interventions to support students with executive function impairments
- In behavior management to minimize behavioral problems in the classroom and other school settings and support the development of self-regulation skills
- In differentiating instruction to reach and teach diverse learners and the wide range of skill proficiency and developmental levels of students in the classroom

Teaming and Sharing with Colleagues

- Most students with ADHD will be educated in general education classrooms. Some will be receiving special education services, and others will not. Classroom teachers benefit from collaboration and consultation with special educators and school support staff regarding effective strategies and accommodations to address individual students' needs.
- Buddying with a partner teacher is often helpful for exchanging ideas and reenergizing each other, and for disciplinary purposes (for example, sending a student for a brief "time-out" in the buddy teacher's class).
- Coteaching and team teaching opportunities can be very beneficial in sharing instruction and management and being able to provide more support to students in the classroom.
- Both students and teachers benefit when teachers have opportunities for grade-level teams or other colleagues to exchange and share with each other (information, lessons, materials, instructional and behavioral strategies and techniques).

Administrative Support

Administrators can help teachers and other staff members by

- Providing teachers and support staff with the time and opportunity (for example, through creative scheduling) to meet, plan, team up, and collaborate with each other
- Providing teachers with professional development that builds their awareness and understanding of students with "hidden disabilities" such as ADHD and learning disabilities and that strengthens their skills and instructional toolkit to better reach and teach their students
- Providing assistance for teachers who are overloaded with more than their fair share of "challenging" students (for example, fewer students in the class, more prep time, scheduling preferences, more push-in help and extra support in the classroom)

- Encouraging teachers to "experiment" with various strategies and techniques to find what works for an individual child
- Creating a lending library of materials teachers can access, including books, DVDs, and other resources for teaching students with ADHD

Support Team Members

Teachers are best supported by team members who

- Are knowledgeable about students with ADHD
- Are responsive and helpful when teachers express concerns and seek assistance
- Strategize and help teachers plan appropriate actions and interventions for students
- Follow through and provide timely feedback and assistance

Other Supports

- Teachers need to be able to access academic interventions within general education for students in need (such as tier 2 and tier 3 RTI supports). These also serve as prereferral interventions that teachers can try prior to referring a student for special education.
- It is helpful for teachers to have the opportunity to observe other teachers and receive mentoring or peer coaching assistance if needed or requested.
- Teachers need to be cheered on to keep on learning and growing. The best support is being able to associate with positive, upbeat, and enthusiastic colleagues who love to teach, are committed to their students and profession, and want to keep advancing their skills and knowledge.
- Teachers must be treated as professionals whose opinions and input are solicited and listened to for site-based decision making.
- We all need to know that our efforts are recognized and appreciated. A thoughtful "thank you" or positive comment from a colleague, parent, administrator, or student means a lot to teachers.

Keep in Mind

- Regardless of whether parents are able to attend a meeting (for example, an SST initial meeting), they should always be kept well informed, and every effort should be made by the school to include them and receive their input.
- Parents are key members of any team meetings involving their child—an SST, 504, or IEP team meeting. Realize how intimidating it can be for a parent to attend any such meeting—sitting around a table with a number of school people discussing their child. Hearing about how one's son or daughter is struggling in school is not easy for any parent; and it often raises one's defenses, anxiety, anger, and fears. It is important to be sensitive and empathetic to what parents may be feeling, and really take the time to listen to what they have to say. We must clearly communicate that the school is committed to working together in any way possible to help their child succeed.
- Teachers must communicate observations and provide (with parental permission granted in writing and on file with the school district) any requested information to clinicians involved in the diagnosis or treatment of the student.

The Clinicians' Role in the Collaborative Team Process

Medical and mental health professionals must obtain information and data from parents and educators in order to determine whether the child meets the *DSM-5* diagnostic criteria for ADHD. It is important that the clinician has a clear picture and understanding of the child's or teen's issues, challenges, and functional levels at home, school, and other key environments. If medical or mental health intervention is provided, treatment goals and effects must be monitored regularly by seeking feedback from parents and teachers.

Cultural Sensitivity in Communication with Parents

School personnel and clinicians need to be aware of cultural factors that are barriers to communication—for example, cultural differences and interpretations of nonverbal communication (eye contact, gestures, and proximity), which may be viewed as hostile or disrespectful in some cultures. Of course, language barriers must be bridged to communicate with parents who are not English proficient, such as by providing a translator, simplifying language verbally and in written reports, and providing more visuals and other supports to make information clearer.

With regard to diagnosis and intervention for ADHD, the cultural view of normal children's behavior differs, and beliefs or cultural attitudes about disabilities and mental health conditions are factors that influence parents' decision to have their child evaluated and treated. Parents may fear having their child labeled as having a disorder or disability, and may have a mistrust of intervention (mental health services, medication, special education) because of views held by immediate and extended family members and their community. School, medical, and mental health professionals need to be sensitive to these issues when communicating with parents—listening to their concerns, answering questions thoroughly, and sharing information and resources to help them make informed decisions about what is needed to help their child.

The Role of the School's Multidisciplinary Team

A multidisciplinary team of school professionals is used to support classroom teachers and students in various ways. There are multidisciplinary teams and processes (such as SST and RTI) that are designed for identifying and providing appropriate intervention to any student in need—part of the general education process. The Response to Intervention (RTI) model and team process is described in Section 3.2 of this book, which covers research-based instructional approaches and interventions. There are also IEP teams, which are involved in the evaluation, diagnosis, and provision of services for students with disabilities qualifying for special education. There is often overlap, with some of the same school staff serving on different teams in their school.

The Student Support Team (SST) Process

Most schools have a team process for assisting teachers in devising instructional and behavioral strategies and supports for students experiencing difficulties in general education. This process and team are referred to by many names:

- SST can stand for student support team, student study team, or student success team.

- In some districts, the team is called the SAT (student assistance team), SIT (student intervention team), IST (instructional support team), or TAT (teacher assistance team).
- In others, it may be called the CT (consultation team), CGT (child guidance team), CST (child study team), MIT (multidisciplinary intervention team), and so forth.
- More recently, the SST has sometimes been referred to as the RTI team (Response to Intervention team).

When concerned about a student's academic or behavioral performance, teachers and parents need to initiate efforts to work together on behalf of the student. The first step should always be a parent-teacher conference to discuss and plan strategies for the student's success. It is recommended that parents always take their concerns directly to the teacher as a first step, as well. This is proper protocol in most schools, and is often communicated to parents at the beginning of the school year by the administration.

Once parent-teacher contact has been made, agreed-on strategies and actions should be implemented. If the problem is not resolved and more intervention is needed, the next step in most schools is to proceed through a multidisciplinary team process, whatever the team may be called in that school district. Throughout this section (and book), this team will be referred to as the student support team (SST).

The SST is part of a schoolwide general education process for problem solving and supporting students in need of additional assistance. The intent of the SST process is to provide support and strategies to teachers in their efforts to help individual students who are at risk or struggling academically, behaviorally, or with social-emotional issues. The SST is a forum for teachers to request help from the team and to meet with a variety of school professionals to share concerns and strategize together a targeted plan of intervention for that student. It also serves as protocol in many districts for examining student needs and trying to resolve issues as part of the prereferral to the special education process. SSTs have been in place in most schools for a number of years.

The process and SST protocol vary from district to district and school to school. The SST meetings, which meet on a regularly scheduled basis, should be designed to efficiently discuss concerns about individual students, strategize appropriate interventions, monitor progress, and follow up with further action for those particular students on the agenda.

Depending on the staff available at the school (and their schedules), members of the team vary. For example, the team generally includes a school administrator; special educator (resource teacher); guidance counselor, social worker, or psychologist; and classroom teacher(s). Other school or district staff with various roles and expertise may be regular team members or participate in meetings as needed (such as the school nurse, speech-language therapist, reading or other subject area specialist, adapted PE teacher). Parents are generally requested to attend the SST meeting because their input is extremely important in the problem-solving and strategy-planning process for their child.

The Role of the School

When implemented well and functioning as it should, the SST (and the RTI) process is a highly effective method for early intervention, providing much-needed support to struggling students and their teachers.

The SST process benefits the school in the following ways:

- Provides the teacher with access to a group of colleagues who share information and expertise in order to help the teacher better meet the individual needs of students
- Assists the teacher in problem solving, strategizing, and developing a plan of appropriate classroom interventions
- Facilitates student access to additional school-based interventions and perhaps community-based supports and interventions (as needed)
- Provides teachers with an expanded toolkit or repertoire of instructional and behavioral strategies and adaptations that are useful not only for the targeted student but also for others with similar learning and behavioral challenges in their classroom
- Provides the necessary prereferral intervention documentation if a formal referral for special education is required
- Enhances the home-school partnership in efforts to collaboratively address student needs

Schools may have more than one team in a building, particularly those with a large population or high percentage of students in need of support. To be effective, schools must be creative in finding ways to meet more frequently and consistently, as well as expand on the resources and personnel in the building who can contribute and participate in the SST. For example:

- Establishing a few teams in the building with different members of support staff, administration, and teachers assigned to each team.
- Using a layered or tiered SST process and structure. For example, students are first discussed and a plan of action with strategies is designed in grade-level teacher teams, cluster teams, or house teams; if problems are not resolved at this level, then a school-level SST is scheduled with parents and other SST members.

The Role of Teachers

It is very helpful for teachers to follow through on preliminary steps prior to the SST meeting:

- Implement some strategies and interventions to address the areas of concern, and document their effectiveness
- Communicate with previous teachers
- Review the cumulative records and student data
- Collect work samples
- Share concerns and action taken with appropriate SST members at the informal level as appropriate, and submit a request for an SST meeting
- Establish communication with parents—notifying them of observations, concerns, attempts to assist, and so on

With such preliminary steps taken, the SST meeting is more productive. The team is in a position to recommend next-step interventions. Teachers should be prepared when meeting with the team to do the following:

- Describe the student's strengths, interests, and positive traits
- Identify and clearly describe their areas of concern about the student's functioning (academic, behavioral, social-emotional)
- Share data and documentation regarding the student's areas of weakness, and strategies and supports that have been tried so far

At the SST meeting, after the teacher and others (including parents if in attendance) share relevant information and observations about the student, the team then spends time problem-solving. They brainstorm possible supports, interventions, and strategies that can be tried to assist the student, as someone from the team records all ideas. A plan of action is developed with a few strategies and interventions decided on to try for a period of time, with a follow-up date to examine the effectiveness of the plan. This may involve either a follow-up SST meeting (for example, scheduled in a specified number of weeks) or a less formal follow-up meeting attended by the teacher, parents, and one or two members of the team, as appropriate.

SSTs may recommend and form an action plan that involves a number of possible interventions. The classroom teacher(s) may be asked to implement a few recommended strategies or accommodations and to keep data. Often particular team members will be assigned responsibilities, such as to help design and reinforce a behavior contract, consult and collaborate with the teacher on various strategies, arrange for more individual or small-group assistance to the student, observe the student in different settings, or meet with parents to further share and discuss concerns and strategies.

The SST members are also frequently the 504 team members. A good SST action plan for a student with ADHD (or displaying such symptoms) is often very similar to a 504 plan. After assessing and determining eligibility, many 504 accommodation plans involve basically rewriting the SST intervention strategies that are proving to be effective and adding any other additional agreed-on accommodations, supports, and information onto a district 504 form.

If parents are not attending the SST meeting, it is recommended that the school obtain their input by phone interview or by sending home a parent questionnaire or input form prior to the meeting. Regardless of whether a parent is able to attend the meeting, schools should communicate with parents and seek their input, as well as share a summary of the meeting and plan of action.

Multi-Tier System of Supports (MTSS)

Many schools are implementing Response to Intervention (RTI) and Positive Behavioral Interventions and Supports (PBIS) in their buildings. These are both very powerful and effective multi-tier systems of support. RTI is explained in Section 3.2, and PBIS is described in Section 2.7.

In some schools, the RTI process has replaced the SST process, or what was once the SST evolved and was restructured to become incorporated under the RTI model. In other schools, there may be both the SST and RTI teams and processes occurring. And some schools, unfortunately, have very inefficient systems of any kind to strategize about and support their struggling students and teachers.

Response to Intervention (RTI)

RTI is a single, integrated system for providing systematic, research-based instruction and a continuum of tiered interventions to students (tiers 1, 2, 3). Students in need of support are to be matched to the appropriate level of intervention, which is based on objective data from frequent progress-monitoring measures. This data guides the team's decision making as to the intensity of intervention necessary to address the students' educational needs.

Positive Behavioral Intervention and Supports (PBIS)

PBIS, also referred to as SWPBS (Schoolwide Positive Behavior Supports), is a framework or approach for school personnel to organize and provide evidence-based behavior supports and interventions through an integrated continuum. It is basically the same as RTI, but with a behavioral rather than instructional focus—a structure for creating a positive climate throughout the school with strategies and supports for all students to prevent behavior problems, and provision of progressively more intensive levels of support and intervention (tiers 1–3) to students in need, which is driven by data.

More about MTSS

These multi-tiered systems of support are powerful vehicles for transforming schools and improving outcomes for all students—particularly those with ADHD and learning disabilities or others who can easily slip through the cracks and fail to have their educational needs met. Creating and implementing systems such as RTI and PBIS in schools takes a great deal of teamwork and collaboration—involving the participation and commitment of multiple parties within the school and community committed to working simultaneously (not piecemeal) on several components.

The National Center for Learning Disabilities developed the NCLD School Transformational Model (NCLD, n.d.). This model identifies the following seven essential components to transforming schools through MTSS, all of which are proven by decades of research to be necessary and effective:

1. *Leadership.* Improve achievement for all students by improving education for students with learning disabilities.
2. *Professional learning.* Ensure that all teachers are comfortable implementing effective, evidence-based practices with fidelity.
3. *Empowering culture.* Involve the students and their families in the students' education; establish a problem-solving approach within the school; encourage collaboration.
4. *Curriculum.* Select basals, textbooks, and interventions that have an evidence base demonstrating effectiveness with the intended population.
5. *Instruction.* Implement strategies shown to be effective with the intended population.
6. *Assessments.* Determine special education eligibility with a range of assessments from informal, formative assessments through formal comprehensive evaluations.
7. *Data-driven decision making.* Commit to making decisions based on data throughout the problem-solving process.

Note: *For more information, see the RTI Action Network (a program of NCLD) website at http:// www.rtinetwork.org and NCLD's school transformation resources in Part 6 Additional Sources and Resources.*

Additional Points

- For the SST or RTI process to be effective, it has to be a priority in the school. Administrators must make every effort to resolve scheduling issues by taking such measures as providing coverage for classroom teachers if the meetings take place during school hours.

- For any plan to be effective (whether it is one generated at an SST or RTI meeting, a 504 plan, or an IEP), there must be measurement of results and follow-up for accountability. The best of plans fails if we don't revisit it in a timely manner and assess how effective it is.
- Recommendations for referrals for special education or an ADHD evaluation are best initiated through the SST or RTI team. Proceeding through the SST and RTI process prior to an evaluation for special education is not a requirement, but is highly recommended. It is an efficient means of communicating and problem solving. In the meeting, teachers, parents, and other members of the team are able to share information and observations with each other—discussing and strategizing ways to help the student. Parents can be provided with resources and recommendations when indicated regarding any screening or evaluations (clinical or school based), and team members can share with parents what will be involved if they choose to do so.
- Parents have the right to request a school-based evaluation at any time to determine if their child is eligible for special education, related services, or accommodations under federal laws protecting children with disabilities (IDEA and Section 504). Sometimes a school evaluation to determine educational needs and possible services and supports is initiated concurrently with a clinical evaluation for ADHD.
- Be aware that the law specifies that a referral for special education and a comprehensive evaluation may be made at any time. If a disability is suspected, regardless of the RTI tier (if the school uses the RTI model) or SST meetings that have or have not taken place, parents and teachers or other school personnel may refer a student for a special education evaluation.
- Parents need to be informed of their rights to request such a referral for evaluation, as well as be provided with written notice of IDEA procedural safeguards.

When parents request an evaluation under IDEA or Section 504 of the Rehabilitation Act of 1973, keep the following in mind:

- Parents may be asked whether they are willing to first discuss their concerns at an SST or RTI meeting (which should be scheduled very quickly and timely).
- Parents cannot be denied the immediate initiation of the IEP process if they choose it and make that request/referral.

If You Suspect a Student Has ADHD: Recommendations for Teachers and Other School Personnel

When you observe a student displaying symptoms of ADHD in the classroom, you should automatically attempt to deal with those behaviors by using strategies known to help with those issues. These strategies include, for example, environmental structuring, more cueing, prompting and external supports, organization and study skills assistance, and behavior modification techniques. Obviously this is simply good teaching practice, because all students who display the need should be provided with behavioral and academic help and support.

Teachers should always communicate with parents about difficulties the student may be experiencing. It is also good practice if concerned about a student to keep records on strategies and interventions you are using in your attempt to help the student, anecdotal records regarding the student's behaviors and classroom performance, work samples, as well as any phone contacts, conferences, or other communication you have had with parents.

It is suggested when concerned about a student to consult informally with appropriate support staff (such as school counselor, school nurse, psychologist, or special education teacher) for their advice and any assistance as needed. You may also want to communicate with the previous year's teacher(s) to see if your areas of concern were also of issue the prior year and, if so, to find out what strategies and interventions were used successfully or unsuccessfully by that teacher.

The next step in most schools is to bring your concerns about a student to your SST or RTI team—following whatever is your school's protocol for requesting the team meeting—to strategize about your student. If the school team feels that an ADHD evaluation should be recommended to parents, the SST or RTI team may do so at this time or in a follow-up meeting (after SST or RTI interventions have been implemented to determine the student's response to those interventions). The team members can inform parents of the school's role and responsibilities in an ADHD evaluation.

Caution and Tips for Teachers

It is important that school professionals be careful how they express to parents their concerns that a student might have ADHD, because there are liabilities that may be incurred if those concerns are not communicated properly. For example, school districts do not want teachers telling parents that their child needs to have a medical evaluation, because the district may be asked to pay for it. It is, however, an astute and helpful teacher who alerts parents to problems that often lead to the successful diagnosis and treatment of students with ADHD. Teachers do have a professional obligation to inform parents of their observations and concerns.

It is generally best to discuss with parents through a team forum the possibility that their child may have a medical issue or disorder causing the problems he or she is experiencing. Whether this occurs during an SST or RTI meeting or at some other time, it is recommended that at minimum, one other school professional (the school nurse, guidance counselor, administrator, or school psychologist, for example) should join the classroom teacher in having this conversation.

- Do not tell parents that you think their child has ADHD or make statements that sound as if you have concluded the child must have this disorder.
- Do not attempt to diagnose ADHD. You are not qualified to do so.

- Do not tell parents that their child needs to be evaluated for ADHD.
- Never tell parents that their child needs medication for ADHD.
- Share with parents the positives about the student (strengths, talents, character traits, behaviors), not just your concerns.
- Emphasize the difficulties (learning, academic, social) the symptoms or behaviors are causing *their child*, not the problems they are causing *you*.
- Be very explicit in describing objectively the behaviors of concern, and ask parents if they have seen any of the same behaviors at home.

Following are some possible statements to use in communicating with parents:

> "These are the behaviors I have been observing that have been causing your child difficulty at school and affecting his learning and relationships with the other children . . ."

> "Sometimes there are physiological reasons or medical causes for these kinds of difficulties [with paying attention, self-control, impulsive behavior, being highly active and restless . . .]. You may want to share these concerns with your child's doctor or consider an evaluation."

It is usually OK to make a statement such as, "I have had students in the past with similar behaviors, and some of them were diagnosed with ADHD. The only way to know if that's the case for your child would be through a professional evaluation."

School-Based Assessment for ADHD

In some school districts, a school-based evaluation is conducted for ADHD—for educational purposes and interventions. Schools that do such evaluations generally follow certain procedures and steps, which are completed in stages, and described in more depth by Anne Teeter Ellison (Dendy, Durheim, & Ellison, 2006). The evaluation generally begins with referral and information documented about presenting concerns.

A screening process may take place next, with the teacher sharing information briefly about the student's performance and some strategies that have been tried so far. Sometimes the teacher is asked to complete an ADHD behavior rating scale to measure the number of presenting symptoms of inattention, hyperactivity, and impulsivity. If there are a sufficient number of presenting ADHD symptoms on the rating form, a comprehensive assessment would then be initiated. This involves multiple measures, such as the following:

- Parent interview for obtaining information about the child's developmental, medical, and academic history, and family history, eliciting parents' input regarding their child's functioning, when they started noticing symptoms, and the degree to which those symptoms are affecting the child's or teen's life
- Teacher interview to obtain information about the student's academic, behavioral, and social functioning at school. The teacher may be asked to share information such as how and to what degree the symptoms and behaviors are causing the student impairment and interfering with success; the most problematic times and environments (for example, transition times, the playground); the child's strengths, interests, and motivators; and the interventions that have been tried and their degree of success.
- Behavior rating scales and other scales or questionnaires filled out by parents, teachers, and others who know the child well or who observe and interact with the child frequently, such as a school counselor or special education teacher
- Direct observation of the student in the classroom (by someone other than the classroom teacher) and in other school settings (such as the playground or cafeteria)
- Review of cumulative school records (including report card grades and teacher comments, standardized assessments, diagnostic reports, school behavioral referrals)

- Academic measures, such as curriculum-based assessments, observation of student independent work performance, and checking for number of assignments missing or incomplete
- Vision and hearing screening
- Other assessments, as indicated

Interpreting the Data and Next Steps

Once the data is gathered, it needs to be reviewed and interpreted—looking to see if *DSM-5* diagnostic criteria for ADHD have been met. For educational purposes, such as eligibility for a 504 accommodation plan, that is often sufficient. The ADHD screening and assessment procedures previously described are sufficient for determining if a student has "a physical or mental condition that significantly limits a major life activity," which would meet the criteria under Section 504 to offer reasonable accommodations.

ADHD is a clinical diagnosis. In some school districts, the school psychologist or other professional is qualified to make the diagnosis for the purpose of determining eligibility for special education and related services under the special education law IDEA. Other school districts require a physician's statement in writing that the child has ADHD in order to be considered eligible for special education under OHI—other health impaired—criteria. In that case, the school's assessment data and summary are sent to the physician, who then makes the official ADHD diagnosis. The physician may also be asked to describe how the symptoms that led to the diagnosis might impair the student's school functioning.

If the school team (which includes parents) determines that the ADHD symptoms are having an adverse impact on the student's educational performance, the student would qualify under the federal law IDEA to special education and related services. See more on eligibility criteria for special education in Section 6.4.

School Documentation and Communication with Medical Providers and Others

Communication with Physicians

School personnel can provide valuable input (observations, insight, data) regarding a student that is very useful to a clinician in the diagnostic process and in the management of any medical or psychosocial treatments initiated. Sections 1.3 through 1.6 describe the type of information that is recommended from teachers and other school staff who work with the student. The following are some examples of school communication to physicians that help inform the clinician about the student's functioning in the school environment and about steps that the school has taken so far. These communications are helpful in facilitating a collaborative effort between the school and clinicians.

> **No such communication is permitted without first obtaining written consent from parents enabling the school and clinicians to share information about their child.** Check with your school administration regarding any consent forms that need to be signed by parents before providing information about a student to the doctor.

Typically when a child is being evaluated by his or her physician for ADHD, the practice (doctor's office) sends ADHD rating scales, such as the

Vanderbilt or Conner's, to the school (or via the parent) for the teacher(s) and sometimes others who work with the student to fill out. In addition, it is recommended that the school consider sending additional information that is succinct and easy for a busy doctor to read through. Such information, such as in the sample letters that follow here, summarizing concerns and actions taken so far to address those issues, is helpful.

In the following example, Steven is a third-grade boy who was evaluated by the school district in second grade and found eligible for special education. He has an IEP and is receiving resource services (a combination of pull-out and push-in support in his classroom). Behaviors symptomatic of ADHD had been significantly affecting his educational performance since kindergarten. The school team had shared their concern that Steven needs more intervention and recommended that parents pursue a clinical evaluation.

Steven's parents agreed and granted the school permission (in writing) to communicate with Steven's physician and to share school data and information that may be helpful. The school team compiled the following for parents to give to the doctor:

- School testing results and reports from his psychoeducational evaluation
- A copy of Steven's IEP

- A one-page summary of information from the cumulative records that indicated his school history and interventions that had taken place in the past

- A one-paragraph teacher statement of her direct input
- The following letter, written by Steven's special education (resource) teacher

School Letter to Steven's Physician

Date: xx/xx/xx

Dear Dr. *Name*,

I am very concerned about Steven's ability to function at school, both in the large classroom and in the small-group settings. It has been my observation that Steven is unable to maintain attention or remain seated for more than a few minutes. His excessive movement and impulsivity (talking out inappropriately in class, frequently falling from his chair, difficulty keeping his hands and feet to himself, doing flips in the class when the teacher turns her back) are extremely disruptive. His behaviors impact his academic performance and also his social success.

His classroom teacher has already moved Steven several times because he is unable to sit near the other children without bothering them constantly. He typically cannot complete assignments without someone sitting directly with him and keeping him on-task and focused. Steven has been given preferential seating in the classroom (right near the teacher for direct instruction). We have been letting Steven use a study carrel (partitioned office area) to help block out distractions and give him more "space" for independent work times of the day. We have also recently begun use of a behavioral chart in his classroom for monitoring specific behaviors and communicating with parents on a daily basis. Our school counselor will be assisting the teacher with this, and providing rewards for successful days.

In the small-group setting, I have been using a great deal of structuring and cueing. Steven is also on an incentive program in the resource room, with positive behaviors earning him points (which are later applied toward a bank of rewards/privileges). Even with these interventions, and only four other students in the group, Steven is having significant difficulty attending to task and controlling his behavior.

Steven is a very charming, likable, friendly boy, who unfortunately has been struggling in school. We are willing and eager to do whatever is necessary and possible to help him succeed. We are pleased that Mr. and Mrs. X are pursuing a medical evaluation at this time to determine whether Steven has ADHD (in addition to his learning disabilities in visual-motor integration and auditory memory).

Enclosed you will find: the results of the psychoeducational evaluation conducted last spring by our school team, Steven's IEP, a couple of current work samples with a scoring guide (rubric) showing grading criteria, and a summary of Steven's school history (based on past report cards and other school records). We will be happy to provide any other information/data you need for your evaluation.

Our team is committed to working closely with his parents and with you to help coordinate efforts on behalf of this child. Please feel free to contact me at any time.

Sincerely,
Name, Title
School name
School phone
Email address

The following are other examples of letters sent to the student's doctor, along with other appropriate documentation, records, and reports.

School Letter to Lucas's Physician

Date: xx/xx/xx

Regarding Lucas Z.

To whom it may concern:

Lucas was referred to our school's student support team (SST) in first and second grades. He was also evaluated for special education in first grade, with an IEP held on [date]. Enclosed are copies of his IEP, assessment reports, and referral forms. He was referred for testing in first grade due to academic difficulty in all areas—reading, math, and written language, and significant difficulty staying on-task and controlling impulsive behaviors.

My notes from the SST meeting on [date] include the following comments from Lucas's first-grade teacher: "Lucas is very inconsistent in his attention to task. He seems to have an auditory strength and is bright. He is lovable, with an outgoing personality. His behavior is erratic and impulsive. He flits from one idea to the next. He is always blurting out answers, very active—can't stay still." His kindergarten teacher also described Lucas as needing to "develop self-control."

As a result of this meeting, the team worked with Lucas and the teacher. Recommended strategies were shared with his teacher. Lucas was to continue with small-group instruction from the reading teacher, speech-language services for articulation needs, peer/cross-age tutoring, and working with the counselor as well as the teacher on specific behaviors (with behavior charts and positive reinforcement). Our guidance counselor was to recommend some free or affordable parenting classes to his mother.

Later that year, the school tested Lucas. He did not qualify for special education because he did not meet the eligibility criteria for having a disability. (See psychoeducational testing and reports.)

This year (second grade) Lucas was referred again on [date] to the SST by his teacher, [name]. She was and is still concerned about the same behaviors. Lucas is noted as having a very high activity level, lack of self-control, and impulsive behavior. He is continuing to receive interventions of school counseling, small-group assistance, academic supports/tutoring, and many in-class interventions (change of seating, behavior modification, close communication between teacher and parent, a lot of direct assistance for much of the day). The team has met with Lucas's mother and discussed our recommendation that she share these concerns with you to see if a medical evaluation is indicated.

We are very concerned about Lucas. He continues to receive maximum intervention within general education. His behaviors are continuing to interfere with his success in the classroom. We appreciate your assistance in helping this child.

Please feel free to contact me, his classroom teacher, or other members of our team. We are happy to provide any other information you need. Our contact information is below. Thank you.

Sincerely,
Name, Title
School phone / email

School Letter to Christina's Physician

Date: xx/xx/xx

Dear Dr. *Name*:

I am writing this letter regarding Christina T. to provide you with past and current school observations, concerns, and most recent diagnostic information. Christina has attended Parker Elementary School since kindergarten, and is currently in second grade. She was evaluated last year due to her academic difficulties, and was found to have specific learning disabilities in visual processing skills (visual sequential memory, visual perception, and visual-motor integration). Christina was certified into special education and has been receiving services and supports through the resource program for the past year and a half.

Christina is a beautiful, very sweet little girl who tries hard, has a positive attitude, and wants to please. She is motivated and likes school. All teachers working with Christina since kindergarten observe that she is also very distractible, has significant difficulty focusing and attending to task, and has a high activity level. Christina talks/jabbers incessantly, is in constant motion, and has great difficulty remaining in her seat or sitting on the rug (sliding, rolling, tapping hands and feet, and so on). With gentle reminders and cues, she tries to control her behavior, but clearly it is not something she is able to do.

As Christina is one of my students, I work with her in small group daily for forty minutes three times a week (in the resource room), and in the classroom setting twice a week. She has an outstanding classroom teacher, who is very skilled at teaching children with attention and learning difficulties and willingly implements several accommodations to address her special needs. For example: Christina receives in her classroom:

- Preferential seating and many opportunities for movement provided by her flexible teacher
- Prompts/cues/reminders
- Use of timers and incentives/rewards to increase on-task behavior
- Modified/adjusted assignments
- Extra help and support on reading and writing tasks
- Behavior modification approaches

We have requested that Mr. and Mrs. T. bring this to your attention, so that you are aware of Christina's school functioning. Our school team will be happy to provide any further information you may need.

Sincerely,
Name, Title
School
Phone number

Communication between Schools

The following letter is a communication from an elementary school to the "feeder" middle school that will be receiving this particular student the following September. The purpose of this letter is to alert the middle school team of an incoming student with very significant needs. The letter is also a plea for the school to do whatever is possible to keep trying to obtain the needed help for this boy. It also illustrates the frustration and reality that, unfortunately, teachers and schools have to deal with: children with severe needs that we cannot effectively meet because "our hands are tied." Frequently (due to lack of funds), programs don't exist or the child doesn't qualify for them. In this case, the parent did not agree to school recommendations for program placement. Without parental approval, the school cannot act.

Letter Regarding Damien

Date: xx/xx/xx

Student: Damien N.
Birth date: xx/xx/xx
Grade: xx

Dear *[name of resource/special education teacher at the middle school]*,

Having worked intensively with Damien over the past few years, I would like to share my observations and recommendations at this time. Our team's concern for Damien is that he may very likely have a difficult time adjusting and coping next year in middle school. Our hope is that he will receive a great deal of assistance in his transition to the middle school setting, especially with his social and emotional needs.

Damien has been medically diagnosed as having ADHD, as well as having learning disabilities. He displays all of the classic behaviors associated with ADHD, including high activity level/great need for mobility, extreme distractibility and impulsive behavior, difficulty staying seated, always touching and playing with objects around him and invading others' space, very sensitive to noises around him, and oblivious to social cues—resulting in difficulty functioning with adults and peers.

Damien has episodes of out-of-control behavior during which he is unable to remain in the classroom. On these days, he typically has not received his medication upon coming to school. Teachers need to be aware of and sensitive to his needs. Usually, when Damien receives his medication, he is capable of far more self-control, and the above-mentioned behaviors are more manageable.

Damien is a bright, capable boy with a lot of potential. He has a strong interest in and aptitude for math and science. We would like to see him have every opportunity to participate and advance in math and the sciences. Damien has always been weak in reading and language skills (writing and oral expression), due to a learning disability in auditory sequential memory skills and phonological processing. In spite of some difficulty, Damien still has the ability to do most of the work at his grade level (with some modification and assistance).

He underachieves in his classes every year. Due to his low tolerance for frustration, Damien often resists or refuses to do work that he perceives as too difficult. Often days go by when he will not produce

(continued)

any work in class or only a minimal amount. Great care has always gone into placing Damien in classes with teachers who are nurturing, sensitive, and skilled in working with children with special needs.

Damien is a kind and affectionate boy. He is very good with younger children and is sweet and warmhearted. He is also quick to anger and is often upset and tearful. Adults who know him well can see beyond his behaviors, which are often disruptive and inappropriate. He is very vulnerable and likely to be "led into trouble" if the opportunity arises.

Our school team has been concerned about the strong social and emotional factors that impede his functioning at school. He is very easily frustrated and "shuts down" frequently in class and in the resource room. When he doesn't feel like working or participating (which occurs frequently and unpredictably), he will not open books, join the rest of the class, or respond when the teacher speaks to him or asks him questions.

Damien is very moody, and it is impossible to predict how he will function on any particular day. His moods and behavior fluctuate drastically. He very rarely smiles or shows signs of being happy at school. He is quiet, soft-spoken, and rather shy. Often he appears sullen and possibly depressed.

Socially, he has a very difficult time and has few friends at school. Other children basically tolerate him, but don't seek him out as a friend. Damien does not pick up on social cues (facial expressions, tone of voice, and so forth) as most children do. This causes him trouble and conflict with others. He is often in the middle of a conflict and frequently is not aware of his part in it. Damien has received a great deal of counseling in school, including training/assistance in conflict resolution, dealing with anger and frustration appropriately, social skills groups, and so on. However, his needs are such that in-school counseling is not sufficient.

We have spoken to Damien's mother on several occasions regarding the importance of having him see his physician for a medical follow-up. His medication may need to be regulated or changed. We feel he needs outside counseling and more assistance/intervention than we have been able to provide at school to address his behavioral and social-emotional needs.

As you can see (attached assessments, IEPs, recommendations), our team has been very concerned about Damien for several years. Every school year, we have had several team meetings regarding how to best meet his needs. Damien's mother is very difficult to get in touch with and often does not speak to us when we call. We have written and sent certified letters, have made every effort to accommodate his mother's requests in scheduling meetings, and involved a parent facilitator. Damien has had extensive assessment. In addition to annual review meetings, we have conducted a few "review of placement" IEP meetings, as well. Damien has qualified and been eligible for more intensive special education services in smaller class settings that may have better addressed his needs. However, his mother has never agreed to nor permitted a change of placement or followed team recommendations for more intervention.

We hope that Damien will be able to make a smooth transition to middle school, and that you will be successful in helping Damien obtain the appropriate care and assistance he needs. Please feel free to contact me at any time.

Sincerely,
Name, Title
Phone number
Email address

Teacher Documentation

Teacher documentation of specific behaviors exhibited by the student is very helpful to a diagnostician. Examples include emotional or behavioral outbursts, frustration exhibited by tearing up papers, inability to stay on task and work independently as noted by completing only one or two math problems during a twenty-minute independent seatwork period, and so on.

Teachers use a number of systems for jotting down notes to themselves to save as "mind joggers" for documentation, reasons for referrals, parent-teacher conferences, and other purposes.

Some teachers have a ring of index cards with each student's name on a different card. Whenever something occurs in class that the teacher wants to recall, he or she jots down the incident and the date on that student's card. Some teachers carry pads of sticky notes in their pockets. When they want to write themselves a note regarding a student, they use the sticky note and place it in their lesson plan book. Later, they transfer all of these notes into a folder that they maintain on each student. Others enter notes electronically. These anecdotal records, together with a collection of work samples, are very useful sources of documentation.

Letter Requesting Teachers to Complete ADHD Behavioral Rating Forms

This is an example of a letter that accompanied ADHD behavior rating forms that were provided by the parent to teachers.

Dear _____ (lists all teachers),

To help us track Adam's in-class behavior, and to ensure he is receiving appropriate medications, would you please be good enough to observe his behavior daily over a week's time and mark your observations on the attached Vanderbilt Scale?

If you would kindly return it in the attached self-addressed stamped envelope, I would be most appreciative. As Adam grows and changes in his new middle school environment, our goal is to help him achieve continued success in your classroom. Many thanks for your cooperation.

Sincerely,
Parent's signature
Cc: *Physician*

Sample Letters for Parents Requesting an Evaluation from the School District

If requesting an educational evaluation from the school district to determine whether or not their child is eligible for services and supports under Section 504 or IDEA, parents are advised to send a letter to the school's principal or the director of special education. It is best to send the letter certified with a return receipt requested.

The following components should be in the letter:

1. Your (parents') name, address, and other contact information (phone and email)
2. Date

3. School principal's/administrator's name and address (include school district and school name and street address)
4. Your child's full name, date of birth, school name, and grade/class
5. Your statement requesting the school district to evaluate your child under the Individuals with Disabilities Education Act (IDEA) and Section 504 of the Rehabilitation Act of 1973 to determine whether or not your child meets eligibility criteria under those laws for special education programs/services or accommodations and supports
6. Statement of your concerns regarding your child's struggles in school and reasons you suspect your child may have a disability impacting or interfering with his or her school success (learning, behavioral) and may be in need of special help. *Note:* Give some examples, such as your child's difficulty staying on task and focused, completing assignments without direct one-to-one support, controlling impulsive and disruptive behaviors, poor writing skills, or other academic areas. You may also want to include some of the steps or strategies that have been tried so far to help with these concerns.

7. Information, if it exists, regarding previous evaluations and diagnosed disorders. For example, if your child was evaluated by a medical or mental health professional and has a clinical diagnosis of ADHD, state that in the letter. Let the school know that the records/documentation of the disability can be provided on request.
8. Closing. You may want to say that you look forward to receiving the required paperwork or that you look forward to hearing from them soon to begin the evaluation process.

There are a variety of sample letters that you can use as templates. See links to such sample letters found in Part 6 Additional Sources and Resources.

A very basic letter would simply state something such as the following:

Dear_____,

My (son/daughter) attends (name of school) and is in the _____ grade, in Mr./Mrs. _____'s classroom. I am requesting that the school district evaluate my child to determine if he/she meets eligibility criteria for special education services (or a 504 accommodation plan). My child has been struggling with _____, and I am concerned that _____.

If you have any questions, please do not hesitate to contact me. I look forward to hearing from you.

Sincerely,

Federal Laws and Educational Rights of Students with ADHD

Some of the information in this section related to education laws may change when future IDEA amendments and regulations are implemented. This section is meant as a brief overview for reference. I recommend that you obtain more information about the current law and regulations from your state and local school district and other sources (such as those listed in the Part 6 Additional Sources and Resources).

There are two main laws protecting students with disabilities, which include ADHD:

- Individuals with Disabilities Education Act (known as IDEA or IDEA 2004)
- Section 504 of the Rehabilitation Act of 1973 (known as Section 504)

IDEA is the federal special education law that protects the educational rights of students with disabilities and governs special education. This law has been in effect since 1975, but it has been amended by Congress numerous times over the years. It was reauthorized by Congress in 2004, and the final regulations clarifying how the law is to be implemented by state and local education agencies were issued by the US Department of Education in 2006 (and others at the end of 2008). Section 504 is a federal civil rights statute that prohibits discrimination against individuals with disabilities and is enforced by the US Office of Civil Rights.

Another law that protects individuals with disabilities is the Americans with Disabilities Act (ADA), a federal civil rights law that was amended in 2008 and went into effect in 2009. The Americans with Disabilities Amendments Act of 2008 (ADAA) made significant changes that affected students with ADHD in that it expanded the eligibility criteria under Section 504.

There are different criteria for eligibility, services, and supports available, and procedures and safeguards for implementing the laws. Therefore, it is important for parents, educators, clinicians, and advocates to be well aware of the variations between IDEA and Section 504 and to be fully informed about their respective advantages and disadvantages.

Individuals with Disabilities Education Act (IDEA)

Overview

IDEA requires school districts to provide children with disabilities with a free and appropriate public education (FAPE), which means provision of special education and related services necessary for the child to benefit from his or her education. The FAPE is to be delivered in the least restrictive environment (LRE). This means that students should be educated and included to the maximum extent appropriate to their individual needs with their typically developing peers. IDEA includes rules and requirements for special education and providing specially designed instruction and related services to meet the individual needs of qualifying children with disabilities at no cost to parents.

An Individualized Education Program (IEP), tailored to the specific needs of the individual student, must be developed for each student who is classified with a disability and who meets eligibility criteria for special education and related services. It is a detailed plan that specifies the specialized programs, supports, services, and supplementary aids that are to be provided to the student, and requires measurable annual goals.

There are thirteen categories of disabilities under which a student who meets the eligibility criteria may qualify for special education and related services. Students with ADHD most commonly are found eligible under the category of other health impaired (OHI). Those with coexisting learning disabilities often qualify under the category of specific learning disabilities (SLD), and some with emotional and behavioral disorders may qualify under the category of emotional disturbance (ED). The IEP that is developed by the multidisciplinary team must address all of the identified areas of need. So, if a student with ADHD is found eligible under OHI, SLD, or ED, the IEP should include goals, supports, and accommodations that address the child's identified learning, behavioral, and functional needs. To determine eligibility, the school district must provide a nondiscriminatory comprehensive evaluation, which includes information obtained about the student's developmental and functional skills as well as academics.

IDEA requires that the disability adversely affect the student's educational performance (that it impairs learning or other areas of functioning) in order for the student to qualify for special education. IDEA 2004 makes it clear that eligibility is not based on academic impairment alone. The student is not required to have failing grades or test scores or to have been retained in a course or grade to qualify for special education and related services. Other factors related to the disorder that are impairing the student's educational performance to a significant degree (social, behavioral, executive function–related difficulties) must be considered as well when determining eligibility.

Chris A. Zeigler Dendy (2011) points out the important fact that students with ADHD may be passing classes primarily because of medication or herculean efforts of the student, parent, or tutors. If those supports are withdrawn, academic performance may decline significantly. Educators need to take that into consideration.

IDEA provides a broad array of protections for students with disabilities and their parents. There are a number of rules, regulations, procedural safeguards, and timelines that govern the referral and IEP processes. There are rules and regulations regarding how disputes between parents and the school district are to be handled with regard to the referral, evaluation, or any part of the IEP process or placement. Many state laws and rules go beyond the requirements of IDEA. Parents should become familiar with disability laws in their own state because there is some variance among states. There are extensive rules and procedures regarding how schools should promote positive behavioral strategies and interventions (as a preventive measure to avoid behavioral problems) and for how to respond when a student with a disability requires disciplinary action for more serious behaviors and breaking of school rules. For more on this topic, see the information in the section "Disciplining Students with Disabilities under IDEA 2004."

Parents have many rights under the law, such as the rights to access to their child's educational records (including all testing results), to be notified of any proposed change in programs or services, to revoke consent at any time to their child's participation in special education, and to due process and other ways to resolve disputes when in disagreement with the school. To avoid litigation, the law gives parents and schools the right to request an impartial hearing and a resolution session, which is an alternative to mediation, prior to a due process hearing. Parents have a right to file a due process complaint with their local school district when issues cannot be resolved. An impartial hearing officer hears these cases.

IDEA requires provision of services and supports for the child to benefit from his or her education, not to maximize the child's potential. Special education is a service, not a place, which may include many settings (the regular classroom, a resource room, a special education class placement, or alternative setting). Most students with ADHD who qualify for special education are served in the general education classroom for at least most of the school day. Placement is a team decision based on the student's needs.

IDEA provides eligible students with related services that are developmental and corrective, and other supportive services necessary for them to benefit from special education. These services include the following: speech-language pathology, occupational therapy, counseling services, psychological services, transportation, medical services, school health services, parent training and counseling, and social work services.

The IEP Process

The IEP process begins when a student is referred for evaluation because of a suspected disability, and a process of formal evaluation is initiated to determine eligibility. The IEP does not go into effect until parents sign and thereby agree to the plan.

Referral and Evaluation

- Parents or school personnel may refer a child, requesting an evaluation to determine eligibility for special education and related services. Requests for evaluation should be made in writing to the school or district (usually to the principal or director of special education). A referral may be made by parents, school personnel, school district staff, or other persons with knowledge about the student.

- Once a referral is made, the school staff review the child's functioning and school performance to determine whether they believe that an evaluation is needed. If the staff does agree that an evaluation is necessary, parents are given written notification of the referral, proposed testing, timelines, and other information. The assessment plan developed by the school's multidisciplinary team must address all areas of suspected disability. Parents must give informed and written consent to any testing.

- After parents or guardians are informed of their rights and have given consent to the assessment plan, the child receives a comprehensive evaluation by the multidisciplinary team of school professionals. A variety of nondiscriminatory assessment tools and strategies must be used to gather relevant functional, developmental, and academic information about the child, including information provided by the parent. This information may include any independent educational evaluations by competent professionals that the parents provide.

- Under IDEA 2004, schools are given sixty calendar days to complete the evaluation from the date parents give their written consent (unless the state law provides otherwise). When more intensive interventions are being implemented as part of the RTI process and early intervening services (EIS), generally there is agreement among parents and teachers to delay opening the sixty-day timeline for evaluation. As noted earlier, parents have the right to request an evaluation at any time—even within an RTI system.

- IDEA 2004 added the requirement that the evaluation is to be conducted in the "language and form most likely to yield accurate information."

- Reevaluation occurs every three years unless the parent and school district agree that a reevaluation is not necessary at that time. IEPs are to be reviewed annually (or sooner if needed).

- If there is disagreement about whether a child needs an evaluation, parents or the district have a right to a due process hearing.

The Individualized Education Program (IEP)

If the student is found to have a qualifying disability that is causing an adverse educational impact to the degree that special education and related services are needed, the IEP is then developed. The IEP, developed by a multidisciplinary team, including the child's parents, is tailored to meet the individual needs of the student and is the guide for every educational decision made.

IEP Team Members

Writing the IEP is a collaborative effort by the IEP team, composed at a minimum of the following people:

- The child's parents or guardians
- Not fewer than one regular education teacher of the child (if the child is, or may be, participating in the regular education environment)
- Not fewer than one special education teacher or provider of the child
- An individual (usually the school psychologist) who can interpret the instructional implications of the evaluation results
- A local school representative who is qualified to provide or supervise the provision of special education to the child and is knowledgeable about the general education curriculum and about the availability of resources
- Others (at the discretion of the parent or agency) who have knowledge or special expertise regarding the child
- The student with the disability, when appropriate

IEP Contents

IDEA has very specific requirements as to the content of the IEP:

- A statement identifying the child's disability or disabilities

- Present levels of educational performance (academic, developmental, and functional) provided in each area of need, which should be described in such a way that it is a baseline for measuring and determining progress over time
- A statement of how the child's disability affects his or her learning, participation, and progress in the general education curriculum
- Measurable annual goals designed to enable the student to be involved in and make progress in the general education curriculum and meet other needs resulting from the disability
- A description of how the child's progress toward meeting the annual goals will be measured
- A statement of the special education and related services, supplementary aids and services (based on peer-reviewed research to the extent practicable), and any program modifications or supports to be provided to the child or on behalf of the child (such as support for the classroom teacher)
- The extent (if any) to which the child will not participate with nondisabled children in the regular class and other school activities
- A statement of any individual accommodations or modifications that are necessary to measure the academic achievement and functional performance of the child on state and district-wide assessments
- The starting date, frequency, duration, and location of services of all special education, related services, and supplementary aids and supports
- A statement of the assistive technology and assistive technology services the child may need to benefit from his or her education
- Transition goals and services that must be in place no later than by the time the student is sixteen years of age—that is, education and training goals to help students with disabilities make a transition to work or further education and independent living after high school

Other Points Regarding IEPs

- When developing an IEP, the team needs to consider the student's strengths, not just deficits, and the parents' concerns and input about the student's functioning at home and school.
- The team needs to discuss and consider special factors depending on the needs of the child—for example, if the child's behaviors are interfering with his or her learning or the learning of others.

Eligibility for Students with ADHD under OHI or SLD Categories

Most students with ADHD who will qualify for special education will meet eligibility criteria under the disability category *other health impaired* (OHI).

OHI Eligibility Criteria

- The child has a chronic or acute health problem. (ADD and ADHD are chronic health problems that are specifically listed in IDEA, among others, such as diabetes, epilepsy, and Tourette Syndrome.)
- This health problem causes "limited strength, vitality, or alertness" in the educational environment, which includes limited alertness to educational tasks because of heightened alertness to environmental stimuli.
- This disabling condition results in an adverse effect on the child's educational performance to the extent that special education is needed. *Note:* The adverse effect on educational performance is not limited to academics. It can also include impairments in other aspects of school functioning, such as behavior.

Some states and school districts require a physician's medical diagnosis or confirmation of ADD or ADHD to qualify a student under OHI; others do not require it. Check with your local school district regarding specific requirements for an OHI diagnosis. The school's multidisciplinary team will gather relevant information and determine through their evaluation process and school-based assessment whether the student meets OHI criteria.

The Office of Special Education and Rehabilitative Services (OSERS) in the US Department of Education, in response to requests to clarify IDEA regulations, did so in "Q and A: Questions and Answers on IEP's, Evaluations, and Reevaluations." The following is OSERS' answer to the question of whether assessments and other evaluation measures used to determine eligibility for special education and related services include a doctor's medical diagnosis, particularly for children suspected of having autism or ADD/ADHD:

Under 34 CFR §300.306(c)(1)(i), in interpreting evaluation data for the purpose of determining whether the child is a child with a disability under Part B of the IDEA and the educational needs of the child, the group of qualified professionals and the parent must draw upon information from a variety of sources, including aptitude and achievement tests, parent input, and teacher recommendations, as well as information about the child's physical condition, social or cultural background, and adaptive behavior. Under 34 CFR §300.306(c)(1)(ii), the public agency must ensure that information obtained from all of these sources is documented and carefully considered. There is nothing in the IDEA or the Part B regulations that would prevent a public agency from obtaining a medical diagnosis prior to determining whether the child has a particular disability and the educational needs of the child. Also, there is nothing in the IDEA or the Part B regulations that would prohibit a State from requiring that a medical diagnosis be obtained for purposes of determining whether a child has a particular disability, such as attention deficit disorder/attention deficit hyperactivity disorder or autism, provided the medical diagnosis is obtained at public expense and at no cost to the parents and is not used as the sole criterion for determining an appropriate educational program for the child. (US Department of Education, 2011)

Specific Learning Disability (SLD) Eligibility Criteria

Many children and teens with ADHD have coexisting learning disabilities (approximately 25 to 50 percent), and those students often meet eligibility criteria under the category of specific learning disability (SLD).

IDEA 2004 and the regulations issued by the Department of Education in 2006 and 2008 changed the way schools can identify students with learning disabilities and find them eligible for special education and related services. According to the law, a state

- Must not require the use of a severe discrepancy between intellectual ability and achievement for determining whether a child has a specific learning disability
- Must permit the use of a process based on the child's response to scientific, research-based interventions
- May permit the use of other alternative research-based procedures for determining whether a child has a specific learning disability, as defined in 34 CFR 300.8(c)(10)

IDEA 2004 provided an option for states and school districts to use Response to Intervention (RTI), instead of the traditional discrepancy formula between IQ test scores and achievement test scores, as part of the process for determining whether a child has an SLD and is eligible for special education. In addition to an RTI option, the 2006 regulations also gave school districts the option of determining a learning disability based on a pattern of strengths and weaknesses in performance, achievement, or both, relative to the child's age, state-appropriate grade-level standards, or intellectual development. (This is an alternative research-based procedure.)

Another part of the criteria is that the child does not achieve adequately for his or her age or to meet state-approved grade-level standards in one or more of the following areas, when provided with learning experiences and appropriate instruction: oral expression, listening comprehension, written expression, basic reading skills, reading fluency skills, reading comprehension, mathematics calculation, and mathematics problem solving.

Section 504 of the Rehabilitation Act of 1973

Section 504 of the Rehabilitation Act of 1973 (known as Section 504) is a federal civil rights law that prohibits discrimination against people with disabilities. It protects the rights of individuals with disabilities against discrimination in programs and activities that receive federal financial aid, which includes all public schools and many charter schools, private schools, and others; it is enforced by the US Office of Civil Rights (OCR).

Students with ADHD who may not be eligible for services under IDEA (and do not qualify for special education) are often able to qualify under Section 504 to receive accommodations, supports, and related aids or services depending on need, under a Section 504 plan. Even though there is no funding for providing services or supports required under Section 504, the OCR can withhold federal funds to any programs or agencies (for example, school districts) that do not comply.

Students who qualify for services under IDEA eligibility criteria are automatically covered under Section 504. However, the reverse is not true. Under Section 504, eligible students are entitled to reasonable accommodations in the educational program, commensurate opportunities to learn as nondisabled peers, and appropriate interventions within the general education program.

Section 504 is intended to level the playing field for students with disabilities so that their educational needs are met as adequately as those of nondisabled students. As noted earlier, Section 504 has different criteria for eligibility, procedures, safeguards, and services available to students than IDEA. However, many of the same protections mandated under IDEA are also mandated under Section 504:

- A free and appropriate public education (FAPE) to every qualified person with a disability, provided in the least restrictive environment (LRE) with his or her nondisabled peers to the maximum extent appropriate to their individual needs

- Supports (adaptations, accommodations, modifications, related and supplementary aids and services), based on his or her educational needs, to enable each student an equal opportunity to participate and learn in the general education program
- Equal opportunity to participate in all academic, nonacademic, and extracurricular activities the school has to offer
- A free, nondiscriminatory evaluation
- Procedural due process
- A plan to support the student in general education

Section 504 Eligibility Criteria

- Eligibility for protections under Section 504 is based on the existence of an identified physical or mental condition or impairment that "substantially limits a major life activity." Section 504 defines an individual with a disability as any person who (1) has a physical or mental impairment, (2) has a record of, or (3) is regarded as having such an impairment.
- The physical or mental impairment substantially limits one or more major life activities, which includes activities such as learning, concentrating, reading, and thinking.

Americans with Disabilities Act Amendments Act of 2008 (ADAAA)

Another federal law that protects individuals with disabilities is the Americans with Disabilities Act (ADA), a civil rights law that was amended in 2008 and called the ADA Amendments Act of 2008 (ADAAA). These amendments made significant changes to the ADA of 1990. Because the two civil rights statutes (Section 504 and ADAAA) are interpreted together, these 2008 amendments also apply to Section 504's rules, definition of who has a disability, eligibility criteria, and other factors. These changes under ADAAA had a direct impact on Section 504 and students with ADHD.

Changes to Section 504 as of ADA Amendments Act of 2008 (ADAAA)

There have been significant changes to Section 504 eligibility criteria as of the ADAAA:

- "Major life activity" has been expanded to include additional examples of major life activities, such as reading, concentrating, thinking, communicating, interacting with others, and major bodily functions. These include neurological and brain functions.
- ADAAA also provided for a broader and more inclusive interpretation of "substantially limits" that affects determining if a student has a disability under Section 504. Language was added: "An impairment that is episodic or in remission is a disability if it would substantially limit a major life activity when active." In other words, the limitation of a major life activity doesn't need to be constant.
- ADAAA also added that "mitigating measures" that offset the effects of an impairment (such as use of medication, hearing aids, and learning adaptations—including assistive technology or accommodations and services) can no longer be used when evaluating whether a student has a disability (except for the use of contact lenses or glasses that correct a vision problem). Schools must now evaluate under Section 504 without considering the impact of these mitigating measures in determining whether a student has a disability.

These changes broadened the definition of *disability* and enable more people with disabilities to be found eligible for protections under this civil antidiscrimination law, including students with ADHD.

Additional Important Information about Section 504

- As with IDEA, there must be a substantial negative impact of the disorder on the student's learning and school functioning in order for the student to be found eligible for a 504 accommodation plan. This is a school team determination after assessment of whether or not the student's disability is causing a substantial negative impact.

- As with IDEA, under Section 504 a student does not need to have failing grades or low academic achievement to show that the disability is substantially limiting learning or other major life functions. Other factors, such as a low rate of work production, significant disorganization, off-task behavior, and social or behavioral issues can indicate the substantial negative impact of the disorder on the student's learning and school functioning.
- The implementation of the 504 plan is primarily the responsibility of the general education school staff.
- A 504 plan is much simpler than an IEP—often very similar to an intervention plan that is created for a student at a SST or RTI team meeting, as described in Section 6.1.

504 Accommodations

Section 504 plans are to include some accommodations that are deemed most important for a student to have an equal opportunity to be successful at school. They do not include everything that might be helpful for a student, just reasonable supports that generally the teacher is to provide. Throughout this book, I describe many possible accommodations and supports that can be included in a 504 plan. Following are a few examples of some possible 504 plan accommodations:

- Preferential seating (near the teacher or a good role model, away from distractions)
- Breaking long-term projects and work assignments into shorter tasks
- Audio recordings of books
- Reduced homework assignments
- Extended time on tests
- Receiving a copy of class notes from a designated note taker
- Cueing and prompting before transitions and changes of activity

- Frequent breaks and opportunities for movement
- Assistance with organization of materials and work space
- Assistive technology, such as access to a computer or portable word processor for written work and a calculator for math computation
- A peer buddy to clarify directions
- A peer tutor
- Use of daily and weekly notes or a monitoring form between home and school for communication about school performance

> The 504 plan can also involve accommodations that are provided during nonacademic times and in school environments outside of the classroom, such as the lunchroom, recess, and physical education. Supports under Section 504 might also include the provision of such services as counseling, health, organizational assistance, and assistive technology.

Which Is More Advantageous for Students with ADHD: An IEP or a 504 Plan?

This is a decision that the team (parents and school personnel) must make considering eligibility criteria and the specific needs of the individual student. For students with ADHD who have more significant and complex school difficulties, receiving an IEP under IDEA is usually preferable for the following reasons:

- An IEP provides more protections (procedural safeguards, monitoring, accountability, and regulations) with regard to evaluation, frequency of review, parent participation, disciplinary action, and other factors.
- Specific and measurable goals addressing the student's areas of need are written in the IEP and regularly monitored for progress.
- There is a much wider range of program options, services, and supports available.
- IDEA provides funding for programs and services. The school district receives funds

for students being served with an IEP. Section 504 is nonfunded, and the school district receives no financial assistance for implementation.

- Generally speaking, an IEP carries more weight and is taken more seriously by school staff.

For students with ADHD who have milder impairments and do not need special education, a 504 plan is a faster, easier procedure for obtaining accommodations and supports. A 504 plan can be highly effective for those students whose educational needs can be addressed through adjustments, modifications, and accommodations in the general curriculum and classroom. In contrast to the IEP, the 504 process is simpler, has less bureaucracy and fewer regulations, is generally easier in terms of evaluation and the determination of eligibility, and requires much less with regard to procedures, paperwork, and so forth.

Disciplining Students with Disabilities under IDEA 2004

IDEA addresses the disciplinary actions that schools are allowed to take when a child with disabilities violates a local code of student conduct. There are protections for students with disabilities when certain criteria are met under the law. Because students with ADHD often have behavior difficulties resulting in disciplinary action, such as school suspensions, it is important for parents and school personnel to be aware of and understand this section of the law.

The information provided here is a summary of what is current regarding IDEA's regulations on discipline. I highly recommend that you read more in-depth information directly from the law in Part B of IDEA from 300.530 through 300.536, and in sources such as those listed at the end of Part 6. Also, because codes of conduct vary, parents should be familiar with the policies of their child's school district with regard to codes of conduct and consequences for breaking them.

> The law refers to school districts as local education agencies (LEA). *Schools, school districts,* and *LEAs* are terms used interchangeably in the following discussion.

Removal from School (Suspensions and Expulsions)

The following applies to students with disabilities:

- A student with disabilities may be removed to an appropriate interim alternative educational setting or another setting or be suspended for not more than ten school days in a row—to the extent applied to children without disabilities. During a removal of up to ten school days in one school year, schools do not need to provide the child with special education services as long as they also do not provide educational services to children without disabilities who are similarly removed.
- Schools have the authority to make additional removals of the child as long as it is not for more than ten school days in a row in a school year and if those removals do not constitute a "change of placement."
- A change of placement means that the removal is for more than ten consecutive school days or that the child has had a series of removals that constitute a pattern (which is determined on a case-by-case basis by the school district).
- A pattern of removals exists in these circumstances:
  — The series of removals total more than ten school days in a school year.
  — The child's behavior is substantially similar to the child's behavior in previous incidents that resulted in the series of removals.
  — Additional factors exist, such as the length of each removal, the total amount of time the child has been removed, and the proximity of the removals to one another.
- On the date when the decision is made to make a removal that constitutes a change of

placement because of a child's violation of a code of student conduct, the parents must be notified by the school district of that decision and provided with the procedural safeguard notice.

- The parent may request a due process hearing if there is disagreement with the LEA about the removal of a student.

Manifestation Determination Review

A manifestation determination review is a formal review by the LEA, the parent, and relevant members of the child's IEP team that needs to take place no later than ten school days from the time that the school makes the decision to change a student's placement. The LEA must reach a manifestation determination within those ten school days. The purpose of the manifestation review is to determine whether or not the child's conduct that resulted in the recommendation for suspension or expulsion (1) was caused by or substantially linked to his or her disability or (2) was a direct result of the school district's failure to implement the child's IEP.

The manifestation determination review team makes its decision based on a review of all relevant information in the student's file, including the child's IEP, any teacher observations, and any relevant information provided by the parents. In making its determination, the review team should consider such factors as the child's school program; environmental factors; home factors; the child's mental, physical, and developmental challenges; and the child's discipline history.

If the team determines that the behavior resulting in violating the code of conduct was a direct result of the school's failure to implement the child's IEP, it must take immediate steps to remedy those deficiencies. If the team finds that the child's misconduct was because of or had a direct and substantial relationship to his or her disability, then the team needs to immediately conduct a functional behavioral assessment (FBA) if one had not already been conducted and to write a behavioral intervention plan (BIP), unless one already exists. If the BIP does already exist, then the team needs to review and modify it as needed.

Placement for the student with disabilities when the review does determine that one of these two conditions occurred requires that the child be returned to the placement from which he or she was removed except when (1) the behavioral infraction involved special circumstances of weapons, drugs, or serious bodily injury or (2) the parents and school agree to change the child's placement as part of the modification of the BIP.

When the manifestation determination review finds that the behavior resulting in removal was not a direct result of the LEA's failure to implement the child's IEP, and the violation of the code of conduct is not substantially linked to the child's disability, then school personnel have the authority to apply the same disciplinary procedures as would be applied to a child without disabilities (although any special education and related services that are required must still be provided).

FBA and BIP

Section 2.4 of this book discusses functional behavioral assessments (FBAs) and behavioral intervention plans (BIPs). Briefly, the FBA is a problem-solving process of gathering and analyzing information for determining the causes and functions of a student's problem behaviors, the settings or environments most likely for those specific behaviors to occur, and the consequences that result from the misbehaviors. Once the IEP team has conducted the FBA, the information is used to develop a BIP that specifies what behaviors are being targeted for change and how that plan will be carried out.

More Rights and Requirements under the Law

School personnel and parents should also be aware of the following specifications under IDEA 2004 with regard to implementing a change of placement.

Case-by-Case Determination

School personnel may consider any unique circumstances on a case-by-case basis when determining whether a change of placement is appropriate for a child with a disability who violates a code of student conduct.

Services for Students with a Change of Placement

A student with a disability who is removed from his or her current placement (long-term suspension or expulsion) must continue to receive educational services so as to enable the child or teen to continue to participate in the general education curriculum (although in another setting) and to progress toward meeting the goals set out in his or her IEP.

What Are "Special Circumstances" under the Law?

School personnel may remove a student to an interim alternative educational setting for not more than forty-five school days without regard to whether the behavior is determined to be a manifestation of the child's disability if the child does one of the following:

- Carries a weapon to or possesses a weapon at school, on school premises, or to or at a school function under the jurisdiction of a state or local education agency
- Knowingly possesses or uses illegal drugs or sells or solicits the sale of a controlled substance while at school, on school premises, or at a school function under the jurisdiction of a state or local education agency
- Has inflicted serious bodily injury on another person while at school, on school premises, or at a school function under the jurisdiction of a state or local education agency

> There is more clarification directly in the law regarding the definition of serious bodily injury and dangerous weapons.

The Right to Due Process and Appeal

The parent of a child with a disability who disagrees with a school district's decision regarding change of placement may appeal the decision by requesting a hearing. Whenever a hearing is requested, the parents or the LEA involved in the dispute must have an opportunity for an impartial due process hearing.

The state or LEA is responsible for arranging the expedited due process hearing, which must occur within twenty school days of the date the complaint requesting the hearing is filed. Resolving disputes through alternative means is recommended when possible, such as through a resolution meeting or mediation.

Protections for Students Who Do Not Have IEPs

The discipline procedures under IDEA 2004 also contain the provision of a "basis of knowledge" that would apply under certain circumstances for a student who has not been determined to be eligible for special education and related services. If that child or teen engaged in behavior that violated a code of student conduct, he or she may be protected under this section of the law if the situation was such that the LEA had knowledge that he or she was a child with a disability before the behavior that resulted in the disciplinary action occurred. This basis of knowledge would apply under the following circumstances:

- The parent of the child expressed concern in writing to supervisory or administrative school district personnel, or a teacher of the child expressed concern that the child is in need of special education and related services.
- The parent of the child requested an evaluation of the child.
- The teacher of the child or other school personnel expressed specific concerns about a pattern of behavior demonstrated by the child directly to the director of special education or to other supervisory personnel of the LEA.

This would not apply if the parent has not allowed an evaluation or has refused services, or if the child has been evaluated and determined not to be a child with a disability.

Part 6 References

Section 6.2

Dendy, C.A.Z., Durheim, M., & Ellison, A. T. (2006). *CHADD educator's manual.* Landover, MD: CHADD.

National Center for Learning Disabilities. (n.d.). NCLD's school transformation model: Seven components essential to whole system reform. Retrieved at http://www.rtinetwork.org/about -us/school-transformation

Section 6.4

Dendy, C.A.Z. (2011). *Teaching teens with ADD, ADHD and executive function deficits* (2nd ed.). Bethesda, MD: Woodbine House.

US Department of Education. (2011, September). Q and A: Questions and answers on IEP's, evaluations, and reevaluations. Retrieved from http://idea.ed.gov/explore/view/p/%2Croot%2C dynamic%2CQaCorner%2C3%2C (See Question B-2 under the category "Initial Evaluation Timelines and Determination of Eligibility.")

Part 6 Additional Sources and Resources

Cohen, M. (2009). *A guide to special education advocacy: What parents, clinicians, and advocates need to know.* London, UK: Jessica Kingsley.

Cohen, M. (2013). *AD/HD under IDEA: What you need to know about AD/HD under IDEA.* Retrieved from www.childadvocate.net/adhd_and_idea.htm

Dabkowski, D. M. (2004, January/February). Encouraging active parent participation in IEP team meetings. *Teaching Exceptional Children, 36*(3), 34–39.

Dendy, C.A.Z., & Zeigler, A. (2003). *A bird's-eye view of life with ADD and ADHD: Advice from young survivors* (2nd ed.). Cedar Bluff, AL: Cherish the Children.

Durheim, M. (2003). *Making the system work for your child with ADHD.* New York, NY: Guilford Press.

Hallam, S. (2008). Help teachers help your child. *ADDitude, 8*(5), 52–53.

Hallowell, E. (2007). Dr. Ned Hallowell on . . . Building rapport with teachers. *ADDitude, 7*(3), 21. Retrieved from www.additudemag.com/adhd/article/2494.html

Jensen, P. S. (2004). *Making the system work for your child with ADHD.* New York, NY: Guilford Press.

Klatz, M. B. (2006). Response to intervention (RTI): A primer for parents. National Association for School Psychologists. NASP Resources. Retrieved from www.nasponline.org/resources /factsheets/rtiprimer.aspx

Lamorey, S. (2002, May/June). The effects of culture on special education services. *Teaching Exceptional Children, 34*(5), 67–71.

Martín, J. L. (n.d.). Legal implications of Response to Intervention and special education identification. RTI Action Network. Retrieved from www.rtinetwork.org/learn/ld /legal-implications-of-response-to-intervention-and-special-education-identification

McIntyre, T. (2014). Functional behavioral assessments (FBA). Retrieved from www .behavioradvisor.com/FBA.html

Morin, A. (n.d.). Sample letters for requesting evaluations and reports. Retrieved from https:// www.understood.org/en/school-learning/evaluations/evaluation-basics/toolkit-for-parents -sample-letters-for-requesting-evaluations-and-reports

Morin, A. (2014). *The everything parent's guide to special education.* Avon, MA: Adams Media.

National Center for Learning Disabilities. (n.d.). NCLD's school transformation model: Helping all students succeed. Retrieved from http://www.rtinetwork.org/about-us/school-transformation

National Dissemination Center for Children with Disabilities (NICHCY). Sample letters: Requesting an initial evaluation for special education services. Retrieved from http://www .ldonline.org/article/14620/

National Resource Center on ADHD (n.d.). Sample letter requesting educational evaluation of child diagnosed with ADHD. Retrieved from http://www.help4adhd.org/sampleletter.cfm

Quinn, P., & Stern, J. (2009). *Putting on the brakes: Understanding and taking control of your ADD or ADHD* (2nd ed.). Washington, DC: Magination Press.

Richmond County School System Department of Psychological Services. (2014–2015). *Response to intervention/Student support team manual.* Augusta, GA: Richmond County Board of Education. Retrieved from Richmond County School System, August, GA, at http://www.rcboe.org /download.axd?file=54584e8b-df71-4096-876e-ada0761ab657&dnldType=Resource

Rief, S. (2008). *The ADD/ADHD checklist: A practical reference for parents and teachers* (2nd ed.). San Francisco, CA: Jossey-Bass.

Rief, S. (2015). *The ADHD book of lists: A practical guide for helping children and teens with attention deficit disorders* (2nd ed.). San Francisco, CA: Jossey-Bass.

Rief, S., & Stern, J. M. (2010). *The dyslexia checklist: A practical reference for parents and teachers.* San Francisco, CA: Jossey-Bass.

Sample letter to request accommodations for ADHD students. (n.d.). *ADDitude.* Retrieved from http://www.additudemag.com/adhd/article/792.html

San Francisco Unified School District Student Support Services Division. (2008). *Student success team manual.* Retrieved from http://www.sfusd.edu/en/assets/sfusd-staff/programs/files/special-education/SSTManualRev2008.pdf

Taylor-Crawford, K., Richardson, J., & Madison-Boyd, S. (2003, June). AD/HD: Cultural attitudes & perceptions. *Attention, 9*(6), 38–45.

Torres, D., Gill, M., & Taylor-Klaus, E. (2013). The parent's role makes a difference. [First of a three-part series, "Parents as Case Managers: A Roadmap for ADHD Management"]. *Attention, 20*(5), 14–21. Retrieved from http://www.chadd.org/Membership/Attention-Magazine/Attention-Magazine-Article.aspx?id=29

Tudisco, R. M. (2007). The four ATES of effective student advocacy: Evaluate, educate, communicate, and advocate. *Attention, 14*(3), 12–17.

US Department of Education. (2011). Building the legacy: IDEA 2004. Identification of specific learning disabilities. Retrieved from http://idea.ed.gov/explore/view/p/%2Croot%2Cdynamic%2CTopicalBrief%2C23%2C

US Department of Education, OSEP. (n.d.). Building the legacy: IDEA 2004. Retrieved from http://idea.ed.gov

Zirkel, P. A. (2009). What does the law say? New section 504 student eligibility standards. *Teaching Exceptional Children, 41*(4), 68–71.

Websites

ADDitude magazine has a "Your Legal Rights" section in every issue, which provides expert advice and answers to questions about ADHD and the law.

Center for Effective Collaboration and Practice, http://cecp.air.org/fba/

Center for Parent Information and Resources (CPIR), http://www.parentcenterhub.org. This website now contains the information formerly available at the National Dissemination Center for Children with Disabilities (NICHCY) and Technical Assistance Alliance for Parent Centers, which no longer exist.

Center on Instruction, www.centeroninstruction.org

Center on Response to Intervention at American Institutes for Research, www.rti4success.org/related-rti-topics/special-education

CHADD and the National Resource Center on ADHD, as well as *ADDitude* magazine, have free webinars from experts on a variety of topics, including the educational rights of students with ADHD. CHADD has a large number of resources for parent advocacy at www.chadd.org/Advocacy.aspx and its Parent to Parent training program (http://chadd.org/Training-Events/Parent-to-Parent-Program.aspx). CHADD and National Resource Center on ADHD information on educational rights of students with ADHD can be found at http://chadd.org/Advocacy/Education.aspx.

Council for Exceptional Children, www.cec.sped.org

Council of Parent Attorneys and Advocates, www.copaa.org

Family and Advocates Partnership for Education, www.fape.org

Federation for Children with Special Needs, http://fcsn.org

IDEA Partnership, www.ideapartnership.org

IDEA and US Department of Education, http://idea.ed.gov/. Federal site for information about the Individuals with Disabilities Education Act (IDEA).

IDEA Partnership (funded by the US Department of Education Office of Special Education Programs) informs families and educators about IDEA and strategies to improve educational outcomes for students with disabilities, www.ideapartnership.org

Individuals with Disabilities Education Act (IDEA), www.ed.gov/offices/OSERS/IDEA/regs.html

IRIS Center Peabody College Vanderbilt University, http://iris.peabody.vanderbilt.edu/

LD Online, www.ldonline.org

Learning Disabilities Association of America, http://ldaamerica.org/

National Association of State Directors of Special Education, www.nasdse.org

National Center for Learning Disabilities, www.ncld.org

National Resource Center on ADHD, http://www.help4adhd.org/, a program of CHADD, is the nation's clearinghouse for the latest evidence-based information on ADHD. It is an excellent source of information on Section 504, IDEA, and the educational rights of students with ADHD. See http://help4adhd.org/Understanding-ADHD/About-ADHD/Fact-Sheets-on-ADHD. aspx and http://help4adhd.org/Portals/0/Content/CHADD/NRC/Factsheets/Education%20 Rights.pdf.

Parent Advocacy Coalition for Educational Rights (PACER Center), www.pacer.org

Pinterest links on RTI, www.pinterest.com/sandrarief/response-to-intervention-rti/

Pinterest links on PBIS, www.pinterest.com/sandrarief/pbis-schoolwide-positive-behavior-support/

Positive Behavioral Interventions and Supports. US Department of Education's Office of Special Education Programs (OSEP) Technical Assistance Center on PBIS, www.pbis.org

RTI Action Network (a program of the National Center for Learning Disabilities), www .rtinetwork.org

RTI Central, www.rtictrl.org

RTI Classification Tool and Resource Locator (RTI CTRL), www.rtictrl.org

Wrightslaw, www.wrightslaw.com

Appendix: Forms

A.1: ___'s Daily Report

A.2: My Behavior Report

A.3A: Daily Report

A.3B: Daily Report Card

A.3C: Daily/Weekly Report Card

A.3D: Daily Behavior Report

A.4: Daily Monitoring Report

A.5: Self-Monitoring Behavior Log

A.6: Notebook Check

A.7: Homework Assignments

A.8: Homework Tracking Sheet

A.9: Book Club Roles

A.10: Book Club Culminating Activities

A.11: Five-Paragraph Persuasive Essay Rubric

A.12: Research Log

_____'S DAILY REPORT

Date_____

Times or Subjects	stays seated No more than __ warning(s)		on task No more than __ warning(s)		follows directions No more than __ warning(s)	
	+	−	+	−	+	−
	+	−	+	−	+	−
	+	−	+	−	+	−
	+	−	+	−	+	−
	+	−	+	−	+	−
	+	−	+	−	+	−
	+	−	+	−	+	−
	+	−	+	−	+	−
	+	−	+	−	+	−
	+	−	+	−	+	−
	+	−	+	−	+	−

My goal is to earn at least ___ pluses (+) by the end of the day (or ___% of the day showing great behavior and effort).

If I meet my goal, I will earn a reward/privilege of:

_____
Teacher signature

_____
Parent/guardian signature

MY BEHAVIOR REPORT

Name: _____

Teacher: _____

Week of: _____

BEHAVIOR	MONDAY		TUESDAY		WEDNESDAY		THURSDAY		FRIDAY	
	Before recess	After lunch	Before recess	After lunch	Before recess	After lunch	Before recess	After lunch	Before recess	After lunch
I followed the rules and my teacher's directions.										
I did my work.										

_____ smileys per day earns _____

_____ smileys per week earns _____

Parent signature _____

Yes, I did!

DAILY REPORT

STUDENT NAME_____   **DATE**_____

Teachers: Please write Y (yes) or N (no) by each behavior at end of class, and sign/initial. You may also write comments.

1st Period   Comments & Signature/Initials
_____ **ON TIME TO CLASS**
_____ **HOMEWORK TURNED IN**
_____ **USED CLASS TIME PRODUCTIVELY**
_____ **FOLLOWED CLASS RULES (no more than 2 warnings)**

2nd Period   Comments & Signature/Initials
_____ **ON TIME TO CLASS**
_____ **HOMEWORK TURNED IN**
_____ **USED CLASS TIME PRODUCTIVELY**
_____ **FOLLOWED CLASS RULES (no more than 2 warnings)**

3rd Period   Comments & Signature/Initials
_____ **ON TIME TO CLASS**
_____ **HOMEWORK TURNED IN**
_____ **USED CLASS TIME PRODUCTIVELY**
_____ **FOLLOWED CLASS RULES (no more than 2 warnings)**

4th Period   Comments & Signature/Initials
_____ **ON TIME TO CLASS**
_____ **HOMEWORK TURNED IN**
_____ **USED CLASS TIME PRODUCTIVELY**
_____ **FOLLOWED CLASS RULES (no more than 2 warnings)**

5th Period   Comments & Signature/Initials
_____ **ON TIME TO CLASS**
_____ **HOMEWORK TURNED IN**
_____ **USED CLASS TIME PRODUCTIVELY**
_____ **FOLLOWED CLASS RULES (no more than 2 warnings)**

6th Period   Comments & Signature/Initials
_____ **ON TIME TO CLASS**
_____ **HOMEWORK TURNED IN**
_____ **USED CLASS TIME PRODUCTIVELY**
_____ **FOLLOWED CLASS RULES (no more than 2 warnings)**

7th Period   Comments & Signature/Initials
_____ **ON TIME TO CLASS**
_____ **HOMEWORK TURNED IN**
_____ **USED CLASS TIME PRODUCTIVELY**
_____ **FOLLOWED CLASS RULES (no more than 2 warnings)**

Total number of yeses received today _____.

A minimum of ___ Yeses are required in order to earn agreed upon reward/privilege.

A successful day of meeting the goal will result in:

Student Signature_____   Parent/Guardian Signature _____

A.3A

DAILY REPORT CARD

	Monday	Tuesday	Wednesday	Thursday	Friday
8:25-9:45 am On-Task Self-Control Best Effort	1 2 3 4 1 2 3 4 1 2 3 4	1 2 3 4 1 2 3 4 1 2 3 4	1 2 3 4 1 2 3 4 1 2 3 4	1 2 3 4 1 2 3 4 1 2 3 4	1 2 3 4 1 2 3 4 1 2 3 4
10-11:20 am On-Task Self-Control Best Effort	1 2 3 4 1 2 3 4 1 2 3 4	1 2 3 4 1 2 3 4 1 2 3 4	1 2 3 4 1 2 3 4 1 2 3 4	1 2 3 4 1 2 3 4 1 2 3 4	1 2 3 4 1 2 3 4 1 2 3 4
12-1 pm On-Task Self-Control Best Effort	1 2 3 4 1 2 3 4 1 2 3 4	1 2 3 4 1 2 3 4 1 2 3 4	1 2 3 4 1 2 3 4 1 2 3 4	1 2 3 4 1 2 3 4 1 2 3 4	1 2 3 4 1 2 3 4 1 2 3 4
1-2 pm On-Task Self-Control Best Effort	1 2 3 4 1 2 3 4 1 2 3 4	1 2 3 4 1 2 3 4 1 2 3 4	1 2 3 4 1 2 3 4 1 2 3 4	1 2 3 4 1 2 3 4 1 2 3 4	1 2 3 4 1 2 3 4 1 2 3 4
2-3 pm On-Task Self-Control Best Effort	1 2 3 4 1 2 3 4 1 2 3 4	1 2 3 4 1 2 3 4 1 2 3 4	1 2 3 4 1 2 3 4 1 2 3 4	1 2 3 4 1 2 3 4 1 2 3 4	1 2 3 4 1 2 3 4 1 2 3 4
Homework: Completed Turned in Written down	Yes/Some/None Y S N Y S N Y S N	Yes/Some/None Y S N Y S N Y S N	Yes/Some/None Y S N Y S N Y S N	Yes/Some/None Y S N Y S N Y S N	Yes/Some/None Y S N Y S N Y S N
Teacher Comments: 1-Didn't demonstrate 2-Needs some work 3-Good Job 4-Excellent!					
Parent Signature:					

DAILY/WEEKLY REPORT CARD

Name: _____   Week of: _____   Daily Goal: _____   Points: _____ Points (total for day)

Period	MONDAY		TUESDAY		WEDNESDAY		THURSDAY		FRIDAY	
	Conduct	Classwork	Conduct	Classwork	Conduct	Classwork	Conduct	Classwork	Conduct	Classwork
1										
2										
3										
4										
5										
6										
7										
Total Points →										
Any teacher comments										
	Parent's Signature		Parent's Signature		Parent's Signature		Parent's Signature		Parent's Signature	

CONDUCT:
- Was respectful to adults and classmates
- Followed teacher directions
- Raised hand to speak (didn't blurt or interrupt)
- Stayed in assigned place (received permission to leave seat)

CLASSWORK:
- Participated in lessons & activities
- Started on assignments right away
- Came to class prepared (with homework and materials)
- Stayed on task with little redirection

Teacher Directions: Please enter a conduct score (0-4 points) and a classwork score (0-4 points) at the end of the class period. Base your score on how many of the four specific conduct/classwork behaviors the student demonstrated in your class that day.

Reward/Privilege earned for meeting daily goal: _____
Reward/Privilege earned for a successful week (A minimum of __ days of meeting the daily goal): _____
Parents, please sign nightly and have your son or daughter return the form to school each day. It is your child's responsibility to bring the form from class to class and to bring this report to and from school daily.

Daily Behavior Report for _____

	Stays in Assigned Place	Uses Class Time Effectively	Respectful to Adults & Classmates
Morning	😊 Keep trying	😊 Keep trying	😊 Keep trying
Recess			😊 Keep trying
Afternoon	😊 Keep trying	😊 Keep trying	😊 Keep trying
Specials	😊 Keep trying	😊 Keep trying	😊 Keep trying

Notes:

Daily Behavior Report for _____

	Stays in Assigned Place	Uses Class Time Effectively	Respectful to Adults & Classmates
Morning	😊 Keep trying	😊 Keep trying	😊 Keep trying
Recess			😊 Keep trying
Afternoon	😊 Keep trying	😊 Keep trying	😊 Keep trying
Specials	😊 Keep trying	😊 Keep trying	😊 Keep trying

Notes:

A.3D

Daily Monitoring Report

Student's Name _____ Date _____

Time/subject	Had needed materials yes=1 no=0 1 0	Stayed in assigned place yes=1 no=0 1 0	Showed good effort yes=1 no=0 1 0	Raised hand to speak yes=1 no=0 1 0	Followed rules and directions Rate 4-0 (see key below)	points
						/8
						/8
						/8
						/8
						/8
						/8
						/8
						Total /56 _____ %

Key: 4- Great job!, 3-Good - tried hard, 2-OK/Most of the time, 1- Had difficulty and needed lots of redirection, 0-Very uncooperative

Daily goal (number of points or %): _____

Teacher comments:

Parent/Guardian comments:

Parent/Guardian signature _____

SELF-MONITORING BEHAVIOR LOG FOR _____

(fill in the behavior)

STUDENT'S NAME _____ WEEK OF _____

How well did I do today?   5 – Great   4 – Very good   3 – Pretty good   2 – Not so good   1 – Poor

Subjects/Periods	MONDAY	TUESDAY	WEDNESDAY	THURSDAY	FRIDAY
_____	1 2 3 4 5	1 2 3 4 5	1 2 3 4 5	1 2 3 4 5	1 2 3 4 5
_____	1 2 3 4 5	1 2 3 4 5	1 2 3 4 5	1 2 3 4 5	1 2 3 4 5
_____	1 2 3 4 5	1 2 3 4 5	1 2 3 4 5	1 2 3 4 5	1 2 3 4 5
_____	1 2 3 4 5	1 2 3 4 5	1 2 3 4 5	1 2 3 4 5	1 2 3 4 5
_____	1 2 3 4 5	1 2 3 4 5	1 2 3 4 5	1 2 3 4 5	1 2 3 4 5
_____	1 2 3 4 5	1 2 3 4 5	1 2 3 4 5	1 2 3 4 5	1 2 3 4 5
_____	1 2 3 4 5	1 2 3 4 5	1 2 3 4 5	1 2 3 4 5	1 2 3 4 5

Directions: Rate yourself by circling 1–5 using a pencil. Your teacher should also rate how well he/she thinks you did (using pen). See if you agree or almost agree about your behavioral performance.

Comments: _____

_____

_____

NOTEBOOK CHECK

Student's Name: _____   Date: _____

Evaluator's Name: _____

_____ Your notebook organization is outstanding. Thank you for being responsible in keeping your notebook orderly.

_____ Your notebook is in satisfactory order.

_____ Your notebook is not in satisfactory order. Please organize it tonight. You may have it rechecked again tomorrow.

Homework Assignment

WEEK OF _____

Teacher's signature _____ **Parent's signature** _____

ASSIGNMENT	CLASS/ TEACHER	ASSIGNED DATE	DUE DATE

Homework Tracking Sheet

Name: _____   Date: _____

Class	Completed Classroom Assignments?		Homework	Upcoming Projects or Exams	Teacher Initials
	Yes	No			
Period 1	**Yes** **or** **No**			Date:	
Period 2	**Yes** **or** **No**			Date:	
Period 3	**Yes** **or** **No**			Date:	
Period 4	**Yes** **or** **No**			Date:	
Period 5	**Yes** **or** **No**			Date:	
Period 6	**Yes** **or** **No**			Date:	

Parent/Guardian Signature: _____

MISSING ASSIGNMENTS/NEEDS TO COMPLETE

Period 1: _____

Period 2: _____

Period 3: _____

Period 4: _____

Period 5: _____

Period 6: _____

Book Club Roles

Note to the student: These are examples of roles you might be asked to assume during book clubs. Read through each role and discover which kinds of things you might prefer to do. Of course, you might think of more innovative ways to perform your role.

Basic Roles All group members keep a record of their findings on sticky notes or other paper. This written account should be neat and contain few errors in spelling or grammar. All sticky notes should be completed on your scheduled meeting date. Group members may assist each other in finding pertinent evidence to support your points. The roles marked with an asterisk (*) are required, whereas the other roles may be assigned as needed or when ideas for more conversation are needed.

*Discussion Director Your responsibility is to think of good questions to ask during the discussion of the chapters that you just read. The questions should be open ended. Each person should be able to add on to the discussion. It is a good idea to have each person talk about something that he or she has marked in his or her book, such as a question, wondering, response back to the author, confusion, or a favorite or interesting part.

*Illustrator You are responsible for creating a visual picture of three different scenes from the reading selection and illustrating one on the sticky note provided. Prepare an illustration and write a brief summary of what you have drawn and why you drew it. What events led up to this picture, and what happened afterwards? Ask your group to guess what your picture is about before you tell them. Help your group members talk about the event.

*Connector You will use sticky notes to save places in the story that you or other members of the group can connect with or relate to. Think of things that you have in common with the main character. What do other characters from books you have already read this year have in common with this character? You should look for text-to-text, text-to-self, and text-to-world connections that are important to you as a reader and will help you hold on to the gist of the story and make meaning.

*Summarizer You are responsible for briefly summarizing what the group has just read. Make sure you share the key or main events from the reading. Use bullets to identify the main events. Ask your group members to agree or disagree with your account.

Conflict Connector Conflict is the main struggle that takes place in the story. Most stories center around four basic types of conflict:

- Character versus character
- Character versus nature (storms, forest fires, or tornadoes)
- Character versus himself or herself (being afraid, lonely, unhappy, or angry)
- Character versus the laws or customs of a society

In your role, you are to decide which conflict was the dominant one in the story. Identify three different ways the main character tried to resolve the conflict. If you were the main character, would you have tried to resolve the conflict the same way or in a different way? Explain your answer.

(Continued)

Reprinted from: Heimburge, J., & Rief, S. (2007). *How to Reach & Teach All Children through Balanced Literacy*. Jossey-Bass.

Book Club Roles (*Continued*)

Literary Element Locator   You are to mark places in the chapter where the author has used story elements such as similes, metaphors, flashbacks, foreshadowing, conflict, writing style, voice, point of view, and so on. Page numbers should be marked with sticky notes. Other elements, such as italics, conversation, chapter titles, themes, and special writing techniques, may also be discussed. Your group should be encouraged to locate these elements within the story too. You might ask them to find the element on page ___.When someone finds it, ask him or her to tell the rest of the group if it is at the top, middle, or bottom of the page. You might ask someone else to read it back to the group. You can also take the group back into the story where there is descriptive language or other memorable parts.

*Word Wizard   Your job is to look for special words in the story that are difficult, unfamiliar, funny, or unusual. The words should be marked with sticky notes, defined by looking them up in the dictionary, and used correctly in a sentence. You might ask the group to locate the word on the page you found it and have someone read the sentence aloud to the group. Have one group member try to define the word and use it in a sentence. Use sentence strips so that all of your group members can see the word. Put the word on the word wall when you are finished with your group.

*Character Investigator   Your role is to help your group better understand the characters in the book. You should be watching for any changes in personal growth in the characters. Think of at least three characteristics of the main character. Look for ways that the character reveals himself or herself to you. Support these character traits with an example or evidence from the text. Consider what might happen to the character as the story progresses.

Passage Picker   Your job is to pick parts of the story that you want to read aloud to your group. You can choose parts that are funny, scary, interesting, powerful, sad, or engaging. Have your group follow along as you read the section to them. Then ask your group questions about their feelings about those passages. You might want to try different voices for each of the characters and read with the voice that you think the character would really use. You should practice your reading several times aloud so that you are fluent in your delivery.

Reprinted from: Heimburge, J., & Rief, S. (2007). *How to Reach & Teach All Children through Balanced Literacy*. Jossey-Bass.

Book Club Culminating Activities

Oral Language Activities

- Read aloud **key passages** using the voice of the character and your voice as the reader and tell why you chose those parts.
- Develop a **book talk**.
- Make an audio recording of your group members reading different parts of the book. Use **different voices for the characters** you choose.
- Choose **ten things from your houses** that represent the story. Bring them in a special box. Pull one out at a time and explain why the item is important to the story. Display the items on a table and label each one.
- **Impersonate the characters** in costume with props.
- Present a **newscast** reporting the events that happened in the book.
- Present a **debate** about one of the issues in the book.
- Put one of the characters in the book on the **trial of a crime**. Prepare your case, giving all your arguments and supporting them with facts.
- Pretend you are a **TV or radio interviewer**. Prepare an audio or video interview with a character in the book.
- Have a **group discussion** about why the author might have written this book. Did he or she have something that he or she wanted children to think about more deeply? If so, what was the message the author was trying to convey?

Word Study

- Create a **word challenge**. Find eight to ten words that might cause someone to have difficulty.
- Find **ten new words** from the text that you might be able to teach to others. Write them on sentence strips and put them on a chart. Read the word from the text. See if classmates can figure out the meaning.
- Create a **word game** to challenge your classmates to learn several new words or create a Word of the Day section for the word wall, bulletin board, or classroom whiteboard based on the new words that you encountered in your book.
- If you are reading a book with **foreign words** in it, such as *Esperanza Rising,* make a chart of at least ten of these words. Put the foreign word in one column, the pronunciation in another column, and the meaning in the last column. Make sure you know how to pronounce the words and practice them with the help of the class.
- Prepare a **crossword puzzle** using questions from the book.

Performance Activities

- Create a radio show or a talk show audio recording interviewing people about their feelings about the book, interviewing the characters, or interviewing the author about reasons for writing the book. Make sure you prepare eight to ten questions **before** the show.
- Compose a **skit** based on a part of the book.
- Create a **readers theater** script and act it out.
- Perform **hotseat**: one member of the group poses as a character. The other members ask the character meaningful questions about his or her behavior, actions, feelings, reasons for doing things, and so on.

(Continued)

Reprinted from: Heimburge, J., & Rief, S. (2007). *How to Reach & Teach All Children through Balanced Literacy.* Jossey-Bass.

Book Club Culminating Activities (*Continued*)

- Create a *video* of one of the scenes. Bring it to school for your classmates to enjoy.
- Produce a *live performance* using props and costumes.
- Role-play a *phone conversation or conference call* between two or more characters.
- Write and act out an *advertisement or commercial* for the book using a video camera.

Music and Art Activities

- Create a *song or dance* about the book.
- Create a *scene in the book* inside a cereal box, shoebox, or other type of box. Include a written paragraph to explain what is going on in the scene you have chosen.
- Use a camera to shoot *photographs* that retell the story.
- Create a *piece of art* to represent the book using painting, photography, collage, or other art media.
- Create a *set of puppets* or *character sticks* and perform one of the scenes from the book.
- Make up a *board game* to represent a part of the story or all of it.
- Create a *poster board*.
- Create a *musical representation* of the book. It might be a song, chant, or jingle. You might also have musical accompaniment.
- Make a *banner or mural*. You might want to divide it into sections.

Research Activities

- Look up information in books or on the Internet about the *history of the period or the setting* of the book. Inform your classmates about your findings.
- Research the author of the book. Inform your class about your discoveries.

Games

- Create a *Twenty Questions* game about the book.
- With your group, plan a *Jeopardy-type game* with $10, $20, $30, $40, and $50 questions. Also include a Daily Double.

Miscellaneous Activities

- Present a *book talk* in your native language.
- Create a *memory basket* with items representing events or themes in the story.

Activities Using Graphic Organizers, Diagrams, or Charts

- Make a list of the *major and minor problems* faced by the characters in this book. Talk about the solutions.
- Make a *sequence chart* with sentence strips to show the main events in the story. Paste them onto a large piece of paper.
- Create a *time line* of the events in the story. Consult your social studies book for the correct form.
- Create a *Top Ten chart* of what you should know about this book.
- If your book is in movie form, *see the movie or watch the video* with your group. Discuss how it resembled and how it differed from the book. Make a Venn diagram poster showing your thinking.
- Use two different *graphic organizers* to retell, sequence, or compare the story with another one.

Reprinted from: Heimburge, J., & Rief, S. (2007). *How to Reach & Teach All Children through Balanced Literacy.* Jossey-Bass.

Five-Paragraph Persuasive Essay Rubric

Organization and Content

- First paragraph includes a hook to capture reader's attention and interest.
- Thesis statement in first paragraph clearly states writer's position on issue and why reader should agree with writer's point of view.
- Body paragraphs include three main ideas or reasons defending position on issue.
- Each main idea or reason is backed up with supporting details or evidence to defend writer's side of the argument.
- The counterargument or rebuttal on the issue is also given to address reader's concerns.
- A satisfying concluding paragraph restates thesis statement and writer's case for or against the topic.
- Smooth flow and transitions between paragraphs.
- A convincing case is presented for writer's side of the argument.

Scoring Guide

4-Demonstrates seven to eight of the above criteria.
3-Demonstrates five to six of the above criteria.
2-Demonstrates three to four of the above criteria.
1-Demonstrates less than three of the above and/or contains less than five paragraphs.

Language Usage, Spelling, Mechanics, and Neatness

- Complete sentences throughout that make sense (no run-ons)
- Descriptive vocabulary and word choice
- A variety of sentence beginnings and lengths
- Correct spelling most of the time
- Correct punctuation most of the time
- Correct use of capitalization most of the time
- Effort made to edit and correct mechanics and spelling errors
- Neat and legible final product

Scoring Guide

4-Demonstrates seven to eight of the above criteria.
3-Demonstrates five to six of the above criteria.
2-Demonstrates three to four of the above criteria.
1-Demonstrates less than three of the above criteria.

RESEARCH LOG

Name: _____

Research topic: _____

Keep a daily record of the time you spend working on your research project. Keep an accurate account of what you accomplish during your time at work.

Date	Time Begun	Time Ended	Tasks/Accomplishments

Index

AAAmath.com, 327

AAP. *See* American Academy of Pediatrics

ABC Cursive Writing, 315

ABC Teach, 269

Academic challenges, 8; EF and, 24; instructional clarity addressing, 57–58

Academic skills, of kindergarten children, 68

Academic supports, 38

Academic testing, 30–31

ACCEPTS: The Walker Social Skills Curriculum (Walker), 54, 157

Accommodations, 37

Accountability, 201

Accuracy, in reading fluency, 269

Achieve 3000, 204

Acting out behaviors, 12

Activate program, 39, 240

Activation, 22

Active participation, student attention maintenance through, 179

Activity rewards, 101–102

ADA. *See* Americans with Disabilities Act

ADAA. *See* Americans with Disabilities Amendments Act of 2008

ADAAA. *See* Americans with Disabilities Act Amendments Act of 2008

ADD. *See* Inattentive attention-deficit disorder

Adderall, 43, 44

Adderall XR, 44

ADDES. *See* Attention Deficit Disorders Evaluation Scale

ADDitude, 77, 216

ADHD. *See* Attention-deficit/hyperactivity disorder

ADHD Rating Scale-IV, 30

Administrative support, 61

Adolescence: ADHD-related challenges, 74–75; challenges of, 74; coexisting disorders in, 75; LDs warning signs in, 78; mentor for, 79; needs of, 74–75; school supports for, 75–76; school transition for, 76–77; self-advocacy, 78–79; warning signs (red flags), 77–78

Aggressive behaviors, 12

Alert Program, 188

Alphabet Learning Center Activities Kit (Fetzer and Rief), 68, 268

AlphaSmart, 351, 352

American Academy of Pediatrics (AAP), 27, 35–36, 66; preschool children and, 66

American Sign Language, 177

Americans with Disabilities Act (ADA), 415, 421

Americans with Disabilities Act Amendments Act of 2008 (ADAAA), 421–422

Americans with Disabilities Amendments Act of 2008 (ADAA), 415

Amitriptyline (Elavil), 46

Amphetamines, 43–44

Anchor charts, 273

Anger, prevention of, 149–150

Animal Discovery, 288

Anne (case study): concern areas for, 380–381; follow-up for, 383–384; function level of, 380–381; intervention plan for, 381–383; profile of, 379; school history of, 379–380

Antecedents, 135

Antidepressants, 46

Antihypertensives, 46

Anxiety disorders, 10, 11, 12, 75

Apps: for handwriting, 315; for writing, 293; for writing difficulties, 306–307; for written expression, 299

Argumentative behavior, dealing with, 150–152

Arkive, 288

ARMS mnemonic, 303

Arousal, 22

Art activities, in book club, 445

ASD. *See* Autism spectrum disorder

Aspire Public Schools, 204

Assignment modification, 60

Assignment sheets, 214–215

Atomoxetine (Strattera), 46

Attention Deficit Disorders Evaluation Scale (ADDES), 30

Attention problems: mathematics and, 328; in preschool children, 65; in writing process struggles, 264

Attention-deficit disorder (ADD). *See* Inattentive attention-deficit disorder

Attention-deficit/hyperactivity disorder (ADHD), 3–6; behavioral rating form, 413; causes of, 15; clinical evaluation for, 27–29; clinical interview for, 29; coexisting disorders of, 10–12; complementary interventions for, 38–40; comprehensive evaluation components for, 29–31; conditions resembling, 12; current school functioning information and, 32–33; evaluation pursuing for, 31–32; knowledge of, 13–14, 57; labels clarification of, 3; observations for, 30; ODD and, 142; presentations of, 8–9, 28; professional evaluation in, 32; qualified diagnosis of, 31–32; qualities positive in, 18–19; risk factors for, 10; school history information and, 33; school-based assessment for, 404–405; statistics of, 9–10; strengths and interests development for, 40; student school success with, 57–61; suspected, 403–404; understanding of, 57

Audible, 288

Audio Bookshelf, 288

Auditory techniques: for multiplication tables, 243; for student attention, 177

Auman, Maureen, 297

Autism spectrum disorder (ASD), 11

Aventyl. *See* Nortriptyline

BADDS. *See* Brown Attention Deficit Disorder Scales

Barkley, Russell, 10, 21, 53, 55, 114, 152, 154, 237, 258

Barkley Deficits in Executive Functioning Scale–Children and Adolescents (BDEFS-CA), 24, 30

Barkley's Model, of EF and ADHD, 23

Barton Reading and Spelling System, 261

Bassarear, T., 325

Battelle Developmental Inventory/Screening Tool, 2nd ed. (BDI-ST), 67

BDEFS-CA. *See* Barkley Deficits in Executive Functioning Scale–Children and Adolescents

BDI-ST. *See* Battelle Developmental Inventory/ Screening Tool, 2nd ed.

BeeLine Reader, 271

Behavior charts, 70

Behavior expectations: of kindergarten children, 69; of preschool children, 69

Behavior management techniques, for preschool and kindergarten children, 69–71

Behavior modification, 52

Behavior problems: classroom transitions, 111–112; home, outside of, 113–114; out-of-classroom activities transitions, 112; out-of-classroom school settings, 112–113; in preschool children, 65

Behavior Rating Inventory for Executive Function (BRIEF), 24, 30

Behavior report form, 435

Behavioral intervention plans (BIPs), 54, 136, 137–138, 152, 157, 424

Behavioral interventions, 51–52

Behavioral rating form, 413

Behavioral standards, 98–99

Behavioral therapy, 37

Behavioral treatment: child-based, 54–55; home-based, 52–53; school-based, 53–54

Behaviors: ABCs of, 135; argumentative, 150–152; hyperactivity (*See* Hyperactivity behaviors); impulsive (*See* Impulsive behaviors); positive reinforcement, 100–102

Best Multiplication Songs Ever, 243

Biederman, Joseph, 17

Biffle, C., 102

Bingo board, 117–118

Bipolar disorder, 10, 11

BIPs. *See* Behavioral intervention plans

Birth complications, 16

Black, Beth, 294–295, 299–301

Blended learning, 203; benefits of, 203–204; models of, 204; technology, 204

Bodily-kinesthetic intelligence, 193

Book club: activity culmination, 444–445; roles in, 442–443. *See also* Classroom book club

Bookshare, 275

BOTEC mnemonic, 294

Boyles, Nancy, 283

Brain: birth injury of, 16; chemical (neurotransmitter) inefficiency, 15; delayed maturation of, 14–15; diminished activity in, 15; executive functions and, 23; lower metabolism in, 15; structural differences of, 14–15

Brain Gym, 188

Brainology, 39

Brainstorming, 291

Brain-training technologies, 39

BRIEF. *See* Behavior Rating Inventory for Executive Function

Brigance Screens-II, 67

Brown, A. L., 284

Brown, T. E., 15

Brown ADD Rating Scales for Children, Adolescents and Adults, 24

Brown Attention Deficit Disorder Scales (BADDS), 30

Brown's Model, of EF and ADHD, 23–24

Buddy reading, 270; cross-age, 271

Bull's Eye Game, 134

Bupropion hydrochloride (Wellbutrin), 46

Buron, K. D., 147

Calendars, 214–215

Calming strategies, 148

Case studies. *See* Anne; Chloe; Vincent

CASL Handwriting Program, 315

CAST. *See* Center for Applied Special Technology

Catapres. *See* Clonidine

CCSS. *See* Common Core State Standards

CCSSO. *See* Council of Chief State School Officers

CD. *See* Conduct disorder

CDI. *See* Child Development Inventory

CEFI. *See* Comprehensive Executive Function Inventory

Center for Applied Special Technology (CAST), 191–192

CHADD, 32, 40, 53, 55, 66, 347, 383, 390

Chamot, A., 229, 233

Character webs, 281

Chart Jungle, 131

Chart moves, 116

CHECK (Change, Have, Establish, Create, Keep), 233

Check-in-check-out (CICO), 130–131

Chemical (neurotransmitter) inefficiency, 15

Chess, Stella, 365

Child Development Inventory (CDI), 67

Child Find, 67

Child Study Team (CST), 32

Child-based behavioral treatment, 54–55

Children: educational rights of, 391; school-based social skill interventions impact on, 154; symptoms of ADHD, 5–8. *See also* Adolescence; Kindergarten children; Preschool children

Chloe (case study): behavior of, 376; intervention plan for, 376–378; outcomes desired for, 376; parents of, 379; profile of, 375; reading level of, 375–376; school staff and, 378–379; work completion level of, 376; writing level of, 376

Choral reading, 270

Choral responses, 181

Chromebook, 204

CICO. *See* Check-in-check-out

Class Dojo, 199–120

Classmates, positive attention from, 70

Classroom: oral reading in, 271; school-based social skill interventions, 155–156. *See also* Group reinforcement systems

Classroom behaviors, disruptive, 12; addressing, 105–106; triggers or antecedents to, 104–105

Classroom book club, 285–286; benefits of, 286; etiquette, 286; folders for, 287

Classroom management: auditory and visual cues in, 99–100; effectiveness, 58; environment in, 97–98; environmental distraction limitation in, 103–104; environmental supports, 102–104; misbehavior in, 104–106; movement and, 102; music in, 104; positive reinforcement, 100–102; procedures and routines in, 99; rules for, 98–99; student accommodation, 102–104; student seating, 102–103

Classwide peer tutoring, 199–200

Clonidine (Catapres), 46

Clonidine, extended-release (Kapvay), 46

Cluster maps, 280

Clustering, 293

Coaching, 38

Cogmed Working Memory Training Program, 39, 240

Cognition disorders, in preschool children, 64

Cognitive flexibility, in writing process struggles, 264

Cognitive learning strategies, 231; auditory representation, 231; CHECK, 233; deduction/induction, 231; grouping/classifying, 231; imagery, 231; inference making, 231; note taking, 231; POW + TREE, 232; prior knowledge elaboration, 231; RAP, 232–233; RCRC, 232; resourcing, 231; S2TOP, 233; SCORER, 233; SQ3R, 232; SQ4R, 232; summarizing, 231

Cognitive strategies, 229

Cognitive working memory training (CWMT) programs, 240

Cognitive-behavioral curricula, 157

Collaboration, 59

Collaborative for Academic, Social, and Emotional Learning, 158

Collaborative Problem Solving (CPS) model, 142, 150

Common Core State Standards (CCSS), 68, 277, 323; English Language Arts Literacy Speaking and Listening Standards, 286

Communication: clarity of, 57–58; between home and school, 58; between schools, 411

Community Parent Education Program (COPE), 53

Comparison charts, 280

Compliment cards, unsolicited, 117

Comprehensive Executive Function Inventory (CEFI), 24, 30

Concerta, 43, 44

Conduct disorder (CD), 10, 11, 75

Confidentiality, 61

Conners Parent and Teacher Rating Scales, 30

Consequence, 135

Consistency, 69–70

Context clues, 272

Contingency contracts, 124–125

CoolMath4Kids.com, 327

Cooperation in the Classroom, 158, 203

Cooperative learning: ADHD and, 203; five elements of, 200–201; social skill teaching through, 202; structuring to achieve positive interdependence, 201

COPE. *See* Community Parent Education Program

Copeland, L. A., 147

COPS (capitalize, overall, punctuation, spelling), 304

Council of Chief State School Officers (CCSSO), 323

Counseling, 37

Co:Writer, 307

CPS. *See* Collaborative Problem Solving model

Cross-age buddy reading, 271

CST. *See* Child Study Team

Cultural sensitivity, in parent communication, 398

Curtis, M. B., 147

CWMT. *See* Cognitive working memory training programs

Daily monitoring report form, 437

Daily report cards (DRCs), 125–130, 156

Daily report form, 434, 436

Dawson, P., 77

Daytrana patch, 43, 44

DBRs. *See* Direct behavior ratings

"Default mode" network (DMN), 14

Defiant Children: A Clinician's Manual for Assessment and Parent Training (Barkley), 53

Dendy, Chris A. Zeigler, 22, 25, 49, 76, 77, 416

Denver-II Developmental Screening Test, 67

Depression, 10, 11, 12

Deshler, D., 284

Desipramine (Norpramin), 46

Dexedrine, 43, 44

Dexedrine Spansule, 44

Dexmethylphenidate, 44

Dextroamphetamine, 44

DextroStat, 44

Diagnostic and Statistical Manual of Mental Disorders (DSM-5): for ADHD diagnosis, 27; ADHD diagnosis in, 4; criteria, 27–29; diagnosis of ADHD, 4; symptoms of ADHD, 4, 5–6

Diamond, Adele, 69

Diet, 39–40

Differentiated instruction, 37, 192–194

Digital response tools, 181

Direct behavior ratings (DBRs), 131

Directed reading-thinking activity (DRTA), 283

Discipline: under IDEA, 423–425; BIPs, 424; case-by-case determination, 424–425; FBAs, 424; manifestation determination review, 424; school expulsion, 423–424; school suspension, 423–424; positive, 58

Discovery Education, 288

Diversionary tactics, 70

Dixon, E. B., 49

DMN. *See* "Default mode" network

Documentation, by teachers, 413

Dopamine, 15

Double-entry journal, 230

Draft, in writing process, 263

Draft composition, 298

DraftBuilder, 299

Dragon Naturally Speaking, 299, 307

DRCs. *See* Daily report cards

Dreambox Learning, 204

DRTA. *See* Directed reading-thinking activity

Dyscalculia, 319

Dysgraphia, 265, 313–314, 359

Dyslexia, 12, 64, 68, 75, 108–109, 258, 267; parents and, 260–261; signs of, 259; student instructions with, 259–260

Early intervention services (EIS), 197, 417

Echo reading, 270

Ed Helper, 293

Editing, in writing, 263, 303

Educational interventions, 37–38; special, 37

Educational rights, of children, 391

EF. *See* Executive function

EIS. *See* Early intervention services

ELA. *See* English Language Arts

Elavil. *See* Amitriptyline

Electronic devices, 181

Electronic feedback point system, 119–120

Electronically capturing ideas, 291

Ellis, E., 284

Emergent literacy skills, in preschool children, 64

Emotional regulation and control: calming strategies, 148; escalation avoidance, 148; prevention strategies for teachers, 146–148

Emotional self-control, 22

Emotional symptoms, 7

Empowering Writers, 297

English Language Arts (ELA), 68

Environmental factors, 16; for inattentive, distractible students, 184

Environmental modifications and accommodations, 58

Environmental structuring, 70

Escalation avoidance, 148

Essay Express, 294

Essay Information, 298

Execution function related reading errors, 262

Executive function (EF), 21; analogies of, 21–22; brain and, 23; components of, 22–23; dysfunction of, 23; impairment in, 23–24; metaphors of, 21–22; parents and, 24–25; teachers and, 24–25

Executive skills, 8

Exercise, 38–39, 70

Expository text structure, 281

Expulsion, from school, 423–424

Families: ADHD impact on, 19–20; counseling for, 37; school-based social skill interventions impact on, 154

FAPE. *See* Free and appropriate public education

FBAs. *See* Functional behavior assessments

Fetzer, Nancy, 234

Figurative language, 273

Fine motor skills, 314, 364

First Steps to Success Preschool Edition (Voyager Sopris Learning), 69

Fisher, D., 280, 282, 283

Fit Brains, 240

504 Plan: IEPs *versus*, 422–423. *See also* Rehabilitation Act of 1973, Section 504

5W charts, 281

Five-Finger Check, 271

Five-paragraph persuasive essay rubric, 446

Flash cards, for multiplication tables, 244

Flex models, 204

Flexibility, 22

Flowcharts, 280

Fluency Formula Program, 271

Focalin, 44

Focalin XR, 44

Forest, 222

Forms: behavior report, 435; daily monitoring report, 437; daily report, 434, 436; homework assignments, 440; homework tracking sheet, 441; notebook check, 439; research log, 447; self-monitoring behavior log, 438; social skill lesson plan, 160–163; weekly progress report, 225

Framed outlines, 280

Frames, 292, 297

Free and appropriate public education (FAPE), 415–416

Free Printable Behavior Charts.com, 131

Frey, N., 280, 283

Friedlander, B., 232

Frustration, prevention of, 149–150

Fuchs, Douglas, 200

Fuchs, Lynn, 200

Fuel the Brain.com, 269, 327

Fun Way, 241

FunBrain.com, 269, 327

Functional behavior assessments (FBAs), 54, 136–137, 152, 157, 424

FunFonix, 269

Games, in book club, 445

Gardner, Howard, 193

GBG. *See* Good Behavior Game

Genre structures, 297

Ghotit, 303, 307

Girls, with ADHD, 17–18

GIST (generation, interaction, between, schemata and text), 283–284

Goal directed persistence, 22

Goal setting tips, 158

Goal sheets, 124

Gojak, L., 325

Good Behavior Game (GBG), 119

Google Docs, 302

Graham, Steve, 232, 294

Grandma's Rule, 345

Graphic organizers, 235, 280–281

Graphomotor skills: difficulties with, 327–328; in writing process struggles, 265

Graphophonic cues, 268

Gray, Carol, 135

Greene, Ross, 142, 147, 150, 152

Gregory, G. H., 230

Gross motor skills, 364

Group processing, 201

Group reinforcement systems: bingo board, 117–118; chart moves, 116; compliment cards, unsolicited, 117; electronic feedback point system, 119–120; Good Behavior Game, 119; group response cost, 119; lottery grid, 117–118; mystery motivator, 118; 100 chart, 117–118; points, table or team, 115; praise and positive attention, 115; raffles or lotteries, 116–117; scoreboards, 120; stamp cards, individual, 117; student interference with, 121; target goals, 115; T-charts, 120; teacher-student points, 120; token economy system, 118–119; tokens in jar, 116

Group response cost, 119

Guanfacine (Tenex), 46

Guanfacine, extended-release (Intuniv), 46

Guare, C., 77

Guare, R., 77

Guided writing, 296–297

Hand signals, for whole-group responses, 181

Handwriting, 359–360; apps for, 315; improvement in, 313–317; programs for, 315; tactile-kinesthetic techniques for, 315–316

Handwriting Without Tears, 315, 378

Harris, K. R., 232, 294

Harris, Z., 307

Heimburge, J. A., 203, 227, 298

Heredity, 13, 15–16

High school children. _See_ Adolescence

Hiltel, Terri, 188–190

Hinshaw, Stephen, 17

Holubec, E., 200–201

Home-based behavioral treatment, 52–53

Homework assignments form, 440

Homework limitation, 60

Homework Now, 227

Homework Planet, 223

Homework survival kits, 369

Homework tips: for parents, 219–223; helping during, 221–222; motivation, 222; preparation, 221; routine and schedule development, 220; structure, 221; supply organization, 220–221; teacher communication, 223; work environment, 220; work production, 222; for teachers, 223–226; communication clarity, 224; monitoring, 224, 226; motivation, 226; perspective, 226; support, 224, 226

Homework tracking sheet form, 441

Horner, R. H., 157

Hot seat, in reading comprehension, 285

Houghton Mifflin's Education Place, 293

How to Reach and Teach All Children through Balanced Literacy (Rief & Heimburge), 286

Human developmental theory, 365

Humphreys, C., 325

Hunter and His Amazing Remote Control, 147, 149

Hyperactive child syndrome. _See_ Attention-deficit/hyperactivity disorder

Hyperactive-impulsive attention-deficit/hyperactivity disorder: inattentive ADD combined with, 3, 9, 28; predominantly, 3, 9

Hyperactivity, 4, 5–7; girls with, 18

Hyperactivity behaviors, 143–146; feedback for, 144; management tips for, 143–144; reinforcement for, 144; self-regulation strategies and supports, 144

I Can Problem Solve, 147, 158

iCanWrite, 315

IDEA. _See_ In federal education law

IEPs. _See_ Individualized education programs

IKL.com, 327

Illes, Terry, 219–220

Imagery, in reading comprehension, 283

Imipramine (Tofranil), 4

IMPACT (Investigating the Mindset of Parents about ADHD and Children Today), 154

Impulsive behaviors, 143–146; feedback for, 144; management tips for, 143–144; reinforcement for, 144; self-regulation strategies and supports, 144

Impulsivity, 5–7; girls with, 18

Impulsivity-related reading errors, 261

In federal education law (IDEA), 3, 32, 33, 67, 76, 152, 197; disciplining disabled students with, 423–425; IEP process, 417–419; OHI eligibility criteria, 419; overview of, 415–417; SLD eligibility criteria, 420

Inattention, 4–5, 12

Inattention-related reading errors, 261

Inattentive attention-deficit disorder: girls with, 17–18; predominantly, 3, 9

Inattentive attention-deficit/hyperactivity disorder, hyperactive-impulsive ADHD combined with, 3, 9, 28

inClass, 216

Incredible Years Parenting Program, 53, 157, 158

Individual counseling, 37

Individualized education programs (IEPs), 67, 75, 76, 79, 416; 504 Plan *versus*, 422–423; contents of, 418; evaluation in, 417–418; process of, 417–418; referral in, 417–418; student protection without, 425; team members in, 418; for Vincent (case study), 351

Individualized interventions, 123–131; check-in-check-out, 130–131; contingency contracts, 124–125; daily report cards, 125–130; direct behavior ratings, 131; goal sheets, 124; response costs, 132–133; self-monitoring, 133–134; social stories, 135; token economy, 125; token programs, 125

Informational text structure, 281

Inhibition, 22; in writing process struggles, 264

Inner Body, 288

Inspiration, 293

Instructional factors, for inattentive, distractible students, 186

Intelligence testing, 30–31

International Dyslexia Association, 259

Internet-4Classrooms, 269

Interpersonal intelligence, 193

Interpersonal skills, 201

Interventions. *See* Individualized interventions

Interviews, 50, 55–56, 61–62, 72, 79–81, 108–109, 205, 236, 288–289

Intrapersonal intelligence, 193

Intuniv. *See* Guanfacine, extended-release

iPad, 204

iReady, 204

iWriteWords, 315

Jamestown Timed Reading, 271

Johnson, David W., 200–201

Johnson, Roger T., 200–201

Journal: entries, 285; metacognitive, 230–231; responses, 230–231

Jungle Rangers, 39

Kagan, L., 202–203, 326

Kagan, M., 202–203, 326

Kagan, S., 202–203, 326

Kalikow, K. T., 47

Kapvay. *See* Clonidine, extended-release

Katz, Mark, 69

Kaufman, C., 262, 268, 294

Keyword mnemonics, 241

Kid Pointz, 131

Kids Memory, 243

Kidspiration, 293

Kidwize Multiplication Songs, 243

Kindergarten children: academic skills of, 68; ADHD in, 63–72; behavior expectations of, 69; behavior management techniques for, 69–71; expectations of, 68; research-supported intervention programs for, 69; teacher strategies for, 71–72

Knoff, H. M., 157

Kutscher, Martin, 22, 213

Kuypers, L., 147

KWHL, 283

KWL, 283

KWL Plus, 283

Landau, S., 154

Language: figurative, 273; in writing process struggles, 265

Language disorders, 8, 11; in preschool children, 64

Lapp, D., 280

LDs. *See* Learning disabilities

Learning Ally, 275

Learning Break-through, 188

Learning disabilities (LDs), 8, 10, 11, 75; in adolescence, 78; coexisting, 258–260; dyslexia, 259–260; red flags for, 64–65

Learning log, 230–231

Learning strategies, 229

Learning style preferences, 193, 369–370

Learning styles, 61

Learning Toolbox, 233

Learning Works for Kids, 216, 243

LEAs. *See* Local education agencies

"Lecture Notes," 234–235

Legibility, 313

Lenz, B., 284

LetterSchool, 315

Levine, Mel, 262

Light-bulb strategy, 189–190

Lindamood-Bell, 268

Linguistic intelligence, 193

Linsin, Michael, 140

Lisdexamfetamine dimesylate, 44

Literature, mathematics and, 330

Literature Circles. *See* Classroom book club

Literature logs, in reading comprehension, 285

Littman, Ellen, 17–18

Living Letters, 315

Local education agencies (LEAs), 423

Logical-mathematical intelligence, 193

Lotteries, 116–117

Lottery grid, 117–118

Mahone, E. M., 64

Management factors, for inattentive, distractible students, 184–186

Manifestation determination review, 424

Marriages, ADHD impact on, 19

Mason, L., 232

Mastropieri, M. A., 241

Math Cats.com, 327

Mathematics: attention problems and, 328; attention weaknesses in, 319; challenge of, 323–324; executive function weaknesses in, 320; fine motor weaknesses in, 321; focus and, 328; graphomotor difficulties and, 327–328; instruction in, 323, 324–327; language weaknesses in, 321; literature and, 330; memory weaknesses in, 319–320; metacognitive strategies in, 328–329; motivation and, 327; parents and, 329; practice and, 328; review and, 328; self-monitoring and, 328–329; sequencing weaknesses in, 320–321; spatial-organization weaknesses in, 321; standards of, 321–324; student expectations of, 321–324; visual-motor weaknesses in, 321; word problem in, 324–325; writing and, 330; written expression weaknesses in, 321

Mathletics.com, 327

Math-Play.com, 327

McConnell, M. E., 135

Medication, for Vincent (case study), 354

Medication therapy, 36

Medications: nonstimulant, 46; stimulant, 43–46

Meditation practices, 39

Melt-downs, prevention of, 149–150

Memory Joggers, 241, 246

Mendeley, 293

Metacognition, 22–23, 229–230; questions, 230

Metacognition-related reading errors, 262

Metacognitive journal/learning log, 230–231

Metacognitive knowledge, 229

Metacognitive strategies, 229, 229–230, 328–329; journal responses, 230–231; reading logs, 231; think-aloud, 231

Metadate CD, 44

Metadate ER, 44

Metaphors, 298

Methylin, 43, 44

Methylin ER, 44

Methylphenidates, 43–44

Middle school children. *See* Adolescence

Mikami, A. Y., 55

Mind mapping, 293

Mindfulness, 39

Minimal brain dysfunction. *See* Attention-deficit/hyperactivity disorder

Misbehavior, in classroom: addressing, 105–106; triggers or antecedents to, 104–105

Mixed amphetamine salts, 44

Mnemonics: acronym examples, 241; acrostics examples, 241; ARMS, 303; BOTEC, 294; keyword, 241; for multiplication tables, 245–246; OSWALD, 298–299; pegword, 241–242; PLEASE, 294; RIDE, 325; STAR, 325; for writing, 294; writing proofreading strategies, 304; writing strategies for, 294

Moats, Louisa, 274

Modeled writing, 292, 296

Morris, Rick, 177

Motor skill disorders, in preschool children, 65

Movement, 70

Mr.Nussbaum.com, 327

MTSS. *See* Multitiered system of support

Multi Rap HD, 243

Multimodal interventions, 36–40

Multiple intelligences, 193

Multiplication Rock, 243

Multiplication tables, learning technologies for, 243; arrays, 244; auditory, 243; conceptual, 246; flash cards, 244; grids, 244; manipulatives, 244;

mnemonic devices, 245–246; patterns, 244–245; tactile, 244; tech games and programs, 245; typing, 245; verbal, 245; visual, 244; writing, 245

Multisensory instruction, 193

Multitiered system of support (MTSS), 53, 401–403; PBIS, 402; RTI, 402

Muschla, G. R., 326

Muschla, J., 326

Muschla-Berry, E., 326

Music, 242; in classroom management, 104; lessons, 40; therapy, 40

Music activities, in book club, 445

Musical intelligence, 193

Musically Aligned, 242

MyHomework, 216

Mystery motivator, 118

MyStudyLife, 216

Nadeau, Kathleen, 17–18, 49

Narrative text structure, 281

NASA, 288

National Center for Learning and Disabilities (NCLD), 402

National Center on Accessible Educational Materials, 192

National Center on Birth Defects and Developmental Disabilities, Centers for Disease Control and Prevention, 67

National Center on Universal Design for Learning, 192

National Council of Teachers of Mathematics (NCTM) Principles and Standards, 321–322

National Geographic for Kids, 288

National Governors Association Center for Best Practices (NGA Center), 323

National Institute of Mental Health, 15, 65

Naturalist intelligence, 193

NCLD. See National Center for Learning and Disabilities

NCLD School Transformational Model, 402

NCTM. See National Council of Teachers of Mathematics Principles and Standards

Neurofeedback (EEG biofeedback), 39

Neurotransmitters. See Chemical (neurotransmitter) inefficiency

New York University and Child Study Clinic, 154

NGA Center. See National Governors Association Center for Best Practices

Nonstimulant medications, 46

Nonverbal working memory, 238

Norepinephrine, 15

Norpramin. See Desipramine

Northern Nevada Writing Project, 293

Nortriptyline (Pamelor; Aventyl), 46

Note taking, 231, 233–235

Notebook check form, 439

Number Talks, 325–326

Obsessive-compulsive disorder (OCD), 10, 11

OCD. See Obsessive-compulsive disorder

ODD. See Oppositional defiant disorder

Office of Special Education and Rehabilitative Services (OSERS), 419

OHI. See Other health impaired category

Olsen, Jan, 315

O'Malley, J., 229, 233

100 chart, 117–118

Online-Stopwatch, 178

Onomatopoeia, 298

Oppositional defiant disorder (ODD), 10, 11, 75; ADHD and, 142; dealing with, 150–152

Oral language activities, in book club, 444

Organization, 7–8, 22, 59; materials, 208–209, 211–212; memory cues, 209–210, 212; monitor, 210–211; motivation, 210–211; parents and, 211–213; planning, 211; support, 210–211; teachers and, 208–213; thinking, 211; visual reminders, 209–210, 212; workspace, 208–209, 212; in writing process struggles, 264

Orton-Gillingham methodology, 259–260, 261

OSEP Technical Assistance Center on Positive Behavioral Interventions and Supports, 157

OSERS. See Office of Special Education and Rehabilitative Services

OSWALD mnemonic, 298–299

Other health impaired (OHI) category, 199, 416; eligibility criteria of, 419

Output speed and production, in writing process struggles, 265

Palincsar, A. S., 284

PALS. See Peer Assisted Learning Strategies

Pamelor. See Nortriptyline

Paragraph construction, 296

Parent Child Interaction Training, 66

Parent to Parent program, 66

Parent-Child Interaction Therapy, 53

Parents: ADHD training for, 36; child listening and following directions, 140–141; composing stage and, 301; counseling for, 37; cultural sensitivity in communication with, 398; drafting and, 301; dyslexia and, 260–261; EF and, 24–25; helping inattentive, distractible students, 186–188; homework tips for, 219–223; helping during, 221–222; motivation, 222; preparation, 221; routine and schedule development, 220; structure, 221; supply organization, 220–221; teacher communication, 223; work environment, 220; work production, 222; mathematics and, 329; organization and, 211–213; preschool children concerns, 66–67; reading comprehension and, 287; reading disability and, 260–261; reading motivation by, 287–288; reading strategies for, 274–275; stimulant medication administration by, 49; support groups for, 40; time management and, 216–218; writing and, 295–296

Parents' Evaluation of Developmental Status (PEDS), 67

Parker, R., 325

Parry, T., 230

Participation, active, student attention maintenance through, 179

Partner reading, 270

Partner responses, 182–183

PASS (preview, ask, summarize, synthesize), 284

PATS. *See* Preschool ADHD Treatment Study

PBIS. *See* Positive Behavioral Interventions and Supports model

PeaceBuilders, 158

PEDS. *See* Parents' Evaluation of Developmental Status

Peer Assisted Learning Strategies (PALS), 200

Peer-mediated instruction and intervention: classwide peer tutoring, 199–200; cooperative learning, 200–203

Pegword mnemonics, 241–242

Pelham, William, 55

Performance activities, in book club, 444–445

Performance deficits, skill deficits *versus*, 154

Performance tests, 31

Personal story telling, 292

PFC. *See* Prefrontal cortex

Physical activity, 38–39

Physical exam, 30

Physicians: school communication with, 407; school letter examples to, 408–411

Pinterest, 211, 220, 246, 291

Planning, 22; in writing process struggles, 264

Planning forms, for writing, 292–293

Play Attention, 39, 240

Play Kids Games, 243

PLEASE mnemonic, 294

Plot charts, 280

Points, table or team, 115

Positive Behavioral Interventions and Supports (PBIS) model, 53, 112, 145, 156–157, 197

Positive incentive programs, 131–132

Positive interdependence, 200–201; structuring to achieve, 201

Positive Parenting Program (Triple P), 53

POW (Pick, Organize, Write), 232

Prediction charts, 280

Prefrontal cortex (PFC), 23, 25

Premade response cards, 181

Preschool ADHD Treatment Study (PATS), 65

Preschool children: ADHD in, 63–72; attention problems in, 65; behavior expectations of, 69; behavior management techniques for, 69–71; behavior problems in, 65; cognition disorders in, 64; competencies for, 67–68; diagnosis in, 66–67; emergent literacy skills in, 64; evaluation in, 66–67; intervention in, 66–67; language disorders in, 64; learning disability red flags, 64–65; motor skill disorders in, 65; parents concerns of, 66–67; research-supported intervention programs for, 69; signs and symptoms in, 63–64; social behavior disorders in, 65; teacher strategies for, 71–72

Prewrite, in writing process, 263

Prewriting techniques: brainstorming, 291; electronically capturing ideas, 291; explicitly taught strategies, 292; frames, 292; modeled writing, 292; personal story telling, 292; quick writes, 291; reference books, 292; sample topic sentences, 292; sharing exemplary pieces, 292; talking through, 292; verbalizing ideas into recording device, 292; writing prompts, 292; writing topic folders, 291

Primary (universal) intervention, 197–198

Prioritizing, 22

Privacy, 61

Private speech, 23

Privileges, 101–102

ProCentra, 44

Processing speed, in reading fluency, 269

Processing speed-related reading errors, 262

Project Read Language Circle, 261

Promoting Alternative Thinking Strategies-PATHS, 158

Promotive interaction, 201

Prosody, in reading fluency, 269

Psychosocial interventions, 37

Psychotherapy, 37

Publish, in writing process, 263

Question-answer relationships (QAR), in reading comprehension, 284–285

Quick Reads, 271

Quick writes, 291

Quiet space, 70

Quillivant XR, 44

Quinn, Patricia, 17–18, 49

Rabiner, David, 154

Rafferty, L. A., 135

Raffles, 116–117

Raising Healthy Children, 158

RAP (Read, Ask, Paraphrase), 232–233

Rate, in reading fluency, 269

Ratey, J. J., 38

Rating scales, 29–30

RCRC (Read, Cover, Recite, Check), 232

Read, 204

Read 180, 204

Read Naturally, 270, 271

Read Naturally, 377

Read Works, 279

Read & Write, 299

Readers theater, 270, 285

Reading comprehension: after-reading strategies, 279; anticipation guide in, 283; before-reading strategies, 277–278; close reading in, 282–283; directed reading-thinking activity in, 283; during-reading strategies, 278–279; expository text structure in, 281; GIST, 283–284; graphic organizers in, 280–281; hot seat in, 285; imagery in, 283; informational text structure in, 281; journal entries in, 285; KWL, 283; literature logs in, 285; narrative text structure in, 281; parents and, 287; PASS, 284; question-answer relationships in, 284–285; readers theater in, 285; reciprocal teaching in, 284; retelling in, 285; summarizing in, 281; teacher modeling of strategic reading, 280; visualization in, 283

Reading disability, parents and, 260–261

Reading errors and weaknesses, 261; execution function related, 262; impulsivity-related, 261; inattention-related, 261; metacognition-related, 262; processing speed-related, 262; working memory-related, 261–262

Reading fluency, 269–272; accuracy, 269; automaticity, 269; buddy reading, 270; choral reading, 270; contributing factors to, 269; correct practice, 269; cross-age buddy reading, 271; echo reading, 270; fluency-building strategies, 269–271; independent reading tips, 271–272; online programs for, 270; oral reading in classroom, 271; partner reading, 270; practicing to perform, 270–271; processing speed, 269; prosody, 269; rate, 269; readers theater, 270; reading volume, 269; recording-assisted reading, 270; remediation challenge, 271; software programs for, 270; student-adult reading, 269–270; timed repeated reading and charting, 271; vocabulary, 269

Reading logs, 231

Reading process, 257–258

Ready, Start, School: Nurturing and Guiding Your Child through Preschool and Kindergarten (Rief), 68

Reciprocal teaching, in reading comprehension, 284

Recording device, verbalizing ideas into, 292

Recording-assisted reading, 270

Reference books, 292

Rehabilitation Act of 1973, Section 504, 32, 33, 420–421, 422; eligibility criteria, 421

Reinforcement systems. *See* Group reinforcement systems

Relationship skills, 158

Report Form, 158, 163

Rescue Time, 222

Research activities, in book club, 445

Research log form, 447

Research-supported intervention programs, for preschool and kindergarten children, 69

Resource materials, 235

Response costs, 132–133

Response to Intervention (RTI) team, 32, 37, 53, 156, 196–199, 399; components of, 197; IDEA and, 199; MTSS and, 402; PBIS and, 402; three-tiered model of intervention, 197–199

Responsible decision making, 158

Retelling, in reading comprehension, 285

Retrieval, in writing process struggles, 264

Review games, 235

Revise, in writing process, 263

Revisions, in writing, 302–303

Rewards, 70
Rhyme, 242
RIDE mnemonic, 325
Rief, S., 203, 227, 298, 369, 373
Riley, D. A., 142
Ritalin, 43, 44
Ritalin LA, 44
Ritalin SR, 44
Rotation models, 204
RTI. *See* Response to Intervention team
Rubrics, 297; five-paragraph persuasive essay, 446

S2TOP (Set, See, Touch, Organize, Proceed), 233
Sandler, M., 304
SAT. *See* Student assistance team
Schedules, 69–70
School communication, 32; with physicians, 407;
    between schools, 411
School district: evaluation from, 392–393, 413–414;
    evaluation of, 67
School supports, for adolescence, 75–76
School transition, for adolescence, 76–77
School-based behavioral treatment, 53–54
Schoolwide Positive Behavior Supports (SWPBS),
    156–157, 197, 402
Schusteff, A., 64
SCOPE (spelling, capitalization, order of words,
    punctuation, express complete thoughts), 304
Scoreboards, 120
SCORER (Schedule, Clue, Omit, Read, Estimate,
    Review), 233
Scruggs, T. E., 241
Seatwork, on-task during, 183–184
Second Step (Committee for Children), 54, 157
Secondary (targeted) intervention, 198
SEL. *See* Social-emotional learning programs
Self Control, 222
Self-awareness, 158
Self-correction, 230
Self-direction, 230
Self-evaluation, 230
Self-management, 158
Self-monitoring, 22–23, 133–134, 230; attention,
    188–190; behavior log form, 438; mathematics
    and, 328–329; teaching, 298–299; in writing
    process struggles, 264–265
Self-Regulated Strategy Development Approach
    (SRSD), 232

Self-regulatory techniques, 188–190
Self-talk, 23
Semantic cues, 267–268
Semantic maps, 280
Semantic webs, 272
Semple Math, 246
Sentence structure, 297–298
Sentences starters, 297
Shaw, Philip, 15
Shellenberger, S., 147
Sheridan, Susan, 154
Shifting, 22; in writing process struggles, 264
Shure, Myrna, 147, 152
Similes, 298
Simonsen, B., 157
Skill deficits, performance deficits *versus*, 154
Skillstreaming the Elementary School Child
    (McGinnis and Goldstein), 54, 157
SLD. *See* Specific learning disability category
Sleep disorders, 11, 75
Slingerland, 261
Small-group responses, 182–183
Small-group skills, 201
Smart Classroom Management, 140
SNAP-IV-C. *See* Swanson, Nolan, and Pelham
Social awareness, 158
Social behavior disorders, in preschool children, 65
Social rewards, 100–101
Social skill interventions, school-based: ADHD-
    related difficulties, 153; children impact from, 154;
    in classroom, 155–156; families impact from, 154;
    schoolwide programs and interventions, 156–158;
    skill deficits *versus* performance deficits, 154
Social Skill Lesson Plan, 158, 160–162
Social skills training, 37
Social stories, 135
Social symptoms, 7
Social-emotional learning (SEL) programs, 158
Software: for writing, 293; for written expression, 299
Songs for Learning, 242
Songs for Teaching, 242
Sounds in Syllables, 261
Sousa, D., 284
Space, increased, 60–61
Spatial intelligence, 193
Special education, 37
Specific learning disability (SLD) category, 199, 416;
    eligibility criteria for, 420

Speech disorders, 11

Speech recognition software, 299, 307

Speech-to-text software, 307

Spelling: checkers, 307; multisensory techniques for, 311–313; in writing process struggles, 265

Spelling challenges, 309–310

Spelling instruction, 310–311

SPORTS (sentence structure, punctuation, organization, repetition, tenses, spelling), 304

Sports Illustrated for Kids, 288

SQ3R (Survey, Question, Read, Recite, Review), 232

SQ4R (Survey, Question, Read, Recite, Write, Review), 232

SRSD. *See* Self-Regulated Strategy Development Approach

SST. *See* Student support team

Stamp cards, individual, 117

STAR mnemonic, 325

Starfall, 269

STARS (Safety first, Teamwork, Always respectful, Ready to learn, Sharing and caring), 98–99

STEM (science, technology, engineering and mathematics), 323

Step Up to Writing, 297

Stern, Judith, 49

Stimulant medications, 43–46; immediate-release formulas, 44–45; longer-acting, extended-release formulas, 45; mechanism of action, 44; parent administration of, 49; short-acting formulas, 44–45; side effects of, 45; teacher administration of, 47–48; titration process of, 45–46; types of, 44–45

Stop and Think Social Skills Program (Knoff), 54, 157

Stoplight Clock, 178

Story frames, 280

Story maps, 280, 293

Story Place, 288

Storyboards, 280

Storytelling, 242–243

Strattera. *See* Atomoxetine

Strong Kids Curricula, 158

Structure, 57–58

Struggling learners, intervention design for, 204–205

Student assistance team (SAT), 32

Student attention: anticipation, 178; auditory techniques for, 177; curiosity, 178; maintaining of, 179–183; on-task during seatwork, 183–184; personalization and, 178; student thinking organization, 179; with technology, 178; visual techniques for, 177–178

Student learning style/interest interview, 194–196

Student planners, 214–215

Student support team (SST), 32, 76, 399–401; schools role in, 400; teachers role in, 401

Student thinking organization, 179

Student-adult reading, 269–270

Students: accommodation of, 102–104; belief in, 61; dyslexia and, 259–260; engagement of, 179–181; feelings, 61; group reinforcement systems interference by, 121; inattentive, distractible, 184; on-task during seatwork, 183–184; school success, 57–61; seating, 102–103; strengths, 59

Study skills, 59

Sugai, G., 157

Summarizing, 281

Superheroes Social Skills: A Multimedia Program, 157

Suspension, from school, 423–424

Sustaining attention, 22

Swanson, Nolan, and Pelham (SNAP-IV-C), 30

SWPBS. *See* Schoolwide Positive Behavior Supports

Syntactic cues, 268

Tactile techniques, for multiplication tables, 244

Taking Charge of ADHD (Barkley), 53, 114

Tales2Go, 288

Target behaviors, 123

Target goals, 115

Taylor, J. K., 152

T-charts, 120

Teacher Support Force, 243

Teachers: ADHD training for, 38; attention-getting strategy for, 139; bad behavior and, 71–72; child trouble sitting and, 71; clear directions and communication by, 139–140; compliance increase by, 141–142; documentation by, 413; EF and, 24–25; feedback from, 140; flexibility, 57; follow-through by, 140; handling disappointments, 71; helping inattentive, distractible students, 184–186; homework tips for, 223–226; communication clarity, 224; monitoring, 224, 226; motivation, 226; perspective, 226; support, 224, 226; homework tips for parents from, 223; motivation of, 140; organization and, 208–213; positive attention from, 70; positive attitude, 57; SST and, 401; stimulant medication administration by, 47–48; strategies for kindergarten children, 71–72; strategies for preschool children, 71–72; tactile-defensive child and, 71; time management and, 213–218; Vincent (case study) and, 353–354; writing difficulties and, 305–306

Teacher's College assessment, 375

Teacher-student points, 120

Teaching Pyramid, 53

Teaching strategies, 58

Team approach, 389–390; advocating and, 391–392; clinicians' role in, 397–398; educators' role in, 394–397; parents role in, 390–394; record maintenance and, 392

Teamwork, 59

Technology, student attention with, 178

Teens, symptoms of ADHD, 5–8

Teeter, P. A., 63

Tenex. *See* Guanfacine

Tertiary (intensive) intervention, 198–199

Text-to-speech software, 299, 307

ADHD Book of Lists (Rief), 131

Alert Program, 147

Dyslexia Checklist: A Practical Reference for Parents and Teachers (Rief and Stern), 68

Incredible Five-Point Scale, 147

Think-aloud, 231

30/30, 216

Thomas, Alexander, 365

Tics, 11

Time, increased, 60–61

Time awareness, 22, 213–214, 216

Time lines, 280

Time management, 7–8; assignment sheets, 214–215; calendars, 214–215; long-term projects, 215, 217–218; parents and, 216–218; schedules, 215, 217; student planners, 214–215; teachers and, 213–218; time awareness, 213–214, 216

Time Timer, 100, 178

Time Tracker, 178

Timed repeated reading and charting, 271

Times Tables, 241

Times Tables the Fun Way, 245

Tofranil. *See* Imipramine

Token economy, 118–119, 125

Token programs, 125

Tokens in jar, 116

Tolisano, Silvia Rosenthal, 283

Tomlinson, Carol Ann, 192

Tools of the Mind, 24, 69

Topic sentences, 292, 297

Touch and Write, 315

Tourette Syndrome, 10, 11

Toxemia, 16

Toxin exposure, 16

Treatments, alternative, 41

TREE (Topic, Reasons, Explanation, Ending), 232

Triple P. *See* Positive Parenting Program

Tumble Books, 288

Turtle Diary, 269

Tutoring supports, 38; classwide peer, 199–200

Typing and keyboarding software, for writing difficulties, 306–307

UCLA's Mindful Awareness Research Center, 39

UDL. *See* Universal Design for Learning

Unison responses, 181

Universal Design for Learning (UDL), 191–192

Vanderbilt Parent and Teacher Assessment Scales, 29–30

Venn diagrams, 280

Verbal working memory, 237

Victoria. *See* Vincent (case study)

Vincent (case study): ADHD diagnosis, 347, 349–350; assistive technology for, 352–353; behavioral plan, 354–356; college and, 367–369; coping strategies, 370–371; discipline and, 351–352; in drama class, 353; educational history of, 344–347; educational supports for, 347–351; good communication with, 354; IEP for, 351; learning styles of, 369–370; medical history of, 343–344; medication for, 354; note taking, 353; power struggle avoidance with, 352; professional development of, 367–369; school supplies, 371–372; social history of, 344–347; stress and, 370–371; success and, 356, 357–358; teachers and, 353–354; therapeutic interventions for, 356–357

Visual organizers, for writing, 292–293

Visual prompts, 70

Visual techniques: for multiplication tables, 244; for student attention, 177–178

Visualization, in reading comprehension, 283

Visualizing and Verbalizing for Language Comprehension and Thinking, 283

Vocabulary, 273; anchor charts, 273; context clues, 272; figurative language, 273; games, 273;

mapping unknown words, 273; multiple meanings, 272; in reading fluency, 269; semantic webs, 272; teaching words directly, 272; text preview and frontload, 273; word lists, 273; word play, 273; word precision, 273; word root teaching, 273

Vocabulary Cartoons, 241

Vocational counseling, 37

Voice volume scale, 145

Volume, reading, 269

Voyager Sopris Learning, 69

Vyvanse, 43, 44

Walker, Hill, 69

Wallace, I., 154

WBT. *See* Whole Brain Teaching

Webmath.com, 327

Webs, 280

Weekly progress report, 224, 225

Wellbutrin. *See* Bupropion hydrochloride

Wet-Dry-Try Suite, 315

Whole Brain Teaching (WBT), 120, 134, 140, 152

Whole Brain Teaching for Challenging Kids, 134

Whole-group responses, hand signals for, 181

Wikki Stix, 312

Williams, M. S., 147

Wilson Fundations, 261

Wilson Reading, 261

Wired for Reading, 378

WM. *See* Working memory

Wolraich, M. L., 66

Word decoding, 268–269

Word lists, 273

Word play, 273

Word precision, 273

Word predictors, for writing difficulties, 307

Word problem, 324–325

Word processing, for writing difficulties, 306

Word recognition, 268–269

Word root teaching, 273

Word Sorts, 268

Word study, in book club, 444

WordQ, 307

Working memory (WM), 22, 237–238; accommodations for, 239–240; deficits, 238; descriptions of, 237–238; difficulties associated with, 238; mathematics and, 319–320; nonverbal, 238; reading errors related to, 261–262; support

for, 239–240; verbal, 237; in writing process struggles, 264

Workspace organization, 208–209, 212

Wowzers, 204

Write-on tools, 181

Write:Outloud, 299

Writing: apps for, 293; clustering, 293; editing in, 303; mathematics and, 330; mind mapping, 293; mnemonic proofreading strategies, 304; mnemonic strategies for, 294; parents and, 295–296; planning forms for, 292–293; revisions in, 302–303; software for, 293; story maps, 293; thinking and questioning, 293–294; visual organizers for, 292–293. *See also* Prewriting techniques

Writing difficulties: apps for, 306–307; assistive technology for, 306; online programs for, 306–307; speech-to-text software, 307; spelling checkers for, 307; teachers and, 305–306; text-to-speech software, 307; typing and keyboarding software for, 306–307; word predictors for, 307; word processing for, 306

Writing Fix, 293

Writing process steps, 263

Writing process struggles: attention, 264; cognitive flexibility, 264; graphomotor skills, 265; inhibition, 264; language, 265; organization, 264; output speed and production, 265; planning, 264; retrieval, 264; self-monitoring, 264–265; shifting, 264; spelling, 265; working memory, 264

Writing prompts, 292

Writing topic folders, 291

Writing Wizard, 315

Written expression, building skills in: apps for, 299; draft composition, 298; frames, 297; genre structures, 297; guided writing, 296–297; instructional approaches, 296–297; instructional programs, 297; modeled writing, 296; paragraph construction instructions, 296; rubrics, 297; self-monitoring teaching, 298–299; sensory descriptions, 297; sentence structure teaching, 297–298; sentences starters, 297; software for, 299; student examples, 296; topic sentences, 297

Written workload modification, 60

Zones of Regulation, 147

Zoo-Phonics, 268

Zumpfe, H., 54

Zylowska, Lidia, 39

Notes

Notes

Notes

Notes

Notes

Notes

Notes

Notes

Notes

Notes

Notes

Notes

Notes